Philosophical Perspectives, 9
AI, Connectionism and
Philosophical Psychology, 1995

Previously Published Volumes
Volume 1, Metaphysics, 1987
Volume 2, Epistemology, 1988
Volume 3, Philosophy of Mind and Action Theory, 1989
Volume 4, Action Theory and Philosophy of Mind, 1990
Volume 5, Philosophy of Religion, 1991
Volume 6, Ethics, 1992
Volume 7, Language and Logic, 1993
Volume 8, Logic and Language, 1994

Forthcoming Volumes
Additional Titles to be announced.

Philosophical Perspectives, 9
AI, Connectionism and
Philosophical Psychology, 1995

Edited by
JAMES E. TOMBERLIN
California State University, Northridge

Ridgeview Publishing Company   Atascadero, California

Paper Text: ISBN 0-924922-23-0
Cloth Text: ISBN 0-924922-73-7

All the typesetting and many of the illustrations in volumes 1 through 8 were done by Robert Olsen. The editor and the managing editor always appreciated Bob's skill, thoroughness, and commitment to producing fine typesetting. Bob's accidental death this year has deprived us of a much liked and valued co-worker.

Published in the United States of America
by Ridgeview Publishing Company
P. O. Box 686
Atascadero, California 93423

Printed in the United States of America
by Thomson-Shore, Inc.

Philosophical Perspectives, 9, AI, Connectionism, and
Philosophical Psychology, 1995

Contents

Editorial Preface

The Third Philosophical Perspectives Lecture

WILLIAM G. LYCAN   Consciousness as Internal Monitoring, I   1

AI

JOHN L. POLLOCK   Practical Reasoning in Oscar   15

WILLIAM J. RAPAPORT   Understanding Understanding: Syntactic
Semantics and Computational Cognition   49

Connectionism

ANDY CLARK   Moving Minds: Situating Content in the
Service of Real-time Success   89

ROBERT CUMMINS   Connectionism and the Rationale Constraint
on Cognitive Explanation   105

TERENCE HORGAN and   Connectionism and the Commitments
JOHN TIENSON   of Folk Psychology   127

Representation

MARTIN DAVIES   Two Notions of Implicit Rules   153

RUTH GARRETT MILLIKAN   Pushmi-Pullyu Representations   185

GEORGES REY   A Not "Merely Empirical" Argument
for a Language of Thought   201

MICHAEL TYE   A Representational Theory of Pains
and Their Phenomenal Character   223

Consciousness

COLIN McGINN   Consciousness Evaded:
Comments on Dennett 241

KIM STERELNY   Basic Minds 251

ROBERT VAN GULICK How Should We Understand the
Relation Between Intentionality
and Phenomenal Consciousness? 271

Consciousness and Moore's Paradox

BERNARD W. KOBES Telic Higher-Order Thoughts
and Moore's Paradox 291

DAVID M. ROSENTHAL Moore's Paradox and Consciousness 313

Psychological Attitudes, States and Content

FELICIA ACKERMAN The Concept of Manipulativeness 335

STEVEN E. BOËR   Propositional Attitudes and
Compositional Semantics 341

MARK CRIMMINS   Contextuality, Reflexivity,
Iteration, Logic 381

DERK PEREBOOM   Conceptual Structure and
the Individuation of Content 401

Causation and Properties

LOUISE ANTONY   Law and Order in Psychology 429

DAVID BRAUN   Causally Relevant Properties 447

STEPHEN YABLO   Singling Out Properties 477

Corrections to "Hop, Skip, and Jump: the Agonistic Conception of Truth"
by Stephen Yablo which appeared in *Philosophical Perspectives, 7,
Language and Logic, 1993* 503

PREFACE

Consciousness, machine and practical reasoning, connectionism and folk psychology, understanding and implicit rules, the language of thought, representation, Moore's paradox, propositional attitudes and content, causation and properties—these are some of the central issues addressed in twenty-two original essays in this volume devoted to AI, connectionism, and philosophical psychology.

A series of topical philosophy studies, *Philosophical Perspectives* aims to publish original essays by foremost thinkers in their fields, with each volume confined to a main area of philosophical research. The intention is to publish volumes annually.

Philosophical Perspectives could not have come to fruition without the precious encouragement it received from administrative officials at California State University, Northridge. I am particularly grateful to Dr. Blenda J. Wilson, President of this institution, and Dr. Luanne Kennedy, Provost and Vice President for Academic Affairs, who provided essential support. I also thank Dr. Jorge Garcia, Dean, School of Humanities, and Dr. Daniel Sedey, Chair, Department of Philosophy, for their consistent efforts in advancing this project. Patricia D. Hackl, Manager of Academic Resources, School of Humanitites, maintained logistical supervision and arranged for many valuable services. Linda S. Carlson, Head Secretary of the department, and Deidre Dowling-Mertz contributed ever so many hours of invaluable clerical assistance and support.

Finally, I am pleased to observe that the present volume includes the third *Philosophical Perspectives* lecture presented by William Lycan at California State University, Northridge in Fall, 1994.

August 1995   **JAMES E. TOMBERLIN**

Philosophical Perspectives, 9, AI, Connectionism, and
Philosophical Psychology, 1995

CONSCIOUSNESS AS INTERNAL MONITORING, I

The Third *Philosophical Perspectives* Lecture

William G. Lycan
University of North Carolina, Chapel Hill

Locke put forward the theory of consciousness as "internal Sense" or "reflection"; Kant made it "[i]nner sense, by means of which the mind intuits itself or its inner state."[1] On that theory, consciousness is a perception-like second-order representing of our own psychological states and events.

The term 'consciousness' of course has many distinct uses.[2] My concern here is with that use according to which much of one's mental or psychological activity is unconscious or subconscious even when one is wide awake and well aware of other goings-on both external and internal. I shall argue that what distinguishes conscious mental activity from un- and subconscious mental activity is indeed second-order representing.

Locke's idea has been urged in our own time by philosophers such as D.M. Armstrong and by psychologists such as Bernard Baars; I have previously defended it too.[3] But some interesting criticisms have been raised against the view by a number of theorists. My most urgent task in this paper is to overcome an objection due to Georges Rey.[4]

1. Armstrong states the Inner Sense doctrine as follows.

> Introspective consciousness...is a perception-like awareness of current states and activities in our own mind. The current activities will include sense-perception: which latter is the awareness of current states and activities of our environment and our body.[5]

As I would put it, consciousness is the functioning of internal *attention mechanisms* directed upon lower-order psychological states and events. I would also add (or make more explicit) a soupçon of teleology: Attention mechanisms are devices which have the *job* of relaying and/or coordinating information about ongoing psychological events and processes.[6]

Armstrong offers a plausible Just-So Story to explain the prevalence of introspective consciousness:

> [T]he biological function of introspective consciousness...is to sophisticate our mental processes in the interests of more sophisticated action.
>
> Inner perception makes the sophistication of our mental processes possible in the following way. If we have a faculty that can make us aware of current mental states and activities, then it will be much easier to achieve *integration* of the states and activities, to get them working together in the complex and sophisticated ways necessary to achieve complex and sophisticated ends.
>
> ...[C]o-ordination [of many parallel processes] can only be achieved if the portion of the computing space made available for administering the overall plan is continuously made "aware" of the current mental state of play with respect to the lower-level operations that are running in parallel, Only with this feedback is control possible... . It is no accident that fully alert introspective consciousness characteristically arises in *problem* situations, situations that standard routines cannot carry one through.[7]

A slightly deflated version of this idea will figure in my own defense of the Inner Sense theory.

The Lockean thesis is a component of a wider project of mine: that of establishing the *hegemony of representation*. I am concerned to maintain a weak version of Brentano's doctrine that the mental and the intentional are one and the same. Weak, because I am not sure that intentionality suffices for representation; but my claim is strong enough: that the mind has no special properties that are not exhausted by its representational properties. It would follow that once representation is (eventually) understood, then not only consciousness in our present sense but subjectivity, qualia, "what it's like," and every other aspect of the mental will be explicable in terms of representation, without the positing of any other ingredient not already well understood from the naturalistic point of view.[8]

I should repeat and emphasize that my concern in this paper is solely with the notion of conscious awareness, with the distinction between conscious mental states and un-, sub- or otherwise non-conscious mental states. In particular, I am not here addressing issues of qualia or phenomenal character, which I have resolved almost entirely satisfactorily elsewhere.[9] There may be Inner Sense theorists who believe that their views solve problems of qualia; I make no such claim, for I think qualia problems and the nature of conscious awareness are mutually independent and indeed have little to do with each other.[10]

2. The Inner Sense view of consciousness has a number of advantages, the first of which is that it does distinguish awareness from mere psychology, and conscious states/events (in the sense indicated above) from mere mentation. We may plausibly suppose that many lower animals have psychologies and mentation, or at least internal representation, without awareness. Second, the view affords some *grades* of un- or subconsciousness; e.g., a state/event may be unconscious just because it is unattended, but a Freudian wish to kill one's father may have been rendered unattend*able* by some masterful Censor. —And further distinctions are available, both for animals and for human beings.

Third, the Inner Sense account affords the best solution I know to the problem of subjectivity and "knowing what it's like," raised by B.A. Farrell, Thomas Nagel and Frank Jackson; Georges Rey and I hit upon that solution independently a few years ago.[11] It involves the behavior of indexical terms in the proprietary vocabulary mobilized by the relevant attention mechanisms. But there is no time to rehearse it here.

Fourth, the Inner Sense view sorts out a longstanding issue about sensations and feeling: Consider pain. A minor pain may go unfelt, or so we sometimes say.[12] Even quite a bad pain may not be felt if attention is distracted by sufficiently pressing concerns. Yet such assertions as my last two can sound anomalous; as David Lewis once said, meaning to tautologize, "pain is a feeling." When one person's commonplace sounds to another contradictory on its face, we should suspect equivocation, and the Inner Sense model delivers: Sometimes the word 'pain' is used to mean just the first-order representation of damage or disorder, a representation which can go unnoticed. But sometimes "pain" means a conscious feeling or mode of awareness, and on that usage the phrase "unfelt pain" is simply self-contradictory; it comprehends both the first-order representation and the second-order scanning together. Thus the equivocation, which gave rise to the issue; the issue is dissolved.

3. In correspondence, Fred Dretske has asked a good pair of questions about the Inner Sense view:[13] Why is consciousness (or just representation) of certain physical states enough to make those states *themselves* "conscious"? And more specifically, what is it that is so special about physical states of that certain sort, that consciousness of them makes them—but not just any old physical state—conscious? After all, we are conscious *of* (what are in fact) physical states of our stomachs; for that matter, through ordinary perception we are conscious of physical states of our skins, such as their being freckled, but no one would distinguish between "conscious" *stomachs* and "unconscious" stomachs, or between "conscious" and "unconscious" frecklednesses.

Indeed, why does the concept work that way (assuming it does work that way)? It may have something historically to do with the fact that until the 20th century the mental/psychological was simply identified with the conscious, and so only recently have we had to adopt a taxonomic distinction between states we are aware of holding and states we are not. (I am assuming that there is such a distinction in reality, and I believe—what is not uncontroversial—that the distinction in theory applies to any ordinary mental state, not counting states described as "being consciously aware of [such-and-such].")

What is it that is so special about physical states of that certain sort, that consciousness *of* them makes them "conscious"? That they are themselves mental. Stomachs and freckled patches of skin are not mental. It seems psychological states are called "conscious" states when we are conscious of them, but nonpsychological things are not.

Given the reality of the distinction between states we are aware of being in and states we are not aware of being in, the only remaining question is that of why the *word* "conscious" is thus dragged in as an adjective to mark it. My bet is that there is a grammatical answer. Maybe it is a transferred epithet: We begin with the adverbial form, as in "consciously thought" or "consciously felt," and when we make the verb into a noun the adverb automatically becomes an adjective—as in the move from "meditatively sipped" to "took a meditative sip." That is fairly plausible; at any rate it is the best I can do for now.

In any case, it is important to see that the question pertains to the notion of conscious awareness itself; it is not a problem for or objection to the Inner Sense theory of awareness in particular.

4. An initial flaw in the version stated so far is that it makes a Cartesian assumption recently highlighted by Dan Dennett:[14] that there is some determinate stage of information-processing that constitutes the locus of conscious mental states/events. More specifically, "Cartesian materialism" is the (usually tacit) assumption that there is a *physically realized* spatial or temporal turnstile in the brain, a stage where "it all comes together" and the product of pre-processing is exhibited "to consciousness."

Dennett attacks that assumption. However natural it may be, it is gratuitous and empirically implausible: First, it is a priori unlikely that Mother Nature has furnished the human brain with any central viewing-room or single monitor to do the viewing; nor is there any positive neurophysiological sign of such an organ. Second, Dennett argues at length that the famous "temporal anomalies" of consciousness discovered by psychophysical research, such as color phi, the cutaneous rabbit and Libet's "backward referral" of sensory experiences,[15] are anomalous only so long as Cartesian materialism is being assumed; jettison the assumption, and the phenomena are readily explained. Dennett's analyses of the experimental data are not completely uncontroversial,[16] but I find them convincing on the whole, and it is hard to think how anyone might defend Cartesian materialism on purely neurophysiological grounds.

The point is not just that there is no *immaterial audience* in the brain, nor just that there is no undischargeable homunculus, but that there is no such locus at all, however physically characterized—no single Boss Unit or even CPU within the brain, to serve as chief executive of my utterings and other actions. The central nervous system is as central as it gets. There is, if you like, a "stream of consciousness": "We are more-or-less serial virtual machines implemented—inefficiently—on the parallel hardware that evolution has provided for us," "Joycean" machines that formulate synthesized reports of our own passing states,[17] though the reports are never entirely accurate.

The Inner Sense theory has it that conscious awareness is the successful operation of an internal scanner or monitor that outputs second-order representations of first-order psychological states.[18] But an "internal scanner" sounds very much as though it presupposes an internal audience seated in a Cartesian Theater, even if it and the Theater are made of physical stuff. Is the Inner Sense view not then committed to Cartesian materialism?

It is not hard to come up with a pretty damning collection of direct quotations. Armstrong spoke (above) of "*the* portion of the computing space made available for administering the *overall plan.*" And (just to save you looking) I myself wrote of an internal scanner's "delivering information about...[a first-order] psychological state to one's *executive control unit.*"[19] For shame. There may be an "executive control unit" in some functional sense, but very probably not in the sense of being: that agency, arrival at which makes information conscious.

But it should be clear that the Inner Sense view is not *per se* committed to Cartesian materialism. For even if an internal scanner resembles an internal audience in some ways, the "audience" need not be seated in a Cartesian Theater: There need be no *single*, executive scanner, and no one scanner or monitor need view the entire array of first-order mental states accessible to consciousness. Accordingly, there need be neither a "turnstile of consciousness" nor one central inner stage on which the contents of consciousness are displayed in one fixed temporal order. An internal monitor is an attention mechanism, that presumably can be directed upon representational subsystems and stages of same; no doubt internal monitors work selectively and piecemeal, and their operations depend on control windows and other elements of conative context. On this point, the Inner Sense theory has already parted with Cartesian materialism.

A qualification: We should not throw out the integration-and-control baby with the Cartesian bathwater. The operation of an internal monitor does not *eo ipso* constitute consciousness. For we can imagine a creature that has a panoply of first-order states and a rich array of monitors scanning those states, but in such a way that the monitors' output contributes nothing at all to the creature's surrounding psychology, maintenance, or welfare; the outputs might just go unheard, or they might be received only by devices that do nothing but turn patches of the creature's skin different colors. For consciousness-constituting, we must require that monitor output contribute—specifically to the integration of information in a way conducive to making the system's behavior appropriate to its input and circumstances. Though the latter formulation is terribly vague, it will do for present purposes; the requirement rules out the ineffectual monitors without falling back into the idea of a Cartesian Theater or single CPU.

(This is a good juncture at which to underscore and deepen the teleological cast I am imparting to the Inner Sense theory. I said that for an internal monitor to count in the analysis of consciousness, in the present sense of 'conscious', the monitor must have monitoring as its function, or one of its functions. But that is not all. To count in the analysis of *my* consciousness, the monitor must do its monitoring *for me.* A monitor might have been implanted in me somewhere that sends its outputs straight to Reuters and to CNN, so that the whole world may learn of my first-order psychological states as soon as humanly possible. Such a device would be teleologically a monitor, but the wire services' monitor *rather than* mine. More importantly, a monitor functioning within one of my subor-dinate homunculi might be doing its distinctive job for that homunculus rather than for me; e.g., it might be serving the homunculus' event memory rather than my own proprietary event memory.[20] This distinction blocks what would otherwise be obvious counterexamples to the Inner Sense view as stated so far.)

Rejection of Cartesian materialism is not only compatible with the Lockean view. In an important way, it supports the Inner Sense theory: It predicts introspective fallibility of two characteristic sorts. First, as Dennett emphasizes, the result of an introspective probe is a *judgment* made by the subject, which judgment does not (or not eo ipso) simply report a "presentation" to an inner audience. And the "temporal anomalies" alone should have made us question the reliability of introspective reports. Introspection gets small temporal details wrong. That tends to confirm rather than to impugn the Inner Sense view of consciousness. If conscious awareness is indeed a matter of introspective attention and if introspection is the operation of a monitor or self-scanner, then such anomalies were to be expected—for monitors and scanners are characteristically fallible on details, and Dennett shows admirably how such devices might corporately mix up temporal sequence in particular.

Second, if there is no single Cartesian Theater, then there should be no single optimal time of probing a first-order process. More strongly, Dennett argues that probing "changes the task," i.e., interferes with the very process it purports to be monitoring. That too is good news for the Inner Sense theory. For if introspection is the operation of a monitor or self-scanner, then revisionary effects of the present sort are again just what we should have expected; monitoring instruments (such as ammeters) typically do affect the values of the magnitudes they measure.[21]

Thus the Inner Sense theory of consciousness survives the collapse of Cartesian materialism, and is even strengthened by it.

5. On at last to Rey's objection. It is that if all it takes to make a first-order state a conscious state is that the state be monitored by a scanner that makes integrative use of the information thus gleaned, then consciousness is a lot more prevalent than we think. Any notebook computer, for example, has devices that keep track of its "psychological" states. (If it be protested that no computer has genuinely psychological states—e.g., because it has neither authentic intentional states nor sensory states—that is inessential to the point. Once we had done whatever needs to be done in order to fashion a being that does have first-order intentional and sensory states, the addition of an internal monitor or two would be virtually an afterthought, a trifling wrinkle, surely not the sort of thing that could turn a simply nonconscious being into a conscious being.) For that matter, individual subsystems of our own human psychologies doubtless involve their own internal monitors, and it is implausible to grant that those subsystems are themselves conscious.

Several replies may be made to this. First, for consciousness we should require that our monitor emit a genuine representation, not just physical "information" in the Bell-Telephone sense or a simple nomological "indication" in the Wisconsin sense. But that is of little help, since surely our subsystems do contain monitors that output genuine representations.

Second, it should trouble no one that s/he has proper parts that are conscious. The proper part of you that consists of you minus your left arm is conscious, as is the part consisting of you minus your skin and most of your musculature. Other (individually) expendable chunks include: your entire gastrointestinal tract, your auditory system, much of your cortex, and possibly much of a hemisphere. Each of your respective complementary proper parts is conscious, even as we speak.

But (it may be said) the second reply is of little more help than the first. For each of the large proper parts I have mentioned would qualify, mentally speaking, as being *you*, if taken on its own. Its consciousness is your consciousness; at least, there is nothing present to its consciousness that is not also present to yours. But the sort of case that worries Rey is one in which self-monitoring is performed by a *silent*, subterranean subsystem, perhaps one of "all those unconscious neurotic systems postulated in so many of us by Freud, ...[or] all those surprisingly intelligent, but still unconscious, subsystems for perception and language postulated in us by contemporary cognitive psychology" (p. 11). What troubles Rey is that he or you or I should contain subsystems that are conscious on their own though we know nothing of them, and whose conscious contents are not at all like ours.

It does sound eerie. But I am not so sure that the individuation of consciousnesses is so straightforward a business. For one thing, that the contents of one consciousness coextend with those of mine hardly entails that the first consciousness *is* (=) mine; they still may be two. For another, the commissurotomy literature has raised well-known thorny questions about the counting of consciousnesses in the first place,[22] and it is abetted in that by thought-experiments such as Dan Dennett's in his classic "Where Am I?" and a more recent one by Stephen White.[23] My own preference is to doubt there to be any fact of the matter, as to how many consciousnesses live in a single human body (or as to how many bodies can be animated by the same consciousness).

A third reply to the argument: In his own essay on Rey's objection,[24] Stephen White enforces a distinction that Rey himself acknowledged but slighted: the difference between consciousness and *self*-consciousness. Rey had argued that if we already had a nonconscious perception-belief-desire machine, the addition of a "self" concept would be trifling (just as would be that of a simple internal monitor); one need only give the machine a first-person representation whose referent was the machine itself, i.e., add the functional analogue of the pronoun 'I' to the machines language-of-thought. But White argues on the basis of an ingenious group-organism example that the matter is hardly so simple, and that the difference between consciousness and self-consciousness is far larger and more important than Rey allowed. Surprisingly, having a functional inner 'I' does not suffice for being able to think of oneself as oneself; nor does mere consciousness as opposed to self-consciousness confer personhood or any moral status. And it turns out on White's analysis that although subsystems of ours might count as conscious, they would not be self-conscious in the way we are.

That difference helps to explain and assuage our reluctance to admit them to our own country club.[25] I find White's defense of these claims quite convincing.[26]

But I do not invest much in these second and third meditations as replies to Rey's objection. I have presented them mainly for the purpose of softening you up.

6. So I turn to my fourth and (*chez* me) most important reply. It is: emphatically to deny (what John Searle has recently asserted with unsurprising boldness[27]) that consciousness is an on-off affair, that a creature is either simply Conscious or simply not conscious. (If Searle did not exist I would have to invent him, for he actually puts it that way: "Consciousness is an on/off switch; a system is either conscious or not" (p. 83).) I maintain that consciousness comes in degrees, which one might describe as degrees of richness or fullness.[28] We human beings are very richly conscious, but there might be more complex and/or more sophisticated organisms that are more fully conscious than we. "Higher animals" are perhaps less fully so; "lower" animals still less, and so forth.

In saying this (you will have noticed), I am shifting my sense of 'conscious' slightly. For there is not obviously any great spectrum of degrees of: whether something has an internal monitor scanning some of its psychological states. (Actually there probably is a *significant* spectrum, based on the extent to which monitor output contributes to integration of information and to control; as was conceded at the time, I did leave the formulation vague. But I will not rest anything on this.) The paronymy works as follows. A thing is conscious, at all, if it is conscious to any degree at all, i.e., if it has at least one internal monitor operating and contributing etc. etc.; we might call this "bare" or "mere" consciousness. The thing may be *more richly or more fully* conscious if it has more monitors, monitors more, integrates more, integrates better, integrates more efficiently for control purposes, and/or whatever.

Actually I have not yet achieved paronymy, for I have located the degrees in the modifers ('richly' and 'fully') rather than in the basic term 'conscious' itself, which so far retains its original sense. But I do still mean to shift its meaning, for I want to allow at least a very vague sense in which some "barely" conscious devices are not really conscious; I take that one to be the ordinary sense of the word. But I would insist that that sense still affords a largeish spectrum of degrees. (Granted, this needs defense, and I shall provide some shortly.)

My principal answer to Rey is, then, to deny his intuition: So long as it contributes in the way aforementioned, one little monitor does make for a little bit of consciousness. More monitors and better integration and control make for fuller and fuller consciousness.[29]

Rey conjectures (p. 24), as a diagnosis of his own chauvinist intuitions about machines, that *if* consciousness is anything, it is like an "inner light" that is on in us but could be off in or missing from other creatures that were otherwise first-order-psychologically and functionally very like us; that is why he finds it so obvious that machines are not conscious even when they have been hypothetically given a perception-belief-desire system like ours. (Naturally given his conditional assumption, he asks why we should believe that *we* are not just very complicated perception-belief-desire machines, and offers the eliminative suggestion that we are therefore not conscious either; consciousness *is not* anything.[30]) But I see no reason to grant the conditional conjecture. I have no problem saying that a device whose internal monitor is contributing integration-and-control-wise is conscious of the states reported by the monitor. There is a rhetorical difference between saying that a device is conscious *of* such-and-such and saying that it, itself, is...conscious! But, I contend, that is *only* a rhetorical difference, barring my slight paronym above. What is special about us is not our being conscious *per se*, but that we monitor so much at any given time and achieve so high a degree of integration and control.

Thus two remarks made by psychologists and quoted by Rey as "astonishing" him by their naïveté do not astonish me in the slightest:

> Perceptions, memories, anticipatory organization, a combination of these factors into learning—all imply rudimentary consciousness. (Peter H. Knapp)[31]

Depending on what Knapp meant by "anticipatory organization," this is not far wrong. If anticipatory organization implies internal monitoring that contributes, or if the "combination of...[the] factors into learning" involves such monitoring, or both, I endorse the statement.

> Consciousness is a process in which information about multiple individual modalities of sensation and perception are combined into a unified, multi-dimensional representation of the state of the system and its environment and is integrated with information about memories and the needs of the organism, generating emotional reactions and programs of behavior to adjust the organism to its environment. (E. Roy John)[32]

No quarrel there either, assuming again that the "combining" is done in part by contributory monitoring.

The main *obstacle* to agreement with my matter-of-degree thesis is that we ourselves know only one sort of consciousness from the inside, and that one is particularly rich and full. We have elaborate and remarkably non-gappy visual models of our environment; we have our other four main sense modalities, which supplement the blooming, bursting phenomenological garden already furnished by vision; we have proprioception of various sorts that orient us within our surroundings; and (most importantly) we have almost complete freedom of attention within our private worlds, i.e., we can at will attend to virtually any representational aspect of any of our sensations that we choose. (All this creates the Cartesian illusion of a complete private world of sensation and thought, a seamless movie theater. There is no such completeness even phenomenologically, what with failings like the blind spot and the rapid decay of peripheral vision, but the illusion is dramatic.) Now, since this is the only sort of consciousness we have ever known from the inside, and since the only way to *imagine* a consciousness is to imagine it from the inside, we cannot imagine a consciousness very different at all from our own, much less a greatly impoverished one. What we succeed in imagining, if we try to get inside the mind of a spider or a notebook computer, is either an implausible cartoon (with anthropomorphic talk balloons) or something that hardly seems to us to deserve the title, "consciousness." It is a predicament: we are not well placed to receive the idea that there can be very low degrees of consciousness.[33]

7. But now, finally, for a bit of argument. (1) consider the total mental states of people who are very ill, or badly injured, or suffering the effects of this or that nefarious drug. Some such people are at some times called "semiconscious." Any number of altered states are possible, many of them severely diminished mental conditions. For some of these, surely, there will be no clear Searlean "Yes" or "no" to the question, "Is the patient conscious?," but only a "To a degree" or "Sort of." (2) We could imagine thousands of hypothetical artifacts, falling along a multidimensional spectrum having at its low end ordinary hardware-store items like record-changers and air conditioners and at its high end biologic human duplicates (indistinguishable from real living human beings save by their histories).[34] Along the way(s) will be robots of many different sorts, having wildly different combinations of abilities and stupidities, oddly skewed and weighted psychologies of all kinds. Which are "conscious"? How could one possibly draw a single line separating the whole seething profusion of creatures into just two groups?

(3) For that matter, the real world provides a similar argument (for those who favor the real world over science fiction); consider the phylogenetic scale. Nature actually contains a fairly smooth continuum of organisms, ranked roughly by complexity and degree of internal monitoring, integration and efficient control. Where on this continuum would God tell us that Consciousness begins? (Appropriately enough, Searle himself declares deep ignorance regarding consciousness and the phylogenetic scale.[35]) (4) If (3) does not move you (or even if (3) does), consider *human infants* as they develop from embryo to fetus to neonate to baby to child. When in that sequence does Consciousness begin?

I do not say that any of these arguments is overwhelming. But taken together—and together with recognition of the imaginative predicament I mentioned prior to offering them—I believe they create a presumption. At the very least, they open the door to my matter-of-degree view and make it a contender. Therefore, one cannot simply assume that consciousness (if any) is an on-off switch. And Rey's argument does assume that.

Thus I do not think Rey has refuted the Inner Sense view.[36]

Notes

1. Locke, *As Essay concerning Human Understanding*, ed. A.C. Fraser (New York:

Dover Publications, 1959), Book II, Ch. I, sec. 3, p. 123; Kant, *Critique of Pure Reason*, tr. Norman Kemp Smith (New York: St. Martin's Press, 1965), A23/B37, p. 67.

2. See my "What is 'The' Problem of Consciousness?," MS.

3. D.M. Armstrong, *A Materialist Theory of the Mind* (London: Routledge and Kegan Paul, 1968), and "What Is Consciousness?," in *The Nature of Mind and Other Essays* (Ithaca, NY: Cornell University Press, 1980). Baars, "Conscious Contents Provide the Nervous System with Coherent, Global Information," in R. Davidson, G.E. Schwartz and D. Shapiro (eds.), *Consciousness and Self-Regulation, Vol. 3* (New York: Plenum Press, 1983), pp.41-79; *A Cognitive Theory of Consciousness*. Lycan, *Consciousness* (Cambridge, MA: Bradford Books / MIT Press, 1987), Ch. 6.

4. "A Reason for Doubting the Existence of Consciousness," in Davidson, Schwartz and Shapiro, *op. cit.*, pp. 1-39.

In a sequel to the present paper, I shall also address criticisms made by Christopher Hill, David Rosenthal, Fred Dretske, and others.

5. "What is Consciousness?," *loc. cit.*, p. 61.

6. There is an potential ambiguity in Armstrong's term, "introspective consciousness": Assuming there are attention mechanisms of the sort I have in mind, they may function automatically, on their own, or they may be deliberately mobilized by their owners. Perhaps only in the latter case should we speak of introspec*ting*. On this usage, "introspective" consciousness may or may not be a result of introspecting. Armstrong himself makes a similar distinction between "reflex" introspective awareness and "introspection proper," adding the suggestion that "the latter will normally involve not only introspective awareness of mental states but also introspective awareness of that introspective awareness" ("What is Consciousness?," *loc. cit.*, p. 63).

7. "What is Consciousness?," loc. cit., pp. 65-66. Robert Van Gulick has also written illuminatingly on the uses of consciousness, though he does not focus so specifically on introspection; see particularly "What Difference Does Consciousness Make?,". *Philosophical Topics* 17 (1989): 211-30.

8. I began this project with respect to subjectivity and qualia respectively in Chs. 7 and 8 of *Consciousness, loc. cit.* Parts of it have also been pursued by Gilbert Harman ("The Intrinsic Quality of Experience," in J.E. Tomberlin (ed.), *Philosophical Perspectives, 4, Action Theory and Philosophy of Mind, 1990* (Atascadero, CA: Ridgeview Publishing, 1990)), Michael Tye ("Qualia, Content, and the Inverted Spectrum," *Noûs*, forthcoming (1994)), and Sydney Shoemaker ("Phenomenal Character," *Noûs*, forthcoming (1994)).

9. In *Consciousness, loc. cit.*; see also my "Functionalism and Recent Spectrum Inversions," unpublished MS, and "True Colors," in preparation.

10. When I made this point emphatically after a presentation of this material at the NEH Summer Institute on "The Nature of Meaning" (Rutgers University, July, 1993), Bill Ramsey responded much as follows: "I see; once you've got the explanandum whittled all the way down, as specific and narrow as you want it, the big news you're bringing us is that what *internal monitoring* really is, at bottom, is...internal monitoring!" That characterization is not *far* wrong. Though the Inner Sense doctrine is not tautologous and faces some objections, I think it is very plausible, once it has been relieved of the extraneous theoretical burden of resolving issues that

are not directly related to the "conscious"/"nonconscious" distinction *per se*.

Incidentally, I do not offhand know of any Inner Sense proponent who does claim that the theory resolves qualia problems. Yet there is a tendency among its critics to criticize it from that quarter; I conjecture that such critics are themselves confusing issues of awareness with issues of qualitative character.

11. Rey, "Sensations in a Language of Thought," in E. Villanueva (ed.), *Consciousness* (*Philosophical Issues, 1, 1991)* (Atascadero, CA: Ridgeview Publishing, 1991), and "Sensational Sentences," in M Davies and G. Humphreys (eds.), *Consciousness* (Oxford: Basil Blackwell, 1992); Lycan, "What is the 'Subjectivity' of the Mental?," in J.E. Tomberlin, *op. cit.*

12. From a current trash novel: "Each step was painful, but the pain was not felt. He moved at a controlled jog down the escalators and out of the building." (John Grisham, *The Firm* (New York: Island Books, Dell Publishing, 1991), p. 443.

    David Rosenthal offers a nice defense of unfelt pain, in "The Independence of Consciousness and Sensory Quality," in Villanueva, *op. cit.* See also David Palmer's "Unfelt Pains," *American Philosophical Quarterly* 12 (1975): 289-98.

13. In "Conscious Experience" (*Mind* 102 (1993): 263-83), he has also made a couple of substantive objections to Inner Sense theory. I shall address those in the sequel to this paper.

14. *Consciousness Explained* (Boston, MA: Little, Brown & Co., 1991); D.C. Dennett and M. Kinsbourne, "Time and the Observer: The Where and When of Consciousness in the Brain," *Behavioral and Brain Sciences* 15 (1992): 183-201.

15. P. Kolers and M. von Grünau, "Shape and Color in Apparent Motion," *Vision Research* 16 (1976): 329-35; F.A. Geldard and C.E. Sherrick, "The Cutaneous 'Rabbit': A Perceptual Illusion," *Science* 178 (1972): 178-79; B. Libet, "Cortical Activation in Conscious and Unconscious Experience," *Perspectives in Biology and Medicine* 9: 77-86.

16. E.g., B.J. Baars and M. Fehling, "Consciousness is Associated with Central As Well As Distributed Processes," *Behavioral and Brain Sciences* 15 (1992): 203-04, and B. Libet, "Models of Conscious Timing and the Experimental Evidence," *ibid.*: 213-15. Dennett and Kinsbourne reply to their critics in "Authors' Response," *ibid.*: 234-43.

17. *Consciousness Explained, loc. cit.*, pp. 218, 225.

18. For convenience, I shall continue to speak of the states that get monitored as "first-order" states, but this is inaccurate, for introspective states can themselves be scanned. This will be important later on.

19. *Consciousness, loc. cit.*, p. 72.

20. On such distinctions, and for more illuminating examples, see Chs. 3 and 4 of *Consciousness, loc. cit.*

21. One might be tempted to infer (something highly congenial to Dennett himself) that introspection is *woefully* fallible, unreliable to the point of uselessness. But that inference would be unjustified. Though the "temporal anomalies" alone should have made us question the reliability of introspective reports, notice that the scope of unreliability exhibited by the anomalies is very small, tied to temporal differences within the tiny intervals involved, a small fraction of a second in each case.

22. For a survey and discussion, see C. Marks, *Commissurotomy, Consciousness and the Unity of Mind* (Montgomery, VT: Bradford Books, 1979).

23. Dennett, "Where Am I?," in *Brainstorms* (Montgomery, VT: Bradford Books, 1978),

reprinted in D.R. Hofstadter and D.C. Dennett (eds.), *The Mind's I: Fantasies and Reflections of Self and Soul* (New York: Basic Books, 1981); see also D.H. Sanford, "Where Was I?," in Hofstadter and Dennett, *op. cit.* White, "What Is It Like to Be a Homunculus?" *Pacific Philosophical Quarterly* 68 (1987): 148-74.

24. "What Is It Like to Be a Homunculus?," *loc. cit.*

25. Moreover, as he observes (p. 168), we have no access to unproblematic examples of consciousness in the absence of self-consciousness, and that fact contributes to an important predicament that I shall expound below.

26. In like wise, he maintains, no notebook computer is self-conscious even if some are conscious in a less demanding functional sense. (I believe White would accept my claim that mere consciousness is more prevalent than philosophers think; see p. 169.) But I do not see that his analysis of self-consciousness generates that result, since his main concern was to argue only that self-consciousness is restricted to the highest level of organization in a *group organism*, which result does not help deny self-consciousness to whole computers. (White has explained in conversation that his analysis alone was not intended to do that; he has other means.)

27. *The Rediscovery of the Mind* (Cambridge, MA: MIT Press, 1992).

28. I have defended this thesis before, in "Abortion and the Civil Rights of Machines," in N. Potter and M. Timmons (eds.), *Morality and Universality* (Dordrecht: D. Reidel, 1985), pp. 144-145.

    It should be noted that Searle himself goes on (*ibid.*) to qualify his "on/off" claim: "But once conscious, the system is a rheostat: there are different degrees of consciousness"; he speaks of levels of intensity and vividness. Thus, it seems, our real disagreement is over, not degrees *per se*, but the question of whether a creature or device could have a much lower degree of consciousness than is ordinarily enjoyed by human beings and still qualify as being conscious at all.

29. I should emphasize again that a monitor makes for consciousness when what it monitors is itself a psychological state or event. My suggestion that notebook computers are after all conscious is conditional upon the highly controversial assumption that such computers have psychological states such as beliefs and desires in the first place.

30. By way of further diagnosis (p. 25), Rey offers the additional conjecture that our moral concern for our living, breathing conspecifics drives us to posit some solid metaphysical difference between ourselves and mere artifacts, as a ground of that concern. He opines that we need no such ground in order to care more for human beings than for functionally similar machines, but he does not say what he thinks *would* ground that difference in care.

31. "The Mysterious 'Split': A Clinical Inquiry into Problems of Consciousness and Brain," in G. Globus, G. Maxwell and I Savodnik (eds.), *Consciousness and the Brain* (New York: Plenum Press, 1976), pp. 37-69.

32. "A Model of Consciousness," in G.E. Schwartz and D. Shapiro (eds.), *Consciousness and Self-Regulation*, Vol. 1 (New York: Plenum Press, 1976), p. 1-50.

33. Samuel Butler said, "Even the potato, rotting in its dank cellar, has a certain low cunning." But I grant the potato has no internal monitors.

34. This is the one argument I gave in "Abortion and the Civil Rights of Machines," loc. cit.

35. "I have no idea whether fleas, grasshoppers, crabs, or snails are conscious" (p. 74). He suggests that neurophysiologists might find out, by a method of apparent-

consciousness-debunking, viz., looking for evidence of "mechanical-like tropism to account for apparently goal-directed behavior in organisms that lacked consciousness" (p. 75); he pooh-poohs "mechanical-like" functional processing as being in no way mental or psychological. On this, see D.C. Dennett's review of *The Rediscovery of the Mind, Journal of Philosophy* 90 (1993): 193-205.

36. This essay was presented as the Third *Philosophical Perspectives* Lecture at California State University, Northridge, in the fall of 1994. I am grateful to James Tomberlin and his colleagues for that invigorating occasion. I am grateful to Joe Levine, Ned Block and Georges Rey for extensive comments and discussion.

Philosophical Perspectives, 9, AI, Connectionism, and
Philosophical Psychology, 1995

PRACTICAL REASONING IN OSCAR

John L. Pollock
University of Arizona

1. Practical Cognition

It has long been my conviction that many of the problems encountered in artificial intelligence research are basically philosophical problems. In particular, in order to build an artificial rational agent, one must first have a clear theory of rationality to serve as a target for implementation. Accordingly, the OSCAR project is aimed at providing such a theory and building an AI system to implement it. In its present incarnation, OSCAR is a programmable architecture for a rational agent, based upon a general-purpose defeasible reasoner. To use this architecture to construct an actual agent, one must fill it out in various ways. This can be regarded as a matter of programming the architecture to implement proposed principles of rationality. For those who are skeptical about the very possibility of interesting AI systems, it is to be emphasized that this system is fully implemented, and available from the author for use by other researchers.

I will begin by giving a very brief sketch of the general architecture, and then I will turn to some questions about practical reasoning that will constitute the main focus of this paper. These are questions that must be answered before OSCAR can become a full-fledged rational agent.

On the conception of rationality embodied in OSCAR (discussed further in my [1993] and [1995]), a rational agent can be regarded as having four basic constituents:

- One or more mechanisms for proposing goals.
- A mechanism for evaluating the "goodness" of plans.
- A mechanism for searching for and adopting plans on the basis of their comparative evaluations by the plan evaluator.
- A mechanism for initiating action on the basis of adopted plans (together, possibly, with built-in or learned plan-schemas).

These mechanisms constitute a system of practical cognition. On any theory of rationality, plan evaluation and adoption will be based in part on what beliefs the agent has about its situation. Accordingly, an important part of a rational agent is a system of epistemic cognition producing such beliefs. As will be seen below, in OSCAR, the bulk of the work involved in finding, evaluating, and choosing plans and directing action is done by epistemic cognition rather than by dedicated special-purpose modules devoted to practical cognition.

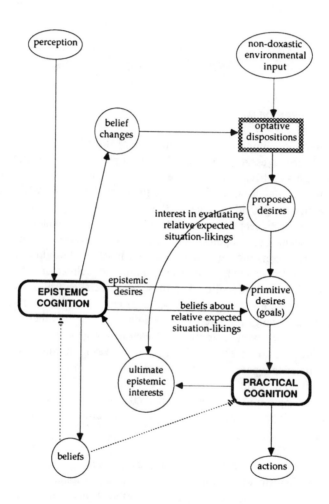

Figure 1. The flow of data in practical cognition

The OSCAR architecture begins with a *situation-evaluator*, which produces a (real-measurable) degree of liking for the agent's current situation. This is presumed to be sensitive to the agent's beliefs about its situation. The *likeability* of a situation is the degree the agent would like it if it had true beliefs about all relevant aspects of the situation. The objective of the agent's reasoning is to put itself in situations that are more likeable than the situations in which it would find itself if it did not take action.

Ideally, plans are evaluated in terms of the *expected likeability* of their being adopted. This is just the mathematical expectation of the likeability of the situation-type consisting of their being adopted. Reasoning about expected likeabilities involves both reasoning about likeabilities and reasoning about probabilities. Such reasoning is computationally difficult, so the OSCAR architecture allows the use of shortcut procedures for producing approximate evaluations of plans. Such shortcut procedures are called *Q&I modules* ("quick and inflexible"). Q&I modules occur throughout rational cognition (in humans, as well as in OSCAR). A mark of rationality, however, is that when the output of Q&I modules conflicts with the output of explicit reasoning, the agent overrides the Q&I modules and adopts the conclusion of the reasoning.

Goals are judged suitable or unsuitable on the basis of their expected likeability. The function of goals is to direct the course of planning. The use of goals and standard techniques of goal reduction constitutes a control mechanism for planning. Without goals, the agent would have to survey plans at random. The chances of finding good plans in that way are minuscule. With the help of goals, planning is constrained, and because suitable goals have high expected likeability, there is a (defeasible) presumption that plans having a high likelihood of achieving suitable goals will also have high expected likeabilities. This provides a defeasible basis for adopting plans without going through the onerous process of computing their expected likeabilities.

Shortcut procedures for the choice of goals are indispensable in any realistic agent, because the agent must be able to live in the world before it acquires the general knowledge that is required for evaluating the suitability of goals. These take the form of Q&I modules called *optative dispositions*, which are dispositions to adopt goals. Some optative dispositions may be built into a rational agent from the beginning, and others can be acquired by conditioning mechanisms. In human beings, such dispositions produce desires. Desiring something constitutes a defeasible ground for choosing it as a goal, but in an ideally rational agent, the belief that the object of desire does not have satisfactorily high expected likeability should override the desire.

The system of epistemic cognition embodied in OSCAR is based upon an "interest-driven" defeasible reasoner. This means, in part, that epistemic cognition is driven by practical cognition. Practical cognition poses queries that are passed to epistemic cognition. These queries constitute the list of ultimate-epistemic-interests. When new queries are inserted into the list of ultimate-epistemic-interests epistemic cognition sets about trying to answer them. For example, when a new goal is adopted, practical cognition will query epistemic cognition about how to achieve that goal, and when epistemic cognition produces a plan for achieving it along with beliefs about the expected value of that plan, these beliefs are sent back to practical cognition, which decides whether to adopt and execute the plan.

I will not say more here about the system of epistemic cognition embodied in OSCAR.[1] For present purposes, all that is important is that the process of actually constructing plans for the achievement of goals is a process carried out by epistemic cognition. It is a complicated task, as is witnessed by the massive literature of AI planning theory. The topic of the present paper is the system of practical cognition that drives this epistemic cognition and uses its output. The combined system has the structure diagramed in figure 1.

2. Decision-Theoretic Planning

In philosophy, decision theory has focused on choosing between acts rather than plans, but I have recently argued [1992] that that is an inadequate approach to practical reasoning. Instead, we must choose between competing plans —complex programs for action—in terms of their expected values, and then choose acts on the basis of the plans prescribing them. I defended this claim by presenting intuitive counterexamples to the alternative approach in terms of acts rather than plans. Without trying to give a full defense of this view, let me illustrate its motivation with a simple example. Suppose we are faced with the simple maze diagramed in figure 2. There are two doors into the maze, and four paths through the maze. The top two paths begin at door A and lead to payoffs of 20 utiles and 0 utiles, respectively. The bottom two paths begin at door B, and lead to payoffs of 12 utiles and 10 utiles, respectively. Which door should we enter? Clearly, we should enter door A and traverse the upper path. Now let us apply the decision-theoretic model. We must compare the expected utility of entering door A with the expected utility of entering door B. But what are these expected utilities? The payoff resulting from entering door A depends upon which plan we adopt for traversing the maze after entering door A. If we take the upper path we will receive 20 utiles, and if we take the second path we will receive 0 utiles. So our choice of a plan determines the payoff. In computing the expected utility of entering door A, we can either assume that we will take the upper path, or assume ignorance of which path we will take. If we assume ignorance, then it seems we should assign a probability of .5 to taking either path, and hence the expected utility of entering door A is 10 utiles and the expected utility of entering door B is 11 utiles. On this calculation, the decision-theoretic model prescribes entering door B, *but that is the wrong answer*! If we instead assume that if we enter door A we will take the upper path, and similarly if we enter door B, then we can compute the expected utilities to be 20 utiles and 12 utiles, respectively, and we get the correct prescription that we should enter door A. However, this assumes that we have some way of knowing that we will choose the upper path if we enter door *A*. This is typically something we do know about ourselves, but we are not entitled to use it here in computing the expected utility of entering door *A* because that would be circular. We only believe that we will traverse the upper path because we believe that is the rational thing to do. If we did not believe the latter then we would not normally believe that we will traverse the upper path. But the object of the exercise is to determine the rational thing to do, so we cannot just assume the solution to the decision problem in the course of computing the probabilities and utilities used in solving the problem.

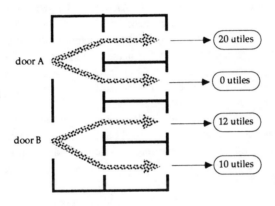

Figure 2. A simple maze

The upshot of this is that the decision-theoretic calculation yields the right answer only if we have some way of choosing between different plans for traversing the maze prior to computing the expected utilities. If we have a way of choosing between different maze-traversal plans, then we can simply choose the best plan overall (not just the best plan that has us entering door *A* and the best plan that has us entering door *B*) and enter the door that plan prescribes. That is the solution to the decision problem. So to recapitulate, if we compute the expected utilities of entering the doors without first choosing which maze-traversal plan to adopt if we enter a given door, then the decision-theoretic model gives the wrong answer. But if we have a way of choosing between maze-traversal plans then there is no need to compute the expected utilities, because we should simply choose the best plan and execute it, and that will determine which door we enter.

There are complicated ways of trying to circumvent this counterexample, and they are discussed at length in my [1992]. Rather than repeat that discussion, I am going to assume here that practical reasoning must proceed in terms of plans rather than individual acts. This enterprise proceeds by applying the machinery of standard decision theory to plans rather than acts, and is accordingly called "decision-theoretic planning" in AI. It is tempting to suppose that we can choose between competing plans by simply picking the plan with the higher expected value, and this has been the standard presumption in AI planning theory. But because plans are structured objects that can embed other plans within themselves, this turns out to be inadequate, as I will now demonstrate.

Consider a planning agent embedded in a realistic world in which both its goals and its knowledge change over time. What this rules out is the kind of toy planning problems often encountered in AI, where the planner has a small fixed set of goals and a fixed knowledge base and is able to plan once for all those goals simultaneously and then stop. As a real agent acquires more knowledge about its situation, it will typically form new goals, and possibly reject earlier goals. New goals may also be produced by internal considerations. For example, human beings get hungry, and batteries run down in robots. Internal sensors may then produce new goals in an automatic fashion.

Such a realistic planning agent exhibits two important characteristics. First, it is never finished planning. As new goals and knowledge arise, new planning will be required, and old plans may have to be revised or withdrawn. This is a continual, ongoing process. Some plans will be acted upon while others are still in the process of formation. The second characteristic is a corollary of the first. This is that the planning agent cannot confine its planning activities to global planning. It cannot be viewed as constructing one big global plan for a fixed set of goals. Instead, it must construct local plans for limited goals, adopting such plans provisionally, and then when conflicts are discovered between provisionally adopted plans, try to fix the conflicts by patching or replacing some of the plans. There are two separate reasons why the planner must engage in such local planning: (1) A real agent acquires a huge number of goals over an extended period of time, and planning for all of them simultaneously is too hard. (2) Having to plan for all of one's goals simultaneously would require continual replanning as goals change. Goals change much more rapidly than global replanning could occur, so the agent might never actually come up with any plans.

The upshot of this is that realistic planning must consist of (1) the provisional adoption of local plans, and (2) patching the set of adopted plans when conflicts are discovered. Now let us look at the application of decision-theoretic-planning to local plans.

The point of choosing plans is to direct activity. In a given situation, the considerations that make it reasonable to choose a plan must also make it reasonable to act upon it. An agent engaged in decision-theoretic-planning will (1) search for plans, (2) choose between competing plans that have been discovered, and (3) direct activity on the basis of the plans thus adopted. It must be emphasized that if it is reasonable to choose a plan, it must be reasonable to act upon it. This simple observation has the consequence that, given two competing plans, it is not automatically reasonable to choose the plan with the higher expected value. This is because a single plan may aim to satisfy several different goals. The conflict may arise from small parts of the plans, and the plan having the higher expected value may get most of that value from other parts of the plan that do not conflict with its competitor. For instance, plan A might be the plan to run two errands on a single trip. The first errand consists of buying paint at a certain store, and the second errand consists of going to the grocery store. Plan B is the plan to buy paint at a different store, located just as conveniently close to the grocery store, but plan B does not include going to the grocery store. Let us suppose that buying paint from the second store would, by itself, be preferable to buying paint from the first store. Nevertheless, plan A may have a higher expected value than plan B just because it also acquires value as a result of the agent's going to the grocery store. Obviously, this would not be a reasonable basis for adopting plan A. Instead, the agent should construct a third plan C out of the parts of plans A and B. C consists of buying the paint at the second store and then going to the grocery store. This plan is preferable to either of A or B. Accordingly, an agent that has uncovered plans A and B should not choose A on the grounds that it has a higher expected value. Instead, the agent should consider the structural relationship between A and B and use that to propound and choose C. Note that this is exactly what a human being would do.

It is important to realize that in a situation like the above, A's having a higher expected value than B does not even give us a defeasible reason for choosing A. It cannot be presumed, without examination, that A's higher expected value is not simply a result of its being a more comprehensive plan, aimed at achieving more goals. No rational choice can be made without examining the structural relationships between the competing plans.

These problems would not arise in a planner that only had to choose between global plans. But that is not an option that is available to a realistic planning agent. Local plans must be constructed and adopted provisionally. By its very nature, local planning can produce plans that vary in comprehensiveness. One local plan may aim at some very specific goal, while another (like the plan of running several errands at once) may aim to achieve several goals. The search for such "composite plans" will be an important part of decision-theoretic-planning. But plans of varying comprehensiveness cannot be compared directly by looking at their expected values. That could be a matter of comparing apples and oranges.

A criterion of choice that accommodates the above considerations can be constructed as follows:

A plan σ *is rationally preferable to* a plan η iff there is a (possibly null) subplan μ of η and a composite $\sigma+\mu$ of σ and μ such that for every subplan ν of σ and a composite $\eta+\nu$ of η and ν, $\sigma+\mu$ is superior to $\eta+\nu$.

I call this "the coextendability criterion". The relationship between the plans referenced in this criterion is diagramed in figure 3. I propose that this criterion should be applied more or less directly by a decision-theoretic planner in choosing between competing plans. The criterion looks complicated, but the message is the fairly simple one that a planning agent cannot compare competing plans blindly by just looking at their expected values. Competing plans will typically vary in comprehensiveness, in which case a comparison of expected value tells us literally nothing. A planner must engage in a more complicated comparison that involves looking at the structures of the competing plans and seeking the best plan that can be constructed out of their subplans. This is a complex process, but no simpler comparison can carry any rational weight in the process of the agent's deciding what actions to take.

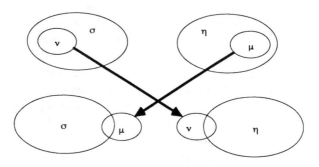

Figure 3. Coextendability.

3. Planning

Having seen how plans are to be compared, what is the process by which a rational agent produces plans and uses this criterion for choosing between them? A rational agent begins with primitive desires produced by epistemic cognition and optative dispositions, and then deliberates about how to satisfy those desires. The agent adopts plans on the basis of that deliberation. We can distinguish two central tasks within practical reasoning: (1) constructing and adopting plans; (2) directing activity *given* our desires and plans. We can think of (1) as being performed by a functional module called *the PLANNER*, and (2) by a functional module called *the PLAN-EXECUTOR*.

Let us begin by looking at the PLANNER. We can usefully distinguish between three levels of planning. We plan for *how to satisfy* a primitive desire, we plan for *how to perform* the operations prescribed by other plans, and for *when to perform* them. I will refer to the first of these three kinds of plans as *top-level plans*, and the others as *subsidiary plans*. Planning for how to do something is *teleological planning*. This consists of means-end reasoning and general problem solving. Planning for when to do something is *scheduling*. Teleological planning and scheduling proceed in importantly different ways. When a teleological subsidiary plan is adopted, it is not integrated into the original plan. It is a separate plan that is called by the original plan. The original plan remains intact. But scheduling proceeds by modifying the original plan, adding timing instructions. The initial planning that transpires in response to the acquisition of primitive desires is top-level teleological planning. Such planning tends to be highly schematic. To focus on a concrete example, suppose I form the desire for my garage to look better. In response to that desire, I may adopt the top-level plan to paint it. Notice just how schematic this plan is. It contains no specification at all of how I will go about painting it or when I will do it. Having adopted this simple top-level plan, I must plan further. The adoption of this plan must somehow initiate subsidiary planning for how to paint the garage. The resulting subsidiary plan might take the following form:

1. Buy the paint.
2. Make sure the ladder is in good condition.
3. When the weather is good, paint each wall of the garage.

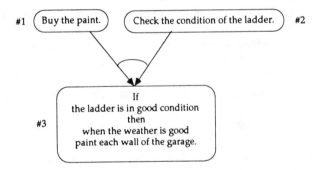

Figure 4. Graphical representation of a plan.

The structure of this plan can be represented more accurately by the graph diagramed in figure 4. Consider each plan-node. Node 1 is going to require further subsidiary planning. I must plan how to buy the paint, i.e., what kind of paint, what color, at what store I should buy it, how I will pay for it, etc. Node 2 illustrates something that is of considerable importance. Although checking the condition of the ladder is a rather complicated procedure, I need not plan for how to do it. This is because I "know how to do it". Such knowledge consists of a stored plan schema that I am able to retrieve and act upon whenever I want to check the condition of a ladder. I will call such stored plan schemas *standing plans*. Node 3 is somewhat similar, because again, I know how to paint the wall of a garage.

Having constructed this subsidiary plan for how to paint my garage, and perhaps a further subsidiary plan for node 1, I am still not ready to paint my garage. That is because nothing in this plan tells me when to do anything. Node 3 does contain a timing-condition, but it is a very indefinite one. As it stands, I can execute this plan at any future time as long as the weather is good when I do the actual painting. This plan cries out for scheduling. I must decide when to buy the paint, when to check the ladder, and when to do the actual painting. This requires further subsidiary planning. It must eventually be determined *exactly* when operations are to be performed, but my initial scheduling may be much more indefinite than that. For example, I may decide to buy the paint tomorrow. That leaves undetermined just when tomorrow I will do it. When tomorrow rolls around, I must do some more specific scheduling. At that point I may decide to buy the paint in the afternoon. But that is still pretty indefinite. As the day progresses and I get a better picture of what I must do during the day, I will be in a position to decide more precisely just when I will buy the paint. Knowing that I am going to the grocery store after lunch, I may decide to pick up the paint on my way to the grocery store. Notice that I may also wait until making this decision to decide just where to buy the paint. Because I am going to buy it while on my way to the grocery store, it may be more convenient to buy it at one paint store (*The Flaming Rainbow*) rather than another, and so I choose my paint store on that basis.

Let me summarize my conclusions so far. First, our top-level plans tend to be very schematic. Adopting a schematic plan must lead to the initiation of further subsidiary planning.[2] Second, our teleological planning typically leaves the scheduling of nodes quite indefinite. At some point, further scheduling must occur. Third, some aspects of teleological planning may depend upon decisions regarding scheduling, so scheduling and teleological planning must be interleaved.

The PLANNER can be viewed as having three components. There must be a component that initiates planning when new primitive desires are acquired; there must be a component that actually does the planning, constructing new plans that thereby become candidates for adoption; and there must be a component that determines whether to adopt a candidate plan. These are *the PLANNING-INITIATOR, the PLAN-SYNTHESIZER,* and *the PLAN-UPDATER*, respectively. As I conceive it, the PLANNING-INITIATOR responds to the acquisition of new desires. It is the trigger that begins the process of planning. As such, it can initiate the operation of the PLAN-SYNTHESIZER. The PLAN-SYNTHESIZER produces new plans that are put in a database of **candidate-plans**. The PLAN-SYNTHESIZER is responsible for both teleological planning and scheduling. The PLAN-UPDATER is responsible for all changes in what plans are adopted. Such a change can consist of either the adoption of a new candidate plan or the withdrawal of a previously adopted plan. This somewhat more detailed understanding of the PLANNER allows us to diagram it as in figure 5.

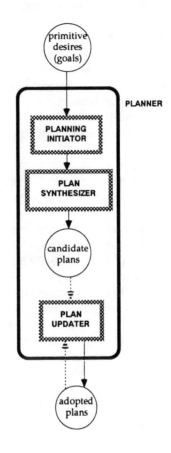

Figure 5. The architecture of the PLANNER

4. The PLAN-UPDATER

From a philosophical point of view, the most interesting problems arising out of this picture concern the PLAN-UPDATER, which is responsible for the adoption and retraction of plans. What are the criteria that should be employed by the PLAN-UPDATER in deciding what plans to adopt? At this point it is useful to distinguish between a theory of *reasoning* and a theory of *warrant*. A theory of reasoning tells us how a rational agent should proceed in drawing conclusions at any given point. Reasoning is *defeasible* in the sense that it can lead to the adoption of a conclusion at one time and then mandate its retraction later, either as a result of additional reasoning, or as a result of the acquisition of new information. If a rational agent has reasoned correctly up to the present time, then in one sense of "justified" its conclusions are justified. As a result of further reasoning, and without any new input, some of those conclusions may become unjustified, and may subsequently become justified again, and so on. *Warranted conclusions* are conclusions that would be justified "in the long run". More precisely, a potential conclusion is *warranted* iff, if reasoning could proceed without limit, a point would be reached where the conclusion would become justified and would never subsequently become unjustified just as a result of further reasoning.

Warrant is an ideal notion. It is, in a certain sense, the target at which a reasoner aims. A theory of practical warrant can reasonably appeal to all possible plans:

> The decision to adopt a plan σ is practically warranted iff there is no (logically constructible) plan that is rationally preferable to σ.

As a theory of warrant, this may be reasonable, but as a theory of practical *reasoning*, it would be preposterous. We cannot require a rational agent to survey all possible plans before deciding what to do. In practical deliberation, epistemic reasoning will produce candidate plans to be considered for adoption, and then a theory of practical reasoning should tell us what conclusions to draw on the basis of the consideration of a limited (usually very small) set of candidate plans. Given that we have tried to construct relevant plans in a reasonable way and have reached justified conclusions about their expected values, how can we make a justified decision about what acts to perform? As a first approximation we might try the following:

> The decision to adopt a plan σ is practically justified iff a rationally satisfactory search for plans has been conducted and it led to the discovery of no plan that we are justified in believing to be rationally preferable to σ.

The main problem with this initial formulation turns upon the fact that we can have two competing plans neither of which is preferable to the other. In such a case, let us say that the two plans are *tied.* Following Bratman [1987], I call such cases "Buridan cases".

To make progress with Buridan cases, we must first understand what it is for plans to compete. Competing plans are plans that in some sense conflict, so that the agent cannot reasonably adopt them both. Standard decision-theory takes the notion of competing alternatives as primitive and unanalyzed, but we must do better if we are to incorporate it into the design of a rational agent. Under what circumstances must the agent choose between plans? It is initially tempting to suppose that plans compete iff it is impossible for both plans to be successfully executed. But this is much too strong a notion of competition. Plans can "interfere" with each other without rendering one another impossible. For example, executing one plan may make it more difficult to execute another. This can happen because the agent becomes tired, consumes resources, is left further from some important location, etc. Executing one plan may also affect the expected values of other plans by changing the values of the goals at which they aim. For example, drinking orange juice becomes less desirable after eating a dill pickle. All of these considerations can make it desirable to choose between two plans rather than executing both. A first attempt at capturing this notion of competition is as follows:

Two plans *A* and *B* *compete strictly* iff every composite of *A* and *B* has a lower expected value than the maximum of the expected values of *A* and *B* alone.

This analysis proceeds in terms of the notion of *composites* of two plans, which I assume to make sense, but its precise definition will turn on the kinds of plans envisioned. I will also help myself to the notion of one plan being a *subplan* of (contained in) another.

The idea behind strict competition is that plans compete just in case it would be better to execute one rather than both. Strict competition would be a satisfactory criterion for competition if we had only global plans to compare, but for rather subtle reasons, it fails for local plans. The difficulty is that if *A* and *B* are multi-step plans, then even though there is a composite *A+B* having a higher expected value than either *A* or *B*, we may still not want to execute both *A* and *B*. This is because there may be a third plan *C* such that (1) *A* is a subplan of *C*, (2) *C* is a subplan of *A+B*, and (3) *C* has a higher expected value than any of *A*, *B*, or *A+B*. For instance, consider a human agent that finds itself in the embarrassing position of having social commitments to have dinner at two different places (and times) the same evening. Plan *A* is the plan to eat a normal dinner at Jones' house, and plan *B* is the plan to eat a normal dinner at Smith's house. The situation may be such that it would be better to do both rather than just one, despite the predictable intestinal discomfort. Thus the two plans do not compete strictly. But perhaps a better alternative is to attend both dinner parties, eating a normal meal at Jones' house, but then eating only desert at Smith's house. This is a plan *C* that is constructed out of plan *A* and just part of plan *B*. The availability of this plan makes it preferable not to adopt *A+B*. On the other hand, because *A* is a subplan of *C*, executing *C* involves executing *A*. So it seems reasonable to say that there is a conflict between *A* and *B*, and that *A* should be chosen (as part of *C*).

This notion of competition can be made precise as follows:

A and *B* *compete* iff there is a composite *A+B* of *A* and *B* and a subplan *C* of *A+B* such that (1) either *A* or *B* is a subplan of *C*, (2) the expected value of *C* is greater than that of either *A* or *B*, and (3) the expected value of *C* is greater than the expected value of every composite of *A* and *B*.

It can be proven that if one plan is rationally preferable to another, in the sense of the coextendability criterion adumbrated above, then they compete in the present sense (see my [1992]). Note that for global plans, this concept of competition reduces to strict competition, because global plans cannot be subplans of one another.

Now let us return to Buridan cases. Buridan cases are cases in which competing plans are tied. The basic observation about Buridan cases is that in deciding what actions to perform, a rational agent chooses at random between the tied plans. However, this is only a remark about the actions performed as a result of the planning, and not directly a remark about the planning process. At some point a random choice must be made, but that could be either (1) a random choice between competing plans, resulting in one of the tied plans being adopted at random, or (2) a random choice between the actions dictated by the tied plans, without either of the tied plans ever being adopted in its own right. This is really a question about the control structure of the rational agent. At what point in the architecture is the random choice made? The simplest suggestion would be that a random choice between plans is made immediately upon producing the competing plans. However, it takes little reflection to see that, in human beings, things are more complicated than that. Returning to the example of painting my garage, a decision had to be made about where to buy the paint. Suppose there were two paint stores between which I could not initially decide. Eventually, I decided on *The Flaming Rainbow*, because it was on my route to the grocery store. That made the plan to buy the paint there preferable to the plan to buy it at the other store. But what happened prior to my deciding to go to the grocery store? I did not initially decide at random to buy the paint at one of the stores, and then later change my mind because I had a better reason to buy it at the other store. What I did was decide to *either* buy the paint at *The Flaming Rainbow* or buy it at *The Chartreuse Flamingo*, but I did not at that point decide arbitrarily to adopt one plan rather than the other. Instead, I stored the set consisting of the two competing plans and waited until I had some basis for choosing between them.

This indicates that if an agent has a set Σ of plans that are tied and between which it cannot decide, the rational decision is the disjunctive decision to execute *one* of these plans. Eventually the agent must decide between the plans, and if there is still no objective basis for doing so then the decision must be made at random. The time at which a decision must finally be made is the time at which one of the plans in Σ first requires something be done. This requires some small changes in the architecture of the PLANNER as it has so far been described. Specifically, the list of **adopted-plans** must either be replaced by or augmented by a list of **disjunctively-adopted-plan-sets**.

The preceding remarks apply to teleological planning, but much the same thing is true of scheduling. Scheduling tends to be a matter of continually refining previous schedules as the agent acquires new information or adopts new plans to be fitted into the schedule. For example, in deciding when to buy the paint for my garage, I schedule the purchase more and more precisely as time passes. First, I planned (yesterday) to buy the paint today. Then I planned to buy it this afternoon. Then I planned to buy it on my way to the grocery store. In this way I generate increasingly precise schedules. But it is important to realize that I may never generate an absolutely precise schedule. As a consequence of this, at any given time it will typically be the case that nodes from many different plans have been called, their timing-conditions are satisfied, and they are waiting to be executed by having their operations performed. For instance, I plan to call my travel agent sometime this afternoon to check on my car rental in New Zealand, I plan to start the barbecue pretty soon to fix dinner, I plan to run out to the mailbox and retrieve my mail before it gets dark, and so forth. All three of these plans have nodes that have been called and are awaiting execution. The timing-conditions are sufficiently broad that I can successfully execute them any time during the next several hours. I *might* engage in further planning and refine my schedule for when to do them, but more likely a time will come when I just decide to do one of them, and then later I will decide to do another, and so on. These decisions are the work of the PLAN-EXECUTOR, not the PLANNER.

The fact that schedules are left flexible until we acquire a good reason for refining them in some way indicates that, like teleological planning, we do not choose arbitrarily between tied schedules until we have to. When we have several competing candidate schedules, we normally select one only if it is preferable to all the others. There is, however, one important difference between tied schedules and tied teleological plans. Usually, tied schedules differ only in their scheduling of some particular node (or nodes) within a continuous temporal interval. For example, I may have good reason to buy the paint between 2 PM and 3 PM, but not have any reason to prefer one time in that interval to any other time. Rather than choosing randomly to buy the paint at some particular instant, I leave unspecified when exactly to buy the paint, deciding merely to buy it sometime between 2 PM and 3 PM. The times between 2 PM and 3 PM are preferable to other times, but tied among each other. In effect, I am undecided between infinitely many absolutely precise schedules, but I can represent that whole set of schedules with one imprecise schedule which can be adopted as a single plan rather than disjunctively adopting the infinite set of more precise plans. This will not always be the case, but it is frequently the case. This is an important difference between tied schedules and tied teleological plans.

These remarks suggest the following principle for rational plan adoption.

(PA)   The decision to disjunctively adopt a set of plans Σ is practically justified iff (1) a rationally satisfactory search for plans has been conducted, and (2) either:

(*i*) Σ has a single member σ, and for every plan μ discovered by the plan search, if we are justified in believing that μ competes with σ, then we are justified in believing that σ is preferable to μ (in this case, σ is adopted outright); or

(ii) (a) Σ has more than one member, and any two members of Σ are justifiably believed to compete,

(b) the plan search has led to the discovery of no plan that we are justified in believing to be rationally preferable to any member of Σ, and

(c) for every plan μ not in Σ, if μ is justifiably believed to compete with every member of Σ, then some member of Σ is justifiably believed to be preferable to μ.

5. Defeasible Reasons for Plan Adoptions

Principle (PA) makes essential reference to the concept of a rationally satisfactory search for plans. Just what does that involve? It might be supposed that a rationally satisfactory search must at least produce all of the "most obvious" candidate plans before the agent is justified in adopting the best candidate plan. But this proposal should be rejected. A crucial feature of reasoning is that it must be "interruptible". In general, there will always be more reasoning that could be done, but the agent may have to take action before it can do more reasoning. Rational thought must be such that, when the agent has to act, it is reasonable to act on the basis of its current justified conclusions, even if there always remains the possibility of those conclusions being retracted at a later time. This is an essential characteristic of justification, either epistemic or practical. This is virtually a definition of justification—justified conclusions are those it is reasonable to act upon at the present time.

A noteworthy fact about human beings is that in many (perhaps most) cases of routine planning, no more than a single plan for achieving a particular goal is ever produced. We do not generate a large number of different candidate plans and then choose between them. We produce a single plan, and if it is "sufficiently good", we are willing to act upon it without engaging in further search. This is essentially Herbert Simon's [1977] observation that we often satisfice rather than maximize. One plan that is always available to us is the null plan (the empty set of instructions), which has an expected-value of zero. For any other plan to be such that it is reasonable to act upon it, the agent must reasonably believe that it is better than the null plan, i.e., that it has a positive expected-value. Let us take this to be our official definition of a plan being *minimally good*. My suggestion is that if, at the time an agent must act, only a single new plan has been uncovered, and to the best of the agent's knowledge it does not compete with any of the previously adopted plans, then it is reasonable to act upon that plan iff the agent justifiably believes that it is a minimally good plan. This suggests in turn that as soon as a plan is discovered and evaluated as minimally good, it becomes defeasibly reasonable to adopt that plan. This practical decision must be defeasible, however, because if another plan is subsequently produced and judged to be preferable to the first, then the adoption of the first plan should be retracted and the new plan adopted in its place.[3]

Given the right structure for rationally satisfactory searches, the following principle captures the preceding observations and can be regarded as a corollary of (PA):

(P1) ⌜σ is a minimally good plan⌝ is a defeasible reason for adopting σ.

Principle (P1) formulates only a defeasible reason for adopting σ. To get a grasp of what the defeaters for (P1) should be, suppose the plan search produces a new candidate plan σ, and the agent must decide whether to adopt it. There are four possibilities: (a) the agent might simply adopt σ; (b) the agent might adopt σ while retracting the adoption of some previously adopted plans or disjunctive set of plans to which σ is rationally preferable; (c) the agent might decline to adopt σ on the grounds that it competes with another plan that is rationally preferable to it; (d) the agent might incorporate σ into a disjunctive set of tied plans and disjunctively adopt the set.

In deciding whether to adopt σ, the agent should first check to see whether σ is minimally good. If it is, then the agent has a defeasible reason for adopting it. If the agent is unaware of any conflicts with previously adopted plans, then σ should be adopted. In other words, the agent is in situation (a). But if the agent notes that a plan α that competes with σ has also been adopted, the agent must investigate whether σ is preferable to α. If σ is judged to be preferable to α, then the agent has a defeasible reason for adopting σ and retracting α. This is situation (b). If the agent judges α to be preferable to σ, then it should decline to adopt σ but retain α. This is situation (c). Situations (b) and (c) could be handled with the help of a single defeater for (P1):

⌜α is justifiably believed to be rationally preferable to σ⌝ is a defeater for (P1).

However, this defeater need not be adopted as a separate principle because it is a consequence of a more general defeater that is needed to handle situation (d):

(P2) ⌜α is justifiably believed to compete with σ and σ is not justifiably believed to be preferable to α⌝ is a defeater for (P1).

When applied to the case of ties, (P2) defeats the adoption of the individual members of the tied plan-sets. In this case, we need a principle supplementing (P1) that governs disjunctive adoption:

(P3) ⌜$α_1,...,α_n$ are justifiably believed to compete pairwise, each is justifiably believed to be minimally good, and none is justifiably believed to be preferable to another⌝ is a prima facie reason for disjunctively adopting $\{α_1,...,α_n\}$.

Note that (P1) is a special case of (P3). Furthermore, the defeater formulated by (P2) should also be a defeater for (P3):

(P4) $\ulcorner \alpha$ is justifiably believed to compete with each of $\alpha_1,...,\alpha_n$ and no α_i is justifiably believed to be preferable to $\alpha \urcorner$ is a defeater for (P3).

Reasoning with principles (P1)–(P4) should lead to the same disjunctive adoptions as reasoning with principle (PA).

6. The PLAN-SYNTHESIZER

In order to use (P1)–(P4), epistemic cognition must supply the PLANNER with suitable plans. The search for plans is directed by the PLAN-SYNTHE-SIZER, which is activated by the adoption of new goals. The PLAN-SYNTHE-SIZER does its job by passing two tasks to epistemic cognition. The *teleological task* is the task of constructing a plan for the satisfaction of that desire which is minimally good.[4] If the desire is an instrumental desire (that is, the desire to perform some step of another plan), the *scheduling task* is the task of looking for ways of improving the plan that generated the desire by inserting timing instructions.

Suppose epistemic cognition concludes that a certain plan is a minimally good one for satisfying some desire. This conclusion is passed to the PLAN-UPDATER. Suppose the PLAN-UPDATER adopts the plan. It is natural to suppose that this should lead to a cancellation of the search for plans aimed at satisfying that desire. However, adopting a plan for the satisfaction of a desire should not make us totally oblivious to better plans if they come along. For example, suppose I need something at the grocery store, and the only way to get there is to walk, so despite the fact that it is raining, I adopt the plan to walk. Then a friend offers me a lift. I am, and should be, able to appreciate the fact that this enables me to construct a better plan for getting to the grocery store and making my purchase. However, if I had no interest at all in finding plans for getting to the grocery store, I would be unable to draw that conclusion. Adopting one plan for getting to the grocery store certainly relieves some of the urgency in looking for other plans, but it should not cancel interest in them altogether. What it must do is simply lower the degree of interest in finding such plans, thus making the search for such plans a matter of lower priority.

At this point it becomes useful to separate subsidiary teleological planning and scheduling and look at each by itself, because the differences between them become important.

Subsidiary teleological planning

If (1) a plan for the satisfaction of a desire were "perfect", in the sense that it is certain to result in the satisfaction of the desire without attenuating its value,

(2) the probability of its successful execution were 1, and (3) its execution were costless, then there could never be a better plan, and so there would be no reason to continue searching. But of course, no plan can ever be perfect in this sense. As long as a plan is less than certain to succeed and has some execution cost, there is always the possibility of finding a better plan. The expected-value of a perfect plan for satisfying a desire is simply the product of the strength of the desire and the estimated probability of the desire not being satisfied without our doing anything. The expected-value of a plan aimed at satisfying several desires is the sum of these products for the different desires. Let the *degree of imperfection* of a plan be the difference between this figure and its expected-value. When the PLAN-UPDATER adopts a plan for the satisfaction of a desire or set of desires, the degree of interest epistemic cognition should retain in finding additional plans for the satisfaction of that desire or set of desires should be determined by the degree of imperfection of the adopted plan. Furthermore, the remaining interest should be changed to an interest in finding plans rationally preferable to the one already found.

Scheduling

Similar observations can be made about scheduling. However, we must be more careful than we have been in formulating the scheduling task the PLAN-SYNTHESIZER passes to epistemic cognition. Let us call the node from which an instrumental desire is derived its *parent node*, and the plan of which it is a node its *parent plan*. As a first approximation, the scheduling task is that of adding scheduling instructions to the parent node in such a way that the resulting plan is rationally preferable to the original parent plan. This account of the scheduling task is a bit simplistic, however. Scheduling usually consists of coordinating steps from different plans, in which case the scheduling links tie together steps from the different plans. In this case the objective should be to produce a composite plan rationally preferable to the union of the originally separate subplans.

Given this understanding of the scheduling task, suppose epistemic cognition produces such a composite plan and the PLAN-UPDATER adopts it. A rational agent will still be sensitive to the discovery of better ways of scheduling the node in question, so adopting this schedule should not result in a complete cancellation of interest in other schedules, but as in the case of subsidiary teleological planning, it should result in diminished interest in such schedules. This degree of interest should be determined by the degree of imperfection of the adopted schedule. It should also change our interest from scheduling the node to scheduling it in a way rationally preferable to the adopted plan.

Scheduling tends to be unstable. This is for two reasons. First, as time passes, an agent acquires new desires. For example, suppose I plan to sit at my desk writing all morning. But then I develop a craving for a cup of coffee. To accommodate this desire, I may change my plan and decide to get up and fix a cup of coffee as soon as I come to a convenient break in my work. This can also lead to reversing previous scheduling decisions. For instance, I might also have planned to make a phone call when I break for lunch, but it may occur to me that I can do that while I am waiting for the coffee to brew, and so I rearrange my schedule accordingly. It is to accommodate new desires that we leave schedules as indefinite as possible and do not choose arbitrarily between tied schedules.

Another way in which scheduling tends to change over time is that it tends to get more precise as I acquire more information. For instance, in planning to paint my garage, I initially planned to buy paint *sometime today*. Then when I acquired the belief that I would be passing close to the paint store on the way to the grocery store, I planned more precisely to buy paint on my way to the grocery store. As the time for action approaches, we tend to learn more and more about what else will be happening, and we can use that to refine our schedule.

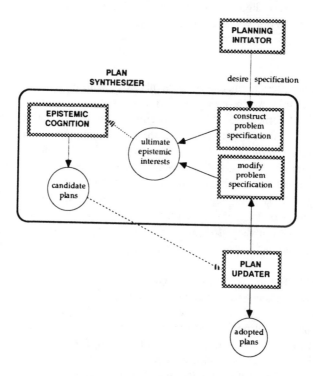

Figure 6. The architecture of the PLAN-SYNTHESIZER.

Both of these kinds of changes will occur automatically as long as epistemic cognition retains interest in finding preferable schedules. When the information becomes available that makes it possible to construct preferable schedules, epistemic cognition will do so as long as it does not have to do more important reasoning that interferes.

The preceding observations can be combined into the rather simple architecture for the PLAN-SYNTHESIZER that is diagramed in figure 6.

7. The Doxastification of Planning

For two different reasons, practical reasoning is defeasible. First, practical decisions are based upon beliefs supplied by epistemic cognition. If those beliefs are retracted, the practical decisions based upon them must also be retracted. Second, plan adoption proceeds in accordance with principles (P1)–(P4), and those are themselves principles of defeasible practical reasoning. This introduces an important complication into the theory of practical rationality. It is insufficient to just state the defeasible reasons and defeaters for practical reasoning. We must also describe the structure of the reasoning itself. This is no simple task. The literature on defeasible epistemic reasoning makes it apparent just how complex this is. Defeasible practical reasoning promises to be equally complex. Must we construct an entire inference engine for defeasible practical reasoning? Reflection on human thought suggests an intriguing way of handling this. Rather than requiring separate computational modules for defeasible epistemic reasoning and defeasible practical reasoning, human cognition sometimes makes do with a single module dedicated to epistemic reasoning, and then integrates practical reasoning into that module using a technical trick. The trick involves "doxastifying" normative judgments. Corresponding to the adoption of a plan is the "epistemic judgment" (i.e., belief) that *it should be an adopted plan*. This judgment can be epistemic in name only. It requires no "objective fact" to anchor it or give it truth conditions. It is merely a computational device whose sole purpose is to allow us to use defeasible epistemic reasoning to accomplish defeasible practical reasoning. Let us abbreviate $\ulcorner\sigma$ should be an adopted plan$\urcorner$ (where this is a practical 'should'—not a moral 'should') as $\ulcorner\sigma$ is *adoptable*$\urcorner$. Similarly, let us say that a set of plans is *disjunctively-adoptable* iff it should be disjunctively adopted. A plan is adoptable iff its unit set is disjunctively-adoptable. Then principles (P1)–(P4) can be rewritten as rules for epistemic reasoning about plans being adoptable and sets of plans being disjunctively-adoptable.

Consider the following array of epistemic prima facie reasons and defeaters:

(E1) $\ulcorner\sigma$ is a minimally good plan$\urcorner$ is a defeasible reason for $\ulcorner\sigma$ is adoptable$\urcorner$.

(E2a) $\ulcorner\alpha$ competes with σ and α is minimally good$\urcorner$ is a defeasible undercutting defeater for (E1).

(E2b) $\ulcorner\sigma$ is preferable to $\alpha\urcorner$ is a conclusive undercutting defeater for (E2a).

(E3) $\ulcorner\alpha_1,...,\alpha_n$ compete pairwise and each is minimally good$\urcorner$ is a prima facie reason for $\ulcorner\{\alpha_1,...,\alpha_n\}$ is disjunctively-adoptable$\urcorner$.

(E4a) $\ulcorner$One of $\alpha_1,...,\alpha_n$ preferable to another$\urcorner$ is a conclusive undercutting defeater for (E3).

(E4b) $\ulcorner\alpha$ is minimally good and competes with each of $\alpha_1,...,\alpha_n\urcorner$ is a defeasible undercutting defeater for (E3).

(E4c) ⌜Some α_i is preferable to α⌝ is a conclusive undercutting defeater for (E4b).

With this array of prima facie reasons and defeaters, the epistemic reasoner will conclude that a plan is adoptable iff a properly constructed defeasible practical reasoner would adopt the plan, and it will conclude that a set of plans is disjunctively-adoptable iff a properly constructed defeasible practical reasoner would disjunctively adopt the set of plans.[5] To illustrate, suppose we have a prima facie reason of the form (P1) for adopting σ, but we also have a defeater of the form (P2). Then we will have a prima facie reason of the form (E1) for concluding that σ is adoptable, and a defeater of the form (E2a) for this prima facie reason, and we will lack a defeater of the form (E2b). The upshot of this is that the same practical reasoning can be accomplished by coupling the defeasible epistemic reasoner with a much simpler practical reasoner that adopts or retracts plans on the basis of epistemic judgments to the effect that they are or are not adoptable.

It is important to realize that the terms 'adoptable' (or 'should be adopted') and 'disjunctively-adoptable' are not given definitions in this account. They are just placeholders in epistemic reasoning. Their purpose is to give the reasoning the right structure to implement the planning architecture. I will refer to this reduction of defeasible practical reasoning to defeasible epistemic reasoning as *the doxastification of practical reasoning*, because it reduces defeasible practical reasoning to epistemic reasoning about beliefs.

The doxastification of practical reasoning has the result that most of the work of plan updating is done by the epistemic reasoner rather than by the PLAN-UPDATER itself. Doxastification is an extremely powerful device, and it has the consequence that the PLAN-UPDATER can be quite simple. The PLAN-SYNTHESIZER poses questions for epistemic cognition regarding the adoptability of plans satisfying certain constraints, and then epistemic cognition goes its merry way. In particular, it will adopt, and sometimes withdraw, beliefs to the effect that various plans are adoptable. All the PLAN-UPDATER must do is respond to *changes* in beliefs of the form ⌜σ is adoptable⌝. When such a belief is adopted, the PLAN-UPDATER adopts σ, and when such a belief is withdrawn, the PLAN-UPDATER retracts the adoption of σ. It was observed earlier that when the adoption of a plan is retracted, this must reinitiate planning for the satisfaction of the desires the retracted plan aimed at satisfying. But this is now automatic. Whenever the epistemic reasoner retracts a belief in which it was originally interested, that has the effect of reawakening interest in it. Similarly, if the epistemic reasoner is looking for a variable-binding that satisfies a certain formula, and it acquires an appropriate belief (a belief in an instance of the formula), then if it subsequently retracts that belief, that will automatically lead it to reopen the search for variable bindings. That latter is what is involved in the search for plans, so the search for plans will automatically be reopened without any new instructions having to be passed to the epistemic reasoner.

8. A Doxastic Implementation of Practical Reasoning

The doxastification of plan adoption has implications for the rest of the planning architecture. The lists of adopted-plans and disjunctively-adopted-plan-sets are encoded as beliefs about adoptability and disjunctive-adoptability. For the rest of the PLANNER to make use of these beliefs, it must either respond to the beliefs directly, or use the beliefs to construct the associated lists and then perform computations on the lists. Reflection upon the latter alternative indicates that it would introduce serious complications into the architecture, because if the adoptability-beliefs are subsequently withdrawn, the lists must be adjusted accordingly, and computations based upon them must also be adjusted. In other words, the rest of the practical reasoner must also operate defeasibly. This suggests a thorough-going doxastification of the entire architecture. The trick to achieving this consists of making use of the full structure of ultimate-epistemic-interests.

First, I have talked about practical cognition sending queries to epistemic cognition by placing the queries in ultimate-epistemic-interests, but that need not be the only source of ultimate epistemic interests. It is compatible with the architecture for there to be a list of permanent-ultimate-epistemic-interests that are in ultimate-epistemic-interests from the start, without having to be placed there by practical cognition. Second, recall that an ultimate epistemic interest encodes a query, together with a degree of interest and an instruction for what to do with an answer. The latter instruction can be of any kind. In particular, it can tell the reasoner to insert another query into ultimate-epistemic-interests. With these observations, suppose we supply epistemic cognition with the following permanent-ultimate-epistemic-interests and supplement (E1)–(E4c) with the following prima facie reasons and defeaters:

permanent-ultimate-epistemic-interests:

(U1) Find a w such that w is an suitable goal.
　　　　When the belief that w is an suitable goal is produced:
　　　　　　　insert ⌜Find an x such that x is a minimally good plan for achieving w⌝ into ultimate-epistemic-interests.
(U2) Find an x such that x is an adoptable plan.
　　　　When this belief is acquired:
　　　　　　　insert ⌜Find a y such that y is a plan for achieving the same goals as x and y is rationally preferable to x⌝ into ultimate-epistemic-interests.
(U3) Find an x such that x is a disjunctively-adoptable plan-set.
　　　　When the belief that x is a disjunctively-adoptable plan-set is produced, for each member of x:
　　　　　　　insert ⌜If x is to be executed, the first step must be performed now⌝ into ultimate-epistemic-interests.
　　　　When this belief is acquired, choose some x in y at random, and have introspection supply the belief that x was randomly chosen for adoption.

forwards directed prima facie reasons:

(E5) Desiring w is a prima facie reason for believing ⌜w is an suitable goal⌝.

(E6) ⌜x is an adoptable plan and w is a situation-type consisting of executing a non-basic node of x if it is called⌝ is a prima facie reason for ⌜w is an suitable goal⌝. (A non-basic node is one whose operation is not a basic act.)

forwards directed conclusive reasons:

(E7) ⌜w is a situation-type having positive relative expected situation-liking⌝ is a conclusive reason for ⌜w is an suitable goal⌝.

(E8) ⌜y is a disjunctively-adoptable plan-set, and x was chosen randomly from the members of y⌝ is a conclusive reason for ⌜x is an adoptable plan⌝.

backwards directed conclusive reasons:

(E9) ⌜x is a situation-type having a non-positive relative expected situation-liking⌝ is a conclusive reason for ⌜x is not an suitable goal⌝.

(E10) ⌜x is a situation-type having a non-positive relative expected situation-liking⌝ is a conclusive undercutting defeater for (E5).

These will combine to give us the reasoning diagramed in figure 7. The large cross-hatched arrows signify that finding an instance of one member of **ultimate-epistemic-interests** leads to the insertion of a new query.

To see how this works, let us step through the operation of a reasoner supplied with these **permanent-ultimate-epistemic-interests** and reasons. The reasoner begins with a permanent interest in finding suitable goals. 'suitable goal' is now treated as an undefined placeholder, just like 'adoptable plan' or 'disjunctively-adoptable plan-set'. It is a paraphrase of 'goal that should (from a practical point of view) be adopted'. The reasoner has three ways of finding suitable goals. If optative dispositions produce the desire for w, by (E5), this constitutes a prima facie reason for concluding that w is an suitable goal. This automatically queries epistemic cognition about whether w is a situation-type having positive relative expected situation-liking, because the defeasible epistemic reasoner always adopts interest in defeaters for its inferences, and (E10) formulates a defeater for (E5). (E7) formulates the "direct epistemic reason" for adopting goals. I will discuss (E6) below.

Once the reasoner concludes that w is a suitable goal, in accordance with (U1), it sends an interest in finding minimally good plans for achieving w to **ultimate-epistemic-interests**. This leads to the epistemic reasoning that constitutes plan synthesis. The reasoning leading to the search for plans will be prioritized by epistemic cognition according to the degree of interest attached to finding the plan, and that will be determined by the importance of the goal.

When the reasoner draws the conclusion that a plan is minimally good, this leads, via (E1) or (E3), to the conclusion that it is adoptable or a member of a disjunctively-adoptable plan-set. In the latter case, in accordance with (U3), a query is sent to **ultimate-epistemic-interests** leading the reasoner to attend to the conditions under which a choice must be made between the members of the plan-set. When the reasoner concludes that a choice must be made, that is done and the information that it was done is supplied via introspection (still in accordance with (U3)) and constitutes a reason (by (E8)) for concluding that the randomly selected plan is adoptable.

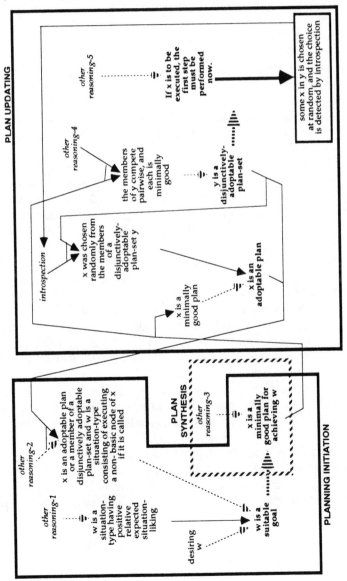

Figure 7. A doxastic implementation of the planning architecture.

When it is concluded that a plan is adoptable, (E6) provides a reason for thinking that executing its nodes if they are called constitutes an suitable goal. This corresponds to the production of instrumental desires.

The upshot of this is that the apparently complex dynamics of plan adoption and modification, and of scheduling, need not be handled in an ad hoc way in a rational agent in which practical reasoning is doxastified. These complex dynamics result in a natural way from the functioning of defeasible epistemic reasoning and its employment in the practical reasoner.

9. The PLAN-EXECUTOR

The PLAN-EXECUTOR is the module that executes plans. It will proceed roughly as follows:

(1) Call initial nodes, and execute them.
(2) Recursively execute nodes called by nodes that have already been executed.

Several complications must be addressed. First, the epistemic reasoning presupposed by plan execution is defeasible, and the PLAN-EXECUTOR must accommodate that. The way to do that is, once more, through the doxastification of practical reasoning. As in the PLANNER, doxastification will allow the bulk of the reasoning involved in plan execution to be done by epistemic cognition. Second, having adopted a plan and begun its execution, a rational agent does not proceed blindly come-what-may. A rational agent monitors the course of plan execution. If things do not go as anticipated, the execution of the plan may be aborted. This monitoring consists of keeping a continual check on whether the part of the plan remaining to be executed (the *tail* of the plan) is, under the present circumstances, an adoptable plan in its own right. The computational module that does this will be called *the TAIL-MONITOR*. As long as the TAIL-MONITOR does not abort plan execution, the PLAN-EXECUTOR will proceed recursively to execute nodes as they are called. A common phenomenon will be that the tail of the plan is modified by further scheduling as plan execution proceeds. Typically, as we see how the execution of a complex plan develops and what is true of our current situation, we will acquire reasons for scheduling the remaining nodes more precisely than we did before plan execution began. This has the effect, via the TAIL-MONITOR, of replacing the tail of the plan by a modification of it that involves further scheduling, adopting that modification, and then beginning its execution. Of course, it too may be modified as execution progresses.

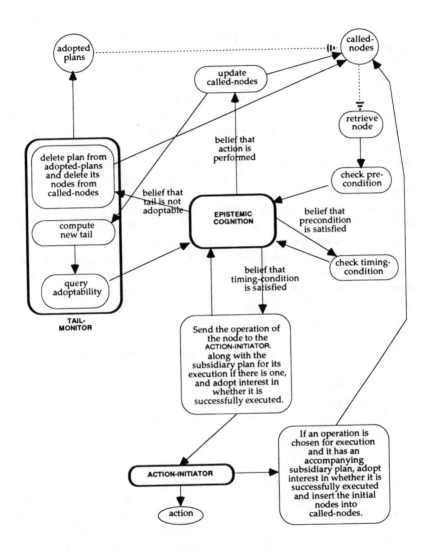

Figure 8. The PLAN-EXECUTOR

Schematically, the PLAN-EXECUTOR can be regarded, as in figure 8, as consisting of a loop. The loop begins by retrieving a node from a list of *called-nodes* (originally the initial-nodes of top-level adopted plans). It checks to see whether the preconditions are satisfied. It does this by passing that question to epistemic cognition. If it is determined that the preconditions are not satisfied, execution of that node terminates. If it is determined that the preconditions are satisfied, the PLAN-EXECUTOR instructs epistemic cognition to become interested (and remain interested) in whether the timing-condition is satisfied. If at some point epistemic cognition produces the belief that the timing-condition is satisfied, it passes this information back to the PLAN-EXECUTOR. The PLAN-EXECUTOR then passes the operation of the node to the ACTION-INITIATOR along with the subsidiary plan for its execution if there is one. The ACTION-INITIATOR will be discussed further below. Among other things, it resolves last-minute scheduling questions. When it chooses an operation for execution, it checks to see whether it is accompanied by an execution plan. If not, the operation is assumed to be a basic act, for the performance of which the agent has hardwired routines. Those routines are then executed mechanically. If instead there is an execution plan, its initial nodes are inserted into the list of called-nodes, and its execution begins. If a time comes when the TAIL-MONITOR decides the plan is no longer executable even if a subsidiary plan is adopted, then execution will be aborted. The ACTION-INITIATOR must monitor the execution of an operation to ensure that it is successful. It does this by querying epistemic cognition. If epistemic cognition concludes that the operation was successfully executed, the PLAN-EXECUTOR concludes that the node was executed, and updates the list of called-nodes and inserts the new tails that begin with each newly called node into the set of adopted-plans. Then the whole routine begins again.

Running in parallel with this is the TAIL-MONITOR. As soon as a node is called, the TAIL-MONITOR instructs epistemic cognition to be continually interested in whether the tail of the plan is adoptable. If at any point epistemic cognition concludes that it is not, the TAIL-MONITOR aborts the plan execution. The epistemic conclusion that the tail is not adoptable may be accompanied by another epistemic conclusion to the effect that a modification of it is adoptable, and then the PLAN-EXECUTOR will automatically begin executing the modification just as it executes other adopted plans.

It would be straightforward to write a program to perform these operations mechanically, but that would not accommodate the defeasability of the agent's access to whether preconditions and timing-conditions are satisfied, operations have been successfully executed, etc. If the agent's beliefs about these matters change, this must alter the course of plan execution. It seems that the best way to handle this is by doxastifying plan execution. In other words, implement the PLAN-EXECUTOR in terms of epistemic reasoning. This can be done by making one addition to the permanent-ultimate-epistemic-interests, and adding the following reason schemas:

permanent-ultimate-epistemic-interests:

(U2*)   Find an x such that x is an adoptable plan.
When the belief that x is an adoptable plan is acquired:
insert ⌜Find a y such that y is a plan for achieving the same goals as x and y is rationally preferable to x⌝ into ultimate-epistemic-interests;

for each initial node *z* of *x*: insert ⌜*x* is executable⌝ in ultimate-epistemic-interests.

(U4)   Find a *v* such that *v* is an executable operation.
        When the belief that *v* is an executable operation is acquired, send *v* to the ACTION-INITIATOR. (The ACTION-INITIATOR will insert ⌜*v* has been executed⌝ into ultimate-epistemic-interests when it tries to execute *v*.)

forwards directed prima facie reasons:

(E11)   ⌜*x* is the tail of *y* with respect to *z* and *z* was an executable node and *z* has been executed⌝ is a prima facie reason for ⌜*x* is an adoptable plan⌝.

forwards directed conclusive reasons:

(E12)   ⌜*y* is the subsidiary plan for *z*, and *z* is an executable node, and *y* has been fully executed⌝ is a conclusive reason for ⌜node *z* has been executed⌝.

(E13)   ⌜Node *z* was executable, *v* is the operation prescribed by node *z*, and *v* was executed during the time *z* was executable⌝ is a conclusive reason for ⌜*z* was executed⌝.

(E14)   ⌜*x* is an adoptable plan and *z* is an initial node of *x*⌝ is a conclusive reason for ⌜*z* is called⌝.

(E15)   ⌜*x* was an executable node of plan *y* and *x* has been executed⌝ is a conclusive reason for ⌜*x* is no longer executable⌝.

backwards directed conclusive reasons:

(E16)   ⌜*z* is called, its preconditions are satisfied, and its timing-condition is satisfied⌝ is a conclusive reason for ⌜*z* is an executable plan-node⌝.

(E17)   ⌜*v* is the operation prescribed by an executable plan-node *z* of expected-value δ⌝ is a conclusive reason for ⌜*v* is an executable operation of strength δ⌝.

(E18)   ⌜*x* is not prescribed by any executable plan-node of expected-value δ⌝ is a conclusive reason for ⌜*x* is not an executable operation of strength δ⌝.

These combine to give us the reasoning diagramed in figure 9 (next page). This constitutes a doxastic implementation of the plan execution architecture diagramed in figure 8. To verify this, let us step through the operation of a reasoner supplied with these **permanent-ultimate-epistemic-interests** and reason schemas. We begin with beliefs of the form ⌜*x* is adoptable⌝, supplied by the planning architecture described above. The pursuit of such beliefs was already among the **permanent-ultimate-epistemic-interests**, but (U2*) adds an instruction to the effect that whenever such a belief is acquired, queries about whether the initial nodes of *x* are executable should be inserted into **ultimate-epistemic-interests**. These queries are answered in terms of (E15) and (E16). If the reasoner concludes that an initial node *z* is executable, and it also concludes that *z* prescribes an operation *v*, then it concludes, by (E17), that *v* is an executable operation, and by (U4), it sends *v* to the ACTION-INITIATOR and that initiates

44 / John L. Pollock

interest in whether *v* has been executed. Information to the effect that various operations have been executed is used to conclude that nodes prescribing them have been executed (by (E12)) and that plans have been fully executed. When it is concluded that an initial node *z* has been executed, it is inferred by (E11) that the tail of *x* with respect to *z* is an adoptable plan, and the loop begins again. Thus we have a doxastic implementation of the PLAN-EXECUTOR.

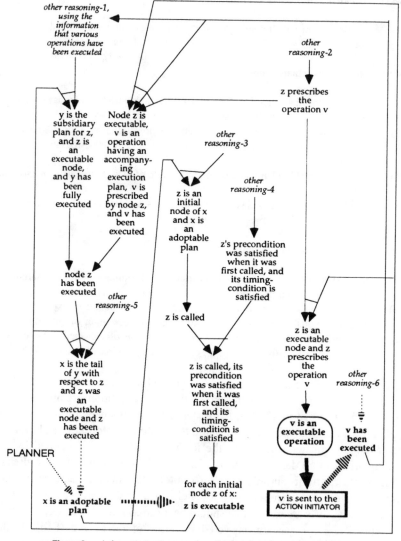

Figure 9. A doxastic implementation of the plan execution architecture.

10. The ACTION-INITIATOR

The PLAN-EXECUTOR places operations awaiting execution in a list of **executable-operations**. The task of the ACTION-INITIATOR is to decide which of these operations to execute at any given time. When it decides to execute one of these operations, it monitors the attempted execution and when it is ascertained that the operation has been successfully executed, that operation is deleted from the list of **executable-operations**.

The fundamental question about the ACTION-INITIATOR is: how does it decide what to do when? The main difficulty in answering this question arises from the fact that the planning architecture adumbrated above leaves an important gap between planning and acting. This is due, in part, to the fact that rationality dictates leaving schedules as flexible as possible to accommodate new plans as they are adopted and to enable the agent to make use of new information that may lower execution costs if plan execution is scheduled in light of it. Return to the example of painting my garage. As the time for buying the paint approaches, I schedule the purchase more and more precisely. First, I planned (yesterday) to buy the paint today. Then I planned to buy it this afternoon. Then I planned to buy it on my way to the grocery store. In this way I generate more and more precise schedules. But I may never generate an absolutely precise schedule. When I actually get into the paint store and stand at the counter, there has to be something that makes me decide to buy the paint *now* (rather than 30 seconds from now, or 5 minutes from now). At any given time, it will typically be the case that nodes from many different plans have been called, their timing-conditions are satisfied, and they are waiting to be executed by having their operations executed. For instance, I plan to call my travel agent sometime this afternoon to check on my car rental in New Zealand, I plan to start the barbecue pretty soon to fix dinner, I plan to run out to the mailbox and retrieve my mail before it gets dark, and so forth. All three of these plans have nodes that have been called and are awaiting execution. The timing-conditions are sufficiently broad that I can successfully execute the nodes any time during the next several hours. I *might* engage in further planning and refine my schedule for when to do them, but more likely a time will come when I just decide to do one of them, and then later I will decide to do another, and so on. These decisions are the work of the ACTION-INITIATOR rather than the PLANNER. To complete the theory of rational plan execution, we need an account of how the ACTION-INITIATOR decides what to do at any given time.

The basis for such a mechanism lies in a distinction between two kinds of primitive desires—desires for the future and desires for the present. Only the former can be the subject of planning. You cannot plan for the present. Planning takes time and you cannot plan ahead for a situation that is already here. In order to play any role in directing action, desires for the present must be desires *to do* something. I will refer to such desires as "present-tense action desires".

What we might call "a reactive agent" (as opposed to a rational agent) guides its actions solely on the basis of built-in and conditioned reflexes generating immediate action. Even in a reactive agents, there can be conflicts that must be adjudicated. More than one reflex can be triggered at the same time, and it may be impossible to perform the actions dictated by them all. A reactive agent must have some mechanism for adjudicating disputes in such cases. The only obvious mechanism is to assign strengths to reflexes, and when two reflexes compete, the stronger wins. We can, at least metaphorically, think of such reflexes as generating present-tense action desires, and in deciding what to do when there is a conflict, all the reactive agent can do is act on the desire that is strongest, i.e., do what it most wants to do.

An agent capable of planning can do better. It can, in many cases, adjust its plans so as to avoid such conflicts. However, planning can never entirely replace reacting to present-tense action desires. Planning is only applicable insofar as we can predict what is apt to befall us. If the unexpected happens, it may be too late to plan for it and all we can do is react. Basic reflexes like withdrawing from pain are going to be essential ingredients in any rational agent. Ratiocination can only supplement such pre-rational mechanisms.

Just as a reactive agent can experience conflicting reflexes, a rational agent can encounter conflicts between plans and reflexes. The plan to retrieve a valuable object that fell into a fire may conflict with the reflex of withdrawing one's hand from the fire. Sometimes, the plan wins out. This requires that there be an adjudication mechanism in a rational agent that can choose not only between actions prescribed by present-tense action desires, but also actions prescribed by plans. This must be done in terms of the value of some parameter of the actions between which the agent is choosing. In the case of actions prescribed by present-tense action desires, the relevant parameter is how much the agent wants to perform the action, i.e., the strength of the desire. Accordingly, we can use the same language in talking about the parameter attaching to actions prescribed by plans. The agent *wants*, more or less strongly, to perform such an action, and it can decide which action to perform by selecting the one it wants most strongly to perform. How badly an agent wants to perform such an action can be regarded as the strength of the agent's desire to perform it, where this desire is the instrumental desire produced by adopting the plan. Plan nodes correspond to instrumental desires, and instrumental desires have strengths associated with them. This strength is inherited by the mandated operation when it is passed to the ACTION-INITIATOR. The executable operations are things the agent "wants to do", and the strength is a measure of how badly the agent wants to do it. The ACTION-INITIATOR selects the one the agent wants most to do (if there is a tie it randomly selects one of the most preferred operations) and then initiates the execution of that operation, deleting it from the list of executable-operations. At the same time it queries epistemic cognition about whether the operation is executed successfully. If the belief is adopted that the operation was not executed successfully then it is reinserted into the list of executable-operations so that the agent can try again.

The ACTION-INITIATOR has the hard-wired ability to initiate basic acts (basic motor skills). If an executable operation is a basic act, and it is not accompanied by an execution plan, then when it is selected for execution, the built-in routines are executed automatically. The built-in routines can be overridden by accompanying the act with an execution plan. For instance, I can normally raise my arm automatically by executing built-in routines for that purpose. But if my arm is anesthetized, I may instead raise it by lifting it with my other arm. Operations that are not basic acts *must* be accompanied by execution plans. Whenever an operation is accompanied by an execution plan and the operation is selected for execution, that subsidiary execution plan is judged adoptable and its initial nodes are judged to be called. The execution of the subsidiary plan is then carried out by the PLAN-EXECUTOR.

This simple model of action initiation explains a great deal. There is a temptation in the theory of practical reasoning to think of the adoption of a plan as beginning a process that grinds inexorably to the execution of the plan unless it is subsequently retracted (i.e., unless the agent changes its mind). But that is inaccurate. Adopting a plan is not like setting a train moving on rigid rails. Even though I plan to do something and never explicitly change my mind, the plan may never be executed just because I never feel like executing it. There may always be other things I want to do more. This can include doing nothing. For example, I might adopt the plan to go to the grocery store this afternoon. As the afternoon progresses, it occurs to me at various times that I planned to go to the grocery store, but each time my reaction is, "Oh, I don't feel like going just now. I will do it later." Finally, the afternoon is over and I have not gone, but there was never a point at which I explicitly retracted my plan to go. I just didn't do it.

It is not only lethargy that can keep plans from being executed. I may have planned to go to the grocery store, but I got engrossed in writing this paper, and every time I thought about going to the grocery store I decided that I would rather keep writing and go later. Eventually, the afternoon was over and I had not gone.

Notice that lethargy and wanting to continue writing are present-tense action desires rather than operations prescribed by plans. That is, they are primitive desires produced by optative dispositions and concern our present behavior rather than our future behavior. Presumably, lethargy is the result of a built-in optative disposition, whereas wanting to continue writing is almost certainly the result of an acquired optative disposition. These examples illustrate the importance of the mechanisms of the reactive agent even in a sophisticated planning agent. Such mechanisms play an extremely important role in "modulating" the behavior of the planning agent.

11. Conclusions

The main conclusion to be drawn from all this is that complex patterns of practical reasoning can be implemented in a suitably constructed rational agent by reducing them to defeasible epistemic reasoning via doxastification. Accordingly, the OSCAR architecture is built around a general purpose defeasible epistemic reasoner. At this time, that architecture has been fully implemented. The architecture is programmable by supplying it with different arrays of conclusive and prima facie reason schemas and defeaters. Work is currently underway to implement planning and plan execution by incorporating the reason schemas described above. OSCAR is available by anonymous ftp from arizona.edu in the directory /ftp/pub/oscar, or on the web at http://aruba.ccit.arizona.edu/oscar.html.

Notes

1. This is described in more detail in my [1992a], [1994], [1995], and [1995a].
2. This is a familiar point in AI planning theory. Such planning is called "hierarchical". (See Sacerdotti [1975] and [1977].)
3. Simon's official definition of satisficing ([1977], pg. 173) does not incorporate defeasibility.
4. Instead of constructing a new plan from scratch, the construction of a plan for a new desire may involve modifying a previous plan so that it aims at satisfying the new desire as well as achieving its original goals.
5. The defeasible epistemic reasoner works by adopting interest in defeaters whenever it makes a defeasible inference. Preference between plans results from relations between composites of subplans of those plans. For rules (E1)-(E4c) to work properly, the reasoner must consider those composite plans that generate preference relations and consider whether they should be adopted in place of the plans that are first proposed. This must be built into the interest rules governing the evaluation of plans.

References

Agre, P.E. and Chapman, D., 1987, Pengi: an implementation of a theory of activity. *Proceedings of AAAI-87*. Seattle, Washington. 268-272.

Bratman, Michael, 1987, *Intention, Plans, and Practical Reason*. Cambridge: Harvard University Press.

Pollock, John L., 1992, New foundations for practical reasoning. *Minds and Machines* 2, 113-144.

Pollock, John L., 1992a, How to reason defeasibly. *Artificial Intelligence* 57, 1-42.

Pollock, John L., 1993, The phylogeny of rationality. *Cognitive Science* 17, 563-588.

Pollock, John L., 1994, Justification and defeat. *Artificial Intelligence*, forthcoming.

Pollock, John L., 1995, *Cognitive Carpentry*. Cambridge: Bradford Books/MIT Press.

Pollock, John L., 1995a, OSCAR—a general-purpose defeasible reasoner. *Journal of Applied Non-Classical Logics*, forthcoming.

Sacerdotti, E.D., 1975, The non-linear nature of plans. IJCAI-75.

Sacerdotti, E.D., 1977, *A Structure of Plans and Behavior*. Amsterdam: Elsevier-North Holland.

Simon, Herbert A., 1977, *Models of Discovery*. Dordrecht: Reidel.

Philosophical Perspectives, 9, AI, Connectionism, and
Philosophical Psychology, 1995

UNDERSTANDING UNDERSTANDING:
SYNTACTIC SEMANTICS AND COMPUTATIONAL COGNITION

William J. Rapaport
State University of New York at Buffalo

John Searle (1993: 68) says: "The Chinese room shows what we knew all along: syntax by itself is not sufficient for semantics. (Does anyone actually deny this point, I mean straight out? Is anyone actually willing to say, straight out, that they think that syntax, in the sense of formal symbols, is really the same as semantic content, in the sense of meanings, thought contents, understanding, etc.?)." *I say:* "Yes". *Stuart C. Shapiro (in conversation, 19 April 1994) says:* "Does that make any sense? Yes: Everything makes sense. The question is: What sense does it make?" This essay explores what sense it makes to say that syntax by itself *is* sufficient for semantics.

1   Computational Natural-Language Understanding and a Computational Mind

1.1   Understanding Language.

What does it mean to understand language? "Semantic" understanding is a correspondence between two domains; a cognitive agent understands one of those domains in terms of the other. But if one domain is to be understood in terms of another, how is the other understood? Recursively, in terms of yet another. But, since recursion needs a base case, there must be a domain that is not understood in terms of another. So, it must be understood in terms of itself. How? Syntactically! Put briefly, bluntly, and a bit paradoxically, *semantic understanding is syntactic understanding.* Thus, any cognitive agent—including a computer—capable of syntax (symbol manipulation) is capable of understanding language.

1.1.1. Computers, programs, and processes.

What does it mean for a computer to understand language? Strictly speaking, neither computers nor programs can do so. Certainly, but uninterestingly, no present-day computers or AI programs do so. Some suitably-programmed computers can process a lot of natural language, though none can do it (yet) to the degree needed to pass a Turing Test. Rather, if a suitably programmed computer is ever to pass a Turing Test for natural-language understanding, what will understand will be neither the mere physical computer (the hardware) nor the static, textual program (the software), but the dynamic, behavioral *process*—the program being executed by the computer (cf. Tanenbaum 1976: 12; Smith 1987, §5).

1.1.2 The real thing.

Such a successful natural-language–understanding process will be an example of "strong AI". First, it will probably be "psychologically valid"; i.e., the underlying algorithm will probably be very similar (if not identical) to the one we use. Second, natural-language understanding is at least necessary, and possibly sufficient, for passing the Turing Test. Thus, anything that passes the Turing Test does understand natural language. But such a process will pass the Turing Test. So, such a process will do more than merely simulate natural-language understanding; it will *really* understand natural language. Or so I claim. What is needed for any cognitive agent—human or computer—to understand language?

1.1.2.1 Robustness. A cognitive agent that understands language must be "open-ended" or "robust", able to deal with "improvisational audience-participation discourse".

Although some "canned" patterns of conversation will be needed, as in theories of "frames", "scripts", etc. (e.g., Minsky 1975, Schank & Riesbeck 1981), it cannot rely solely on these. For we can use language in arbitrary and unforeseen circumstances. Similarly, the language-understanding process must be able to improvise.

Second, monologues are fine as far as they go; but a language-using entity unable to converse with an interlocutor would not pass the Turing Test. Interaction provides feedback, allowing the two natural-language–understanding systems (the two interlocutors) to reach mutual understanding (to "align" their "knowledge bases"). It also provides causal links with the outside world.

Finally, the process must be able to understand not only isolated sentences, but *sequences* of sentences that form a coherent discourse. What it understands at any point in a discourse will be a function partly of what it understood before. (Cf. Segal et al. 1991: 32.)

1.1.2.2 Natural-Language Competencies. A natural-language–understanding process must understand virtually all input that it "hears" or "reads", whether grammatical or not; after all, *we* do. It must remember what it believed or heard before, as well as what it learns during a conversation. It must be able to perform inference on what it hears and believes; revise its beliefs, as needed; and remember what, that, how, and why it inferred. It must be able to plan and to understand plans: In particular, it must be able to plan speech acts, so that it can *generate* language to answer questions, to ask questions, and to initiate conversation. Thus, it must be both a natural-language–*understanding* process and a natural-language–*generation* process; call this natural-language *competence* (Shapiro & Rapaport 1991). And it must be able to understand the speech-act plans of its interlocutors, in order to understand why speakers say what they do. This, in turn, requires the process to have (or to construct) a "user model"—a theory of the interlocutor's beliefs. Last on this list (though no doubt more is needed), it must be able to learn via language—to learn about non-linguistic things (the external world, others' ideas), and to learn about language, including its own language: It must be able to learn its own language from scratch, as we do from infancy, as well as consciously learn the syntax and semantics of its language, as we do (or should) in school.

1.1.3 Mind.

To do all of this, a cognitive agent who understands natural language must have a "mind"—what AI researchers call a 'knowledge base'. Initially, it will contain what might be called "innate ideas"—anything in the knowledge base before any language use begins. And it will come to contain beliefs resulting from perception, conversation, and inference. Among these will be internal representations of external objects.

For convenience and perspicuousness, let us think of the knowledge base or mind as a propositional semantic network, whose nodes represent individual concepts, properties, relations, and propositions, and whose connecting arcs structure atomic concepts into molecular ones (including structured individuals, propositions, and rules). The specific semantic-network theory we use is the SNePS knowledge representation and reasoning system (see §1.2), but you can think in terms of other such systems, such as (especially) Discourse Representation Theory,[1] the KL-ONE family,[2] Conceptual Dependency,[3] or Conceptual Graphs.[4] (Or, if you prefer, you can think in terms of a connectionist system.)

1.1.4 Syntax suffices.

> Philosophy must be done in the first person, for the first person. (Hector-Neri Castañeda, in conversation, 1984)

Meaning will be, *inter alia*, relations among these internal representations of external objects, on the one hand, and other internal symbols of the language of thought, on the other. A cognitive agent, *C*, with natural-language competence understands the natural-language output of another such agent, *O*, "by building and manipulating the symbols of an internal model (an interpretation) of [*O*'s] output considered as a formal system. [*C*]'s internal model would be a knowledge-representation and reasoning system that manipulates symbols" (Rapaport 1988b: 104). Hence, *C*'s semantic understanding of *O* is a *syntactic* enterprise.

Two semantic points of view must be distinguished. The *external* point of view is *C*'s understanding of *O*. The *internal* point of view is *C*'s understanding of itself. There are two ways of viewing the external point of view: the "third-person" way, in which *we*, as external observers, describe *C*'s understanding of *O*, and the "first-person" way, in which *C* understands its own understanding of *O*. Traditional referential semantics is largely irrelevant to the latter, primarily because external objects *can* only be dealt with via internal representations of them. It is first-person and internal understanding that I seek to understand and that, I believe, can only be understood syntactically. I have argued for these claims in Rapaport 1988b. The rest of this essay is an investigation into what kind of sense this makes.

1.2 A Computational Mind.

The specific knowledge-representation and reasoning (KRR) system I will use to help fix our ideas is the SNePS *S*emantic *N*etwork *P*rocessing *S*ystem (Shapiro 1979; Shapiro & Rapaport 1987, 1992, 1995). *As a knowledge-representation system*, SNePS is symbolic (or "classical"; as opposed to connectionist), propositional (as opposed to being a taxonomic or "inheritance" hierarchy), and fully intensional (as opposed to (partly) extensional). *As a reasoning system*, it has several types of interrelated inference mechanisms: "node-based" (or "conscious"), "path-based" (generalized inheritance, or "subconscious"), "default", and belief-revision. Finally, it has certain *sensing and effecting mechanisms*, namely: natural-language competence, and the ability to make, reason about, and execute plans. Such, at least, is SNePS in principle. Various implementations of it have more or less of these capabilities, but I will assume the ideal, full system.

There is no loss of generality in focussing on such a *symbolic* system. A connectionist system that passed the Turing Test would make my points about the syntactic nature of understanding equally well. For a connectionist system is just as computational—as syntactic—as a classical symbolic system (Rapaport 1993).

That SNePS is propositional rather than taxonomic merely means that it represents everything propositionally. Taxonomic hierarchical relationships among individuals and classes are represented propositionally, too. Systems that are, by contrast, primarily taxomonic have automatic inheritance features; in SNePS, this is generalized to path-based inference. Both events and situations can also be represented in SNePS.

But SNePS is intensional, and therein lies a story. To be able to model the mind of a cognitive agent, a KRR system must be able to represent and reason about intensional objects, i.e., objects not substitutable in intensional contexts (such as the morning star and the evening star), indeterminate or incomplete objects (such as fictional objects), non-existent objects (such as a golden mountain), impossible objects (such as a round square), distinct but coextensional objects of thought (such as the sum of 2 and 2, and the sum of 3 and 1), and so on. We think and talk about such objects, and therefore so must any entity that uses natural language.

We use SNePS to model, or implement, the mind of cognitive agents named 'Cassie' and 'Oscar'.[5] If Cassie passes the Turing Test, then she *is* intelligent and *has* (or perhaps *is*) a mind. (Or so I claim.) Her mind consists of SNePS nodes and arcs; i.e., SNePS is her language of thought (in the sense of Fodor 1975). If she is implemented on a Sun workstation, then we might also say that she has a "brain" whose components are the "switch-settings" (the register contents) in the Sun that implements the nodes and arcs of her mind.

We will say that Cassie can represent—or think about—objects (whether existing or not), properties, relations, propositions, events, situations, etc. Thus, all of the things represented in SNePS when it is being used to model Cassie's mind are objects of Cassie's thoughts (i.e., Meinongian objects of Cassie's mental acts); they are, thus, inten*t*ional—hence inten*s*ional—objects. They are not extensional objects in the external world, though, of course, they may bear some relationships to such external objects.

I cannot rehearse here the arguments I and others have made elsewhere for these claims about SNePS and Cassie. I will, however, provide examples of SNePS networks in the sections that follow. (For further examples and argumentation, see, e.g., Maida & Shapiro 1982; Shapiro & Rapaport 1987, 1991, 1992, 1995; Rapaport 1988b, 1991; Rapaport & Shapiro 1995.)

Does Cassie understand English? (This question is to be understood as urged in §1.1.1.) If so, how? Searle, of course, would say that she doesn't. I say that she does—by manipulating the symbols of her language of thought, viz., SNePS. Let's turn now to these issues.

2   Semantics as Correspondence
2.1   *The Fundamental Principle of Understanding.*

It has been said that you never really understand a complex theory such as quantum mechanics—you just get used to it. This suggests the following *Fundamental Principle of Understanding*:

> To understand something is either
> 1.   to understand it *in terms of something else*, or else
> 2.   to "get used to it".

In type-1 understanding, one understands something *relative* to one's understanding of another thing. This is a *correspondence theory* of understanding (or meaning, or semantics—terms that, for now, I will take as rough synonyms). The correspondence theory of truth is a special case.

Type-2 understanding is *non-relative*. Or, perhaps, it *is* relative—but to itself: To understand something by getting used to it is to understand it in terms of *itself*, perhaps to understand *parts* of it in terms of the *rest* of it. The coherence theory of truth is a special case.

Type-1 understanding is *externally* relative; type-2 understanding is *inter-*

nally relative. Type-1 understanding concerns correspondences between two domains; type-2 understanding concerns syntax.

Since type-1 understanding is relative to the understanding of something *else*, one can only understand something in this first sense if one has *antecedent* understanding of the other thing. How does one understand the other thing? Recursively speaking, either by understanding it relative to some third thing, or by understanding it *in itself*—by being used to it. Either this "bottoms out" in some domain that is understood non-relativistically, or there is a large circle of domains each of which is understood relative to the next. In either case, our understanding bottoms out in "syntactic" understanding of that bottom-level domain or of that large domain consisting of the circle of mutually or sequentially understood domains.

'Correspondence' and 'syntactic understanding' are convenient shorthand expressions that need explication. Before doing so, let me make it clear that I use the terms 'syntax' and 'semantics' in Morris's classic sense (Morris 1938: 6-7): *Syntax* concerns the relations that symbols have among themselves and the ways in which they can be manipulated. *Semantics* concerns the relations between symbols, on the one hand, and the things the symbols "mean", on the other. Classically, then, semantics always concerns two domains: a domain of things taken as symbols and governed by rules of syntax, and a domain of other things. Call these two domains, respectively, the 'syntactic domain' and the 'semantic domain'. There must also be a relation between these two domains—the "semantic relation".

Understanding, in the usual and familiar sense of type-1 understanding, is a semantic enterprise in Morris's sense of semantics. But this has some surprising ramifications. Once these are seen, we can turn to the less familiar, type-2 sense of understanding as a syntactic enterprise (§3).

When faced with some new phenomenon or experience, we seek to understand it. Perhaps this need to understand has some evolutionary survival value; perhaps it is uniquely human. Our first strategy in such a case is to find something, no matter how incomplete or inadequate, with which to *compare* the new phenomenon or experience. By thus *interpreting* the "unknown" or "new" in terms of the "known" or "given", we seek analogies that will begin to satisfy, at least for the moment, our craving for understanding. For instance, I found the film, *My Twentieth Century*, to be very confusing (albeit quite entertaining—part of the fun was trying to figure it out, trying to understand it). I found that I could understand it—at least as a working hypothesis—by mapping the carefree character Lili to the pleasure-seeking, hedonistic aspects of 20th-century life; another character—her serious twin sister, Dora—to the revolutionary political activist, social-caring aspects of 20th-century life; and the third main character—a professor—to the rational, scientific aspects of 20th-century life. The film, however, is quite complex, and these mappings—these correspondences or analogies—provided for me at best a weak, inadequate understanding. The point, however, is that I *had to*—I was *driven to*—find *something* in terms of which I could make sense of what I was experiencing.

This need for connections as a basis for understanding, as an anchor in uncharted waters, can also be seen in the epiphenal well-house episode in the life of Helen Keller. With water from the well running over one hand while Annie Sullivan finger-spelled 'w-a-t-e-r' in the other, Helen suddenly understood that 'w-a-t-e-r' meant water (Keller 1905). This image of one hand literally in the semantic domain and the other literally in the syntactic domain is striking. By "co-activating" her knowledge (her understanding) of the semantic domain (viz., her experiences of the world around her) and her knowledge of the syntactic domain (viz., her experiences of finger-spellings), she was able to "integrate" (or "bind") these two experiences and thus understand (cf. Mayes 1991: 111).

Is there an alternative to the classical view of semantics as correspondence? Many philosophers and linguists look with scorn upon formal or model-theoretic semantics. However, as long as one is willing to talk about "pairings" of sentences (or their structural descriptions) with meaning (cf. Higginbotham 1985: 3), there is no alternative. That is, if we are to talk *at all* about "the meaning *of* a sentence", we must talk about *two* things: sentences and meanings. Thus, there must be two domains: the domain of sentences (described syntactically) and the domain of the semantic interpretation.

There is, however, another kind of semantics, which linguists not of the formal persuasion study. Here, one is concerned not with what the meanings of linguistic items are, but with semantic relationships among linguistic items: synonymy, implication, etc.[6] These relationships are usually distinct from, though sometimes dependent upon, syntactic relationships. But note that they are, nonetheless, relationships *among linguistic, i.e., syntactic, items.* Hence, on our terms, they, too, are "syntactic", not "semantic".[7] So, semantics is either correspondence or else syntactic.

2.2 Tarskian Semantics.
2.2.1 Syntactic systems.

On the standard view, the syntactic domain is usually some (formalized) language L, described syntactically. That is, one specifies a stock of symbols and rules for forming well-formed formulas (WFFs) from them. (What I intend by 'symbols' are just marks, (perhaps) physical inscriptions or sounds, that have only some very minimal features such as having distinguished, relatively unchanging shapes capable of being recognized when encountered again.) A *language* is sometimes augmented with a *logic*: Certain WFFs of L are distinguished as axioms (or "primitive theorems"), and rules of inference are provided that specify how to produce "new" theorems from "old" ones. The general pattern should be familiar (see, e.g., Rapaport 1992ab). The point is that all we have so far are symbols and (syntactic) rules for manipulating them either linguistically (to form WFFs) or logically (to form theorems)—syntax in Morris's sense.

2.2.2 Semantic interpretations.

Given a syntactic domain such as L, one can ask purely "internal", syntactic, questions: What are L's WFFs and theorems? One can also ask: What's the meaning of all this? What do L's symbols mean (if anything)? What, e.g., is so special about the WFFs or the theorems? To answer this sort of question, we must go outside the syntactic domain, providing "external" entities that the symbols mean, and showing the mappings—the associations, the correspondences—between the two domains.

Now a curious thing happens: I need to show you the semantic domain. If I'm very lucky, I can just point it out to you—we can look at it together, and I can describe the correspondences ("The symbol A_{37} means that red thing over there."). But, more often, I have to describe the semantic domain to you in... symbols, and hope that the meaning of *those* symbols will be obvious to you.

As an example, let's see how to provide a semantic interpretation of L. Assuming L has individual terms, function symbols, and predicate symbols —combinable in various (but not arbitrary) ways—I need to provide meanings for each such symbol as well as for their legal combinations. So, we'll need a non-empty domain **D** of things that the terms will mean and sets **F** and **R** of things that L's function and relation symbols will mean, respectively. These three sets can be collectively called **M** (for Model). **D** contains anything you want to talk or think about. **F** and **R** contain functions and relations on **D** of various arities—i.e., anything you want to be able to say about the things in **D**. That's our *ontology*, what there is.

Now for the correspondences. To say what a symbol of L means in **M**, we can define an interpretation mapping I that will assign to each symbol of L something in **M**. Again, the general way of doing this should be familiar (cf. Rapaport 1992ab). Typically, I is a homomorphism; i.e., it satisfies a principle of compositionality: The interpretation of a molecular symbol is determined by the interpretations of its atomic constituents in the usual recursive manner. Ideally, I is an *isomorphism*—a 1-1 and onto homomorphism; i.e., *every* item in **M** is the meaning of *just one* symbol of L.[8] (Being onto is tantamount to L's being "complete".) In this ideal situation, **M** is a virtual duplicate of L. (Indeed, **M** could *be* L itself (cf. Chang & Keisler 1973: 4ff), but that's not very interesting or useful for *understanding* L.) Less ideally, there might be symbols of L that are *not* interpretable in **M**: I would be a *partial* function. Such is the case when L is English and **M** is the world ('unicorn' is English, but unicorns don't exist), though if we "enlarge" or "extend" **M** in some way, then we can make I total (e.g., we could take **M** to be Meinong's *Aussersein* instead of the actual world; cf. Rapaport 1981). In another less ideal circumstance, "Horatio's Law" might hold: There are more things in **M** than in L; i.e., there are elements of **M** not expressible in L: I is not onto. Or I might be a relation, not a function, so L would be ambiguous. There is another, more global, sense in which L could be ambiguous: By choosing a different **M** (and a different *I*), we could give the symbols of *L* entirely distinct meanings. Worse, the two **M**s need not be isomorphic.

Suppose that *L* is a language for ordinary propositional logic and that **M** is a model for it consisting of states of affairs and Boolean operations on them. As an experiment, one could devise an exotic formal symbol system *L'* using, say, boxes and other squiggles as symbols, and give it a syntax like—but not *obviously* like—that of *L* (say, with only postfix notation, to make it more disorienting). Not realizing that it was syntactically isomorphic to *L*, one could only understand *L'* by getting used to manipulating its symbols, laboriously creating WFFs and proving theorems: doing grammatical and logical syntax. But one could provide relief by giving a semantic interpretation of *L'* in terms of a model whose domain is *L*'s atomic *symbols*. Of course, I could also have told you what *L'*'s symbols mean in terms of *L*'s model, **M**. In that case, *L'* just *is* ordinary propositional logic, exotically notated. In the first way, the model for *L'* is itself a syntactic formal symbol system (viz., *L*) whose meaning can be given in terms of **M**, but *L'*'s meaning can be given either in terms of *L or* in terms of **M**.

Obviously, the exotic *L'* is not a very "natural" symbol system. Usually, when one presents the syntax of a formal symbol system, one already has a semantic interpretation in mind, and one *designs* the syntax to "capture" that semantics: In a sense that will become clearer, the syntax is a model—an implementation—of the semantics.

We also see that it is possible and occasionally even useful to allow *one syntactic* formal symbol system to be the semantic interpretation of *another*. Of course, this is only useful if the interpreting syntactic system is antecedently understood. How? In terms of *another* domain with which we are antecedently familiar! So, in our example, the unfamiliar *L'* was interpreted in terms of the more familiar *L*, which, in turn, is interpreted in terms of **M**. And how is it that we understand what states of affairs in the world are? Well...we've just gotten used to them.

In our example, *L* is a sort of "swing" domain, serving as *L'*'s *semantic* domain and as **M**'s *syntactic* domain. We can have a "chain" of domains, each of which except the first is a semantic domain for its predecessor, and each of which except the last is a syntactic domain for its successor. To understand any domain in the chain, we must understand its successor. How do we understand the last one? Syntactically. But I'm getting ahead of myself. Let's first look at some "chains".

2.3 *The Correspondence Continuum: Data.*

Let's begin with examples of *pairs* of things: One member of each pair plays the role of the syntactic domain; the other plays the role of the semantic domain.

1. The first example is the obvious one: *L* and **M** (or *L'* and *L*).

2. The next examples come from what I'll call (after Wartofsky 1979) *The Muddle of the Model in the Middle*. There are two notions of "model" in science and mathematics: We speak of a "mathematical model" of some physical phenomenon, by which we mean a mathematical, usually formal, theory of the phenomenon. In this sense, a model is a *syntactic* domain whose intended semantic interpretation is the physical phenomenon being "modeled". But we also speak of a semantic interpretation of a syntactic domain as a "model", as in the phrase 'model-theoretic semantics'. In this sense, a model is a *semantic* domain. We have the following syntax/semantics pairs:

   data/formal theory (i.e., theory as interpretation of the data),

   formal theory/set-theoretic (or mathematical) model (i.e., a model of the theory),

   set-theoretic (or mathematical) model/real-world phenomenon.

   The latter is closely related to—if not identical with—the data that we began with, giving us a cycle of domains! (Cf. Rosenblueth & Wiener 1945: 316.)

3. A *newspaper photograph* can be thought of as a semantic interpretation of its *caption*. But a cognitive agent reading the caption and looking at the photo makes further correspondences: (a) There will be a mental model of the caption—the reader's semantic interpretation of the caption-as-syntax; (b) there will be a mental model of the photo—the reader's semantic interpretation of the photo-as-syntax; and, (c) there may be a single mental model that collates the information from each of these and which, in turn, is a semantic interpretation of the picture+caption unit. (Srihari & Rapaport 1989, 1990; Srihari 1991ab.)

4. A *musical score*, say, Bach's *Goldberg Variations*, is a piece of syntax; a *performance of* it is a semantic interpretation. And, of course, there could be a performance of the *Goldberg Variations* on piano or on a harpsichord. E.g., a piano transcription of a symphony is a semantic interpretation of the symphony (cf. Pincus 1990; conversely, Smith (1985: 636) considers "musical scores as models of a symphony").

5. Similarly, the *script* of a play is syntax; a *performance* of the play is a semantic interpretation. For a performance to be a semantic interpretation of the script, an actual *person* would play the role (i.e., be the semantic interpretation) of a *character* in the play. (Scripts are like computer programs; performances are like computer processes; see example 17; cf. Rapaport 1988a.)

6. A *movie* or *play* based on a *novel* can be considered a semantic interpretation of the text. In this case, there must be correspondences between the characters, events, etc., in the book and the play or movie, with some details of the book omitted (for lack of time) and some things in the play or movie added (decisions must be made about the colors of costumes, which might not have been specified in the book, just as one can *write* about a particular elephant without specifying whether it's facing left or right, but one can't *show*, *draw*, or *imagine* the elephant without so specifying).

7. Consider a narrative text as a piece of syntax: a certain sequence of sentences and other expressions in some natural language. The *narrative* tells a *story*—the story is a semantic interpretation of the text. On this way of viewing things, the narrative has a "plot"—descriptions of certain events in the story, but not necessarily ordered in the chronological sequence that the events "actually" occurred in. Thus, one story can be told in many ways, some more interesting

or suspenseful than others. The story takes place in a "story world". Characters, places, times, etc., in the story world correspond to linguistic descriptions or expressions of them in the narrative. (Cf. Segal 1995.)

8. The reader of the narrative constructs a mental model of the narrative as he or she reads it. This mental story is a semantic interpretation of the syntactic narrative. Or one could view it as a *theory* constructed from the narrative-as-data (cf. Bruder et al. 1986; Duchan et al. 1995).

9. Examples 4-8 suggest a tree of examples: Some *narrative text* might be interpreted as a *play*, on which an *opera* is based. There could be a *film* of a *ballet* based on the *opera*, and these days one could expect a *"novelization"* of the film. Of course, a (different) ballet could be based directly on the play, or a film could have been based directly on the play, then novelized, then re-filmed. Or a symphony might have been inspired by the play, and then have several performances.

10. The *linguistic and perceptual "input"* to a cognitive agent can be considered as a syntactic domain whose semantic interpretation is provided by the agent's *mental model* of his or her (or its) sensory input. (The mental model is the agent's "theory" of the sensory "data"; cf. examples 2, 8.)

11. The *mental model*, in turn, can be considered as a syntactic language of thought whose semantic interpretation is provided by the *actual world*. In this sense, a person's beliefs are true to the extent that they correspond to the world.

12. In Kamp's Discourse Representation Theory, there is a discourse (i.e., a linguistic text—a piece of syntax), a (sequence of) discourse representation structures, and the actual world (or a representation thereof), with mappings from the discourse to the discourse representation structures, from the discourse to the world, and from the discourse representation structures to the world. Each such mapping is a semantic interpretation. One can also consider the correspondences, if any, between the story world and the actual world; these, too, are semantic. (Cf. examples 7, 8, 10, and 11.)

13. The *Earth* is the semantic domain for a global *map*.

14. A *house* is a semantic interpretation of a *blueprint* (cf. Potts 1973, Rapaport 1978, Smith 1985).

15. A *scale model* (say, of an airplane) corresponds to the *thing modeled* (say, the airplane itself) as syntax to semantic interpretation. And, of course, the thing modeled could itself be a scale model, say, a statue; so I could have a model of a statue, which is, in turn, a model of a person. (Cf. Smith 1985, Shapiro & Rapaport 1991).

16. A *French translation* of an *English text* can be seen from the French speaker's point of view as a *semantic* interpretation of the English syntax, and from the English speaker's point of view as a *syntactic* expression of the English (cf. Gracia 1990: 533).

17. A computer *program* is a static piece of syntax; a computer *process* can be thought of as its semantic interpretation. And, according to Smith, one of the concerns of knowledge representation is to interpret *processes* in terms of the actual world: "It follows that, in the traditional terminology, the *semantic domain* of traditional programming language analyses [which "take...semantics as the job of mapping programs onto processes"] should be the knowledge representer's so-called *syntactic* domain" (Smith 1987: 15, 17-18).

18. A *data structure* (such as a stack or a record) provides a semantic interpretation of (or, a way of categorizing) the otherwise inchoate and purely syntactic *bits* in a computer (Tenenbaum & Augenstein 1981, Schneiderman 1993). Suppose we have a computer program intended to model the behavior of customers lining up at a bank. Some of its data structures will represent customers. This gives rise to the following transitive syntax-semantics chain: syntactic bits are semantically interpreted by data structures, which, in turn, are semantically interpreted as customers. (Cf. Smith 1982: 11.)

No doubt you can supply more examples. My conclusion is this:

> Semantics and correspondence are co-extensive. *Whenever* two domains can be put into a correspondence (preferably, but not necessarily, a homomorphism), one of the domains (which can be considered to be the *syntactic domain* can be understood in terms of the other (which will be the *semantic domain*).

2.4 The Correspondence Continuum: Implications.

The syntactic domain need not be a "language", either natural or formal. It need only be analyzable into parts (or symbols) that can be combined and related—i.e., manipulated—according to rules. (Cf. Wartofsky 1979: 6.)

Moreover, *the so-called "syntactic" and "semantic" domains must be treated on a par*; i.e., one cannot say of a domain that it is syntactic except relative to another domain which is taken to be the semantic one, and vice versa: "[T]he question of whether an element is syntactic or semantic is a function of the point of view; the syntactic domain for one interpretation function can readily be the semantic domain of another (and a semantic domain may of course include its own syntactic domain)" (Smith 1982: 10).

Finally, *what makes something an appropriate **semantic** domain is that it be antecedently understood*. This is crucial for promoting semantics as "mere" correspondence to the more familiar notion of semantics as meaning or under-standing. And ultimately such antecedent understanding is syntactic manipulation of the items in the semantic domain.

Suppose that something identified as the semantic domain is *not* antecedently understood, but that the putative syntactic domain *is*. Then, by switching their roles, one can learn about the former semantic domain by means of its syntactic "interpretation" (cf. Rosenblueth and Wiener 1945: 318, Corless 1992: 203).[9]

2.5 The Correspondence Continuum of Brian Cantwell Smith.

What I have referred to as the "correspondence continuum" has received its most explicit statement and detailed investigation in the writings of Brian

Cantwell Smith (from whom I have borrowed the term).

2.5.1 Worlds, models, and representations.

In an important essay on computer ethics, Smith (1985) sets up the Wartofskian "model muddle" as follows:

> When you design...a computer system, you first formulate a model of the problem you want it to solve, and then construct the computer program in its terms. ...
>
> To build a model is to conceive of the world in a certain delimited way. ...[C]omputers have a special dependence on these models: *you write an explicit description of the model down inside the computer*, in the form of a set of rules or...*representations*—...linguistic formulae encoding, in the terms of the model, the facts and data thought to be relevant to the system's behaviour. ...[T]hat's really what computers are (and how they differ from other machines): they run by manipulating representations, and representations are always formulated in terms of models. (Smith 1985: 636.)

The model is an abstraction of the real-world situation. For instance, "a hospital blueprint would pay attention to the structure and connection of its beams, but not to the arrangements of proteins in the wood the beams are made of..." (Smith 1985: 637). The model is itself "modeled" or *described* in the computer program; the model, thus, is a "swing domain", playing the role of syntactic domain to the real world's semantic domain, and the role of semantic domain to the computer program's syntactic—indeed, linguistic—description of it.

Smith calls the process of abstraction (which for him includes "every act of conceptualization, analysis, categorization", in addition to the mere omission of certain details) a necessary "act of violence—[if you] don't ignore some of what's going on—you would become so hypersensitive and so overcome with complexity that you would be unable to act" (Smith 1985: 637). Of course, one ought to do the least amount of violence consistent with not being overwhelmed. This might require successive approximations to a good model that balances abstraction against adequacy. Lakoff's complaints about "objectivism" (1987) can be seen as a claim that "classical" categories defined by necessary and sufficient conditions do too much violence, so that the resulting models are inadequate to the real-world situations.

But I fail to see why complexity makes acting difficult. The real-world situation has precisely the maximal degree of complexity, yet a human *is* capable of acting. Moreover, a complete and complex model of some real-world situation might be so complex that a mere human trying to understand *it* might "drown" in its "infinite richness" (Smith 1985: 637), much as a human can't typically hand-trace a very long and complex computer program. Yet a computer can execute that program without "drowning" in its complexity.

Nevertheless, for Smith, "models are inherently *partial*. All thinking, and all computation, ...similarly *have* to be partial: that's how they are able to work" (Smith 1985: 637). Note that some of the partiality of thinking and computation is inherited from the partiality of the model and then compounded: To the extent that thinking and computation use partial descriptions of partial models of the world, they are doubly partial. Much inevitably gets lost in translation, so to speak. Models certainly need to be partial, at least to the extent that the omitted "implementation" details are irrelevant, and certainly to the extent that they (or their descriptions) are discrete whereas the world is continuous. But does thinking "have to be partial" in order to be "able to work"? A *real* thinking thing isn't partial—it is, after all, part of the real world—though its descriptions of models of the world might be partial. And that's really Smith's point—thinking things (and computing things) work with partial models. They "represent the world *as being a certain way*", "*as being one way as opposed to another*" (Smith 1987: 4, 51n.1): They present a fragmentary point of view, a facet of a complete, complex real-world situation—they are objects under a (partial) description (cf. Castañeda 1972).

So we have the following situation. On one side is the real world in all its fullness and complexity. On the other side are partial models of the world and—embedded in computer programs—partial descriptions of the models. But there is a gap between full reality, on the one hand, and partial models and descriptions, on the other, insofar as the latter fail to capture the richness of the former, which they are intended to interact with: Action "is not partial. ...When you reach out your hand and grasp a plow, it is the real field you are digging up, not your model of it...[C]omputers, like us, participate in the real world: they take real actions" (Smith 1985: 637-638). This holds for programs with natural-language competence, too. Their actions are speech acts, and they affect the real world to the extent that communication between them and other natural-language–using agents is successful.

To see how the "reaching out" can fail to cross the gap, consider a blocks-world robot I once saw, programmed with a version of an AI program (Winston 1977) for picking up and putting down small objects at various locations in a confined area. This robot really dealt with the actual world—it was not a simulation. But it did so successfully only by accident. If the blocks were *perfectly* arranged in the blocks-world area, all went well. But if they were slightly out of place—as they were on the day I saw the demo—the robot blindly and blithely executed its program and behaved as if it were picking up, moving, and putting down the blocks. More often, it failed to pick them up, knocked others down as it rotated, and dropped those it hadn't grasped correctly. It was humorous, even pathetic. The robot was doing what it was "supposed" to do, what it was programmed to do, but its partial model was inadequate. Its *successful* runs were, thus, accidental—they worked only if the real world was properly aligned to allow the robot to affect it in the "intended" manner. Clearly, a robot with a more complete model would do better. The Rochester checkers-playing robot, for example, has a binocular vision system that enables it to "see" what it's doing and to bring its motions into alignment with a changing world (Marsh et al. 1992).

So, computers participate in the real world *without interpretations of their behavior by humans* and without the willing participation of humans.[10] Does a computer with natural-language competence really "use language" or "communicate" without a human interpreter? There are two answers: 'yes' and 'no, but so what?':

Yes: As long as the computer is using the vocabulary of some natural language according to its rules of grammar, it is thereby using that language, even if there is no other language-using entity around, including a human. This is true for humans, too: Even if I talk to myself without uttering a sound, I mean things by my silent use of language; sound or other external signs of language-use are not essential to language (Cho 1992). And, therefore, neither is a hearer or other interlocutor.[11]

No; but so what?: A human might interpret the computer's natural-language output differently from how the computer "intended" it. Or one might prefer to say that the computer's output is meaningless until a human interprets it. The output would be mere syntax; its semantics would have to be provided by the human, *although it could be provided by another natural-language–using computer*. However, interpretation problems can arise in human-to-human communication, too. Nicolaas de Bruijn once told me roughly the following anecdote: Some chemists were talking about a certain molecular structure, expressing difficulty in understanding it. De Bruijn, overhearing them, thought they were talking about mathematical lattice theory, since everything they said could be—and was—interpreted by him as being about the mathematical, rather than the chemical, domain. He told them the solution of their problem in terms of lattice theory. They, of course, understood it in terms of chemistry. Were de Bruijn and the chemists talking about the same thing? No; but so what? They *were* communicating!

It is also important to note that when a natural-language–competent computer interacts with a human or another natural-language–competent computer, both need to be able to reach a more-or-less stable state of mutual comprehension. If the computer uses an expression in an odd way (perhaps merely because it was poorly programmed or did not adequately learn how to use that expression), the human (or other interlocutor) must be able to correct the computer—*not* by reprogramming it—but by *telling* it, in natural language, what it should have said. Similarly, if the human uses an expression in a way that the computer does not recognize, the computer must be able to figure out what the human meant. (Cf. Rapaport 1988b and §§2.6.2, 3, below.)

2.5.2 The model-world gap and the third-person point of view.

The gap between model and world is difficult, perhaps impossible, to bridge:

> ...we in general have no guarantee that the models are right—indeed we have no *guarantee* about much of anything about the relationship between model and world.
>
> ...
>
> ...[T]here is a very precise mathematical theory called "model theory." You might think that it would be a theory about what models are, what they are good for, how they correspond to the worlds they are models of. ...Unfortunately,...model theory doesn't address the model-world relationship at all. Rather, what model theory does is to tell you how your descriptions, representations, and programs *correspond to your model*. (Smith 1985: 638.)

To "address the model-world relationship" requires a language capable of dealing with *both* the model *and* the world. This would, at best, be a "Russellian" language that allowed sentences or propositions to be constructed out of real-world objects (Russell 1903, Moore 1988). It would have to have sentences that explicitly and directly linked parts of the model with parts of the world (recall Helen Keller at the well house). How can such model-world links be made? The only way, short of a Russellian language, is by having *another* language that describes the world, and then provide links between *that* language and the model. (That would have to be done in a meta-language. I am also assuming, here, that the model is a language—a description of the world. If it is a non-linguistic model, we would need yet another language to describe *it*.) But this leads to a Bradleyan regress, for how will we be able to address the relationship between the world and the language that describes it? This parallels the case of the mind, which, insofar as it has no direct access to the external world, has no access to the reference relation.

According to Smith, model theory discusses only the relation (call it R_1) between a model and its description. It does not deal with the relation (call it R_2) between the model and the real-world situation. But if semantics is correspondence, the two cases should be parallel; one ought to be able to deal with both R_1 and R_2, or with neither. Yet we have just seen that R_2 cannot be dealt with except indirectly. Consider R_1. Is it the case that the relation between the computer and the model is dealt with by model theory? No; as Smith says, it deals with the relation between a *description* of the model and the model. After all, the computer is part of the real world (cf. Rapaport 1985/1986: 68). So the argument about the model-world relationship also holds here, for, in the actual computer, there is a physical (real-world) implementation of the model.

Thus, a relation between a syntactic domain and a semantic domain can be understood only by taking an independent, external, third-person point of view. There must be a standpoint—a language, if you will—capable of having equal access to *both* domains. A semantic relation can obtain between two domains, but neither domain can describe that relation by itself. From the point of view of the model, nothing can be said about the world. Only from the point of view of some agent or system capable of taking *both* points of view simultaneously can comparisons be made and correspondences established.

2.5.3 Assymetry.

Smith begins "The Correspondence Continuum" by considering such core semantic or intentional relations as representation and knowledge, "asymmetric" relations that "characterise phenomena that are *about* something, that refer to the world, that have meaning or content" (Smith 1987: 2). What kind of asymmetry is this? Wartofsky has argued that any domain can be used to represent another (cf. our data in §2.3) and that the modeling relation (cognitive agent S takes domain x as a model of domain y) is asymmetric. Yet Wartofsky says that it is not merely that x and y cannot be switched, but rather that in order for S to take x as a model of y, x must (be believed by S to) have fewer relevant properties than y, because if it were "equally rich in the same properties...it would be identical with its object", and if it were "*richer* in properties,...these would then not be ones relevant to its object; it [the object] wouldn't possess them, and so the model couldn't be taken to represent them in any way" (Wartofsky 1979: 5-7).

But it is more appropriate to locate the asymmetry in the fact that the model must be antecedently understood: Suppose an antecedently understood model M of some state of affairs or object O has fewer properties than O, the case that Wartofsky takes to be the norm. Here, the asymmetry between M and O could be ascribed either to M's having fewer properties (as Wartofsky would have it) or to M's being antecedently understood (as I would have it). Suppose, next, that M and O have the same properties. On Wartofsky's view, the asymmetry is lost, but if I antecedently understood M, I could still use M as a model of O: This is the situation of Dennett's Ballad of Shakey's Pizza Parlor (1982: 53-60): Since all Shakey Pizza Parlors are indistinguishable, I can use my knowledge of one to understand the others (e.g., to locate the rest rooms). Finally, suppose that M has *more* (or perhaps merely *different*) properties than O. For example, one could use (the liquidity of) milk as a model of (the liquidity of) mercury (at least, for certain purposes),[12] even though milk has more (certainly, different) properties. These extra (or different) properties are "implementation details"; but they are *merely* that—hence, to be ignored. As long as I antecedently understand M, I can use it as a model of O, no matter how many properties it has. But if I *don't* antecedently understand M, then I *can't* use it as a model (cf. n. 9). And how do I antecedently understand M? By getting used to it.

2.5.4 The continuum.

Smith sees the classical semantic enterprise as a special case of a general theory of correspondence. I see *all* cases of correspondence as being semantic.

Smith distinguishes various types of correspondences. Some semantic relations, e.g., are transitive; others aren't (Smith 1987, e.g., p. 27). Consider, as he suggests, a photo (P_2) of a photo (P_1) of a ship (S). Smith observes that P_2 is not, on pain of use-mention confusion, a photo of S, but that this is "pedantic". Clearly, there are differences between P_1 and P_2: Properties of P_1 *per se* (say, a scratch on the negative) might appear in P_2 and be mistakenly attributed to S. But consider a photo of a map of the world; I *could* use the *photo* as a map to locate, say, Vichy, France. As Smith points out, the photo of the map isn't a map (just as P_2 isn't a photo of S). Yet *information* is preserved, so the photo can be *used as* a map (or: to the extent that information is preserved, it can be so used).

Another of Smith's examples is a document-image–understanding system, which has a knowledge representation of a digital image of a photo (cf. example 3, above). Does the knowledge representation represent the digitized image, or does it represent the photo? The practical value of such a system lies in the knowledge representation representing the photo, not the (intermediate) digitized image. But perhaps, to be pedantic about it, we should say that the knowledge representation does represent the digitized image even though *we* take it *as* representing the photo. After all, the digitized image is internal to the document-image–understanding system, which has no direct access to the photo. Of course, neither do we. Smith seems to agree:

> The true situation...is this: a given intentional structure—language, process, impression, model—is set in correspondence with one or more other structures, each of which is in turn set in correspondence with still others, at some point reaching (we hope) the states of affairs in the world that the original structures were genuinely about.
>
> It is this structure that I call the 'correspondence continuum'—a semantic soup in which to locate transitive and non-transitive linguistic relations, relations of modelling and encoding, implementation and realisation. ...(Smith 1987: 29.)

But can one distinguish among this variety of relations? What makes modeling different from implementation, say? Perhaps one can distinguish between transitive and non-transitive semantic relations,[13] but within those two categories, useful distinctions cannot really be drawn, say, between modeling, encoding, implementation, etc. Perhaps one can say that there are "intended" distinctions, but these cannot be pinned down. Perhaps one can say that it is the person doing the relating who decides, but is that any more than giving different names or offering external purposes? Indeed, Smith suggests (p. 29) that the only differences are individual ones.

He thinks, though, that not all "of these correspondence relations should be counted as genuinely semantic, intentional, representational" (p. 30), citing as an example the correspondences between (1a) an optic-nerve signal and (1b) a retinal intensity pattern, between (2a) the retinal intensity pattern and (2b) light-wave structures, between (3a) light-wave structures and (3c) "surface shape on which sunlight falls", and between (4a) that sunlit surface shape and (4b) a cat. He observes that "it is the cat that I see, not any of these intermediary structures"

(p. 30). But so what? Some correspondence relations are not present to consciousness. Nonetheless, they can be treated as semantic.

Not so, says Smith: "correspondence is a far more general phenomenon than representation or interpretation" (p. 30). Perhaps to be "genuinely semantic" (p. 30) is to be *about* something. But why *can't* we say that the retinal intensity pattern is "about" the light-wave structures? Or that the light-wave structures are "about" the sunlit surface shape? The relation between two of these purely physical processes is one of information transfer, so it is surely semantic. Note that it seems to be precisely when phenomena are information-theoretic that models of them *are* the phenomena themselves: Photos of maps *are* maps; models of minds *are* minds.

In any case, what is important for my purposes is Smith's claim that

> the correspondence continuum challenges the clear difference between "syntactic" and "semantic" analyses of representational formalisms... . ...[N]o simple "syntactic/semantic" distinction gets at a natural joint in the underlying subject matter. (Smith 1987: 38.)

Although he might be making the point that there can be no "pure" syntactic (or semantic) analyses—that each involves the other—his discussion suggests that the "challenge" is the existence of swing domains.

2.5.5 Smith's Gap, revisited.

So we have a continuum, or at least a chain, of domains that correspond to one another, each (except the last) understandable in terms of the next. Yet where the last domain is the actual world, Smith's Gap separates it from any model of it. Nonetheless, if that model of the world is in the mind of a cognitive agent—if it is *Cassie's* mental model of the world—then it was constructed (or it developed) by means of perception, communication, and other direct experience or direct contact with the actual world. In terms of Smith's three-link chain (§2.5.1) consisting of a part of the actual world (W), a set-theoretic model of it (M_W), and a linguistic description (in some program) of the model (D_{M_W}), what we have in Cassie's case is that her mental model of the world is simultaneously M_W and D_{M_W}. It is produced by causal links with the external world. Thus, the gap is, in fact, bridged (in this case, at least). Bridged, but not comprehended. In formalizing something that is essentially *in*formal, one can't *prove* (formally, of course) that the formalization is correct; one can only discuss it with other formalizers and come to some (perhaps tentative, perhaps conventional) agreement about it. Thus, Cassie can never check to see if her formal M_W really does match the informal, messy W. Thus, the gap remains. But, once bridged, M_W is independent of W, except when Cassie interacts with W by conversing, asking a question, or acting. That is the lesson of methodological solipsism. Let us turn to Cassie's construction of M_W.

2.6 Cassie's Mental Model.

How does Cassie (or any (computational) cognitive agent) construct her mental model of the world, and what does that model look like? I will focus on her language-understanding abilities—her mental model of a conversation or narrative. (For visual perception, cf. example 3, above.) Details of Cassie's language-understanding abilities have been discussed in a series of earlier papers.[14] Here, I will concentrate on a broad picture of how she processes linguistic input, and a consideration of the kind of world model she constructs as a result.

2.6.1 Fregean semantics.

Frege wanted to divorce logic and semantics from psychology. He told us that terms and expressions (signs, or symbols) of a language "express" a "sense" and that to some—but not all—*senses* there "corresponds" a "referent". So expressions indirectly "designate" or "refer" (or fail to designate or refer) to a referent. Further, the sense is the "way" in which the referent is presented by the expression. Except for the mentalistic notion of an "associated idea", which he does not take very seriously, all of this is very objective or non-cognitive (Frege 1892).

Something exactly like this goes on in cognition, when Cassie—or any natural-language–understanding cognitive agent—understands language:

1. Cassie perceives (hears or reads) a sentence.
2. By various computational processes (namely, an augmented-transition-network parser with lexical and morphological modules, plus various modules for dealing with anaphora resolution, computing belief spaces and subjective contexts, etc.), she constructs (or finds) a molecular node in the semantic network that is her mental model.
3. That node constitutes her understanding of the perceived sentence.

Now, the procedures that input pieces of language and output nodes are algorithms—*ways* in which the nodes are associated with the linguistic symbols. They are, thus, akin to senses, and the nodes are akin to referents (cf. Wilks 1972). Here, though, all symbols denote, even 'unicorn' and 'round square': If Cassie hears or reads about a unicorn, she constructs a node representing her concept (her understanding) of that unicorn. Her nodes represent the things she has thought about, whether or not they exist—they are part of her "epistemological ontology" (Rapaport 1985/1986).

A very different correspondence can also be set up between natural-language understanding and Frege's theory. According to this correspondence, it is the node in Cassie's mental model that is akin to a sense, and it is an object (if one exists) in the actual world to which that node corresponds that is akin to the referent. On this view, Cassie's unicorn-node represents (or perhaps is) the sense of what she read about, although (unfortunately) there is no corresponding referent in the external world. Modulo the subjectivity or psychologism of this correspondence (Frege would not have identified a sense with an expression of a language of thought), this is surely closer in spirit to Frege's enterprise.

Nonetheless, the first correspondence shows how senses can be interpreted as algorithms that yield referents (a kind of "procedural semantics"; see, e.g., Winograd 1975, Smith 1982). It also avoids the problem of non-denoting expressions: If no "referent" is found, one is just constructed, in a Meinongian spirit (cf. Rapaport 1981).

The various links between thought and language are direct and causal. Consider natural-language generation, the inverse of natural-language understanding. Cassie has certain thoughts; these are private to her.[15] By means of various natural-language-generation algorithms, she produces—directly and causally, from her private mental model—public language: utterances or inscriptions. I hear or read these; this begins the process of natural-language *understanding*. By means of *my* natural-language–understanding algorithms, I interpret her utterances, producing—directly and causally—my private thoughts. Thus, I interpret another's private thoughts indirectly, by directly interpreting her public expressions of those thoughts, which public expressions are, in turn, her direct expressions of her private thoughts. (Cf. Gracia 1990: 495.)

The two direct links are both semantic interpretations. The public expression of Cassie's thoughts is a semantic interpretation (an "implementation" or physical "realization") of her thoughts. And my understanding of what she says is a semantic interpretation of her public utterances. Thus, the public communication language (Shapiro 1993) is a "swing domain".

2.6.2 The nature of a mental model.

Cassie's mental model of the world (including utterances expressed in the public communication language) is expressed in her language of thought. That is, the world is modeled, or represented, by expressions—sentences—of her language of thought (which, for the sake of concreteness, I am taking to be SNePS). There may, of course, be more: e.g., mental imagery. But since Cassie can think and talk about images, they must be linked to the part of her mental model constructed via natural-language understanding (Srihari 1991ab). Hence, we may consider them part of an extended language of thought that allows such imagery among its terms. This extended language of thought, then, is propositional with direct connections to imagistic representations.

In Section 1, I asked how we understand language. This is the challenge of Searle's (1980) Chinese Room Argument: How could Searle-in-the-room come to know the semantics of the Chinese squiggles? One question left open in that debate is whether Searle-in-the-room even knows what their *syntax* is. He could not come to know the syntax (the grammar) just by having, as Searle suggests, a SAM-like program (i.e., a program for global understanding of a narrative using scripts; cf., e.g., Schank & Riesbeck 1981); a syntax-learning program is also needed (see, e.g., Berwick 1979; cf. §1.1.2.2, above). So let us assume that Searle-in-the-room's instruction book includes this.

Given an understanding of the syntax, how can semantics be learned? The meaning of some terms is best learned ostensively, or perceptually: We must see (or hear, or otherwise experience) the term's referent. This ranges from terms for such archetypally medium-sized physical objects as 'cat' and 'cow', through 'red' (cf. Jackson 1986) and 'internal combustion engine', to such abstractions as 'love' and 'think' (cf. Keller 1905: 40f, 300).

But the meaning of many, perhaps most, terms is learned "lexically", or linguistically. Such is dictionary learning. But equally there is the learning, on the fly, of the meaning of new words from the linguistic contexts in which they appear. If 'vase' is unknown, but one learns that Tommy broke a vase, then one can compute that a vase is that which Tommy broke. Initially, this may appear less than informative, though further inferences can be drawn: Vases, whatever they are, are breakable by humans, and all that that entails.[16] As more occurrences of the word are encountered, the "simultaneous equations" (Higginbotham 1989: 469) of the differing contexts, together with background knowledge and some guesswork, help constrain the meaning further, allowing us to revise our theory of the word's meaning. Sooner or later, a provisionally steady state is achieved (pending future occurrences). (See §3.2.2.)

Both methods are contextual. For ostension, the context is physical and external—the real world (or, at least, our perception of it); for the lexical, the context is linguistic (Rapaport 1981). Ultimately, however, the context is mental and internal: The meaning of a term represented by a node in a semantic network is dependent on its location in—i.e., the surrounding context of—the rest of the network (cf. Quine 1951, Quillian 1967, Hill 1994). Such holism has a long and distinguished history, and its share of skeptics (most recently, Fodor and Lepore (1992)). It certainly appears susceptible to charges of circularity (cf., e.g., Harnad 1990), but a chronological theory of how the network is constructed can help to obviate that: Granted that the meaning of 'vase' (for me) may depend on the meaning of 'breakable' *and vice versa*, nonetheless if I learned the meaning of the latter first, it can be used to ground the meaning of the former (for me). Holism, though, has benefits: The meanings of terms get enriched, over time, the more they—or their closest-linked terms in the network—are encountered. For instance, in the research for this essay, certain themes reappeared in various contexts, each appearance enriching the others. In writing, however, one must begin somewhere—writing is a more or less sequential, not a parallel or even holistic, task. Though this is the first mention of holism in the essay, it was not the first in my research, nor will it be the only one.

Understanding, we see again, is recursive. Each time we understand something, we understand it in terms of all that has come before. Each of those things, earlier understood, were understood in terms of what preceded them. The base case is, retroactively, understandable in terms of all that has come later:

> There should therefore be a time in adult life devoted to revisiting the most important books of our youth. Even if the books have remained the same (though they do change, in the light of an altered historical perspective), we have most certainly changed, and our encounter will be an entirely new thing. (Calvino 1986: 19.)

But initially, the base case was understandable solely in terms of itself (or in terms of "innate ideas" or some other mechanism; see Hill 1994 on the semantics of base nodes in SNePS).

But *is* "knowledge of the semantics" (Barwise & Etchemendy 1989: 209) achieved by speakers? If this means knowledge of the relations between word and thing in such a way that it requires knowledge of *both* the words (syntactic knowledge) *and* the things, then: No. For we can't have (direct) knowledge of the things. This is Smith's Gap. It also means, by the way, that ostensive learning is really mental and internal, too: I learn what 'cat' means by seeing one, but really what's happening is that I have a mental representation of that which is before my eyes, and what constitutes the ostensive meaning is a (semantic) link that is established between my internal node associated with 'cat' and the *internal* node that represents what is before my eyes.

Thus, "knowledge of the semantics" means (1) knowledge of the relations *between* our linguistic concepts and our "purely conceptual" concepts (i.e., that correspond to, or are caused by, external input) and (2) knowledge of the relations *among* our purely linguistic concepts. The former (1) is "semantic", the latter (2) "syntactic", as classically construed. Yet, since the former concerns relations among our internal concepts (cf. Srihari 1991ab), it, too, is syntactic.[17]

Barwise and Etchemendy (1989) conflate such an internal semantic theory with a kind of external one, identifying *"content of a speaker's knowledge* of the truth conditions of the sentences of his or her language" with *"the relationship between sentences and non-linguistic facts* about the world that would support the truth of a claim made with the sentence" (p. 220, my italics). I take "the content of a speaker's knowledge of...truth conditions" to involve knowing the relations between linguistic and non-linguistic *internal* concepts. This is the internal, Cassie-approach to semantics. In contrast, giving an "account of the relationship between sentences and non-linguistic facts" (p. 220) is an *external* endeavor, one that *I* can give concerning Cassie, but not one that *she* can give about herself. This is because *I* can take a "God's-eye", "third-person" point of view and see both Cassie's mind and the world external to it, thus being able to relate them, whereas she can only take the "first-person" point of view.

However, a "third person" cannot, in fact, have direct access to either the external world or Cassie's concepts (except as in n. 15). So what the third person is *really* comparing (or finding correspondences between) is the third person's *representations* of Cassie's concepts and the third person's *own concepts* representing the external world. That is, the third person *can* establish a semantic correspondence (in the classic sense) between two domains. From the third person's point of view, the two domains are the syntactic domain of Cassie's concepts and the semantic domain of the external world. But, in fact, the two domains are *the third person's representations* of Cassie's concepts and *the third person's representations* of the external world. These are both *internal* to the third person's mind! And internal relations, even though structurally *seman-tic*—i.e., even though they are correspondences between two domains—are fundamentally *syntactic* in the classic sense: They are relations *among* (two classes of) symbols in the third person's language of thought.

What holds for the third person holds also for Cassie. Since she doesn't have direct access to the external world either, she can't have knowledge of "real" semantic correspondences. The best she can do is to have a correspondence between certain of her concepts and her representations of the external world. What might her "knowledge of truth conditions" look like? Here is one possibility: When she learns that Lucy is rich, she builds the network shown in Figure 1.

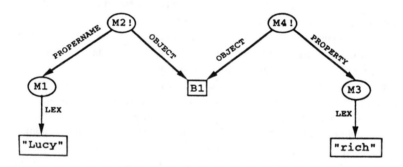

Figure 1: Cassie's belief that Lucy is rich. (Linearly abbreviated: **M4** = **B1** is rich; **M2** = **B1** is named 'Lucy'. Node labels with '!' appended are "asserted", i.e., believed by Cassie.)

Thus, Cassie might think to herself something like: "My thought that [Figure 1] is true iff ($\exists\, x \in$ external world)$[x = $ Lucy & x is rich]". This would require, for its full development, (1) an internal truth predicate (cf. Maida & Shapiro 1982, Neal & Shapiro 1987), (2) an existence predicate (cf. Hirst 1991), (3) a duplication of the network, and (4) a biconditional rule asserting the equivalence (see Figure 2 for a possible version).

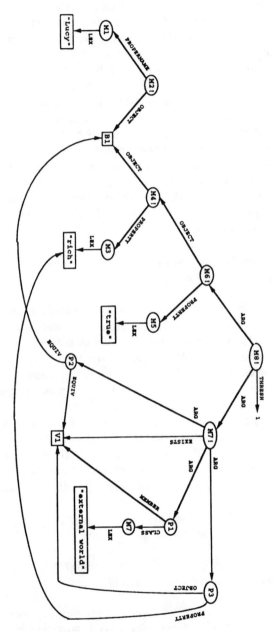

Figure 2: A biconditional rule (**M8**) asserting the equivalence of **M6** = that Lucy is rich is true, and **M7** = something in the external world is Lucy and is rich. (See Shapiro 1979, Shapiro & Rapaport 1987 for the semantics of **thresh**. The truth condition for **M2** is not shown.)

The picture we have of Cassie's mental model of the world (including utterances) is, in part, this: If Cassie hears or reads a sentence, she constructs a mental representation of that sentence qua linguistic entity, *and* she constructs a mental representation of the state of affairs expressed by that sentence. These will be linked by a Tarski-like truth-biconditional (**M8**) asserting that the representation of the sentence (**M7**) is true (**M6**) iff the representation of the state of affairs (**M7**) is believed (**M7 !**). If Cassie sees something, she constructs a mental representation of it, *and* she constructs a mental propositional representation of the state of affairs she sees. These will be linked in ways extrapolatable from §2.3, example 3, above. These networks, of course, are not isolated, but embedded in the entire network that has been constructed so far. What is newly perceived is understood in terms of all that has gone before. This is purely syntactic, since both sides of the biconditional are expressed in Cassie's language of thought. Thus, the best Cassie can do is to have a theory of truth as coherence among her own concepts.

3 Semantics as Syntax.
3.1 The Story So Far.

To understand language is to construct a semantic interpretation—a model—of the language. In fact, we *normally* understand something by modeling it and then determining correspondences between the two domains. In some cases, we are lucky: We can, as it were, keep an eye on each domain, merging the images in our mind's eye. In other cases, notably when one of the domains is the external world, we are not so lucky—Smith's Gap cannot be crossed—and so we can understand that domain *only* in terms of the model. Lucky or not, we understand one thing in terms of another by modeling that which is to be understood (the syntactic domain) in that which we antecedently understand (the semantic domain). But how is the antecedently understood domain antecedently understood? In the base case of our recursive understanding of understanding, a domain must be understood in terms of *itself*, i.e., syntactically.

3.2 Syntactic Understanding.
3.2.1 Familiarity breeds comprehension.

What is type-2, syntactic understanding? What does it mean to "get used to" something? In some sense, it should be obvious:

> In today's chess, only the familiarly shaped Staunton pieces are used. ... [One] reason is the unfamiliarity, to chess players, of other than Staunton pieces....[In Reykjavik, in 1973, two grandmasters] started to play [with a non-Staunton set], and the conversation ran something like:
> "What are you doing? That's a pawn."
> "Oh. I thought it was a bishop."

"Wait! Maybe it is a bishop."

"No, maybe it really is a pawn."

Whereupon the two grandmasters decided to play without the board. They looked at each other and this time the conversation ran:

"D5"

"C4"

"E6"

"Oh, you're trying *that* on me, are you? Knight C3."

And they went along that way until they finished their game. (Schonberg 1990: 38-39.)

In a game played with Staunton pieces, the players are "used to" the pieces. Even in a game played with no physical pieces at all, the players are "used to" the symbolic notation for the pieces. But in a game played with non-Staunton pieces, clearly they are not.

Suppose that the semantic relation is (merely) a correspondence relation. Suppose, further, that it is a homomorphism mapping the syntactic domain into the semantic domain. To understand something in terms of itself would then be to take the syntactic domain as its own semantic domain, treating the homomorphism as an *automorphism*. Such an automorphism would be a relation among the symbols of the syntactic domain, hence a classically syntactic relation. Yet it would also be a *semantic* relation, because it is a correspondence between "two" domains (better: between two roles played by the same domain). Indeed, the very first example of a semantic model in Chang & Keisler 1973 is such a mapping. The syntactic domain, now considered as its own *semantic* domain, is syntactic twice over: once by way of its own, purely syntactic, features, and once by way of the semantic automorphism. (Recall the way some linguists do semantics; cf. §2.1.)

Now, the automorphism is either the identity mapping, or it isn't. If it is, then the symbol manipulations (the syntax) that constitute the semantics are just those of the syntactic domain itself. This is the core meaning of understanding by "getting used to" the system (as in the syntactic way of understanding §2.2.2's *L'*). We do the same thing when we learn how to solve algebraic equations by manipulating symbols (Rapaport 1986).

If the automorphism is *not* the identity mapping, then it must map some elements onto others (or sets of others). So some parts of the syntactic domain will be understood in terms of others. (There may be "fixed points"—symbols that *are* mapped into themselves; see §3.2.3.) Let's see what this means for our central case—natural-language understanding.

3.2.2 Dictionary definitions and algebra.

Dictionary-like definitions are an obvious example of this sort of automorphism. Indeed, this is probably what *most* people mean by "meaning", as opposed to philosophers, logicians, and cognitive scientists—though *some* cognitive scientists are sympathetic: "meanings are, if anything, only other symbols" (Wilks & Fass 1992: 205; cf. Wilks 1971, 1972: 86).

And, as noted earlier (§2.6.2), we learn the meaning of many (if not most) new words in linguistic contexts—either in explicit definitions or "on the fly" in ordinary conversational or literary discourse. The unknown word, like the algebraic unknown, simply means whatever is necessary to give meaning to the entire context in which it appears. The meaning of the unknown word is (the meaning of) the surrounding context—the context "minus" the word. Finding the meaning is, thus, "solving" the context for the unknown: "The appearance of a word in a restricted number of settings suffices to determine its position in the language as a whole" (Higginbotham 1985: 2; cf. Wilks 1971: 519-520). As Wilks 1971 notes, the context must be suitably large to get the "correct" or at least "intended" meaning. But, as the 'vase' example shows (§2.6.2), any context will do for starters. One's understanding of the meaning of the word will *change* as one comes across more contexts in which it is used (or: as the total context becomes larger); ultimately, one's understanding of the meaning will reach a stable state (at least temporarily—everything is subject to revision). Thus, learning a word is theory construction: One's understanding of the word's meaning is a *theory*, subject to revision.

The first time I read the word 'brachet', I did not know what it meant (do you?). Here is the context of that first occurrence:

> [T]here came a white hart running into the hall with a white brachet next to him, and thirty couples of black hounds came running after them with a great cry. (Malory 1470: 66.)

My first hypothesis (believe it or not) was that a brachet was a buckle on a harness worn by the hart. Although this hypothesis goes beyond the algebraic picture I've been painting, the algebraic metaphor is still reasonable if we extend the notion of context to include the background knowledge ("world knowledge" or "commonsense knowledge") that I bring to bear on my understanding of the narrative (cf. Rapaport 1991, Rapaport & Shapiro 1995). Nor does it matter whether this hypothesis is good, bad, indifferent, or just plain silly; if I never see the word again, it won't matter, but, if I do, I will have ample opportunity to revise my beliefs about its meaning. Indeed, after 18 more occurrences of the term,[18] I stabilized on the following theory of its meaning: A brachet is a hound or hunting dog, perhaps a lead hound. Not bad, considering that the *Oxford English Dictionary* defines it as "A kind of hound which hunts by scent". (For details and further references, see Rapaport 1981; Ehrlich & Rapaport 1992; Ehrlich, 1995.)

This is purely syntactic: First, there is no external semantic domain: I did not see a brachet (or a picture of one). Second, when I read the word (or when Cassie does), I build a mental representation of that word embedded in a mental representation of its context. These mental representations are part of the entire network of mental representations in my mind. Thus, the background knowledge I contribute is part and parcel of the mental representation of the new word in context. It is that system of mental representations that constitutes the syntactic domain in which is located "the meaning" of—i.e., my understanding of—the word.

Representing meaning in such a dictionary-like network goes back at least to Quillian 1967, though he was more concerned with merely representing the information in a dictionary, whereas I am concerned with representing meaning as part of a cognitive agent's entire complex network of beliefs. This is a brand of holistic, conceptual-role semantics, since I take the meaning of a word to be, algebraically, the role it plays in its context.

3.2.3 Understanding the parts.

Another thing that using parts of the syntactic domain to understand the rest of it might mean is that those parts are primitives. How are *they* understood? What do *they* mean?

They might be "markers" with no intrinsic meaning. But such markers *get* meaning the more they are used—the more roles they play in providing meaning to *other* nodes. A helpful analogy comes from Wartofsky:

> '[M]ental' objects, or 'internal representations' are derivative, and have their genesis in our primary activity of representing, in which we take external things,—most typically, what we also designate as physical objects—as representations. Moreover, I take our *making* of representations to be, in the first place, the actual praxis of creating concrete objects-in-the-world, *as* representations; or of taking the made objects as representational. (1979: xxi-xxii.)

In this *primary* activity, what do we take the external physical object to be a representation *of*? Its use and history? What does that have to do with the common properties in terms of which one thing can represent another? More likely, it is that, once made, it can *remind us* of its use or of its manufacture and therefore represent those things for us. The *first* time we see an unfamiliar object, it is a meaningless thing (except insofar as it shares any properties with anything familiar, allowing us to form hypotheses about it and to place it in our semantic network). The *second* time we see it, it can remind us of something, if only of itself on its first appearance. Subsequent encounters produce familiarity, which entrench it in our network, and allow newer objects to be understood in terms of *it*. This is how holism works.

Alternatively, the fixed points or the markers (or—for that matter—any of the nodes) are somehow "grounded" in another domain. This, of course, is just to say that they have meaning in the correspondence sense of semantics, and ultimately we will be led to question the way in which we understand that other domain.

3.2.4 The symbol-grounding problem.

The symbol-grounding problem, according to Harnad (1990), is that without grounding, a hermetically sealed circle of nodes can only have circular meaning. And, presumably, circles are vicious and to be avoided.

It is well known that a dictionary is a closed circle of meanings: Each word is defined in terms of other words. Assuming that all words used in the definitions are themselves defined, we have a circle (in fact, several of them). Now, before agreeing with Harnad that such circles cannot yield meaning or understanding, consider that we do use dictionaries fairly successfully to learn meanings. How can this be? A very small circle may indeed not be informative, especially if we don't antecedently know the meaning of the definiens (e.g., 'being' is defined as "existence", and 'exist' as "have being" in *Webster's Vest Pocket Dictionary*). However, the larger the circumference of the circle, so to speak, the more likely it is that it will be informative, on the assumption that the definition of the word whose meaning we seek, and the definitions of the words in that definition, and so on, will contain *lot* of words that we antecedently understand. So, we can easily "solve" the "equation" for the unknown word—i.e., dictionary definitions are most useful to the extent that they are like '$x = (4 - 3)/2$', rather than like '$x = (4y - 3)/2$' (where there is a further unknown in the definiens).

Nonetheless, some words will still only be poorly defined in terms of other words, notably (but not exclusively) nouns like 'cat' or 'cow'. For these, *seeing* a cat or cow (or for 'love', *experiencing* love) is worth a thousand-word definition. Illustrated dictionaries handle this with a type distinction in the syntax of the definiens: Terms can be of the type *word* or the type *picture*. But although we now have grounding in an extra-linguistic system, *it is still part of the dictionary*. And, of course, the pictures could, with a suitable indexing scheme, themselves be definiendum entries: A picture of a cat could have as its "definiens" the word 'cat', as in a visual dictionary or a field guide to cats. This, of course, only widens the circle. We could widen it further, albeit at some expense and inconvenience: Let every dictionary come with a real cat; ditto for all other better-ostensively-defined terms. We still have a circle, but now, I think, Harnad would have to agree that we've also got grounding—we've merely incorporated the groundings into the dictionary.

The same holds for the mind. Harnad says a link is needed between (some) mental nodes (say, our "cat" node) and items in the external world (say, a cat). Although we can't import such items directly into our minds, we *can* have mental representations of them. And it is the relation between our "cat" node and a node representing a perceived cat that grounds the former. We saw how in §2.6.2: What we (or Harnad) *think* is the relation between word and world is really a connection between an internal representation of a perceived *word* and an internal representation of the perceived *world*.

Do not misunderstand me: Experience certainly enriches our understanding. Consider "immersion" learning of a foreign language. "Thinking in French" is understanding French holistically, without any correspondences to one's native language (say, English). It is helped immeasurably by living in a francophone community. When we ask "What does the French word '*chat*' mean?", and we give the answer ("cat") in English words, we are doing pure *syntax* (here, relating symbols from one system to those of another) *that is also semantic* (understanding one system in terms of another). This is no different than answering the question in French ("*un chat est un petit animal domestique, dont il existe aussi plusieurs espèces sauvages*")[19]—except for choice of language for the definiens. Giving the definition in English is just as much symbol grounding as pointing to a cat would be. Symbol grounding, thus, does *not* necessarily get us out of the circle of words—at best, it widens the circle. That is my point: Syntactic understanding—the base case of understanding—is just a *very* wide circle.

Surprisingly, Harnad's own examples of grounding are internal in just the ways we have been considering. He distinguishes between "symbolic" and "non-symbolic" representations (Harnad 1990: 335, Abstract). But *both* are *internal* representations. Harnad says that non-symbolic "*iconic representations...are* **internal** analog transforms of the projections of distal objects on our sensory surfaces" (p. 342; Harnad's italics, my boldface). Such a projection could be a retinal image, say. So an iconic representation is some "analog transform" of *that*, stored (or created) somewhere further along the optic pathway. Thus, it could be part of our semantic network (cf. Srihari 1991ab). Furthermore, the symbolic and non-symbolic representational systems must be linked; hence, because of Smith's Gap, they must all be internal.

One would *expect* internal items to be "grounded" in *external* ones. But in Harnad's hierarchy (p. 335, Abstract), symbolic representations are "grounded" in "elementary symbols", which are "names" of "categories", which categories are "assigned on the basis of" categorical representations, which representations are "derived" from sensory projections; and iconic representations are "analogs" of those sensory projections. In fact, the only actual use of the term 'grounding' is between symbolic representations and elementary symbols, *both of which are internal.* Indeed, *all* the items on this hierarchy are internal!

Curiously, Harnad only mentions "grounding in the world" in a footnote:

> If a candidate model [for a cognitive system] were to exhibit all...behavioral capacities, both *linguistic* ["produce" and "respond to descriptions of...objects, events, and states of affairs"]...and *robotic* ["discriminate,...manipulate,...[and] identify...the objects, events and states of affairs **in the world they live in**]..., it would pass the "total Turing test". ... A model that could pass the total Turing test, however, would be **grounded in the world**. (Harnad 1990: 341fn13; Harnad's italics, my boldface.)

Recall the blocks-world and checkers-playing robots (§2.5.1). The former is blind and methodologically solipsistic. The latter can see. But is it grounded? Could it be fooled as the blind robot was? Possibly: by Cartesianly deceiving its eyes. It would then "live in" a world in which to be was to be perceived. Of course, such a Berkeleyan robot *would* be grounded *in the world that it lives in*, which happens not to be the actual world, but a purely intensional one. (In this case, note that the grounding system *and* the grounded one are *both* internal, hence part of a single network.) What would such a robot's symbols mean *to it*? Here, internal semantic interpretation would be done by internal links only.

Even more curious is the fact that grounding for Harnad—even grounding in the external world—does not seem to serve a semantic function:

> Iconic representations no more "mean" the objects of which they are the projections than the image in a camera does. Both icons and camera images can of course be *interpreted* as meaning or standing for something, but the interpretation would clearly be derivative rather than intrinsic. (p. 343.)

Harnad seems to be saying here that the causal connection of the iconic representations with its real-world counterpart is irrelevant to its intrinsic meaning. In that case, Harnad owes us answers to two questions: (1) what does such a causal grounding *do* in his theory, and (2) what *is* the intrinsic meaning of an iconic representation? Harnad may have identified an interesting problem, but he doesn't seem to have solved it.

My position is this: The mind-world gap cannot be bridged by the mind. There are causal links between them, but the only role these links play in semantics is this: The mind's internal representations of external objects (which internal representations are caused by the external objects) *can* serve as "referents" of other internal symbols, but, since they are *all* internal, meaning is in the head and is syntactic.

A purely syntactic system is ungrounded, up in the air, self-contained. But there are arbitrarily many ways to ground it; that is, there are infinitely many possible interpretations for any syntactic system. By "communicational negotiation", we (agree to) ground our language of thought in equivalent ways for all practical purposes (cf. Bruner 1983). Harnad seeks a *natural* grounding (cf. "intended interpretation"). Some candidates, such as the (human) body, are convenient.[20] But such natural groundings are merely one or two among many. The only one that is non-arbitrary is the "null" grounding, the "self" grounding: the purely syntactic, "internal" mode of understanding. "'Explanations come to a stop' as...Wittgenstein would put it; 'there is a last house in the lane'" (Leiber 1991: 54; cf. Wittgenstein 1958: §1, p. 3e, and §29, p. 14e). The last semantic domain in a correspondence continuum is the "last house in the lane". It can only be understood syntactically. Hence, all understanding rests on syntactic understanding.

This is one of the flaws in Searle's Chinese-Room Argument. Part of his argument is that computers can never understand natural language because (1) understanding natural language requires (knowledge of) semantics, (2) computers can only do syntax, and (3) syntax is insufficient for semantics. I take *my* argument to have shown that (3) is false (and that, therefore, (2) is misleading, since the kind of syntax that computers do *ipso facto* allows them to do semantics).

4   Summary

We understand one domain recursively in terms of an antecedently understood one. The "base" case is the case in which a domain is understood in terms of itself. When a syntactic domain is its own semantic domain, the semantic interpretation function either maps the symbols to themselves or else to other symbols. In the former case, we understand the domain by "getting used to" its syntax. In the latter case, if there are no fixed points—if each symbol is mapped to a different one—then we have the situation we face when using a dictionary. The difference is that since all external items are also mapped into internal ones, the symbol-grounding problem can be avoided. If there *are* fixed points, then they come to be understood either retroactively in terms of the role they play in the understanding of other terms, or else by "grounding" them to "non-linguistic"—albeit *internal*—symbols.

In any case, we have a closed network of meaning—a holistic, "conceptual-role semantics". And that is how semantics can arise from syntax.

Notes

1.   Kamp 1984, Kamp & Reyle 1993.
2.   Brachman & Schmolze 1985, Woods & Schmolze 1992.
3.   Schank & Rieger 1974, Schank & Riesbeck 1981, Hardt 1992, Lytinen 1992.
4.   Sowa 1984, 1992.
5.   Cassie is the Cognitive *A*gent of the *S*NePS *S*ystem—an *I*ntelligent *E*ntity. Oscar is the *O*ther *S*NePS Cognitive *A*gent *R*epresentation. Shapiro & Rapaport 1985; Rapaport, Shapiro, & Wiebe 1986.
6.   Kean Kaufmann and Matthew Dryer helped me see this.
7.   Kaufmann says that *cognitive* linguistics is not to be included here, presumably because it pairs sentences with meanings "in the head" ("cognitive" meanings), in which case, of course, it is a correspondence theory of semantics.
8.   Perhaps isomorphism is less than ideal, at least for the case of natural languages. When one studies, not isolated or made-up sentences, but "real, contextualised utterances...it is often the case that all the elements that one would want to propose as belonging to semantic structure have no overt manifestations in syntactic structure. ...[T]he degree of isomorphism between semantic and syntactic structure is mediated by pragmatic and functional concerns..." (Wilkins 1992: 154).
9.   If one understands *neither* domain antecedently, then one might be able to learn both together, either by seeing the same structural patterns in both, or by "getting used

to" them both. (Although, possibly, this contradicts the second observation, above.) In this case, neither is the syntactic domain—or else both are!

10. This has *moral* implications, too, as Smith emphasizes in his essay.

11. Though without an interlocutor, it could not pass the Turing Test; cf. §1.1.2.1.

12. Not for understanding its meniscus; the example is due to Kripa Sundar.

13. "In a case where the elements of syntactic domain S correspond to elements of semantic domain D_1, and the elements of D_1 are themselves linguistic, bearing their own interpretation relation to another semantic domain D_2, then the elements of the original domain S are called *metalinguistic*. Furthermore, the semantic relation is taken to be *non-transitive*, thereby embodying the idea of a strict use-mention distinction, and engendering the familiar hierarchy of metalanguages" (Smith 1987: 9). However, it's not clear that S really *is* linguistic (although D_1 *is*), for S will typically consist of *names* of items in D_1, but names are not linguistic in Smith's sense. Second, suppose that S = French, D_1 = English, and D_2 = the actual world. Then the semantic relation *is* transitive, and there is *no* use-mention issue. Here, I am thinking of a machine-translation system, *not* of the case of a French-language textbook written in English (i.e., a textbook whose object language is French and whose metalanguage is English). Clearly, though, there *are* systems of the sort described in this assumption.

14. See, e.g., Shapiro 1982, 1989; Rapaport 1986, 1988b, 1991; Rapaport, Shapiro, & Wiebe 1986; Wiebe & Rapaport 1986, 1988; Almeida 1987; Neal & Shapiro 1987; Shapiro & Rapaport 1987, 1991, 1995; Peters, Shapiro, & Rapaport 1988; Neal et al. 1989; Peters & Rapaport 1990; Wyatt 1990, 1993; Wiebe 1991, 1994; Rapaport & Shapiro 1995.

15. Except, of course, that I, as her programmer and a "computational neuroscientist" (so to speak), have direct access to her thoughts and can manipulate them "directly" in the sense of not having to manipulate them via language. That is, as her programmer, I can literally "read her mind" and "put thoughts into her head". But I ought, on methodological (if not moral!) grounds, to refrain from doing so (as much as possible). I should only "change her mind" via conversation.

16. Example due to Karen Ehrlich.

17. The first time you read this, you either found it incomprehensible or insane. By now, it should be less of the former, if not the latter, since its role in the web of my theory should be becoming clearer.

18. The protocols appear in Ehrlich, 1995.

19. *Dictionnaire de Français* (Paris: Larousse, 1989): 187. Translation: A cat is a small domestic animal of which there also exist many wild species. Hardly an adequate definition!

20. For discussion of various aspects of this, see Leiber 1980, Johnson 1987, Lakoff 1987, Turner 1987, Kirsh 1991, Perlis 1991, Dreyfus 1992.

References

Almeida, Michael J. (1987), "Reasoning about the Temporal Structure of Narratives," *Technical Report 87-10* (Buffalo: SUNY Buffalo Department of Computer Science).

Barwise, Jon, & Etchemendy, John (1989), "Model-Theoretic Semantics," in M. I. Posner (ed.), *Foundations of Cognitive Science* (Cambridge, MA: MIT Press): 207-243.

Berwick, Robert C. (1979), "Learning Structural Descriptions of Grammar Rules from

Examples," *Proceedings of the Sixth International Joint Conference on Artificial Intelligence (IJCAI-79*, Tokyo) (Los Altos, CA: William Kaufmann): 56-58.

Brachman, Ronald J., & Schmolze, James G. (1985), "An Overview of the KL-ONE Knowledge Representation System," *Cognitive Science* 9: 171-216.

Bruder, Gail A.; Duchan, Judith F.; Rapaport, William J.; Segal, Erwin M.; Shapiro, Stuart C.; & Zubin, David A. (1986), "Deictic Centers in Narrative: An Interdisciplinary Cognitive-Science Project," *Technical Report 86-20* (Buffalo: SUNY Buffalo Department of Computer Science).

Bruner, Jerome (1983), *Child's Talk: Learning to Use Language* (New York: W. W. Norton).

Calvino, Italo (1986), "Why Read the Classics?" *The New York Review of Books* (9 October 1986): 19-20.

Castañeda, Hector-Neri (1972), "Thinking and the Structure of the World," *Philosophia* 4 (1974) 3-40; reprinted in 1975 in *Critica* 6 (1972) 43-86.

Chang, C. C., & Keisler, H. J. (1973), *Model Theory* (Amsterdam: North-Holland).

Cho, Kah-Kyung (1992), "Re-thinking Intentionality" (in Japanese), in Y. Nitta (ed.), *Tasha-no Genshogaku (Phenomenology of the Other)* (Hokuto Publishing Co.).

Corless, R. M. (1992), "Continued Fractions and Chaos," *American Mathematical Monthly* 99: 203-215.

Dennett, Daniel C. (1982), "Beyond Belief," in A. Woodfield (ed.), *Thought and Object* (Oxford: Clarendon Press): xvi-95.

Dreyfus, Hubert L. (1992), *What Computers Still Can't Do: A Critique of Artificial Reason* (Cambridge, MA: MIT Press).

Duchan, Judith F.; Bruder, Gail A.; & Hewitt, Lynne (eds.) (1995), *Deixis in Narrative: A Cognitive Science Perspective* (Hillsdale, NJ: Lawrence Erlbaum Associates).

Ehrlich, Karen (1995), "Automatic Vocabulary Expansion through Narative Contexts," *Technical Report 96-09* (Buffalo: SUNY Buffalo Department of Computer Science).

Ehrlich, Karen, & Rapaport, William J. (1992), "Automatic Acquisition of Word Meanings from Natural-Language Contexts," *Technical Report 92-03* (Buffalo: SUNY Buffalo Center for Cognitive Science, July 1992).

Fodor, Jerry A. (1975), *The Language of Thought* (New York: Thomas Y. Crowell Co.).

Fodor, Jerry, & Lepore, Ernest (1992), *Holism: A Shopper's Guide* (Cambridge, MA: Basil Blackwell).

Frege, Gottlob (1892), "On Sense and Reference," M. Black (trans.), in P. Geach & M. Black (eds.), *Translations from the Philosophical Writings of Gottlob Frege* (Oxford: Basil Blackwell, 1970): 56-78.

Gracia, Jorge J. E. (1990), "Texts and Their Interpretation," *Review of Metaphysics* 43: 495-542.

Hardt, Shoshana L. (1992), "Conceptual Dependency," in S. C. Shapiro (ed.), *Encyclopedia of Artificial Intelligence*, 2nd edition (New York: John Wiley & Sons): 259-265.

Harnad, Stevan (1990), "The Symbol Grounding Problem," *Physica D* 42: 335-346.

Higginbotham, James (1985), "On Semantics," reprinted in E. Lepore (ed.), *New Directions in Semantics* (London: Academic Press, 1987): 1-54.

Higginbotham, James (1989), "Elucidations of Meaning," *Linguistics and Philosophy* 12: 465-517.

Hill, Robin (1994), "Issues of Semantics in a Semantic-Network Representation of

Belief," *Technical Report No. 94-11* (Buffalo: SUNY Buffalo Department of Computer Science).

Hirst, Graeme (1991), "Existence Assumptions in Knowledge Representation," *Artificial Intelligence* 49: 199-242.

Jackson, Frank (1986), "What Mary Didn't Know," *Journal of Philosophy* 83: 291-295.

Johnson, Mark (1987), *The Body in the Mind: The Bodily Basis of Meaning, Imagination, and Reason* (Chicago: University of Chicago Press).

Kamp, Hans (1984), "A Theory of Truth and Semantic Representation," in J. Groenendijk, T. M. V. Janssen, & M. Stokhof (eds.), *Truth, Interpretation, and Information* (Dordrecht: Foris): 1-41.

Kamp, Hans, & Reyle, Uwe (1993), *From Discourse to Logic: Introduction to Modeltheoretic Semantics of Natural Language, Formal Logic and Discourse Representation Theory* (Dordrecht, Holland: Kluwer Academic Publishers).

Keller, Helen (1905), *The Story of My Life* (Garden City, NY: Doubleday, 1954).

Kirsh, David (1991), "Foundations of AI: The Big Issues," *Artificial Intelligence* 47: 3-30.

Lakoff, George (1987), *Women, Fire, and Dangerous Things: What Categories Reveal about the Mind* (Chicago: University of Chicago Press).

Leiber, Justin (1980), *Beyond Rejection* (New York: Ballantine Books).

Leiber, Justin (1991), *An Invitation to Cognitive Science* (Cambridge, MA: Basil Blackwell).

Lytinen, Steven L. (1992), "Conceptual Dependency and Its Descendants," *Computers and Mathematics with Applications* 23: 51-73.

Maida, Anthony S., & Shapiro, Stuart C. (1982), "Intensional Concepts in Propositional Semantic Networks," *Cognitive Science* 6: 291-330.

Malory, Sir Thomas (1470), *Le Morte D'Arthur*, ed. and trans. by R. M. Lumiansky (New York: Collier Books, 1982).

Marsh, Brian; Brown, Chris; LeBlanc, Thomas; Scott, Michael; Becker, Tim; Quiroz, Cesar; Das, Prakash; & Karlsson, Jonas (1992), "The Rochester Checkers Player: Multimodal Parallel Programming for Animate Vision," *Computer*, Vol. 25, No. 2 (February 1992) 12-19.

Mayes, A. R. (1991), Review of [*inter alia*] H. Damasio & A. R. Damasio, *Lesion Analysis in Neuropsychology*, in *British Journal of Psychology* 82: 109-112.

Minsky, Marvin (1975), "A Framework for Representing Knowledge," in P. H. Winston (ed.), *The Psychology of Computer Vision* (New York: McGraw-Hill).

Moore, Robert C. (1988), "Propositional Attitudes and Russellian Propositions," *Report No. CSLI-88-119* (Stanford, CA: Center for the Study of Language and Information).

Morris, Charles (1938), *Foundations of the Theory of Signs* (Chicago: University of Chicago Press).

Neal, Jeannette G., & Shapiro, Stuart C. (1987), "Knowledge Based Parsing," in L. Bolc (ed.), *Natural Language Parsing Systems* (Berlin: Springer-Verlag).

Neal, Jeannette G.; Thielman, C. Y.; Dobes, Zuzanna; Haller, Susan M.; & Shapiro, Stuart C. (1989), "Natural Language with Integrated Deictic and Graphic Gestures," *Proceedings of the DARPA Speech and Natural Language Workshop* (Morgan Kaufmann): 14.

Perlis, Donald (1991), "Putting One's Foot in One's Head—Part I: Why," *Noûs* 25: 435-455.

Peters, Sandra L., & Rapaport, William J. (1990), "Superordinate and Basic Level

Categories in Discourse: Memory and Context," *Proceedings of the 12th Annual Conference of the Cognitive Science Society (Cambridge, MA)* (Hillsdale, NJ: Lawrence Erlbaum Associates): 157-165.

Peters, Sandra L.; Shapiro, Stuart C.; & Rapaport, William J. (1988), "Flexible Natural Language Processing and Roschian Category Theory," *Proceedings of the 10th Annual Conference of the Cognitive Science Society (Montreal)* (Hillsdale, NJ: Lawrence Erlbaum Associates): 125-131.

Pincus, Andrew L. (1990), "The Art of Transcription Sheds New Light on Old Work," *The New York Times*, Arts and Leisure (Sect. 2) (23 September 1990).

Potts, Timothy C. (1973), "Model Theory and Linguistics," in E. L. Keenan (ed.), *Formal Semantics of Natural Language* (Cambridge, Eng.: Cambridge University Press, 1975): 241-250.

Quillian, M. Ross (1967), "Word Concepts: A Theory and Simulation of Some Basic Semantic Capabilities," *Behavioral Science* 12: 410-430.

Quine, Willard Van Orman (1951), "Two Dogmas of Empiricism," reprinted in W. V. Quine, *From a Logical Point of View* (Cambridge, MA: Harvard University Press, 2nd ed., revised, 1980): 20-46.

Rapaport, William J. (1978), "Meinongian Theories and a Russellian Paradox," *Noûs* 12: 153-180; errata, *Noûs* 13 (1979) 125.

Rapaport, William J. (1981), "How to Make the World Fit Our Language: An Essay in Meinongian Semantics," *Grazer Philosophische Studien* 14: 1-21.

Rapaport, William J. (1985/1986), "Non-Existent Objects and Epistemological Ontology," *Grazer Philosophische Studien* 25/26: 61-95.

Rapaport, William J. (1986), "Logical Foundations for Belief Representation," *Cognitive Science* 10: 371-422.

Rapaport, William J. (1988a), "To Think or Not to Think," *Noûs* 22: 585-609.

Rapaport, William J. (1988b), "Syntactic Semantics: Foundations of Computational Natural-Language Understanding," in J. H. Fetzer (ed.), *Aspects of Artificial Intelligence* (Dordrecht, Holland: Kluwer Academic Publishers): 81-131.

Rapaport, William J. (1991), "Predication, Fiction, and Artificial Intelligence," *Topoi* 10: 79-111.

Rapaport, William J. (1992a), "Logic, Predicate," in S. C. Shapiro (ed.), *Encyclopedia of Artificial Intelligence*, 2nd edition (New York: John Wiley): 866-873.

Rapaport, William J. (1992b), "Logic, Propositional," in S. C. Shapiro (ed.), *Encyclopedia of Artificial Intelligence*, 2nd edition (New York: John Wiley): 891-897.

Rapaport, William J. (1993), "Cognitive Science," in A. Ralston & E. D. Reilly (eds.), *Encyclopedia of Computer Science*, 3rd edition (New York: Van Nostrand Reinhold): 185-189.

Rapaport, William J., & Shapiro, Stuart C. (1995), "Cognition and Fiction," in J. F. Duchan, G. A. Bruder, & L. Hewitt (eds.), *Deixis in Narrative: A Cognitive Science Perspective* (Hillsdale, NJ: Lawrence Erlbaum Associates).

Rapaport, William J.; Shapiro, Stuart C.; & Wiebe, Janyce M. (1986), "Quasi-Indicators, Knowledge Reports, and Discourse," *Technical Report 86-15* (Buffalo: SUNY Buffalo Department of Computer Science).

Rosenblueth, Arturo, & Wiener, Norbert (1945), "The Role of Models in Science," *Philosophy of Science* 12: 316-321.

Russell, Bertrand (1903), *The Principles of Mathematics* (New York: W. W. Norton,

1937).

Schank, Roger C., & Rieger, Charles J. (1974), "Inference and the Computer Understanding of Natural Language," *Artificial Intelligence* 5: 373-412.

Schank, Roger C., & Riesbeck, Christopher K. (eds.) (1981), *Inside Computer Understanding: Five Programs Plus Miniatures* (Hillsdale, NJ. Lawrence Erlbaum).

Schneiderman, Ben (1993), "Data Type," in A. Ralston & E. D. Reilly (eds.), *Encyclopedia of Computer Science*, 3rd edition (New York: Van Nostrand Reinhold): 411-412.

Schonberg, Harold C. (1990), "Some Chessmen Don't Make a Move," *New York Times* (15 April 1990), Sect. 2, pp. 38-39.

Searle, John R. (1980), "Minds, Brains, and Programs," *Behavioral and Brain Sciences* 3: 417-457.

Searle, John R. (1993), "The Failures of Computationalism," *Think* (Tilburg, The Netherlands: Tilburg University Institute for Language Technology and Artificial Intelligence) 2 (June 1993) 68-71.

Segal, Erwin M. (1995), "Stories, Story Worlds, and Narrative Discourse," in J. F. Duchan, G. A. Bruder, & L. Hewitt (eds.), *Deixis in Narrative: A Cognitive Science Perspective* (Hillsdale, NJ: Lawrence Erlbaum Associates).

Segal, Erwin M.; Duchan, Judith F.; & Scott, Paula J. (1991), "The Role of Interclausal Connectives in Narrative Structuring: Evidence from Adults' Interpretations of Simple Stories," *Discourse Processes* 14: 27-54.

Shapiro, Stuart C. (1979), "The SNePS Semantic Network Processing System," in N. Findler (ed.), *Associative Networks* (New York: Academic Press): 179-203.

Shapiro, Stuart C. (1982), "Generalized Augmented Transition Network Grammars for Generation from Semantic Networks," *American Journal of Computational Linguistics* 8: 12-25.

Shapiro, Stuart C. (1989), "The CASSIE Projects: An Approach to Natural Language Competence," *Proceedings of the 4th Portuguese Conference on Artificial Intelligence (Lisbon)* (Springer-Verlag): 362-380.

Shapiro, Stuart C. (1993), "Belief Spaces as Sets of Propositions," *Journal of Experimental and Theoretical Artificial Intelligence* 5: 225-235.

Shapiro, Stuart C., & Rapaport, William J. (1987), "SNePS Considered as a Fully Intensional Propositional Semantic Network," in N. Cercone & G. McCalla (eds.), *The Knowledge Frontier: Essays in the Representation of Knowledge* (New York: Springer-Verlag): 262-315.

Shapiro, Stuart C., & Rapaport, William J. (1991), "Models and Minds: Knowledge Representation for Natural-Language Competence," in R. Cummins & J. Pollock (eds.), *Philosophy and AI: Essays at the Interface* (Cambridge, MA: MIT Press): 215-259.

Shapiro, Stuart C., & Rapaport, William J. (1992), "The SNePS Family," *Computers and Mathematics with Applications* 23: 243-275.

Shapiro, Stuart C., & Rapaport, William J. (1995), "An Introduction to a Computational Reader of Narrative," in J. F. Duchan, G. A. Bruder, & L. Hewitt (eds.), *Deixis in Narrative: A Cognitive Science Perspective* (Hillsdale, NJ: Lawrence Erlbaum Associates).

Smith, Brian Cantwell (1982), "Linguistic and Computational Semantics," *Proceedings of the 20th Annual Meeting of the Association for Computational Linguistics (University of Toronto)* (Morristown, NJ: Association for Computational Linguistics):

9-15.

Smith, Brian Cantwell (1985), "Limits of Correctness in Computers," in C. Dunlop & R. Kling (eds.), *Computerization and Controversy* (San Diego: Academic Press, 1991): 632-646.

Smith, Brian Cantwell (1987), "The Correspondence Continuum," *Report No. CSLI-87-71* (Stanford, CA: Center for the Study of Language and Information).

Sowa, John F. (1984), *Conceptual Structures: Information Processing in Mind and Machine* (Reading, MA: Addison-Wesley).

Sowa, John F. (1992), "Conceptual Graphs as a Universal Knowledge Representation," *Computers and Mathematics with Applications* 23: 75-93.

Srihari, Rohini K. (1991a), "PICTION: A System that Uses Captions to Label Human Faces in Newspaper Photographs," *Proceedings of the 9th National Conference on Artificial Intelligence (AAAI-91, Anaheim)* (Cambridge, MA: AAAI/MIT Press): 80-85.

Srihari, Rohini K. (1991b), "Extracting Visual Information from Text: Using Captions to Label Faces in Newspaper Photographs," *Technical Report 91-17* (Buffalo: SUNY Buffalo Department of Computer Science.

Srihari, Rohini K., & Rapaport, William J. (1989), "Extracting Visual Information From Text: Using Captions to Label Human Faces in Newspaper Photographs," *Proceedings of the 11th Annual Conference of the Cognitive Science Society (Ann Arbor, MI)* (Hillsdale, NJ: Lawrence Erlbaum Associates): 364-371.

Srihari, Rohini K., & Rapaport, William J. (1990), "Combining Linguistic and Pictorial Information: Using Captions to Interpret Newspaper Photographs," in D. Kumar (ed.), *Current Trends in SNePS—Semantic Network Processing System, Lecture Notes in Artificial Intelligence, No. 437* (Berlin: Springer-Verlag): 85-96.

Tanenbaum, Andrew S. (1976), *Structured Computer Organization* (Englewood Cliffs, NJ: Prentice-Hall).

Tenenbaum, Aaron M., & Augenstein, Moshe J. (1981), *Data Structures using Pascal* (Englewood Cliffs, NJ: Prentice-Hall).

Turner, Michael (1987), *Death is the Mother of Beauty* (Chicago: University of Chicago Press).

Wartofsky, Marx W. (1979), *Models: Representation and the Scientific Understanding* (Dordrecht: D. Reidel).

Wiebe, Janyce M. (1991), "References in Narrative Text", *Noûs*, 25: 457-486.

Wiebe, Janyce M. (1994), "Tracking Point of View in Narrative," *Computational Linguistics* 20: 233-287.

Wiebe, Janyce M., & Rapaport, William J. (1986), "Representing *De Re* and *De Dicto* Belief Reports in Discourse and Narrative," *Proceedings of the IEEE* 74: 1405-1413.

Wiebe, Janyce M., & Rapaport, William J. (1988), "A Computational Theory of Perspective and Reference in Narrative" *Proceedings of the 26th Annual Meeting of the Association for Computational Linguistics (SUNY Buffalo)* (Morristown, NJ. Association for Computational Linguistics): 131-138.

Wilkins, David P. (1992), "Interjections as Deictics," *Journal of Pragmatics* 18: 119-158.

Wilks, Yorick (1971), "Decidability and Natural Language," *Mind* 80: 497-520.

Wilks, Yorick (1972), *Grammar, Meaning and the Machine Analysis of Language* (London: Routledge & Kegan Paul).

Wilks, Yorick, & Fass, Dan (1992), "The Preference Semantics Family," *Computers and Mathematics with Applications* 23: 205-221.

Winograd, Terry (1975), "Frame Representations and the Declarative/Procedural Controversy," in D. G. Bobrow & A. M. Collins (eds.), *Representation and Understanding* (New York: Academic Press): 185-210.

Winston, Patrick Henry (1977), *Artificial Intelligence* (Reading, MA: Addison-Wesley).

Wittgenstein, Ludwig (1958), *Philosophical Investigations: The English Text of the Third Edition*, trans. by G. E. M. Anscombe (New York: Macmillan).

Woods, William A., & Schmolze, James G. (1992), "The KL-ONE Family," *Computers and Mathematics with Applications* 23: 133-177.

Wyatt, Richard (1990), "Kinds of Opacity and Their Representations," in D. Kumar (ed.), *Current Trends in SNePS—Semantic Network Processing System*, Lecture Notes in Artificial Intelligence, No. 437 (Berlin: Springer-Verlag): 123-144.

Wyatt, Richard (1993), "Reference and Intensions," *Journal of Experimental and Theoretical Artificial Intelligence* 5: 263-271.

Philosophical Perspectives, 9, AI, Connectionism, and
Philosophical Psychology, 1995

MOVING MINDS: SITUATING CONTENT
IN THE SERVICE OF REAL-TIME SUCCESS

Andy Clark
Washington University in St. Louis

0. Two Takes on Internal Representation.

Much is expected of the familiar construct of internal representation. On the one hand, internal representations are supposed to encode information about how we take the world to be. On the other hand such encodings, to be of any use, must be bound to the service of situated activity and real-time response. Internal representations seem thus burdened with a dual role[1]: the passive encoding of information abut how the world is, and the internal origination of appropriate and speedy action in response to information transduced. For brevity we may call the first (passive, reflective) role 'encoding' and the second (action-originating) role 'control'[2]. Historically, cognitive science has focussed more on issues of encoding than on issues of control. But change is in the air.

The one-time emphasis on encoding had several roots. Some were pragmatic: in the absence of advanced robotic technology, the cognitive scientists notion of 'action' was often restricted to the production of appropriate quasi-linguistic responses or the selection of virtual movements within a very constrained space of options—see e.g. work reviewed in Boden (1987) and revisited in Cliff (1994). But there were plausible-sounding theoretical reasons too. Perhaps the step from good reflective encodings and inferential practices to action would be trivial, or merely present some mechanical (i.e. not cognitive) hurdles. Surely the hard tasks are knowing how the world is and reflectively computing a course of action in the light of that knowledge? Turning that thought into real-world motion in real-time is mere mechanics. Or so it was hoped.

This emphasis on encoding and inference over action characterized the bulk of work in so-called 'classical A.I'. Work on planning, story-understanding, scientific creativity and much else besides all shared a pre-occupation with the flow of disembodied reason. This pre-occupation helped, in turn, to determine the form of the internal representational systems constructed. Such systems were modelled on the grammar-and-symbol systems of public language—itself an artifact whose written form, at least, is largely dedicated to the role of passively encoding knowledge. Classical A.I., however, rapidly encountered a series of profound difficulties, largely centered around the difficulties of search, movement and update within a large body of stored quasi-linguistic encodings (see e.g. the collection of papers on the so-called frame problem in Pylyshyn (1987), Oaksford and Chater (1991) and even Fodor (1983)).

One of the guiding intuitions behind the explosion of interest in Connectionism in the last decade[3] was, precisely, the perceived urgency of exploiting alternative ways of encoding and accessing information. The combination of parallel processing architectures with new ways of encoding information and some powerful learning rules looked set to revolutionize cognitive science. But the revolution I shall argue, was sadly incomplete. Connectionism provided a valuable new set of cognitive scientific tools. But much of the new research remained locked into the same basic take on representation (representation as encodings) as classical A.I.

Recent work in Artificial Life and situated robotics challenges the persistent bias towards an encoding-based understanding of internal representation. In its place we find a refreshing emphasis on issues of control, action and real-time intervention. But the fine details of the marriage between these concerns and a general understanding of internal representational systems remains unclear. Indeed, some radical proponents of the situated vision evince skepticism about the value of internal representation as an explanatory construct no matter how it is understood.[4] The alternative to a reflection-based take on internal representation, they contend, is to abandon the commitment to internal representation tout court.

In what follows I shall argue in favor of re-thinking, but not abandoning, the notion of internal representation. I shall concede (section 1) that Connectionism does indeed constitute a kind of unfinished revolution. But I argue (section 2) that the best way to complete the revolution is not to give up on the very idea of internal representation but rather to re-cast it in a way which makes control and intervention basic. Some concrete examples of such re-casting are reviewed. I go on (section 3) to consider some possible relations between control-based and encoding-based notions of representation, and to speculate on evolutionary and developmental trajectories linking the two. I end by briefly noting some of the broader consequences of the proposed re-orientation in favor of a control-based notion of representation. These consequences concern the philosophical treatments of folk-psychology and content and the explanatory ambitions of cognitive science.

1. Connectionism: An Unfinished Revolution?

Connectionist research has done much to clarify the practical possibility of alternatives to an encoding-based conception of internal representation. The defining characteristics of encoding-based approaches are (1) their identification of the fundamental problem of cognition as one of reflecting (internally) an external structure of objects and properties and (2) conceiving the origination of actions as the outcome of sequences of inner inferences defined over the information and goals thus represented. Described at this level of abstraction, it should be clear that what I am calling the encoding-style take on internal representation aligns closely (though not exclusively) with Fodor's (1975, 1987) philosophical systemization of (much—not all) work in classical artificial intelligence under the umbrella of the Language of Thought hypothesis, and with Newell and Simon's (1976) abstraction of the 'Physical Symbol System Hypothesis' as the theoretical underpinnings of classical cognitive science.

Connectionism is now widely accepted as having successfully challenged the one-time hegemony of the passive-encoding-and-inference model of internal representation. It has done so in virtue of three key features of broadly connectionist-style internal representations. These are;

1. The connectionist amalgamation of data-storage and processing.
2. The replacement of inference defined over quasi-linguistic items with vector-to-vector transformations.
3. The abstraction of task-specific 'dedicated representations' in connectionist learning.

In expanding upon these features I must take for granted a basic understanding of connectionist architectures and processing (Clark (1989), Churchland (1989) and Bechtel and Abrahamsen (1991) all contain accessible introductory expositions). But recall that a typical 3 layer connectionist network consists of a set of input units (each capable of encoding varying numerical activation values), a set of 'hidden units' which mediate the processing, and a set of output units (able to specify a response in terms of another set of varying numerical activation values). The layers of units are connected by weighted links and a non-linear function (e.g. the logistic function) describes the activation-passing behavior of the mediating units. Knowledge is encoded in the weighted connections, and it is these which are adapted during learning. Processing involves the propagation of activity throughout the network in response to the presentation of a specific set of activation values for the input units. In such a milieu stored knowledge is deeply intertwined with processing characteristics. For to adjust the weights is at one and the same time to *register* information and to determine the way that information is to be *used* in subsequent problem solving. Information is not a passive commodity to be stored in some canonical form and then utilized by distinct and independent processing operations. Instead, the knowledge-base and the processing profile develop simultaneously and depend on a single and common resource, the set of units and weights. The import of this is that:

> The representation of...knowledge is set up in such a way that the knowledge necessarily influences the course of the processing. Using knowledge in processing is no longer a matter of finding the relevant information in memory

and bringing it to bear: it is part and parcel of the processing itself. McClelland, Rumelhart and Hinton (1986) p. 32.

The second divergent feature of connectionist representation follows directly from the first. Given the profound inter-penetration of knowledge and processing, it is not fruitful to conceive of connectionist problem solving by imagining some set of separately defined inference rules being applied to a body of passive and text-like syntactic items. Instead, connectionists treat inference as a case of complex transformations between vectors of activation values: transformations whose nature is *not* determined independently of the informational contents to which the network has been adapted. (For a full account of this model of inference as vector-to-vector transformation, see Churchland (1989) ch. 9.) This is so because connectionist style learning (and here we pass on to our third and final feature) involves finding a representation (an encoding) for a body of knowledge *in the concrete context* of trying to perform a specific task. The representations which the network acquires thus reflect the specific demands of the task.

As a brief illustration of this, consider NETtalk (Sejnowski and Rosenberg (1987)). NETtalk was trained to turn coding for text into coding for phonemes. And in so doing it dedicated a significant cluster of related activation patterns to responding to *vowels* and a distinct cluster to responding to consonants. In a sense it thus came to 'resonate' (in Gibson-talk—see section 2 following) to vowel-hood and to consonant-hood. But this resonance falls interestingly short of constituting a passive, detached representation of *vowel-hood* etc. For it is a fully task-specific response. The knowledge is encoded in a way dedicated to its use in the specific task of text-to-phoneme conversion. It could not, for example, be easily deployed so as to subserve some other purpose such as counting the number of vowels in an input sequence. (See Clark (1993), Clark and Karmiloff-Smith (1993) for a full discussion of this phenomenon of 'dedicated representation'.)

Basic connectionist representations thus offered a significant departure from a passive-encoding vision. The representations are selected in a way dictated by the demands of a concrete task, and are encoded in a way which leaves no gap between the knowledge and its use in processing. Reasoning using such representations is not usefully conceived as traditional inference, since the recall of information and its use in processing are no longer conceptually distinct events. The image of rules being applied to distinct data-structures simply gets no grip[5].

But Connectionism, as I have just described it, retains a significant chunk of the classical approach to internal representation. In particular, many connectionist treatments have inherited task-specifications and task-abstractions which seem natural given the encoding vision of internal representation, but methodologically suspect once that vision is challenged.

Thus consider the question of inputs and outputs. If we assume that cognitive operations draw on a central knowledge store whose basic format is use-independent, then we may make significant headway in cognitive science by investigating such representations in the context of just about any input/output coding which will serve to set up some problem. But once we take seriously the connectionist's proposed intermingling of representation and specific use, we can no longer afford to be sanguine about our choice of inputs and outputs. It may be that very different systems of representation develop according to whether we (a) fix the inputs as transduced physical signals and the outputs as real action commands or (b) abstract away from these two 'real-world' poles and work with artificial constructs such as coding for letters as input and coding for phonemes as output. (See also Dennett (1986)).

Abstracting away from the real-world poles of biological cognition also deprives our artificial systems of the opportunity to simplify or otherwise transform their information-processing tasks by the exploitation of real world structure and action. This is a theme which will figure prominently in our subsequent discussion. Examples of such exploitation include using the world as its own model (see e.g. Brooks (1991)) and physically re-structuring the environment so as to reduce the computational complexity of problem solving.

Abstracting away from the real world anchors of sensing and acting will also encourage a certain choice of task domains. Connectionists, like their classical predecessors, have tended to focus on isolated fragments of a human-level cognitive competence. Thus we encounter networks dedicated to modelling the production of the past tense (Rumelhart and McClelland (1986)), to grammar acquisition (Elman (1991)), to block balancing tasks (McClelland (1989), Plunkett and Sinha (1991)) etc. etc. In all such cases the inputs are carefully constructed at a large remove from real sensory input data. And the required outputs either fall far short of generating actions of the type found in biological cognition (such as movements of arms and blocks) or else they mimic only special, highly restricted sub-classes of actions such as the production of the strings of phonemes characteristic of a past tense utterance.

Finally, and perhaps most importantly, the standard methodology of bracketing real-world sensing and acting encourages researchers to marginalise or ignore the *timing* of cognitive phenomena. By conceiving of tasks independently of realistic input devices and output requirements, we make it all too easy to forget that the time taken to arrive at a solution, and the relative time-courses of various actions and cognitive episodes, constitute crucial parameters for biological cognition.

In contrast to all this, a growing wave of researchers now believes that it is more fruitful to study whole (albeit simple) systems capable of orchestrating a range of adaptive behaviors in a real-time and real-world setting. Work in situated robotics and autonomous agent theory (see below) takes seriously the thought that the form of our inner resources has been shaped and moulded in unexpected and counter-intuitive ways by our physical embodiment and by the real-world demands of fast, robust action in response to direct sensory inputs. It is this 'embodied, embedded' perspective[6] on cognition which, I will next suggest, offers an alternative perspective on internal representation itself.

2. Representation and Control.

2.1 Representation and Action

The defining characteristics of a control-based conception of internal representation are (1) that it identifies the fundamental problem of cognition as the production of appropriate actions, in real-time, in response to realistic environmental stimuli, and (2) that it conceives the internal origination of such adaptive behavior not as the outcome of classical inferential procedures but as the outcome of an action-oriented coupling between the organism and the world. This latter characteristic is obviously in need of some careful elaboration and illustration.

We can make a start by considering what might be called the Problem of the Encoding Homunculus. Thus suppose some agent has a highly detailed internal representation of its local environment as the encoding theorist suggests. A familiar problem then arises: to exploit the information contained in the representation the system requires some further intelligent homunculus to inspect the representation and arrive at decisions concerning action. Classical computational approaches are, of course, dedicated to solving exactly this problem. The encoded information, on such approaches, does indeed stand in need of careful retrieval and use. But this is achieved by an army of less intelligent homunculi—the problem of intelligent action is thus not fully recapitulated in the inner arena (see e.g. Dennett (1980)).

For all that, the classical solution often looks unnecessarily baroque, at least as far as local problem-solving is concerned. Why posit a detailed internal recapitulation of the environment at all? An alternative option is to turn the computational resources which would in any case need to be applied to the internal representation directly onto the external world itself. Instead of generating and updating a detailed inner model of the world, why not allow the world itself to 'store' the information, and retrieve what we need when we need it, by intelligent perception? In a certain light, the step of positing an inner world model intervening between perception and action can thus seem absolutely spurious. (See e.g. Brooks (1991) and more moderately, Ballard (1991). The latter is discussed in detail below.) Naturally, such a solution is restricted in application; it will not work when the real world is unavailable for inspection due to distance or temporal dislocation, and it needs careful work (see e.g. Malcolm, Smithers and Hallam (1989)) to see how to do anything like counterfactual planning within such a framework. But it is a step in an interesting direction, the direction of treating internal representations as first and foremost tools for action and not ends in themselves.

The most clear-cut forerunner of such a take on internal representation is the work of J.J. Gibson on so-called 'direct perception'. This work is sometimes ignored or downplayed in computational cognitive science, largely because of some ill-chosen anti-representational and anti-computational rhetoric. Despite this (and see Hatfield (1990) for a nice defense of the same claim), Gibsonian approaches are probably best seen as opposing only what we have termed the encoding view of internal representation.

Gibson's central claim (see e.g. Gibson (1979)) was that perception is not generally mediated by internal representations which themselves stand in need of further inspection or computational effort (by some inner agency) before issuing in appropriate action. Perception is *in that sense* direct—it is not mediated by action independent inner states; ones which require additional cognitive operations to drive appropriate behavior. But this, of course, is not to deny that mediating inner states exist and are both essential to successful behavior and worthy objects of study. It is rather to question a certain vision of the nature of those intervening states. In place of positing a system of action-independent internal representations (e.g. objective world models depicting the environment as a set of objects and properties) Gibson treats perception as exploiting inner states which are keyed to detecting ('resonating to') the so-called 'affordances' of the distal environment. These affordances (see Gibson (1979) are nothing other than the possibilities for use, intervention and action which the physical world offers to a given agent. They are thus profoundly keyed to the agent's own physical structure (embodiment) and capacities of action. Chairs are directly perceived (by us) as affording sitting; but a hamster would not share that perception. What the world affords to the hamster will determine its own specialized Umwelt (see Von Uexkull (1957)).

According to the Gibsonian model, then, we directly (in the sense defined above) perceive the world as a complex of possibilities for action. We do not first represent the presence of a chair and then compute or infer its suitability for sitting; instead, to perceive a chair is, at one and the same time, to detect the opportunity of sitting. Likewise, as Millikan (1995) nicely points out, we may sometimes represent our environment *as* a set of potentials for action (for running, grasping, climbing, etc.). Millikan's focus is on what she terms Pushmi-pullyou representations. These are representations which serve both to say how the world is (an encoding function) and, at one and the same time, to specify a response or action (a control function). Such representations are, as she puts it, both descriptive and directive. Since no further computational effort is needed to yield the prescription for action, such inner states fall squarely under the alternative approach to internal representation described above. They consist in an action-oriented coupling between organism and world. Such a coupling obtains whenever the internal state which stands for some external item, property or event *itself* prescribes an adaptive response.

(Notice that classical data-structures which contain explicit action-relevant information fail to meet this condition. The data-structure concerning 'cups' may contain the explicit information 'used for drinking'. But activation of that data-structure does not in and of itself control the action of drinking. Control-oriented representations close the gap between encoding information and selecting actions. They thus avoid the inferential step characteristic of standard representation-based A.I.)

A useful example invoked in Hooker, Evans and Penfold (1992) is the connectionist crab of Churchland (1986). The crab registers the location of a food item by simple ocular displacement across two eyes. A two-layer network transforms the visual input into an output which specifies claw positions for grasping the food. The visual input, in the inner context thus created, thus directly specifies a reaching procedure. Compare this to the expensive option of using the visual input first to create an objective internal world model displaying the location of food and other items, and then defining a procedure which takes this model as input and generates the action commands as output. The connectionist crab sidesteps (sic) the need for such an inner model, and directly perceives the food as affording a certain kind of reaching. (Of course, someone might insist that the transduced visual input itself constitutes an inner model. But this surely trivializes the notion of an internal model. And in any case, it would not constitute a classical mediating inner model (representing the world as a set of objects, properties and locations) of the kind under discussion.)

Control-oriented inner states thus constitute a genuine alternative to the kind of inner economy celebrated by encoding-style approaches. But are they genuinely representational? The topic is difficult (see Clark & Toribio (1994) for an extended treatment) but I think the short answer is 'Yes'. They are internal representations because (1) they are inner states which have been selected so as to obtain when the distal environment is of a certain disposition, and (2) they are used by the organism to negotiate the environment in the light of that information. Surely the neural network in the connectionist crab represents food location and ways of reaching—for our best understanding of the net's functional role adverts directly to its ability to embody these two types of information. One sign of this is the ease with which we treat the occasional failures of such a system (e.g. when the objects to which it responds are hidden behind a distorting lens) as cases of misrepresentation (see Hatfield (1990), Dretske (1988), Millikan (1984)).

Inner states dedicated directly to the control of action *represent* by specifying interventions whose adaptive value depends precisely upon the world's being a certain way. There need be no action-independent representation of how the world is. Instead, the inner state activated by the transduced sensory information is *itself* the recipe for action. By providing a means of encoding information in which knowledge and use are simultaneously specified (see section 1), Connectionism constitutes an existence proof of the viability of such control-oriented representation. In a sense, it provides the mechanism of direct perception required to implement the Gibsonian model (see Clark (1990), Hatfield (1991)).

It may seem that such control-oriented approaches import an undesirable rigidity into the responses of the cognizing agent. To represent e.g. the presence of food in a way which leads directly to the activation of reaching and chewing seems, on the face of it, to leave no room for intelligent thought and choice: should I eat this small meal now, or walk towards a larger food source elsewhere? Notice, however, that control-oriented systems can be much more flexible. They can take rich, detailed and temporally extended contextual features into account, so that one and the same gross external stimulus will select very different inner states (and hence directly select very different actions) on different occasions. All that matters, for the classification of the inner states as control-oriented, is that there be no gap between the current representation of the state of the world and the recognition of that world-state as constituting a certain possibility for action.

It will be useful to end the present sub-section by considering some on-going research which takes as its starting point a control-oriented perspective on cognition. I have in mind work in the so-called 'Animate Vision' paradigm (Ballard (1991), P.S. Churchland, V.S. Ramachandran and T.J. Sejnowski (1994)). This work reconstructs the basic task of vision in a control-oriented way, and in addition bases itself firmly in the particular capacities (of motion, physical search, etc.) of the embodied and environmentally embedded cognizer. Where Marr (1982) depicts the primary computational task of vision as one of building a 3-D world model on the basis of 2-D sensory inputs, Ballard depicts it as, simply, producing adaptive responses (actions), in an ecologically realistic context, at the lowest possible computational cost.

A crucial feature of embedded, embodied visual systems is the capacity for repeated scanning and intelligent search for perceptual inputs. Evolution seems, in humans, to have economized on visual resolution (over wide areas) by building mechanisms dedicated to getting the most benefit from a relatively small area of high resolution vision (the fovea). Human vision thus exhibits multiple gaze control mechanisms which determine saccades to and fro within the visual field. In addition, we exploit coarse mechanisms of intelligent gaze control e.g. orienting our whole head towards a patch of color detected at the low-resolution peripheries of our vision. The embodied, embedded agent, armed with a little, well-chosen stored world knowledge can often succeed using a combination of such strategies and quite minimal resources of world-modelling and storage. To repeat Ballard's own simplest example, we may locate the 35mm film display in the drug store not by storing or creating an inner map marking its location, but by responding to the low-resolution cue of 'kodak yellow', orienting towards it, and then saccading in on the film display. 'Planned sensing' is thus a cost-efficient strategy available to the embodied, embedded agent capable of real physical motion and in genuine sensory contact with its world. But note that it is a strategy which seems to call for at least a modicum of 'detached', action-independent stored knowledge. The association of kodak-yellow with film displays should not *always* result in our orienting towards the film display on detecting the color cue—instead it should do so only in the context of particular current needs and goals. But, as we noted earlier, it remains possible to conceive of this further flexibility as merely a function of a larger context and hence in principle itself amenable to a context-sensitive extension of the control-oriented approach. Exactly where to draw the line between genuinely action-independent stored knowledge and highly context-sensitive but action-specifying inner states is thus a surprisingly delicate question.

The central lesson of the Animate Vision work, in any case, is just that by exploiting multiple kinds of on-the-spot search embodied embedded agents may often avoid the need to construct and update detailed internal models of their surroundings. Instead, like good research scientists, they may store only knowledge about how to find the information they need by consulting canonical sources (in this case the world) as and when the need arises. As P.S. Churchland et al (1994) suggest, the phenomenological fact that we seem to maintain a detailed understanding of the structure of our surroundings may be a kind of illusion—an illusion generated by the ease with which we recover specific items of information as and when required. (See also Dennett (1991)). Churchland, Ramachandran, and Sejnowski (1994) report some fascinating data supporting such a hypothesis. The data comes from psychological experiments using a so-called "moving window" paradigm (O'Regan (1990), McConkie (1979)). Two such experiments are

(1) Subjects view a picture on a computer screen. *Between* saccades, objects are added, exchanged, colors altered, etc.. These changes are very seldom noticed—in fact, concentrated attention on selected elements is required before we see the changes!

(2) Subjects read text off of a computer screen. The real text occupies only an 18 character window and is surrounded by junk text, i.e. random characters. But the window of real text moves as the subject scans the screen left to right. The phenomenological impression is very strongly one of 'seeing' a whole screen of real words and persists even once subjects are told what is going on.

Perhaps, then, our internal representations of the world are much more partial and more transient than our experience suggests. The historical emphasis on enduring, passive, objective world models may be grounded more in the shallow phenomenology of our perceptual contact with the world than in its computational roots.

2.2 Representation and Time.

Action-oriented 'deictic' internal representations fulfil many of the requirements of a control-oriented conception as outlined at the start of section 2.1. But they do not, in and of themselves, do justice to the concern with *time* which also figures prominently in that characterization. The notion of representations as inner control elements is supposed to build in both action selection *and* the timing of interventions in the world. Such representations are not *merely* deictic; they are deictic representations generated and put to work within temporal parameters established by (a) the speed of sensing and response required for adaptive success and (b) the relative timing of various internal events in systems capable of multiple coordinated responses.

These timing issues import into our discussions elements which go far beyond standard conceptions of representation and even of computation. Two systems which are built of different materials may be said to implement one and the same computation and to go through exactly the same sequence of representational states. Yet the real-time performance may differ widely. As a result one may be fit to function as e.g. an arm controller in a given robot sensing task and the other not. Internal states which are identified as representational in virtue of the regular contributions they make to the generation and control of real action are thus identified in an essentially temporalized context. They merit their functional characterizations partly *in virtue* of the timing of their contributions. Timing and ascribed representational content thus go hand in hand.

Motor emulation provides a nice example. Motor functions such as skilled reaching seem to depend (in humans and higher mammals) on internal systems ('emulators') which provide a kind of *virtual* proprioceptive feedback. Instead of waiting for position indicating signals to arrive back from distant bodily peripheries, we seem to generate faster error-correcting feedback by exploiting internalized models of our own bodily dynamics. This trick (of using an internal model to generate virtual 'feedback' for use in on-line error-correcting activity) is used widely in industrial robotics, and seems both neurally plausible and mandatory given what we know about the speed of nervous conduction and human response timings. (See Grush (1994), Kawato et al (1987), Kawato (1990), Dean, Mayhew and Langdon (1994)). Emulators thus provide for a kind of responsive hyper-acuity, enabling us to generate smoother and more accurate reaching trajectories than would otherwise be possible given the speed of conduction of signals back from the real sensory peripheries. Such devices constitute internal representational systems of a transparently time critical variety. *Merely* modelling the relation between action-commands and subsequent proprioceptive feedback is obviously not sufficient to fix their adaptive role. What counts is that the motor model provide virtual feedback *within* established temporal parameters i.e. sufficiently fast to 'beat' the real sensory signals and hence provide a genuine benefit.

It seems plausible (see e.g. papers in Port and Van Gelder (to appear)) to suppose that this time critical profile is characteristic of *most* of the representational functions underlying daily on-line cognition and problem solving. (Think of skilled typing, tennis, conversational interactions etc. etc.) The upshot, if this is so, must be that standard conceptions of representation and computational states lack the full resources necessary to specify the relevant equivalence classes of cognitive subsystems. The equivalence class of e.g. motor emulators (for human cognition) is determined both by the contents and sequence of representational/computational states generated *and* the real-time profile of their generation. Most computational models fix only the first of these conjuncts. Yet the second is every bit as critical to adaptive success.

3. Conclusions: From Control to Encoding.

Sections 1 and 2 set out to chart a fundamental contrast between two species of internal representation. The first ('encoding') species aims at representing the world as a complex of objects, orientations and action-independent properties (such as shape, weight, color). To thus know the world is not yet to be disposed to act in the world in any given way. The selection of action requires further computational effort. The second ('control-oriented') species represents the world directly as a complex of possibilities for action. To represent the location of the cup, on this model, is at once to know how to reach out and grasp it. The location is given *as* a point in 'reaching space'. To thus know the world is at once to know what possibilities it affords for action and intervention. The contrast is between systems which use transduced information to generate an inner, conceptualized model of the world and *then* go on to compute actions, and systems (like Churchland's crab) which directly exploit the transduced data to select appropriate (potential) actions. This way of specifying the contrast invites two important questions—(1) how far can we realistically expect to get using *only* control-oriented representations and (2) if other resources are needed, how might they be acquired and deployed?

As far as I can tell, the limits on the power of control-oriented representations are purely practical ones (though no less potent as a result!). In principle (given unlimited time and processing power) a system could rely solely on a fantastically context-sensitive mass of control-oriented representations. Such a system would look, for all the world, as if it incorporated a stored, objective world model. But such a vision, like the giant look-up tables of yore, is probably a philosopher's fantasy. If one piece of information (e.g. the association between kodak and yellow) is fit to play a role in multiple different kinds of cognitive episode, then it seems sensible to store it as a 'passive, detached' knowledge structure available for use as *input* to a variety of action-oriented on-board networks. Likewise, if knowledge about an object's location is to be used for a multitude of different purposes, it would be economical to generate a single, action-independent inner map which can be used as input by multiple more dedicated devices.

Nonetheless it seems reasonable to suppose, following Millikan (1995), that the control-oriented species of internal representations (what she terms Pushmi-pullyou representations) are more evolutionarily and perhaps developmentally, basic. A real crab, much like Churchland's crab, probably makes only a few, quite specific uses of transduced data indicating the location of food. There would seem to be no pressure here to introduce an intervening world-model into the sense-act cycle. And what is thus evolutionary basic often turns out to be developmentally basic too. In this vein, Annette Karmiloff-Smith has conjectured that human infants may initially specify problem-solving information in a highly context-dedicated manner and only subsequently go on to re-code that knowledge in a sequence of less restrictive ways: ways which make the knowledge available for a wider variety of uses. (See Karmiloff-Smith (1979, 1992), Clark and Karmiloff-Smith (1993), Clark (1993).) What Karmiloff-Smith is proposing, in our terms, is a developmental progression from pure control-oriented internal representations to increasingly detached, multiply useable, encoding-style modes of storage. Moreover, according to Karmiloff-Smith, the early control-dedicated knowledge-structures are not destroyed. Rather, they are preserved alongside the more detached re-codings, and may be invoked to subserve fast, familiar on-line activity as and when required. This corresponds directly to Millikan's proposal that Pushmi-pullyou representations may persist and play important roles in adult human thought. (See Millikan (1995)).

The presence of an important and persisting body of control-oriented representations in human thought would have two major theoretical consequences. First, folk-psychology, in separating out action-selecting states (desires) and information—encoding ones (beliefs), may be fundamentally unsuited as a model of the more basic ('deictic', Pushmi-pullyou...) kind of internal representation we have been discussing. Indeed, it may even be part of the *role* of folk psychological talk to help us pull apart information and action-selection in a way which does not echo but rather *augments* our most primitive representational resources! (For further discussion of these issues, see Millikan (1995)).

Second, cognitive science, if it is to explain and describe basic internal representational resources of a broadly deictic nature, must itself beware the folk psychological image of content. For it is an image which invites a heavily *inferential* and essentially *atemporal* model of cognition. These properties, though endemic in traditional cognitive scientific practice, may yet be anathema to the bulk of natural on-line problem solving[7].

In sum, Connectionism was indeed an unfinished revolution. The first wave of connectionist research showed clearly the power and value of non-classical kinds of internal representation and processing. But the full import of this demonstration was obscured by a persisting bias in favor of classical task-abstractions and time-lenient simulations. The future progress of cognitive science looks set to involve ever-increasing efforts to anchor research to the real world poles of sensing and acting. Thus anchored, time, world and body emerge as significant players in the cognitive arena. How could we ever have forgotten them?

Notes

1. Two recent treatments which clearly distinguish these roles are Millikan (to appear) and Hooker, Penfold and Evans (1992). Thanks especially to Ruth Millikan for encouraging me to think in these terms.
2. The notion of representation as control is suggested and pursued in Hooker, Penfold and Evans (1992), and it is implicit in many treatments due to P.M. Churchland, e.g. P.M. Churchland (1989, ch. 5). See also Churchland, P.S., Ramachandran, V.S. and Sejnowski, T.J. (1994).
3. See McClelland, J., Rumelhart, D. and the PDP Research Group (1986) vols. I and II, Clark (1989)(1993), P.M. Churchland (1989), Bechtel and Abrahamsen (1991).

4. See e.g. Brooks (1991), Beer (1995), Beer and Gallagher (1992), Wheeler (1994).
5. For better or for worse—see Fodor and Pylyshyn (1988) for a discussion of the dark side of all this.
6. See Haugeland (to appear).
7. In this context, see the discussion of 'fitting mode' problem solving in Hooker et al (1992) pp. 533-535. The infamous 'Eliminativism' of Churchland ((1989) and elsewhere) is perhaps a (misguided) response to the perceived lack of fit between the folk-based image and natural modes of problem-solving and internal representation—see also Clark (1989).

References

Ballard, D. (1991) "Animate Vision" *Artificial Intelligence* 48, 57-86.
Bechtel, W. and Abrahamsen, A. (1991) *Connectionism and the Mind*, Oxford: Basil Blackwell.
Beer, R. (1995) "A Dynamical Systems Perspective on Environment Agent Interactions". *Artificial Intelligence*, 72: 173-215.
Beer, R. & Gallagher, J.C. (1992) "Evolving dynamical neural networks for adaptive behavior", *Adaptive Behavior*, 1, pp. 91-122.
Boden, M. (1987) *Artificial Intelligence & Natural Man* (MIT Press; Cambridge).
Brooks, R. (1991) "Intelligence without representation", *Artificial Intelligence*, 47, pp. 139-159.
Churchland, P. M. (1989). *The Neurocomputational Perspective.* (Cambridge, MA: MIT/Bradford Books.) (1981).
Churchland, P. S., Ramachandran, V. S. and Sejnowski, T. J. (1994) "A Critique of Pure Vision" in C. Koch and J. Davis (eds.) *Large-Scale Neuronal Theories of the Brain* (MIT Press, Cambridge, MA).
Clark, A. (1989). *Microcognition: Philosophy, Cognitive Science and Parallel Distributed Processing.* (MIT Press; Cambridge, MA).
Clark, A. (1990) "Perception, Construction and Developmental A.I." in *CCAI-The Journal for the Integrated Study of Artificial Intelligence, Cognitive Science and Applied Epistemology*, 7, 2, 171-184.
Clark, A. (1993). *Associative Engines: Connectionism, Concepts and Representational Change.* (MIT Press; Cambridge, MA).
Clark, A. & Karmiloff-Smith, A. (1993) "The Cognizer's Innards: A Psychological & Philosophical Perspective on the Development of Thought" *Mind & Language*, 8: 4, 487-519.
Clark, A. & Toribio, J. (1994) "Doing Without Representing?" *Synthese* 101, 401-431.
Cliff, D (1994) "AI and A-Life: Never Mind the Blocksworld" AISB, 87, 16-21.
Dean, P., Mayhew, J. and Langdon, P. (1994) "Learning and Maintaining Saccadic Accuracy: A Model of Brainstem-Cerebellar Interactions" *Journal of Cognitive Neuroscience* 6:2 117-138.
Dennett, D. (1978). *Brainstorms* (Harvester Press: Sussex).
Dennett, D. (1980). "The Logical Geography of Computational Approaches: A View from the East Role" in M. Harnish & M. Brand (Eds.) *Problems in the Representation of Knowledge* (Univ. of Arizona Press: Tucson, AZ) 59-79.
Dennett, D. (1991) *Consciousness Explained* (Little Brown & Co.: New York).

Dretske, F. (1988) *Explaining Behavior* (MIT Press: Cambridge).

Elman, J. (1991) "Incremental learning or the importance of starting small," *Technical Report 9101, Center for Research in Language*, University of California, San Diego.

Fodor, J. (1975) *The Language of Thought* (Crowell: New York).

Fodor, J. (1983) *The Modularity of Mind: An Essay on Faculty Psychology* (MIT/Bradford: Cambridge).

Fodor, J. (1987) *Psychosemantics: The problem of meaning in the Philosophy of Mind* (MIT Press: Cambridge).

Fodor, J. & Pylyshyn, Z. (1988) "Connectionism and cognitive architecture: A critical analysis", *Cognition*, 28, pp. 3-71.

Gallistel, C. (1992) (Ed.) *Animal Cognition* (MIT/Bradford Books: Cambridge)

Gibson, J. (1979) *The Ecological Approach to Visual Perception* (Boston; Houghton Mifflin).

Grush, R. (1994) "Motor models as steps to higher cognition" *Behavioral and Brain Sciences* 17, 2, pp. 209-210.

Hatfield, G. (1990) "Gibsonian Representations and Connectionist Symbol Processing: Prospects for Unification" *Psychological Research*, 52, 243-252.

Hatfield, G. (1991) "Representation in Perception & Cognition: Connectionist Attendances" in W. Ramsey, S. Stich & D. Rumelhart (Eds.) *Philosophy & Connectionist Theory* (Erlbaum: NJ) p. 163-196.

Haugeland, J. (to appear) "Mind Embodied and Embedded" in Yu- Houng Houng (ed) *Mind and Cognition: Proceedings of the First International Conference on Mind and Cognition* (Academia Sinica, Taipei, Taiwan).

Hooker, C., Penfold, H. and Evans, R. "Control, Connectionism and Cognition: Towards a New Regulatory Paradigm". *British Journal for the Philosophy of Science* Vol. 43, no. 4 Dec. 1992 p. 517-536.

Karmiloff-Smith, A. (1992) *Beyond modularity: a developmental perspective on cognitive science*. Cambridge, MA: MIT Press/Bradford Books.

Kawato, M. (1990) "Computational schemes and neural network models for formation and control of multijoint arm trajectory." In: *Neural Networks for Control* ed W.T. Miller III, R. Sutton and P. Werbos (1990) MIT Press.

Kawato, M., Furukawa, K. & Suzuki, R. (1987) "A hierarchical neural network model for the control and learning of voluntary movement." *Biological Cybernetics* 57:169-185.

McClelland, J. L. (1989) "Parallel Distributed Processing—Implications for Cognition and Development" in R. Morris ed., *Parallel Distributed Processing—Implications for Psychology and Neurobiology*, Oxford: Clarendon Press.

McClelland, J., D. Rumelhart, and G. Hinton (1986) "The Appeal of Parallel Distributed Processing," in McClelland, Rumelhart and PDP Research Group, eds. *Parallel Distributed Processing: Explorations in the Microstructure of Cognition*, vol. II, pp. 3-44, Cambridge MA: MIT/Bradford Press.

McClelland, J., Rumelhart, D. and the PDP Research Group (1986) *Parallel Distributed Processing: Explorations in the Micro-Structure of Cognition*, Vol. I and II, MIT Press, Cambridge, MA.

McConkie, G.W. (1979) "On the role and control of eye movements in reading" in A. Kolers, M. Wrolstad and H. Bouma (Eds.) *Processing of Visual Language* (Plenum Press: New York).

Malcolm, C., Smithers, T. and Hallam, J. (1989) "An emerging paradigm in robot architecture," Edinburgh University Dept. of Artificial Intelligence, Research Paper no. 447, 1989.

Millikan, R. (1995) "Pushmi-pullyou Representations" in Tomberlin, J., this volume, and L. May, M. Friedman & A. Clark (Eds.) *Mind & Morals* (MIT Press: Cambridge).

Newell, A. & Simon, H. (1976) "Computer Science as Empirical Enquiring" in J. Haugeland (Ed.) *Mind Design* (MIT Press, Cambridge, MA, 1981).

Oaksford, M. & Chater, N. (1991) "Against Logicist Cognitive Science" *Mind & Language* vol. 6, no. 1, 1-38.

O'Regan (1990) "Eye Movements and Reading" in Kowler, E. (Ed.) *Eye Movements and Their Role in Visual and Cognitive Processes* (Elsevier: Amsterdam).

Plunkett, K. and C. Sinha (1992) "Connectionism and developmental theory," *British Journal of Developmental Psychology*, 10, pp. 209-254.

Pylyshyn, Z. (1987) (Ed.) *The Robots Dilemma: The Frame Problem in Artificial Intelligence* (Ablex: Norwood, NJ).

Rumelhart, D., and McClelland, J. (1986) "On learning the past tenses of English verbs." In *Parallel distributed processing: Explorations in the microstructure of cognition*, volume 2, ed. D. Rumelhart et al MIT Press, Cambridge, MA 216-271.

Sejnowski, T. and Rosenberg, C. (1986) "NETtalk: a parallel network that learns to read aloud," Johns Hopkins University Technical Report JHU/EEC-86/01.

Von Uexkull, J. (1957) "A Stroll through the Worlds of Animals and Men" in C. Schiller & K. Lashley (Eds) *Instinctive Behavior* (International Univ. Press: New York) p. 5-80.

Wheeler, M. (1994) "From Activation to Activity: Representation, Computation, and the Dynamics of Neural Network Control Systems" *AISB Quarterly*, 87, 36-42.

Philosophical Perspectives, 9, AI, Connectionism, and
Philosophical Psychology, 1995

CONNECTIONISM AND THE RATIONALE CONSTRAINT
ON COGNITIVE EXPLANATION

Robert Cummins
University of Arizona

I. The Rationale Constraint

Cognitive Science wants to explain cognitive capacities. Capacities are dispositions, specified by articulating what Ruth Millikan (1984, p. 20) calls a law *in situ*, a law specific to a particular type of mechanism or system. A *cognitive* capacity is a disposition to satisfy some set of epistemic constraints that define "correct" or "good" performance. The capacity to play chess, to recognize faces, to find one's way home, to learn a language, and to perceive the local environment are cognitive capacities in this sense.

There is a tradition going back at least to Aristotle according to which cognitive capacities generally depend on the capacity for reason and inference. Helmholz (1856) held that perception is unconscious inference. Chomsky (1965) spearheaded the cognitive revolution with the idea that speaking and understanding a language is to be explained as the unconscious application of a theory of that language. Fodor (1975) argued that the acquisition of cognitive capacities is a species of scientific inference, the formulation and confirmation of the sort of unconscious theory whose application underlies cognitive performance on the Chomskian model.

The fundamental assumption behind this tradition is that reasoning explains cognition: Where there are epistemic constraints being satisfied, the underlying process is an inferential process. We can express this idea as a constraint on the explanation of cognitive capacities. I call it the *Rationale Constraint*. It says that you haven't explained a cognitive capacity of S—i.e., a capacity of S to satisfy epistemic constraints—unless you have shown that manifestations of the target capacity are caused in S by a process that instantiates a justifying argument—a *rationale*—for those manifestations. In the sense intended, the partial products algorithm is a rationale for the products that are computed by executing it, and a chess program, if it is any good, is a rationale for the moves it generates. Processes that generate cognitive behavior ought, in short, to be mechanized epistemology.

The argument for the Rationale Constraint is simple. A cognitive function,

as I shall understand it, is a function whose arguments and values are epistemo-
logically related.[1] Suppose the causal process that mediates between the arguments and values of such a function is not the execution of a Rationale. Then it
would seem that either (i) the capacity has been unmasked as non-cognitive, e.g.,
as the result of a look-up procedure (cf., Block, 1978, pp. 281-2), or (ii) we are
left with no idea how the underlying causal process could guarantee that the
characteristic epistemic constraints get satisfied, and explanation fails. Failure to
satisfy the Rationale Constraint, in short, is either evidence that we aren't dealing
with genuine cognition, or that we have an unexplained coincidence on our
hands. Imagine, for example, a device that consistently generates outputs interpretable as reasonable conclusions given an input interpretable as a set of
premises about some domain. There seem to be only two viable explanations. (i)
The thing is reasoning. (ii) The thing is a fake: We are looking at the results of
a perhaps elaborate look-up table, and not at the manifestations of a truly
productive capacity. What appears to be ruled out is the possibility that a truly
productive capacity to satisfy some set of epistemic constraints requires nothing
like argument generation. For it seems that the selection of appropriate implications in an unbounded number of different cases would have to involve generating intermediate conclusions in an argument-like way. At least in the productive
case, justified outputs appear to be a mystery (or a cosmic coincidence) in the
absence of a justifying process that produces them. I'll have more to say about
the argument for the Rationale Constraint as the discussion progresses, but, for
now, I take it that the *prima facie* case for the Rationale Constraint is strong
enough to shift the burden of justification or criticism to those would deny it.

II. Connectionism and the Rationale Constraint

Cognitive capacities are difficult to specify with any precision. No one
knows how to specify a law *in situ*, satisfaction of which is sufficient for having
the ability to plan a party, eat in a restaurant, or comfort a friend. Even formal
domains present difficulties. What, after all, does a good chess player do? More
than obey the rules, of course. But what more, exactly? It seems the only way
to specify an interesting chess function is to write a chess program, i.e., to give
a precise formulation of a rationale for making chess moves.[2] This "specification
problem" (Cummins, 1989, p. 111ff) makes a difficulty for orthodox computationalism whose methodology is basically the same as that of any programmer:
Given a specification of a function, find an implementable algorithm for computing it.[3] If you are *not* given a specification of a function to compute, you have
to fall back on some form of the Turing test: make a machine that is indistinguishable from humans *in the relevant respects, when they are exercising the
target capacity.* Not hopeless, perhaps, but a swamp on anyone's view. One of
the reasons the study of language has become so predominant in cognitive science is that the capacities to speak, understand and acquire a natural language are
(i) clearly cognitive, (ii) complex enough to be challenging, and (iii) specifiable

with a great deal of precision. A good strategy in science is to attack problems to which your methodology happens to apply.

Connectionists can, in principle, finesse the specification problem because it is possible to "train" a network to have a cognitive capacity without having even the beginning of an analysis of it; one simply needs a good training set. A successful network, however, is not, by itself, an explanation. A working network may be nearly as difficult to understand as a brain in at least this respect: No rationale will typically be discernable in the spread of activation. Orthodox computationalists, on the other hand, can only succeed by writing a program that articulates a rationale for the target capacity. Unlike connectionists, they cannot succeed as engineers yet fail as scientists.

One natural and inevitable connectionist response to this situation is to point out that the orthodox approach is hamstrung by the specification problem: Better let the network solve the problem, the argument goes, and afterwards study the working result in an attempt to figure out how the magic is done. But there is a more radical connectionist response that I want to discuss, which is to deny the Rationale Constraint itself. This is, for example, an implication of the line that Paul Smolensky and his colleagues have been developing (e.g., 1988, 1992), and it raises some issues in the philosophy of psychology that deserve to be surfaced.

The basic argument I want to consider, then, is this:

- The Rationale Constraint is incompatible with connectionism in its most interesting form.
- Connectionism is a viable framework for the explanation of cognition.
- Hence, the Rationale Constraint must be abandoned.

Of course, one person's *modus ponens* may be another's *modus tollens*: Someone (not me) may choose to see this as an argument against connectionism rather than an argument against the Rationale Constraint. However that may be, the focus of this discussion will be on the first premise, which I'll call the incompatibility thesis.

As I see the geography of this issue, there are two general lines of thought that might underlie the incompatibility thesis. I'll begin by setting them out briefly and uncritically, then turn to discussion.[4]

The semantic arguments. The fundamental idea here is that the explanation of a cognitive capacity and its specification take place on different semantic dimensions.[5] I've seen three ways of working out this idea:

Version A: When a fully distributed[6] connectionist system satisfies a cognitive function, the causal process that mediates the argument-to-value connection is defined over "sub-symbols". For present purposes, the point about sub-symbols is that they are manipulated locally by processes that have no access to the "big picture". These micro-processes operate at the single node (activation) or single connection (weight) level and therefore have no access to the distributed representations over whose semantic contents the target cognitive function is defined.

Version B: When a connectionist system satisfies a cognitive function, it computes over representations that have no interpretation in the domain in which the target cognitive capacity is specified. Whatever it is that a set of weights or an activation pattern means, neither have meanings in the semantic space in which the target cognitive function is defined. This is supposed to follow directly from (i) the claim that connectionist representation and symbolic representation are more or less incommensurable, and (ii) the claim that target cognitive capacities are specified symbolically.

Version C: A connectionist system satisfies a cognitive function only approximately. Only under idealization do the values actually computed correspond to the values of a properly specified cognitive function. The causal process that actually mediates the argument to value connection in a network therefore cannot be interpreted as a Rationale for the values of the target cognitive function because these are not the values that are actually computed.

The computational arguments. The second general line of argument that has been leveled at the Rationale Constraint is that connectionist computation has a fundamentally different form than reasoning. I've see this argument run in a variety of ways, but I think they all boil down to one of the following.

Version A: Connectionist computation is essentially a matter of discovering or exhibiting statistical correlations, whereas most rationales are not.

Version B: Connectionist systems can mimic classical rationalizers by computing over encodings of classical representations. Since the encodings do not preserve the constituent structure of the representations they encode, network computations cannot be executions of the rationales they mimic.

Let's look now at each of these lines of argument in some detail.

III. The Semantic Arguments

What I am calling the semantic arguments for the incompatibility of connectionism and the Rationale Constraint are based on the idea that connectionist representations don't represent rationales, or anyway, not the right rationales—not the rationales that rationalize the system's cognitive capacities.

III.1: The "sub-symbols" argument. The term "sub-symbols" was introduced by Smolensky (1988) to describe the semantic role of an individual unit in a distributed representational scheme. A scheme for representing a domain D is fully distributed just in case every unit involved in the representation of one member of D is also involved in the representation of every other member of D. What we have, in short, is each element in D represented by a different pattern of activation on the same pool of units. To see why Smolensky calls the individual units in a distributed scheme sub-symbols, think of each representation of an element of D as a symbol. Since the scheme is distributed, these representations will be patterns of activation over a pool of units. No single unit represents any element in D though it does make a contribution to the representation of each element in D. Thus, the individual units in the pool can be thought of as sub-symbols, parts of a symbol, if you like.

What I am calling the sub-symbols argument is a semantic argument because it attempts to drive a wedge between the causal organization of a network and the semantic interpretation under which it satisfies a cognitive function. The crucial premise is that connectionist computation is local in a way that entails that it operates on sub-symbols but never on the symbols themselves that are the arguments and values of a cognitive function. On this assumption it would follow that connectionist systems don't execute rationales, because their computational processes are insensitive to the relevantly significant states. The assumption that the system is fully distributed amounts to the assumption that the relevant rationale cannot be defined over the contents (if any) represented by the individual units. The assumption that computation is local, however, amounts to the claim that the causal structure of the system is discernable only in terms of the interaction of individual units. The two assumptions together decouple the causal structure from the cognitively relevant representational states, with the consequence that the relevant causal structure cannot be seen as an implementation of a rationale for the cognitive function satisfied.

The sub-symbol argument evidently stands or falls with the assumption of local computation. In a nutshell, the problem with the assumption of local computation is that the causal dynamics of a network is specified as a function on activation *vectors*, not at the individual unit level. Connectionist computation consists in computing output activation vectors from input activation vectors and weights, and this is just to say that the representation computed—output vector—is a function of the input representation—input vector—and stored representations—the weights.[7] We think of the dynamics in terms of vectors because it is the entire activation vector at t, not the activation of any particular unit, that, together with the weights, determines the activation of each unit at t', and hence the activation vector at t'. The assumption of local computation, as it figures in the sub-symbol argument, appears patently false.

And yet, the idea hangs on.[8] I think what keeps the assumption of local computation alive is the intuitive sense that activation vectors are rather artificial. Unlike velocities and accelerations, they seem to be simply a notational artifact: One speaks of activation vectors to save ink, but it is just a gimmick for talking about each individual unit in turn. In the case of velocity, for example, we use the coordinates to specify a speed and direction. Some object is actually moving at a certain speed in a certain direction, and we pick coordinates in a way that makes for convenient representation. The coordinates are conventional. In the connectionist case, however, the coordinates are not conventional, for they are the activations of individual units, and the actual values of these matters. We can, for convenience, put activation values in a standard order and treat them as coordinates, but there is no direction or net magnitude out there that we are trying to capture. We are trying to capture the individual activations.

To neutralize this intuition completely would require a healthy chunk of metaphysics that I'm in no position to provide. But we can get a sense of what is wrong by contrasting the connectionist case with an uncontroversial case of the sort the sub-symbol argument contemplates. Imagine, then, that you are given a set of instructions for crossing a field. They specify a start position and time, and consist of a series of instructions from the following set: {go left, go right, go straight, go back, go n steps}. Every step is to be exactly one yard, and you are to take one step per second. Now if we give a lot of people instructions like this, they can be made to spell out various things on the field like a marching band at a football game. Imagine we arrange things so that they spell out proofs. These will be intelligible from the stands, but not to the individual marchers. Indeed, it is obvious that nothing anyone does is sensitive to the representations relevant to the proof; no one's actions are sensitive to the epistemic constraints whose satisfaction makes the process a proof. Causally speaking, though, the individual actions are all there are. Each person follows their instructions and that's all there is to it.

Now, we *could* specify the states of this system in vector notation: the state of the system is given by a vector whose elements are the positions of the various persons on the field. To transform one vector into another, however, we need the instructions for each marcher. Can we, as it were, aggregate these instruction sets into one function that effects the needed transformations? Of course. But—and here is the crucial point—the resulting combined function is a fraud, because the position of person A does not, by hypothesis, depend on the prior positions of any other marchers, and hence does not depend on the prior position vector. Since it is only position vectors that have interpretations in the proof, it follows that proof states don't determine other proof states, though they do predict them. Proof states are artifacts, and the "law" that predicts later ones from earlier ones is an artifact as well. (See Cummins, 1978, for the notion of an artifactual regularity.) This contrasts with connectionist systems precisely because the activation of output units does depend on the entire input vector and hence on something that *does* have a relevant representational significance.[9]

What I'm calling the sub-symbol argument, then, fails to undermine the Rationale Constraint because its attempt to demonstrate that connectionist causal structure is insensitive to distributed representation depends on the indefensible assumption of local computation.

III.2: The incommensurability argument. Version B of the semantic argument concedes that connectionist networks compute over distributed representations, but alleges that those representations are not representations of the arguments and values of cognitive functions. I'll call this argument the incommensurability argument, because it is based on the "incommensurability thesis", namely that distributed connectionist representational schemes are incommensurable with the (typically symbolic) schemes that must be used to specify cognitive functions.

As it stands, the incommensurability argument is incoherent because it assumes that connectionist systems can satisfy cognitive functions, even though they cannot represent the arguments and values of those functions. To be sure, one could reconcile the thesis that symbolic representation and connectionist representation are incommensurable with the thesis that connectionist systems satisfy cognitive functions by abandoning the view that cognitive functions must be specified symbolically. I have some sympathy with this view. But the result leaves us with no argument against the Rationale Constraint unless we add a premise to the effect that rationales can only be specified symbolically. This premise is worth examining in some detail, for it would, together with the incommensurability thesis, make connectionism and the Rationale Constraint incompatible.

Why might one think that a rationale can only be specified symbolically? Let's begin by getting some bad reasons out of the way.

"Epistemic constraints are defined over propositions, not over things like images." This just turns on an ambiguity in "proposition". As philosophers use the term, a proposition is not itself a representation but something represented, a set of possible worlds, say. In this sense, it is at least arguable that epistemic constraints are defined over propositions, for one might hold that epistemic constraints only make sense when applied to things with truth conditions.[10] Evidence, for example, is evidence for the truth of something, so a process cannot be constrained by the evidence unless that process traffics in propositions somehow. But holding that epistemic constraints are defined over propositions in this sense doesn't yield the conclusion that rationales can only be specified symbolically unless you *also* hold that only symbolic schemes can represent propositions. But surely there is no reason to believe this. A picture, for example, can hold in some possible worlds and not others just as well as a sentence.

As psychologists use the term, a proposition is a symbolic representation. In this sense of the term, it simply begs the question to suppose that epistemic constraints can only be defined over propositions. Either way you understand "proposition," then, we have no argument here for thinking that rationales have only symbolic specifications.

"To be epistemically discriminating you have to be logically discriminating. But logical relations are defined over symbolic structure." Again, we have an ambiguity. If "logical relations" is understood semantically, then they are relations among propositions, and hence independent of how the propositions are represented. If "logical relations" is understood syntactically, the question is begged, since syntax is, of course, particular to a representational scheme. The relations of interest among the formulas of symbolic logic are, of course, defined over symbolic syntax. But the relations of interest among the representations in a non-symbolic system like that of Barwise and Etchemendy (1990a, 1990b) are defined over properties of those non-symbolic representations.[11]

Indeed, the existence of non-symbolic representational schemes for reasoning seems to refute outright the idea that rationales can only be specified symbolically. But the symbolist might reply that non-symbolic reasoning is limited in a way that unsuits it for cognition generally. Only symbolic schemes, they will say, allow for (i) content independent reasoning, and (ii) unbounded reasoning competencies. The alleged boundedness of connectionist competencies will come up for discussion later on when we consider computational arguments against the rationale constraint. I'll restrict my attention here to the claim that non-symbolic representational schemes don't allow for content-independent reasoning.

There are two questions we need to ask about content independence. First, *is* reasoning content independent? And second, is it true that non-symbolic representational schemes cannot support content independent reasoning? The answer to both questions, I think, is "no."

Is reasoning content independent? In logic, we teach our students that deductive validity turns on form, not content. Although we usually temper this message with warnings about non-deductive inference and about inferences like that from being red to being colored, the central message remains that the sort of semantic relations that are central to inference can be seen to be invariant across contents. For most of us, *modus ponens* and simplification are paradigms of good reasoning, and they are content-independent.[12]

But logic, as many people have pointed out, is not a theory of reasoning, it is a theory of validity. One of the few really clear lessons of the last three decades of research in artificial intelligence, I suppose, is that reasoning needs to be domain specific to be effective, because it needs to be driven by lots of contingent knowledge—the more the better, so long as it can be efficiently accessed. While the jury is admittedly still out on this question, it surely cannot be simply assumed at the current time that human reasoning is or even can be content independent.

We needn't worry too much about it in the current context, however, because it simply isn't true that only symbolic schemes can support content independent reasoning. A now familiar example is the Galilean geometrical scheme for reasoning about relations between distance, velocity and time. In this scheme, vertical lines represent time, with time increasing from top to bottom and horizontal lines beginning at a vertical line and projecting left represent velocities, with velocity increasing from right to left. The area of the rectangle in figure one represents the distance traveled by a body that travels at uniform velocity v for a time t_1. The area of the triangle in figure one represents the distance traveled by a body that begins at rest at t_0 and achieves a velocity v at time t_1.[13] Galileo used this scheme to reason about motion, as just described. But the scheme can be used to reason about the relations of any three quantities that are related as base, height and area. And, of course, it can be used to reason geometrically, as it was before Galileo adapted it to mechanical problems.

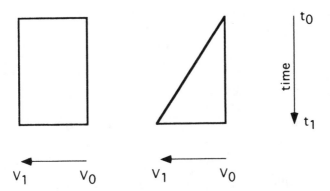

Figure one: the area of the rectangle represents the distance traveled by a body moving at uniform velocity V_1 for a time t_1; the area of the triangle represents the distance traveled by a uniformly accelerated body beginning at rest and traveling for a time t_1 when it achieves a velocity of V_1.

A final point before we leave the incommensurability argument. People do engage in symbolic reasoning. A connectionist who accepts the incommensurability thesis must somehow account for this fact. The obvious strategy here is to think of symbolic reasoning not as an explanans, but as an explanandum on a par with, or perhaps parasitic on, language use. According to this line of thought, people don't have cognitive capacities because they can reason symbolically; they rather have the cognitive capacity to reason symbolically because they can reason non-symbolically.[14] Whether connectionism can handle the capacity for language and other symbolic tasks is an open and difficult question. But it is somewhat peripheral in the current context. Given the incommensurability thesis, making connectionism *prima facie* consistent with the Rationale Constraint requires only that there be non-symbolic rationales.

The incommensurability argument, then, fails to demonstrate any incompatibility between connectionism and the Rationale Constraint. Even if we grant that connectionist representation and symbolic representation are incommensurable, there is no reason to think that non-symbolic reasoning is either impossible or an inaccurate picture of the inferential processes that underlie human cognitive capacities.

III.3: The approximation argument. Think about those XOR networks you cut your teeth on: They don't compute XOR no matter how long they are trained. First, the outputs aren't ones and zeros, but stuff like 0.9s and .11s. Here is a typical trace of performance after training:

Inputs		Values
1	1	.10
1	0	.90
0	1	.92
0	0	.09
0	.5	.76
.4	0	.59
.4	.7	.88
.3	0	.38

Table One: performance of typical XOR network after training.

What we are calling a "true" isn't even always the same number. More seriously, as the table shows, the network is quite happy with any numerical inputs, not just ones and zeros. Lines five and six of the table do not correspond to arguments and values to XOR.

"Now, then," the argument I have in mind continues, "what goes for XOR goes for connectionist computation generally. You don't get cognitive functions computed, but only approximations to them; more or less close simulations, if you like. The causal process that mediates the argument-to-value connection in the connectionist system cannot realize a rationale for the target cognitive function, for the system doesn't compute that function."

I call this the "approximation" argument because I want it to remind you of certain passages in Smolensky (1988). But the argument I've given is somewhat misnamed, for the idea is not that connectionist systems compute approximations to XOR, but that XOR can be viewed as a normalized (high numbers become ones, low numbers zeros) and restricted (only one and zero inputs count) version of the function the network actually computes. Moreover, the argument as I've presented it is self-defeating in the same way that the incommensurability argument is self-defeating. You can't argue against the Rationale Constraint on the grounds that connectionist systems cognize but don't satisfy the constraint, if part of your argument is that connectionist systems don't compute cognitive functions. We can rescue the argument from this embarrassment by supposing that, contrary to the appearances our symbolically biased epistemology generates, cognitive functions are actually like the functions connectionist systems compute in being more or less continuous.[15] Indeed, I have more than a little sympathy for this line. But it evidently lets the Rationale Constraint off the hook, unless we add the premise, lately scouted, that rationales can only be formulated for the normalized and restricted functions we *thought* were the targets. Since, as we've seen, there is no reason to believe that connectionists cannot have rationales in, as it were, their own terms, the present argument fails to show that successful connectionism is an embarrassment to the Rationale Constraint.

So much for the "semantic arguments." They don't work. The computational arguments, though not conclusive, do better.

IV. The Computational Arguments

The fundamental idea behind this form of argument is that connectionist computation has a fundamentally different form than reasoning. Connectionist principles of computation, then, could not be principles of rationale execution. I'll discuss two versions of this line of thought, the second far more serious than the first.

IV.1: The correlation-engine argument. The thought here is that connectionist systems are, in their "learning" phase, simply correlation detectors. A trained network is then simply a correlation table with the added wrinkle of being able to automatically extrapolate between entries. No doubt connectionist networks can be used to implement other processes, but, so the argument goes, that is beside the point: At the dimension of analysis where the system is distinctively connectionist, it is simply a correlation engine. Since, however, it is obvious that rationales of the sort that rationalize cognitive performance are not typically (or ever?) algorithms for the discovery and exhibition of correlations, it follows that connectionist systems violate the Rationale Constraint.

Remember when people used to say, "All computers really do is manipulate ones and zeros,"? The reply we all learned was this: True enough, but irrelevant, because orchestrated manipulation of ones and zeros amounts to the execution of any symbolic algorithm you like. One then points out that, on the assumption (rather more suspect these days than in the golden age when we learned all this) that cognitive functions are computable functions, computers can have cognitive capacities.

It is tempting to reply to the correlation-engine argument in a similar vein: "Maybe, at bottom, connectionist systems are just correlation-engines, but who cares what happens *at bottom.*" The correlation-engine argument anticipates this reply, however, by insisting that it is precisely at the dimension of analysis where the system is distinctly connectionist that it is a correlation-engine. It is conceded in advance (for the sake of argument) that connectionist systems can implement rationales of the sort that the Rationale Constraint requires. The argument insists, quite correctly, that the issue is not whether cognitive processes can be *implemented* as connectionist processes, but whether cognitive processes are properly *analyzed* as connectionist processes. The claim on offer is that rationale execution does not boil down to the discovery or exhibition of correlations. Since connectionist systems are correlations engines, either they don't compute cognitive functions, or the Rationale Constraint must be abandoned.

This argument is generally taken to be a knock on connectionism, but it could just as well be taken, by a convinced connectionist, as a refutation of the Rationale Constraint. Either way you take it, however, the argument suffers from a terminal naivete about connectionist computation. Connectionist systems do, of course, correlate inputs and outputs, but so does every computational system. The claim that connectionist systems are correlation engines must come to more than this triviality. In the light of the fact that connectionist systems are able to solve quite general parsing problems, as we will see in the next section, there appears to be no reason to accept the bald claim that connectionist systems are *mere* correlation engines.

IV.2: The SLM argument. The correlation-engine argument is naive, but it is based on a promising strategy: Show that rationale execution and connectionist computation are fundamentally different. To establish this difference, one needs some fix on the form of rationales and on the form of connectionist computation. The idea that connectionist systems are correlation engines fills the bill nicely, because no one seriously supposes that rationales boil down to the discovery or exhibition of correlations. That idea fails because no one is in a position to argue that connectionist systems are correlation engines in the relevant sense. But there are other routes one might take to the conclusion that rationale execution and connectionist computation don't mix. The most interesting one is found in Smolensky, LeGendre and Miyata (1992; hereafter "SLM").

The cornerstone of the SLM approach is Smolensky's well-known tensor product (tp) scheme for encoding classical representations. The notion of an encoding is crucial to what follows. Let R be a representational scheme. <E, f> is an encoding of R iff f:E→R, but E does not preserve the formal structure of the elements of R. Gödel numbers are a familiar encoding scheme. Morse code, however, is not, since it preserves form, being just a different spelling of an alphabet-based scheme in which spelling is irrelevant anyway. The tp scheme is an encoding in this sense since it does not preserve the constituent structure of the classical (in the sense of Fodor and McLaughlin, 1990) representations it encodes. SLM reports development of a LISP-like programming language, TPPL, which allows for the expression of classical rationale-embodying algorithms. One takes the representations computed over by a TPPL algorithm and constructs a tp encoding. A network is then constructed, using a variation of back-propagation, that can be proved to be weakly equivalent to the TPPL algorithm. Since the tp encoding does not preserve the constituent structure of the classical representations employed by TPPL, it follows that the network does not execute a rationale defined over those representations.

SLM constitutes a serious challenge to the Rationale Constraint. It appears to establish that a connectionist system can mimic a classical rationalizer computing over representations that merely encode, but are not isomorphic to, the representations computed by that classical rationalizer. How are we to square this result with the Rationale Constraint? There are, I think, just three possibilities:

- Find some flaw in the SLM argument.
- Argue that the connectionist system does execute a rationale for the target capacity, though not one defined over the representations whose encodings the network utilizes. The network somehow finds its own rationale.

- Abandon the Rationale Constraint, and find some way to defuse the argumentation that supports it.

Is the SLM argument sound? A rationale typically defines a competence that is unbounded under idealization away from resource constraints. Idealization away from resource constraints, however, is possible only for systems whose architecture supports a distinction between the algorithm executed and the memory/time it utilizes. Consider adding machines: They do not compute plus, but a finite restriction of plus. Nevertheless, they are said to compute the full infinite function because the restriction is due to a resource limitation. Add more memory, and you relax the restriction, because the algorithm the device executes is perfectly general: It is defined for the representations of any addends whatever. A look-up table, by contrast, is inherently finite. If you are using a look-up table, adding scratch paper and patience won't help you with addends not covered explicitly in the table.[16]

The idea that a finite device can have the sort of unbounded competence typically characterized by a rationale, then, depends on a distinction between the algorithm executed on the one hand, and the resources—time and memory— available to it on the other. Schwarz (1993) argues, however, that connectionist networks do not support this distinction, and hence cannot be genuinely productive. His argument is simple. There are only two ways to add memory to a connectionist network: add units, or add precision to units already available. Since physical networks are finite, and since physical units have bounded precision, to idealize away from memory constraints in a network amounts to asking how the network would behave where more units or more precision added. If we add units to a fully distributed network that computes f, however, it will, in general, no longer compute f. For, when we add a unit, we must, in general, re-adjust all the weights. But, to alter the weights is to alter the algorithm. You haven't added memory to an existing network, the original network has been replaced by a different one. The same point holds for adding precision. To add precision requires altering the weights to allow for distinctions among previously indistinguishable activations. And altering weights amounts to substituting a new network.

A crucial and controversial assumption of Schwarz' argument is that weight change in a connectionist framework is analogous to algorithm change (reprogramming) in a classical framework, and hence that changing weights amounts to building a different system. This will seem odd to those used to thinking about networks that learn, for, when a network learns, the weights change, yet surely the network retains its identity through learning. To understand what Schwarz has in mind, therefore, it is important to distinguish learning functions, which are functions from input vectors (and, in supervised learning, targets) to weight changes, from I/O functions whose domains and ranges are sets of activation vectors. Training alters the latter functions, but preserves the former. Schwarz' assumption, then, is that we should individuate connectionist systems by I/O function, at least for purposes of assessing the productivity issue.

The argument for this assumption appears to be as follows. Classical systems are individuated by algorithm. When we add memory to an adding machine, we don't change the way inputs are processed, we just make space for bigger ones. But when we add memory to a network, we change the way every input is processed, and this amounts to reprogramming the system. This argument is seriously flawed, however, by a misconception of classical systems. The function determined by a classical algorithm is a function from input and internal state (i.e., the state of memory), to output and internal state. It is important to see things this way because we want to be able to say that a change in stored knowledge, while it changes the input-output properties of the system, does not change the algorithm executed. When we program a classical system, we program it to behave differently as a function of different stored knowledge. This is what allows us to describe learning coherently as a change in the stored knowledge of a system that persists through that change. If we think of things this way, we shall be forced to admit that there is a sense in which, when stored knowledge is altered, the processing of every input is altered too, for, since the algorithm executed is sensitive to stored knowledge, a change in stored knowledge makes the processing of each input subject (at least in principle) to different constraints. But this is evidently not to say that changing stored knowledge amounts to writing a new algorithm and hence to building a new system.

We should think of connectionist systems analogously. If we do, we will think of a point in weight space as a point in stored knowledge space. A connectionist algorithm, then, is a recipe for computing a function from an input vector and a point in weight space to an output vector and a point in weight space.[17] From this point of view, we do not build a new network when we change weights any more than we build a new classical system when we change its stored knowledge, and this is what allows us to coherently describe learning as a change in the stored knowledge of a persisting system.[18]

The productivity issue, as we've seen, turns on whether it makes sense to idealize away from memory constraints, and, for connectionism, this depends on how connectionist networks are individuated. Schwarz is quite right in supposing that if we make identity of computational route from input to output a necessary condition of system identity, then we cannot coherently idealize away from memory constraints in connectionist systems.[19] But the argument proves too much, for, if we make identity of computational route from input to output a necessary condition of system identity, we cannot coherently describe learning in either classical or connectionist systems. Schwarz is right to point out that there is, in connectionist systems, an internal relation between how large memory is and what is in it, while the relation between memory size and memory content is external in classical systems. But you cannot, so far as I can see, promote this into an argument against productivity in connectionist systems.[20]

Schwarz' argument bears on our question only on the assumption that finite competencies—capacities that are finite even under idealization from resource constraints—are not genuinely cognitive. The underlying idea is that finite competencies can be mimicked by a look-up table, and hence are always subject to "unmasking". I'm not at all sure we should find this persuasive. Even in the finite case, it seems that output could bear any or all of the standard epistemological relations to input and initial state, and hence qualify as cognitive behavior under the only standard of cognitiveness that we have, namely epistemic constraint satisfaction. But we are right to concentrate on unbounded competencies when discussing the bearing of SLM on the Rationality Constraint, for a network that is weakly equivalent to a *finite* TPPL rationale *might* well be simply a look-up device, hence not cognitive at all. The cognitiveness of a finite system seems to depend on the presence of a rationale. An SLM-based attack on the Rationale Constraint cannot rest on the existence of finite networks that are only weakly equivalent to TPPL rationalizers, since such an attack cannot presume the cognitiveness of a finite system while at the same time arguing that it executes no discernable rationale.

Fond as I am of the Rationale Constraint, I'm prepared to concede that the encoding argument shows that the SLM strategy works: You can design a network that is weakly equivalent to a classical rationalizer by having it compute over non-structure preserving encodings of the representations utilized by the classical rationalizer. There is, however, still a way that a defender of the Rationale Constraint can assimilate this result, for it is still open to defenders of the Rationale Constraint to suppose that systems like those proposed by SLM do in fact execute rationales, though not, of course, the same rationales as their TPPL counterparts.

To get this line of defense off the ground, it is helpful to begin with an idea of Haugeland's (1991), namely, that symbolic representational schemes and activation vector/weight matrix schemes belong to different genera of representational schemes. For present purposes, the essential point is that schemes from different *genera* are semantically more or less disjoint, only very approximate translation being possible.[21] The incommensurability argument, scouted above, made use of this idea to support the claim that connectionist systems cannot execute rationales defined over symbolic representations. We can accept this point, I argued, without prejudice to the Rationale Constraint, provided we could make room for rationales defined over activation vectors and weight matrices. But which rationales are those?

I don't know. We know so little about non-symbolic representational schemes, and our epistemological concepts are so closely wedded to the linguistically expressed and hence symbolic rationales they were developed to evaluate, that we can only speculate at present. Non-symbolic rationales are possible, as the work of Barwise and Etchemendy (1990a, 1990b) demonstrates. Taking heart from this, friends of the Rationale Constraint may take a major goal of connectionist research to be the articulation of such principles of connectionist representation as will make possible the formulation and study of connectionist rationales. In the meanwhile, those who, like me, are friendly to both the

Rationale Constraint and to connectionism, needn't be dismayed by a showing of mere weak equivalence between a symbolic rationalizer and a connectionist network, for it is demonstrable that not all reasoning is symbolic, and it is at least possible that we will, one day, be able to discern non-symbolic reasoning in the disciplined spread of activation. I hope so. It is uncontroversial that there is reasoning in the brain, and that there is spreading activation there. But it is increasingly controversial to suppose that the brain is a symbol-cruncher in (very deep) disguise. *We* are symbol users, of course, but we should recognize our symbol use for what it is: An astounding bit of cultural technology. The fact that we can use symbols no more *entails* that our brains are symbol users than the fact that we use can-openers entails that our brains use them. If you think that the brain is in the spreading activation business, and you also think that it is reasoning that explains epistemic constraint satisfaction, then you had better take seriously the possibility of a connectionist epistemology.

Why not simply abandon the Rationale Constraint? Because it is very compelling. It says simply that a process cannot preserve an epistemological virtue V (or any other, for that matter) without being sensitive in some way to V-making factors. Bugs that cannot detect drawn lines cannot consistently run drawn mazes. If you design a bug that embarrasses my principle, I will take it as a research problem, not a refutation. I will do this because it is very dangerous to abandon compelling constraints on explanation. We can always respond to a theory that doesn't deliver the kind of understanding we want by training ourselves and our students to be more easily amused, but this will only trivialize science and produce hollow scientific successes. No doubt the progress of science can and should inform our conception of scientific explanation. But we should not repeat the mistake of the deductive-nomological model of explanation and confuse predictive or deductive success with explanatory success.[22]

SLM, it is interesting to notice in passing, wears its D-N patch on its sleeve:

> Now we see that the principles of SSP [sub-symbolic paradigm] do indeed provide a non-Classical explanation for the systematicity and productivity of higher cognition. To recapitulate, less formally: the patterns of activity which are mental representations have a combinatorial (tensor product) structure which mental processes are sensitive to; the constituents in these representations figure crucially in the statement of certain high-level regularities (e.g., systematicity and productivity) in behavior; the combinatorial structure of the representations figures centrally in the explanation of this behavior (*via* mathematical deduction); but the constituents do not have causal power in the sense of figuring in mental algorithms for generating behavior: These causal algorithms can *only* be stated at a level lower than that of mental constituents, the level of individual connectionist units. (SLM, p. 44)

SLM has demonstrated (mathematically deduced) a weak equivalence, but the absence of a strong equivalence, between a classical rationale and a process of spreading activation. Should we say: *that explains how the network gets the correct answers*? Or should we ask: *How in the name of heaven does the spreading activation get it right*? I'm inclined to think I'm not alone in thinking we should be pressing this second question, for it is this question that motivates the very considerable research devoted to understanding the so-called "hidden representations" in connectionist systems. (E.g., Hinton, 1986; Rosenberg, 1987; Sanger, 1989.)

Notes

1. Broader, or just plain different, definitions of cognitive functions are defensible. Nothing hangs on this terminological issue. I'm just interested in the class of functions, whatever they are called, that have the property indicated.
2. Part of the problem is that different players, or the same player on different occasions will do different things faced with the same board position. There is, therefore, no function from board-positions to board-positions, which constitutes *the* function chess players satisfy, in the way that there is a function from number pairs to numbers that is *the* function multipliers satisfy. But this is distinct from the problem I want to focus on here which is that there appears to be no way to formulate a chess function at all without articulating a rationale, hence no way of specifying the explanadum prior to the discovery of an explanans.
3. This is the "classic" methodology described by Marr (1982). He somewhat misleadingly calls specifying a cognitive function giving a computational theory. (It's misleading because what Marr calls a computational theory specifies a function to compute, but not how to compute it.)
4. This isn't a literature review. I've tried to cover all the arguments I know about, but I've organized the various points in my own way to facilitate exposition and discussion.
5. See Haugeland (1978) for the distinction between dimensions and levels of analysis. The fundamental point about the level-dimension distinction is that levels within a dimension are semantically homogeneous, a lower level simply a being more refined analysis of the level above, while dimensions differ in their semantic interpretations. A LISP program and its assembly code implementation are typically on different dimensions because the LISP is about lists and things listed, whereas the assembly code is about memory locations.
6. By a 'connectionist system' I shall generally mean a fully distributed system. Exceptions will be explicitly noted in the text.
7. By "input" and "output" here I don't mean just final input or output, but also intermediate input and output, i.e., input and output to on a given processing cycle.
8. I point no fingers. If the shoe fits... .
9. Some dialectics.

    (1) Later proof states do depend on earlier ones. Delay a few people, and all subsequent states will be different.

    Reply. True enough. But *strategically* delay several marchers so that they you get, e.g., "p&p" rather than "p&q" and the result will not be *relevantly* different: you won't, except by wild coincidence, get something that follows from the previous steps, you'll get garbage. This shows that the interpretation does not individuate states in a way that tracks their causal significance.

(2) In a connectionist system, the activation of unit A at t depends on *its* entire input vector. But A's input vector may be only a part of the vector that has a relevant interpretation. And,

(3) All an individual unit can know is a weighted sum of the activations of the units to which it is connected. Even neglecting differences in weights, if I am connected to two neighbors, A and B, I cannot tell the difference between both of them having an activation of 1 and A having an activation of 2 while B has an activation of 0. Hence, I am insensitive to differences in the input vector that make a representational difference.

Reply. Both (2) and (3) are quite right, but beside the point. It is the output *vector*, not some single unit, that needs to be sensitive to differences in input vectors. Moreover, there needn't be sensitivity to every difference; what's wanted is sensitivity to differences that matter. The test of whether there is enough discrimination is in performance: If performance is good enough, then so is the capacity to discriminate different representational states.

10. I am aware of at least one reason why one might deny even this. It goes back to Locke and Hume who held that epistemic relations are relations among ideas, and also (according to some recent commentators—see e.g. Owen (1993)) that ideas don't express propositions. Perhaps, then, reasoning can be understood as a process that traffics in things subpropositional, i.e., in things with satisfaction conditions rather than truth-conditions.

11. Our epistemological concepts have been developed in a symbolic framework. We want to hold people accountable to epistemological norms, and this means that those norms have to be applicable to, and articulated in, language. Moreover, decades of positivist and neo-positivist epistemology were couched explicitly in symbolic terms. Indeed, for many years, articulation of epistemological principles in the language of symbolic logic was a more-or-less explicit requirement for serious research. Non-symbolic epistemology is even rarer than non-symbolic logic. But these may be just what's required to understand human cognition at its most fundamental level.

12. That content independence inference is seen as the base case is brought out by the fact that there is a whole literature in psychology on content effects in reasoning. (See D. Cummins, under review; J. St. B. Evans, 1989.) The underlying assumption is that content effects are somehow deviations from proper reasoning. Often, they are treated outright as errors.

13. For further details, see Haugeland, 1985, pp.19-23.

14. If there is a language of thought, why do only humans have language? On the view that basic cognition is non-symbolic, this question has a straight-forward answer: language and other symbolic processing are very special achievements; they are *very hard* for brains. Hence, only the very best brains can do them.

15. This appears to be the line taken in Smolensky, LeGendre and Miyata (1992). If I understand them rightly, they argue that grammaticality is really a matter of degree, but that this is masked (to some extent, though not as much as MIT high churchers would have you believe) by the fact that the system always opts for the parsing with the maximum harmony. Like XOR networks, things only begin to look black and white when you ignore everything that doesn't reach some threshold.

16. It is important to distinguish idealizing away from resource constraints from idealizing away from attention lapses and the like. Performance may differ from competence—there may be errors, in short—because of factors like interruptions. But idealizing away from these sorts of error at most makes for correct computation of some finite function.

    Strictly speaking, to get an unbounded competence, you not only have to idealize away from resource constraints, you have to idealize away from physical breakdown as well.

17. Strictly speaking, it is a function from a point in activation space and a point in weight space to another point in activation space and another point in weight space. An input or output vector needn't specify the activation of every unit, yet the activation of any unit can affect subsequent performance.

18. It is instructive to see how the same confusion can arise in thinking about production systems. We think of programming a production system as a matter of writing productions, and this makes it seem that adding or subtracting productions amounts to building a new (though related) system. But if we think of things this way, we shall have to say that any change in stored knowledge amount to changes in the system, and it will be impossible to describe a system that learns. We should rather think of the productions we write as items in the long term memory of a system that consists of a production interpreter, a working memory, and a conflict resolution system. Construed thus, two production systems that differ only in which productions they incorporate are the same system with different stored knowledge.

19. This claim depends on the assumption that there is, in general, no point in weight space that will produce correct behavior for all real valued activations. When there is such a point, the required idealization will go through even on Schwarz's assumption about how connectionist systems should be individuated, since adding precision would not require a move away from this point. A corresponding point cannot be made about adding units, however. To see this, imagine an indefinite supply of units fully connected to existing units with zero weights. Adding units amounts to making some of these weights non-zero, and hence amounts to changes in weight space. In the special case in which old connections remain the same, and the new ones simply add scratch space, as in SIMPLIFIER (Cummins, 1991), it is arguable that we haven't built a new system, but this will hardly be the standard case.

    A possibility not considered by Schwarz is that outputs might be given as a finite but unbounded temporal sequence of activation vectors. This allows, in principle, for functions with infinite ranges. But, again, the crucial issue is whether there is some point in weight space that would, given enough time, suffice for the computation of any value in an infinite range. For many functions, such as addition, this presents no problem because the digits can be processed sequentially, with only enough memory required to handle carries. In effect, the system satisfies a finite function—sum two digits and carry—which amounts to an infinite function when the inputs and outputs are read as temporal sequences. But this trick won't work in general. Many other functions, such as speech production, will require idealization from memory constraints because early outputs in the temporal sequence can depend on later ones. (Think, for example, of verb agreement in English questions.)

20. There is another line of thought that seems to be influencing Schwarz. It goes like this. Identity of I/O function is a necessary condition of identity of algorithm computed. Changing the weights changes the I/O function computed, hence changes the algorithm, hence amounts to introducing a new system.

   We have to be careful how we think of an I/O function here. Evidently, when we add memory to an adding machine, it produces outputs it didn't produce before, from inputs it didn't accept before. If we think of I/O functions this way, then adding memory changes the I/O function of an adding machine, hence (by the argument on offer) the algorithm it executes, and this is not the conclusion Schwarz wants. To avoid this, we have to think of the I/O function as the one that would be computed but for resource limitations. But if we do that, identity of I/O function is no longer an independent condition on algorithm identity.

   As remarked above, Schwarz is apparently thinking that when we change the weights in a network, all the outputs are then computed in a new way, whereas, when we add memory to an adding machine, the computation isn't changed at all. But this is an artifact of the example. In general, when we change stored knowledge, we do change how each output is computed, in that the computational path from input to output is, at least in principles, different for each input-output pair. Imagine adding to the look-up table in an adding machine to handle 1 + 10 directly. Assuming the table is searched sequentially, and that this is the first entry, the contemplated change will alter the computational path initiated by every input. But it doesn't alter the algorithm at all.

21. Simple example: you cannot, as Locke and Berkeley agreed (*Essay concerning human understanding*, IV, vii, 9; *The principles of human knowledge, Introduction*) represent triinguality pictorially, though you can symbolically. Conversely, any verbal description of me is bound to hold in a different set of possible worlds than a picture of me.

22. We'd all love a hidden variable solution in quantum mechanics, because that would allow us to satisfy a fundamental constraint on explanation that currently goes begging. There is no hidden variable solution to be had, but we haven't all simply abandoned the constraint. It's the tension this situation generates that makes one of the main employment opportunities for philosophers in the middle of physics.

References

Barwise, J., and Etchemendy, J., (1990a) "Visual information and valid reasoning," in *Visualization in mathematics*, ed. W. Zimmerman. Washington, DC: Mathematical Association of America.

Barwise, J., and Etchemendy, J., (1990b) "Information, infons, and inference," in *Situation theory and its applications*, ed. R. Cooper, K. Mukai, and J. Perry. Stanford, CA: CSLI Publications.

Block, N. (1978) "Troubles with functionalism," in *Readings in the philosophy of psychology*, v.1, pp. 268-305.

Chomsky, N. (1965) *Aspects of the theory of syntax*. Cambridge, MA: M.I.T. Press.

Cummins, D. (under review) "Pragmatics, logical form, and human defeasible reasoning."

Cummins, R. (1978) "Explanation and subsumption." PSA 1978, 1, pp. 163-75.

Cummins, R. (1983) *The nature of psychological explanation*. Cambridge, MA: M.I.T.

Press, A Bradford Book.

Cummins, R. (1989) *Meaning and mental representation.* Cambridge, MA: M.I.T. Press, A Bradford Book.

Cummins, R. (1991) "The role of representation in connectionist models of cognition," in Rumelhart, Stich and Ramsey, *Connectionism and Philosophy*, Erlbaum, 1991, pp, 91-114.

Evans, J. St. B. (1989) *Bias in human reasoning.* London: Erlbaum.

Fodor, J. (1975) *The language of thought.* New York: Thomas Y. Crowell.

Haugeland, J. (1978) "The nature and plausibility of cognitivism," *The Behavioral and brain sciences,* 1: 215-226.

Haugeland, J. (1985) *Artificial intelligence: The very idea.* Cambridge, MA: M. I. T. Press, A Bradford Book.

Haugeland, J. (1991) "Representational genera," in Rumelhart, Stich and Ramsey, *Connectionism and Philosophy*, Erlbaum.

Helmholtz, H. von (1856) *Handbook of physiological optics,* ed. J. P. C. S. Southhall. New York: Dover Reprint, 1963)

Hinton, G. (1986) "Learning distributed representations," *Proceedings of the Seventh International Joint conference on Artificial Intelligence.* Vancouver, British Columbia.

Millikan, R. (1984) *Language, thought and other biological categories.* Cambridge, MA: M. I. T. Press, A Bradford Book.

Owen, D. (1993) "Locke on reason, probable reason and opinion." *The Locke Newsletter.* 24: 33-79.

Rosenberg, C. (1987) "Revealing the structure of NETtalk's internal representations," *Proceedings of the ninth annual meeting of the cognitive science society.* 537-554. Seattle, Washington.

Sanger, D. (1989) "Contribution analysis: A technique for assigning responsibilities to hidden units in connectionist networks. *Technical Report CU-CS-435-89.* Department of computer science, University of Colorado at Boulder.

Schwarz, G. (1993) "Connectionism, processing, memory," *Connection Science,* v. 4, 3-4: 207-226.

Shiffer, S. (1987) *Remnants of meaning.* Cambridge, MA: M. I. T. Press, A Bradford Book.

Smolensky, P., LeGendre, G., and Miyata, Y. (1992) "Principles for an integrated connectionist/symbolic theory of higher cognition," Tech. Report 92-08, Institute of Cognitive Science, University of Colorado.

Smolensky, P. (1988) "On the proper treatment of connectionism." *The behavioral and brain sciences.* 11:1-74.

Philosophical Perspectives, 9, AI, Connectionism, and
Philosophical Psychology, 1995

CONNECTIONISM AND THE COMMITMENTS
OF FOLK PSYCHOLOGY

Terence Horgan and John Tienson
The University of Memphis

Many philosophers believe that connectionism is incompatible with folk psychology, and hence that the success of connectionism would support eliminativist conclusions about propositional attitudes. Some philosophers actually *argue* that (certain brands of) connectionism has such eliminativist implications. In this paper we examine two such arguments, due to Ramsey, Stich, and Garon (1990; hereafter, RSG). Their principal argument centers around a feature of the propositional attitudes they call functional discreteness. RSG's second argument centers on the question whether the predicates of common sense psychology are projectable.

We conclude that their arguments are not successful. Common sense psychology, properly understood, is not incompatible with connectionism, properly understood—at least not in the way that RSG allege. But we are not simply concerned to refute another eliminativist argument, even though RSG's paper has been quite influential.[1] RSG's arguments are a useful vehicle for getting clearer about the issues on which their arguments turn, concerning both folk psychology and connectionism.

1. The Functional Discreteness Argument.

RSG's main argument is that common sense psychology has commitments that are not satisfied by an important class of connectionist models. Thus, if the correct models of human cognition lie within that class, common sense psychology will be shown to be seriously in error.

In this Section we lay out RSG's argument in four steps: the commitment of common sense psychology to functional discreteness, a class of connectionist models that are held to lack functional discreteness, an example of a model from that class, and the explicit argument that such models lack functional discreteness. In Section 2 we look at common sense functional discreteness in more detail. We argue that common sense is committed only to certain paradigm cases of functional discreteness, and that connectionist models of the class RSG identify *do* exhibit discreteness of that kind. We also point out that connectionist models in this class can exhibit other kinds of functional discreteness which common sense recognizes as possible, but to which it is not committed.

1.1 A Commitment of Common Sense Psychology.

RSG base their main argument on three commitments of common sense psychology concerning propositional attitudes: propositional attitudes are *semantically interpretable*; they have a *causal role*; and they are *functionally discrete*. RSG call this cluster of features *propositional modularity* (504). The first two are familiar. Propositional attitudes are the sorts of things that can be true or false, satisfied or unsatisfied, and the like; in the current term of art, they have content. And propositional attitudes influence behavior, belief fixation, etc. in ways that are appropriate to their content. To say that propositional attitudes are functionally discrete is to say that they can have effects singly (or in content-based structures, as when a conclusion is drawn from two premises, with no other propositions playing a role). RSG hold that distributed connectionist models do not satisfy the common sense demand for functionally discrete states because in such models all information is encoded holistically—hence inseparably—throughout the network.

They mention two different ways in which common sense propositional attitudes are functionally discrete. First, they can be acquired or lost individually (nearly enough). For example, "Henry...had completely forgotten that the car keys were hidden in the refrigerator," (504-5) although he had forgotten nothing else. And if you are told that the keys are in the refrigerator, you will acquire a small cluster of new beliefs, but most of your beliefs will be not be altered.

The second kind of functional discreteness is more important in the argument. Sometimes a person has a total set of beliefs and desires that provide more than one reason for performing an action, A. And sometimes it happens that the person does A for one of those reasons, with the other possible reason not figuring in the etiology of the action at all. Likewise, sometimes a person has several sets of beliefs that could lead her to infer a particular new belief, p, and she infers p from one of those sets, with the others not figuring in her thinking at all. Thus, according to common sense psychology, it is a determinate question *which* potential reasons for an action or change in belief were the actual or operative reasons.

According to common sense psychology, then, the same state is semantically evaluable and has a content-appropriate, functionally discrete, causal role. Such states have what RSG call propositional modularity. Functional discreteness is the feature on which the argument turns. Since semantic evaluability and some kind of causal role are taken for granted for the most part, we will usually speak of functional discreteness, reserving 'propositional modularity' for contexts in which semantic evaluability (or causal role) might be an issue.

1.2 A Class of Connectionist Models.

RSG claim that distributed connectionism must deny propositional modularity. They characterize a class of connectionist models, which, they claim, are incompatible with propositional modularity, in particular with functional discreteness of semantically evaluable states. The models in this class are characterized by three properties:

i.   Their encoding of information in the connection weights and in the biases on units is *highly* distributed rather than *localist*.
ii. Individual hidden units in the network have no comfortable symbolic interpretation; they are *subsymbolic*....
iii. The models are intended as *cognitive*, not merely as *implementations* of cognitive models. (p. 508)

Features (i) and (ii) are meant to insure that it is not possible to associate specific information with particular local parts of the model. Connections and nodes are not to be semantically evaluable individually or in small sets. Information in the model is encoded holistically throughout the network or throughout large portions of the network. Furthermore, each node contributes to representing many different propositions, and each connection weight contributes to storing many different propositions. Thus, information is contained in the network holistically and globally, not locally. And this means, RSG argue, that all of the information in the network is involved in all of its processing, so that it is not possible to single out certain bits of information as operative—and others as inoperative—in a token process, as folk psychology requires.

As RSG note, feature (iii) is not about the network as such, but about how it is to be interpreted. The idea is that the model is supposed to tell us something about how the *mind* works, not how it might be embodied. Consider, for instance, a classical parser—a classical computer program which is meant to take natural language sentences as input and yield structural descriptions of the input sentences as output. Such a program can be considered a hypothesis about the cognitive processes, knowledge structures, and so forth, involved in recognizing the grammatical structure of sentences. The program can be run on many different computers, with different machine languages; the hypothesis about cognition is the same in each case. The machine language of the computer that the program happens to be running on is irrelevant to the cognitive story the program proposes.

One could attempt to use a connectionist network to implement the operation of such a classical program. This would be to attempt to use the network as an *implementation* of the classical model—as an alternative, unorthodox kind of machine language. There would still be no difference in the hypotheses put forward about *cognition*. This is the kind of construal of connectionist models that (iii) rules out.

But a connectionist model—for instance, a parsing model such as Berg (1992)—can also be construed as offering an *alternative* story about the *cognitive* processes involved in recognizing the grammatical structure of sentences, a story that is in competition with the classical model. This would be to construe the model as a cognitive model, as required by (iii). When understood in this way, RSG hold, distributed connectionist models are incompatible with the propositional modularity of folk-psychological states.

1.3 An Example.

RSG describe a simple three-layered, feedforward connectionist network, which they describe as "a connectionist model of memory." The network, called Network A, has sixteen input nodes, one output node, and a hidden layer of four nodes. Input consists of encodings of sixteen propositions, for example,

> Dogs have fur.
> Cats have fur.
> Dogs have gills.
> Fish have gills.

Eight input nodes are used to encode the subject of the proposition, eight to encode the predicate.

Network A was trained up so that its output node is on (> .9) when the input proposition is true, and off (< .1) when the input proposition is false. Thus, the network has memorized the answers to a true/false test. The network is capable of generalizing; it responded correctly to encodings of 'cats have legs' and 'Cats have scales,' which were not in the training set.

1.4 The Argument

RSG observe that

> [t]he information encoded in Network A is stored holistically and distributed throughout the network. Whenever information is extracted from Network A, by giving it an input string and seeing whether it computes a high or a low value for the output unit, *many* connection strengths, *many* biases and *many* hidden units play a role in the computation. And any particular weight or unit or bias will help encode information about *many* different propositions. (513)

This is certainly a correct description of the workings of the network. Whenever the truth or falsehood of a proposition (i.e., high or low output node activation) is computed from an input proposition, all of the hidden units and many of the weights are involved in the computation. RSG argue that this holistic computation is incompatible (they say, "radically incongruent") "with the propositional modularity of common sense psychology."

> For as we saw in Section 3, common sense psychology seems to presuppose that there is generally [sic] some answer to the question of whether a particular belief or memory played a causal role in a specific cognitive episode. But if belief and memory are subserved by a connectionist network like ours, such questions seem to have no clear meaning. (513)

2. Critique of the Functional Discreteness Argument.

The overall structure of our critique is as follows. We distinguish three different ways that intentional mental properties (state-types) can be possessed by a cognitive system (section 2.1). On the basis of this tripartite distinction we distinguish several different possible forms of functional discreteness; we then argue that common sense psychology is committed to only one of these forms of functional discreteness, and that common sense psychology leaves it an open empirical question whether or not any of the other forms are manifested by propositional attitudes in humans (section 2.2). With this discussion as background, we press three separate replies to RSG's argument.

First, connectionist models, including RSG's Network A, typically exhibit the only kind of functional discreteness to which common sense psychology is committed. Thus, even if connectionism does preclude some or all of the other kinds, this fact would not generate an incompatibility with common sense psychology; rather, it would mean that connectionism answers in the negative certain empirical questions about functional discreteness that common sense psychology itself leaves open (section 2.3).

Second, even if common sense psychology *were* committed to those other kinds of functional discreteness, and even if human cognition failed to exhibit them, these facts would only show that common sense psychology is somewhat mistaken about propositional attitudes; they would not show that propositional attitudes don't exist (section 2.4).

Third, we argue that connectionism does not really preclude any of the other kinds of functional discreteness anyway. In principle, any or all of them could be manifested in a connectionist system in which information is embodied holistically and distributedly in weights and in activation patterns across nodes. Such functional discreteness normally would not involve distinct *physical* components of the network's causal evolution; instead it would be discernible only at a more abstract, mathematical, level of description in which the network is characterized as a high-dimensional "dynamical system" (section 2.5).

2.1 Psychological States: Occurrent, Dispositional, and Morphological.

There are three different ways in which intentional content or intentional state-types can be possessed by humans and other cognizers. The first two are standardly mentioned in the literature of philosophy of mind; the third is not. First, a person can possess the intentional property *occurrently*. This means, at least roughly, that a token of the relevant psychological state-type occurs as a concrete event or state within the person. In connectionist models, representations are certain patterns of activation—those patterns that are interpreted as having intentional content. Patterns of actual, occurrent activation in the network are the concrete states that constitute its token representations, and that thus play the role (in the model) of occurrent mental states.

Second, a person can possess the intentional state-type *dispositionally*. This means, at least roughly, that the cognitive system is disposed to generate a token of that type under appropriate circumstances, a token which will then have suitably content-appropriate effects on the system's cognitive processing and behavior. In connectionist models, dispositional intentional state-types thus are a matter of a network's (weights being set to produce a) tendency to generate occurrent representations under appropriate circumstances.

Third, a person can possess intentional content *morphologically* (as we will put it). Morphological possession of intentional content M is a matter of the cognitive system's being disposed, by virtue of its persisting structure rather than by virtue of any occurrent states that are tokens of M, to undergo state transitions that are systematically appropriate to content M—and to do so, at least much of the time, without generating a token of M during the process. Morphological content differs from occurrent representational content (e.g., occurrent belief) because it involves the cognitive system's persisting structure, rather than occurrent tokening of M. Morphological content differs from dispositional representational content (e.g., dispositional belief) as standardly understood (and as characterized in the preceding paragraph) because the relevant dispositions associated with morphological content involve tendencies other than the tendency to generate token representations with that content.

Consider, for example, a cognitive system which treats all members of a certain class, R, of representations similarly. It tends to make the same kinds of inferences from representations in R. When it acquires a new representation in the way it acquired the members of R, it tends to make the same kinds of inferences with that new representation. But it has other representations from which it does not make similar inferences. The system thus *treats* members of R as representations of the same type; in effect, it treats the kinds represented by the members of R as species of the same genus. But the system may have no representation for the genus itself. Thus, the system cannot represent the fact that (the kinds represented by) two members of R are species of the same genus, though it treats them as such. (*We* can say R is a class of representations; the system cannot.) This is the kind of thing that would count as (in this case purely) morphological content.

In connectionist models, morphological possession of intentional content is a matter of information being embodied "in the weights." (The tendency to generate occurrent mental states when appropriate is, of course, also something that's "in the weights." So dispositional intentional states can be seen as a special case of morphological content.)

Common sense psychology attributes both occurrent and dispositional modes of possession for the various kinds of state-types it posits, including beliefs and desires. Dispositional beliefs, desires, etc., as such, are *unconscious* states; any conscious mental state is an occurrent state. On the other hand, common sense psychology does leave open the conceptual possibility of occurrent beliefs and desires that are unconscious. There is no apparent reason why an intentional psychological theory could not posit morphological content, in addition to occurrent and dispositional state types. As far as we can see, morphological content is consistent with common sense psychology, but common sense psychology is not committed to morphological content.[2]

2.2 Types of Functional Discretenes, and their Status within Common Sense Psychology.

With these distinctions in mind, let us reconsider common sense psychology's commitment to functional discreteness. Consider, for instance, RSG's example of Clouseau. Clouseau has heard that the hotel is closed for the season and that the train is out of service. The Butler says that he spent the night at the hotel and took the train back to town in the morning. Common sense reckons that Clouseau might have inferred that the butler is lying from his belief that the hotel is closed for the season, or from his belief that the morning train has been taken out of service, or from both. From the perspective of common sense there is—often—a determinate answer to the question which it was. RSG believe that no determinate answer to this question is possible if human cognitive systems are relevantly like their Network A.

Why does common sense reckon this a determinate question? The first thought of the common sense psychologist is that it depends upon which relevant beliefs *consciously occurred* to Clouseau (and which logical connections he was aware of). If he consciously thought of the hotel closing and consciously realized that its being closed meant that the Butler couldn't have spend the evening in the hotel, but didn't remember the train at all at the time, well—its obvious which one was operative.

Consider also RSG's example of Alice the E-mailer. Alice had two reasons to go to her office. She wanted to talk to her research assistant, and believed that he would be at the office. And she wanted to send some E-mail messages, which she believed she could do from the office. "Common sense psychology assumes that Alice's going to her office might have been caused by either one of the belief/desire pairs, or by both, and that determining which of these options obtains is an empirical matter." (p. 505) In RSG's rendition, Alice's desire to send some E-mail messages was causally inert. Why might that be? The most natural explanation is that it did not *consciously occur* to her in the relevant time frame while her desire to talk to her research assistant did. The relevant time frame is not, of course, just the period immediately preceding her departure for the office. She might have had a thought early in the morning which she could have expressed out loud by saying, "Oh, I've got to talk to Fred today about...." She might then have taken care of some household chores, read the paper, gotten ready to go to the office and departed, without Fred ever again entering her consciousness.

Thus, the paradigmatic cases of propositional modularity recognized by common sense psychology are cases in which the causally active mental state is occurrent and conscious, whereas the causally dormant mental state is dispositional but not occurrent. That is, the type of functional discreteness to which common sense psychology is clearly committed is the following.

1. S1 is occurrent; S2 is dispositional but not occurrent.
    (Subcase: S1 conscious/S2 unconscious)
    (Here and below, S1 is the state that is causally active; S2 is a state that could have led to the same action or thought but did not do so in this case.)

We will call this subcase of type 1 functional discreteness *paradigmatic* functional discreteness.

Common sense also recognizes that one might make use of information that does not rise to consciousness, or arrive at a conclusion without conscious inference, especially in rapid physical activity.[3] Thus we should add a second subcase to type 1 functional discreteness: unconscious/unconscious.

It is not contrary to common sense to consider possible complications of paradigmatic functional discreteness, especially in the case of explanation of actions, decisions, choices, etc. Perhaps Alice is more deeply interested in her E-mail conversations than she cares to admit to herself. So her "real" reason for going to the office is to send some E-mail messages, but she "tells herself" (as we might say) that she is going to the office to talk to Fred. Her desire to send E-mail messages was occurrent and causally efficacious, but she suppressed awareness of its efficacy, and perhaps of the desire itself. This seems to be a case in which *both* desires are tokened, but in which only one, the one that is not consciously considered, is the actual cause. Thus, common sense clearly recognizes the possibility of a second type of functional discreteness.

2. S1 is occurrent and S2 is occurrent.
    (Conscious/conscious; conscious/unconscious; unconscious/conscious; unconscious/unconscious.)

All four subcases are conceptually possible although the first is perhaps questionable from the point of view of common sense. It seems odd to suppose that Clouseau thought of the hotel closing, thought of the train being taken out of service, understood that each was incompatible with something the Butler had said, and inferred that the Butler was lying from one of these beliefs but not the other.

Dispositional possession of an intentional state-type does not make a direct causal contribution to an outcome the state-type could cause; rather, dispositional states enter the causal fray indirectly via the exercise of the disposition, i.e., via the occurrence during processing of an occurrent token of that state-type. Case 1 involves a situation where the disposition to produce a token of S2 does *not* get exercised during processing, so it is, in a sense, a *degenerate* type of functional discreteness. It needs to be stated because it is the one case of functional discreteness to which common sense is clearly committed. Given that intentional state-types that remain merely dispositional do not play a causal role, three further cases are worth distinguishing.

3. S1 is occurrent; S2 is morphological.
   (Conscious/unconscious; unconscious/unconscious.)
4. S1 is morphological; S2 is occurrent.
   (Unconscious/conscious; unconscious/unconscious.)
5. S1 is morphological; S2 is morphological.

Common sense allows for the conceptual possibility of each of Cases 3 through 5, because one can make intelligible, from the point of view of common sense, the idea that there is morphological content that has a causal role. For instance, here is the transcript of an actual conversation:

J: The Parkers are at their place; the red flag is up on their mailbox.
N: Yeah, I saw their golden [retriever dog] last night.
J: Oh, yeah; you told me that. I forgot.

Clearly, J inferred the Parkers' presence from the flag, not from the dog. The flag is the thing he thought of. Had he remembered the dog, he might have realized that he did not have to tell N about the Parkers. So far, this story illustrates Type 1 functional discreteness.

But it illustrates something more. To infer that the Parkers were home from the raised flag on their mailbox, J must rely on something like (F) the flag is up on the Parkers mailbox only when they are here to raise it. Likewise, when N inferred that the Parkers were home, she relied on something like (D) the Parkers' golden is here only when they are here. Thus, we have instances of (F) and (D) exhibiting functionally discrete causal roles.

But it is quite unlikely that either (F) or (D) consciously occurred to either J or N. And, we submit, it is quite intelligible from the point of view of common sense to suppose that neither (F) nor (D) was tokened subconsciously either; indeed, that neither was tokened subconsciously seems more likely to us than not. If it was not, this is not a case of Type 1 or of Type 2 functional discreteness. If the information (F) that played a role in J's inference was not tokened consciously or unconsciously, then it was morphological rather than occurrent or merely dispositional.[4] This seems, then, to be construable by common sense as a case of Type 5 functional discreteness. So common sense evidently does permit the possibility of morphological content and Type 5 functional discreteness. (In Section 5 we offer an example construable as Type 4 functional discreteness, plus variants of RSG's Clouseau example for each of Types 2-5.)

But our main point in this Section is that common sense is only *committed* to the paradigm case of functional discreteness, Type 1 functional discreteness where the causally active state is conscious. The other cases we have distinguished are recognized by common sense as possibilities, some as the quite serious possibilities.

In Section 2.5 below, we argue that all five types of functional discreteness are possible in models that fall within the class of models characterized by RSG.

2.3. First Reply: Folk Psychology and Distributed Connectionism Are Compatible.

The most immediate reply to RSG's functional discreteness argument is now quite straightforward. The only kind of functional discreteness to which common sense psychology is committed is paradigmatic functional discreteness. Connectionist models have no trouble at all manifesting this degenerate kind of functional discreteness. For, on one hand, the occurrent beliefs of common sense psychology correspond most naturally to certain tokened activation patterns in a connectionist network; and activation patterns have a causal influence on processing. Processing in a connectionist network *is* spreading activation. On the other hand, the dispositional beliefs of common sense psychology correspond most naturally to a connectionist network's dispositions to generate the activation patterns that function in the system as representation-tokens; and when such a disposition remains dormant, so that the relevant activation pattern does not get tokened during processing, then the pattern does not affect the system's processing (since it is not *there*). Thus, paradigmatic functional discreteness is easily accommodated within the relevant class of connectionist models: an activation pattern can occur that constitutes a token representation that causes a certain subsequent outcome, while at the same time the system has a dispositional representation which would bring about the same outcome were it activated and yet remains dormant on this particular occasion. Therefore, the connectionist models considered by RSG do not preclude the kind of functional discreteness to which common sense psychology is committed.

In the remainder of this subsection we will amplify this reply, by discussing (i) the Network A described by RSG and their remarks about it, (ii) RSG's replies to certain objections they themselves consider, and (iii) recent remarks about RSG's modularity argument by Stich and Warfield (forthcoming).

There are two kinds of representations in Network A. The input layer is interpreted as representing questions concerning the truth or falsity of certain propositions. And the trained up network represents answers to those questions. That is, it represents certain propositions as being true or false in the pattern of activation in the set of nodes consisting of input nodes plus the output node.

Activation of the encoding of a proposition in the input layer *causes* the output node to record true or false. The occurrent representation of the proposition causes the recollection of its truth value. Potential but non-occurrent representations *do not exert any such influence*. Thus Network A, like connectionist models generally, exhibits paradigmatic functional discreteness: occurrent representations have an effect, whereas non-occurrent representations that the system is disposed to produce, but has not produced on a given occasion, do not have an effect.

Of course, what RSG actually have in mind as analogues of beliefs, in Network A, are not occurrent representations in the input layer (or in the hidden layer), but rather the propositional information which is holistically embodied "in the weights". They argue,

> Since information is encoded in a highly distributed manner...with information regarding any given proposition scattered throughout the network, the system lacks functionally discrete, identifiable sub-structures that are semantically interpretable as representations of individual propositions. (514.)[5]

Functional discreteness does not obtain, they contend, for propositional information embodied holistically in the network's weights (and biases). Rather,

> There is a real sense in which *all* the information encoded in the network's connectivity matrix [weights] is causally implicated in *any* processing in which the network engages. (O'Brien, 1991, p. 173; quoted with endorsement by Stich, 1991, p. 180)[6]

But the common-sense psychologist can grant that all the information in the weights is implicated in any processing in which the network engages, and deny that this goes contrary to the kind of functional discreteness to which common sense psychology is committed (viz., the paradigmatic kind). Information in the weights is, if anything, the connectionist analog of *morphological* content. And common sense psychology simply is not committed to claiming that morphological content in humans exhibits functional discreteness. Whether it does or not is an open empirical question, as far as common sense psychology is concerned. Thus, if (some) distributed connectionist models do not have functionally discrete morphological content, that doesn't make them incompatible with common sense psychology; rather, it answers the empirical question negatively (for those models).

RSG do discuss the objection that (i) connectionist representations are patterns of activation, and (ii) activation patterns are functionally discrete states. They reply that the identification of beliefs with activation patterns is "singularly implausible," because "in common sense psychology beliefs and propositional memories are typically of substantial duration; and they are the sorts of things that cognitive agents generally have lots of even when they are not using them" (p. 518). But the appropriate counterreply is straightforward: it is only *occurrent* beliefs that are appropriately regarded, within connectionist modeling, as activation patterns.

RSG also discuss the suggestion that "long standing beliefs might be identified not with activation patterns, but with *dispositions to produce activation patterns*," and the related suggestion that "the familiar philosophical distinction between dispositional and occurrent beliefs might be captured, in connectionist models, as the distinction between dispositions to produce activation patterns and activation patterns themselves" (pp. 518-9). They reply that dispositions to produce activation patterns "are not the discrete, independently causally active states that folk psychology requires" (p. 519). Once again the counterreply is straightforward: folk psychology recognizes a distinction between occurrent and dispositional belief, and is not committed to the functional discreteness of dispositional beliefs qua dispositional; it is only committed to paradigmatic functional discreteness. (Dispositions to re-create beliefs, memories, etc. are in the weights holistically. But the (recreatable) *activation pattern* is not in the weights when it is not active. It is nowhere. Thus, there really is no question of the functional discreteness of dispositional beliefs. It is not that all of the dispositional beliefs are directly implicated in processing; none of them are.[7])

So connectionist representations have, by and large, functionally discrete causal roles. Those representations that get activated in a process play a causal role in that process; those not activated do not. And the specific causal roles of the ones that get activated depend upon patterns of spreading activation.[8]

Stich and Warfield (forthcoming) reply to a similar observation by Andy Clark (1990). Clark suggests that it is only a "belief-in-action" (as opposed to a long-standing belief, which may be just a disposition to produce an occurrent belief-in-action) that needs to be capable of functionally discrete causal potency (p. 96). Stich and Warfield's relevant argument is that the proposal is too weak,

> for on the interpretation of propositional modularity..., no deterministic system that stores propositional information could fail to satisfy propositional modularity. If this is right, there is nothing at all we could learn about the workings of such a system that would show that it violates modularity and thus does not really have beliefs. (Section 2.2)

We take 'and thus' in the last line to mean 'and for this [lack of propositional modularity] reason'. Other deep commitments of common sense psychology might be violated even if propositional modularity is not.

Thus, the operative complaint in this passage is that, on the proposed interpretation of propositional modularity (which requires discrete causal potency only for tokened representations), no system could fail to satisfy propositional modularity, in particular, no system could fail to exhibit functional discreteness.

Our reply is fourfold. First, Network A is a model of a single, immediate cognitive step—in this case, rote recall. There are no representation-level intermediaries. Given that the input and output of such a one-step process are (interpreted as) representations, and that representations are entered singly, nothing could show that the system lacks Type 1 functional discreteness. The occurrent representation in the input layer is causally active. Dispositional representations—ones that could be in the input layer but are not—are not causally active.

But second, this is surely nothing to complain about. Any cognitive process which is immediate for a system,[9] and which receives only one relevant input at a time must, obviously, exhibit Type 1 functional discreteness. (It does not even depend upon the system being deterministic.) This just means that the commitment of common sense psychology to functional discreteness of propositional attitudes is a very weak commitment.

However, third, it is easy to imagine other sorts of connectionist models that might not exhibit functional discreteness for tokened representations. A model of some task that involves multiple simultaneous soft constraint satisfaction, for instance, must allow many representations to be active at once. It might often, perhaps even typically, be impossible to determine which representations were causally responsible for the solution to a problem, especially if the representations are widely distributed. Furthermore, some systems with distributed representations in which each node contributes to many different representations can have many representations active at once by *superposition* of representations, in which case it may be—though it need not be (cf. section 2.5 below)—impossible to separate the causal contribution of distinct representations. Thus, there may be models of these kinds, with sensible representation level interpretations that do not exhibit Type 2 functional discreteness.

Finally, fourth, common sense psychology is not committed to Type 2 functional discreteness anyway. The only kind of functional discreteness to which it is actually committed *is* trivially satisfiable.

2.4 Second Reply: Ontologically Conservative Theory Change.

Suppose, for the sake of argument, that we are wrong in claiming that common sense psychology is only committed to the kind of functional discreteness that involves a conscious occurrent belief and a non-activated dispositional belief, and that it is actually committed to some or all of the other kinds delineated in section 2.1 above. Suppose too (although we will argue against this in the next subsection) that distributed connectionist models of the sort sketched by RSG are incompatible with the further kinds of functional modularity. Do these suppositions sanction RSG's key claim, viz., "If connectionist hypotheses of the sort we will sketch turn out to be right, so too will eliminativism about propositional attitudes" (p. 500)?

Surely not. RSG themselves draw a distinction between "ontologically conservative" theory changes (which preserve the key theoretical entities posited by of an original theory while altering or replacing that theory's claims *about* those entities), and "ontologically radical" theory changes (in which the entities posited by the old theory are repudiated as well). Even if common sense psychology happens to be committed to one or more kinds of functional discreteness of Type 2 through Type 5, altering the theory by dropping this commitment would be a rather conservative change—especially since these are not *paradigmatic* cases of functional discreteness. Such a change would not even approach entailing that there are no beliefs.[10]

2.5 Third Reply: Strong Forms of Functional Discreteness Are Not Precluded.

Distributed connectionist models embody information holistically, rather than containing discrete items of propositional information in physically discrete internal states, structures, or processes. Information that is not occurrently represented is distributed throughout the network, and each part of the network contributes to storing much or all of its information. So it appears plausible that distributed connectionist models are incompatible with functional discreteness of Types 3-5. This appearance motivates RSG's argument. But the appearance is misleading, as we now briefly explain. We begin by describing a way of thinking about morphological content in connectionism. We then discuss a common phenomenon that is plausibly regarded as involving Type 4 functional discreteness—that is, a situation in which morphological content trumps occurrent content. Then we revisit Clouseau and the butler.

The natural mathematical framework for describing connectionist networks is the body of mathematical concepts, techniques, and results known as dynamical systems theory. To describe a network as a dynamical system is to specify in a certain way its temporal evolution, both actual and hypothetical. Each node in the network is assigned a separate dimension, or axis, in a high-dimensional hyper-space; the possible activation values the node can take are points along that axis. Each possible *total* state of the system is thus represented by a unique point in the system's "state space" (in the case of connectionist networks, often called "activation space"). The dynamical system, as such, is essentially the full collection of temporal trajectories the network would follow through its state space—with a trajectory emanating from each point it can occupy in state space.

The dynamical system can be thought of as a high-dimensional geometrical/topological object. A useful geometrical metaphor for dynamical systems is the notion of a *landscape* (in the case of networks, an *activation landscape*). Think of the network's n-dimensional activation space as a contoured n-dimensional surface, oriented "horizontally" in (n+1)-dimensional space. For each point p, the temporal trajectory that the network itself would follow through its activation space if it were to evolve (without perturbation) from p is the path "downhill" along the landscape that a ball would follow if positioned at p and then allowed to "roll."

Each point on the activation landscape corresponds to a total activation state of the network. Certain of these points are representation-realizing points: when the network is in the total activation state corresponding to the given point, one or more representations are tokened as activation patterns. In general, representations are multiply realizable in connectionist models. Representations are identified with activation vectors, typically with activation vectors that specify activation values for only a relatively small portion of the nodes of the network. Such a vector thus specifies values for some, but not all dimensions of activation space. All points that satisfy these values will realize the given representation.[11] Also, several distinct representations can, in general, be realized by a single point in activation space: the point's coordinates simultaneously satisfying the coordinate-specifications of several different vectors, each of which is identified with a distinct representation.[12]

From the dynamical systems point of view, cognitive-level state transitions in a connectionist network are trajectories along the activation landscape from one representation-realizing point to another. These transitions depend jointly on two interrelated factors: (i) the relative positions on the activation landscape of the representation-realizing points, and (ii) the topography of the landscape itself. Landscape topography is determined by the connections among the nodes and the weights on those nodes. "Training up" a network, by progressively altering its weights in accordance with some learning algorithm (e.g., backpropagation of error), amounts to the progressive *molding* of the activation landscape in a way that results in systematically content-appropriate trajectories from one representation-realizing point to another.[13] Learning thus involves modification of the existing activation landscape, in a way that accommodates new information while leaving intact the information to which what is learned is irrelevant.

Learning to make a certain class of inferences, for instance, produces a slope or incline on the activation landscape. From every point realizing a (possibly complex) representation of a certain kind, the system is inclined to proceed to a point realizing a corresponding representation of a different kind. The landscape also has other inclines, subserving potentially conflicting inferences one has learned to make. And many other inclines too, subserving various potentially conflicting tendencies to evolve from one representational point to another in various *non-inferential* content-appropriate ways. So the activation landscape is a very high dimensional, subtly contoured, space with inclines upon inclines upon inclines. (Think of the disorientation and contortion of earlier geological strata by rising new land.) Thus, being inclined to make an inference does not mean that one will make the inference.

In any particular cognitive trajectory along the activation landscape, information that is part of the content of representation-realizing points along that trajectory is the information that becomes occurrent—i.e., gets explicitly represented—during the cognitive process corresponding to that trajectory. On the other hand, information that is accommodated by the trajectory *without* being part of the content of any representation-realizing point on it is (relative to that trajectory, anyway) morphologically embodied rather than explicitly represented. The local topographical features of the landscape—i.e., the various different, superimposed inclines present in the immediate vicinity of a given representation-realizing point—are what determine the content-appropriate trajectory from any such point to another one.

One special case of inclines in activation space comes up fairly often in connectionist discussions. Representations are thought of as *attractor* points or regions in activation space, and one speaks of the *basin* of the attractor—viz, the set of all points in activation space from which the system will evolve to the attractor. A basin is, of course, an incline all individual slopes of which lead to the same place.

For a different kind of example of an incline, consider a system that has learned to make a class of Humean inferences. Whenever it encounters an A, it expects a B. But it has never occurrently represented the proposition that A's are B's, and it is not currently disposed to do so. Perhaps if it is sophisticated enough, it could come to occurrently believe that A's are B's by reflecting on its own inferential tendencies. But it has not reflected in that way.

In such a case, the information that A's are B's is contained in the system morphologically (but not dispositionally or occurrently). That is, there is an incline in its activation space connecting A-realizing points to B-realizing points, but there is no point in its current activation space that realizes the belief that A's are B's.

Consider now the phenomenon of prejudice. A person is strongly inclined to come to certain kinds of judgments, J, about anyone (or anything) he classifies as being of a certain type, K.[14] On occasion he feels a need to explain one of those judgments, sometimes from external prodding, sometimes not. On these occasions he comes up with an explanation of the particular judgment that does not refer to type K. And typically, the explanations he gives are rather different in different cases.

The prejudice consists in an incline in that person's activation space from points realizing representations of individuals as being of kind K to points realizing J judgments about those individuals. The person may have little or no inclination to (occurrently) believe the generalization connecting K to J. (Being a human being, he has, of course, the capacity to *entertain* that generalization.)

Often when a J judgment is made, it is preceded by an occurrent representation, R, that the person puts forward—to himself or others—as the reason for his J judgment on a particular occasion. But in fact, R is causally inert. There is no path in activation space from points realizing R but not realizing a representation of an individual as of kind K to the J judgment. At the network level, there is no spreading of activation from R to J.

The incline (in activation space), i.e., morphological content, plays an actual causal role in bringing about the J judgment; the occurrent representation, R, does not. Thus, we have here a conceptually possible case of Type 4 functional discreteness. Representation *R* might be a complex representation that fully justifies *J*—in the easiest case, the premises of a valid argument for *J*. Yet *K* leads to *J* only in conjunction with the (mis)information morphologically embodied in the incline from *K*-realizing points to *J*-realizing points; and *K* leads to *J* in that case whether or not the inferential trajectory commences from an *R*-realizing point. Furthermore, the person need not consciously represent the fact that the individual is of kind *K* for his prejudice concerning *K*'s to come into play. (It is an interesting empirical question whether such a representation must be occurrent at all, even unconsciously.)

Consider, in light of the foregoing discussion, RSG's example of Clouseau. Suppose that Clouseau's internal network is at a point p in activation space that realizes the state-type B:

(B)   believing that the butler said he spent the night at the village hotel, and that he said he arrived back on the morning train.

Suppose that Clouseau's activation landscape has distinct, determinate, inclines within it that respectively subserve trajectories appropriate to belief-types H and T, respectively:

(H)   believing that the village hotel is closed for the season.
(T)   believing that the morning train has been taken out of service.

(We will call these inclines the *H*-incline and the *T*-incline, respectively.) In the immediate vicinity of the point p on Clouseau's activation landscape that his cognitive system currently occupies, the local topography is a complex contouring consisting of the superposition of various different inclines, including the H-incline and the T-incline. Suppose that at point p, the T-incline and certain other inclines (not including the H-incline) effectively "cancel each other out"; i.e., when superimposed together, the T-incline and these other inclines jointly make no net contribution to the local topography in the vicinity of p. Finally, suppose that the *dominant* net effect, locally at point p, is contributed by the H-incline. So an inferential trajectory commences, emanating from p and terminating at a point p' which realizes the state-type L:

(L)   believing that the butler is lying.

This is a scenario in which Clouseau believes that the village hotel is closed for the season, he also believes that the morning train has been take out of service, and he infers that the butler is lying on the basis of the first belief but not the second.

This scenario can be further elaborated in several ways, corresponding to Type 2 through Type 5 functional discreteness. If the content of both belief H and belief T is only embodied morphologically in the H-incline and T-incline respectively, but neither content gets occurrently represented during Clouseau's inferential process, then we get morphological/morphological functional discreteness: Type 5. But there are three other variants or the scenario, where the content of one or both beliefs also becomes occurrent, i.e., is part of the representational content of point p, or of some other point along the inferential trajectory commencing from p: H and T both occurrent (Type 2); H occurrent but not T (Type 3); T occurrent but not H (Type 4).

So the upshot of this subsection is that all four of these kinds of functional discreteness are open conceptual possibilities, under distributed connectionism. RSG are mistaken to suppose that functional discreteness of cognitive states can only occur if the content of those states is embodied, in weights and/or in activation patterns, in a physically discrete way.[15]

3. The Projectable Predicates Argument.

RSG briefly offer a second argument for the radical incompatibility of connectionism and common sense psychology. Network A learned the truth values of sixteen propositions. RSG describe a second model, Network B, which learned the truth values of those sixteen propositions plus one more. The weights, biases, and internal activation values in processing are not similar in Networks A and B, and the differences between them do not correlate in any way with the difference in what they have "learned". Both of these networks represent the proposition that dogs have fur, among others. There are indefinitely many other connectionist networks that represent the information that dogs have fur, which differ in indefinitely many ways from Networks A and B.

From these observations, RSG argue as follows.

> ...common sense psychology treats predicates expressing the semantic properties of propositional attitudes as projectable. Thus 'believes that dogs have fur' or 'remembers that dogs have fur' will be projectable predicates in common sense psychology.... [But] though there are *indefinitely* many connectionist networks that represent the information that dogs have fur just as well as Network A does, these networks have no projectable features in common that are describable in the language of connectionist theory. (514)

Thus, we take it, the conclusion is that common sense psychology treats as projectable a huge class of predicates that connectionism renders non-projectable. (Projectable predicates, say RSG, are "the sort of predicates that are appropriately used in nomological or law-like generalizations" (p. 504).) Hence, if connectionism turns out to be correct, there will be no states of the kind that these common-sense psychological predicates purport to ascribe.[16]

RSG profess not to find "features in common that are describable in connectionist theory" in Networks A and B. We suppose that they are thinking of connectionist theory as the theory of networks: activation levels and the equations that determine them, weights, biases, and learning algorithms. There are indeed no projectable predicates *here* that correspond to the projectable predicates of common sense psychology.

But the projectable predicates of common sense psychology are "predicates expressing the semantic properties of propositional attitudes." Connectionist theory also has predicates expressing the semantic properties of representations— e.g., the predicate, 'representation that dogs have fur.' A large part of connectionist theorizing consists of talk about *representations*. Read the description of any connectionist model! Read RSG's description of Network A! Prominent in the description of any connectionist model is an account of the representations in the model and of how they are realized in the network. The connectionist models on which RSG's argument centers are, they insist, to be construed as *cognitive* models. Surely, if a model is construed as a cognitive model, then representations will be a central part of the theory of that model.

Thus, Network A and Network B do have a feature in common that is describable in the language of connectionist theory: they both represent the proposition that dogs have fur. And, of course, they share this feature with all those other actual and potential connectionist models that have a representation of the proposition that dogs have fur.

Furthermore, connectionist representation predicates are projectable. For any reasonably successful connectionist model that has a representation of the proposition that dogs have fur, 'representation that dogs have fur' will be a projectable predicate. If the alleged representations of a model are not projectable relative to the cognitive task being modeled, the model doesn't work. Exactly how representation predicates are projectable relative to a model will depend upon the cognitive task being modeled. But that is what one would expect, since cognitive models tend to be aimed at modeling a single cognitive task or small cluster of tasks, and the causal role of a representation relative to one cognitive task will be different from its causal role relative to different cognitive tasks.[17]

When the same network is trained up on the same task more than once, there are differences in weights, biases, and activation levels of hidden nodes, but generalizations involving representation-level connectionist predicates are typically projectable from one trained up network to the other. Representation-level generalizations are similarly projectable when distinct networks are implementations of the same cognitive model, and when similar networks are trained up on different but similar tasks (as were RSG's Network A and Network B).

Generalizations involving representation-level connectionist predicates are not, in general, projectable from one connectionist model to others devoted to different cognitive tasks; the terms of such a generalization are often not even applicable to the other model. But that is a result of the nature of cognitive modeling. In any case, it is not a difference from common sense. From the point of view of common sense psychology, the degree of projectability of generalizations involving propositional attitude predicates to other cognizers and other kinds of cognizers is quite variable and context dependent. Thus, connectionism has projectable predicates—predicates assigning representations to network models—that line up quite nicely with the projectable predicates of common sense psychology.

When RSG say "these *networks* have no projectable features in common" (our emphasis), there is a sense in which what they say is true. The networks *as such* have no projectable features in common. The models—the networks interpreted as performing a cognitive task—do have projectable features in common. Cognitive science is a branch of scientific theory that spans and interconnects several levels of description. Within classical, pre-connectionist, cognitive science, the canonical articulation of the multi-level nature of the enterprise was given by David Marr, who wrote:

> At one extreme, the top level, is the abstract computational theory of the device, in which the performance of the device is characterized as a mapping from one kind of information to another, the abstract properties of this mapping are defined precisely, and its appropriateness and adequacy for the task are demonstrated. In the center is the choice of representation for the input and output and algorithm to transform one into the other. At the other extreme are the details of how the algorithm and representation are realized physically—the detailed computer architecture, so to speak. (1982, 24-25)

Thus, Marr identifies three theoretically significant levels of description. The top level, the level of the mental *qua* mental, specifies a cognitive function: a transition-function that pairs cognitive states with the appropriate cognitive successor-states.[18] The middle level specifies the algorithm by which that function is computed. And the lowest level specifies the physical device in which the algorithm is implemented.[19]

An algorithm, or program, is a mathematical object, a set of rules for manipulating symbols or data-structures purely on the basis of their formal/structural properties, independent of any intentional content they might have. Symbols and data-structures, so described, are also mathematical objects. Thus, the middle level in Marr's typology is a mathematical level of organization. This level of organization mediates between intentional mental states and their physical realization. Intentional mental states and state-transitions are realized by certain mathematical states and state-transitions, which in turn are realized by certain physical states and state-transitions.[20] The mathematical level is the appropriate one for characterizing the abstract system of functional/organizational features that constitutes Nature's engineering design for human cognition.

However, the discrete mathematics of algorithms is not common to all approaches to cognition. As discussed in Section 2.5, the natural mathematical framework for connectionism is the theory of dynamical systems. And if cognitive transitions are not determined by algorithms over symbols, then it need not be assumed that the potential cognitive transitions of a cognitive system constitute a tractably computable function. Marr's tri-level typology for cognitive science can thus be seen as a species of a more generic tri-level typology:

Cognitive State-Transitions. The level of the mental *qua* mental.
Mathematical State-Transitions. The level of functional organization.
Physical Implementation. The level of the physical *qua* physical.

Connectionist cognitive models are another species of this generic typology, with the mathematics of dynamical systems as the natural mathematical framework at the middle level of description, and with connectionist networks (often as simulated on conventional computers) as the prototypical devices for physical implementation.[21]

In both classical and connectionist cognitive science, then, theorizing involves the cognitive, the mathematical, and the physical levels of description and the interconnections among them. In both classical and connectionist cognitive science, predicates at each level of description are projectable, even though the state-types they express are multiply realizable at lower levels of description.[22] To claim, as RSG do, that connectionist models that differ in the manner of their Network A and Network B "have no projectable features in common that are describable in the language of connectionist theory," is to ignore the fact that connectionist cognitive science includes two levels of description above the level of the physical qua physical.

4. Conclusion.

RSG argue that common sense psychology is incompatible with a certain brand of connectionism because common sense psychology is committed to the functional discreteness of propositional attitudes, while that brand of connectionism precludes functional discreteness. We distinguished three ways in which a cognitive system may possess intentional content: occurrently, dispositionally, or morphologically. Mixing and matching these ways of possessing content leads to several conceptually possible types of functional discreteness. We argued that common sense psychology is committed to only the most innocuous kind of functional discreteness—Type 1 functional discreteness, in which occurrent representations make a causal contribution and merely dispositional ones do not. Virtually any system that has representations, including the systems of RSG's brand of connectionism, will exhibit Type 1 functional discreteness.

Common sense also recognizes the possibility of the other types of functional discreteness that we distinguish, and some of these possibilities suggest interesting ways to think about cognition. We suggested (in Section 2.5) that these other types of functional discreteness could be found in distributed connectionist models. Thus, even if common sense psychology is more deeply committed to functional discreteness than we believe, RSG would not have shown that common sense psychology is incompatible with distributed connectionism.

We also argued (Section 3), contrary to RSG, that connectionist theory does have projectable predicates comparable to the propositional attitude predicates of common sense psychology.

Even if we have succeeded in showing that RSG's arguments are not successful, this constitutes only a limited defense of the compatibility of connectionism and common sense psychology. There are other arguments afoot (e.g., Davies 1991) that purport to demonstrate an incompatibility between connectionism and common sense.[23] But addressing such arguments and the issues they raise is a task for another occasion.

Notes

1. The paper has been anthologized at least four times (see the entry for it in the bibliography), and has been widely discussed in the recent philosophical literature.
2. We leave open the question of what sorts of conditions must be met by morphological content in order for it to count as the morphological possession of a *belief* (or of some other state-type of common sense psychology). Here is one plausible-looking requirement: in order to be a belief, the state-type must be one that can become an occurent thought within the cognitive system. Morphological content only counts as a belief if that content is also possessed dispositionally.
3. Whether arriving at a conclusion without conscious inference is properly called inference at all from the point of view of common sense is not clear. But it does not matter for present purposes.
4. This sort of thing—non-tokened information playing an essential role in cognitive processing—appears to be ubiquitous. If it really does occur, as the phenomenology of conscious experience suggests, then any adequate theory of cognition needs to be able to account for it.
5. This argument as stated is clearly fallacious. It has the same logical form as: since there are non-cows in the pasture, there are no cows in the pasture. (Since network A has states that embody propositional information indiscretely, it lacks states that embody propositional information discretely.) But what RSG obviously mean is that the propositional information embodied in the system's weights is not embodied by functionally discrete substructures of weighted connections.
6. O'Brien says here that the information is *encoded* in the network's connectivity matrix, and this is not an uncommon way to speak. We would choose, however, not to say that the weights themselves en*code* information, though they may be said to *embody* (RSG's word) information. Information is not *represented* in the weights; it's represented in the representations. The weights do not constitute a code.
7. In traditional, pre-connectionist, models of memory in cognitive science, memories are full-fledged representations; they reside in a mental "file cabinet," in the same form as when they become occurrent by being fetched back into the system's central processing unit. But the idea of *stored* (in-the-head, or in-the-soul) memories is not presupposed by common sense psychology (even though if it might seem so to some philosophers educated in classical cognitive science). Common sense is not committed to any particular view about the ontology of memory; hence it is not contrary to common sense to say that beliefs and memories are no where when not

active. Cf. Locke: "Memory, signifies no more but this, that the Mind has a Power, in many cases to revive Perceptions... . And in this Sense it is, that our *Ideas* are said to be in our Memories, when indeed, they are actually no where, but only there is an ability in the Mind, when it will, to revive them again... ." (*Essay*, II.X.ii.)

8. There are many ways in which activated representations might be involved in a process. Some might, for example, be false starts that are overruled by further information or processing. But in such cases it is often possible, by following out paths of spreading activation, to determine which active representations made a positive casual contribution in bringing about the end result, and which active representations got overruled.

9. A particular type of cognitive transition might be traversed in several cognitive steps by one connectionist system but leapt in a single bound by another. Cf. Lloyd 1991.

10. Stich and Warfield (forthcoming) make essentially the same point (without, however, distinguishing between paradigmatic functional discreteness and the other kinds). Needless to say, this is a change of position for Stich.

11. A more familiar source of multiple realizability in connectionist models is that often many different vectors—all vectors meeting some condition—count as realizing the same representation. E.g., the representation is considered activated when all members of a certain set of nodes have activation level > .85.

12. Sometimes when two or more distinct representations are realized by a single point on the activation landscape, each occurrent representation will correspond to a physically discrete sub-pattern of activation within the overall activation state of the network; but sometimes the total complex representation will instead be a physical superposition of physical sub-patterns, with certain nodes participating simultaneously in several sub-patterns. (In Bach's piano music, often a note played on a single key belongs simultaneously to several superimposed, contrapuntal, melodies.)

13. Certain sophisticated learning techniques employ what is called the "moving target" strategy, which in effect brings about a controlled co-evolution of weights and representations; in dynamical systems terms, this amounts to the simultaneous molding of the activation landscape and re-positioning of representational points *on* that landscape. We discuss specific examples in Horgan and Tienson (1992a, 1993).

14. The term 'prejudice' has negative associations. But there are prejudices that incline one to make positive judgments, as well as evaluatively neutral judgments.

15. Forster and Saidel (forthcoming) present a simple network that arguably exhibits some of the kinds of functional discreteness we have been describing (and also illustrates some of the ways that functional discreteness is related to various counterfactual conditionals true of the network's performance).

16. RSG state the alleged connectionism/common sense contrast in another way:

> From the point of view of the connectionist model builder, the class of networks that might model a cognitive agent who believes that dogs have fur is not a genuine kind at all, but simply a chaotically disjunctive set. Common sense psychology treats the class of people who believe that dogs have fur as a psychologically natural kind; connectionism does not. (514-5)

This suggests a rhetorically stronger eliminativist conclusion: if connectionism is correct, then certain *natural kinds* of common sense psychology do not exist (though it seems odd to say that common sense psychology treats the class of people who believe that dogs have fur, as opposed to the belief itself, as a natural kind). We will discuss the argument in terms of projectable predicates, although what we say applies equally to natural kinds.

17. Most any connectionist cognitive model will exhibit certain non-accidental generalizations at the representational level of description. For instance, in Chapter 1 of Rumelhart and McClelland (1986), one finds the following remarks about a model of memory retrieval that embodies information about the members of two gangs, the Sharks and the Jets:

> The model...tends to retrieve what is common to those memories which match a retrieval cue which is too general to capture any one memory... . In this way the model can retrieve the typical values that members of the Jets has on each dimension—even though no one Jet has these typical values. (p. 30)

18. Marr labels the top level 'the theory of the computation'. This refers to *what* is to be computed. How it is computed is to be determined at the middle level.

19. In general, the interconnections between these three levels involve a variable number of intervening levels. Flow charts specify levels of description between the top and the middle—increasingly specific determinations of the algorithm by which the cognitive function is computed. There may be several levels between an AI program in a familiar programming language—Marr's middle level—and the machine language of the computer on which it is running—which is not yet a physical implementation, but rather is the abstract specification of the computational processes that literally get physically implemented. The specification of a network, including weights and activation equations and levels, occupies a similar role in connectionism.

20. *Multiple* realizability is possible between each level and one below it. This point is commonly recognized with respect to the physical realization of computational processes, but it is equally true for the computational realization of intentional state-transitions. For further elaboration of this point, see Horgan (1992, pp.454-6) and Horgan and Tienson (1993, pp. 160). On p. 162 of the latter we quote a passage from Marr (1977) indicating that he himself evidently appreciated the point quite clearly.

21. This generic framework and the possible virtues of its connectionist species are discussed in detail in Horgan and Tienson (1994, forthcoming a).

22. For a discussion of multiple realizability of higher-level states and processes in connectionist models, see Bickle (in preparation).

23. Davies argues (i) that common sense psychology requires a language of thought, in order to accommodate the distinctive causal roles that common sense posits for semantic constituents of propositional attitudes, but (ii) that connectionism with distributed representations is incompatible with a language of thought. We agree with Davies that syntax is necessary to support the kind of causal role of semantic constituents that common sense psychology implies. But we maintain that connectionism does not preclude either syntactic structure in mental representations or structure-sensitive processing; nor does it become mere implementation of classicism by incorporating these features. Cf. Horgan and Tienson (1988, 1989, 1992a, 1992b, forthcoming a, forthcoming b).

References

Berg, G. (1992). "A Connectionist Parser with Recursive Sentence Structure and Lexical Disambiguation," *Proceedings of the American Association for Artificial Intelligence.*

Bickle, J. (in preparation). "Connectionism, Reduction, and Multiple Realizability."

Clark, A. (1990). "Connectionist Minds," *Proceedings of the Aristotelian Society*, 90. Reprinted in C. and G. MacDonald (eds.), *The Philosophy of Psychology* (Blackwell, forthcoming).

Davies, M. (1991). "Concepts, Connectionism, and the Language of Thought," in W. Ramsey, S. Stich, and D. Rumelhart (eds.), *Philosophy and Connectionist Theory*, Earlbaum.

Forster, M. and Saidel, E. (forthcoming). "Connectionism and the Fate of Folk Psychology: A Reply to Ramsey, Stich, and Garon," *Philosophical Psychology.*

Horgan, T. (1992). "From Cognitive Science to Folk Psychology: Computation, Mental Representation, and Belief," *Philosophy and Phenonemological Research*, 52.

Horgan, T. and Tienson, J. (1988), "Settling into a New Paradigm," *Southern Journal of Philosophy*, 24, Supplement. Reprinted in T. Horgan and J. Tienson (eds.), *Connectionism and the Philosophy of Mind* (Earlbaum, 1991).

Horgan, T. and Tienson, J. (1989). "Representations without Rules," *Philosophical Topics*, 17.

Horgan, T. and Tienson, J. (1992a). "Cognitive Systems as Dynamical Systems," *Topoi*, 11.

Horgan, T. and Tienson, J. (1992b) "Structured Representations in Connectionist Systems?" in S. Davis (ed.), *Connectionism: Theory and Practice*, Oxford.

Horgan, T. and Tienson, J. (1993). "Levels of Description in Nonclassical Cognitive Science," in C. Hookway and D. Peterson (eds.), *Philosophy and Cognitive Science*, Cambridge.

Horgan, T. and Tienson, J. (forthcoming a). "A Nonclassical Framework for Cognitive Science," *Synthese*, issue on connectionism and philosophy.

Horgan, T. and Tienson, J. (forthcoming b). *Connectionism and the Philosophy of Psychology: Representational Realism without Rules.* M.I.T.

Lloyd, D. (1991). "Leaping to Conclusions: Connectionism, Consciousness, and the Computational Mind," in T. Horgan and J. Tienson (eds.), *Connectionism and the Philosophy of Mind*, Earlbaum.

Marr, D. (1977). "Artificial Intelligence—A Personal View," *Artificial Intelligence*, 9. Reprinted in J. Haugeland (ed.), *Mind Design*, (M.I.T., 1981).

Marr, D. (1988). *Vision*, Freeman.

O'Brien, G. (1991). "Is Connectionism Commonsense?", *Philosophical Psychology*, 4.

Ramsey, W., Stich, S., and Garon, J. (1990). "Connectionism, Eliminativism and the Future of Folk Psychology," *Philosophical Perspectives, 4, Action Theory and Philosophy of Mind, 1990*, edited by J. E. Tomberlin. Reprinted in W. Greenwood (ed.), *The Future of Folk Psychology* (Cambridge, 1991); in W. Ramsey, S. Stich, and D. Rumelhart (eds.), *Philosophy and Connectionist Theory* (Earlbaum,); in S. Christensen and D. Turner (eds.), *Folk Psychology and the Philosophy of Mind* (Earlbaum, 1993); and in C. and G. MacDonald (eds.), *The Philosophy of Psychology* (Blackwell, forthcoming).

Rumelhart, D. and McClelland, J. (1986). *Parallel Distributed Processing: Explorations in the Microstructure of Cognition. Volume 1: Foundations*, M.I.T.

Stich, S. (1991). "Causal Holism and Commonsense Psychology: A Reply to O'Brien," *Philosophical Psychology*, 4.

Stich, S. and Warfield, T. (forthcoming). "Do Connectionist Minds Have Beliefs?—A Reply to Clark and Smolensky," in C. and G. MacDonald (eds.), *The Philosophy of Psychology*, Blackwell.

Philosophical Perspectives, 9, AI, Connectionism, and
Philosophical Psychology, 1995

TWO NOTIONS OF IMPLICIT RULES

Martin Davies
Corpus Christi College, University of Oxford

In popular accounts of the differences between connectionism and the ('Classical') rules and representations paradigm, it is often said that connectionist networks perform cognitive tasks without knowledge of rules. Thus, for example (Rumelhart and McClelland, 1986, p. 218):

> We would...suggest that parallel distributed processing models may provide a mechanism sufficient to capture lawful behaviour, without requiring the postulation of explicit but inaccessible rules.

Equally, when the stress is upon the way that networks learn, it is said that networks learn to perform cognitive tasks without learning rules (McClelland, Rumelhart and Hinton, 1986, p. 32):

> [W]e do not assume that the goal of learning is the formulation of explicit rules. Rather, we assume it is the acquisition of connection strengths which allow a network of simple units to act *as though* it knew the rules.

Likewise (Norman, 1986, p. 536):

> [A]lthough the system develops neither rules of classification nor generalizations, it *acts* as if it had these rules... . It is a system that exhibits intelligence and logic, yet that nowhere has explicit rules of intelligence or logic.

These three quotations all come from early expositions of the connectionist programme (indeed, from the PDP 'Bible'), but such claims recur frequently enough. We find something similar, for example, in a more recent description of a connectionist model of the cognitive task of reading single words aloud (Seidenberg and McClelland, 1989).

In this case, the connectionist model stands in contrast to a 'dual route' model of reading aloud, a model in which one route—crucial for the pronunciation of irregular words like 'pint' and 'have'—makes use of a lexicon, while the other route is able to achieve the correct pronunciation of regular words ('mint', 'slave') and of non-words ('slint', 'mave') by way of letter-sound, or grapheme-phoneme, or more generally sub-word level orthographic-to-phonological *rules* (Coltheart, 1985). Mark Seidenberg says of the connectionist reading aloud model (1989, p. 40):

> In contrast to the dual-route model, there are no rules specifying the regular spelling-sound correspondences of the language and there is no phonological lexicon in which the pronunciations of all words are listed.

But it also worth noting that Seidenberg says later (1989, pp. 66-7):

> What the model shows is that certain simple, intuitive notions of what is meant by 'rule' fail to capture relevant generalizations about naming [reading aloud] behaviour. ... It is valid to ask whether a particular notion of 'rule' is adequate as a means of capturing generalizations of a particular sort. ... However, it is vacuous to ask whether behavior is rule governed if the notion of 'rule' is unconstrained. Much of the debate over 'rules' to this point...has little force because no explicit notion of rule is at stake.

Seidenberg says 'explicit notion of rule', not 'notion of explicit rule'; and the difference is important. If we restrict attention to the idea of an explicit rule ('certain simple, intuitive notions of what is meant by "rule"') then, although even that idea needs to be made more precise (Section 1.2 below), we can agree already that there are no spelling-sound rules in the Seidenberg and McClelland reading aloud network. But what Seidenberg invites is an attempt to make explicit some other notion, or notions, of rule for which it would at least be sensible to ask whether the network knows or embodies spelling-sound rules.

Scanning the connectionist literature, we may come upon sentences that seem, at first glance, flatly to contradict the 'Biblical' orthodoxy about networks and rules. Consider, for example (Bates and Elman, 1993, p. 634): 'Contrary to rumor, it is not the case that connectionist systems have no rules.' What notion of rules is at stake here? The answer from Bates and Elman is that (ibid.):

> the 'rules' in a connectionist net include the connections that hold among units, i.e. the links or 'weights' that embody all the potential mappings from input to output across the system as a whole. This means that rules (like representations) can exist by degree, and vary in strength.

So, on this account, each weighted connection—from an input unit to a hidden unit, or from a hidden unit to an output unit—embodies a rule; and a network with thirty, or fifty, or a hundred units embodies hundreds or thousands of rules.

The Seidenberg and McClelland network with 400 input, 200 hidden, and 460 output units would, by this reckoning, embody 172,000 rules. Whatever might be the content of these rules, we can be confident that they will not all be sub-word level orthographic-to-phonological conversion rules of the kind envisaged in the dual route model. There are simply too many of them. And, in fact, we can see that none of these rules—embodied in the connection between, say, a single input unit and a single hidden unit—can be a letter-sound rule, or a grapheme-phoneme rule, or any other kind of sub-word level orthographic-to-phonological rule. In the Seidenberg and McClelland model, the system for coding the orthographic input proceeds by, first, converting a word, such as 'cat', into a set of Wickelgraphs (trios of letters and spaces)—in this case, the set {#CA, CAT, AT#}. Then, each of the 200 input units is correlated with 1,000 Wickelgraphs, in such a way that each Wickelgraph activates about 20 input units. So, in short, no input unit corresponds to a letter, or to a grapheme, or to any sub-word unit that might be the subject of a spelling-sound rule.

Bates and Elman go on to say (1993, p. 634-5):

> [I]t is possible for several different networks to reach the same solution to a problem, each with a totally different set of weights. This fact runs directly counter to the tendency in traditional cognitive and linguistic research to seek 'the rule' or 'the grammar' that underlies a set of behavioral regularities.

It is certainly true that the Bates and Elman notion of rule returns only a trivial answer to the question whether two versions of the Seidenberg and McClelland reading aloud network—the results of training runs from different random initial weights, say—embody the same spelling-sound rules. The trivial answer is that neither network embodies any such rules, in the Bates and Elman sense. And if two networks were to embody spelling-sound rules by the Bates and Elman criterion, then they would embody *different* rules, simply in virtue of having different weight matrices. But Bates and Elman speak tantalizingly of the possibility that two networks might reach 'the same solution to a problem', even though the actual weights in the networks are quite different. What is this notion of 'the same solution'?

Now, it may be that all that Bates and Elman have in mind here is that two networks can achieve the same input-output relation on a training set, even though the networks are internally very different. But, what would be more interesting would be the idea that, amongst networks all of which achieve the correct input-output relation to solve a problem, the networks can be classified into groups on the basis of having reached *the same solution*—having adopted the same way of achieving the input-output relation, despite having different weights. This would be an interesting idea because it would suggest a level of classification of networks that would discriminate more finely than mere input-output relations, but more coarsely than weight matrices—a level of classification that might conceivably be inhabited by a new notion of rule.

Let us pause to review the situation thus far. Connectionist networks typically do not contain explicit rules in the way that classical AI systems do. Nevertheless, there is an invitation (Seidenberg, 1989) to develop new notions of rule so that we can raise the question whether a connectionist network embodies spelling-sound rules, for example. We might begin with the idea that rules are embodied in weights on individual connections (Bates and Elman, 1993). But at that fineness of grain, we shall not find spelling-sound rules in the Seidenberg and McClelland network—nor, generally, shall we uncover in typical connectionist networks the kinds of rules that figure in 'traditional cognitive and linguistic research'. What would be interesting would be a notion of rule that allows that a rule might indeed be embodied in a single weighted connection, but which also permits one and the same rule to be embodied in different configurations of weights in different networks.

Gary Hatfield has remarked that (1991, p. 90):

> Connectionist approaches to cognition afford a new opportunity for reflection on the notions of *rule* and *representation* as employed in cognitive science.

In this paper, I shall be taking up that opportunity, so far as rules are concerned. The remainder of the paper is in four main sections. In Section 1, I review two extreme notions of knowledge of rules. In Section 2, I introduce an intermediate notion which makes use of the idea of a causally systematic process. This is my first notion of implicit rule. In Section 3, I distinguish this from a second notion of implicit rule, which imposes fewer requirements upon the causal processes taking place inside a system. Finally, in Section 4, I use the distinction between the two notions of implicit rule to shed light upon a recent dispute about *structure-sensitive processes*, between Jerry Fodor, Zenon Pylyshyn, and Brian McLaughlin on the one hand (Fodor 1987; Fodor and Pylyshyn, 1988; Fodor and McLaughlin, 1990), and Paul Smolensky on the other (Smolensky, 1991a, 1991b).

1. Two extreme notions of knowledge of rules

The two notions of knowledge of rules from which I begin are, at one extreme—the strong end of the spectrum—the idea of a rule that is *explicitly represented* within a system and, at the other extreme—the weak end of the spectrum—the idea of a rule to which the input-output relation of a system *conforms*, whether by design or by happenstance. The orthodoxy about connectionism is that networks achieve conformity to rules without explicit representation of rules. Let us take some time over each of these extreme notions.

1.1 Knowledge in the weak sense: Conformity

The notion of conformity to a rule is simple; but still, there is one possible misunderstanding to be avoided. Someone might say, naturally enough, that a wooden block sliding along a smooth surface conforms to the rule 'F = m.a' ('force equals mass times acceleration'), or equivalently 'a = F/m' ('acceleration equals force divided by mass'). But this is *not* the notion of conformity to a rule that we need to have at the weak end of our spectrum.

We are considering information processing systems, and a system that possesses knowledge of a rule—whatever exactly that turns out to be—is a system that has a resource enabling it to perform inference-like transitions between input and output states that are states of information, that have content or meaning. Knowledge of the rule 'a = F/m' would permit the transition from an input state that means (contains or encodes the information) that the force is n units to an output state that means that the acceleration is n/m units. If we are asking about the presence or absence of that knowledge, then the relevant input-output transitions are not from an input state that *is* a force to an output state that *is* an acceleration, but from an input state that *represents* a force to an output state that *represents* an acceleration.

At the weak end of our spectrum of notions of knowledge of rules, then, we have the idea of a system that performs such input-output transitions, and does so in such a way that the resulting input-output pairs are, in point of their meaning, in conformity with the rule.

In a similar way, we can consider a spelling-sound rule, perhaps that an initial 'c', coming before 'a', 'o', or 'u', is pronounced /K/. A system that is performing the reading aloud task is presented with a token of a written word—a letter string—say 'cat', and produces a pronunciation—a phoneme string—say /KAT/. In some theoretical contexts, we might consider the written word token to be the input and the utterance to be the output. For our purposes, though, we shall take as the input state a state of the system that represents the orthographic item 'cat', and as the output state a state of the system that represents the pronunciation /KAT/. The transitions that interest us are then transitions from such input states to such output states. To the extent that the system yields input-output pairs that conform to the rule in point of their meaning—a representation of the letter string 'cod' gives rise to a representation of the phoneme string /KOD/, and so on—we shall say that the system has knowledge of the rule in the weak sense.

In order to raise the question whether a system possesses knowledge of a rule, even in this weak sense, we already have to presume upon the idea that the input and output states of the system have meaning—that they are representational states. In the Seidenberg and McClelland network, the input state that represents the written word 'cat' is a pattern of activation over about 60 of the input units. Similarly, the output state that represents the pronunciation /KAT/ is a pattern of activation over some of the output units. Hatfield suggests (1991, p. 90) that we need to reflect upon the notion of representation as well as the notion of rule; and that is right. We need some philosophical account of what it is, in virtue of which a pattern of activation counts as having meaning, or representing something. But for the purposes of this paper, and our reflections upon the notion of a rule, I shall take for granted the idea of input and output states that have representational properties.

1.2 Knowledge in the strong sense: Explicit representation

The notion of explicit representation of a rule is not entirely simple, since different theorists have chosen to label rather different ideas with the term 'explicit' (versus 'implicit' or 'tacit').

Michael Dummett says (1991, p. 96):

> Someone has explicit knowledge of something if a statement of it can be elicited from him by suitable enquiry or prompting...

And (1991, p. 97):

> A body of knowledge, however explicit, is obviously not continuously before our consciousness, being a store of items available, save when our memory betrays us, for use when needed. How the storage is effected is of no concern to philosophy: what matters to it is how each item is presented when summoned for use.

So, in Dummett's usage, explicitness is a matter of the subject being able to present information in linguistic form, and is not a matter of how the information is stored in between presentations. Explicit knowledge is *ipso facto* accessible knowledge—'save when our memory betrays us'.

The orthodoxy about connectionism says that networks lack explicit representations of rules, and contrasts the connectionist programme with 'the *explicit inaccessible rule* view' (Rumelhart and McClelland, 1986, p. 217). Since in Dummett's usage, 'explicit' and 'inaccessible' are contradictory, we must look elsewhere for help with the notion of explicit representation that is under discussion here.

In a rather similar way, the distinction in experimental psychology between explicit and implicit memory tests does not help us. In an implicit memory test (Schacter, 1989, p. 695):

> memory for a recent experience is inferred from facilitations of performance, generally known as repetition or direct priming effects, that need not and frequently do not involve any conscious recollection of the prior experience.

In contrast, explicit memory tests (ibid.):

> make explicit reference to and demand conscious recollection of a specific previous experience.

Given that we are considering human information processing much of which is unconscious, and that we also want our notions of knowledge of rules to be applicable to systems—such as small connectionist networks—for which the question of conscious recollection does not even arise, this second usage of 'explicit' is of no help to us either.

The notion of explicit representation of rules that underwrites the connectionist orthodoxy—that networks do not contain explicit representations of rules—has at least two components. One component is the idea of a syntactically structured representation that encodes the rule. The second component is the idea of a state of knowledge whose presence in a system by itself falls very far short of explaining the input-output transitions for which the knowledge is logically adequate.

Thus, imagine that a system contains a representation of the rule 'a = F/m' in a linguistic format: the rule is written down on a sheet of paper, stored in one of many pigeon holes. And suppose that the system goes into an input state that encodes the information that F = 10 units and m = 5 units. The proposition that a = 2 units follows logically from the propositions that a = F/m, that F = 10 units, and that m = 5 units. But, in the system, a great deal needs to happen if an output state encoding the information that a = 2 units is to be produced. The relevant sheet of paper needs to be located in its pigeon hole (search), and it needs to be brought together with the input representations in the workspace (access). There, some inferences need to be carried out, and those inferences require the arithmetical information that $10 \div 5 = 2$. Perhaps that information is somehow 'built into' the mechanism that subserves the inference process; but on the other hand, it might itself be stored on a sheet of paper in a pigeon hole; or it might have to be inferred from some generalization that is stored in that way. However the details may go, it is clear that, in order to make use of the knowledge that is stored in it, the system must go through processes of search and access, as well as logical and arithmetical processes.

Both components of the idea of explicit representation are present in the example that I have described. There is a syntactically structured representation of the rule (it is written down on paper); and there is a considerable gap between having the knowledge (stored in a pigeon hole) and using it (to derive the result that a = 2 units). But the presence of this kind of gap (the second component) does not depend essentially upon what is stored being a representation in a linguistic format (the first component).

To see this, just imagine a variant of the example where what is stored in the pigeon hole is not a sheet of paper with 'a = F/m' written on it, but instead a little machine. If the representations of the force and the mass are plugged into this machine, it produces a representation of the acceleration. But merely having representations of the force and the mass as input states of the overall system is not, by itself, enough to engage the little machine; first, it has to be located and moved into position. If there were a problem in finding the little machine in its pigeon hole, then the overall system would not produce an output state representing the acceleration. So, in this variant example, there is still a gap between having the knowledge (embodied in the stored machine) and using it to mediate input-output transitions.

In describing the variant example, I have helped myself to the notion of the stored machine embodying knowledge of the rule 'a = F/m'. That notion cries out for explanation, of course. But the point of highlighting the gap between having knowledge and using it is that it leads us to a contrasting feature of connectionist networks. For in networks there is no such gap (McClelland, Rumelhart and Hinton, 1986, p. 32; italics added):

> The representation of the knowledge is set up in such a way that the knowledge *necessarily* influences the course of processing. Using knowledge in processing is no longer a matter of finding the relevant information in memory and bringing it to bear; it is *part and parcel of the processing itself.*

So, the connectionist orthodoxy that networks do not contain explicit representations of rules itself has two elements. First, networks do not contain stored representations of rules in a linguistic format. Second, and more generally, networks store their knowledge in a way that does not present any problem of search and access; rather, it is 'part and parcel of the processing'.

The strong notion of knowledge of rules as explicit representation enables us to draw a distinction within the class of systems whose input-output transitions are in conformity with a rule (that is, which have knowledge of a rule in the weak sense). On one side of this distinction, we can place symbol manipulation devices which make use of a stored syntactically structured representation of the rule in question—*rule-explicit* symbol manipulation devices. On the other side of the distinction we find a heterogeneous collection of systems. There are symbol manipulation devices that do not make use of a syntactically structured representation of the rule. There are connectionist networks. And there are look-up tables that simply store all the input-output pairings independently.

In the case of models of the reading aloud task, we would have on one side of the distinction those models that make use of syntactically structured representations of spelling-sound rules. Within such a model, there would need to be additional machinery to locate the correct rules to apply given a particular input, and then to draw out the logical consequences of those rules for that input. The implementation of the non-lexical part of the dual route model by Coltheart, Curtis, Atkins and Haller (1993) is essentially of this type.

On the other side of the distinction, we would have models containing a host of little processing mechanisms corresponding to grapheme-phoneme conversion rules. (Once again, there would need to be extra machinery to bring the correct mechanisms into operation upon any given input.) We would have interactive activation models (McClelland and Rumelhart, 1981; Taft, 1991; also the implementation of the lexical route of the model envisaged by Coltheart et al., 1993), and also connectionist models, such as the Seidenberg and McClelland network and the earlier NETtalk of Sejnowski and Rosenberg (1987). And finally, we would have systems that operate by table look-up.

1.3 The next step

Many different information processing systems might achieve conformity to a rule, or to a set of rules, over some domain of examples. That is, many systems might have knowledge of the rule or rules in the weak sense. Within that class of systems, some might operate by having knowledge of the rule or rules in the strong sense: they might be rule explicit. What we are seeking is a new notion of knowledge of rules which would allow us sensibly to ask whether a connectionist network has knowledge of spelling-sound rules, for example. We are looking to make a distinction within the class of connectionist networks, and more generally within the class of systems that achieve conformity to the rules without being rule explicit.

Fodor and Pylyshyn remark (1988, p. 60):

> [O]ne should not confuse the rule-implicit/rule-explicit distinction with the distinction between Classical and Connectionist architecture. ...
>
> The one thing that Classical theorists do agree about is that it *can't* be that *all* behavioral regularities are determined by explicit rules; at least some of the causal determinants of compliant behavior *must* be *im*plicit...
>
> Classical machines can be *rule implicit* with respect to their programs,...

Unfortunately, Fodor and Pylyshyn are not absolutely explicit about what 'rule implicit' means, but they do talk about some of the functions of a computer being 'wired in'—we might say, being 'part and parcel of the processing'. So there is at least the suggestion here of a notion of rule implicit system that might include some classical symbol manipulation devices and also some connectionist networks.

Perhaps all that Fodor and Pylyshyn intend by 'rule implicit' is a machine that achieves input-output transitions in conformity with certain rules without explicitly representing those rules. But, however that may be, my plan is to introduce two notions of implicit rules that are intermediate between the strong and weak notions of knowledge of rules. They are intermediate in the sense that to say that a rule is implicit in a system will require more than mere conformity to the rule but less than explicit representation of the rule.

2. The first notion of implicit rules

The notion of implicit rules to be introduced in this section makes use of the idea of a *causally systematic process*. Although many refinements would be needed in a full treatment, the core of this idea is very simple. (For some of the complications, see Davies, 1987. For applications of the idea to connectionist networks, see Davies, 1989, 1990a, 1990b, 1991.)

2.1 Causally systematic processes

To begin with, we note that the weak notion of knowledge of rules—the notion of conformity—can be formulated in terms of a rule's describing a pattern in a system's input-output relation. In our earlier example, an information processing system performs transitions from input states that represent a force and a mass to output states that represent an acceleration. Where the input-output transitions are in conformity with the rule 'a = F/m', that rule describes a pattern in the input-output relation. To say that there is this pattern in the input-output relation is to say nothing, yet, about the way in which the input-output transitions that instantiate the pattern are performed—nothing about the structure of the processing that takes place inside the system.

The crucial diagnostic question for the first notion of implicit rules concerns the causal explanation of these input-output transitions. Do the transitions that instantiate the pattern have a *common causal explanation*? A roughly equivalent way of asking the same question is this. Is there, within the system, a component mechanism, or processor, or module that operates as a *causal common factor* to mediate all the input-output transitions that instantiate the pattern described by the rule? If so, then the rule is said to be implicit in the system (or the system is said to have implicit or tacit knowledge of the rule).

We can add two small points of clarification here. First, it might be better to say that, if the answer to our question is 'Yes', then the rule is *at least* implicit in the system, for the case where the rule 'a = F/m' is explicitly represented is intended to be one case in which the question is answered affirmatively. Second, it is important that the causal common factor really does mediate the transitions from input state through to output state. It is certainly not sufficient for implicit knowledge of a rule that there should merely be some tiny component that figures somewhere in all the transitions.

Consider, then, the system that we described earlier, in which the rule 'a = F/m' is written down on a sheet of paper and stored in a pigeon hole. When the system goes into the input state that encodes the information that F = 10 units and m = 5 units, the resulting output state encodes the information that a = 2 units. When the input state means that F = 12 units and m = 4 units, the resulting output state says that a = 3 units. These two input-output pairs instantiate the pattern described by the rule. Do the two transitions have a common causal explanation? The answer is 'Yes' because the core of the explanation of both transitions is afforded by the presence of the stored representation of the rule. In each case, the representation of the rule is located, brought together with the input state, and subjected to inferential procedures. In fact, all the input-output transitions that are in conformity with the rule have the same causal explanation.

The answer would be 'No' in the case of a system that operated by table look-up. In such a case, the explanations of the two input-output transitions would be utterly different. Given the first input state, a search procedure would operate to locate a sheet of paper with 'F = 10, m = 5 ∴ ___ ' written on it, and what follows the ' ∴ '—namely, 'a = 2'—would be used to generate the output state. The presence of that sheet of paper in its pigeon hole would be fundamental in the causal explanation of the first input-output transition, but would be explanatorily irrelevant to the performance of the second transition.

Thus, we have three notions of knowledge of rules: the strong notion, the weak notion, and the intermediate notion—our first notion of implicit rules. But the two examples that we have just described are not enough to show that the first notion of implicit rules is genuinely intermediate between the two extreme notions. For, on those two examples, the answer to our diagnostic question goes in step with the presence or absence of an explicit representation of the rule. What we need is an example where the answer to our diagnostic question is 'Yes' even though the rule is not explicitly represented.

2.2 Three configurations

In effect, we have already indicated an example of the type that we need, in our discussion of models of reading single words aloud. Along with a model that contains explicit representations of spelling-sound rules, and a model that operates by table look-up, we mentioned the possibility of a model containing processing mechanisms corresponding to the various grapheme-phoneme conversion rules. However, in order to be more explicit about an example, and also to indicate how the first notion of implicit rules allows us to make a distinction within the class of connectionist networks, let us consider a very simplified version of the reading aloud task.

The task domain consists of just twenty five items, each of which is a two-letter string. In each string, the first letter is one of the consonants, 'b', 'd', 'f', 'h', 'k', and the second letter is one of the vowels 'a', 'e', 'i', 'o', 'u'. The pronunciation of these twenty five items is completely regular, and we indicate the phonemes corresponding to the ten letters by using capital letters. There are ten letter-sound rules that characterize this reading aloud task, and we shall consider three models that achieve conformity with those ten rules. One model, which we shall not describe in any more detail, is a rule-explicit system—as it might be, a much simplified version of the Coltheart et al., (1993) model.

The rule-explicit system, we may suppose, performs in conformity with the ten letter-sound rules, so it has knowledge of those rules in the weak sense. Since it is a rule-explicit system, it also has knowledge of the rules in the strong sense. And since the presence of an explicit representation is sufficient for an affirmative answer to our diagnostic question, the rules are implicit (or at least implicit) in the system according to our first notion of implicit rules. The other two models are both very simple connectionist networks.

The first network has ten input units, in two pools of five, and likewise ten output units. A two-letter string is represented by a pattern of activation involving two of the ten input units, one from each pool. The string 'ba' is represented by the vector of activations <1, 0, 0, 0, 0, 1, 0, 0, 0, 0> across the ten input units. Similarly, a two-phoneme string is represented by activation at two of the output units. There are no hidden units, and each input unit is connected (with a weight of 1) to exactly one output unit. Figure 1 shows the input state that represents the letter string 'ba' and the output state that represents the phoneme string /BA/ in this network—which we call the *modestly modular* configuration.

The second network has twenty five input units, corresponding to the items in the task domain, and likewise twenty five output units. Each two-letter string is thus represented by activation at just one input unit. Each input unit is connected to just one output unit, activation at which represents the corresponding phoneme string. Figure 2 shows the input state that represents the letter string 'ba', and the output state that represents the phoneme string /BA/ in this network—which we call the *madly modular* configuration.

Each network performs an input-output transition for each of the twenty five items in the task domain, and the twenty five input-output pairs conform to the ten letter-sound rules. So, although neither network has knowledge of those ten rules in the strong sense, each has knowledge of the rules in the weak sense. Each of those ten rules describes a pattern that is instantiated five times amongst the twenty five input-output pairs. Thus, for example, the letter-sound rule that says that any two-letter string 'b_' is pronounced /B_/ describes a pattern instantiated by the five pairs: <'ba', /BA/>, <'be', /BE/>,..., <'bu', /BU/>. So, we can ask our diagnostic question about those five input-output transitions. Do they, in the respect in which they conform to the letter-sound rule for 'b', have a common causal explanation?

In the case of the modestly modular configuration, the answer is 'Yes'. The connection between the input unit for 'b' and the output unit for /B/ figures as a causal common factor in the five transitions. In the madly modular configuration, the answer is 'No'. The connection that is causally responsible for the input-output transition for 'ba' is explanatorily quite irrelevant to the other four transitions.

The madly modular configuration is essentially a connectionist version of table look-up, and we already had an example to illustrate that where there is table look-up there are no implicit rules (except the trivial rules that have only one instance each). But it is the modestly modular configuration that provides the example that we needed: the answer to our diagnostic question is 'Yes' for each of the ten letter-sound rules, although none of those rules is explicitly represented in the network. That is enough to show that the first notion of implicit rules is genuinely intermediate between the two extreme notions of knowledge of rules. And, despite the fact that the two networks are exceedingly simple—particularly in that they lack hidden units—they do illustrate that the first notion of implicit rules can, in principle, make distinctions within the class of connectionist networks.

Configuration	Strong	Intermediate	Weak
Rule explicit	Yes	Yes	Yes
Modestly modular	No	Yes	Yes
Madly modular	No	No	Yes

Table 1: Knowledge of rules in the three configurations

2.3 Adding hidden units

We can, in fact, move quite simply from the modestly modular network to a network with hidden units which has the same spelling-sound rules implicit in it. Figure 3 shows a network that uses the same input and output coding schemes as the modestly modular network, but also includes ten hidden units. The input activation pattern that represents the letter string 'ba', results in activation at just two hidden units, and then at the corresponding output units, yielding the output pattern that represents /BA/. There are various different ways in which this pattern of hidden unit activation might be achieved. In one variation, each of the hidden units has a level of activation that is simply equal to the total activation coming into it (a linear activation function). The connection strengths from each input unit to just one hidden unit, and from that hidden unit to the corresponding output unit are one, and all other connection strengths are zero. An alternative would be for the hidden units to be simple threshold units, turned on by net incoming activation of more than 0.5, say. In that case, the connection strengths that were zero in the first variation could be non-zero, so long as they remained small. And the connection strengths that were one could now be less than one, so long as they remained large enough.

Whatever the details, the two input-hidden connections and two hidden-output connections that are shown in bold explain the input-output transition for 'ba'. And it is clear that the connections with large weights from the input unit for 'b' to one hidden unit, and from that hidden unit to the output unit for /B/ make up a component mechanism that is a causal common factor in the five 'b_'-to-/B_/ transitions.

We can also give a simple example of a network that uses the same input and output coding schemes but does not have implicit letter-sound rules. Figure 4 shows a network in which one hidden unit is dedicated to each of the twenty five letter strings in the task domain. The input unit for 'b' has connections of strength 0.5 leading to five hidden units (for 'ba', 'be', ...,'bu'), and the input unit for 'a' likewise has connections of strength 0.5 to five hidden units, including the unit for 'ba'. The hidden units themselves are simple threshold units (and this non-linearity is an important aspect of the example). The threshold is set to 0.75, so that a hidden unit is switched on if and only if both the corresponding input units are active. Each hidden unit passes activation to the two corresponding output units. The two input-hidden connections and two hidden-output connections that are shown in bold explain the input-output transition for 'ba'. But now, there is nothing in common between these connections and the four connections that are involved in the transition for 'be'.

The first notion of implicit rules thus permits us to ask whether a network (with or without hidden units) embodies spelling-sound rules; to that extent it is just the kind of notion that Seidenberg (1989) invited us to develop. Much more work would need to be done, of course, before we could sensibly pose the question in cases where the hidden units are neither linear units nor threshold units but use the standard sigmoid activation function, or cases where complicated schemes of distributed input or output representations are employed.

The first notion of implicit rules also allows that a rule can be embodied in the weight on an individual connection, just as Bates and Elman (1993) said. What we were aiming at, though, was a notion that would also permit one and the same rule to be embodied in different configurations of weights in different networks. It should now be clear that the first notion of implicit rules does meet this requirement. The diagnostic question concerns the structure of causal explanations of input-output transitions rather than the fine-grained detail of how each transition is achieved. Thus, a connectionist network with hidden units, a network without hidden units, and a classical symbol manipulation device can have the same rules implicit in them.

2.4 Two consequences

In the next section, I shall introduce a second notion of implicit rules. But to conclude this present section, I shall note two consequences of the first notion of implicit rules.

2.4.1 Systematicity and syntax

One consequence follows from the fact that causal systematicity of process imposes requirements upon the causal properties of input states. Suppose that we define a syntactic (or formal) property of a representational state to be (i) a physical property of the state that is both (ii) systematically related to the state's semantic properties and (iii) a determinant of the state's causal consequences (Fodor, 1987, pp. 16-21). Then it is possible to show that implicit rules in a system require a measure of syntactic articulation in the system's input states (Davies, 1989, 1991). In particular, the presence of implicit rules about the pronunciation of individual letters requires that the input states that represent letter strings should have internal syntactic structure corresponding to the individual letters in the represented string. This requirement is met in the modestly modular network (Figure 1) by the articulation within the patterns of activation that represent the letter strings. All the input states that represent strings 'b_', for example, have the property of involving activation of the first unit in the first pool. This is surely a physical property of those input states—(i). It is a property that is correlated with a semantic property, namely that the state represents a string beginning with 'b'—(ii). And it is a property which, in the presence of the connections between input and output units in the network, is a determinant of the input state's causal consequences—(iii). There is, of course, no such syntactic articulation in the input states that represent letter strings in the madly modular network (Figure 2). The input states of the network in Figure 4 are no less articulated than those in the modestly modular network, but still the spelling-sound rules are not implicit there. In essence, the structure that is present in the input states is thrown away at the hidden unit layer. Syntactic articulation in input states is a necessary, but not a sufficient, condition for causal systematicity of process in input-output transitions.

2.4.2 Formal theories and causal processes

The other consequence of the first notion of implicit rules concerns formal theories of a cognitive task. The rules that characterize a task, such as the reading aloud task, can be stated by the axioms of a formal theory. The particular consequences of those rules, such as statements of the pronunciations of particular letter strings, can be derived from those axioms as theorems of the theory. Furthermore, it is possible to specify a canonical proof procedure that is to be followed in deriving those theorems from the axioms. An individual axiom can then figure as a derivational common factor in the (canonical) proofs of several theorems. For example, the axiom stating the letter-sound rule for 'b' would figure as a derivational common factor in the proofs of the five theorems that state the pronunciations of the strings 'ba', 'be',...,'bu'.

There is then a very evident parallel between formal theories and causal processes. If the rules stated by the axioms of a formal theory of a task are implicit in a processing system, then the causal structure of the processing in the system mirrors, or follows the contours of, the derivational structure of the (canonical) proofs in the formal theory. Where an axiom functions as a derivational common factor in the proofs in the theory that concern certain items in the task domain, a component processor functions as a causal common factor in the processing in the system that begins from input states representing those items.

3. The second notion of implicit rules

The notion of implicit rules to be introduced in this section imposes fewer requirements upon the causal processes taking place inside a system. The core of this second notion is the idea of a rule that could be extracted or derived from information that is present in the system.

3.1 *What is present and what can be derived*

In a discussion of explicit, implicit, and tacit representation, Daniel Dennett suggests (1983, p. 216):

> [L]et us have it that for information to be represented *implicitly*, we shall mean that it is *implied* logically by something that is stored explicitly.

Applied to the case of a rule, Dennett's account would have the result that an implicit rule is one that is logically implied by information that is explicitly represented in the system. The second notion of implicit rule that I am introducing is a generalization or relativisation of that idea. Relative to any given notion of information being present in a system—of which, information being explicitly represented is one—a rule is implicit in the system if it can be derived from information that is already present in the system. This is not to say that the system itself contains mechanisms for performing these logical derivations.

There is scope for a second relativisation in this notion of an implicit rule. For we might consider the use of different resources for deriving rules from a body of information. Dennett speaks of what is 'logically implied', but we might also permit broadly inductive methods of rule derivation (extraction), for example. However, this second relativisation will not concern us here.

Suppose now that, instead of taking the notion of information that is explicitly represented as our baseline, we make use of the intuitive idea that the information that 'ba' is pronounced /BA/, and the information that 'be' is pronounced /BE/, and so on, is present in all three of the systems that we considered in Section 2.2—the rule-explicit system, the modestly modular network, and the madly modular network. As well as being an intuitive idea, this is an idea that is underwritten by the first notion of implicit rules. The twenty five trivial (one-case) rules are implicit in all three systems according to that first notion. Then, relative to that starting point, the ten letter-sound rules may be implicit (according to the second notion of implicit rules) even in a madly modular network.

To see this, consider two formal theories of some cognitive task. Our simplified reading aloud task can serve as an example. The first formal theory, T_1, is a structured theory with axioms stating the ten letter-sound rules. The second formal theory, T_2, is a 'listiform' theory. Its axioms simply state the twenty five one-case rules for pronouncing the twenty five items in the task domain. According to the first notion of implicit rules, the rules of the structured theory, T_1, are implicit in the modestly modular system (Figure 1) but not in the madly modular system (Figure 2). But, as we have just noted, the one-case rules of the listiform theory, T_2, are implicit in both the modestly and the madly modular systems.

In certain cases, two theories related as T_1 and T_2 are logically equivalent. The axioms of T_2 are theorems of T_1 in any case. But, where the two theories are logically equivalent, the structured rules can actually be derived from the one-case rules of the listiform theory. This is the case with the two theories of the reading aloud task. Or rather—to be properly delicate—this is the case provided that T_2 is augmented by a theory of the task *domain* that says that there are just the five consonants that can occur in the first position in a string and just the five vowels that can occur in the second position. So—with that proviso—the ten letter-sound rules of T_1 appear to be implicit (according to the second notion) even in the madly modular system. Since the one-case rules that we are taking to be present in the system are themselves implicit (according to the first notion) rather than explicitly represented, we might say that the ten letter-sound rules are doubly implicit in the madly modular network.

3.2 Articulation in the input representations

The conclusion that the letter-sound rules are doubly implicit in the madly modular network (Figure 2) is almost correct, but we have to face up to a complication that will be important in Section 4.

I said that the letter-sound rules can be derived from statements about the pronunciations of individual letter strings. Thus, for example, the rule for the letter 'b', which we can state as:

> any two-letter string 'b_' (that is, any string that begins with the letter 'b') is pronounced /B_/ (that is, has a pronunciation that begins with the sound /B/)

is to be derived from five of the axioms of the listiform theory:

> 'ba' is pronounced /BA/
> 'be' is pronounced /BE/
> 'bi' is pronounced /BI/
> 'bo' is pronounced /BO/
> 'bu' is pronounced /BU/

along with the background assumption that there are just the five vowels 'a', 'e', 'i', 'o', 'u' that can go together with 'b' to make up a two-letter string. But now we should consider carefully the nature of the terms that are used in the theory to designate the two-letter strings in the task domain—the term "'ba'" for example. It is crucial that these terms should be structural descriptions of letter strings and not just unstructured names of those strings.

If the term "'ba'" is just a label for the two letter string made up of 'b' followed by 'a', then the axioms of the listiform theory are tantamount to:

> #1 is pronounced /BA/
> #2 is pronounced /BE/

and so on. And from these axioms, absolutely nothing about letter strings beginning with the letter 'b' follows logically, since these axioms do not tell us, for example, that string #1 begins with 'b'. What is needed is that the axioms of the listiform theory should state that;

> the two-letter string made up of 'b' followed by 'a' is pronounced /BA/
> the two-letter string made up of 'b' followed by 'e' is pronounced /BE/

and so on. From such axioms we certainly can derive conclusions about letter strings beginning with 'b'.

We said that what is stated by the axioms of the listiform theory is information that is present even in the madly modular network. But now we see that more care is required. Are the rules stated by the axioms of the structured theory implicit in that network (according to the second notion of implicit rules)? The answer is highly sensitive to whether the information present in the madly modular network is the information that the two-letter string made up of 'b' followed by 'a' is pronounced /BA/ or merely the information that string #1 is pronounced /BA/. Does the madly modular network contain any information about the internal structure of the twenty five twp-letter strings in the task domain?

To this question it is only possible to give an intuitive answer, since we are making use of an intuitive notion of information being present in a system—a notion only partially underpinned by the first notion of implicit rules. But the intuitive answer is surely that the madly modular network as it stands does *not* contain information about the structure of the objects in its task domain. It is difficult to see how a system can contain the information that string #1 has 'b' as its first letter, if the system has no way of representing the letter 'b'.

One way—arguably the most natural way, though certainly not the only conceivable way—of making it more plausible that the madly modular network contains the information from which the ten letter-sound rules can be derived is to incorporate some structure or articulation into the input representations that it uses. We can add extra input units to represent the constituent letters of the strings, make appropriate connections between those letter units and the input units that represent the letter strings themselves, and set appropriate activation thresholds for the letter string units. Then, even if the network's way of representing the string 'ba' (activation at the letter string input unit) is just an unstructured label, still we can plausibly credit the network with the information that the string thus labelled contains 'b' and 'a'. Consequently, we really can say that the letter-sound rules are implicit in this network (according to the second notion of implicit rules). Figure 5 depicts the madly modular network augmented in this way. (Similar augmentation is provided at the output end of the network.)

It should be clear that, despite our tinkering with the input and output representations, this network still does not license an affirmative answer to the diagnostic question for the first notion of implicit rules. The articulation in the input representations is not utilized in the transition from the letter string input unit to the phoneme string output unit. The connection whose presence is crucial to the explanation of the 'ba'-to-/BA/ transition is still explanatorily irrelevant to the 'be'-to-/BE/ transition, for example.

In preparation for the next section, there are two points to notice about the network in Figure 5. The first point is that the scheme of input representation is a simple case of *tensor product coding*. The units for the letter strings are *binding* units, while the separate units for the consonants and vowels in first and second position in the strings are *filler* and *role* units (see e.g. Smolensky 1987; 1990, pp. 147-53).

The second point is that once a binding unit—say, the unit for the string 'ba'—is activated, the presence of the filler and role units—the units for 'b' and 'a'—is causally irrelevant to the subsequent feed-forward processing. The causal consequences of activation at the 'ba' unit are exactly the same whether that unit is switched on by activation passed from the 'b' and 'a' units or is clamped on by external intervention.

3.3 Summary: The two notions

In this section and the previous one, I have introduced two notions of implicit rules. The first notion is defined in terms of causally systematic processes (or causal common factors in processing), and is genuinely intermediate between the strong and weak notions of knowledge of rules discussed in Section 1. Implicit rules do not need to be encoded in syntactically structured representations, but there is a connection with syntactic structure nevertheless: implicit rules require syntactic articulation in the system's input states. The second notion is defined in terms of the derivation of a rule from information that is present in the system. This notion imposes fewer requirements on the causal processes that take place within the system, as witness the fact that implicit rules may be present according to this second notion where they are absent according to the first notion. But the second notion of implicit rules arguably requires some articulation in the system's input representations, such as the structure provided by tensor product coding. In the final section, I shall use these two notions to shed some light upon a dispute about structure-sensitive processes.

4. Structure-sensitive processes

There are many things at issue between the advocates and opponents of connectionism. In the debate between Fodor (and Pylyshyn and McLaughlin) and Smolensky, a great deal seems to rest upon the question whether the processing in connectionist networks is structure-sensitive. Fodor claims that mental (generally, psychological) processes are structure-sensitive, and that connectionist networks are not good models of mental processes since processing in networks is not structure-sensitive. Clearly, there are two ways for an advocate of connectionism to respond to this challenge. He can deny that mental processes are structure-sensitive, or he can insist that processing in connectionist networks can be structure-sensitive. On the face of it, Smolensky takes the second course, but his claim to have delivered connectionist structure-sensitivity by way of tensor product coding has been greeted with incredulity by Fodor (1991, p. 279):

> As for Smolensky's 'tensor product' defense of connectionism... . As far as I can tell, the argument has gone like this: Fodor and Pylyshyn claimed that you can't produce a connectionist theory of systematicity. Smolensky then replied by not producing a connectionist theory of systematicity. Who could have foreseen so cunning a rejoinder?

My suggestion in this final section is that the parties to this debate are talking past each other to some extent, since they are using different notions of structure-sensitivity. What Smolensky is offering is significant in its own right; but it is not what Fodor was asking for.

4.1 Fodor's notion of structure-sensitive processes

What is the notion of structure-sensitive processes that Fodor is working with? To begin with, a psychological process involves operations over representations. An information processing system can, obviously enough, be described in terms of the information that is being processed. A system progresses from having the information that a certain presented item is (a token of) the letter string 'ba' to having the information that the presented item is to be pronounced /BA/. The basic idea of information processing psychology is that this progression occurs because of two things. There is some state of the system—whether an occurrence of a formula in some linguistic format, or a pattern of activation over units—that represents the letter string 'ba'. And there is some operation—whether symbol manipulation or passing activation forward along weighted connections—that gives rise to a second representational state, this time representing the pronunciation /BA/. Thus Fodor says (1987, p. 145):

> If you think of a mental process—extensionally, as it were—as a sequence of mental states each specified with reference to its intentional content, then mental representations provide a mechanism for the construction of these sequences; they allow you to get, in a mechanical way, from one such state to the next *by performing operations on the representations*.

This idea of psychological processes as achieved by operations performed upon representations applies to all the models that we have considered, whether rule-explicit or rule-implicit, modestly or madly modular, with or without hidden units. Structure-sensitive psychological processes require something more (Fodor and Pylyshyn, 1988, p. 13):

> Because Classical mental *representations* have combinatorial structure, it is

possible for Classical mental *operations* to apply to them by reference to their form. The result is that a paradigmatic Classical mental process operates upon any mental representation that satisfies a given structural description, and transforms it into a mental representation that satisfies another structural description.

In a structure-sensitive process, the representations over which the operations are performed have syntactic structure, and the operations make use of that syntactic structure.

Suppose that the system's representations of the strings 'ba', 'be',...,'bu' have syntactic structure. In the case of the representation of 'ba', this means that there are two physical properties—(i), that are correlated with the semantic properties of designating a string containing 'b' and designating a string containing 'a'—(ii), and that are determinants of the causal consequences of the occurrence of that representational state within the system—(iii). Considering the five representations of the 'b_' strings, we can see that they have a physical and causal property in common; namely, the physical property corresponding to the semantic property that they share (they all designate strings containing 'b'). This common causal property of the five input representations certainly invites the application of a single operation in order to make a systematic contribution to the production of output representations of the pronunciations of the five strings. Syntactically structured input representations lend themselves perfectly to causally systematic input-output transition processes, although (Figure 4) structure in the input representations does not guarantee causally systematic processing thereafter.

I have already said—though I did not give the argument in this paper (see Davies 1989, 1991)—that causally systematic processes require syntactic structure in a system's input representations. And we have just seen that the syntactic properties of representations are made for—they go hand in glove with—causally systematic processes. In short, Fodor's notion of a structure-sensitive process is essentially the same as the idea of a process in which a rule is implicit according to the first notion of implicit rules.

4.2 Smolensky's notion of structure-sensitive processes

One of the examples that Fodor and Pylyshyn (1988) give of a process that would certainly be treated as structure-sensitive within a Classical framework is the process of logical inference, such as the inference from P&Q to P. Smolensky addresses this case in terms of tensor product coding (1991a, p. 216):

> I have talked so far mostly about representations and little about processing. If we are interested, as [Fodor and Pylyshyn] are, in inferences such as that from *P&Q* to *P*, it turns out that with tensor product representations, this operation can be achieved by a simple linear transformation upon these representational vectors,... . Not only can this structure-sensitive process be achieved by

> connectionist mechanisms on connectionist representations, but it can be
> achieved through the simplest of all connectionist operations... .

In tensor product coding, patterns of activation over the role units and the filler units produce a pattern of activation over the binding units. It is a general feature of this technique that—subject to certain conditions—given a pattern of activation over the binding units and the original pattern of activation over the role units it is possible to recover the original pattern of activation over the filler units. This is called unbinding (the filler from the role), and it could be used as Smolensky says to recover a representation of the left conjunct from a tensor product representation of a conjunction.

Smolensky goes on to say (1991a, p. 217):

> [T]he agenda for connectionism should [be]...to develop formal analysis of
> vectorial representations of complex structures and operations on those
> structures that are sufficiently structure-sensitive to do the required work. This
> is exactly the kind of research that, for example, tensor product representations
> are being used to support.

But Fodor can reply that, however things may be with tasks that can be treated as cases of unbinding, tensor product coding does not, in general, address the issue of structure-sensitivity as he conceives it.

The reason is that, for Fodor, structure-sensitivity is a causal matter—an operation engages causally with the syntactic or formal properties of the representations upon which it is performed. But, if tensor product coding is used for the input representations in some system, and if the forward connections run from the binding units, then the backward connections from the binding units to the filler and role units are not causally relevant to the operations that produce the system's outputs.

Consider once again the input representation of the string 'ba' in the network in Figure 5. Activation at the 'ba' letter string input unit has the properties of being partly caused by activation at the 'b' unit and being partly caused by activation at the 'a' unit. These physical properties of the input representation are correlated with its semantics: it designates a string containing 'b' and 'a'. But, as we noted towards the end of Section 3, these backward-looking causal properties are not themselves determinants of the causal consequences of the activation of the 'ba' unit. In fact, the causal irrelevance for feed-forward processing of the activation at the filler and role units can be dramatized by noting that in some examples of tensor product coding it is only the binding units that are really present in the network; the filler and role units are merely virtual. All this is in sharp contrast to the input representation of the string 'ba' in the modestly modular network in Figure 1. In that case, the pattern of activation that represents the string 'ba' has the properties of being partly constituted by activation at the 'b' unit and being partly constituted by activation at the 'a' unit.

These properties are correlated with the semantics of the input representation, but they are also clearly determinants of the causal consequences of the overall pattern of activation which they jointly constitute. Thus Fodor and McLaughlin (1990, p. 200):

> The relevant question is whether tensor product representations...have the kind of constituent structure to which an explanation of systematicity might appeal. But we have already seen the answer to *this* question: the constituents of complex activity vectors typically aren't 'there', so if the causal consequences of tokening a complex vector are sensitive to its constituent structure, that's a miracle.

4.3 Complications and confounds

There are similarities between the network in Figure 5 and the one in Figure 4. We could turn the network in Figure 5 into the network in Figure 4 by just collapsing the phoneme string output units with the letter string input units. In neither network are the letter-sound rules implicit. But we are using the two networks to make different points.

The network in Figure 4 shows that syntactic structure in input representations (patterns of activation over letter units) might not be utilized for causally systematic processing. The network in Figure 5 shows that input representations (activation of letter string units) may have physical properties that correlate with semantics, without those physical properties being determinants of the causal consequences of those input states. This is generally illustrated by the backward-looking causal relational properties of the activation of binding units.

There are points at which Smolensky seems to embrace the thought that he is not offering the kind of structure-sensitivity that Fodor is asking for. For example (Smolensky, 1991a, p. 222): 'Are the vector constituents in physical and connectionist systems causally efficacious? It would appear not...' However, there are two confounds that make it difficult to assess the import of this apparent concession.

The first confound is that, in this brief remark, Smolensky is not, in fact, talking about the 'constituents' in tensor product representations. That is, he is not talking about the patterns of activation over filler and role units that give rise to a pattern of activation over binding units. Instead, he is talking about components in a vector sum. It is a familiar point that, in connectionist theory, activation over a pool of n units is often represented as an n-place vector. So, suppose that we have a pattern of activation, represented in that way. Then, since there is no unique way to decompose a vector into components, there will be many different ways to see the pattern of activation as a sum of sub-patterns. Smolensky's point is then that the component sub-patterns are not causally efficacious, even though decomposing activation vectors in certain ways may be crucial 'in order to understand and explain the regularities in the network's behavior' (1991a, p. 221). Whether or not this claim about causal efficacy is correct (in fact, it arguably is not), it is clear that Smolensky's remark does not straightforwardly address Fodor and McLaughlin's concerns.

The second confound concerns a claim that Smolensky appears to make (p. 222), namely that it is safe to make his concession about the lack of causal efficacy in the case of connectionist constituent structure, since there is arguably no more efficacy of constituent structure in the Classical case. The problem is that the argument for this claim depends upon an analogy with software (ibid.):

> When we write a Lisp program, are the symbolic structures we think in terms of causally efficacious in the operation of the computer that runs the program?

The answer to this question (which we may suppose to be negative) is not strictly relevant, since Fodor and McLaughlin are concerned with the syntactic properties of the representations that are actually implicated in the operation of an information processing system, not the syntactic properties of a programme that may be removed from that operation by many steps of compiling.

Smolensky's explicit mention of the question of causal efficacy seems only to muddy the waters. It really is not quite clear what he takes the requirement of structure-sensitivity to amount to. But we can make a sympathetic proposal for reducing the mutual incomprehension that characterizes this debate.

4.4 Implicit rules and structure-sensitive processes

Having introduced two notions of implicit rules, we have already observed that Fodor's notion of structure-sensitive processes corresponds to the first notion of implicit rule. ('F' for 'Fodor', and for 'first'.) The F-notion of implicit rules requires causally systematic processing—as assessed by the diagnostic question of Section 2.1—and this in turn requires syntactic articulation in the system's input representations.

We can introduce another notion of structure-sensitive processes corresponding to the second notion of implicit rules. The sympathetic proposal is simply that this is the notion of structure-sensitive processes that Smolensky is employing, whether intentionally or not. ('S' for 'Smolensky', and for 'second'.) The S-notion of implicit rules arguably requires some articulation in input representations, for example, the kind of articulation that is provided by tensor product coding (Section 3.2); hence Smolensky's focus upon this style of input representation. But nothing that is required by the S-notion guarantees causally systematic processing (as the network in Figure 5 illustrates); hence Fodor's remark about 'so cunning a rejoinder'.

Smolensky reckons himself to have delivered; but Fodor pronounces himself unsatisfied. No wonder: Fodor is asking for F-structure-sensitivity, while Smolensky is offering S-structure-sensitivity. That, by my lights, is the source of the mutual incomprehension. But to diagnose is not yet to resolve.

Armed with our distinctions, we can see that the debate should be reconfigured. When it comes to structure-sensitivity, the agenda for connectionist research needs to have two aspects. On the one hand, it needs to develop tensor product representations as inputs to S-structure-sensitive processes. On the other hand, it also needs to explore what limitations there may be upon F-structure-sensitive processes in networks. Certainly, F-structure-sensitivity is not ruled out altogether; the networks in Figures 1 and 3 illustrate that. The significance of the results of this research will then be conditioned by findings from (human) psychological research that addresses the question whether mental processes are really F-structure-sensitive or only S-structure-sensitive.

Putting this in terms of implicit rules, we can say that the research agenda is to discover whether connectionist networks and human mind/brains embody implicit rules. But to ask that question productively, we must distinguish two notions of implicit rules.

References

Bates, E.A. and Elman, J.L. 1993: Connectionism and the Study of Change. In M.H. Johnson (ed.), *Brain Development and Cognition: A Reader*, Oxford: Blackwell Publishers, 623-42.

Coltheart, M. 1985: Cognitive Neuropsychology and the Study of Reading. In M.I. Posner and O.S.M. Marin (eds), *Attention and Performance XI*, Hillsdale, NJ.: Lawrence Erlbaum Associates, 3-37.

Coltheart, M., Curtis, B., Atkins, P. and Haller, M. 1993: Models of Reading Aloud: Dual-Route and Parallel-Distributed-Processing Approaches. *Psychological Review*, 100, 589-608.

Davies, M. 1987: Tacit Knowledge and Semantic Theory: Can a Five per cent Difference Matter? *Mind*, 96, 441-62.

Davies, M. 1989: Connectionism, Modularity, and Tacit Knowledge. *British Journal for the Philosophy of Science*, 40, 541-55.

Davies, M. 1990a: Knowledge of Rules in Connectionist Networks. *Intellectica* nos.9-10: D. Memmi and Y.M. Visetti (eds), *Modèles Connexionnistes*, 81-126

Davies, M. 1990b: Rules and Competence in Connectionist Networks. In J.E. Tiles, G.T. McKee and G.C. Dean (eds), *Evolving Knowledge in Natural Science and Artificial Intelligence*, London: Pitman, 85-114.

Davies, M. 1991: Concepts, Connectionism, and the Language of Thought. In W. Ramsey, S.P. Stich and D.E. Rumelhart (eds), *Philosophy and Connectionist Theory*, Hillsdale, NJ.: Lawrence Erlbaum Associates, 229-57.

Dennett, D.C. 1983: Styles of Mental Representation. *Proceedings of the Aristotelian Society*, 83. Reprinted in D.C. Dennett, *The Intentional Stance*, Cambridge, MA.: MIT Press, 1987, 213-25.

Dummett, M. 1991: *The Logical Basis of Metaphysics*. Cambridge, MA.: Harvard University Press.

Fodor, J. 1987: *Psychosemantics*. Cambridge, MA.: MIT Press.

Fodor, J. 1991: Replies. In B. Loewer and G. Rey (eds), *Meaning in Mind: Fodor and His Critics*, Oxford: Basil Blackwell, 255-319.

Fodor, J. and McLaughlin, B.P. 1990: Connectionism and the Problem of Systematicity: Why Smolensky's Solution Doesn't Work. *Cognition*, 35, 183-204.

Fodor, J. and Pylyshyn, Z. 1988: Connectionism and Cognitive Architecture: A Critical Analysis. *Cognition* 28, 3-71.

Hatfield, G. 1991: Representation and Rule-Instantiation in Connectionist Systems. In T. Horgan and J. Tienson (eds), *Connectionism and the Philosophy of Mind*, Dordrecht: Kluwer Academic Publishers, 90-112.

Hinton, G.E., McClelland, J.L. and Rumelhart, D.E. 1986: Distributed Representations. In D.E Rumelhart, J.L McClelland and the PDP Research Group, *Parallel Distributed Processing: Explorations in the Microstructure of Cognition Volume 1: Foundations*, Cambridge, MA.: MIT Press, 77-109.

McClelland, J.L. and Rumelhart, D.E. 1981: An Interactive Activation Model of Context Effects on Letter Perception, Part 1: An Account of Basic Findings. *Psychological Review*, 88, 375-407.

McClelland, J.L., Rumelhart, D.E. and Hinton, G.E. 1986: The Appeal of Parallel Distributed Processing. In D.E Rumelhart, J.L McClelland and the PDP Research Group, *Parallel Distributed Processing: Explorations in the Microstructure of Cognition Volume 1: Foundations*, Cambridge, MA.: MIT Press, 3-44.

Norman, D.A. 1986: Reflections on Cognition and Parallel Distributed Processing. In J.L. McClelland, D.E. Rumelhart and the PDP Research Group, *Parallel Distributed Processing: Explorations in the Microstructure of Cognition Volume 2: Psychological and Biological Models*, Cambridge MA.: MIT Press, 531-46.

Rumelhart, D.E. and McClelland, J.L. 1986: On Learning the Past Tenses of English Verbs. In J.L McClelland, D.E Rumelhart and the PDP Research Group, *Parallel Distributed Processing: Explorations in the Microstructure of Cognition Volume 2: Psychological and Biological Models*, Cambridge, MA.: MIT Press, 216-71.

Schacter, D.L. 1989: Memory. In M.I. Posner (ed.), *Foundations of Cognitive Science*, Cambridge, MA.: MIT Press, 683-725.

Seidenberg, M. S. 1989: Visual Word Recognition and Pronunciation: A Computational Model and its Implications. In W. Marslen-Wilson (ed.), *Lexical Representation and Process*, Cambridge, MA.: MIT Press, 25-74.

Seidenberg, M. S. and McClelland, J.L. 1989: A Distributed, Developmental Model of Word Recognition and Naming. *Psychological Review*, 96, 523-68

Sejnowski, T.J. and Rosenberg, C.R. 1987: Parallel Networks that Learn to Pronounce English Text. *Complex Systems*, 1, 145-68.

Smolensky, P. 1987: A Method for Connectionist Variable Binding. Technical Report CU-CS-356-87, Department of Computer Science, University of Colorado at Boulder.

Smolensky, P. 1990: Representation in Connectionist Networks. *Intellectica*, nos.9-10: D. Memmi and Y.M. Visetti (eds), *Modèles Connexionnistes*, 127-65.

Smolensky, P. 1991a: Connectionism, Constituency, and the Language of Thought. In B. Loewer and G. Rey (eds), *Meaning in Mind: Fodor and His Critics*, Oxford: Basil Blackwell, 201-227.

Smolensky, P. 1991b: The Constituent Structure of Connectionist Mental States: A Reply to Fodor and Pylyshyn. In T. Horgan and J. Tienson (eds), *Connectionism and the Philosophy of Mind*, Dordrecht: Kluwer Academic Publishers, 281-308.

Taft, M. 1991: *Reading and the Mental Lexicon*. Hove, Sussex: Lawrence Erlbaum Associates.

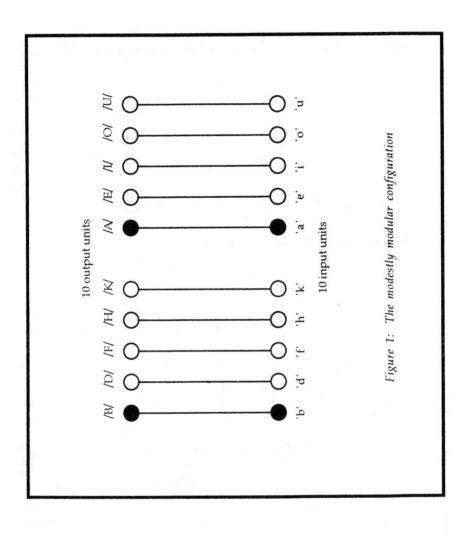

Figure 1: The modestly modular configuration

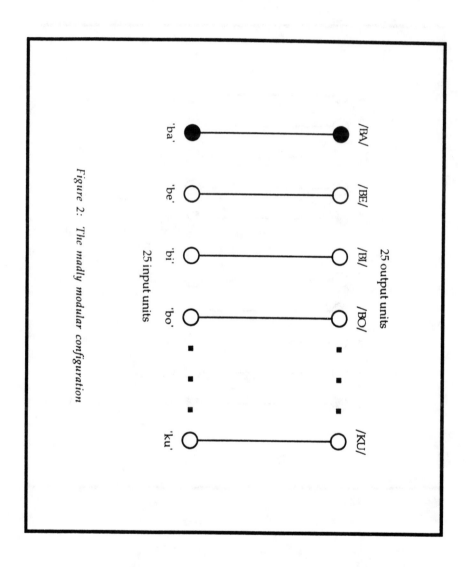

Figure 2: The madly modular configuration

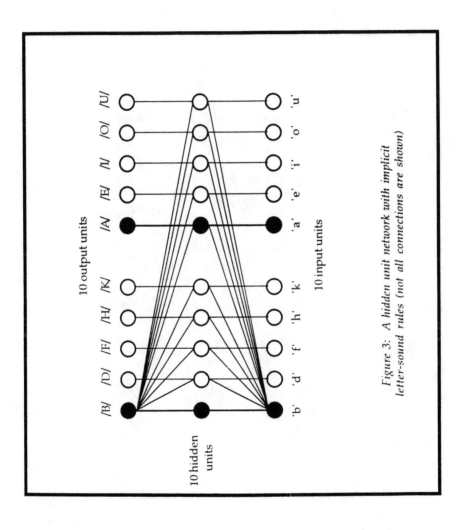

*Figure 3: A hidden unit network with implicit
letter-sound rules (not all connections are shown)*

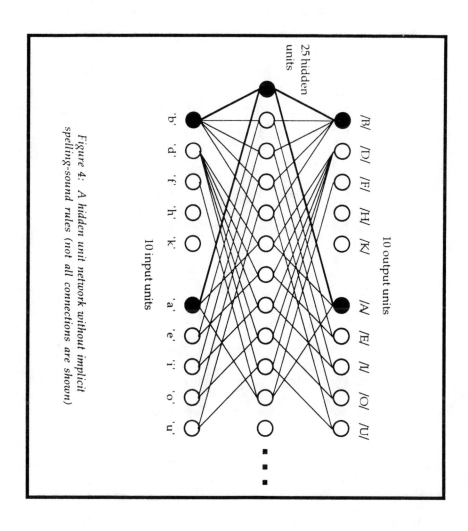

Figure 4: A hidden unit network without implicit spelling-sound rules (not all connections are shown)

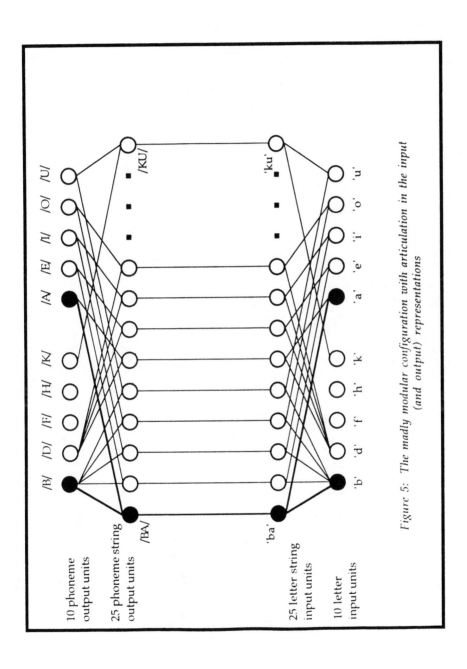

Figure 5: The madly modular configuration with articulation in the input (and output) representations

Philosophical Perspectives, 9, AI, Connectionism, and
Philosophical Psychology, 1995

PUSHMI-PULLYU REPRESENTATIONS

Ruth Garrett Millikan
University of Connecticut and
University of Michigan

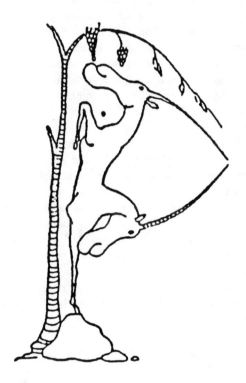

I. Introduction

A list of groceries, Professor Anscombe once suggested, might be used as a shopping list, telling what to buy, or it might be used as an inventory list, telling what has been bought (Anscombe 1957). If used as a shopping list, the world is supposed to conform to the representation: if the list does not match what is in the grocery bag, it is what is in the bag that is at fault. But if used as an inventory list, the representation is supposed to conform to the world: if the list does not match what is in the bag, it is the list that is at fault. The first kind of representation, where the world is supposed to conform to the list, can be called "directive"; it represents or directs what is to be done. The second, where the list is supposed to conform to the world, can be called "descriptive"; it represents or describes what is the case. I wish to propose that there exist representations that face both these ways at once. With apologies to Dr. Doolittle,[1] I call them pushmi-pullyu representations or PPRs.

PPRs have both a descriptive and a directive function, yet they are not equivalent to the mere conjunction of a pure descriptive representation and a pure directive one but are more primitive than either. Purely descriptive and purely directive representations are forms requiring a more sophisticated cognitive apparatus to employ them than is necessary for these primitives. Purely descriptive representations must be combined with directive representations through a process of practical inference in order to be used by the cognitive systems. Purely directive representations must likewise be combined with descriptive ones. The employment of PPRs is a much simpler affair.

Perhaps the most obvious PPRs are simple signals to conspecifics used by various animals—bird songs, rabbit thumps, and bee dances, for example. But PPRs also appear in human language and probably in human thought. Illustrations in language are "No Johnny, we don't eat peas with our fingers" and "The meeting is adjourned" as said by the chair of the meeting. Human intentions are probably an example of PPRs in thought, serving at once to direct action and to describe ones future so that one can plan around it. Our inner representations by which we understand the social roles that we play as we play them are probably also PPRs. The natural way that we fall into doing "what one does," "what women do," "what teachers do," and so forth, suggests this. I suspect that these primitive ways of thinking are an essential glue helping to hold human societies together.

I view PPRs from within a general theory of representations developed in other places (Millikan 1984, 1993). I will start by sketching just a little of that theory (though not nearly enough to defend it).

II. The background theory of representation

Brentano took the essence of intentionality to be the capacity of the mind to "intend" the nonexistent. In recent years it has become generally accepted that he was right in this sense: the core of any theory of representation must contain an explanation of how misrepresentation can occur. I have argued that misrepresentation is best understood by embedding the theory of intentionality within a theory of function that allows us to understand, more generally, what malfunction is. For this we use a generalization of the biological notion of function as, putting things very crudely, the survival value of a reproduced type of entity. I call functions of this generalized kind "proper functions" (Millikan 1984, 1993).

Think of the proper function of a type as what it has been doing to account for its continued reproduction. The possibility of misrepresentation is derived from the possibility that a token may fail to perform a function that has been accounting for continued reproduction of its type. In some cases, failure to function properly may be even more common, statistically, than proper functioning. For example, many biological mechanisms fail much of the time to have those occasional propitious effects that have nonetheless accounted for their proliferation in the species. Thus the eyeblink reflex, exhibited when any object moves too close to the eye, may be triggered uselessly many times for every time it actually prevents foreign matter from entering the eye. In order to proliferate, often a type needs to perform properly only in a some critical but small proportion of cases, a proportion that varies widely depending upon other factors that enter into the mechanisms of evolution by natural selection.

We can apply the notion *proper function* directly to natural languages. Whole sentences are not usually reproduced, but phonemes and words are reproduced, and the syntactic forms in which they are placed are reproduced. They are copied from one generation of speakers to the next, and reproduced by the same speaker on various occasions. If some theory of Universal Grammar is correct, then certain very general grammatical features are also reproduced via the genes. But more immediately, it is clear that speakers of a given language reproduce words patterned into certain concrete syntactic forms, rather than certain other forms, because the effects these patterns have had upon hearers, in some critical proportion of cases, are effects the speakers wish to reproduce. These effects are described with reference to the semantic and conventional pragmatic rules of the language.

The proper effects upon hearers of language forms—the proper reactions of hearers to these forms—are also reproduced. This is not necessarily because hearers directly copy one another's reactions, though this may sometimes happen. These reactions are reproduced because hearers, at least often enough, benefit from reacting properly to the sentences they hear. By moving from sentences into belief or into action in conformity with the rules of the language, often enough hearers gain useful knowledge, or their actions find a reward, hence they reproduce conformity to these rules. Thus each generation of hearers learns to accord in its reactions with the expectations of the previous generation of speakers, while each generation of speakers learns to expect those same reactions from a previous generation of hearers—with sufficient frequency, that is, to keep the language forms in circulation. Similarly, the proper reaction of a bird to the song of a conspecific, though not for most species an imitated response, is also reproduced—in this case, genetically reproduced. In both cases, the proliferation of representations and the proliferation of proper reactions to them are each dependent on and tailored to the other.

The proper function (or functions) of an expression in a public language may contrast with the function that a speaker intends for it on a given occasion. In (Millikan 1984, chapter 3) I have shown how the speaker's intention in use can lend tokens of a language device additional proper functions, as in the case of Gricean implicature. These additional functions are not functions of the *public* language forms, however. Indeed, the two layers of function, public and private, can sometimes conflict, as in the case of purposeful lying and of certain parasitic uses of language. We will not need to consider this sort of complexity here, but it is well to warn in advance that if there are pushmi-pullyu forms existing in the public language, as I will argue there are, these should not be confused with the well known phenomenon of Gricean implicature. Public pushmi-pullyu forms are double-aspected on the first layer of function, the public language layer. It is not merely the user's intention that produces the pushmi-pullyu effect.

To understand what *inner* representations are (percepts, thoughts), we apply the notion of a proper function not directly to the representations themselves, but to the mechanisms whose function it is to produce and to use inner representations. When functioning properly, inner-representation-producing mechanisms produce representations in response to, and appropriate to, situations in which the individual organism finds itself. In humans, these mechanisms are exceedingly complex, including mechanisms of belief and desire formation, and also mechanisms of concept formation, inference, decision making and action. When the entire system functions properly, the belief-forming mechanisms produce true beliefs and the desire-forming mechanisms produce desires the fulfillment of which would benefit the organism. But it is possible also to sharpen the notion "proper function" in such a way that inner representations themselves are seen to have proper functions, as follows.[2]

Many biological mechanisms are designed to produce alterations in the organism in response to some aspect of the environment, so as to adapt or "match" the animal to that aspect, hence to serve some further function within that environment. A simple example of this is the mechanism in the skin of a chameleon that rearranges its pigment so that its color will match that of its environment. This then serves the further function of concealing the chameleon from predators. Each *particular* coloring of the chameleon produced is naturally said to have a function too—the same function: concealing the chameleon from predators. Similarly, any state constituting a *stage* in a (proper-) functional process, when the shape of the process and hence of the state is determined by input from and as a function of certain features of the environment, can be viewed as itself having proper functions. The proper functions of this state are to help in the production of various further stages in the process to which this state will give rise if the whole system continues to function properly. In this way, specific inner states—even quite unique inner states, unique because induced by unique organism-environment relations—may have proper functions. In this way, even such representations as someone's desire to climb Mount Everest backward, or someone's belief that persimmons cure mumps, can be considered to have proper functions.

But I have not yet said what any of these proper functions are, what it is that representations, either inner or outer, properly do.

III. Descriptive and directive representations

Elsewhere I have defended a proposal to explain how the content of a representation—its satisfaction condition—is derived. The explanation takes time, and it is different for descriptive and for directive representations. Here I will assume the notion of content, explaining only what I take the difference between descriptives and directives to be.

A representation is *directive* when it has a proper function to guide the mechanisms that use it so that they produce its satisfaction condition. Like a blueprint, it shows what is to be done.

Desires are directive representations. To see how this might be so, it is important to remember that the proper function of an item can be a function that it is unlikely to perform. Perhaps the sad fact is that an overwhelming majority of our desires never become satisfied. Many (e.g., the desire to square the circle) may even be incapable of becoming satisfied, or (e.g., the desire that it rain tomorrow) may be incapable of being satisfied by normal operation of those mechanisms that are designed to help fulfill desires. This has no bearing on the claim that desires are satisfied when things proceed "properly," that is, when things proceed in the ideal sort of way that accounted for the survival and proliferation of those integrated systems whose job it is to make and use desires. Surely the job of these systems is, first, to produce desires that would benefit one if fulfilled and then, second, given certain additional propitious inner and outer circumstances, to be moved by them to their fulfillment.

Sentences in the imperative mood are, paradigmatically, directive representations. They proliferate in the language community primarily insofar as they (often enough) help to effect the fulfillment of their satisfaction conditions.

Unlike directive representations, what makes a representation *descriptive* is *not* its function. Rather, the descriptive representation's truth condition is a condition to which it adapts its interpreters or users in the service of *their* proper functions (Millikan 1984 chapter 6, 1993 chapters 4-6). It is a condition that must hold if the interpreter's (proper) way of being guided by the representation is to effect fulfillment of the interpreter's functions in accord with design. For example, beliefs are descriptive representations. If my belief that there is an umbrella in the hall closet is to help guide my decision-making and action-guiding apparatus (i.e., the belief's "interpreter") such that it serves its function of helping to fulfill my desires, for example my desire to keep off the rain, then there needs to be an umbrella in the hall closet. If it is to help me make a correct inference concerning, for example, whether or not Susan returned my umbrella, one that yields truth not by accident but in accordance with the good design of my cognitive systems, still there needs to be an umbrella in the hall closet—and so forth.

Typical sentences in the declarative syntactic pattern have, perhaps, a descriptive function. Their function is to produce hearer beliefs or, more precisely, to produce *true* hearer beliefs. For it is only when a certain proportion of what hearers are told is true, hence is interpreted by them into *true* beliefs, that they are encouraged to continue to conform to certain rules of interpretation from English (from the public language) into beliefs. One could not learn to understand a language if too large a proportion of the sentences one heard in it were false. Because its function is to produce *true* beliefs in hearers, the declarative syntactic pattern is descriptive. Roughly speaking, sentences in this pattern affect their interpreters in a proper way only under the conditions that are their truth conditions.

Earlier I remarked that I was not pausing to explain how the satisfaction conditions of representations are determined. But it will be important to grasp this much. On the analysis I have given, the satisfaction condition of a representation is derived relative to its function. The content of the representation turns out to be an abstraction from a fuller affair intrinsically involving an embedding mood or propositional attitude. Put simply, there is no such thing as content without mood or attitude; content is an aspect of attitude. A corollary, as we will soon see, is that it is possible for the very same representation to carry at once two different contents, one relative to each of two different attitudes or moods which simultaneously embed it.

IV. Pushmi-pullyu representations

Consider first a very primitive representation: the food call of a hen to its brood. A proper function of this call is to cause the chicks to come to the place where the food is and so to nourish them. Assume, what is reasonable, that this is the only proper effect that the call has on chicks, the only effect the call has been selected for. Then the call is directive, saying something like "come here now and eat!". But it is also a *condition* for proper performance of the call that there be food there when the hen calls. So the call is also descriptive, saying something like "here's food now". (Note that the descriptive and the directive contents of this representation are different.) Assume further, what is again reasonable, that the effect of the call on the chicks is not filtered through an all-purpose cognitive mechanism that operates by first forming a purely descriptive representation (a belief that there is food over there), then retrieving a relevant directive one (the desire to eat), then performing a practical inference and, finally, acting on the conclusion. Rather, the call connects directly with action. *Its function is to mediate the production of a certain kind of behavior such that it varies as a direct function of a certain variation in the environment, thus directly translating the shape of the environment into the shape of a certain kind of conforming action:* where the hen finds food, there the chick will go. The call is a PP representation.

Other examples of primitive PPRs (probably) are other bird calls, danger signals used by the various species, the various predator calls used by chickens and vervet monkeys, the dance of the honey bee, and so forth. For example, the bee dance tells at once where the nectar is and where to go. Functioning properly it produces variation in behavior as a direct function of variation in the environment. Actually, there is evidence that the bee has a map in its head of its environment and that the dance induces it, first, to mark the nectar location on this map (Gallistel 1990).[3] Still, assuming that the only use the bee ever makes of a mark for nectar on its inner map is flying to the marked position to collect the nectar, then the nectar on the bees' inner map is itself a PPR. And it seems reasonable to count a representation whose only immediate proper function is to produce an inner PPR as itself a PPR.

James J. Gibson did not advocate speculating about inner representations. Yet his notion that in perception we perceive certain affordances (opportunities for action) suggests that perceptual representations are PPRs. Think of perceptual representations simply as states of the organism that vary directly according to certain variations in the *distal* environment. The perceived layout of one's distal environment is, first, a representation of how things out there are arranged—a descriptive representation. It is also a representation of possible ways of moving within that environment: ways of passing through, ways of climbing up, paths to walk on, graspable things, angles from which to grasp them, and so forth. Variations in the layout correspond to variations in possible projects, and in the paths of motion needed to achieve them. The representation of a possibility for action is a directive representation. This is because it actually *serves* a proper function only if and when it is acted upon. There is no reason to represent what *can* be done unless this sometimes effects its *being* done. Compare desires, which serve a function only insofar as they occasionally help to produce their own fulfillment. In the case of perceived affordances, action toward their fulfillment is, of course, directly guided by the percept, variations in the environment, hence in the percept, translating directly into variations in the perceiver's movement.

There are cells in the inferior premotor cortex of monkeys (informally, "monkey see monkey do cells") that fire differentially according to the immediate ends (e.g., grasping small pieces of food with the fingers) of the manual manipulations the monkeys are about to execute, and which also fire when the monkeys see other monkeys perform these same manipulations for the same ends (Rizzolatti et al. 1988). Imitative behaviors in children show up extremely early. One infant was observed in the laboratory to imitate facial expressions (opening the mouth, sticking out the tongue, etc.) at the age of forty minutes (Meltzoff and Moore 1983). We might speculate, on analogy with the monkeys, that these primitive mechanisms of imitation in children employ PPRs, which picture what the other is doing at the same time that they serve to direct what the self is to do. Compatibly, Jeannerod (1994) cites evidence that imagining oneself performing certain movements and actually performing them involve, in part, the same dedicated area of the brain, hence that picturing what one might do and intending to do it may be two sides of numerically the same representing coin. Indeed, one of his suggestions is that imagining an action without at the same time performing it is accomplished by inhibition of normal connections to motor pathways.

It is important to see that PPRs are not merely conjunctions of a descriptive plus a directive representation. PPRs are more primitive than either purely directive or purely descriptive representations. Representations that tell only what the case is have no ultimate utility unless they combine with representations of goals and, of course, representations that tell what to do have no utility unless they can combine with representations of facts. It follows that a capacity to make mediate inferences, at least practical mediate inferences, must already be in place if an animal is to use purely descriptive or purely directive representations. The ability to store away information for which one has no immediate use (pure description), and to represent goals one does not yet know how to act on (pure direction), is surely more advanced than the ability to use simple kinds of PP representations.

V. PP representations in human thought

Organisms often evolve in complexity by modifying less differentiated multipurpose structures into more differentiated dedicated ones. Thus we would expect beliefs (dedicated to facts) and desires (dedicated to goals) to be a later evolutionary achievement than inner PPRs. On the other hand, if there are purposes that could be served as well or better by PPRs than by more differentiated representations, our first hypothesis should be that that is how these purposes still *are* served. I think that there are some such purposes.

One obvious hypothesis is that human intentions are PPRs. If intentions are inner representations, surely they are at least directive ones. They perform their proper functions when they issue in the intended actions. But it is also a common and plausible assumption that a person cannot sincerely intend to do a thing without believing she *will* do it. If one starts in a rather traditional way, assuming that there are only two basic sorts of cognitive representations, purely descriptive ones (beliefs) and purely directive ones (desires), then whether "intending" must involve harboring a descriptive as well as a directive thought may appear to be a matter of "analysis of the concept 'intention.'" But if intentions are PPRs, then the dual nature of intentions is no conceptual truth but a biological or neurological truth. And there is reason to suppose they might be PPRs.

Suppose that my brain already harbors, for purposes of guiding my action, a representation of what I am definitely going to do. And suppose there is need to take this settled future into account when making further decisions about what else I can compatibly do. It would surely waste space and introduce unnecessary mechanisms for evolution to duplicate the representation I already have. Better just to use it over again as a descriptive representation as well. Notice, however, that this kind of PPR differs from the kinds we have previously discussed in this way. Rather than functioning as do, say, perceptual PPRs, which map variations in the organism's world directly into (possible) actions, it maps variations in goals directly onto the represented future world. It differs also in that the contents of the directive and descriptive aspects of the representation are not different but coincide.

A second kind of PPRs that may be fundamental in human thought are primitive representations of social norms and roles. I suggest not that this is the *only* way humans can cognize these norms and roles, but that it may be the primary *functional* way, and that this way of thinking may serve as an original and primary social adhesive. There are good reasons for thinking that humans and other social animals have designed into them mechanisms leading to the coordination of behaviors.[4] Coordinated behaviors are behaviors that benefit each individual involved in the coordination given that the others also play their assigned roles. Some of the principles governing evolution of such behaviors are now well known. Allan Gibbard suggests that "[s]ystems of normative control in human beings...are adapted to achieve interpersonal coordination (1990, p.64)." His ultimate aim is to cast light on the origins and function of the language of ethics and the thought it communicates, including especially the function of normative discussion in originating what he calls "normative governance." My project here is less ambitions. My speculations concern only a mechanism for stabilizing and spreading coordinative behaviors that are already in place, and for coordinating expectations.

I have in mind two basic sorts of social coordinations. The first might be called "common norms." They apply equally to all members of a given society: we drive on the right; we speak at meetings only when duly recognized; we wait in orderly queues; we are quiet at concerts; we honor our contracts; we see to our families first, then to our relatives, then to our friends; and so forth. The second might be called "role norms." These apply to a person only in so far as he or she is filling a certain role: children obey adults while adults direct children; the chair of the meeting calls it to order and so forth, but does not introduce or speak to motions or vote, while the members do introduce motions, speak to them and vote; pupils raise hands to be called on while teachers speak freely; guests and hosts behave in assigned ways, and so forth.

The norms just mentioned undoubtedly all have coordinating functions. On the other hand, the distinction between common norms and role norms could be applied as well to norms lacking coordinating functions. For example, not eating peas with one's fingers and not picking one's nose in public may be noncoordinating common norms, whereas wearing a skirt if you are female and trousers if you are male may always have been a noncoordinating role norm. A mechanism whose biological function is to transmit coordinating norms might well have as a mostly benign side effect the transmission of a good number of non-coordinating norms as well. Thus humans tend to be creatures of convention, exhibiting many patterns of both solo and interactive behavior that are handed on quite blindly, seeming to serve no purpose at all. It may be that our propensity to play games is another side effect of a mentality built to effect coordinations.

The mechánism for stabilizing coordinative patterns of behavior that I propose is simple. It is the capacity and disposition to understand social norms in a way that is undifferentiated between descriptive and directive. What one does (or what *das Mann* does—remember Heidegger?), what a woman does, what a teacher does, how one behaves when one is married or when one is chair of the meeting, these are grasped via thoughts, PPRs, that simultaneously describe and prescribe. In the primitive mind, these PPRs describe and prescribe what is understood to be The Moral Order, an order taken as totally objective, noninstrumental (absolute) and real, but understood at the same time as stringently prescribed. (In primitive thought, self and others have Sartrian essences with a vengeance!) But it may also be that without the general disposition to think in this way during much of the unreflective parts of our lives, the social fabric would be weakened beyond repair. Yes, I am seriously proposing this as a possible neural mechanism, although supplemented, of course, with more sophisticated mechanisms by which we moderns may also dissect the relevant norms to reveal two faces.

VI. PP representations in human language

If human thought contains PPRs, arguably human languages should contain them as well. Just as they contain forms, on the one hand, whose function is to implant ideas about what is the case, and on the other, to implant ideas about what to do, one would expect them to contain forms whose function is to implant mental PPRs in hearers. For example, if the inner vehicles of our intentions and of our unreflective graspings of social norms are PPRs, it is reasonable that there should be linguistic forms to correspond. There do not seem, however, to be any *dedicated* syntactic arrangements to do these jobs. And indeed, granted PPRs really exist in thought, this lack of a form of expression dedicated entirely to PPRs may do much to explain their near invisibility. PPRs, I believe, are imparted by use of the declarative syntactic pattern. At least this is true for English. That is, the declarative pattern has more than one function. Sometimes it is descriptive, and sometimes it expresses a PP mood.

In the PP mood we say, for example to children, "We don't eat peas with our fingers" and "Married people only make love with each other." The job of this mood is to describe and to prescribe, producing at the same time both true expectations and coincident behaviors, the one as a direct function of the other. Notice that the mechanism here is not that of Gricean implicature. Both functions are explicit or literal; the mood is proliferated precisely because it serves both functions at once; both functions are fully conventional.

Strict orders are standardly delivered in the English declarative pattern, which then functions directively: "You will report to the CO at 6 am sharp"; "You will not leave the house today, Johnny, until your room is clean." This use, I suggest, is more than just directive; it is not just another imperative form.[5] Its function is to impart an *intention* to a hearer and to impart it directly, without mediation through any decision-making process, for example, without involving first a desire and a practical inference. This is the PP mood, undifferentiated between directive and descriptive, serving to impart PPRs.

The PP mood may also be used to impart intentions to a group, thus serving a coordinating function. "The meeting will now come to order," when it functions properly, imparts to each member of the group both intentions concerning their own behavior and expectations concerning the behavior of others. The PP mood statement in the university catalog, "Professors will hold office hours every day during registration week," informs both students and faculty, and imparts intentions to faculty.

I would like finally to introduce two more kinds of PPRs that I believe occur in public language but that will require somewhat more lengthy discussions. The first is a variety of explicitly performative sentence. The second are terms expressing "thick concepts."

VII. Performatives

Many performative utterances, I believe, are in the PP mood.[6] When viewed incorrectly as simple present-tense descriptives, they are puzzling in that they seem to create facts *ex nihil*, making something to be the case simply by *saying* that it is the case. Suppose, for example, that the chair of the meeting says "The meeting is adjourned," but that nobody pays any attention and three more motions are debated. There does seem to be a sense in which these motions will have been debated not just after the meeting was *called* adjourned but after it *was* adjourned, that is, a sense in which "The meeting is adjourned" is self guaranteeing. Similarly, once the chair has said "The meeting will now come to order" the meeting has been brought to order even if everyone keeps talking loudly. And if the right person says to the right couple at the right time "I now pronounce you man and wife" then these two are man and wife, even if they don't act that way and even if nobody, including the legal authorities, is disposed to treat them that way. On the other hand, if nobody pays any attention when the chair says "The meeting is adjourned" or, say, "The meeting will now come to order," there is also a tug that says these sentences somehow were *not* true. Let me try to explain why this tension occurs.

Many conventionally or legally molded patterns of activity allow or require the making of, as I will call them, conventional or legal "moves," under designated circumstances, by participants playing designated roles. Examples are performing a marriage ceremony, making a move in a game, appointing someone to a position, making a motion in accordance with parliamentary procedure, legally closing a road, and so forth. These are acts that, once performed, place restrictions on what may or must follow after if things are to accord with convention or law. Moves of this sort may or may not be made with the aid of articulate language forms. For example, in some contexts a bid may be made by saying "I bid," but in others, merely by raising a finger, a vote may be made by raising a hand, and so forth. Most such moves are themselves in essence PPRs.[7]

Their proper function is to channel behaviors that follow so that they take certain forms and not others (directive), and to coordinate expectations accordingly (descriptive). Functioning properly in the usual way, they produce inner PPRs in the various participants which guide them in coordinating their expectations and actions.

The implications of such moves for ensuing behavior are often quite complex, involving complicated mandates or the limiting of options for a variety of affected people playing a variety of roles. For this reason, these implications often could not easily be spelled out in an explicit formula, for example, by saying something simple like "The meeting will now come to order." Imagine the minister trying to fill in all the blanks in this formula: "You, Jane, and you, John, will now...and the guardians of law will now...and your parents and friends will now..." and so forth, spelling out all that marriage entails. However, there usually are names for conventional or legal moves, or for the situations consti- tuted by their having been performed: "bidding six diamonds," "checking the queen," "being married," "being chairman," "appointing a chairman," "voting for a candidate," "a road being legally closed," "making a motion," and so forth. These names are not names for the "shapes" of the moves—not names like "raising one's finger" or "raising one's hand." Rather, they are names or descriptions that classify moves according to their conventional outcomes—by what sorts of things follow after them in accordance with convention or law.

Now there is an obvious and very general meta-convention by which one may use the name of any move in order to make that move. For, assuming that the conventional "shape" that the move has is *merely* conventional, as it generally is, any other shape might be substituted for this shape, so long as everyone understands what move is being made. Saying that I perform the move will generally be enough to perform it, then, granted that the vehicle that usually performs it is arbitrary, and granted that I am the fellow whose move it is to make. For example, even "I move my queen to Q5" may be quite enough to perform that move in chess, especially if circumstances are such as to make an actual board move awkward or impossible (e.g., chess by mail, or while also trying to get dinner).

In English, present-tense declaratives are used in making such moves: "I bid three diamonds," "I pronounce you man and wife," "I move that the meeting be adjourned," "The meeting is adjourned," "This road is legally closed," and so forth.[8] This use of the declarative pattern proliferates because it serves the func- tion of producing the conventional outcomes of the moves named, channeling ensuing activities (a directive function) and coordinating relevant expectations (a descriptive function) at the same time. The proper function of the declarative in each of these cases is thus exactly the same as the function of the move named or described, indeed, the move IS the utterance, in the right circumstances, of the sentence naming it, just as raising ones hand in the right circumstances IS voting. It is a matter of convention that one can vote by raising one's hand, and it is a matter of (very sensible) convention that one can make almost any conventional move by embedding its name in this way in the declarative pattern. These embeddings are called "performative formulas." Such performative formulas are PPRs. They produce conventional outcomes and they coordinate expectations accordingly, standardly by producing relevant inner PPRs in participants.

But there is another detail. One can, of course, make a conventional move with a performative formula that names that move only granted that one is the right person in the right circumstances to make that move. I cannot, for example, adjourn a meeting by saying "The meeting is adjourned" unless I am chair and we are in the right kind of a meeting and the right time has come. Another function of the performative formula—another thing it does when functioning properly—is to produce true beliefs that the named conventional move is in fact being performed. In this respect the performative is just (is also) an ordinary descriptive. It is true if it is in fact being uttered by an appropriate person in appropriate circumstances, that is, if the move it claims is performed is in fact being performed. Nor does this hang on whether or not it in fact effects its conventional outcome.

Suppose, for example, that I put up a sign on my road saying "This road is legally closed." If I have reproduced this token of the declarative pattern on the model merely of descriptive sentences I have previously heard rather than copying my use from the cultural pattern of performative uses, then it is not, of course, a sentence in the PP mood at all. It is merely descriptive and, assuming the town has not in fact closed my road, it is plain false. If I have reproduced it instead on the model of PP sentences I have previously heard, perhaps supposing myself to have the legal right to close my own road in this way, then it is in the PP mood. Still, just as if it were a simple descriptive, it is, minimally, false. It is not true that my road is legally closed.

Integrating this now with the previous theme, besides this last sort of truth condition, a performative sentence of this kind also has a directive satisfaction condition and a *second* truth condition as well. It directs that a certain conventional outcome should ensue, and it induces expectations to accord with this. Returning to "the meeting is adjourned," one of its truth conditions is fulfilled by the fact that it is the chair who says it and at an appropriate time. Whether or not three more motions are debated afterwards, once the chair has said these words, the meeting is in fact adjourned. There is a second truth condition, however, namely, that the proceedings should then actually draw to a close. For only if this happens, will the coordinated expectations which it is the proper job of the performative sentence to induce be true expectations. Last, like any PP mood sentence whose job is to impart intentions, it has the meeting's actually drawing to a close as a directive satisfaction condition as well.

VIII. Thick concepts

I wish now to speculate about one last example of PPRs in public language. These are sentences that contain words expressing "thick concepts." Thick concepts are concepts such as *rude, glorious, graceful,* that seem to describe a thing and to prescribe an attitude toward it at the same time. Recently there have been absorbing and complex discussions about these concepts that I cannot enter into here. But I would like make a suggestion that might be fruitful to explore.

I hesitate to take any strong position on thick concepts in part because I am not sure, within the framework I have been using, how to understand the nature of those states or dispositions that ordinary speech calls "attitudes."[9] It is not likely, for example, that an adequate description of the attitude involved in thinking something rude could be given by reference only to the notions "directive" and "descriptive". But let us suppose this much: if the function of a term in the language is in part to induce an attitude, then this part of its function is not entirely descriptive. That is, attitudes are other than or more than mere (descriptive) beliefs. If I can make plausible, then, that one function of a term expressing a thick concept is to produce an attitude but that these terms are also descriptive, I shall have shown at least that these terms are close kin to PP representations.

Suppose that certain (perhaps highly disjunctive) configurations of primary qualities tend to produce in us certain attitudes towards their bearers when perceived or contemplated. This might be due to native dispositions, or due to the influence of culture. Secondary qualities are traditionally thought of as powers to produce sensations, but powers to produce attitudes are perhaps similar enough to be called secondary qualities too—"attitudinal secondary qualities". Secondary qualities are such only relative to a kind of perceiver or, in this case, a kind of reactor. Nonetheless, relative to a certain group or class of reactors, attitudinal secondary qualities are objective properties.

My suggestion is that words expressing thick concepts may, first, *describe* attitudinal secondary qualities relative either to our species as a whole or to the culture of speaker and hearer. That is, declarative sentences using these words attributively will not serve their proper functions in a normal way unless the objects of attribution indeed have certain attitudinal secondary qualities relative to a community encompassing both speaker and hearer. But, second, *this is because their proper function is a directive one,* namely, to produce in the hearer the relevant attitudes. Their function is to cause the hearer to take these attitudes towards these items. That is, these words continue to produce in hearers these attitudes towards designated objects only because the attitudes induced turn out, in a large enough proportion of cases, to be independently "true" by the hearers' own lights. The objects described are such as actually to *produce,* on direct inspection, or given a more detailed description, *those* attitudes. Words expressing thick concepts thus face two ways at once, describing their subjects and at the same time inducing attitudes towards these subjects. Indeed, perhaps the inner representations induced by these words themselves face two ways at once. Perhaps they are inner PPRs.

Notes

1. And Hugh Lotfing: *The Story of Doctor Dolittle: being the history of his peculiar life at home and astonishing adventures in foreign parts.*
2. Also see, especially, (Millikan 1884) chapter 2, (Millikan 1993) chapter 11 and (Millikan 1994).
3. If the dance says there is nectar at a location where the bee's experience has previously shown there is a large body of water, the bee will be unmoved by the dance (Gallistel 1990).
4. A good informal summary of these reasons is given in (Gibbard 1990).
5. This is a correction of the remarks on army orders in (Millikan 1984) chapter 3.
6. The performative sentences most obviously referred to in the following discussion are those that perform what Strawson (1964) termed "essentially conventional illocutionary acts" or, more accurately I believe, "K-II illocutionary acts" as these are described in (Millikan forthcoming) section VI. The relation of these performatives to those that perform explicit "K-I illocutionary acts" is interesting, but too involved to pursue in a general paper of this sort.
7. I say "most" because some conventional patterns have no functions at all. See (Millikan forthcoming).
8. Some have argued that performatives function by contextual implicature. However, explicit performatives like "I order you to", "I promise that," and so forth, are lacking in some languages, "particularly those with a more developed system of sentence types or those spoken in societies that seem to have less cultural need for formulaic discourse of the kind represented by performative sentences" (Sadock 1988, p.186).
9. Philosophers' "propositional attitudes" of belief and desire are not "attitudes" in ordinary speech at all.

References

Anscombe, G.E.M. 1957. *Intention*. Ithaca: Cornell University Press.

Gallistel, C.R. 1990. *The Organization of Learning*. Cambridge: Bradford Books/MIT Press

Gibbard, A. 1990. *Wise Choices, Apt Feelings* Cambridge: Harvard University Press.

Jeannerod, M. 1994. "The representing brain: neural correlates of motor intention and imagery". *Behavioral and Brain Sciences* 17:187-245.

Meltzoff, N. and Moore, K. 1983. "Newborn Infants Imitate Adult Facial Gestures". *Child Development* 54:702-709.

Millikan, R.G. 1984. *Language Thought and Other biological Categories*. Cambridge:MIT Press.

Millikan, R.G. 1993. *White Queen Psychology and Other essays for Alice*. Cambridge: MIT Press.

Millikan, R.G. 1994. "A Bet With Peacocke". In C. Macdonald and G. Macdonald, *Philosophy of Psychology: Debates on Psychological Explanation*. Oxford:Oxford University Press

Millikan, R.G. (forthcoming). "Proper Function and Convention in Speech Acts". In L.E. Hahn ed., *The Library of Living Philosophers*, Strawson Volume. Open Court

Rizzolatti, G., Carmada, R., Fogassi, L., Gentilucci, M., Luppino, G., & Matelli, M. 1988. "Functional organization at area 6 in the macaque monkey. II. Area F5 and the control of distal movements." *Experimental Brain Research* 71:491-507.

Sadock, J.M. 1988. "Speech act distinctions in grammar". *Linguistics: the Cambridge Survey, vol. II.* Cambridge: Cambridge University Press.

Strawson, P. F. 1964. "Intention and Convention in Speech Acts." *The Philosophical Review* 73(4): 439-60.

*Philosophical Perspectives, 9, AI, Connectionism, and
Philosophical Psychology, 1995*

A NOT "MERELY EMPIRICAL" ARGUMENT
FOR A LANGUAGE OF THOUGHT

Georges Rey
University of Maryland, College Park

I.

The "Language of Thought" ("LOT") hypothesis ("LOTH") is the hypothesis that thinking involves states that have (semantically valuable) logico-syntactic constituents that are causally available to the thinker.[1] It has been advanced in recent decades largely as an empirical hypothesis about the character of much human cognition. While this kind of defense of that hypothesis is perfectly reasonable and, I think, very promising, it has the unfortunate side-effect of inviting philosophers to regard the hypothesis as "merely empirical," a kind of Rube-Goldberg conjecture showing (perhaps contrary to Descartes) how a material mind *conceivably might* work, but not a serious hypothesis about how one actually *does* (much less *must*) work. Questions of this latter sort are the business of ("mere") psychologists and computer scientists, not philosophers.

Now, there are, to be sure, "merely empirical issues" in discussions of mind, as in any concrete domain, issues that can be settled only by going out and looking: for example, what strategies people actually use in reasoning, the fallacies to which they are susceptible, how their amygdalas are implicated in anger. But there are also theoretical issues in this domain, as in any other, which I submit are not happily classified as either "purely philosophical" or "merely empirical." They are a mixed bag of methodological reflections, very general constraints on possible theories, and commitments that may turn out to run fairly deep in our understanding of the world. For example, the atomic theory of matter, the theory of natural selection, the theory of genetic inheritance: these theories strike me as too deep to be classified as "merely empirical." For no notion of "observation," however loose and theory-laden, do we just "observe" them to be true. But nor do they all seem to be establishable "by pure reason alone." We can *imagine* some of them being false; they may even be *possibly false*. *Mere* imaginings and possibilities, however, can come to seem idle and uninteresting the more we appreciate the fundamental role these hypotheses play in our general theories and taxonomies of the world.[2]

The LOTH strikes me as just such a case in point. Although there are many "merely empirical" considerations that can be marshalled on its behalf, there are also deeper ones that should not be so regarded. Some philosophers, e.g. Maloney (1989), Davies (1991), Lycan (1993), have already proposed some *a-priori*-style arguments (Lycan calls his "deductive"), to many parts of which I'm quite sympathetic. I worry, though, that the premises of their arguments may not be all that *a priori* or unproblematic, and that, in any case, they may be far too strong for many readers.[3] In §II of this paper I want to advance what I believe to be, if not an *a-priori*, at least a not "merely empirical" argument of my own, based on weaker premises. Whether it is in fact *a-priori*—whether the premises are in some sense analytic or apodeictic or otherwise "philosophical"—is not something I want to decide here. For reasons I discuss elsewhere (Rey 1993), these further philosophical distinctions seem to me highly theoretic ones, whose clarification seems to me to await a more detailed psychology than we yet possess. But I do think the argument I will present is close to many that have been regarded as "purely philosophical" in the past, and is, I hope, based upon extremely weak premises that most anyone on a little reflection ought to accept.

One thing I hope to accomplish by providing such an argument is to indicate just how weak and natural the LOTH need be. Many discussions of the LOTH make it seem as though the issue is whether people are Turing machines; or whether thought isn't often imagistic; whether people's *everyday* mental processes are "formal" and abstract in the fashion of symbolic logic, or somehow more ingrained in their understanding of real examples; whether our brains have a "classical" von Neumann architecture or a connectionist/"dynamical" one. Many of *these* questions do turn on quite specific empirical details about which a philosopher need and perhaps ought not make any claims. In §III I will show how my argument frees the LOTH from a stand on these further issues, and so can tolerate much of the evidence and argument that has been raised by connectionists and others against a Classical View. It may well be that many people's *actual* mental processes involve images, metaphors, analogies and all manner of computational tricks, as well as massive parallel processing that is distributed far and wide in the brain. My argument will try to establish only that, if people are genuinely thinking things, they must *also* have *available* to them the resources of an LOT.

There is afoot, however, a general resistance to *any* philosophical (or not "merely empirical") conjectures about the internal structures of our brains, a resistance that has its roots in Twentieth Century abhorrence of philosophy committing itself to any substantive claims about the world. This has resulted in what I call a "superficialism" about mental concepts that is evident in much phenomenological, behavioristic and even more recent "commonsense" accounts of such concepts. In §IV I shall argue that the arguments on behalf of these accounts are fallacious, and that they miss the important, internal explanatory role that the phenomena picked out by many mental concepts are designed to play. If this is true, then it can be no objection to my argument for LOTH that it involves speculations about internal structures that are ordinarily hidden from view.

II. Argument T

What might be called "the argument from thought"—what I will call "argument T"—proceeds as follows:

> (1) There are thinking things (e.g. oneself) that are capable of rational thought, involving at least first-order logical thought.
>
> (2) Anything that is capable of rational thought is capable of making *logical transitions* in thought; i.e. it is *psychologically possible* that it pass from one thought to another *by virtue of logical properties* of its thought.
>
> (3) First-order logical properties are in part constituted by (semantically valuable) logico-syntactic constituent structure.
>
> (4) For transitions between thoughts to occur by virtue of logico-syntactic constituent structure, those constituents must be *causally available* features of the thinker.

From these premises, it follows that:

> (5) A thinking thing is a thing some of whose states have (semantically valuable) logical syntactic constituents that are causally available to the thinker.

and so:

> (6) There are things (e.g. oneself) some of whose states have (semantically valuable) logico-syntactic constituents that are causally available to it; i.e. there are things whose states entoken sentences in a LOT.

The essential idea is that one can know that there are things (e.g. oneself) that have a language of thought almost as well as one can know that there are things (e.g. oneself) that are *capable* of *processes* of logical thought. I shall discuss the premises one by one.

Premise (1) **There are thinking things (e.g. oneself) that are capable of rational thought, involving at least first-order logical thought.**

'Thinking' can, of course, be used in a loose sense for most any mental process, but presumably a system qualifies for this loose sense only if it is capable of thought in some more specific sense, a sense we often capture ordinarily when we contrast thinking with mere dreaming, free association, rote memorization.

At least part of what I think we mean to capture by this more specific sense is *rational thought*, or *reasoning* (and unless otherwise noted I shall have this sense in mind in my uses of 'thought', 'thinking' and related forms[4]).

So understood, premise (1) should, of course, be acceptable to anyone the least bit moved by Descartes. Although he didn't have the resources of modern logic, I take it he and his followers would think those resources do capture an essential *core* of the thoughts of which he thought himself capable by virtue of being a thinking thing—even if they don't capture them *all*. This core includes at least some truth-functional (e.g., "Either I exist or I don't exist") and some quantificational thoughts (e.g., "If I exist, then something exists").[5]

To be sure, Descartes regarded (at least his personal instance of) premise (1) as an absolute certitude on which he hoped to base a great deal of the rest of his knowledge. Argument T has no such ambitions, and can even treat premise (1) as dubitable, at least in principle, even by a live and thinking thing. There might, for example, be some specific feature of the concept [thinking] that could turn out to be problematic (we shall see in discussing the next premise what one such feature might be); or it may be that *no* intentional notion is scientifically or metaphysically respectable. Many philosophers and radical connectionist opponents of the LOTH have, of course, taken this latter view. For example, Daniel Dennett (1978) defines mental (or "intentional") systems as being "stance relative":

> What do two people have in common when they both believe that snow is white? I propose this:
>> (x)(x believes snow is white iff x can be predictively attributed the belief that snow is white). (1978: xvii)

reiterating a little later: "There is no objectively satisfiable sufficient condition for an entity's *really* having beliefs" (1978: 285). Fine: this then simply denies premise (1), that anything is a thinking thing—that anything (e.g. oneself) *really* is one.[6] The present argument is not addressed to such a person. But I do presume that such a view is extremely implausible, shown to be so by the overwhelming failure of eliminativist efforts (e.g. methodological behaviorism) to explain obvious regularities in much human and animal behavior.[7] That's at least one reason on which one could rely to reassure oneself of premise (1). In any case, if you like, assume premise (1) merely for the sake of my argument (and, if not yourself, since perhaps you find the relevant regularities more easily observable in others, use some other example you find more plausible).

Premise (2) **Anything that is capable of rational thought is capable of making *logical transitions* in thought; i.e. it is *psychologically possible* that it pass from one thought to another *by virtue of logical properties* of its thought.[8]**

The claim here is that it is not enough that a thinking thing *have* logical thoughts: it must be at least *capable* of undergoing a *particular sort of process* (or set of processes). At this point in the development of psychology it would be rash to try to specify precisely what the process(es) must be, as rash as it would have been to try to specify exactly the relevant processes that count as digestion or metabolism prior to an adequate theory of physiology. But, as would have been true in the case of digestion, it's not impossible to suggest some plausible *necessary* conditions.[9]

Rational thought has something to do with *reasoning*, reasoning with the *provision of reasons*; and, as I've already suggested in premise (1), the core cases of reasons are provided by *logic*. But, contrary to behaviorism,[10] not just any process that produces as output logical consequences of input premises would count as thinking or reasoning. As the contrast with rote memorization and free association suggests, someone who merely memorized steps of a proof, or associated premises with conclusions as one does "salt" with "pepper," is not someone who is thinking in our non-loose sense, i.e. *genuinely reasoning*. Nor would it do for the process to consist of merely a "look-up" procedure, whereby a table was consulted in which sentences were paired, one by one, with some consequences.[11] What these examples strongly suggest is that, in a case of genuine thinking, it must also be possible for the thought of the consequences to have come about in a certain way *by virtue of* the thought of the premises; and, then, not by virtue of just *any* arbitrary property of the premises—say, a certain pattern of rhyme—but by virtue of their *logical* properties. It would certainly seem to be the most basic fact about thinking things that they are things that are sensitive to such properties.[12] Transitions between thoughts that occur by virtue of the logical properties I shall call "logical transitions." If something were psychologically *incapable* of making *any* such logical transitions, it is hard to see what point there would be in regarding it as a *genuinely* thinking thing, as opposed to something that, like the objects of Dennett's stances, could be conveniently or instrumentally so regarded.

There are, of course, heaps of problems with spelling out just what the nice phrase "by virtue of" means. I do presume that it is metaphysically legitimate, that premise (2) is as intelligible as "He died by virtue of inhaling the smoke, not by virtue of being consumed by the flames (had there been no smoke he would have escaped in time)." Whatever problems attach to such a phrase, I assume, however, that they are in no way peculiar to the mental, or beg the question of the LOTH. Although I won't hazard a general account, perhaps what I have in mind will become clearer by discussion of related cases, both here and in the discussion of the other premises (particular premise (4)).

Consider, at least by way of analogy, Davidson's (1963) similar insistence on a distinction between *real* and mere *rationalized* reasons:

> [A] person can have a reason for an action, and perform the action, and yet this reason not be the reason why he did it. Central to the relation between a reason

and an action it explains is the idea that the agent performed the action *because* he had the reason. (1963/1979: 9)

In a later article, Davidson (1973/1979) observes that a lot here depends upon the *way* in which a reason brings about an act:

> A climber might want to rid himself of the weight and danger of holding another man on a rope, and he might know that by loosening his hold on the rope he could rid himself of the weight and danger. This belief and want might so unnerve him as to cause him to loosen his hold, and yet it might be the case that he never *chose* to loosen his hold, nor did he do it intentionally. (1980: 79)

I leave to premise (4) the question whether the 'because' in the previous quote, and the 'cause' in this one actually involve *physical causation*. The point of the present premise is merely that, however we spell out the ultimate metaphysics, we want to preserve a *quite specific way* in which mental states come about (to put it neutrally) by virtue of other states: otherwise we would seem to have no basis for claiming something was the *real* reason for an act. Similarly, premise (2) could be seen to be based on the insistence of a distinction between *genuine* and only *apparent* thinking: a genuine thinking thing is something that is able to enter into a *process* of *genuine*, and not merely apparent thought, i.e. a process whose results depend in the right way upon the logical properties of the thoughts involved.

Davidson (1980: 80), himself, despairs of spelling out the appropriate way that would distinguish genuine intentional action from the behavior of the climber. And we might readily agree that there may be no *a priori* way of doing so. But our confidence that there *is* a difference may be justified even though we don't know how to *specify* it. We may, after all, be in the position with respect to the distinction between the intentional and unintentional that Grice (1961/65) urged we were in with regard to perception, and Putnam (1975) argued we were in with regard to other explanatorily interesting distinctions, e.g. between chemical kinds, where we leave "a blank space to be filled in by the specialist" (Grice (1961/65: 463).

Someone could insist, however, that there is a usage of 'believe' and 'desire' that *is* indifferent to any facts about *how* any states come about. This was, of course, the view of analytic behaviorism; but it might also, less dramatically, be the view of a decision theorist, who might be interested in merely the thoughts—the beliefs and preferences—agents have *at specific points in time, irrespective of how they happened to arrive at them*. Predictions about game play or market behavior might be derivable from such an abstract theory, and even be illuminating about many regularities in those domains. Such systems might be said to "have *thoughts*" without actually "*thinking*"; we might call them mere "*thoughters*," not *thinkers*. Now, I don't know whether such creatures are genuinely possible; but it's not hard to see why decision theorists often might not care which they are dealing with.

What is good for behaviorism and decision theory, however, may not be enough for premise (1), which is the claim that there are genuinely *thinking* things.[13] As I've emphasized, that claim (and, I submit, most of our interest in psychology) seems to be committed not merely to individual attitude states, but to the character of the *processes* by which those states can and sometimes do come about.

Premise (3) **First-order logical properties are in part constituted by (semantically valuable) logico-syntactic constituent structure.**

Substantial support for this premise is, of course, provided by the enormous success of so-called "formal" methods in logic.[14] For example, at least a core set of logical truths (e.g. 'P v ~P', 'Fa ⊃ (∃x)Fx', '(∃x)(y)Rxy ⊃ (y)(∃x)Rxy') can be shown to be so by virtue of the way in which their semantically valuable constituents—e.g. predicates, operators—are *syntactically* composed. So far as we know, this kind of account is the *only* adequate *kind* of account of logical thoughts that we have (cf. Maloney 1989: 7).

There is an interesting question about how to characterize precisely the class of formalisms necessary to capture quantificational theory. In addition to the usual Frege/Peano/Russell and Polish notation(s), there is the lambda calculus, Tarski's cylindrical algebras, and the variableless, combinatory logic of Curry and Feys (1958).[15] I venture that what is essential to all such formalisms is that they involve a set of *operators* (such as connectives, quantifiers, abstractors) that *operate in an ordered way on the referential devices of the language* (such as predicates, variables, singular terms): the sentences of such systems involve specific orderings of operators and referential devices; the logical truths are those sentences whose truth does not depend upon the reference of the referential devices. It is these orderings of such constituents that constitute what I have been calling "logico-syntactic structure." The burden of premise (3) is that such structure is not an *accidental* feature of logical properties.

Note that this premise is relying only on *logical* properties of thoughts being constituted by logico-syntactic structure. Though it seems to me a perfectly natural assumption that those properties (though not depending upon the reference of the referential devices) are also *semantic*, the present argument does not require their being so. Certainly premise (1) would be ordinarily understood as entailing that there are things with contentful states. But if one wanted to insist, as does Stich (1983), that syntax is determinate but semantics is not, the whole of argument T could be read as establishing only a *syntactic* LOTH.[16]

There are some (e.g. Stalnaker 1984) who might claim that it is really *propositions* that have entailments, and that it is the inclusion relations among *them*, not logico-syntactic form that is relevant. Now, if propositions are construed as sets of possible worlds, as Lewis and Stalnaker propose, then such an account will not distinguish *logical* truths and entailments from other necessary truths and (strictly speaking) valid arguments, as might arise in mathematics or (given necessary constitutions) even chemistry. In any case, we would still be owed an account of how it is possible for thoughts to give rise to other states *by virtue of* their logical structure, if that logical structure were confined to patterns among possible worlds alone (I will consider a more sentential account of propositions in defending premise (4)).

A possibility that many find attractive is that thought might have no *logical syntax* at all: images, maps, diagrams would suffice. Thus, David Lewis (1994) argues that our ordinary talk of thought is not committed to being seriously language-like, involving logico-syntactic constituents, but could be merely map-like:

> A serious issue, and one on which I take folk psychology to be agnostic, concerns the relation between the whole and the parts of a representation. Suppose I have a piece of paper according to which, *inter alia*, Collingwood is east of Fitzroy. Can I tear the paper up so that I get one snippet that has exactly the content that Collingwood is east of Fitzroy, nothing more and nothing less? If the paper is covered with writing maybe I can; for maybe 'Collingwood is east of Fitzroy' is one of the sentences written there. But if the paper is a map, any snippet according to which Collingwood is east of Fitzroy will be a snippet according to which more is true besides. ...If our beliefs are 'a map...by which we steer', as Ramsey said...then they are to that extent not language-like. (p. 422)

But surely Ramsey's remark was only intended as a useful metaphor; just how thoughts about non-spatial matters could literally be *maps* is left entirely unclear. Indeed, it is revealing that Lewis considers here only a case of a *logically simple 2-place spatial predication*, such as 'Collingwood is east of Fitzroy.' He is certainly right that in such a case a map might suffice as a representation instead of a sentence with a logico-syntactic structure, and that one indication of that fact would be the lack of a specific propositional content to assign a specific representation. Indeed, such maps might well afford a way of capturing certain systematicities: they can represent Collingwood as east of Fitzroy iff they can represent Fitzroy as east of Collingwood. And perhaps many thoughts that people have are representable by maps and other sorts of imagistic representations in this way. But premises (1) and (2) include *quantificational* thoughts, and transitions between them by virtue of their *logical structure*: how are we to exploit maps or images for such a purpose unless we can *also* represent those thoughts as possessing logico-syntactic structure? How are maps alone to represent *negations, conditionals, nested quantifications, modals,* and the combinations of them that are required for the logical transitions demanded by premises (1) and (2)? In any case, until someone provides an *imagistic* system of logic as *expressively powerful* as a logico-syntactic one, I submit we are entitled to suppose that premise (3) captures a deep fact about the nature of logical properties.

Premise (4) **For transitions between thoughts to occur by virtue of logico-syntactic constituent structure, those constituents must be *causally available* features of the thinker.**

So far as premises (1)-(3) are concerned, we could be talking about the thinking capacities of angels. The further question arises as to how *ordinary mortals, creatures in space and time*, can make such transitions between states by virtue of logical structure. Descartes, of course, was skeptical that any material object could make such transitions:

> it is morally impossible that a machine should contain so many varied arrangements as to act in all the events of life in the way that reason enables us to act. (1637/1954: 42).

But his skepticism was begun to be met by Alan Turing, when he supplemented Frege's and Russell's work with his account of *mechanical* computation of, *inter alia*, logical functions.

But while Turing might be regarded as having shown how a spatio-temporal device might *possibly* manage to think, he can't be taken to have shown how something *must* think. And I don't intend to offer any such apodeictic argument here. But I do think, continuing with the reasoning I've advanced so far, that there is the following not "merely empirical" thing to be said.

For the question arises as to how, given the kind of physical/causal world in which we live, we are to make sense of premise (2): how can one thing happen "by virtue of" something else, if not as a result of physical causation? In particular, insofar as it must be possible for states to arise *by virtue of the logical structure* of thought, and, by premise (3), that structure involves semantically valuable syntactic constituents, it would certainly seem as if *those constituents had better be causally efficacious*.

In the very passages of Davidson (1963, 1980) that we already cited on behalf of premise (2), it is clear that Davidson presumes that the only way to e.g. distinguish a real from a rationalized reason is by relying on *physical* causation. But, ironically enough, those and other later writings might suggest to someone that one could understand the "by virtue of" (and "because") claims of premise (2) not as involving *causal* relations between states, but simply a *conceptually constitutive* relation imposed by the demands of intentional interpretation. After all, Davidson (1973/1984) insists:

> If we cannot find a way to interpret the utterances and other behavior of a creature as revealing a set of beliefs largely consistent and true by our own standards, we have no reason to count that creature as rational, as having beliefs, or as saying anything. (p. 137)

Depending upon precisely how one spells out "largely consistent and true by our own standards," someone's being prepared to make logical transitions might be regarded as simply constitutive of their having any thoughts at all.[17]

But such a *constitutive* "by virtue of" claim has the agent *already* believing the logical consequences of any belief merely by virtue of *having* it: the agent doesn't have to *do*, or be disposed to *engage* in any sort of *process* of thought. But it was precisely the possibility of a particular *process* of thought to which I have argued premise (2) commits us. Of course, if the constitutive claim is to be understood as also involving just such a possibility, then it is simply another way of expressing premise (2)—a *far stronger* way, one should note, than argument T or the LOTH requires. If it doesn't commit us to a process, then, I submit, we are back to a form of Dennett's instrumentalism, or, again, merely to *thoughters*, not *thinkers*.[18]

But *thoughts* could be causally efficacious without their *constituents* being so. The objects of thoughts could be identified with merely *abstract objects* that have syntactic structure—indeed, merely *type* sentences, say, in some preferred language of the theorist, who then simply pairs states of people onto them: a person's thought that a is F is to be paired to the structure type [Fa]; her thought that something is F, with [(∃x)Fx]. The (interpreted) sentence with which the person's state is associated could be regarded as providing the *content* of that state. And the theorist might claim that for there to be "a logical transition between these states in virtue of form" is for there simply to be a *law* relating the paired states by reference to those structured entities: e.g. whenever someone is in a state paired to [Fa], she makes a transition to a state paired to [(∃x)Fx]. And so, for her to be a thinking thing, it is enough that it is psychologically possible for her transitions to be governed by such a law. On this view, it would appear that there is no need for the logico-syntactic constituents of those thoughts to be causally available.[19]

This view would seem, however, to fail to capture the kind of "by virtue of" claim that is reasonably intended in premise (2). Consider again Davidson's "climber" case: it might be a *law* about the climber that whenever he finds he wants to loosen his hold this so unnerves him that he does so; but that still presumably wouldn't make the loosening *deliberate*. Similarly, in the case of reasoning, not only do we want to rule out *accidental* transitions in thought, we want to rule out even non-accidental transitions that occur *in the wrong way*. Merely some nomological *association* between one thought and another that happens to be a consequence of it doesn't constitute genuine logical thinking: a student who merely *memorizes* some of the consequences of a claim may well make transitions in thought capturable by a law relating sentences; but he isn't engaged thereby in genuine logical thought. Or imagine that we condition a young child to think and say "Two" whenever he sees that his cat, Alice, is purring, to say "Three" whenever he sees that *anything* is purring, and, where both are to be said, to attend first to Alice, and say "Two." Suppose, indeed, such a pattern of conditioning were applied across a wide variety of cases (dogs, people, teddy bears). If it were successful, there would be a *law* relating the child's thought states that would refer to the syntactic structure of the sentences that express the contents of the child's states: for a wide range of values of 'P' and 'a', whenever the child thinks [Pa] he then thinks [(∃x)Px]. But the transitions here would not occur *by virtue of* the logico-syntactic properties of these thoughts. The child might never notice that Alice's purring *entails* that *something* is purring. We can even suppose that the child's inferential ability is too poor even to unself-reflectively sustain the inference (imagine the child is quite retarded, though still conditionable). So merely satisfying the law would not seem to be a way of satisfying the transition condition of premise (2). In this sort of case it is extremely difficult to see how to capture the requisite *right way by virtue of which* an event is brought about without appealing to *the right sort of causal chains*: such causal details would seem to supply precisely the very fine- grained distinctions needed to distinguish both Davidson's climber from someone more culpable, and our conditioned child from someone more genuinely thoughtful. If premise (3) is correct, these causal details will quite plausibly include logico-syntactic properties.[20]

Someone might reply that, for such a child, the proposed pairing to predicative sentences isn't the right one; rather, it ought to be something more holophrastic like "Alice-purrs" and "It-purreth" (like "It-raineth," cf. Quine 1960: ch 2). But note that (1) there would still *be* a law relating the child's states that *did* advert to sentences paired with those states; and (2) in order to insist on the *right* pairing, distinguishing among necessarily equivalent sentences, one would presumably need to ascertain just which inferences the child *was* disposed to make; which is just to concede that there merely being a law relating states characterizable by sentences isn't sufficient for the transitions between those states to count as genuine inference, i.e. genuine thinking, indeed, not even for having the genuine *thought* at all! What is required for *that*? Well, it would certainly seem that the only way to motivate a *structured* vs. merely *holophrastic* content would be for the constituents of the structure to be causally available to the agent. So premise (4) is established merely with a detour through a theory of content.

Aficionados of the literature in this area will recognize in the example of the child a thinly disguised version of Smolensky's (1991: 212ff) proposed codings of mental states as tensor product sums.[21] As he points out (p. 225fn7), such a coding is like Gödel numbering of logical formulae, but with the possible advantage that the transitions between the states that realize the code needn't depend upon any of the coded state's logical constituents being causally efficacious.[22] However, what the above examples strongly suggest is that, insofar as such codings are possible, the transitions that would occur on their basis would not count as *logical* transitions in the sense of premise (2): they wouldn't occur *by virtue of logical structure*. Of course, along the lines of the previous paragraph, a genuine thinker might *exploit* such a procedure as a perhaps economical heuristic, much as a medieval monk might recall the *Barbara Celarent* mnemonic in deciding whether a syllogism was valid, or someone might report the cosine of an angle by looking it up in a book. But if a creature could *only* make transitions between thoughts in this way and *couldn't* also do it by exploiting logical properties (i.e., by premise (3), constituent structure), then it would no more be a thinking thing than would a student who could *only* do logic by the mnemonics be capable of logic, or someone who could only look up cosines in a table be competent at trigonometry.

Note that premise (4) does not require that the logico-syntactic constituents be constituents of the *very* thought state *itself*: someone might think that Alice is purring merely by using an image of a smiling cat, or a Gödel number or a sum of tensor products. What is required is that, insofar as this state is capable of entering into logical transitions, there be *available* to the agent the requisite constituents.[23] The agent would have to be able to move from the image of the smiling cat to representations with the logico-syntactic structure required for logical thought (or from the Gödel numbers or tensor products to their factors).

In any event, a defender of the complete dispensibility of causally efficacious constituents owes us some account of how, without them, *genuine thought* is to be distinguished from merely a behavioristic simulation. What constraint, if any, is being placed on internal processing? Need there be *no* connection between *thought* and *reasoning*, between *reasoning* and *the thinking of reasons*, or between the thinking of *reasons* and *logical properties*? Again, we would seem to be left with no distinction between *thinkers* and mere "thoughters."

The Conclusions

The above premises entail:

>   (5) A thinking thing is a thing some of whose states have (semantically valuable) logical syntactic consitiuents that are causally available to the thinker.

which, in conjunction with premise (1), that there are thinking things, entails:

>   (6) There are things (e.g. oneself) some of whose states have (semantically valuable) logico-syntactic constituents that are causally available to it; i.e. there are things whose states entoken sentences in a LOT.

For example, my thought that I think is capable of giving rise to the thought that something thinks by virtue of the fact that 'I think' has a certain structure, the constituents of which, 'I' and 'think', are both semantically valuable and causally efficacious. The LOTH is in this way very nearly as plausible as Descartes' *cogito*, or, at any rate, *that* claim, and the claim that thinking involves logical transitions that are essentially capturable by logico-syntactic structure.

III. What Argument T Doesn't Show

It is important to see what Argument T does *not* establish.

(1) Argument T is not committed to the usual claims about systematicity, productivity and generality of thought that other authors—e.g. Fodor and Pylyshyn (1988), Davies (1991), Lycan (1993)—have emphasized on behalf of the LOTH. That is, my argument does not require that, for any thought someone can think, she can think it iff she can think all logical permutations of it (systematicity), or all logical combinations of it and other thoughts, no matter how long and complex (productivity, generality). Although I think there is in fact quite a sufficiency of instances to warrant the LOTH on these grounds, I suspect there are limits: we're notoriously dreadful at understanding certain sorts of iterated nestings of especially the *same* operator (negations, modals, propositional attitudes), and it's by no means clear that everyone can really understand arbitrary combinations of concepts that they understand separately (e.g.[Space-time is curved]; [The world is 11-dimensional], [The reddish thing is greenish]).[24] In any case, if argument T is sound, a defender of the LOTH need not be committed to a stand on these questions.

(2) T does not entail that we are Turing Machines (i.e. that our psychology is best regarded as a realization of one). In arguing for premise (3), I relied on Turing's work to establish that logical features are mechanically computable, and that, given my other premises, anything that could think must have causal *access* to logical constituents. But a person could be a lot *less* than a Turing machine for that to be true (for example, there might be nomologically determined limitations on her memory); and, of course, she conceivably might even have access to a great deal *more*: perhaps some methods of computation of which such people as Penrose (1989: ch 4) dream, when they dream that Gödel's theorem shows we aren't Turing machines. In any case, T is certainly not committed to supposing that our mental architecture remotely resembles that of a Turing Machine, or a von Neumann architecture, or any deterministic or serial automaton. LOTH presents only a quite weak *constraint* on possible architectures, viz. that logico-syntactic properties be causally efficacious; and this is compatible with an indefinitely rich variety of architectures, for example, ones that might implement those properties in connectionist and/or massively parallel processors.

(3) T does not establish that *all* or even *most* ordinary mental activities involve an LOTH. The above argument rests upon premises about the *capacities* or, in Chomsky's phrase, *competencies* of a creature, not its *actual* activities or *performance*. For all that T establishes, everyone might in reality use short-cut heuristics that save them the effort of genuine thought, just as most of us use simple mnemonic algorithms, not careful deductive reasoning, in doing our daily sums.

The word 'process' that I have used to describe thinking might of course mislead in this connection: it might appear as though I *am* committing the LOTH to claims about actual processing and performance. However, my claim is not that *all*, or even most, or, come to think of it, even *any* of our *actual* mental processes of thought involve logical transitions; only that, insofar as they are processes of thought, that they involve states for which it is at least *psychologically possible* that they are capable of entering into logical transitions. Someone's being a thinking thing requires that she be *capable* of undergoing certain processes of thought, not that she ever actually has or ever will (most people, after all, may well "live lives of quiet desperation" performing mindless connectionist tasks).[25]

This point—a Chomskyean insistence on competence instead of performance—seems to me to get missed so often in the connectionist debate that it is worth pounding the table a bit about it. Van Gelder and Niklasson (1994), for example, recently attack systematicity, claiming that the well-known "selection task" data of Wason (1966) belie Fodor and Pylyshyn's (1988) claim that minds are systematic: people seem to understand "All Fs are Gs," but not to infer from it that "All not Gs are not Fs."

Put aside the question of whether this latter failure has actually anything to do with systematicity.[26] Van Gelder and Niklasson do consider interpreting Fodor and Pylyshyn's systematicity claims as making a claim about an agent's competence, but make the startling claim that

> Fodor and Pylyshyn *explicitly declined* to rely on competence/performance distinctions, acknowledging that the hypothesis of ideal competence was held in suspicion in the opposing camp (connectionists). (p. 908)

But this misreads Fodor and Pylyshyn's concession. They claim that systematicity "doesn't require the idealization to *unbounded* competence" (Fodor and Pylyshyn 1988: p. 37, italics mine), not that it doesn't require idealization to any sort of competence at all! Of course, it does; as does any interesting claim about the mind's abilities.

(4) Given then that the LOTH, and certainly the premises of T, are claims only about a certain competence, they are compatible with proposals that:

(a) People often exploit the resources of "images, prototypes, schemata, semantic frames, metaphors and metonymy" (Johnson 1993: 152; see also Kosslyn 1980). They may—indeed they should—use whatever works. The only constraint demanded by (T) is that, insofar as the agent is a genuine thinker, she had better have available to her the constituents required for logical transitions;

(b) In particular, people may well often reason according to "models," and not by employing the predicate calculus. Thus, Johnson-Laird (1983) claims:

> The models that people use to reason are more likely to resemble perception or conception of the events (from a God's-eye view) than a string of symbols directly corresponding to the linguistic form of the premises and then applying rules of inference to them in order to derive a conclusion. (pp. 53-4)

Now, it's not altogether clear what contrast Johnson-Laird means to be drawing here: even if people don't ordinarily use the Frege/Russell predicate calculus in reasoning syllogistically, they presumably have to use *some* mechanical, representational medium when they "perceive or conceive" events. But it may well be that people often reason far more efficiently by mapping statements in some logico-syntactic formalism to some imagistic system, perhaps a spatial-reasoning module that happens to be especially efficient in human beings and other navigating animals. The only commitment of argument T and the LOTH is that such heuristics do not *exhaust* people's reasoning abilities: in order to be *thinking* things they must also be *capable* of making the transitions by virtue of logico-syntactic structures as well;

(c) Much pattern recognition and other mental processes may be due to a connectionist—even "dynamical"—architecture. As many have pointed out, connectionism could afford an implementation of an LOT; but even where it didn't, such processes might well co-exist and interact with LOT states. Indeed, for rapid statistical analyses, connectionist systems seem quite plausible.[27]

IV. Resisting the Lure of Superficialism

I have been concerned to show in this paper how the LOTH can be regarded as a consequence of quite weak and plausible assumptions about what it is to be a thinking thing. But, against all of these assumptions, it might be felt that there is an even weaker and more plausible idea, that there mustn't be anything "hidden" about the mind: the application of folk mental concepts should be exhausted by the evidence of introspection and/or overt behavior. I call this view "superficialism," in contrast to the kind of "internalist" account I have been urging here, and fear it is endemic to much 20th Century thought about the mind.[28] One finds it not only in introspectivist and behaviorist approaches to the mind, but even, as we saw in discussing premise (4), lurking in recent connectionist proposals.

Superficialism can be motivated in a number of ways: an extreme verificationist theory of meaning; a philosophical reluctance to speculate about the structure of the brain or, indeed, to make any substantive, possibly false claims about the world.[29] But it can also be motivated by a quite tenacious intuition emphasized by many philosophers concerning the ordinary irrelevance of any facts about the brain, given our ordinary ignorance about it, and what would appear to be our liberality in what we might count as thinking things. Imagine a person who behaved in a way genuinely indistinguishable from a normal person, but whose skull turned out to be empty or full of oatmeal, or whose processing were very different from ours: would we really claim that such a creature had no mental life? In a recent article, Jackson and Pettit (1993: 304), for example, have argued that our ordinary psychological idiom couldn't be committed to "a distinctive style of information processing," since

> it would be unduly chauvinistic to insist that in order to count as a believer a
> creature must solve the informational processing problems a world sets its
> inhabitants in the same general way that we do, or in anything like the way we
> do...but any science-fiction buff knows that our concept of belief does not
> thereby preclude [differently constructed] Vesuvians from having beliefs, say,
> about the location of objects around them. (pp. 304-5)

Leaving aside for a moment, the vagaries of the phrase "information
processing," it's instructive to become clear about what precisely "any science-
fiction buffs knows." Why should we suppose that it makes no difference to our
mental concepts what goes on at *any* psychological level that might be hidden
in the brain? As I noted earlier in citing Davidson (1980) and Grice (1961/65)
in defense of premise (2), distinctions between *genuine* and *merely apparent*
intentional action and perception, seem to depend upon speculations about hidden
causal connections in the brain. Other examples abound: spontaneous vs. feigned
feelings, insincerity vs. self-deception, strong wills vs. weak appetites, courage
vs. foolishness, distraction vs. inconsideration:[30] these distinctions plausibly can
occur only in systems organized in a certain way, and would seem to depend
upon distinctions among very specific sorts of causal processes. This was, of
course, the claim of premises (2) and (4) with regard to *thinking*.

But what then about people (or Vesuvians) whose behavior is indistinguishable from ours but whose skulls are empty or full of oatmeal? It's open to the
internalist simply to claim that those structures must be hidden elsewhere than
in the usual place: maybe it's in their toes, or in some yet unexamined special
ghost stuff. In *some* cases, of course, such as beings remotely controlled from
Mars or Block's (1990) "Blockhead," it is in fact perfectly open to the internalist
to claim that such beings don't really have any minds at all.

So is argument T an *a priori* argument after all? There is this reason to
think it isn't: if it really were to turn out that *none* of even what we take to be
the *best examples* of logical thought in human beings actually involved an LOT,
then that would be some reason to begin to doubt the LOTH.[31] We would be in
something like the position of ancients learning that fire just wasn't *any* sort of
"substance," nor stars any sorts of holes. Thus, if it were to turn out that it really
was oatmeal in *all* our heads that was responsible for (what appeared to be) our
thoughtful ways, or that we were in fact "Blockheads" or radical connectionist
machines, then it would perhaps be overly reactionary to hold onto premises (2)-
(4) and insist that no one has ever engaged in any thought at all. But it is
important to appreciate just how extraordinary such a discovery would be. It
would involve not only giving up some of premises (2)-(4), but a massive
reconsideration of the distinctions between e.g. thinking and mere memorization,
between cogent reasoning and mere association, and the role of these distinctions
in our understanding of people. It would be a little like finding out that there is
no basis for the distinction between deliberate and unintentional action; between
intending and wanting; between real and rationalized reasons for action; or

between the experiences of sight and smell (indeed, one wonders how a radical connectionist proposes to capture *these* distinctions as well). It therefore may not be *logically impossible* that these distinctions are groundless, or grounded other than by inner causal structures. So it may not be *a priori* that our brains have a certain structure. But it does seem improbable in the extreme that they don't, about as improbable as finding out, to return to examples with which I began, that animals really haven't evolved, or that there are no genes. In this way, the postulation of inner causal structure seems to me not "merely empirical" either.

Given that superficialism seems generally unwarranted with regard to our mental concepts, there can be no objection to the LOTH, or to my argument on its behalf, that it involves folk speculations about mental processes not open to ordinary folk inspection. The folk know that. They defer to experts and/or the nature of things in the case of the mind as in the case of any other explanatorily interesting region of the world. Indeed, if argument T is correct, they ought to be quite friendly to the suggestion of an LOTH whose details will be revealed by psychology. For if that argument is correct, the LOTH is as natural as the hypothesis that there are genuine thinking things, for example, themselves.[32]

Notes

1. What counts as "logico-syntactic" will be discussed in due course. I prefer the term "semantically *valuable*" to the more common "semantically *evaluable*" in order to avoid the conventionalist and instrumentalist suggestions of the latter. However, as the parentheses here are meant to indicate, in order to keep the premises of the argument of the present paper as weak as possible, I will try to remain neutral on the issue of semantic realism: I will understand a "LOT" to be a set of logico-syntactic structures available to a thinker, with or without semantic values.

2. I have been influenced here by discussions with Karen Neander of her (forthcoming); see also Lycan's (1993: 412) discussion of "inferences to the *only* explanation". Note that I am not committing myself here to any particular *explanation* of the status of these hypotheses: indeed, one needn't subscribe to a distinction between the philosophical and empirical, much less the analytic and the synthetic, to regard some claims as not "merely empirical": a Quinian could regard the kinds of deep claims I have in mind as simply being more deeply enmeshed in the continuous web of our beliefs.

3. Maloney's (1989) rich discussion is closest to my own (see esp. his §§1.2, 1.4 and 3.1). I contrast my account with these others at various points (see fns. 16, 19 and 20, as well as the beginning of §III).

4. In keeping with my general reluctance to claim my argument is *a priori*, I don't intend, however, to be basing any premises of my argument on any "analytic" claims about (the ordinary use of) the word 'thinking' or its various forms. I use the word only because its traditional associations are closer to my modest intentions than the more formidable 'reason' and its forms.

5. Not that all representations in the predicate calculus represent some thought: some are too long to do so, and some are quite unintuitive (e.g. '$(\exists x)(Fx \supset Gx)$').

6. Dennett's views over the years actually present a number of exegetical difficulties

that need not detain us here; see my (1995).

7. For discussion of non-tendentious empirical reasons for believing in a mind (and in a LOT), see my (1991).

8. For present purposes, I will take what is psychologically possible to be what is compatible with an explanatorily adequate description of a thinker's system of thought under suitable idealization. Spelling out this idealization adequately would require a more complete psychology than is presently available.

9. Let me stress that I do not take myself in what follows to be providing *sufficient* conditions.

10. Or, more generally, "superficialist" ones of the sort I address in §IV below.

11. It's not at all unlikely that there were medieval monks who actually relied for much of their logic on the "*Barbara Celarent*" mnemonic method of traditional syllogistic. Presumably they were not genuinely engaged in (the corresponding) logical thought when they did so, any more than would something that passed the Turing Test merely by coordinating conversational moves by means of a lookup table, as in the case of what has come to be called "The Blockhead," cf. Block (1990).

12. Cf. Fodor and Pylyshyn's (1988: p. 50) and Fodor and McLaughlin's (1991: 348-9) insistence that systematicity be *no accident* of the architecture of the brain; and Davies' (1991: p. 236) insistence on the presence of a "common mechanism." In view of the kinds of case that will emerge in my defense of premise (4), I don't think these claims are sufficient.

13. Thus, another way that premise (1) could turn out to be false is if it turned out that no one was *capable* of logical transitions in thought. It strikes me as an interesting question whether Descartes would have been unnerved by this, and whether he's entitled to as much certitude about his being a thinker as a thoughter (cf. Lichtenberg's quip that Descartes is only entitled to claim not, "I think," but only "there is a thought").

14. As Michael Devitt (1991) has rightly stressed, partly because of the effect of the combined work of Frege, Russell and Turing, the word "formal" is exasperatingly ambiguous in the modern literature between "logico-syntactic" and "physical" (as in "shape"). I suspect it has come to mean something like "physical feature implementing a logico-syntactic one." So as to help distinguish premise (3) and (4), I shall try to avoid the term.

15. See Quine (1966) for a short, lucid discussion of combinatory logic, and his (1970/76) for a review of such systems more generally.

16. Similarly, although my argument here is certainly cousin to the argument of Davies (1991: p. 243-7), it doesn't depend in the way Davies' does on the assumption that possession of a concept depends upon either "appreciating" certain *analytic* transitions, like that between 'bachelor' and 'unmarried' (p. 244), much less upon finding them "primitively compelling" (p. 246-7). I doubt that this approach to conceptual possession conditions in general is promising, and, *pace* p. 236, am skeptical that even if it worked, that there would be a notion of "form" on which it could rely (cf. Rey (1993) and (forthcoming-a)). The only "form" on which the present argument is relying is strictly *logico-syntactic* structure (cf. fns. 19 and 20 below).

17. John O'Leary-Hawthorne pressed this argument on me. Clark (1991: 202-5) makes a similar argument against Fodor and Pylyshyn's (1988) causal understanding of systematicity. I won't attempt to address whether these later views of Davidson's are

compatible with the earlier ones we quoted; see Antony (1989) for an excellent discussion.

18. Indeed, I suspect that the kind of "interpretative" views one finds in Davidson may well arise from the kind of interest he has always had, not in psychology *per se*, but in a fairly abstract decision theory. Thus he writes that, when he found that subjects in experiments didn't make decisions in accordance with Ramsey's theory, he "gave up [his] career as an experimental psychologist" (1974/1980: p. 236).

19. I am indebted to Jerry Fodor for defending this view (against his own—better?—inclinations). Note that Davies' (1991: 236) right insistence that "to each [semantically coherent] pattern there should be a common mechanism whose presence explains the aspect of input-output transitions that is captured in that pattern" is open to this possibility, particularly since the patterns he cites seem to be *essentially* semantic (and not also logico-syntactic, cf. fns. 16 and 20).

20. Putting aside "primitive compulsions," and limiting "form" to logical syntax (fn 14 above), this is perhaps a way of spelling out Davies' (1991: 246) suggestion that "mirroring the commonality in the inferences that are primitively compelling—namely their form—there should be a commonality in the causal processes that explain their being so." Indeed, it provides a basis otherwise unavailable to Davies (see fns. 16 and 19 above) for insisting as he does that the "common mechanism" responsible for inference be one that does indeed *mirror* the logico-syntactic structure: merely *arithmetic* or other *domain specific* inferences *don't* seem "formal"; it would seem enough merely that one's reasoning *respect* certain truths, no matter *how* that respect is realized. Maloney (1989: 17, §3.1) quite rightly stresses the importance of *how* e.g. beliefs cause action, but relies only on inferences being sensitive to *content*, which, again, could arise without causally available logico-syntactic structure (without "inference" being "computation" (p. 18)).

21. See also Smolensky (1990 and forthcoming) for further development of this suggestion. I am indebted to Smolensky for fruitful discussions of this issue, despite (but also because of) our differences with regard to it.

22. It would be miraculous were there to be a machine that operated on Gödel numbers to realize logical relations without the factoring into prime constituents on which Gödel's proof depends. However, I emphasize that, as things presently stand, it is only (epistemically) *possible* that tensor coding is any better off, since it's by no means yet clear that that coding *doesn't* in fact involve causally efficacious constituents. See McLaughlin (this volume) for discussion.

23. For the need of this hedge, I am indebted to Mark Greenberg.

24. That is, there may be limits to what Evans (1982: p. 85) calls the "Russell Principle" on which Davies (1991: p. 240) relies, the principle that to have the concept of being an F, a thinker must know what it is for an arbitrary object (that can be F) to *be* F. The interesting example of "the red thing is green" is raised by an experiment of Crane and Piantanida (1983; cited by Hardin 1988: p. 124-5) in which, as a result of an unusually stable image on their retinas, *some* subjects report having a color experience they are (nearly enough) inclined to describe in this way. All such possibilities seem to me to undermine Clark's (1991: 205) claim that such properties as systematicity in thought are *conceptual* requirements on any thought ascriptions at all.

25. Lest I be thought a "mere competence" extremist on this issue, I should say that I do think people actually do think, quite often logically, and that LOTH seems to me

an excellent hypothesis about how they manage to do so; see §IV for more discussion.

26. Note that all the systematicity needed to establish LOTH is of a "*can* think form: there is no need to claim anything about what a subject "*will* infer". Note also that the Weson selection task involves a question about *confirmation*, which, as Hempel's "raven paradox" shows, is immensely sensitive to form, notoriously to contraposition!

27. Although it's interesting to note in this regard that the alleged superiority of connectionist over classical architectures has evidently been exaggerated. McLaughlin and Warfield (forthcoming) show that, for a large selection of well-known tasks, there is a classical machine comparable in efficiency to any connectionist one.

28. In Rey (1993) I criticize its role in Russell's and Quine's theories of meaning, in Rey (1994), its role in Wittgenstein's thought, and in Rey (forthcoming-b) in the work of Dennett.

29. In his own "deductive" argument for the LOTH, Lycan (1993) seems to me to present a nice antidote to such superficialist temptations, comparing our mentalistic ways of thinking with the way someone (perhaps a Martian) might think about automobiles whose interiors she thinks she can't inspect: from her observation of the details of a car's motion, he points out, she might be able to formulate fairly rich and accurate hypotheses about its inner structure. Essentially, I want to defend this way of thinking about the matter against an objection Lycan didn't consider.

30. In Rey (forthcoming-b) I discuss a particularly striking example in reply to Dennett's (1991: 395-6) superficialist discounting of the puzzle many of us have in the case of the taste of beer: we wonder whether in coming to like it since childhood, it's our experiences or our preferences that have changed. Suppose that there is in fact no behavioral or introspective way to tell; but that it turns out that children have more taste buds than adults. One might have independent evidence that both children and adults have the same *preferences* for bitter titillation, but that consequently children reach a painful threshold sooner with the same quantity of a bitter substance. It *tastes* differently, since, arguably, more intense sensation is caused by their tongues.

31. I am indebted to Ramon Das for pressing me on this issue.

32. Argument T emerged in my mind partly in response to discussions with Murat Aydede of his dissertation (1993), which examines the systematicity arguments of Fodor and Pylyshyn (1988), and partly in response to defenses of superficialism by David Braddon-Mitchell, Frank Jackson and Philip Pettit at the Australian National University (for whose warm hospitality I want to express my appreciation). I am also grateful to James Tomberlin for the invitation to write the argument up (and for his patience while I did so), as well as to Ned Block, Michael Devitt, Mark Greenberg, Karen Neander, and the students of my cognitive science seminar at the University of Maryland for comments on drafts.

References

Antony, L. (1989), "Anomalous Monism and the Problem of Explanatory Force," *Philosophical Review*, pp. 153-87.

Aydede, M. (1993), *Syntax, Functionalism, Connectionism, and the Language of Thought,*

Ph.D. dissertation, Dept. of Philosophy, University of Maryland.

Block, N. (1990), "Computer Model of the Mind," in *An Invitation to Cognitive Science*, ed. by D. Osherson & E. Smith, Vol. 3, pp. 247-289.

Clark, A. (1991), "Systematicity, Structured Representations and Cognitive Architecture: a Reply to Fodor and Pylyshyn," in T. Horgan and G. Graham, *Philosophy and Connectionism*, Dordrecht: Kluwer, 1991, pp. 198-218.

Crane, H. and Piantanida, T. (1983), "On Seeing Reddish Green and Yellowish Blue," *Science* 221, 1078-80.

Curry, H. and Feys, R. ((1958), *Combinatory Logic*, Amsterdam: North Holland.

Davidson, (1963/1979), "Actions, Reasons and Causes," in *Essays on Actions and Events*, Oxford: Clarendon Press, pp. 3-20.

Davidson, D. (1970/1979), "Mental Events," in *Essays on Actions and Events*, Oxford: Clarendon Press, pp. 207-25.

Davidson (1973/1979), "Freedom to Act," in *Essays on Actions and Events*, Oxford: Clarendon Press, pp. 63-81.

Davidson, D. (1973/1984), "Radical Interpretation," in *Inquiries into Truth and Interpretation*, Oxford: Clarendon Press, pp. 125-40.

Davies, M. (1991), "Concepts, Connectionism, and the Language of Thought," in *Philosophy and Connectionist Theory*, ed. by W. Ramsey, S. Stich, and W. Rumelhart; Hillsdale (NJ): Erlbaum, pp. 229-256.

Dennett, D. (1978), *Brainstorms*, Cambridge (MA): Bradford (MIT).

Dennett, D. (1991), *Consciousness Explained*, New York: Little Brown.

Devitt, M. (1991), "Why Fodor Can't Have It Both Ways," *Meaning in Mind: Fodor and his Critics*, B. Loewer and G. Rey, eds., Oxford: Basil Blackwell, pp. 95-118.

Fodor, J. and McLaughlin, B. (1991), "Connectionism and the Problem of Systematicity: Why Smolensky's Solution Won't Work," *Cognition*, 35(2): 183-204.

Fodor, J. and Pylyshyn, Z. (1988), "Connectionism and Cognitive Architecture," in *Connectionism and Symbols*, Cambridge (MA): MIT Press, pp. 3-72.

Gallistel, C. (1990), *The Organization of Learning*, Cambridge (MA): MIT Press.

Gleitman, H. (1992), *Psychology*, New York: Norton & Co.

Grice, H.P. (1961/1965), "The Causal Theory of Perception," in *Perceiving, Sensing, and Knowing*, ed. by R. Swartz; New York: Doubleday.

Hardin, C. (1988), *Color for Philosophers*, Indianapolis: Hackett.

Johnson, Mark (1993), *Moral Imagination*, Chicago: Univ. of Chicago Press.

Kosslyn, S. (1980), *Images and Mind*, Cambridge: Harvard Univ Press.

Lewis, D. (1994), "David Lewis," in Guttenplan, S. (ed.), *A Companion to the Philosophy of Mind*, Oxford: Blackwell's.

Lycan, W. (1993) "A Deductive Argument for the Representational Theory of Thought," *Mind and Language*, Vol. 8(3): pp. 404-22.

Maloney, J. (1989), *The Mundane Matter of the Mental Language*, Cambridge: Cambridge University Press.

McLaughlin, B. (this volume), "Connectionism and Mental Constituents".

McLaughlin, B. and Warfield, T. (forthcoming), "The Allure of Connectionism Re-Examined," *Synthese* (forthcoming).

Neander, K. (forthcoming), "Swampman Meets Swampcow".

Peacocke, C. (1992), *A Study of Concepts*, Cambridge: MIT Press.

Penrose, R. (1989), *The Emperor's New Mind*, Oxford: Oxford Univ Press.

Putnam, H. (1975), "The Meaning of 'Meaning'," *Philosophical Papers*, vol. II, Cambridge: Cambridge University Press.

Quine, W. (1966), "Variables Explained Away," in his *Selected Logical Papers*, New York: Random House, pp. 227-35.

Quine, W. (1970/76), "Algebraic Logic and predicate Functors," in his *The Ways of Paradox and Other Essays*, revised and enlarged edition, Cambridge (MA): Harvard University Press; pp. 283-307.

Rey, G. (1991), "An Explanatory Budget for Connectionism and Eliminativism," in T. Horgan and G. Graham, *Philosophy and Connectionism*, Dordrecht: Kluwer, 1991, pp. 219-240.

Rey, G. (1993), "The Unavailability of What We Mean: a Reply to Quine, Fodor and LePore," *Grazer Philosophiphe Studien*, 46, pp. 61-101.

Rey, G. (1994), "Wittgenstein, Computationalism and Qualia," in *Philosophy and the Cognitive Sciences*, ed. by R. Casati and G. White.

Rey, G. (forthcoming-a) "Resisting Primitive Compulsions," contribution to symposium on C. Peacocke, *A Study of Concepts, Philosophy and Phenomenological Research*, (forthcoming).

Rey, G. (forthcoming-b), "Dennett's Unrealistic Psychology," *Philosophical Topics*.

Smolensky, P. (1991), "Connectionism, Constituency and the Language of Thought," in *Meaning in Mind: Fodor and His Critics*, Oxford: Blackwell.

Smolensky, P. (forthcoming), "Constituent Structure and Explanation in an Integrated Connectionist/Symbolic Cognitive Architecture," in C. Macdonald and G. Macdonald, eds., *The Philosophy of Psychology: Debates on Psychological Explanation*, Oxford: Basil Blackwell.

van Gelder, T. and Niklasson, L. (1994), "Classicism and Cognitive Architecture," in *Proceedings of the Sixteenth Annual Conference of the Cognitive Science Society*, Hillsdale, NJ: Lawrence Erlbaum and Associates, pp. 905-9.

Philosophical Perspectives, 9, AI, Connectionism, and
Philosophical Psychology, 1995

A REPRESENTATIONAL THEORY OF PAINS
AND THEIR PHENOMENAL CHARACTER

Michael Tye
Temple University and King's College, London

The fundamental assumption of cognitive psychology is that the cognitive mind is a *representational* system which mediates between sensory inputs and behavioral outputs. The primary task for the cognitive psychologist is one of explaining how the various cognitive capacities operate by reference to the structure of the salient parts of this representational system. The explanations offered are both functional and decompositional: they decompose the relevant capacities into their basic representational components and show how those components function together to produce the capacities. Theories are evaluated by how well they account for the behavior observed in psychological experiments and, at the lowest level, by how well they fit with knowledge gleaned from neurophysiology about the physical bases of the capacities.

Philosophers have usually assumed that pain cannot lie within the domain of cognitive psychology. Pains, it has been supposed, are not like images or memories or visual percepts: they have no representational content. So, there can be no explanation of the desired sort. To understand the various facets of pain, we need to look elsewhere, perhaps to the realm of neurophysiology. Cognitive psychology cannot help us. This, I now believe, is, a mistake: pains *do* have representational content. So, the view that pain is not a proper object of study for cognitive psychology is not well founded.

My discussion begins with an old objection to the token identity theory in connection with after-images, and a modern response to it which has become widely accepted. This response, I maintain, is unsatisfactory, as it stands. But, with one key revision, it is, I believe, defensible, and it has ramifications for our understanding of pain. In particular, it points to the conclusion that pains have representational content, as does at least one other facet of our everyday conception of pain. In the third section of the paper, I consider the question of what sorts of representations pains are most plausibly taken to be. Are they sentences in an inner language, like beliefs and desires, on the usual computational conception of the latter states? Or are they representations of a different sort? I suggest that a purely sentential approach is difficult to reconcile with some of the neuropsychological data on pain, and I make an alternative hybrid proposal. Pains, I propose, are representations of the same general sort as mental images:

they are arrays to which sentences are appended. So, pain, I urge, is a proper object of study of cognitive psychology. In the final section, I take up some questions concerning the phenomenal character of pain.

I

In the 1950's J.J.C. Smart raised the following objection to the identity theory for sensations: After-images are sometimes yellowy-orange; brain processes cannot be yellowy-orange.[1] So after-images are not brain processes. The reply that Smart himself made to the objection was to deny that after-images exist, there really being, in Smart's view, only experiences of *having* after-images, which are not themselves yellowy-orange.

Another less radical response is available on behalf of the identity theory. It is on this response which I wish to focus here. Why not say that in predicating color words of images we are not attributing to them the very same properties which we attribute to external objects via our use of color language. So, after-images are not literally green or blue in the way that grass or the sky have one or the other of these features. Now it is no longer obviously true that brain processes cannot be yellowy-orange in the relevant sense.

The obvious problem which this response faces is that of explaining how it is that color vocabulary is applied at all to after-images, given that they do not really have the appropriate colors. One solution proposed by Ned Block is to say that color words are used elliptically for expressions like "real-blue-representing", "real-green-representing," and so on, in connection with images generally.[2] In my view, this solution has a number of important virtues.[3] For one thing, brain processes can certainly represent colors. So, the identity theory is no longer threatened. For another, as Block has noted,[4] terms like "loud" and "high-pitched" are standardly applied directly to oscilloscope readings used in connection with the graphical representations of sounds. In this context, these terms evidently do not name real sounds made by the readings. One possibility, then, is that they pick out representational properties such as loud-representing and high-pitched-representing. If this is so, then there already exists an established usage of terms which conforms to the one alleged to obtain in the case of color terms and after-images.

There is a serious difficulty, however. Mental images are not literally square any more than they are literally blue. So, extending the above proposal to shape, we get that a blue, square after-image is simply an after-image that is square-representing and also blue-representing. But intuitively this seems too weak. Surely, a blue, square image cannot represent different things as blue *and* square. Unfortunately, nothing in the above proposal rules this out. "Blue," then, in application to after-images, does not mean "blue-representing." Likewise "square."

This difficulty is not peculiar to images. Precisely the same problem can be raised in connection with oscilloscope readings. The way out, I suggest, is to appreciate that there is nothing elliptical about the meanings of terms like "blue" or "loud" in the above contexts. Instead it is the contexts themselves that need further examination. Let me explain.

The contexts "Hopes for an *F*" and "Hallucinates a *G*" are typically intensional. Thus, I can hope for eternal life and hallucinate a pink elephant, even though there are no such things. Similarly, I can hope for eternal life without hoping for eternal boredom, even if in reality the two are the same. It seems evident that the terms substituting for "*F*" and "*G*" in these contexts retain their usual meanings. The above peculiarities are due to the fact that hoping and hallucinating are representational states, and to the special character of representation itself.

Now precisely the same peculiarities are present in the case of the context "an *F* image," where "*F*" is a color or shape term. Thus, in a world in which nothing is really triangular, I can still have a triangular image. Also, if I have a red image, intuitively it does not follow that I have an image the color of most fire-engines even given that most fire-engines are red. The explanation, I suggest, is straightforward: An *F* image is an image which *represents that something* is *F*.[5]

Likewise, an *F, G* image is an image *which represents that something* is both *F* and *G*. My suggestion, then, is that there is nothing elliptical or peculiar about the meanings of the terms "*F*" and "*G*" in the context "An *F, G* image." Rather the context itself is an intensional one, having a logical structure which reflects the representational character of images generally.

It may still be wondered why we *say* that the image itself is *F* and *G*, for example, blue and square. This is, I suggest, part of a much broader usage. Frequently when we talk of representations, both mental and non-mental, within science and in ordinary life, we save breath by speaking as if the representations themselves have the properties of the things they represent. In such cases, in saying of a representation that it is *F*, what we mean is that it represents that something is *F*. So, when it is said of some given oscilloscope reading that it is loud and high-pitched, what is being claimed is that loud and high pitched are features that the reading represents some sound as having. "Loud" and "high-pitched" mean what they normally do here. The context itself is intensional.

The above proposal solves the problem of the blue, square image. Here the image represents that something is both blue and square, not merely that something is blue *and* that something is square.[6]

The claim that after-images are representational, I might add, does not entail or presuppose that creatures cannot have after-images unless they also have the appropriate concepts (at least as "concept" is frequently understood). Having the concept *F* requires, on some accounts, having the ability to use the linguistic term '*F*' correctly. On other accounts, concept possession requires the ability to represent in thought and belief that something falls under the concept. But after-images, like other perceptual sensations, are not themselves thoughts or beliefs; and they certainly do not demand a public language. They are, if you like, pre-conceptual, or non-conceptual representations.

The broad picture I have here very briefly is this. Processes operating upon proximal stimuli generate certain sorts of visual representations via mechanical procedures. Categorizations of various sorts occur along the way. The representations, so generated, form the outputs of a specialized visual module, and stand ready to produce conceptual responses via the action of the central executive. So, perceptual sensations, feed into the conceptual system, without themselves being a part of that system.

In admitting that after-images are non-conceptual representations, I am not thereby granting that they do not really have *intentional* content, that they are representations of a non-intentional sort. In my view, intentionality does not require concepts. As I use the term "intentionality", the key features are representation (and hence the possibility of *mis*representation) along with the possibility of substitution failures in the associated linguistic contexts. These features, I have argued, are present in the case of after-images. So, after-images are intentional. Those philosophers who want to insist that there cannot be full-blooded intentionality without concepts (or that intentionality is restricted to the central executive) are entitled to their use of the term. But any disagreement here is, I suggest, purely verbal. Nothing of substance hangs upon which usage is adopted.

We are now ready to turn to the case of pain.

II

It is often supposed that terms applied to pain which also apply to physical objects do not have their ordinary meanings. Ned Block, who takes this view, says the following (in his 1983, p. 517):

> There is some reason to think that there is a systematic difference in meaning between certain predicates applied to physical objects and the same predicates applied to mental particulars. Consider a nonimagery example: the predicate '---in---'. This predicate appears in each premise and the conclusion of this argument:
>
> > The pain is in my fingertip.
> > The fingertip is in my mouth.
> > Therefore, the pain is in my mouth.
>
> This argument is valid for the "in" of spatial enclosure..., since "in" in this sense is transitive. But suppose that the two premises are true in their *ordinary* meanings...The conclusion obviously does not follow, so we must conclude that "in" is not used in the spatial enclosure sense in all three statements. It certainly seems plausible that "in" as applied in locating pains differs in meaning systematically from the standard spatial enclosure sense. (Block 1983, p. 517).

This seems to me quite wrong. There is no more reason to adopt the strange position that 'in' does not mean spatial enclosure in connection with pain than there is to say that 'orange' in connection with images has a special meaning.

With the collapse of the latter view, the former becomes unstable. And the inference Block cites does *not* establish his claim. To see this, consider the following inference:

I want to be in City Hall
City Hall is in a ghetto
Therefore, I want to be in a ghetto.

The term 'in' has the same meaning in both premises and the conclusion. But the argument is invalid: I might want to be in City Hall to listen to a particular speech, say, without thereby wanting to be in a ghetto. The same is true, I suggest, in the case of Block's example, and the explanation is the same. In both the first premise and the conclusion, the term 'in' appears in an intensional context. Just as when we say that an image is blue, we are saying that it represents that something is blue, so when we say that a pain is in my fingertip, we are saying that it represents that something is in my fingertip.

It is perhaps worth noting here that the invalidity of the inference involving pain has nothing to do with the fact that mouths are cavities of a certain sort, and hence items whose ontological status might itself be questioned. If I have a pain in my fingertip, and I slit open a small portion of my leg, into which I then thrust my finger, still it does not follow that I have a pain in my leg. Suppose, for example, that my leg has been anaesthetized. In this case, I feel a pain in my finger, but not in my leg.

Nor does it help to say that what the inference failure really shows is that pains themselves are ontologically suspect. For even if it were true that there are no pains, only people who are pained, still this gives us no account of why the inference fails. After all, if 'in' means inside, and I am pained in my fingertip, then I am also pained in my mouth, assuming my fingertip is in my mouth.

That there is a hidden intensionality in statements of pain location is confirmed by our talk of pains in phantom limbs. We allow it to be true on occasion that people are subject to pains in limbs that no longer exist. How can this be? Answer: You can have a pain in your left leg even though you have no left leg, just as you can search for the Fountain of Youth. Again the context is intensional: specifically, you have a pain that represents that something is in your left leg.[7]

Of course, there is some temptation to say that if you don't have a left leg, then you can't really have a pain in it. But that is no problem for my proposal. For there is a *de re* reading of the context, namely that to have a pain in your left leg is for your left leg to be such that you have a pain in *it*. Now a left leg *is* required.

But doesn't a pain in the leg represent more than just that something is in the leg? To answer this question, it is necessary to make some more general remarks about pain. To have a pain is to feel a pain, and to feel a pain is to experience pain. Thus, if I have a pain, I undergo a token experience of a certain sort. This token experience is, I suggest, the particular pain I have.

The identification of pains with token experiences explains why no-one else could feel the *particular* pain I am feeling, and moreover why pains are necessarily owned by *someone* or other. Token experiences are events (in the broad sense, which includes token states), and, in general, events are individuated in part via the objects which undergo them. So, laughs cannot exist unowned, and neither can screams. Likewise, killings, births, and explosions. In each of these cases, there must be a subject for the event: a killer, a creature that is born, an object which explodes. Moreover, the subject is essentially related to the event. No-one else can die my death or laugh my laugh, although, of course, someone else can certainly undergo qualitatively very similar deaths or laughs.

Now *what* I experience or feel, in having a pain in a leg, is that there is some disorder in the leg, some damage that is painful or hurts. So, a pain in the leg, I suggest, is a token sensory experience which represents that something in the leg is damaged, something moreover that is painful or hurts.[8]

This proposal may seem to encounter an immediate difficulty. Token experiences, including pains, are themselves located in the brain. So, there really are no pains inside legs. So, the above experience, in representing that something in the leg is painful, must be *mis*representing what is going on. And this is highly counter-intuitive. Surely, a person who feels a pain in the leg, in normal circumstances, is not subject to an *illusion*.

This objection contains a non-sequitur. From the fact that there are no pains in legs it does not follow that a pain which represents that some disturbance in a leg is painful is a misrepresentation. When it is said that a cut in a finger or a burn or a bruise is painful or hurts, what is meant is (roughly) that it is *causing* a feeling, namely the very feeling the person is undergoing, and that this feeling elicits an immediate dislike for itself together with anxiety about, or concern for, the state of the bodily region where the disturbance feels located. So, a pain in the leg is a pain that represents accurately if, and only if it is caused by damage in the leg and causes the immediate desire that it cease, together with anxiety about the state of the relevant portion of the leg. Since pains in legs are normally caused by tissue damage of one sort or another inside legs, such pains do not normally misrepresent.

This account seems to me intuitively very plausible. A man who reports to his doctor that he has a pain in his left arm is not taken to have lied, if it is discovered that the real cause of his pain lies in his heart. Such a man has a pain in his left arm, but in this case he *is* under a kind of illusion: there really is nothing *in his left arm* which is hurting him.

There is one objection worth mentioning here. Perhaps it will be said that a person who experiences a pain in a certain bodily part does not experience that something inside the relevant part is *causing* any experience or any reaction of dislike. Such a proposal is too complicated to fit the phenomenology of experiences of this sort. If, for example, I have a pain in my left thumb, I surely do not actually feel that something in my thumb is causing the pain experience I am undergoing.

This objection is not compelling. It is true that when I have a pain in my left thumb, what I experience is simply that something is wrong in my left thumb, something that hurts. But this can be accounted for by noting that the context 'experiences that' is highly intensional: not even analytically equivalent expressions may be safely substituted *salva veritate*.

There is another feature of my account which deserves comment. Pains, I claim, represent correctly if, and only if, they are caused by bodily damage and cause an immediate reaction of dislike. Pains, then, misrepresent when there is no damage and also when they fail to elicit a reaction of dislike. But they nonetheless remain pains. So, unlike standard functionalist accounts, my proposal preserves the intuition of many 'qualia freaks' that it is not necessary for pains to occupy their standard causal role in order for them to count as pains. It does so, however, without the introduction of non-intentional qualia.[9]

In my view, the intentionalist treatment I have proposed can be extended to pains of more specific sorts. A twinge of pain is a pain that represents a mild, brief disturbance. A throbbing pain is one that represents a rapidly pulsing disturbance. Aches represent disorders that occur *inside* the body, rather than on the surface. These disorders are represented as having volume, as gradually beginning and ending, as increasing in severity and then slowly fading away.[10] The volumes so represented are not represented as precise or sharply bounded. This is why aches do not feel to have precise locations, unlike pricking pains, for example. A stabbing pain is one that represents sudden damage over a particular well-defined bodily region. This region is represented as having volume (rather than being two-dimensional), as being the shape of something sharp-edged and pointed (like that of a dagger).[11] In the case of a pricking pain, the relevant damage is represented as having a sudden beginning and ending on the surface or just below, and as covering a very tiny area. A racking pain is one that represents that the damage involves the stretching of internal body parts (e.g., muscles).

In each of these cases, what one experiences, in being the subject of the pain, is that some bodily region not only hurts but also has some more specific features. Consider, for example, a pricking pain in the leg. Here, it seems phenomenologically undeniable that pricking is experienced *as* a feature tokened within the leg, and not as an intrinsic feature of the experience itself. What is experienced as being pricked is a part of the surface of the leg. This is nicely accounted for by the above proposal. It should also be noted that since pricking pains do not represent pins, my account does not have the implausible consequence that creatures who live in worlds without pins cannot have pricking sensations or that in these worlds creatures undergoing such sensations are misrepresenting what is going on in them.

Pains, I conclude, like after-images, have representational content. Unlike images, however, they have bodily locations (in the representational sense I have elucidated).[12] So, although pains, in my view, are really constituted by physical processes in the head, it is also true to say that they can occur anywhere in the body.[13]

III

The language of thought hypothesis is an empirical hypothesis about how the representational contents of mental states are, in fact, encoded in the head. It is not an a priori philosophical analysis. So, it is not intended to cover the contents of mental states of all actual and possible creatures. In its most general form, it concerns the coding of *all* actual mental contents. The basic thesis, stemming from the computer model of mind, is that such contents are encoded in symbol-structures in an inner language.

In the case of the so-called "propositional attitudes"—that is, those mental states like belief and desire whose contents are standardly expressed in 'that' clauses—it has typically been supposed that the relevant symbol-structures are sentences.[14] The apparent need to acknowledge inner sentences in an account of the propositional attitudes (hereafter the PAs) derives from several different sources.

To begin with, the PAs are systematic: there are intrinsic connections between certain thoughts. Consider, for example, the thought that the boy is chasing the dog and the thought that the dog is chasing the boy. Anyone who has the capacity to think the former thought also has the capacity to think the latter and vice-versa. Secondly, the PAs are productive: we have the capacity, it seems, to think indefinitely many thoughts and to think thoughts we have never thought before. The PAs are also fine-grained: I can think that you know something important without thinking that you justifiably and truly believe something important, even if the correct analysis of "know" is "justifiably and truly believe." Finally, the PAs have truth-values: my belief that the English pound is worth less in dollars than it was two years ago is either true or false.

Facts exactly parallel to these obtain in the case of sentences in public languages. According to adherents to the language of thought hypothesis, these parallels are best explained by supposing that the PAs themselves have a sentence-like structure.[15]

What sorts of representations, then, are pains? Are they too inner sentences? It may be tempting to suppose that if they have representational content, as I have urged, and if the language of thought hypothesis is true, then they must be sentences. This would be much too quick, however. For a commitment to an inner language within which cognition occurs is not a commitment to sentences in each and every case of mental representation. After all, computers—symbol manipulators, par excellence—operate on all sorts of symbol structures (for example, lists, sentences, arrays) ; and, to mention one example, there are well known theories of mental imagery which fall within the computational approach, but which reject the thesis that images are sentences.[16] Moreover, it is certainly not obvious that the language of thought hypothesis in its unrestricted form is true. Perhaps some mental representations are not coded in our heads in linguistic symbols at all.

So, a simple appeal to the general language of thought hypothesis does not justify the claim that pains are sentences. Do the considerations adduced above in connection with the PAs support the sententialist view of pains? It seems to me that, to some extent, they do. There are some systematic connections between pains: the capacity to feel a burning pain in the leg and (at the same or another time) a stinging pain in the arm seem connected to the capacity to feel a stinging pain in the leg and a burning pain in the arm. Moreover, if pains are representations then they can misrepresent.[17] So, there is a sense in which some pains may be characterized as false: what they represent is not, in fact, the case. Finally, pain experiences are fine-grained: as I remarked earlier, not even analytically equivalent expressions can be safely substituted salva veritate within the context 'experiences that'.

It must be admitted that the first two considerations cited above are not very compelling on their own. Systematic connections between pains are limited and can easily be accounted for on a model of pains as maps, for example. And the possibility of misrepresentation does not *require* that pains be true or false, any more than the fact that maps or paintings are sometimes inaccurate requires that they be true or false. Still, the third consideration, when added to the other two, does strongly suggest a linguistic character to pain representation.

Are there any pieces of evidence which count against a purely sententialist view of pain? It seems to me that there are. We know that in visual perception, the retinal image is reconstructed in the visual cortex so that in a quite literal sense adjacent parts of the cortex represent adjacent parts of the retinal image. There is, then, an orderly topographic projection of the retinal image onto the brain. This has been established from experiments in which a recording electrode is placed inside the visual cortex. Greater neural activity is picked up by the electrode when light is shone onto a particular spot on the retina. Moving the electrode a little results in the continued registration of greater activity only if light is directed onto an adjacent part of the retina.

Topographic organization of this sort is also found in the somatosensory cortex. There is, for example, an orderly topographic representation of the surface of the human body which is dedicated to touch. Here adjacent regions of the body surface are projected onto adjacent regions of the cortex. Enhanced activity in one of the relevant cortical regions represents that the region of body surface projected onto it is being touched. Some relatively small portions of the body, e.g., the hands and face, provide input to more neurons than do some relatively large portions, e.g., the trunk. This is why when people are asked to say whether there are two separate points that are both being touched on their faces or just one, the smallest distance between the points at which both can be felt is much less than the smallest distance when the points are located on the trunk.

There are further representations of the human body in the somatosensory cortex which are similarly structured. It has been established that the experience of pain is associated with activity in this cortex.[18] Now the fact that the somatosensory cortex is topographically organized and that it is the primary locus of pain raises doubts about the sentential view of pain. For sentences do not have the requisite map-like representational structure.[19]

It appears, then, that the evidence points in two different directions. On the one hand, certain logical features of pain discourse suggest that pain experiences, like the PAs generally, represent in the manner of sentences. On the other hand, there is neuropsychological data which suggests that pains have a topographic structure. The way to reconcile these apparently conflicting strands of thought is, I suggest, to hold that pains have a *complex* representational structure, one component of which is sentential and another map-like. In my view, pains are patterns of active cells occurring in topographically structured 3-D arrays to which sentences are attached. This proposal may be unpacked as follows.

For each pain, there is an array made up of cells corresponding to irregularly-sized portions of the body, with adjacent cells representing adjacent body regions.[20] Each cell, when active, may be conceived of as representing that something painful is occurring at the corresponding body region. The irregularity of the grain in the array is partly responsible, I suggest, for variations in our experience of pain when the same degree of damage occurs in different bodily regions of the same size (for example, the face versus the torso).

Since the cells within the pain array itself are individually concerned only with arbitrary body regions, there is no representation in the array of natural body parts. Segmentation of the body regions into such parts occurs via inspection processes that examine patterns of active cells in the array, and assess them, on the basis of their location, as pains in arms, legs, etc. It is here that sentences are appended to the array, sentences which represent that in such and such a body part, something is hurting. I speculate that further modifiers are introduced into the sentences which represent whether something in the associated body region is burning, stinging, and so on. I conjecture that the modifiers are attached via further inspection routines which work over the array and extract at least *some* of the relevant information from its contents. For example, in the case of a stabbing pain, we may suppose that there is a sudden pattern of activity in the array, beginning at a part of the array representing a narrow region of body surface and extending in the proper temporal sequence to cells representing adjacent deeper internal regions (so that a roughly dagger-shaped volume is marked out). The inspection routines process this activity and assign an appropriate descriptive term.[21] In the case of a stinging pain, we may suppose that certain cells in the array representing contiguous regions of body surface along a narrow band are strongly activated, more or less simultaneously, for a brief period of time. This activity is noted by the inspection routines, and the relevant term again affixed. Whether these suppositions are along the right lines is a matter for investigation by cognitive psychology.

This crude model is, of course, very sketchy indeed. What it gives us, I suggest, is an alternative way of thinking about pains as representations, one which seems to me more promising than the purely sentential view. Pains, I believe, represent in something like the way that maps represent which contain additional descriptive information for salient items ("treasure buried here," "highest mountain on island"). In this respect, they are very like mental images, as I conceive them.

There is strong evidence that images and visual percepts share a medium which has been called "the visual buffer." This medium is functional in character: it consists of a large number of cells, each of which is dedicated to representing, when filled, a tiny patch of surface at a particular location in the visual field. For visual percepts and after-images, the visual buffer is filled, in normal cases, by processes that operate on information contained in the light striking the eyes. For mental-images (other than after-images), the visual buffer is filled by generational processes that act on information stored in long-term memory about the appearances of objects and their spatial structure.

Images and percepts, I have argued elsewhere, are interpreted symbol-filled patterns of cells in the visual buffer. The symbols within each cell represent at least some of the following local features: presence of a patch of surface, orientation of the surface, color, texture, and so on. Interpretations are affixed to the patterns of filled cells in the form of sentences which provide a more specific content, for example, whether the imaged object is a circle or a square, or, in more complex cases, a duck or a rabbit. I have elaborated this view in detail in another work.[22] So, I shall not pursue it here. I conjecture that bodily sensations generally, perceptual experiences, and imagistic experiences all have their contents encoded in arrays of the sort I have described.

I should perhaps emphasize here a point I made earlier in connection with after-images. On my view, although the processes responsible for filling the arrays in both bodily and perceptual sensation do not essentially require belief or thought, they certainly involve categorization. Consider, for example, the sorts of categorization that go on in very early vision, for example, the detection of edges and the computation of distance away—categorizations that are relevant to how the visual buffer is filled. These categorizations are automatic. They do not demand that the creature have beliefs or thoughts about the properties of visual stimuli that are represented in such categorizations. Much the same is true, I maintain, in the case of bodily sensations. So nothing in the proposed account entails that a very small child or an animal could not feel pain. Their relative conceptual impoverishment does not preclude them from undergoing processing and representations of the sort necessary to fill some portion of the appropriate array.

What about the sentences that are appended to the arrays? Is thought or belief involved here? Again I am inclined to suppose that in at least *some* cases, the further categorizations that take place here do so without the creatures applying any concepts (understood as involving a public language or thought). Consider, for example, the case of simple shapes in perceptual experience. Nothing looks square to me, unless the appropriate processes have operated upon the filled cells in the visual buffer and categorized them as representing a square shape.[23] But it is not necessary that I think (or believe) of the object I am seeing that it is square. Indeed, I need not have any thought (or belief) at all about the real or apparent features of the seen object.

Perhaps it will now be said that it is not clear how the model I have out-lined accommodates the well established fact that pain is susceptible to top-down influences. For example, in one experiment, joggers were found to run faster in a lovely wooded area than on a track. Apparently, they experienced less pain in their arms and legs while viewing the trees and flowers, and as a result, ran at a quicker pace.[24] There is also the interesting case of some Scottish terriers raised in restricted environments. Upon being released, Melzack tells us, they behaved as follows:

> They were so frisky and rambunctious that inevitably someone would accidentally step on their tails. But we didn't hear a squeak from them. In their excitement, they would also bang their heads with a resounding smack on the building's low water pipes and just walk away. I was curious, and lit a match to see how they would respond to the flame. They kept sticking their noses in it, and though they would back off as if from a funny smell, they did not react as if hurt.[25]

Anxiety, by contrast, increases the experience of pain, as, for example, when one compares a present injury to some past one.

These facts about pain are no threat to the proposal I have made. They may be explained by supposing that the pain receptor pathway in the spinal column leading to the somato-sensory cortex has a gate in it which is controlled by input from the higher brain centers (the gate control theory).[26] When this gate is partly closed, less information gets through and the feeling of pain diminishes. As it opens further, more information is enabled to pass. Anxiety, excitement, joy, concentration, and other higher level activities affect the orientation of the gate. So, the fact that the experience of pain is, *in the above sense*, cognitively pene-trable presents no real difficulty for my proposal.

Still, there is one very important feature of pain on which I have as yet made only a couple of passing comments: its phenomenal character. In what does the phenomenal character of pain consist? What is the relationship of phenomenal character to representational content?

These are questions I shall address in the final section. My concern so far has been simply to establish the thesis that pains have representational content and to make plausible my contention that pains, like images, are a proper object of study for cognitive psychology. Whether pains have phenomenal features which cannot be representationally or intentionally grounded is a further issue (just as in the case of mental images).

IV

It is usually held that pains have intrinsic, introspectively accessible proper-ties which are wholly non-intentional and which are *solely* responsible for their phenomenal character. Such properties are often called "qualia," although the term is sometimes used in a broader way to refer to subjective or phenomenal features, however they are analyzed or understood. As a general view about the phenomenal character of pain, this view seems to me clearly mistaken.

Consider the following case. As I write, I have a backache. There is something it is like for me to be the subject of this backache. What it is like to be the subject of this backache is, of course, the same as what it is like to be the subject of this backache. But what it is like to be the subject of this backache is not the same as what it is like to be me, even though I am the subject of this backache. Why not?

The answer, I suggest, is that the 'what it is like' context is intensional. Co-referential expressions cannot always be safely substituted without change of truth-value. What creates the intensional context is the intentional nature of phenomenal character or 'feel'. The specific phenomenal character of a state—what it is like to undergo it—is none other than the state's intentional content, or more accurately, in my view, an aspect of that content.

Consider again the above case of a backache. What I experience, in having the backache, is *that* something is wrong in my back, something that is painful. The qualities I experience are experienced *as* features instantiated in some region of my back and not as intrinsic features of my experience. Since it could be the case that there really is nothing wrong with my back, the qualities need not be actual features of my back. Rather they are features my experience *represents* as being tokened in my back (for example, the feature of being such-and-such a sort of disturbance). Moreover, these features are not intrinsic properties of my experience which I mistakenly project onto part of my body. There is no general error embedded in pain experiences.

Now the phenomenal character of my pain intuitively is something that is given to me via introspection of *what* I experience in having that pain. But what I experience is intentional. Witness the 'that'-clause used in the specification of the experience in the second sentence of the last paragraph. So, phenomenal character is intentional.

Consider next the phenomenon of transparency.[27] Why, when you turn your gaze inward and try to focus your attention on *intrinsic* features of your pain experiences, do you always seem to end up attending to *what* you experience, namely that such and such a body part hurts in such and such a way? Suppose you have a pain in a thumb. Whether or not there is anything wrong with your thumb, you experience a painful disturbance in it. Careful introspection of your experience reveals only further aspects of *what* you experience, further aspects of its representational content. The experience itself is transparent. Why? The answer, I suggest, is that your experience has no *introspectible* features that distinguish it from other experiences over and above those implicated in its intentional content. So, the specific phenomenal character of your experience—itself something that is introspectibly accessible—is identical with, or contained within, its overall intentional content.

Still, if the distinctive phenomenal character of pains is an aspect of their intentional content, just which aspect is this? What is *phenomenal content*? This is a complex question which I take up fully in a forthcoming work (see Tye forthcoming 1995). In the present essay, I can make only some very schematic remarks.

In my view, phenomenal content is abstract, nonconceptual, intentional content that is poised for use by the cognitive centers. The claim that contents relevant to the phenomenal character of pains (and other sensory experiences) must be *poised* is to be understood as requiring that these contents attach to the output representations of the relevant sensory module(s) and stand ready and in position to make a *direct* impact on the belief/desire system.

This view entails that no belief could have phenomenal character. A content is classified as phenomenal only if it is nonconceptual and poised. Beliefs aren't nonconceptual; and they aren't appropriately poised. They lie within the cognitive system, rather than providing inputs to it. Beliefs aren't sensory representations at all (although on given occasions they may certainly be accompanied by such representations).

The claim that the contents relevant to phenomenal character must be *abstract* is to be understood as demanding that no concrete objects enter into these contents. The reason for this requirement is straightforward. Whether or not you have a left leg, you can feel a pain in your left leg; and in both cases, the phenomenal character of your experience can be exactly the same. So, the existence of that particular leg is not required for the given phenomenal character. What matters rather is the conjunction of general features or properties the experience represents. The experience nonconceptually represents that there are such and such co-instantiated locational and non-locational features, and thereby it acquires its phenomenal character.

The claim that the contents relevant to phenomenal character must be *nonconceptual* is to be understood as saying that the general features entering into these contents need not be ones for which their subjects possess matching concepts. I have already made some remarks pertinent to this requirement.

Exactly which features represented by pains are elements of their phenomenal contents? There is no a priori answer. Empirical research is necessary. The relevant features will be the ones represented by the output representations of the sensory module for pain. We might call features that are so represented in connection with the outputs of the various sensory modules "*observational features*". Since the receptors associated with the modules and the processing that goes on within them vary, features that are observational for one module need not be observational for another.[28] What gets outputted obviously depends upon what gets inputted, and how the module operates. In my view, it is the representation of a certain class of observational features by our pain experiences, and the role that they play, which gives pains their phenomenal character.

Many questions remain here, of course, not the least of which concern the supervenience of phenomenal character upon what is in the head, and the issue of absent qualia.[29] But I hope that I have said enough to show that a wholly representational approach to pains is a promising one.[30]

Notes

1. See Smart 1959.
2. See Block 1983, esp. p. 518.
3. These virtues led me to accept the proposal until very recently. See Tye 1991.
4. See Block 1983, 516-517.
5. There is, I might add, a possible de re reading of this context as follows: F-ness is such that an F image represents that something has *it*. Now, from "I have a red image" and "Red is the color of most fire-engines," "I have an image the color of most fire-engines" *may* be inferred.
6. I might add that, in my view, a necessary condition of any image representing that something is both F and G is that it represent that something is F. So, if I have an F, G image, I must have an F image. The argument for the premise here is straightforward: In having a blue, square image, I experience blue *as* a feature of something or other, a feature co-instantiated with square. *What* I experience, in part, is *that* something is blue. So, my image, in part, represents that something is blue.
7. Phantom limb pain shows that pains do not essentially involve relations between persons and parts of their bodies. This seems to me a decisive objection to the relational view presented in Aune 1967, p. 130.
8. In my view, the representation of damage here is nonconceptual. So, I can certainly see that my leg is damaged without feeling any pain there. In the case of seeing-that, my state involves a belief about damage (and hence the exercise of concepts).
9. According to pain researchers, people who have been given prefrontal lobotomies, or certain other treatments, often report that they feel pain but that they do not mind it or that it does not really bother them. See here Melzack 1961, 1973. These reports, even if taken at face value, are compatible with the proposal in the text. For what they entail, on a literal reading, is that pain can occur without the desire to be rid of it.
10. Cp. Armstrong 1962.
11. I do not mean to suggest here that one cannot have a stabbing pain unless one has the concept of a dagger. Pains, in my view, are non-conceptual sensory representations.
12. I deny that so-called "psychological pains," for example, pains of regret or embarrassment, are really pains. I think it plausible to hold that such states are labelled 'pains' because, like (normal) pains, people are aversive to them. But this usage of 'pain' is, I suggest, metaphorical or analogical. This is not to deny, of course, that real pains may have psychological causes. Embarrassment may certainly *cause* burning facial pain. See here Stephens and Graham 1987, p. 413.
13. The constitution relation is weaker than the relation of identity. A can be constituted by B even though A and B differ in some of their modal properties. See here Tye 1992a.
14. See here Fodor 1975 and 1978.
15. For a detailed development of the above points concerning systematicity and productivity, see Fodor and Pylyshyn, 1988.
16. One such theory is Stephen Kosslyn's Pictorialism. See Kosslyn 1980.

17. Cases of misrepresentation are not rare. Pains in the upper left arm are often due to disturbances in the heart.
18. This is not to deny that other neural regions also play a role in some pain experiences. In particular there are pain pathways which terminate in both the posterior parietal cortex and the superior frontal cortex.
19. For a discussion of the representational differences between sentences, pictures, and maps, see Tye 1991.
20. The characteristics of arrays are examined further in Tye 1991.
21. It need not be assumed that the proper temporal sequence referred to in the last sentence of the text *necessarily* corresponds to the real world temporal sequence. The fact that the inspection routines treat the activity in one cell C as representing a later local bodily disturbance than the activity in another cell C' does not necessitate an implementation via an arrangement in which C is active after C'. For some illuminating comments on the representation of time which can be brought to bear upon this point, see Dennett 1991, Chapter 6.
22. See Tye 1991.
23. For one possible sketch of these processes, see David Marr 1982.
24. See Pennebaker and Lightner 1980.
25. R. Melzack, quoted in Warga 1987.
26. See Melzack and Wall 1965.
27. Transparency has been discussed by a number of philosophers. See, for example, Harman 1990.
28. Moreover, in classifying a feature as observational, I am not supposing that it has that status for all possible species of creatures. Observationality, in my view, is relative to creatures with a certain sort of sensory equipment. Thus, some features that are observational for us might not be for other possible creatures (and vice-versa).
29. See here Tye forthcoming 1995.
30. I would like to thank Ned Block, Gabriel Segal, and especially Sydney Shoemaker for helpful comments.

References

Armstrong, D. 1962 *Bodily Sensations*, London: Routledge and Kegan Paul.

Aune, B. 1967 *Knowledge, Mind, and Nature*, New York: Random House.

Block, N. 1983 "Mental Pictures and Cognitive Science," *Philosophical Review*, 93, 499-542.

Dennett, D. 1991 *Consciousness Explained*, Boston: Little, Brown and Company.

Fodor, J. 1975 *The Language of Thought*, New York: Thomas Crowell. Fodor, J. 1978 "Propositional Attitudes," *Monist*, 61, 501-523.

Fodor, J. and Pylyshyn, Z. 1988 "Connectionism and Cognitive Architecture: A Critical Analysis," *Cognition*, 28, 3-71.

Harman, G. 1990 "The Intrinsic Quality of Experience," in *Philosophical Perspectives*, 4, J. Tomberlin, ed., Northridge: Ridgeview Publishing Company.

Kosslyn, S. 1980 *Image and Mind*, Cambridge, Mass: Harvard University Press.

Lycan, W. 1990 "What is the "Subjectivity" of the Mental?" in *Philosophical Perspectives, 4, Action Theory and Philosophy of Mind, 1990*, J. Tomberlin, ed.,

Northridge: Ridgeview Publishing Company.

Marr, D. 1982 *Vision*, San Francisco: W.H. Freeman and Company.

McGinn, C. 1991 *The Problem of Consciousness*, Oxford: Blackwells. Melzack, R. 1961 "The Perception of Pain," *Scientific American*, 204.

Melzack, R. 1973 "How Acupuncture Can Block Pain," *Impact of Science on Society*, 23, 1-8.

Melzack, R. and Wall, P. 1965 "Pain Mechanisms: A New Theory," *Science*, 150, 971-979.

Pennebaker, J. and Lightner, J. 1980 "Competition of Internal and External Information in an Exercise Setting," *Journal of Personality and Social Psychology*, 39, 165-174.

Smart, J. 1959 "Sensations and Brain Processes," *Philosophical Review*, 68, 141-156.

Stephens, L. and Graham, G. 1987 "Minding Your *P*'s and *Q*'s: Pain and Sensible Qualities," *Noûs*, 21, 395-406.

Tye, M. 1991 *The Imagery Debate*, Cambridge, Mass: The MIT Press, Bradford Books.

Tye, M. 1992a "Naturalism and the Mental," *Mind*, 101, 421-441.

Tye, M. 1992b "Visual Qualia and Visual Content," in *The Contents of Experience*, T. Crane, ed., Cambridge: Cambridge University Press, 1992, 158-176.

Tye, M. 1994 "Qualia, Content, and the Inverted Spectrum," *Noûs*.

Tye, M. forthcoming 1995 *Ten Problems of Consciousness*, Cambridge, Mass: The MIT Press, Bradford Books.

Warga, C. 1987 "Pain's Gatekeeper," *Psychology Today*, August Issue, 51-56.

Philosophical Perspectives, 9, AI, Connectionism, and
Philosophical Psychology, 1995

CONSCIOUSNESS EVADED:
COMMENTS ON DENNETT[1]

Colin McGinn
Rutgers University

Several hundred pages into Daniel Dennett's *Consciousness Explained* (Little, Brown and Company, 1991) I found myself wondering why I still had no clear idea about exactly what Dennett was saying. What was being proved and how was the proof meant to go? I had, I suppose, got some idea of the agenda, the drift, the rhetorical intention: but it would be hard for me to teach a class explaining what Dennett was for in the book and what he was against. I could see no plain answers to plain questions, at least on the major issues. The science was explained clearly enough, by and large, but when the philosophy came in everything went fuzzy. Then, on the very last page of the book (before the appendices), appeared a startling admission, which helped explain my former perplexity:

> 'My explanation of consciousness is far from complete. One might even say that it was just a beginning, but it *is* a beginning, because it breaks the spell of the enchanted circle of ideas that made explaining consciousness seem impossible. I haven't replaced a metaphorical theory, the Cartesian Theater, with a *non*metaphorical ("literal, scientific") theory. All I have done, really, is to replace one family of metaphors and images with another, trading in the Theater, the Witness, the Central Meaner, the Figment, for Software, Virtual Machines, Multiple Drafts, a Pandemonium of Homunculi. It's just a war of metaphors, you say—but metaphors are not "just" metaphors; metaphors are tools of thought. No one can think of consciousness without them, so it is important to equip yourself with the best tools available. Look what we have built with our tools. Could you have imagined it without them?' (p. 455)

Assuming that he means this business about metaphors literally, and not metaphorically, we are being told that the earlier theses and arguments were not intended to state the literal truth; nor was the view attacked a literal statement of a factual claim; nor was the attack a form of direct argument. Rather, an 'enchanted circle' was being breached by setting up one class of non-literal images and 'trading it in' for another class of non-literal images. And indeed, to my mind, much of the earlier formulation looked like hyperbole and caricature at best and sheer unintelligibility at worst. Since I find it impossible to discuss theoretical issues in the figurative way Dennett practices, I propose to do something very plodding instead: I shall give what I take to be a literal sober description of the salient facts about consciousness, doing little more than articulating common sense, and then try to determine whether any of Dennett's metaphors and tropes fit or omit any of this dull stuff. That is, I shall try (i) to see whether his targets correspond to anything in this literally true description, and (ii) to see whether his positive view is adequate in the light of it. Not to keep you in suspense, I think that he caricatures the correct view, so that only the caricature, not the view, is shown faulty, and also that his own account of consciousness is very inadequate. So I suppose I am saying—with the caveats noted above—that there is a middle ground, which is not done justice to in Dennett's Battle of the Metaphors. But a lot of this will involve guessing and paraphrase on my part, since, as I said, I don't really understand most of what Dennett is saying most of the time. In fact, I found *Consciousness Explained* about the most baffling philosophy book I have ever read; quite unpindownable. Whether any of this will prove useful depends upon how gripped you are by Dennett's way of dealing with these issues.

So, let us state some simple truisms about consciousness. First, it is literally the case that people and some animals have bodily sensations and perceptual experiences and conscious thoughts. You can tell from your own case that this is so, and (barring scepticism about other minds) you have good reason to think it is true of others. These can be called 'states of consciousness,' and if we want a handy term with some generality we can say they are cases of 'seemings'. These states can exist whether any one else ascribes them to the subject who has them, so that you can have a pain even if no one else says or thinks that you do. They can also be possessed, in principle, whether or not the subject himself does or can self-ascribe them: an animal can be in pain even if it lacks the concept of pain and so cannot formulate the thought *that* it is in pain. The experience, then, is not the same as the belief that you have the experience.

Not only are there such states and episodes; there is also, literally, a subject who has them—a self or person in the human case. When a pain is experienced *someone* experiences it. When the subject of a conscious state has the concept of that state, and things are otherwise normal, he almost invariably knows that he has the state; so when a normal human being has a sharp pain he is pretty much guaranteed to know that he does at the time of having it. Others are not in this enviable position since the subject might, by behavioural suppression, conceal his possession of the state from others. The knowledge that we have about these states—often called 'introspective knowledge'—is not based on a form of sensory observation. This is shown in the obvious fact that we do not have characteristic modality-specific experiences *of* these conscious states; so we don't *perceive* them in the way (say) vision makes us perceive things around us. The subject of the experience comes to know, introspectively, that he is having the experience; but this does not consist in the operation of any kind of 'inner eye' that perceives the states of consciousness in question, since if that were so there would have to be quasi-visual states corresponding to this inner organ—and there aren't any such.

The states that we thus know about are preceded and followed by other states that are not similarly states of the subject's consciousness; they are states purely of the nervous system, described at different levels, and we don't know about these by introspection. So some of our brain states correspond to states of consciousness while others do not. Moreover, not everything we are conscious of is at the same level of focal attention: some things are centrally attended to, while others are more peripheral. There can also be some vagueness as to whether we are in one sort of conscious state rather than another—as with sensations of intermediate shades of colour. Still, it is typically quite clear whether we were in a certain conscious state during a certain time interval— about as clear as the onset and duration of other sorts of event or process. Conscious states like pain begin at a particular time and end some time later.

The range of concepts we have for experience is quite sensitive to the kinds of experience we actually have, so that it is very difficult—in some cases it may be impossible—to frame concepts for experiences that we don't have, or have nothing similar to. This is connected to the fact that what we can imagine in the way of experience is rather strongly constrained by the kinds of experience we have, these providing the raw materials for our experiential imaginings.

We have discovered that conscious states are affected by neural states of the brain, in that changes in the latter give rise to changes in the former. However, our concepts of conscious states are not themselves neural concepts, so that there is a real question about whether the reference of the two sorts of concept might be the same; and this question looks pressing when we notice that conscious states appear to have many properties apparently not possessed by neural states generally. How it feels to the person in pain is certainly not the same as how his brain looks to an observer. Hence there is a mind-body problem. At present we have no real understanding of how the firings of neurons could subserve conscious states—or whether indeed this is true in any interesting sense. This lack of understanding then naturally fuels dualistic thinking, despite the unappealing aspects of that position. In any case—not to get too theoretical about it—mind certainly *seems* very different from matter, which is why we find it puzzling from a materialist perspective. Yet, whether or not this appearance is illusory, we can be confident of the existence of conscious states: we talk to each other about the ones we are in; we notice their onset and cessation; we cite them in explanations of behaviour. Waxing mildly philosophical, we assert that the existence of conscious states is one of life's few certainties.

So far, so boring. How much, if any, of this is Dennett contesting? It is hard to say. But, I suspect, quite a bit, by implication at least. He seems to think these platitudes are, or are based upon, a dispensable piece of Cartesian baggage—covert reflections of the myth of the pineal interface. He holds that lurking in the kinds of things I said above is a commitment to something called the Cartesian Theater. This phrase gets a number of different definitions, mostly scare-quoted and metaphorical, but I take the operative idea to be that there exists an inner sense that perceives our conscious states—an 'audience' that gazes upon an 'internal stage'. This is admitted to be a view that no one explicitly holds, though Dennett assures us that it lies behind much of what people do hold—including, apparently, the kinds of tame things I said above. *Apparently*, he thinks it lies behind the idea that there is a distinguished subset of neural events that correspond to one's current state of awareness; even behind the idea that a certain event took place within my consciousness during some given time interval. In other words, these innocuous-sounding claims are tainted with the myth of the inner observer.

Well, I fail to see that any of that is so. I myself find the idea of an inner spectator perceiving my conscious states to be plainly absurd, and I don't think anything I said above is committed to it. In particular, to allow that we have introspective knowledge of our conscious states is not to be committed to it: that is just one (bad!) theory of how such knowledge comes about. To repeat what I said earlier: we do not have sensory states whose content represents what is going on in our consciousness; so we don't *perceive* these states. We know about them *without observation* (as Wittgenstein insisted)—plausibly, by virtue of a direct causal link between the state and the belief that we are in it. If a perceptual model of introspective knowledge is the Cartesian Theater, then clearly there is no such thing. But not much follows of interest from this. Certainly it does not follow that there is no firm boundary between conscious and unconscious events; nor that consciousness is not subserved by some discrete locus of neural activity in the brain. Indeed, I don't see how rejection of such a boundary, or denial of such a locus, is incompatible with the myth of the inner observer. That entity might well be neurally dispersed and blurry of vision. Actually, the Cartesian Theater metaphor, so construed, looks to me like an exceptionally scarlet herring serving no useful theoretical purpose. I don't know why we are even considering it. Nobody believes it; it is absurd; and nothing worth taking seriously presupposes it. Its only purpose appears to be that of polemically tarring non-absurd views with the same brush by the method of sloppy definition. Let us be clear, then, that the notion of a well-defined stream or field of consciousness in no way implies that there has to be an inner observer who perceives it; though there may well have to be a subject who *has* such a stream or field—he whose states are at issue. I could not rid myself of the feeling that Dennett roundly conflates these two ideas throughout the book, making illusory hay from the conflation.

Dennett seems to think that he has another metaphor or theory that stands opposed to the Cartesian Theater—the Multiple Drafts view. As far as I under-stand it, this says that the brain produces many representations in its processing activities, revising them in the usual partly bottom-up partly top-down way. It does this in parallel and collates its results. This seems to me quite fine and dandy—and indeed to be a fairly standard approach in cognitive science—but I don't see that it has the kinds of theoretical consequence Dennett attaches to it.

First, why should the multiplicity of the drafts preclude the idea that there is some reading going on by a central homunculus? Not that that is a remotely sensible idea—it's just the inner observer again: my question is why parallel drafts should rule out a chief editor. There is simply no logical opposition here, unless it is just stipulated that there is no single conscious reader of a particular draft. Nor is there any inconsistency with the claim that some of the drafts are conscious while some are not. So Multiple Drafts seems to me a toothless truism, in the present context of dispute, and the Cartesian Theater is a straw man.

What Dennett needs to say—and I am still not sure that he is willing to say it—is that among all the informational states present in the brain at a given time there is just no distinction, firm or loose, between those that reach consciousness and those that do not. This strikes me as obviously false empirically, but in case it is necessary to establish the point just consider vision. According to the usual computational conception, the brain generates many representations as it processes retinal input, where there is no awareness of these representations. After a short time you see something: you are aware, say, of a red sphere in front of a blue curtain. This latter is a conscious state, while most of what led up to it was not conscious. Isn't this perfectly obvious? If MD is inconsistent with this, then MD is mistaken.

Second, I don't see how MD is supposed to be a theory of consciousness at all, i.e. a theory of how the brain contrives to generate specifically conscious states. Either it is silent about what produces conscious states or it flatly denies that there is any distinction between conscious and unconscious states. If the latter, then it is plainly absurd, and amounts to a radical form of eliminativism. If the former, then it is just a claim about how the brain processes data and does not even purport to account for what makes some states conscious and some not. I suspect that what Dennett is really doing is inviting us to make do only with the theoretical resources available from the MD conception—asking us to speak that way alone and forget about whether any of the drafts are conscious, and if so in virtue of what. Well, I reject the invitation, since I think we would miss out on some important facts if we adopted Dennett's linguistic proposal—such as whether a given brain state has the property of being conscious. MD isn't a theory *of* consciousness in Dennett's hands; it is a disinclination to acknowledge consciousness.

Dennett spends many fanciful pages extolling the idea that our first-person reports of conscious states are fictional in import—that the subject-matter of these statements is ontologically on a par with fictional objects like Sherlock Holmes. We are making up characters and episodes as we go along, spinning a fictional tale. This is clearly false, however: when I tell the dentist it hurts I do not intend to spin him a yarn, nor does he take my speech act in that way. If that were the correct interpretation of my utterance, there would be no question of his doing anything to stop the pain. (Compare a child's game in which one pretends to be in pain.) No, my utterances are meant with urgent literality: I really am in pain; I am not engaging in any kind of pretence; I am reporting a simple fact, as straightforward as the cat's being on the mat. Nor am I intending to base a fictional tale around the admittedly real events that are occurring in my brain, like taking a fictional character from real life. And this is not a small point in the Dennett world-view, since he regards this thesis about first-person ascriptions as essential to his position—as one might well agree that it is. He *has* to regard conscious states as fictional or else there would be some real thing that was not explicable within the terms he accepts. Once again, conscious states are being erased not explained.

And it is not just conscious states that are treated as fictional; Dennett also declares that the self is a mere 'centre of narrative gravity'—as it were, a fictional entity of which we are especially fond. Taken literally, this has to be false, of course, on pain of not distinguishing real people from fictional ones. But one assumes that the talk of fiction here is itself metaphorical or non-literal. Perhaps it is only fictionally true that people are fictions, so that literally they are real! This opaque metaphor is never cashed, and I really don't know what it is supposed to imply. Can it be the suggestion that I am to be defined as the fictional character I talk about the *most*, with Humbert Humbert of Nabokov's *Lolita* coming in a close second (I teach a class on him)? Presumably such a doctrine requires no *reductio*. The view appears to go along, in Dennett's mind, with the claim that selves are cultural not biological products: but then it is hardly correct to say that human artifacts in general are *fictional*. More tendentious conflation, it would seem.

Sometimes Dennett expresses himself by saying that consciousness is a 'virtual machine', where I take it he means to adopt the familiar kind of software functionalism. Conscious states are construed as states of a running computer programme; and the property of being a conscious state is identical with the property of being a 'virtual machine' state. Now here we need to make a distinction. Conscious states may well be computational states, in the sense that they play a role in a rule-governed sequence of operations that may be abstractly described using the language of computer science. But of course it is a non-sequitur to infer that their *being* conscious states just consists in this: for they may have two sorts of property—computational and conscious—without there being any reductive or explanatory relation between these distinct properties. Presumably Dennett is holding out for the stronger thesis, though his statements tend to be ambiguous on this (crucial) question. Anyway, I fail to see how he substantiates his claim that conscious states are nothing more than machine states. Obviously this is not in itself sufficient for consciousness, or else you could buy conscious machines at the corner store; and saying that 'complexity' is the missing ingredient is blatant handwaving, no kind of theory at all. Nor does it help to install machine states that monitor other machine states. Nor is it enough to point out that AI specialists have made some machines that do things like some of the things human beings do. Despite some vituperative pages on Searle's Chinese Room argument, Dennett manages not even to state, let alone answer, the core of Searle's point—namely, that programmes are specified purely syntactically but mental states have semantic properties. But, more generally, no serious effort is made to show how the phenomenal features of conscious states can be accounted for in terms of operations on symbols.

And here perhaps the matter comes to a head. For on the crucial question, long deferred by Dennett, of whether he really believes in such phenomenal properties as the smell of a rose, we get a very puzzling answer: that there only *seem* to be such seemings, but really there aren't any. He writes: '*There seems to be phenomenology.* That's a fact the heterophenomenologist enthusiastically concedes. But it does not follow from this undeniable, universally attested fact that there really *is* phenomenology.' (p.366) Well, I would have thought that it did follow, at least if Dennett is using language normally, since it is self-contradictory to say that there are no seemings but that it seems there are. That's like saying there are no feelings such as the feeling of pain but there are feelings *of* feelings of pain; or that there are no beliefs just beliefs in beliefs. One sees here how far Dennett is driven to go by his basic position. Anyway, there surely is phenomenology, if all we mean by that is that people have experiences. I suspect that Dennett denies even this, but he remains obscure on this simple question.

A point to which Dennett attaches considerable importance concerns the proper interpretation of perceptual phenomena in which something is seen in a way that it could only be if the subject had already processed a later stimulus— as with illusions of movement brought about by the successive presentation of stationary stimuli (the 'phi phenomenon'). Dennett wonders whether this happens because the later priming stimulus is consciously perceived but then quickly forgotten, or whether it is preconsciously recognised and then influences conscious events. His suggestion is that there is no fact of the matter about this, since nothing available to the subject himself could settle it; so there is no fact of the matter about whether a given event was conscious. It seems to me very far from clear, however, that no evidence could be brought to bear to decide the question, tricky though it may be to obtain it, and my bets would be on the latter type of interpretation. But the philosophical point I would make is that Dennett's argument appears to have the same form as the following: since no conceivable empirical evidence could decide whether the world came into existence five minutes ago with all our memories intact as opposed to the usual assumption, there is no fact of the matter about it. And I would say there surely is a fact of the matter about whether I had a pain yesterday, whether I can remember it or not. Whether my consciousness contained a certain event is as hard a fact as any (we are not considering vague cases here); my memory of its occurrence is as may be. Dennett appears to want to use his claim about the phi phenomenon (and similar oddities) in order to undermine the idea that there is *ever* a fact of the matter about what my experience contained during a given time interval. But it seems to me perfectly obvious that in standard conditions there is such a fact: I am aware of some things now and not aware of other things. Can this be seriously disputed?

One aspect of the book I applaud: it views the human mind as an evolutionary product—as serendipitously manufactured according to the usual principles of natural selection. It is a kind of hotch-potch of function and side-effect, lucky accident and idle biological junk (not to put too fine a point on it). But Dennett is reluctant to accept that this point of view also applies to the very effort of understanding upon which he is engaged. He proceeds as if his intellect were somehow above the storm, as if it were detached from the usual laws of biology. But our conscious understanding of nature is as much a product of evolution as consciousness itself—indeed, it is simply a special case. (Even Descartes, for all his non-naturalism, recognised that human understanding has limits.) But Dennett cannot stomach psychological naturalism when it threatens to thwart his own desire to explain everything. He never takes seriously the possibility that that bag of evolutionary tricks in our heads might not be capable of explaining everything about itself; indeed, he dismisses any such suggestion as 'mysticism', a perverse wish to keep the mind free from naturalistic scrutiny. It is, of course, the exact opposite of that: it simply applies naturalism to the faculty of human reason, as well as to other aspects of our mental lives. However, this is an axe I have ground sufficiently elsewhere;[2] my point now is merely to note an instructive irony in Dennett's overall perspective. Indeed, I think that his eliminativist tendencies spring precisely from failing to extend naturalism to human theoretical capacities.

Is the generation of new metaphors what we need to make progress in understanding the mind? No, we need literal theories, such as the many now in existence in psychology and associated disciplines. I don't think Chomsky, for instance, would describe his work as mere metaphor. If it turns out that we cannot say anything about certain aspects of mind without the ineliminable use of metaphorical language, then I would take that as a sign that we cannot achieve a proper scientific understanding of the aspects in question. So I suppose I can glimpse a kind of oblique truth in Dennett's metaphorical approach to consciousness, though of course he would not see it that way. In any case, *Consciousness Explained* has a title it nowhere near lives up to.

Notes

Let me take this opportunity to correct a rather gross misrepresentation by Dennett of some remarks of mine about blindsight. In *The Problem of Consciousness* (pp.110-6) I said that a blindsight patient can behave 'much like a sighted person', since such a patient can identify certain stimuli when asked to do so. Dennett bluntly asserts of this remark that it is 'simply false' (p.328, note 4), citing the fact that blindsight patients need to be prompted, unlike normally sighted people. Of course I took it as obvious that they need to be prompted, since (as I noted) they seem to themselves to be blind. My point was simply that *when prompted* they can make visual identifications that are strikingly similar to those of sighted people (though also importantly different)—which is really just to give a canonical description of the phenomenon of blindsight. The lesson I drew from this similarity is that part of their normal visual processing mechanism is intact, a fact I argued to support my claim that ordinary visual perception carries a hidden component.

In any case, Dennett is simply wrong to accuse me of somehow missing the obvious fact that blindsight patients need to be prompted before volunteering their identifications. His glee is therefore misplaced.

1. This paper is a lightly edited version of an invited talk I gave at the APA Eastern Division meetings in Atlanta in December 1993. Brian Loar was my co-commentator on Dennett's *Consciousness Explained*, and Dennett responded. Ned Block encouraged me to publish this talk, about which I had some misgivings, in view of its highly critical content. I hope its photic properties will outweigh its thermal ones.
2. In *The Problem of Consciousness* (Basil Blackwell, 1991), and *Problems in Philosophy: the Limits of Enquiry* (Basil Blackwell, 1993).

*Philosophical Perspectives, 9, AI, Connectionism, and
Philosophical Psychology, 1995*

BASIC MINDS

Kim Sterelny
Victoria University of Wellington

I. Minimal Mentality

Understanding representation in simpler cognitive systems than our own is
important. It is often a good heuristic when interested in some issue to try first
to understand its simple manifestations. Moreover, theories of animal representation are a direct test of theories of human representation: most obviously those
that see a constitutive connection between language and representation. On
plausible assumptions about the limitations of some animal's representational
capacities, theories of animal representation test holist theories of representation,
too. But the issue of animal mental representation is also important in its own
right.

This paper revolves around a distinctive phenomenon and two traditions.
The phenomenon is the break—sharp or gradient—between representing and
merely reactive organisms. The paper focuses on the difference between having
a minimum mind and no mind at all, and on some of the ways minimum minds
can be upgraded. For much animal behaviour is the result of representation of the
world, but not fully intentional representation of the world. For example, Ristau
(1991b) shows that the piping plover's distraction displays are sensitive to
environmental contingencies. She shows the direction of the display is
appropriately linked to the position of the nest and the line of approach of the
intruder and its intensity is linked to the perceived degree of threat both in
closeness of approach and the current and past behaviour of the intruder. Yet
piping plovers obviously are nothing much like a full intention system. Evans
and Marler (1994) show similar restricted but genuine flexibility in chickens'
responses to predators. They respond differently to aerial than terrestrial
predators, and Evans and Marler show experimentally that these responses are not
triggered by a single, simple easily characterised proximal stimulus.

The two traditions are different ways of thinking about representation in the
literature of cognitive ethology. Tinbergen, famously, distinguished the "four
whys" of ecology: evolutionary history, current adaptive function, development
and proximal causation. On one conception, representation is wholly within the

domain of evolution and function. On these views, in attributing representational capacity to an organism, we commit ourselves to very little about the proximal mechanisms of behaviour. Millikan gives an account of representation which counts plants and bacteria amongst the informavores. Jerry Fodor also defends a wholly externalist theory of content. X is a cow representation in virtue of an X-cow relationship. Yet he wants to restrict the class of representation users to organisms whose mechanisms of behavioural control are suitably complex: paramecia do not represent their world (1986, 1990). In a recent paper, Allen and Hauser argue that Millikan's view of representation is at best incomplete on the grounds that it counts acacias as representing their world. On these views, then, representing one's world is something to do with the proximal mechanisms of behaviour. Dretske, in his 1988 restricts representation to learned representation. This is a developmental rather than proximal constraint, but nonetheless implies a different conception of why we talk of representation.

My aim, then, is to evaluate these two traditions of thinking about represen-tation, and through that, explain the distinction between organisms that represent their environment, and those that merely react to it. On the basis of that distinc-tion, I explore one example of upgrading basic minds. One major debate in primate psychology is over the alleged capacities of the Great Apes[1] but not monkeys to represent others' minds. I use the machinery developed to distinguish between representational and other biofunctions to motivate a tentative solution to this debate.

I begin with the simple end of the representation spectrum. When does representation begin? A fruitful set of examples are the complex behavioural patterns amongst the arthropods. The behavioural complexity of the bee's dance is well-known. Distinct components of the dance covary with distance to a nectar source, direction to the source and value of the source. There are many other examples. According to Holldobler and Wilson (1990 pp. 272-273), fire ants have an equally rich system: their odour trails carry information about direction and distance, and the number of ants using the trail carries information about the value of the food resource or of new nest sites. Desert isopods live in family groups densely—sometimes very densely—aggregated in suitable terrain. In natural circumstances, the foraging range of an isopods may include up to 10,000 other individuals. The family share a burrow—an absolutely essential resource—which is vigilantly and rigorously guarded from all others. No alien is ever admitted to a burrow. The burrow guard inspects and recognises kin in virtue of the "chemical badge" of each individual: a mix of individual and acquired traits that signals to the guard that the advancing isopod is kin. The badge in natural circumstances varies very precisely with family membership (Linsenmair 1987).

Communicative behaviour is another good avenue for seeing our way into the problems here. These are often seen as paradigm representations: hence Griffin's slogan (1991 p3) that communication is a "'window' on animal's thoughts". That slogan makes good sense if signals really are representations, and if signalling is information flow. The information that comes out of an animal's mind in communication is a sample—possibly a rich sample—of the information in it. So Ruth Millikan treats communicative signals as representations, even when the communicating organisms are not paradigms of intellectual power. Her paradigm representations (1989) are the beaver's warning splash and the honey bee dance. So what is claimed in claiming that a bee's dance represents the location and value of a food resource, a fire ant's trail the location to a new nest site, or a badge family membership? Is this is claim just about the selective histories of these mechanisms or does it also depend on the proximate mechanisms of behavioural control? I begin with the proximally neutral conception of representation, and shall suggest that even those who are liberal about representation should be cautious about assuming that communication involves representation.

II. Selective History and Proximal Mechanism

Two liberals about representational capacities are Peter Godfrey-Smith and Ruth Millikan. Godfrey-Smith (1991 and forthcoming) revives the Spencer-Dewey hypothesis that representational capacities evolve in response to environmental complexity. Thought is an adaptation to environmental complexity. This hypothesis is not obviously true: we may not have an independent measure of environmental complexity. Moreover, this view of the evolutionary history of cognitive mechanisms does not by itself distinguish representation from other biofunctions. Not every adaptation to complexity is a representation: size or digestive generalisation may be adaptations to complexity without being representations.

But Millikan is the archetype of the teleofunctional liberal. Representational explanation is biofunctional explanation.[2] But what kind of biofunction? She distinguishes between representation producers and representational consumers. Content is determined by use. We have representation when the user can do its job Normally only when the producer goes into a state that covaries with a given environmental condition. The state then represents that condition. So she says "that the representation and the represented accord with one another, so, is a normal condition for proper functioning of the consumer device as it reacts to the representation" (Millikan, 1989, pp. 286-287). For example, the mechanism in our respiratory system that results in panting detects the increase in CO_2 in our bloodstream, but it represents an oxygen shortage, for that shortage is the condition of panting fulfilling its proper function Normally. For something to be representation, there must be something that takes it as a representation, and the content of the representation derives from how it is taken.

So the key idea is that a representation mediates between the producer and consumer in such a way that the consumer cannot fulfil its function Normally, unless the representation is veridical.[3] An ant food recruitment signal means "food" because the recruited ants cannot fulfil their function for the nest, namely of collecting food for the nest, unless the recruitment signal actually signals the existence and location of a sizeable food item. They may of course accidentally stumble on food when following a misinformed ant, but that is not a Normal fulfillment of their function. A similar story assigns content to beaver danger warnings and honey bee food dances.

In my 1990a, I defended a modest version of biosemantics. We should distinguish between a theory of what makes X a representation, and a theory of what X represents, given that it is a representation. I defended a selective history account of what X represents, given that X is a representation. I think part of the problem for Millikan's story is that it collapses these two issues into one. Millikan's theory of representation is beset by serious internal problems. In particular, I think her flagship examples may be misdescribed. For her account of representation sees it as emerging from the interaction of co-operating devices. She may see a representational picture of beaver warnings and the like as unproblematic through a commitment to the classical ethological conception of communication as adapted for the co-ordination of two co-operating individuals. But its at least arguable that picture does not best capture the biofunction of signals, hence will not lead to an appropriate evolutionary theory of signals. In their important 1984 paper, Krebs and Dawkins apply the paradigm of *The Extended Phenotype* to signals, and that leads to problems for Millikan's account.

The Krebs' and Dawkins' conception of communication poses a three way problem for Millikan's conception of bee dance and beaver splashes. Once we see the divergent evolutionary interests between signaller and audience, the idea that communication functions as a flow of information is undercut, and with it the idea that signals are representations. Organisms often alter the behaviour of other organisms. Sometimes this action is direct physical action on the bodies or muscles of an organism. But many organisms make chemicals that act on their audiences' behavioural control mechanisms. Parasites sometimes alter the behaviours of their intermediate hosts in ways that facilitate their move to their definitive hosts. Chemical tools are used within species, not just between species. The suppression of ovulation in subordinate female naked mole-rats is chemically mediated. These chemicals merely function to suppress ovulation: I see no explanatory point in supposing they have the imperative content "Thou Shalt Not Ovulate!". Other operations of one animal on another can have a more benign appearance: food gifts from male to female spiders, or inducing egg formation by extra feeding. Sound can be a tool too, working on an animal's control system through its sensory channels: male canaries induce the development of the partners ovaries by singing (Hinde 1970). Krebs' and Dawkins' picture of communication suggests that we assimilate the canary song to those of extra feeding and other merely chemical causes of behavioural change. If other signals are mere tools like the canary song, the result is an account of communication with no obvious role for representation.

Suppose however that we find principled reasons for resisting collapsing all communication onto mere manipulation. Another problem emerges. Signals do not just pass between co-operating devices. So if we do think that at least some signalling involves representation, it follows that representation is not best understood as involving the interaction of co-operating co-adapted devices. For example, gazelles "stott": they engage in a type of exaggerated and ritualised bounding when they sight an interested predator. If stotting means anything, it means something like "I see you, so don't even try to catch me". Now perhaps we should not think of stotting as communication, or as communication involving representation, at all. But if it fails to be a representation, its not because gazelle and lion are not co-operating. Stotting has as good a claim to being a representation as, say, the ritualised play bows between one coyote and another that take place when one tries to solicit another into the mutually rewarding activity of play.

At first sight, this may seem a problem only for Millikan's choice of examples. But there is another problem that goes deeper. A number of friendly critics of teleofunctional theories of content have pointed out that such theories face indeterminacy problems, for there are more and less specific descriptions of selective regimes and functional outcomes (Bekoff and Allen 1992, Agar 1993, Goode and Griffiths 1994). A different problem for the specification of function arises from the perspective of the *Extended Phenotype*. Adaptations benefit genes, but not necessarily the genes of the adapted organism. Traits are compromises between replicators with at least partially divergent interests, hence their biofunction is less easy to specify. If so, then though signals are a phenotypic expression of the "signalling genes", so too, perhaps, is the behaviour of the audience. The modification in behaviour that is caused by the signal is part of the extended phenotype of the signalling genes. It can be expected to tend to benefit them. It may or may not be beneficial to the receiving organism and its genes. Many interactions are manipulative rather than or as well as mutualistic. Both signal and reception will be consequences of, and hence compromises between, both sets of genes. So when we think, along Millikan's lines, of the Proper Function of the dominant female's pheromones, we must ask: Proper Function for Whom?[4]

In Allen and Hauser's paper, the problem of assigning a function to rhesus monkeys "food calls" emerges very clearly. The reasons to signal are very different from the reasons for responses to signalling. For the respondent, its clear that signals indicate food, and that is the value of responding to calls. Its less clear what the function of giving food calls is, since not calling is a high reward, high risk strategy. Monkeys usually find and punish those that fail to call. But a monkey that gets way with silence gets more. Once we notice that traits can be constructed by the joint operation of replicators whose replication interests are not identical, then assigning functions to those traits becomes much more complex. Moreover, if the perspective of *The Extended Phenotype* is right, it need not just be behavioural traits that are evolutionary compromises between different sets of replicators. This moves the problem of assigning function inside the organism.

Millikan is alive to the danger of an excessively liberal account of representation. She thinks that is one of the problems of indication theories of content. Chameleon skin colour co-varies with background, as does a weasel's fur colour over a year, but neither represent the colour of the animal's background. But Millikan's account is also a very liberal one. It counts ants and plants as representational systems. Acid detectors in the ant represent dead nestmates, for that covariation is the Normal condition for hygienic removal to fulfil its proper function. Plants' daylength detectors represent the approach of spring, for the proper function of those mechanisms that begin spring growth fulfil their proper function only when the triggering condition covaries with seasonal change.

One of the points of this paper is to try to push beyond a clash of intuitions over the liberalism that Millikan recognises and intends. However, I think her account is even more liberal than she intends. It might make any organism a representing system. For all will have some mechanisms tuned to features of their environment on which others depend. Consider, for example nuptial plumage of male birds. These mediate the interaction between male and female. They have the biofunction of attracting mates: perhaps by advertising parasite freedom, good genes or sexy sons. The female can breed successfully only if nuptial plumes veridically represent an acceptable mate. I think its far from obvious that breeding plumes are *representational communications* between the birds: that breeding plumes represent the state of affairs of being a healthy mate even in the same sense that a bee dance represents the location of a good nectar source.

We might bite the bullet on nuptial plumes. But it will turn out that saliva represents food. The production of saliva in the mouth adapts the digestion system to the receipt of food. So it mediates between our mechanisms of ingestion and digestion: our digestive systems can only fulfil their function normally, if saliva is correlated with food. Yet surely this is a nonrepresentational mechanism. I think the relations between many merely physiological mechanisms will meet Millikan's conditions. The cross section of my leg bone will represent my interaction with the gravitational field, for those aspects of my morphology which depend on it for their structural support can only work normally if the cross section is appropriate to the weight it bears.

In a recent paper, Colin Allen and Marc Hauser attempt to repair the liberalism of indicator semantics and biosemantics by distinguishing between "strong" and "weak" senses of information. They believe that the biofunctional and informational readings of signal meaning are too weak for communication to count as a criterion of cognitive complexity. So they propose instead (p. 89) that:

> Signals of type S have strong information content for organism O just in case:
> (i)   tokens of S have weak information content C for O;
> (ii) other structures can have the weak information content for O that a token S has occurred despite the absence of the conditions described by C;
> (iii) other structures can have the weak information content for O that no token

of S has occurred despite the presence of the conditions described by C.

This condition seems too strong. But it is also too weak to demarcate the class of cognitively complex organisms. Any organism that can be conditioned satisfies their conditions, and responsiveness to conditioning is very widespread in the animal kingdom. Consider the growth and decay of the responses of a rat being conditioned to food by the sound of a bell. The fact that this association can decay shows that the rat is sensitive to the pair {bell, no food}. If the rat's rate of spontaneously checking the dispenser is sensitive to the world-head reliability of the bell, then the rat is sensitive to the pair {no bell, food}. Nothing in any of this requires cognitive complexity of any striking nature. There is, after all, no intrinsic reason why their criterion should work. We have no reason to expect a simple strong relationship between the type of phenomenon an organism is behaviourally sensitive to, and cognitive complexity.

I think Millikan's actual specification of biofunction lets in more than anyone should intend. But she has and intends an account in which the evolved systems of behaviour guidance of ants, trees and chimps all count as representation processing devices. These systems represent aspects of the organisms' environment. Fodor, Bennett, Allen and Hauser and others prefer an account of representation in which "reflexlike" organisms do not count as informavores. So let's first characterise the control systems that liberals do and chauvinists do not think of as representation users. I then sketch an argument for a less rather than more liberal account of representation.

In his 1983, Dennett emphasized "performance specifications", characterising different control systems in terms of their different capacities. More recently he has argued that we use the notion of representation to capture "real patterns" exemplified in the behaviour of some systems. The problem however is to say which patterns require representational notions to capture them. Digestive systems exemplify real though noisy patterns. Fodor (1986) and Bennett (1991) have both tried out the idea that representation enables an organism to act, and action is selective response to non-natural kinds. The "real pattern" is a capacity to respond to non-natural kinds, however this capacity is physically realized. This idea puts more strain on the notion of a natural kind that it can bear. Desert isopods can distinguish their relatives through chemical cues, but being a relative of isopod number 47,012 is not a natural kind.

An alternative is to think of the flow of control. On this conception some organisms have a "straight-through" flow, responding to stimuli without contribution from internal storage or feedback. The behavioural mechanisms which produce "vacuum" behaviours—for instance, phantom egg rolling in greyleg geese—look good candidates for behaviours produced without the benefit of feedback loops or input from other sensory modalities. In his 1960, Tinbergen reports elegant experiments which reveal the herring gull's vulnerability to "superstimuli"; they brood oversize dummy eggs in preference to their own, and this might also show simplified control structures. Tinbergen's work on bird behaviour is full of examples of complex behaviours that are triggered by a very simple triggers. Less surprisingly, the same is true of the arthropods. There is a single and simple physical stimulus for nest hygiene, and nest hygiene itself is simple removal. The stimulus can be characterised physically rather than informationally. The behaviour takes place whether appropriate or not, just so long as the simple initiating condition is present. Ants remove dead nest mates when they detect oleic acid the decaying ant releases. Thus a live though acidic ant will be expelled, struggle how she will.

Simple mechanisms result in a fixed though perhaps highly structured response to some stereotypical stimulus. The arthropods provide many examples of organisms capable of a few quite complex behaviours, but capable *only* of those behaviours, and with very little capacity to alter their behaviours when circumstances change. The inputs from these behaviours are "transduced"; there is no internal information contributing to the registration of a stimulus, so a given input produces the same response.

III. Representational Explanation

I think considerations about the explanatory point of appeal to representations support the chauvinist denial that organisms whose behaviour is controlled only by simple mechanisms represent their world. One version of a standard appeal to representation in explanation contrasts the diversity of internal organisations of the mind with the unity of the distal states to which those organisations respond. The internal mechanisms through which we avoid fire, flood and famine may be very different. Yet the behaviours produced are the same, and have the same cause. Despite differences in neural housekeeping, we represent the world in the same way and that is why we behave the same way.

An intuitively useful way of running this idea derives from a distinction drawn by Frank Jackson and Philip Pettit (see e.g. their 1992). They distinguish between **robust-process** and **actual-sequence** explanations.[5] Distinct explanations of the same event can both be important, for they can convey distinct breeds of modal information. In earlier work I have used the origins of the World War I to illustrate this idea. This time, I will illustrate it through a more significant conflict, Australia's victory over England in the 1974-1975 cricket tests. One explanation of this victory would walk us through a play by play description of the tests, detailing each dismissal, run by run and out by out. An alternative would appeal to the strengths and weakness of the opposing sides: in particular, Australia's strengths in fast bowling and fielding. These two explanations do not conflict, and each is of value. The play-by-play explanation is an actual-sequence explanation, for it identifies *the particular possible world* that we inhabit. But if it is true that Australia in that series was much the stronger side, we could know the precise sequence of plays without knowing something very important. Namely, had Australia not won that way, they would have won in another and similar way, with the fast bowlers taking most of the wickets, often to spectacular behind the wicket catches. A robust-process explanation *compares our world to others*. It identifies an important class of counterfactuals. It identifies the feature characteristic of the worlds in which Australia triumphed in the 74/75 series.

When representations are causally relevant, they will be relevant as part of robust-process explanations of behaviour. For example, in two fascinating and convincing books, Franz de Waal charts the shifting balance of power in the Amsterdam chimp colony, and helps himself to richly representational description of chimp mental life on the way. Those representational descriptions are warranted, on this conception, if they are part of a robust process explanation of, for example. Yereon's long struggles to maintain his position. What tracks worlds in which Yereon maintains his central role in the Amsterdam chimp colony? Let proximal stimuli and internal organisation vary as they may, Yereon's worlds will be all—or at least only—those worlds in which he represents and hence responds to nascent alliance between Nikki and Luit. Hence we best explain the patterns in Yeron's behaviour—the alternations of threat and conciliation through which he maintains his position—by attributing to him that representational capacity.

I once argued (Sterelny 1990b; see also Allen 1992) that there was a role for representational notions in comparative psychology, even the comparative psychology of simple organisms. Animals exhibit terrific variation in the structural and computational details of their control mechanisms. Bats and owls hunt the same flying insects at night; possums, bees and honeyeaters forage for nectar; many quite different organisms have enemies in common. Despite differences in internal machinery, their *Umwelts*—their lived worlds—overlap. That overlap explains their behavioural similarities. I am no longer confident of the strength of this argument. In those cases, like the ants, where we do have a genuine biofunctional with different realisations we can recognise the *design* of signals without thereby being committed to the idea that signals represent anything. Though ants differ greatly, the group is unified by both phylogeny and ecology. It is much less obvious that there is a theory of warning behaviour in general. I very much doubt that we have either single cause or single effect in the warning behaviours of arthropods, birds and mammals. The greater diversity in the developmental and proximal mechanisms of behavioural control there is in the group on which we focus, the less likely it is that there is anything that they really share, anything that is a genuine convergence.

Some robust proximal explanations of behaviour require us to identify an organism's represented world. Development points in the same direction. Complex behaviours of even simple organisms involve a developmental trajectory. Since nests may be genetically diverse, "nest smells" are not predictable. Pupa do not emerge with a capacity to recognise nestmates. So virtually all organisms exhibit some form of developmental plasticity. Nevertheless, not all plasticity is alike. Desert isopods learn to recognise nestlings and new instars in a critical period when these hatch or shed their old exoskeletons in the communal burrow. Very likely, this depends on a very specific process.

Consider, in contrast, brushtail possums in New Zealand. These recognise and learn to use a wide variety of foodstuffs. Many initial conditions and proximal histories converge on similar capacities. A robust explanations of their learning history will be representational. A feature of the possum's environment best tracks the worlds in which we get that trajectory. When a very specific proximal stimulus is necessary, then it seems unlikely that a distal property will best track the worlds in which we get that trajectory. Adult vervets fear martial eagles. When they see them, their warning and avoidance behaviours are quite distinctive (Cheney and Seyfarth 1990). If there are a variety of routes through which eagle recognition and appropriate responses to them are constructed, then we should explain this as learning about eagles and how to avoid them. But if the vervet behavioural changes are cued by a few highly specific stimuli, there is nothing about vervet behaviour or change in behaviour that is robustly tracked by a feature of the world which we can take the organism to come to represent.

So there is something right about the idea that developmental plasticity comes in importantly different varieties, and that only some learning is learning to represent the world. Dretske was onto something in suggesting that there are no innate representations. But despite Dretske's use of it, I doubt that the notion of innateness helps demarcate the development of representational from other control systems. The notion itself is foggy, conflating at least the ideas of phylogenetic history, developmental rigidity and genetic control. One notion of innateness does seem to capture something like inflexibility: a capacity is innate when its development is initiated by a minimum and precise triggering experience. A classic example is that of goslings imprinting on Lorenz. These do seem marks of acquisition processes for which a robust process explanation need not rest on a feature of the world which the organism is learning to recognise and respond to. But some "poverty of stimulus" arguments are quite different. Some depend on the capacity of the organism to respond to complex, subtle and degraded information that does not wear its message on its face. The organism could only use that information, the idea runs, if it is cognitively pre-equipped for it. If that is right, there is no conflict between the idea that a developmental process is under the control of innate mechanisms and the idea that its consists in the acquisition of a representational capacity.

A consideration of the point of representation pushes us away from the idea that organisms with simple control systems represent their world. Consider a nest in which an ant has died. Under what circumstances, actual or counterfactual, will that ant be removed. The ant hygiene worlds are not worlds in which ants construct, through various proximal routes, a representation of a dead colleague. Rather, the worlds are tracked by a specific proximal stimulus: ants react to a *particular* decay product. Once initiated, that reaction involves diversity of bodily motions. How an ant removes a corpse, and where it is removed to, depends on the contingencies of individual and nest geography. That is why the ethological description in terms of proximal stimulation and the function of behaviour is robust. Had not an ant removed a corpse then and that way, she or another would have removed it soon and similarly. So a description of the precise sequence of biochemical and neural events would miss something, just as play by play close up of the cricket series does. So Jackson and Pettit's distinction cuts across those of Tinbergen. There is no one "why" of the proximate causes of behaviour. An actual-sequence explanation of (say) chimp behaviour details the transition from stimulus to response, and a robust process explanation turns on what is represented.

So what tracks the possible worlds in which piping plovers feign a broken wing? The flexibility and fine tuning of the display suggests that the worlds are tracked by a representational property: the display worlds are worlds in which the object of the display is a threat to the nestlings. But with reflex-like organisms, the ideas runs, what is robust is proximal stimulus not distal source. What tracks the possible worlds in which isopod number 47,002 is freely admitted to the family nest? Though kinship and badge recognition vary well together, the robust property is the badge, not what the badge is a badge of. Isopods have ingenious mechanisms for kin recognition. But they do not have an equivalent of our perceptual constancy mechanisms. Dretske (in his 1981) pointed out our constancy mechanisms give us multiple routes to stable features of our external environment. That is why our visual systems represent an object's shape not a retinal image. Since isopods have nothing like this, the property that tracks isopod response is proximal stimulus, not the objective property of the world that characterises the selective regime in which the isopod's response mechanism evolved.

Scepticism about isopod representation is not, of course, scepticism about the biological function of the badge. No doubt, that is kin recognition. But just as we could describe the biofunction of ant warning signals without using representational notions, we can do the same for the badge. It functions to admit kin and kin only to the family nest. Indeed, we can use Ruth Millikan's useful distinction between remote and proximal biofunctions to elaborate on them. She applies that distinction to the hoverfly: the proximal function of one of the hoverfly's visual specialisation is (in her view) to locate small moving black dots on its retina; its remote function is to represent the presence of a potential mate (1990). Similarly, the proximal function of the isopod badge is to match a stored chemical sequence; the remote function is to admit only kin to the nest.

So I incline to the view that simple organisms do not represent their world, rather than represent their world crudely. So what then are *representational* biofunctions? They are internal states which do not just have as an effect the detection of features of the environment; they have that effect by design. That internal state is there because, often enough, tokens of the same type enabled its ancestors to respond to that feature in ways that advantaged them by comparison with their less responsive conspecifics. So what is it to *detect* a state of the environment, as distinct from merely reacting by design to a proximal stimulus? It is for there to be sufficient variety in proximal routes, and sufficient stability of distal sources, for the organism's adaptive reaction to the environmental feature to be robust.

IV. Primate Psychologists

In my view, then, we can exploit the notion of a robust explanation to distinguish representation from other internal states that function to guide behaviour. I think the same conceptual tool is useful in identifying not just whether a state is a representation but also what that state represents. One standard worry about teleofunctional theories of content is that selective histories can be specified in a number of ways. (O'Hara 1993). How many times need servals predate vervet ancestors for us to take servals as well as leopards to be part of the selective regime that shaped vervet "leopard" calls? In Sterelny (forthcoming) I recruit the idea of robust explanation to characterise selective regimes. Adaptationist explanation makes a bold empirical bet. Sober and others have characterised it as the bet that other evolutionary forces have been unimportant in the evolution of an adaptation (Sober 1993). In taking the function of ants' formic acid to be defence, we take chance and history to be unimportant in the evolution of that trait. I argue that this mischaracterises the relations between selection and other evolutionary mechanisms: the adaptationist thesis is not that other elements are unimportant, but that the selective regime is robust. Had the variation available to selection, or the developmental or phylogenetic constraints been different, so too would be the evolutionary trajectory of the ant lineage. But if the selective hypothesis is right, so long as we do not vary the selective regime, all these differing trajectories will share a common feature. Adaptationist explanations are appropriate when but only when there is a robust counterfactual feature to be captured, and we capture it when we say what all the ant defence worlds share. So the counterfactual dependence of vervet calling on serval predation is what matters, not its frequency: "leopard" calls mean "leopard or serval" only if the predation by both cats is common to the calling worlds. That is possible: serval predation though rare might push predation to a threshold at which warning calls evolve.

Let's apply this machinery to a central debate in the contemporary primate literature: the idea that chimps and perhaps other close relatives have a theory of mind. The idea is that these primates are aware of themselves, and they are also aware that their fellows represent the world. This second-order representation of other's minds is rich enough to enable them to manipulate other's behaviour by manipulating their minds.

Some of the case histories are very striking. Let me run a few examples to give a sense of the intentional temptations here. Austin and Sherman are two chimpanzees in Savage-Rumbaugh's ape language project. Sherman dominated Austin but was afraid of the dark. Austin was not and would leave their joint cage at night, make strange noises (taping in pipes and windows and the like) then come rushing back into their cage hair bristling. Instead of bossing Austin around Sherman would rush up and embrace for reassurance (Jolly 1988). Some experimental results push us in the same direction. Premack and Woodruff, for example, attempted to test the capacity of chimps to learn a connection between seeing and knowing. After pretrial familiarisation with opaque containers, four chimps were allowed to watch two trainers, as these in turn watched one of two of the containers being baited with food. Only one trainer, however, was in a position to see which container had the food; the chimps were in a position which would have allowed them to see which trainer that was. The chimps were then allowed to a pick a trainer to seek advice from. The right trainer—the one that could see what happened—was always right; by pre-arrangement, the blindside trainer was always wrong. Two of the four chimps mastered the experiment, at least to the extent of a bias towards picking the right trainer and usually following the right trainer's advice (Premack 1988). A key component in the idea that some primates have a "theory of mind" is the social intelligence hypothesis (Byrne and Whiten 1988, 1992; Whiten and Byrne 1988, Byrne forthcoming a and b). The idea is that the evolution of primate intelligence has been driven by the demands of a complex social life. In such a life fitness depends to a very great degree on an appropriate blend of co-operation and competition. Invariant rules of thumb work poorly in social environments. For interaction in social environments is strategic; how others act will depend on your actions and their expectations about your actions. The evolutionary idea, even if right, leaves a good deal open. It is compatible with two views of cognitive architecture. Evolution in a social context may have fuelled an increase in general intellectual and learning capacities. Alternatively, it may have driven the evolution of a specialised capacity to deal with social problems. Moreover, and most importantly for our purposes, the hypothesis has no very direct implications about primate psychologists. Social intelligence requires learning about and representing *the observable social world*: who is aggressive, who can be trusted, who is effective as a coalition partner. These capacities may not require apes to have a theory of mind. The problem that has worried many in this field is that primate knowledge of their social world may be awareness of behavioural conditionals, not mental structures. A solution to this problem requires us to see that the distinction between awareness of behavioural conditions and that of intentional structure is too stark. We should distinguish four hypothesis about the nature of primate mental representation. We can take the Great Apes to have:

i.   The capacity to represent the social organization of, and the relations within their social group—The Weberian Primate Hypothesis.

ii. We can take them to have (only) the capacity to represent a relatively fixed range of behavioural conditionals true of their social partners— The Skinnerian Primate Hypothesis.

iii. We can take them to have the capacity to represent the multi-tracked behavioural dispositions true of their social partners—The Ryleian Primate Hypothesis.

iv. We can take them to have the capacity to represent the complex of motivational and informational states which explain their social partner's behavioural dispositions, and hence, for example, to be able to predict their social partners' behaviours in a wide range of non-stereotypical situations—The Austenian Primate Hypothesis.[6]

There is good evidence that the Weberian Primate Hypothesis is true. But its truth is compatible with any of the ideas represented by (ii) through (iv). The distinction between (ii) and (iii) depends mostly on learning history: as we discover that primates can anticipate conditionals for which they have no specific learning history, we should shift from the Skinnerian to the Ryleian conception of primate capacity. Our conception of the distinction between (iii) and (iv) will depend on general questions in the philosophy of mind. On Dennett's most recent views (Dennett 1991a) metarepresentation is just a threshold of complexity of computational processes involving the social and behavioural relations of self and others. On that view no single functional ability is essential to metarepresentation, or constitutive of it. The distinction between (iii) and (iv) would be one of degree only.[7] A devoted defender of the language of thought (Fodor comes to mind) would take metarepresentation to involve a specific computational mechanism; a particular recursion in the language of thought. Hence there would be a principled distinction between the Ryleian and Austenian hypothesis, however experimentally intractable it was. Either way, the distinction is an important one.

The functional hypothesis that the adaptive value of intelligence is to manage social complexity is compatible with a variety of ideas about the overall architecture of the mind and its representational capacity. It may also be compatible with more than one developmental mechanism. One of the most articulate and vigorous sceptics of the attribution of rich representational capacity to non-human primates is Celia Heyes (Heyes 1993 and b, Heyes 1994, Heyes forthcoming; Heyes and Dickinson 1990). Amongst much else, she argues that many social abilities may be the result of associative mechanisms. For instance, female baboons have been observed to steal meat only from relaxed males and, indeed, to induce this relaxation by grooming. Heyes suggests association may well be sufficient to establish these and similar skills. So she contrasts two conceptions of the baboon. On the one view, the baboon associates relaxation through grooming with the safety of theft; on the other it knows that it is safe to steal when and only when the male is relaxed. But if association is a learning mechanism, it's by no means clear that these are rival views: one is an idea about what the baboon knows; the other, how the baboon has come by this information.[8]

In thinking about primate representational powers, methodological issues are blended with conceptual ones. The central methodological issue is the inference from behaviour to representational capacity. The problem arises for both demoting and promoting hypotheses. The evidence supporting promoting hypotheses—the idea that chimps do have a theory of mind—is typically subject to reinterpretation, with varying degrees of strain, in terms of instrumental knowledge or even conditioning. Similarly, demoting hypotheses can be challenged: our behaviour is far from a perfect reflection of our intentional structures, let alone a perfect reflection of the intentional structures we ought to have: false belief, superstition and weakness of the will intervene. If other primates represent the minds of others, sometimes they will misrepresent them and even when they do not, their behaviour will not perfectly reflect what they know and want. But in practice most of the worry has been about promoting hypotheses: what behaviours enable us to take primates to represent the mental worlds of their conspecifics rather than have mere instrumental knowledge. Cheney and Seyfarth (1991) suggest that though monkeys are sensitive[9] to the behaviour of their conspecifics, they show little sensitivity to what their conspecifics know. In experiments with Japanese macaques, for example, they show that the rates of alarm and food calls are not sensitive to whether the audience is aware of the threats or opportunities. Macaques show not much evidence of a theory of mind.

Heyes thinks that similar considerations apply to the Great Apes. She argues, in my view correctly, that many capacities taken to show a theory of mind can be given a more downbeat reading. Chimps are sometimes alleged to have a theory of not just others' minds but their own: to have introspective self-awareness. One oft-cited item of evidence for this is Gallup's mirror experiments. These purport to show chimps use mirrors to inspect their own bodies, and hence have introspective self-awareness: a capacity to represent their own representations. Even granted the effect is real, they show no such thing. In some sense any organism able to use perceptual input to navigate itself through an environment must be able to represent their own body location. The added sophistication in using a mirror for guidance is not metarepresentation but the ability to use unusual input. Chimps thus may have fewer hard-wired constraints on the sensory input that can be used.

"Perspective-taking" experiments have more potential to persuade. In these, the experimental set-up is supposed to confront a primate with a task whose solution requires the primate to distinguish its perspective on the world from that of another agent. But even these are subject to re-interpretation. In a demanding version of these experiments, chimps watched containers being baited with food in the presence of two trainers. Both were present while a container was filled with food, but Guesser had a paper bag over his head. Both trainers then indicated a container: only the Knower was a reliable guide to the right one. Chimps were allowed to select one container, and two of them managed to learn to (usually) take the one indicated by Knower. The successful chimps were taken to have succeeded in representing the visual world of the trainers (Povinelli 1990). But even here, the chimp may need to know no more than "if he has a bag over his head, take no notice of his guesses". The successful chimps may not know why Guesser's guesses are not accurate. Similarly, Jessie, Premack's chimp who understood enough to remove the blindfold from a trainer rather than simply drag the trainer to the locked container may have understood only the connection between eyes and behaviour, not eyes and the mind. (Premack 1988, pp. 165-165).

Deception also illustrates the problems of inferring from behaviour to capacity. Some of these cases give the Austenian hypothesis terrific psychological pull. A very striking example is that of Nikki and Luit suppressing their signs of anxiety, and concealing their faces until they did, while struggling for control.[10] Engaging tales of sub-ordinate chimps concealing their erections strike a chord. But perhaps all subordinates know is that erections cause attacks. Colin Allen (pers com) made the interesting suggestion that we use pornography to induce erections, and hence test for a theory of mind. If the young chimps have a theory of mind, they should realise that when there are no females around the display of pornography-induced erections will not result in aggression. But even here there is a conjunctive conditioning hypothesis: if I show my erection when there are females around I will be beaten up. When are such suggestions ad hoc? Moreover, we do not want to make the conditions of meta-representation too hard to pass: we can be conditioned in ways that are dissonant with our represented world. A case in point are phobias that the agent knows to be irrational. So Danny might realise he has nothing to fear, but still cover his erection out of a conditioned aversion: a chimp superstition about the ill-luck of showing his erection to his betters.

The cautionary remarks of Heyes are right: many of the deception anecdotes and experiments may show only that primates are good behaviourists rather than good psychologists. But there are a range of increasingly complex appreciations of what others will do. These begin from limited behavioural contingences: if I show my erection he will bite me. A more sophisticated understanding involves a range of conditionals rather than a single one: if I show my erection Mike will be angry, with anger involving quite multi-tracked dispositions. The Ryleian hypothesis, once we distinguish it from the Skinnerian and Austenian ideas, is very plausible. Jolly is surely right in thinking chimp and other primates are aware of others' emotional states, and hence are aware at least of quite complex behavioural contingencies. De Waal's work on primate politics seems to show at least this level of sophistication. Whiten and Byrne point out that some of the most plausible examples of deception involve manipulations of attention, so the Ryleian chimp may be aware of some of the consequences of the fixation of attention and of others' perceptual perspectives. These are all intermediates between mere knowledge of behavioural contingences and paradigmatic representation of others motivational or cognitive states.

Chimps and other primates represent rather than merely react to their social world. The work of Goodall, de Waal, Jolly, and others shows that their response to their circumstances is not under the control of a simple proximal stimulus. They represent their social world in part by representing certain aspects of members of their social group. Let's suppose that selection in social evolution has shaped Darwinian Algorithms in chimps specialised for social life. What is common and peculiar to these selective regimes? What features of their associates have the animals in the chimp lineage responded to over evolutionary time?[11] Birds represent predators, because bird response is tracked best by features of predators, not by features of the proximal stimulus. Similarly chimp behaviour is tuned to dispositions rather than particular stimulus/response conditionals. The perspective-taking experiments do not demonstrate a chimp theory of mind, but they do show that chimps do not need a specific learning history for each circumstance/behaviour pair that they understand. In my view, their representations are Ryleian. Consider Mike, the chimp that invented banging on kerosene tins to make his charges and displays more effective. The interactions around Mike's change in status show both sophistication and its lack. If all Mike knew were a fairly fixed set of behavioural counterfactuals, Mike would have no expectations about the use of kerosene tin banging in display. Equally, his associates would have had no expectations about Mike's jealousy about his new devices. This they would need to learn separately. But equally, the whole story shows a lack of sophistication too. Banging a tin does not make Mike any more powerful. His associates were either superstitious or rather easily tricked. As Dennett has occasionally mentioned, genuinely Austenian primates ought to be puzzled by the behaviour of the trainers. Trainers are weird. Why don't they pull their own blindfold off, or discard the paper bag from their head. The behaviour of the trainers—Trainer Right and Trainer Wrong—in the perspective experiments is pretty odd: standing an equi-distance from the bins with the hidden food, not moving until as string is pulled, then simply handing over food. What could they be doing? What are they up to? An Austenian primate ought be deeply suspicious about these regimes. So I think our best guess is that the selective regime is one in which chimps have acquired a sensitivity to, and the capacity to respond to, complex dispositions of their fellows.[12]

Notes

1.   I apologise for this biologically unsound term: the only group that includes orangs, gorillas, and the two chimps also includes us.
2.   See especially her 1984, 1989 and 1990; I will draw especially on her 1989, as it is the most accessible of her accounts of her ideas.
3.   A second condition is that a signal be part of a representational system; it have a "syntax". But it is easy to meet this condition, since the time and place of the signal—as in the warning slap—can satisfy it.
4.   See Sterelny, Smith and Dickison forthcoming for an attempt to extend the notion of biofunction to cases where traits are influenced by replicators with divergent interests.
5.   They use the terms "comparative" and "contrastive", but this terminology invites confusion, for "contrastive" has been pre-empted by Dretske.
6.   I refer of course to the famous English primatologist, Jane Austen.
7.   Byrne and Whiten, building on the work of Leslie, have argued for a constitutive connection between metarepresentation and other abilities. They think that the capacities for "symbolic play" and for attributing thoughts to others are not distinct

functional capacities but the same capacity differently described. I am very sceptical. For one thing, the category of symbolic play itself strikes me as subject to over-interpretation. Some of the primate anecdotes have terrific appeal: Vicky pretending to pull a toy, and pretending to unsnag it gets a real grip on our intentional imaginations. Leslie (and following him Byrne and Whiten) argue that a chimp pretending that a banana is a telephone involves both representation of a banana and a meta-representation. In my view, pretend play involves two representations—straight and "as if"—of a single object, not a representation of a banana, and a representation of "banana" as a telephone. Moreover, I see no clean difference between these cases and standard mammalian exuberance. The kitten in chasing leaves, say, has dual representations of the leaf, for it does not try to eat the leaf. It does not *just* represent a leaf as prey. And kittens often chase tiny/imaginary gnats—their play does not have to be triggered by a real object.

8. We can drive a wedge between the two ideas if we have a very tight definition of association. So we might define learning as the result of an associative mechanism if there is stimulus generalisation only to physically similar proximal stimuli. Unless there is a specific trigger (as there is in the feeding responses of gull chicks and the like) in the social scene, it is surely unlikely that association narrowly defined will play a major role in primate interactions, as the number, shape, orientation and relations between the interactants will vary considerably from social setting to social setting. So unless there is a specific invariant feature across these social settings (as there might be in male-male displays: distinctive teeth bearing and the like) the social actors need to be sensitive to socio-functional similarities from situation to situation (the alpha male is restless, or aggressive, or distracted) rather than proximate similarities.

9. Sometimes. Vervets continue to give alarm calls long after everyone has responded and fled to safety. So on the assumption that alarm calls mean (ed) "leopard" rather than "I'm scared" even sensitivity to behaviour is rough and ready.

10. De Waal, quoted in Jolly 1991 pp. 239-240.

11. I have presented these arguments in the context of a teleosemantic view of representation. I think, however, that if chimps have their representations of each other in virtue of ontogenetic causation, then the ideas here can be written as a claim about the robustness of causal processes in ontogeny.

12. Thanks to Marc Bekoff and Jack Copeland for their comments on an earlier draft of this paper.

References

Agar, N. "What Do Frogs Really Believe?" *Australasian Journal of Philosophy*, 71, pp. 1-12, 1993.

Allen, C. "Mental Content and Evolutionary Explanation" *Biology & Philosophy*, 7, 1992, pp. 1-13.

Allen, C. & Hauser, M. "Communication & Cognition: Is Information the Connection?" in Hull, D; Forbes, M and Okruhlik, K (eds) *Proceedings of the Philosophy of Science Association*; Volume 2, East Lansing, Michigan 1992.

Bennett, J. "How is Cognitive Ethology Possible" in *Ristau 1991a*.

Bekoff, M. & Allen, C. "Intentional Icons: Towards an Evolutionary Cognitive Ethology" *Ethology*, 91, 1992, pp. 1-16.

Byrne, R. "The Evolution of Intelligence" in P.J.B. Slater and T.R. Halliday (eds) *Behaviour and Evolution*; Cambridge University Press, (forthcoming a).

Byrne, R. "The Ape Legacy" in Goody, E (ed) *Social Intelligence and Interaction*; Cambridge University Press, (forthcoming b).

Byrne, R. "The Meaning of 'Awareness'" *New Ideas in Psychology*, (forthcoming c).

Byrne, R. & Whiten, A. (eds) *Machiavellian Intelligence*, Oxford University Press, Oxford 1988.

Byrne, R. & Whiten, A. "Cognitive Evolution in Primates: Evidence from Tactical Deception" *Man*, 27, pp. 609-625, 1992

Cheney, D. & Seyfarth, R. *How Monkeys See the World*, Chicago University Press, Chicago, 1990.

Cheney, D. and Seyfarth, R. "Reading Minds or Reading Behaviour? Tests for a Theory of Mind in Monkeys" in *Whiten 1991*.

Dawkins, R. *The Extended Phenotype*; Oxford University Press, Oxford, 1982.

Dennett, D.C. "Intentional Systems in Cognitive Ethology: The 'Panglossian Paradigm' Defended" *Behavioural and Brain Sciences*, 6, pp. 343-390, 1983.

Dennett, D.C. *Consciousness Explained*; Little, Brown and Co., Boston, 1991a.

Dennett, D.C. "Real Patterns" *Journal of Philosophy*, 88, pp. 27-51, 1991b.

de Waal, F. *Chimpanzee Politics: Power and Sex amongst Apes*; Harper and Row, New York, 1982.

de Waal, F. *Peacemaking Among Primates*; Harvard University Press, Cambridge, 1989.

Dretske, F. *Knowledge and the Flow of Information*; Blackwell, Oxford, 191.

Dretske, F. *Explaining Behavior: Reasons in a World of Causes*; MIT Press, 1988.

Evans, C.S. and Marler, P. "Language and Animal Communication: Parallels and Contrasts" forthcoming in Roitblat, H. & J. Arcady-Meyer, J. (eds) *Comparative Approaches to Cognitive Science*; MIT Press Cambridge.

Fodor, J.A. "Why Paramecia Don't Have Mental Representations" *Midwest Studies in Philosophy* 10, pp. 3-24, 1986.

Fodor, J.A. *A Theory of Content and Other Essays*; MIT Press, Cambridge, 1990.

Godfrey-Smith, P. "Signal, Decision, Action." *Journal of Philosophy*, 88, pp. 709-722, 1991.

Godfrey-Smith, P. *Complexity and the Function of Mind in Nature*; Cambridge University Press, forthcoming.

Goode, R. & Griffiths, P.E. "The Misuse of Sober's Selection of/Selection for Distinction" *Biology and Philosophy*. forthcoming, 1995.

Griffin, D. "Progress Towards a Cognitive Ethology" in *Ristau 1991a*.

Heyes, C.M. "Anecdotes, Training, Trapping and Triangulating: Do Animals Attribute Mental States?" *Animal Behaviour*, 46, pp. 177-188, 1993.

Heyes, C.M. "Imitation, Culture and Cognition" *Animal Behaviour*, 46, pp. 999-1010, 1993.

Heyes, C.M. "Reflections on Self-Recognition in Primates" *Animal Behaviour*, 47, pp. 909-919, 1994.

Heyes, C.M. "Social Cognition in Primates" in Mackintosh, N.J. (ed) *Handbook of Perception and Cognition, volume 9*, Academic Press, forthcoming.

Heyes, C.M. and Dickinson, A. "The Intentionality of Animal Action" *Mind and Language*, 5, pp. 87-104, 1990.

Holldobler, B. & Wilson, E.O. *The Ants*; Harvard University Press, Cambridge, 1990.

Jackson, F. & Pettit, P. "In Defence of Explanatory Ecumenicalism" *Economics and Philosophy*, 8, pp. 1-21, 1992.

Jolly, A. "The Evolution of Purpose" in *Byrne and Whiten 1988*.

Jolly, A. "Conscious Chimpanzees? A Review of Recent Literature" in *Ristau 1991a*.

Krebs, J.R. & Dawkins, R. "Animal Signals: Mind-Reading and Manipulation" in Krebs, J.R. and Davies, N.B. *Behavioural Ecology: An Evolutionary Approach*; Blackwell Scientific, Oxford, 2nd edition, 1984.

Linsenmair, K.E. "Kin Recognition in Subsocial Arthropods, in particular, the Desert Isopod *Hemilepistus reaumuri*" in Fletcher, D.J. and Michener, C.D. (eds) *Kin Recognition in Animals*; John Wiley and Sons, Chirchester, 1987.

Millikan, R. *Language, Thought, and Other Biological Categories*; MIT Press, Cambridge, 1984.

Millikan, R. "Biosemantics" *Journal of Philosophy*, 86, pp. 281-297, 1989.

Millikan, R. "Truth Rules, Hoverflies and the Kripke-Wittgenstein Paradox" *Philosophical Review*, 94, pp. 323-353, 1990.

O'Hara, R.J. "Systematic Generalization, Historical Fate and The Species Problem" *Systematic Biology* 42, pp. 231-246, 1993.

Povinelli, D., Nelson, K. & Boysen, S. "Inferences about Guessing and Knowing by Chimpanzees" *Journal of Comparative Psychology*, 104, pp. 203-210, 1990.

Premack, D. "'Does The Chimpanzee Have A Theory of Mind' Revisited" in *Byrne and Whiten 1988*.

Premack, D. & Woodruff, G. "Does the Chimpanzee Have a Theory of Mind" *Behavioral and Brain Sciences* 4, 1978, pp. 515-629 (includes commentaries).

Ristau, C. (ed) *Cognitive Ethology* LEA Press, Hillsdale, 1991 (Ristau 1991a)

Ristau, C. "Aspects of Cognitive Ethology of an Injury-Feigning Bird, The Piping Plover" in *Ristau 1991a*. (Ristau 1991b)

Sterelny, K. *The Representational Theory of Mind*; Blackwell, Oxford, 1990a.

Sterelny, K. "Animals and Individualism" in Hanson, P (ed) *Information, Language and Cognition: Vancouver Studies in Cognitive Science*, 1, pp. 323-339, 1990b.

Sterelny, K. "Explanatory Pluralism in Evolutionary Biology" forthcoming in *Biology and Philosophy*.

Sterelny, K., Smith, K. and Dickison, M. "The Extended Replicator" forthcoming in *Biology and Philosophy*.

Sober, E. *The Philosophy of Biology*; Oxford University Press, Oxford, 1993

Tinbergen, N. *The Herring Gull's World*; Basic Books, New York, 1960.

Whiten, A. *Natural Theories of Mind: Evolution, Development and the Simulation of Everyday Mindreading*; Blackwell, Oxford, 1991.

Whiten, A. & Byrne, R. "Tactical Deception in Primates" *Behavioral and Brain Sciences*, 11, 1988, pp. 233-273.

Philosophical Perspectives, 9, AI, Connectionism, and Philosophical Psychology, 1995

HOW SHOULD WE UNDERSTAND THE RELATION BETWEEN INTENTIONALITY AND PHENOMENAL CONSCIOUSNESS?

Robert Van Gulick
Syracuse University

Intentionality and phenomenal consciousness are the two traditional defining characteristics of the mental. Paradigmatically mental states have both, and both serve to anchor our basic concept of what it is for something to be mental. When I have a visual experience of my office laid out before me, my mental state is clearly *about* something or *directed at* something in the intentional sense. My experience is an experience *of* my office. My experience also has a subjective phenomenal aspect; in Thomas Nagel's evocative phrase, there is "*something that it is like*" to have such a experience[1]. From my first person perspective as the one having or undergoing the experience, my office is present to me in a way that involves a rich array of phenomenal qualities.

Thus anyone interested in offering a naturalistic account of mind, that is an account that explains how the mind fits into the natural world without any recourse to magical or unexplained processes, must be prepared to offer both a naturalist theory of intentionality and also one of phenomenal consciousness. However, among analytic philosophers there has been a somewhat schizoid attitude about the status and prospects of the two projects. Many philosophers have treated the two as independent problems and taken a optimistic attitude with regard to naturalizing intentionality while remaining profoundly pessimistic (or at best agnostic) about doing the same for phenomenal consciousness. There has been a great deal of philosophical activity directed at developing naturalistic theories of intentional content with promising results—including teleological theories[2], functional role theories[3], and causal theories[4]. At the same time, the problem of phenomenal consciousness has remained largely intractable and has been regarded by some as not susceptible to naturalistic explanation. Although this dual attitude is widespread, it is far from clear that it defines a viably consistent position. As the philosopher Colin McGinn has observed it is questionable that one can divide the project of naturalizing the mind into two independent projects dealing with intentionality and phenomenal consciousness in isolation from each other[5]. Given the fact that some mental states are conscious, it seems unlikely that we could account for their intentional properties without taking their phenomenal features into account. It does not seems that I could account for the content of my present visual experience as being *of* my office without factoring in how my experience is phenomenally present to me. Nor does it seems likely that I could account fully for its subjective aspect—for what it's like to have such an experience—without regard for its intentional content; that it is an experience of the room where I have worked for the past seven years is an essential part of what it's like for me now to be having this experience. Thus at least with respect to conscious mental states, it is hard to see how one could hope to deal adequately with either of the two defining aspects of mind without also dealing with the other. From which it would seem to follow that if one aspect can not be naturalized then neither can the other. And if we have at present little idea of how to naturalize the phenomenal aspect of mind, how can we be optimistic about naturalizing intentionality?

This problem brings me to the central question of my paper, "If one wants to be a naturalist about the mind, how should one understand the relation between intentionality and consciousness?" I will first consider what I take to be two incorrect answers to the question before offering a more positive reply. The proposed solutions that I will reject both have a certain initial appeal and both have been prominently championed in the recent literature, the first by John Searle[6] and the second by Daniel Dennett[7].

Searle has argued that no state can have intentional content in a genuine and nonmetaphoric sense unless it is at least in principle the sort of state that could become phenomenally conscious. From his perspective, any attempt to provide an account of intentionality that does not bring phenomenal consciousness in right from the start as an essential and ground level property is thoroughly wrongheaded. He argues that we can understand the mind and intentionality naturalistically only when we have discovered how consciousness is caused by and realized in the biochemical structure of the brain, which he believes science will at some point do.

Dennett's view of the relation is pretty much the polar opposite of Searle's. He argues first that intentionality can be explained without any appeal to consciousness, second that there is far less to the phenomenal aspect of mind that is commonly believed, and third that everything real about it can be fully explained in terms of intentional states, mainly in terms of judgements. According to Dennett, the qualitative aspect of my mental state when I look at a red apple in front of me is completely a matter of content fixations that occur within me and judgements I make or would be disposed to make about how the apple compares with other objects and about how my present perceptual state similarly compares with others.

The two views are each extreme in their own way. Searle elevates phenomenal consciousness to an absolutely central role in the entire economy of mind; without it there can be nothing genuinely mental or intentional. Dennett on the other hand marginalizes it as an entirely derivative feature of the mind, one which can be entirely explained in terms of a prior and independent theory of intentionality. The truth I believe lies at neither extreme.

Let us first consider Searle's position and the argument he offers for it. In

The Rediscovery of the Mind he denies the existence, and even the possibility, of mental states that are in principle closed to consciousness. As he puts it, "The claim I will make can be stated in one sentence: *The notion of an unconscious state implies accessibility to consciousness.* We have no notion of the unconscious except as that which is potentially conscious." (italics original)[8] This view is of course in conflict with an enormous amount of contemporary model-building in psychology. Psychologists and linguists regularly appeal to unconscious mental states to explain language comprehension, visual perception, problem solving and a host of other human abilities. And the unconscious states they invoke are often not the sort of which we could become conscious. This conflict does not at all bother Searle because he wishes to discredit such models, at least in so far as the states they invoke are supposed to be mental states. Searle acknowledges that complex psychological processes such as vision will involve many intermediate steps, but he denies that such steps can be mental steps or have intentional content in so far as they cannot be made conscious.

In support of this radical claim he offers his connection argument in seven numbered steps.[9]

1. There is a distinction between intrinsic intentionality and as-if intentionality; only intrinsic intentionality is genuine.
2. Unconscious mental states are intrinsic.
3. Intrinsic intentional states, whether conscious or unconscious, always have aspectual shape.
4. The aspectual feature cannot be exhaustively or completely characterized solely in terms of third-person, behavioral, or even neurophysiological predicates.
5. But the ontology of unconscious mental states, at the time they are unconscious, consists entirely in the existence of purely neurophysiological phenomena.
6. The notion of an unconscious intentional state is the notion of a state that is a possible conscious thought or experience.
7. The ontology of the unconscious consists in the objective features of the brain capable of causing subjective conscious thoughts.

Steps 1-5 are premises intended to support the inference to 6 and 7. According to Searle the first five steps create a conflict or seeming contradiction that can resolved only along the lines provided by 6 and 7. The difficulty as he sees it is that unconscious mental states must have aspectual shapes but their ontology consists entirely in purely neurophysiological phenomena. He argues that steps 6 and 7 offer the only means to ground aspectual shape in neurophysiological fact while accommodating all the facts about the unconscious alleged in steps 1-5.

However, as I have shown elsewhere[10] there are in fact alternative ways of making sense of unconscious intentionality that accommodate everything that is right about steps 1-5. For present purposes, it should suffice to focus on the weakest link in the argument, the notion of aspectual shape which figures in steps 3 and 4.

Aspectual shape is indeed an essential element of intentional states, but just what that involves is less clear. Intentional states represent their conditions of satisfaction in ways that show at least some degree of opacity; specifications of content are not perfectly transparent because intentional states conceptualize and characterize their objects in specific ways. As Searle notes there is a sense in which one can have a desire for water and not have a desire for H_2O even though water and H_2O are one and the same.[11]

However, just how we unpack the notion of aspectual shape can vary widely in application to different types of mental states. Searle's examples involve conscious human states such as seeing a car from a certain angle or wanting a glass of water; such states involve a sophisticated awareness about a finely individuated intentional object. But aspectual shape can apply in cases that involve less determinate content and less self-awareness of content; there need only be facts about the agent or organism that show that it conceptualizes the objects of its states in some ways rather than others. Searle claims that aspectual shape "must matter to the agent"[12] and I agree. But to do so it need only affect how the agent responds or acts. Searle clearly intends more by the claim. He analyzes it in terms of how the agent "experiences a subject matter."[13] But building the notion of experience into aspectual shape would beg the main question at issue. Experiences are conscious, and the dispute is about whether there can be states that genuinely intentional but not conscious.

How we interpret the notion of "aspectual shape" in premise 3 directly affect the plausibility of premise 4. The more we build into aspectual shape; the less plausible we make premise 3. Step 3 is uncontroversial only if we read "aspectual shape" in a weak and general way that does entail any commitment to phenomenal consciousness. However, the weaker we make the notion of aspectual shape the more we undermine premise 4's claim that it cannot be exhaustively characterized in terms of third person facts. Given the crucial importance of this latter claim to Searle's argument, he says surprisingly little to support it. He asserts that behavioral evidence "including even evidence concerning the causation of a person's behavior, no matter how complete, always leaves the aspectual character of intentional states underdetermined"[14] But to back up this claim he merely cites Quine on the indeterminacy of translation[15] and observes that any water-seeking behavior would also be H_2O-seeking behavior. He concludes that there is thus no way behavior could distinguish between wanting water and wanting H_2O. Nor according to Searle would the matter be resolved by appeal to the person's responding "yes" to do "Do you want water?" and "No" to "Do you want H_2O?" since similar problems arise with respect to the agent's use of "water" and "H_2O". Searle implicitly assumes that any account of content based on facts about behavior and its causation must individuate intentional states in a fully transparent way and would thus lack any basis for distinguishing among alternative ways in which an agent might conceptualize the object of his attitudes. But this just isn't so. One might appeal to facts about the overall organization of an agent's behavior and the internal causal structure that produces it to draw just such distinctions, which is just what functionalists do. The reason why it is appropriate to say my six-year old daughter wants a glass of water and not that she wants a glass of H_2O, is that she lacks the many relevant capacities, and behavioral tendencies (both linguistic and nonlinguistic) and internal processing that would constitute understanding the concepts of "hydrogen", "oxygen" and "molecular compounding". At some point she will come to understand those concepts, and when she does it will be in virtue of acquiring the requisite causal organization and behavioral capacities.

Producing a detailed functionalist theory of content would be a difficult task, but fortunately in the present context I don't have to do so. Searle's claim is the very strong one that such facts *can't* provide a basis for distinguishing aspectual shape, and the burden of proof must lie with him. And he has not really shouldered that burden nor shown that contrary to what many believe, no such account can be given.

In evaluating the plausibility of step 4 we must be careful not to let Searle's choice of examples seduce us into reading too much into the notion of aspectual shape. In particular we must not define aspectual shape in such a way that it involves either phenomenal qualities or fully determinate content of the sort associated only with our most sophisticated and linguistically mediated human conscious states. I can desire poached salmon with dill sauce and a glass of 1991 Vouvray, but my cat cannot no matter how much she might enjoy the fish were she to get hold of it. Such finely individuated content is beyond the reach of my cat's intentional repertoire, but she nonetheless has genuinely intentional states that have aspectual shape in their own way. In the same way the unconscious mental states posited by those whom Searle attacks may also lack the finely individuated content associated with my conscious states, but that no more shows they lack aspectual shape than do my cat's desires. Aspectual shape can come in many forms and many degrees; in some cases it involves finely individuated content and phenomenal qualities but in other cases it doesn't. If Searle wishes to claim otherwise, he owes us an argument to show that and I doubt that one can be produced.

Searle thus seems to be caught on the horns of a dilemma: he can use the term "aspectual shape" in a strong sense so that it entails phenomenal representation and fully determinate content or in a weaker sense in which it does not. If he opts for the strong sense, as I believe he does, then premise 3 looks implausible or question-begging. One can agree that intentional states represent their conditions of satisfaction under aspects without needing to assume that in every case those aspects involve phenomenal qualities and fully determinate content. However, if he opts for the second weaker sense and uses "aspectual shape" in a less contentious way, he puts his fourth premise in doubt. Third person facts may be adequate to account for aspectual shape in that weaker sense, especially if they include facts about the multi-level functional organization of the nervous system. What it appears he can not do is read "aspectual shape" in a consistent way that makes both premises 3 and 4 plausible and nonquestion-begging.

If the argument comes apart at this point we need not move to steps 5 and 6 to resolve Searle's alleged apparent contradiction. There need be no conflict between the ontology of unconscious mental states and their status as intentional states with aspectual shape. A functionalist for example could concede that the relevant facts are not sufficient to account for any phenomenal aspect or for fully determinate content while still maintaining that the facts are sufficient to account for how those unconscious states represent and conceptualize their conditions of satisfaction in some range of ways rather than others. Functional facts might thus suffice to account for all there is to account for with regard to aspectual shape in such cases.

In summary, our examination of the connection argument has found that it does not present a sound non-question begging basis for accepting the connection principle. Searle offers a consistent and possible picture of how we might think about unconscious states, but he has not shown that is the *only* way we can coherently think about them. No doubt some unconscious mental states are best analyzed in his favored way as dispositions to produce specific conscious states from which they inherit their content. But Searle has not given adequate reasons to believe that that is the only coherent way in which to understand unconscious mental states. Nor has he shown that the many theorists of the mind who appeal to in-principle unconscious mental states are fundamentally mistaken or confused. Absent some better argument, there is no reason to disavow such states or the many psychological models that incorporate them.

If phenomenal consciousness is not essential for intentionality, just what role should it play in our theory of intentional content. Searle is not alone in holding extreme views on this issue. Though he exaggerates the role of phenomenal consciousness, others surely underrate it. Dan Dennett's view is doubly extreme.

1. First he claims that we can give a complete account of intentionality without any appeal to phenomenal consciousness. His account is in terms of the predictive framework that he calls the intentional stance; to have intentional states with a given content in the most literal and genuine sense it need only be true that your behavior is reliably and voluminously predictable under an interpretation that attributes those states to you and treats you as a close approximation of an ideally rational (or optimally designed) cognitive agent.

2. Second he holds that in so far as there is anything to the phenomenal aspect of mind it can be completely analyzed or explained solely in terms of intentional states—judgements or other types of content fixations—which themselves have no phenomenal qualities. The phenomenal aspect of my mental state when I look at a blue expanse under good light is simply a matter of the sum total of judgements I make and am disposed to make at the moment about the state of the

world and about my own present mental state. He explicitly rejects the suggestion that there could be any facts about how things *seem to me* that are not simply facts about judgements I am disposed to make. If one combines both of these claims then one reaches the extremely surprising (and I would add implausible) conclusion that intentional stance theory is able to account not only for the intentional aspect of mind but the phenomenal aspect as well.

Though few other philosophers are willing to accept the whole of Dennett's quite radical approach, many—indeed perhaps a majority—share his view that phenomenal consciousness is of little if any importance in understanding intentionality. Most mainstream theorists—whether they analyze intentional content in terms of information theoretic relations, teleological relations or functional roles—have little, if anything, to say about the contribution phenomenal consciousness might make to our understanding of intentionality. In some cases they explicitly deny that it plays any significant role[16], though far more often that attitude can be inferred implicitly from the fact that their theories are largely silent on the issue[17]. Few are willing to go as far as Dennett and propose that we can use a nonphenomenal theory of intentional states to completely reduce or explain the phenomenal aspect of mind without a residue. Like Ned Block, they are more inclined to favor a two pronged strategy which explains the intentional and the phenomenal in independent and fundamentally different terms. Block, for example, suggests that intentionality can be explained by a two factor theory that combines internal functional roles with external environmental and social relations[18], but he believes that the explanation of the phenomenal will require a much less abstract appeal to the neurochemistry of the brain.

I suppose that on some principle of academic justice I ought to offer as detailed a critique of Dennett's view as I have of Searle's . Nonetheless I will not do so, since it would require at least the balance of this paper. Moreover, for present purposes the relevant target is not Dennett's specific theory but the more moderate and widely shared general view about the relative unimportance of phenomenal consciousness in understanding intentionality. In brief what I find puzzling about the general strategy is its assumption that we can construct a more or less complete theory of intentionality while shaving off the phenomenal aspect of mind to be handled separately in isolation. As I noted at the outset, it seems unlikely that we can account for the aboutness of conscious phenomenal states without taking into account the subjective aspect of what it's like to be in them. Thus in so far as such states comprise a very major—though admittedly proper—subset of our mental states, we can not hope to arrive at a comprehensive account of intentionality without addressing its relation to the phenomenal.

The general strategy seems to rely implicitly upon what Colin McGinn has called the "medium conception"[20], i.e. the view that phenomenal consciousness is simply one medium among others which might be used to carry or embody intentional content and that any content which it does carry could just as well be carried by some other states devoid of any phenomenal aspect. The medium theory reduces consciousness to the role of merely contingent carrier of a more or less accidentally defined range of intentional contents. As such it would hold little prospect for shedding any real light on the nature of intentionality. McGinn's compares the view with one we might take of sentences; written or spoken sentences have a given shape or sound but they also have a meaning. Those shapes or sounds provide the medium for expressing the meaning, but medium and message can vary along independent dimensions. McGinn puts the point like this,

> The content is *expressed* in a particular conscious medium but we can in principle separate the properties of the medium from the message it carries. What it is like to have the experience is thus fixed by intrinsic features of the medium, whereas what the experience is about is fixed by certain extrinsic relations to the world. ...Consciousness is to be conceived, in effect as a mysterious medium in which something relatively mundane is (contingently) embedded.[21]

I agree with McGinn that once stated explicitly the medium conception retains little plausibility. Though some genuinely intentional states are in principle unconscious, it does not seem that the contents associated with phenomenal states could just as easily be carried by nonphenomenal states; the relation is not nearly that coincidental or accidental. The interplay between a conscious state's intentional and phenomenal aspects is far more intimate and interdependent. The content of my present visual experience is not merely *of this room* it is *of myself as a unified personal agent being aware of this room under quite specific modes of presentation.* I experience it in relation to myself both as a *part of my world* and in terms *of subjective aspects of its presentation to me,* such as the blue green color of my computer screen. It would seem pointless to try to account for this sort of intentional content without taking into account the phenomenal aspects of my mental state. Thus the isolation strategy of trying to give a complete account of intentionality without bringing in the phenomenal seems doomed to failure.

Nonetheless I believe a more modest strategy of partial or temporary isolation holds much greater promise. Though one cannot give a *complete* account of intentionality without bringing in the phenomenal, I believe one can construct a *basic or elementary* account of it without doing so. One need not bring in the phenomenal from the very start; one can instead account for some simple forms of intentionality in purely nonphenomenal terms and then use that account to help understand both the nature of the phenomenal and how it contributes to more sophisticated forms of intentionality. Indeed such a theoretical progression is what one should expect if one takes seriously the biological and evolutionary aspect of the problem, since it seems clear that contentful or representational processes arose long before there was any phenomenal consciousness and continue to exist today in creatures that lack any subjective life (as well as in processes of our own that fall below the level of conscious awareness). I believe this the right strategy. It avoids both extremes discussed above. Contrary to Searle it does not elevate phenomenal consciousness to an essential condition for intentionality, and it recognizes the existence of genuinely intentional states that exist quite independently of consciousness. On the other hand it also rejects the move by Dennett and other mainstream philosophers to marginalize the role of the phenomenal and provide a complete account of the intentional in isolation from subjective consciousness.

For the balance of my paper I would like to sketch—in admittedly limited detail—a few of ways in which such a middle approach might help us understand the relations between these two key aspects of the mind.

First we need a basic account of pre-phenomenal intentionality. Taking the biological nature of intentionality quite seriously, I believe we should analyze intentional content in terms of functional role where the notion of function is read as having a seriously teleological slant.[22] A state's intentional content depends upon the functional role that it plays within the organism with respect to how it contributes to the organism's survival, reproduction and achievement of its ends. I take a very broad view regarding what sorts of functional relations are relevant to content. Some will concern covariance relations of the sort focused on by information-theoretic accounts such as Dretske's[23]. These "tracking relations" are especially important when we are specifying content for informational states such as those involved in perception, belief-acquisition or other forms of learning. However, even in such cases, one must typically look at other aspects of a state's functional role as well to determine what content to attribute to it. Organisms do not merely store information in the passive sense associated with tree rings or fossils, but also possess information in the active sense that they are able to apply it to modify their behavior in ways that are specifically adapted to it. Thus a state's content-fixing role must include the actual and potential effects it has on the organism's behavior either in isolation or in joint action with other states. Since joint action will be much more common the range of interactions with other intentional states into which a given state can enter will also be a primary part of its content determining functional role. Please note that though the notion of functional role includes many internal relations it is most definitely not restricted to them. A functional role account of content can be "wide" in whatever respect one wishes, i.e. it can accommodate distal environmental facts, social facts, or historical facts if the explanatory context in which one is operating requires sensitivity to such factors. They can all be part of what is meant by "functional role". Nor does the sort of functional role theory I envision presuppose that there is a well-defined internal component that can be specified in a systematic and order-revealing way independently of how it is embedded in its world and the nature of the organism-environment interactions into which it enters. Though there obviously must be a physically distinction between what happens within the organism and what happens in the environment we should not expect that there will necessarily be a way of describing what happens internally that exhibits any systematic and illuminating patterns when considered by itself in isolation from context. It may do so only when considered and described in relation to the quite specific contexts within which it operates and the nature of the organism-environment relations that occur within that context.

At this point let me say something that is both ecumenical and heretical: *There is no unique correct theory of content.*

Different theories of content can each have their legitimate uses, and which way of ascribing content is best will vary with the explanatory context. If one is constructing a theory of information flow in a sensory channel, such as the visual pathway, a covariance theory that ties content very closely to "detected" properties of the input may be best; whether the relevant covariance relations reach only as far as the proximal stimulus or to some degree extend out into the environment will depend on one's explanatory interests and the stage of perceptual processing one is trying to model. For example, an environmental detector mode of content may be useful if one is trying to explain the adaptive or evolutionary success of the sensory processing itself. On the other hand, to describe central mechanisms that initiate and regulate behavior, one will probably want a notion of active information content that is more sensitive to a state's effects on outputs and thus reflects what the organism takes its situation to be. From yet another perspective one's interest may be to find formal algorithms that could produce the sequences of contentful states that occur in specific kinds of reasoning, planning or problem solving. If so, one may prefer a purely interpretative notion of content that is neither tied to input nor output, perhaps some sort of conceptual role theory that restricts the content-fixing roles to purely inferential ones. The sole aim would be to find algorithms that generate symbolic transformations mirroring those semantic relations (perhaps as specified model theoretically). This sort of content might be all that is needed for those trying to build formal models of cognition; they need some notion of content that they can use to spell out the contentful relations that they are trying to model formally, but they need not be concerned with how actual states of organisms come to have such contents; that is something they can take for granted and leave for others to explain.

A similar dependence on explanatory interest applies to the dispute between so called "wide" and "narrow" theories of content. Narrow theories determine content solely on the basis of facts about an organism's physical structure and organization in isolation from any facts about its history, its context, or its social, physical or biological environment. Wide theories are wide just because they allow external factors of the sort that narrow theories exclude to play a role in determining content. On a wide theory two creatures might be molecule-for-molecule duplicates of each other but have psychological states with different contents because they are embedded in different contexts.[24] A narrow theory would make that impossible; molecular doppelgängers must be content-identical.

Though there has been fierce debate about which is the right way to give a theory of content, if we look to actual practice we'll see once again that both have legitimate applications and which one is best will depend on what it is we are trying to explain or understand. From a biological perspective an organism's causal powers can be very much dependent on its environmental context. Two lizards may have an identical pattern of coloration, but if they live in two dissimilar natural habitats, one may be superbly camouflaged and the other not. If we are trying to frame explanatory generalizations about the fitness or predator avoidance strategies of lizards we will better served by classifying the well disguised member of our identical pair with other lizards that are similarly hidden in their respective habitats rather than with its "stick out like a sore thumb" twin. On the other hand if we want to explain how skin color derives from underlying pigments, we will likely want to classify the twins as of the same kind. A similar relativity applies to modes of ascribing content. Imagine two organisms, X and Y, that process their visual stimuli along physically identical pathways, but which live in quite different environments. In X's environment moving objects obey Marr's rigidity constraint (that objects retain their shape in motion) in Y's they do not. The processing in X's channel successfully computes the shape of objects from their movement, though the physically identical processing in Y produces only "garbage". If our aim is to explain X and Y's perceptual success or lack there of, we may want to use a wide mode of specifying content that takes into account the different boundary conditions within which their respective visual systems operate. Wide content also seems to be what we want when our aim is to communicate or learn from someone else whose utterances we take to reflect the content of her beliefs and the state of the world as well. On the other hand if we are trying to explain how states of X's and Y's primary visual cortex detect the presence of moving edges on their retina it may be more apt to use a narrow mode to specify the content of the relevant cortical states. I have elsewhere argued that recent metaphysical attempts to show that only narrow content can be invoked in causal explanations don't succeed.[25] I won't repeat those refutations here, though the examples of the camouflaged lizards and the rigidity constraint should serve to show that wide schemes of classification can find use in causal explanations. One would do best to forgo appeal to metaphysics and look instead to actual explanatory practice, and if one does one finds that there is plenty of work for both wide and narrow content. Neither is right for every context; a reasonable pragmatism finds plenty of room in the tent for both.

Thus there is no single right answer to the question, "What's the right way to assign content?" The answer depends on which contentful states and relations one is concerned with, as well what it is about them one is trying to understand. This approach, which might be called content pluralism, is ecumenical because it finds "room in the tent" for all (or at least for most). It is realistic about the complex project of understanding the mind. It recognizes that content plays many different roles in mental processes and that no single theory of content can serve all our explanatory purposes with respect to that diversity. The view is "heretical," or might be regarded as such in the present philosophic context, because so many "true believers" have spent so much ingenuity and mental energy trying to show that their particular theory of content is right and all the others wrong. I doubt my big tent view will find much favor with the faithful of one sect or another; they may well disdain it as so much moderate mush, as is the usual fate of those who try to find merit on all sides. But despite its lack of polemical pizzazz, I think content pluralism is the reasonable way to go if one focuses on the real practice of trying to understand the mind in all complexity.

Given our basic teleological account of content how might we expand it to accommodate and explain more sophisticated forms of content, especially the sort associated with phenomenal consciousness? There are three interrelated developments we need to consider.

First, contentful states can and do differ in the number and diversity of effects they have on the organism's output as well as in the nature and number of interactions they can enter into with other states, a fact that allows us to draw some important distinctions. In some cases content is opaquely embedded within a process or mechanism that makes a limited contribution to behavior and is largely insulated from interactions with other contentful states. Such a state can nonetheless have content, e.g. as an information state, if it satisfies the basic conditions of systematic covariance and production of adaptive response. This is the sort of informational content that one would rightly attribute to evolutionarily acquired stimulus/response mechanisms of simple animals. However, if one moves to the other extreme and considers a highly sophisticated intentional state such as a human belief, both its range of potential adaptive effects on behavior and its range of potential contentfully appropriate interactions with other intentional states is vast, diverse and open-ended. The natural history of intentionality shows a movement toward states with ever increasing sophistication of content based on a process of continually opening up the range of application and interaction. Conscious states fall far along this developmental pathway; they can have a wide range of adaptive effects on behavior and they are what Stephen Stich has called "inferentially promiscuous"[26] i.e. they enter into a wide range of interactions with other contentful states.

A second and directly related development is the movement from representations of the world that are merely implicit in the structure of an organism's behavior regulating mechanisms toward ones that are explicit and available for a multiplicity of internal and external applications. The development of internal structures that function as representations (to be "read", "interpreted", "revised" and "guiding") is a natural design solution to the problem of how to integrate and coordinate a multiplicity of contentful states in some sort of unified and economical structure. (Note I take the existence of representations in this sense to be compatible with all but the most exclusionary versions of connectionism). The content of any such representation will depend upon the same functional role factors that determine content for intentional states with the additional complication that representations will generally have their effects indirectly through processes that can be said in some sense to "interpret" them.[27]

This second developmental strand clearly leads toward phenomenal consciousness. Though representations are employed in many nonconscious processes they are especially prominent in conscious experience. When I have a conscious experience of my office, my awareness involves a unified representation of its spatial arrangement which indicates where each of its components is relative to all the others. A wide range of information about the shape, size, category, color and location of objects is all integrated in a general visual representation.

A third and further element of increasing sophistication involves the extent to which an organism or system can be said to understand the content of the representations that it uses. The more different behaviors it can guide through use of that representation and the more it can situate the information carried by it in the context of other items of information, the more it can be said to understand its significance. Representation-using systems differ greatly along this dimension which I have elsewhere called semantic transparency.[28] The representations associated with phenomenal consciousness again fall far toward the upper end of the continuum; they typically show a very high degree of semantic transparency.

We are now in a position to shed some light on the relation between intentional content and phenomenal consciousness in at least three respects.

First the representations associated with phenomenal consciousness typically involve a very high degree of semantic transparency; for example the representations involved in normal visual experience are such that I am automatically and immediately aware of an enormous wealth of information about the scene that is being represented. This feature of experience allows us to explain in part the intuition that motivates those like Searle who claim that consciousness is essential for genuine intentionality. That intuition relies upon the correct observation that representations processed by a system can be said to be *representations for the system itself* [29] only in so far as the system understands the content of those representations. The representations processed by a weather-forecasting computer have meaning for the people who program it or use to predict the weather, but it would be wrong to say that they have any meaning for the computer itself. Since semantic transparency is just a measure of the degree to which a system understands the content of the representations that it uses, they can be said to be representations *for the system* only in so far as they are semantically transparent.

Because the representations associated with conscious experience are transparent to a high degree we are justified in holding that they are representations *for* the conscious subject who is having the experience; conscious experience is typically *sufficient* for genuine representation-use and intentionality. But contrary to Searle, it does not follow that it is *necessary*. The inference fails for two reasons. First some lesser degree of semantic transparency might be adequate to count representations as having meaning for the system that uses them; conscious representations are semantically transparent to a very high degree and it is not clear that falling short of that extreme must deprive a system of genuine intentionality. A system may have a lesser but nonetheless genuine understanding of the representations that it uses. And secondly it may be possible to achieve even a very high degree of semantic transparency without phenomenal consciousness; in our own human case the two seem to go together, and conscious experience provides us with our paradigm examples of genuinely intentional states. But that coincidence may be just a contingent fact about our particular biological lineage, a fact about one particular design solution that has evolved to produce highly transparent representations. That would leave open the possibility of other systems, whether natural or artificial, that equally understand the content of the representations that they use though they lack any form of phenomenal consciousness. Of course it might be difficult and perhaps impossible for us to imagine what it would be like to be such a system; given their lack of a phenomenal life we could not empathetically project ourselves into their situation. But in so far their functional organization allowed them to connect the representations that they used both with other semantically related representations and with the relevant parts of the external world to a degree that equalled phenomenal experience in its speed and richness, such systems should be regarded as genuinely understanding their meaning. The failure of the empathy test would not justify us in concluding otherwise.

The second respect in which our basic account can shed some light is by helping us understand some of the evolutionary links between intentionality and consciousness. From the teleo-functionalist perspective genuine intentionality arises much earlier in evolutionary history and much lower down the phylogenetical scale than consciousness, which appears only in association with more sophisticated forms of content. Moreover, the process by which it appears involves a continuous growth of meta-intentionality. Organisms become better able to represent features of their environment in part by becoming better informed about the intentional properties of their own nervous systems. Enhanced abilities to interpret and apply the information supplied by input channels, capacities to learn from past environmental encounters by adapting behavior controlling mechanisms to the specific features of one's situation, and the development of increasingly transparent systems of representation are all processes that involve major increases in meta-intentional understanding. In order to better understand its world, an organism must also come to better understand itself. In particular it must come to better understand its own intentional states and representations. The development of phenomenal consciousness is just one very important aspect of this general process.

As I have argued elsewhere, there is a sense in which consciousness essentially involves self-understanding.[30] The highly transparent representations associated with phenomenal consciousness can exist only if a great deal of reflexive meta-intentional understanding is implicitly embedded in the underlying processes that generate, regulate, transform and interrelate those representations. My present visual experience of my office desk contains within its phenomenal structure a great deal of understanding about the scene that is being represented. An understanding that I am looking at a Macintosh LC II computer is at least implicitly present as part of the transparent content of my conscious state. But in what does such understanding consist and how is it functionally realized? It is largely a matter of my ability to automatically and rapidly connect my visual representation with a rich store of other representations that embody my background knowledge and understanding about personal computers, their nature, appearance, function, operation and varieties. My ability in turn is realized by underlying processes that allow me to make the semantically appropriate connections among the many different representations that encode that background information. The fact that my internal organization contains such processes constitutes my having a lot of meta-intentional understanding in so far as it enables me to interrelate my own internal representations in ways that are specifically adapted to their intentional content. It is in this sense that the evolutionary development of increasingly transparent systems of representations has been in large part a matter of a sustained growth in meta-intentional understanding. Thus the evolution of phenomenal consciousness has depended upon a similar growth in reflexive self-understanding. This holds true for relatively simple forms of phenomenal consciousness found in lower animals as well as for the sort of explicitly self-reflexive form of consciousness associated with human beings. A cat, or a mouse or a starling may not engage in any inner monologue reflecting on its state of mind, but in so far as it has unified visual experiences of its surroundings that automatically link up with a store of background understanding about its environment, it possesses a significant degree of meta-intentional understanding implicitly embedded in its functional organization.

Meta-intentionality also underlies the third application of our basic theory, in this case to help explain the fact that our conscious states are experienced as states of a single unified enduring subject of action and experience. The intentional content of my present visual state is not just that there is a LC II computer on my desk, but also that the computer is in front of me and that I am aware of it visually. We experience the world in relation to ourselves and from our perspective as conscious observers within that world. Thus, as Brentano noted, there is always a double aspect to the intentional content of a conscious mental state; on one hand it is directed toward some object outside itself such as my computer, but it is also directed onto itself and onto the fact that it is the state of a given subject. From a Cartesian perspective this might seem to commit us to the existence of an independently existing substantial self which unifies my stream of consciousness by being aware or its elements; on such a view what binds all my thoughts together as the thoughts of a single consciousness is that the same self is conscious of them. But the teleo-functionalist need not go down that road. The natural move for the functionalist is to reverse the order of dependence between the self and the unity of consciousness; it is not that consciousness is unified because a single self if aware of all of it, but rather I constitute a single self because of the way my conscious states are unified. The self is not an illusion. I really am a unified self, but I am so in virtue of how my intentional states interact and coordinate with each other. Rather than being an independently existing thing, the self is a virtual structure that emerges out of the organized flow of intentional states in my internal organization. Thus in pathological cases of dementia or psychosis when the organized structure of thought breaks down, so too does the self; in severe cases the self can literally disintegrate and cease to exist.

The story of how the self the "emerges" from the organized structure of intentional states is not one we can address here in detail. For present purposes, we need only note that the process of becoming a self involves a significant growth in self-understanding and thus in meta-intentionality. From the teleofunctionalist perspective, no system could coordinate and integrate its intentional states and processes in the manner required to constitute a self without at least implicitly understanding a great deal about their intentional content.

To sum up, we have seen how our basic teleofunctionalist account of intentionality can be extended and used to help explain three important features of phenomenal consciousness: its semantic transparency, its evolutionary origin, and its focus from the perspective of a unified self. We saw that each of the three involves a significant element of meta-intentionality which can be analyzed within the framework of our basic theory. Although this sheds a lot of light on consciousness, it falls far short of Dennett's ambition to fully explain everything real about consciousness in terms of an independent theory of intentionality. As I noted above, I do not share that ambition and I doubt it can be achieved. However, understanding how conscious mental states both resemble and differ from other mental states with their respect to their intentionality can provide us with valuable clues about where to look in trying to understand those aspects of consciousness that remain unexplained. For example, we have as yet little real understanding of how phenomenal consciousness arises from the physical operation of the brain; indeed some philosophers including Colin McGinn and Joseph Levine[31] have argued that the psycho-physical link can not be made intelligible and must always remain a mystery to us. If we are to have any hope of refuting this pessimism and bridging the gap we will need to articulate organized structure on both its sides with the aim of forging explanatory connections. It is at this point that intentional features such as the semantic transparency of phenomenal consciousness come into play. A genuinely explanatory account of the brain basis of consciousness will need to explain the functional organization that underlies such transparency. Since it requires the ability to make a rich and nearly instantaneous range of associations among diverse representations, its neural basis will need to subserve just such linkages. Current models suggest that it is more likely a matter of getting the many different areas of the brain that model different aspects of the world to form transient interactive ensembles rather than of constructing total and all-encompassing super representations for review by some all-knowing super homunculus in the Cartesian theater.[32] The competing neural theories—in terms of neural oscillations or the formation of transient Hebb assemblies—are still highly speculative, but at least they offer theories, which if correct, would go a long way toward making the psycho-physical link intelligible. But the neural theories can succeed only if it is clear what needs to be explained and thus it is essential that we have well-developed accounts of the intentional structure of phenomenal consciousness. In the absence of such theories, we wouldn't have a clearly articulated target at which to aim our explanatory project.

Overall I hope thus to have established the three main claims about the relation between intentionality and consciousness that I laid down at the outset.

1. Contrary to Searle, a state need be neither conscious nor accessible in principle to consciousness to have genuine intentional content.
2. Contrary to Dennett, phenomenal consciousness can not be fully analyzed and explained solely in terms of nonphenomenal intentionality.

but

3. One can give a basic account of intentionality that applies to nonphe-nomenal mentality and then expand that account in a way that at least partially explains the nature and basis of phenomenal consciousness.

Notes

1. Nagel (1974).
2. See for example Millikan (1984) or Papineau (1987).
3. See for example Loar (1981) or Harman (1982) or Block (1986).
4. For example in Kripke (1972), Putnam (1975) or Devitt and Sterelny (1987).
5. McGinn "Consciousness and Content" in McGinn (1990).
6. Searle (1992).
7. Dennett (1991).
8. Searle (1992) p. 152.
9. Searle (1992) p. 156.
10. My critical discussion of Searle's position here is heavily indebted to the somewhat longer treatment that I give to the issue in Van Gulick (1995).
11. Searle (1992) p. 158.
12. Searle (1992) p. 157.
13. Searle (1992) p. 157.
14. Searle (1992) p. 158.
15. Searle (1992) p. 164.
16. Block (1978).
17. Fodor (1987).
18. Block (1986).
19. Block (1978).
20. McGinn (1990) p. 34.
21. McGinn (1990) p. 34-35.
22. Van Gulick (1980).

23. Dretske (1981).
24. As in the now classic papers of Putnam (1975) and Burge (1980).
25. Van Gulick (1989a).
26. Stich (1978).
27. Van Gulick (1982).
28. Van Gulick (1988b) and Van Gulick (1989b).
29. Searle (1980).
30. Van Gulick (1988b).
31. McGinn (1990) and Levine (1983) and (1993).
32. Kinsbourne (1988) and Flohr (1992).

References

Block, Ned (1978) Troubles with functionalism. In W. Savage (ed.), *Perception and Cognition, Minnesota Studies in the Philosophy of Science Vol IX* . Minneapolis: 9 University of Minnesota Press.

Block, Ned (1986) Advertisement for a semantics for psychology. In P. French, T. Euhling, and H. Wettstein (eds), *Studies in the Philosophy of Mind.* Vol. 10, *Midwest Studies in the Philosophy.* Minneapolis, University of Minnesota Press.

Burge, Tyler (1979) Individualism and the mental. In P. French, T. Euhling, and H. Wettstein (eds), *Studies in Metaphysics.* Vol. 10, *Midwest Studies in the Philosophy.* Minneapolis, University of Minnesota Press.

Dennett, Daniel (1992) *Explaining Consciousness.* New York: Little Brown.

Devitt, Michael and Sterelny, Kim (1987) *Language and Reality: An Introduction to the Philosophy of Language.* Cambridge, MA: MIT Press.

Dretske, Fred (1981) *Knowledge and the Flow of Information.* Cambridge, MA: MIT Press.

Dretske, Fred (1988) *Explaining Behavior.* Cambridge, MA: MIT Press.

Fodor, Jerry (1987) *Psychosemantics.* Cambridge, MA: MIT Press

Flohr, Hans (1992) Qualia and brain processes. In. A. Beckermann, H. Flohr and J. Kim (eds.) *Emergence or Reduction? Essays on the Prospects of Nonreductive Physicalism.* Berlin & New York: De Gruyter.

Kinsbourne, Marcel (1988) Integrated field theory of consciousness. In A. Marcel and E. Bisiach (eds.) *Consciousness in Contemporary Science.* Oxford: Oxford University Press.

Kripke, Saul (1972) Naming and necessity. In D. Davidson and G. Harman (eds.) *Semantics for Natural Language.* Dordrecht: D. Reidel.

Levine, Joseph (1983) Materialism and qualia: the explanatory gap. *Pacific Philosophical Quarterly* 64.

Levine, Joseph (1993) On leaving out what it's like. In. M. Davies and G. Humphreys (eds.) *Consciousness.* Oxford: Basil Blackwell.

Loar, Brian (1981) *Mind and Meaning.* Cambridge: Cambridge University Press.

McGinn, Colin (1991) *The Problem of Consciousness.* Oxford: Basil Blackwell.

Millikan, Ruth (1984) *Language, Thought and other Biological Categories.* Cambridge, MA: MIT Press.

Nagel, Thomas (1974), What is it like to be a bat? *Philosophical Review* 82.

Papineau, David (1987) *Reality and Representation.* Oxford: Basil Blackwell

Putnam, Hilary (1975) The meaning of meaning. In K. Gunderson (ed.) *Minnesota Studies in the Philosophy of Science.*

Searle, John (1980) Minds, brains and programs. *The Behavioral and Brains Sciences.*

Searle, John (1992) *The Rediscovery of the Mind.* Cambridge: MIT Press.

Stich, Stephen (1978) Beliefs and subdoxastic attitudes. *Philosophy of Science* 45.

Van Gulick, Robert (1980) Functionalism, information and content. *Nature and System* 1. Reprinted in W Lycan (1990) *Mind and Cognition.* Oxford: Basil Blackwell.

Van Gulick, Robert (1982) Mental representation, a functionalist view. *Pacific Philosophical Quarterly* 63

Van Gulick, Robert (1988a) Consciousness, intentionality and self-understanding machines. In A. Marcel and E. Bisiach (eds.) *Consciousness in Contemporary Science.* Oxford: Oxford University Press.

Van Gulick, Robert (1988b) A functionalist plea for self-consciousness. *Philosophical Review* 97.

Van Gulick, Robert (1989a) Metaphysical arguments for internalism and why they don't work. In S. Silvers (ed.) *Rerepresentation* Berlin and New York: Kluwer.

Van Gulick, Robert (1989b) What difference does consciousness make? *Philosophical Topics* 17.

Van Gulick, Robert (1995) What's wrong with the connection argument. *Philosophy and Phenomenological Research* 55.

Philosophical Perspectives, 9, AI, Connectionism, and
Philosophical Psychology, 1995

TELIC HIGHER-ORDER THOUGHTS AND MOORE'S PARADOX

Bernard W. Kobes
Arizona State University

> He had been building one of those piles of thought, as ramshackle and fantastic as a Chinese pagoda, half from words let fall by gentlemen in gaiters, half from the litter in his own mind, about duck shooting and legal history, about the Roman occupation of Lincoln and the relations of country gentlemen with their wives, when, from all this disconnected rambling, there suddenly formed itself in his mind the idea that he would ask Mary to marry him.
>
> Virginia Woolf, *Night and Day*

Introduction.

For all their disconnected character, Virginia Woolf describes Ralph Denham's thoughts as the product of intentional agency ("he had been building"), until the final thought that he would ask Mary to marry him, which Woolf further describes as "so spontaneous that it seemed to shape itself of its own accord before his eyes."[1] Even this last thought, however, if it is to be a goal or plan or intention of his, albeit perhaps a diffident one, requires that he endorse it. The thought may percolate up, but it is an intention only if it meets with approval at the top. Beliefs are like this too, I shall argue, and this helps us understand the oddity of certain Moore-paradoxical thoughts, such as the judgement, "It's raining, but I don't believe it."

I will restrict my attention to thinkers with reflective consciousness, that is to say, thinkers who can think conscious thoughts of the sort usually expressed by sentences of form ⌐I think that p⌐. The goal will be to understand the nature of the belief relation in such thinkers, without denying that the word 'belief' might also have application to more primitive creatures. Conscious reflective believers do not have the phenomenology of mental tokens bumping around; this metaphor does violence to the sense we have of being epistemically engaged, and such engagement is what I want to understand.

My strategy will be as follows. I shall assume that a first-order thought's being conscious, in one centrally important sense of the word 'conscious', consists in the thought's being accompanied by a suitable non-perceptual higher-order thought, a thought about the first-order thought.[2] I shall argue that David

M. Rosenthal's recent version of this account of consciousness requires modifications. One of these is that the mental relation in the relevant higher-order thought should in some cases be seen as "telic", that is, as having desire- or act-like force, rather than as simply assertoric.[3] This helps us explain how it is that the thinker has a certain kind of spontaneous knowledge of what he believes.

It is nevertheless possible, I shall further argue, for a reflective conscious thinker to have sincere Moore-paradoxical thoughts. Looking at the peculiar kinds of violation of integrity involved in some such cases helps us understand the nature of what I shall call epistemic will.

Higher-order thought theory of consciousness.

According to David Rosenthal, a necessary condition of my mental state m's being conscious is that I think a suitable higher-order thought (hereafter, a HOT) to the effect that I am in state m. The first-order state m is not itself intrinsically conscious. Its being conscious is an extrinsic feature, namely, its being accompanied by a suitable HOT. And the HOT is not intrinsically conscious either. In fact, the HOT will typically be unconscious; this is the case in ordinary consciousness, when I am not engaged in deliberate introspection. Only if the second-order thought is accompanied by a still higher-order thought, a third-order thought, will the second-order thought be conscious; this occurs when I deliberately introspect.[4]

In virtue of being in state m, I may be said to be conscious of something in the world, according to Rosenthal. Thus if m is the thought $it's\ raining$, I am conscious of the rain. But in Rosenthal's usage the grammatically transitive predicate 'conscious of' is to be carefully distinguished from the grammatically intransitive predicate 'conscious', as applied to mental states. Thus in virtue of being in m, I am conscious of the rain, even if m is not itself conscious. Similarly, if m is conscious, then in virtue of having a suitable HOT to the effect that I am in mental state m, I am conscious of being in mental state m, even if the HOT is not itself conscious. This aspect of Rosenthal's view is plausible only if 'conscious of' is divorced from its ordinary meaning, but we may grant Rosenthal his use of the grammatically transitive construction as a term of art.[5]

I will not enter into the subtleties of Rosenthal's view or his defense of it. I do want to consider, however, his account of the intuitive immediacy of our awareness of our own mental states. If the presence of a HOT is to explain m's being conscious, it had better not be the case that the HOT is derived solely from third-person observation or inference. If a competent psychotherapist tells me, correctly, that I harbor unresolved and unconscious anxiety about my high school shop class, and I take it on his authority, then my thought that I am in that state of anxiety need not suffice to make the anxiety conscious. At the same time Rosenthal thinks that "non-conscious inference may well underlie the presence of the higher-order thoughts that make mental states conscious".[6] His view then is that my mental state m is conscious only if it is accompanied by a HOT, *not based on any observation or inference of which I am conscious*, to the effect that I am in mental state m.[7]

The italicized proviso will not, however, do the job of restricting our attention to just those HOTs that guarantee and explain the first-order state's being conscious. Consider: I could know about my friend's mental state, say that he is in love, without relying on any inference or observation of which either of us is conscious. I just find myself firmly convinced, though I cannot say why, that he is in love. Perhaps it is something in his voice, or the enlargement of his pupils as he gazes upon his beloved. I am not conscious of my conviction being based on any observation or inference, and what is perhaps more, it is not in fact based on any observation or inference of which I am conscious. Now if this is possible, then it is also possible that I know about my own first-order mental state in precisely the way in which I know about my friend's. But of course my knowing about my friend's mental state in this way does not suffice to make my friend's mental state conscious. Why then should we suppose that my knowing about my own mental state in *just that way* suffices to make my own mental state conscious?

This argument shows that the presence of a HOT to the effect that I am in mental state m does not suffice to explain mental state m's being conscious, even if the subject concept expressible by 'I' achieves its referent in the usual first-person way, and even if the HOT is intuitively immediate in the sense of not being based on observation or inference of which I am conscious. For these conditions are compatible with the HOT's being *segregated* from the first-order state.

We ought to have been suspicious anyway of Rosenthal's proviso. For suppose that my first-order mental state m is conscious in virtue of the presence of a HOT derived by observation or inference of which I am not conscious—a possibility that Rosenthal admits. Now suppose that, by feedback training or neurosurgery, I become conscious of the observation or inference that yields the HOT. Then it follows on Rosenthal's view that m is no longer conscious. But it is not credible that the addition of consciousness of processes whereby the HOT is derived should cause loss of consciousness of the first-order state.

More general worries afflict the HOT view. How could mere *aboutness*, a relation notoriously capable of spanning vast tracts of space and time, do the trick of making the first-order mental state conscious? It seems the wrong sort of relation between a HOT and a first-order mental state to do the job at hand.[8] Some more intimate relation seems required. If a thought about an inner non-mental state ("heart beats, a loose tooth, hiccoughs of a fetus, a cinder in the eye"[9]) does not suffice to make the non-mental state itself conscious, why should it be any different in the case of an inner mental state? Moreover, a first-order mental state m's being conscious is associated with its increased availability for inference and the guidance of action; how could the presence of a HOT that is merely *about* m explain that? It does not help to add that the HOT must be caused by the first-order thought, for that is compatible with the intuitive idea driving these worries that the HOT might be in some relevant sense segregated from the first-order state.[10]

What seems called for to capture the desired more intimate relation between first-order state and HOT is a token-constituency requirement: the first-order mental state or event token must, at the time that it is conscious, be a constituent part of the HOT event token. This rules out the case above in which I am aware of *m* in some way that relevantly resembles my apparently immediate awareness of my friend's being in love. And we need no longer worry that added consciousness of the observation or inference underlying the HOT might cause loss of consciousness of *m*. Finally, the token constituency requirement helps explain why *m*'s being conscious should be associated with its increased availability for inference and action guidance.[11]

A wrinkle in this proposal concerns the idea, which I assume to be correct, that a conscious first-order thought, say a conscious desire that the after-dinner speaker cease talking, consists (at least partly) of both a mental attitude relation—desire, in this case—and a content representation of the state desired. The mental attitude relation consists in the content- representation's playing a certain causal role, or its being disposed to do so. On the proposal so far there must be a HOT with content *I desire that the speaker cease*, whose tokening contains as a proper part a tokening of the desire that the speaker cease. But it seems wrong to require that the HOT itself have, even partly, the force of a desire. Perhaps I do not consciously *endorse* the first-order desire, despite being conscious of it. The HOT itself, in this example, has only assertoric force; the force of desire is attributable to the first-order state alone.

My proposal, then, is that a thinker *S*'s mental state *m* is conscious if and only if (i) *m* is accompanied by a HOT with the content that *S* himself is in mental state *m*, (ii) the HOT token contains as a constituent part the relevant first-order content- representation token, and (iii) the HOT correctly represents the mental attitude relation of *m*. The third clause is added for clarity, but is perhaps redundant in light of the first clause on its most natural construal. Note that the third clause is compatible with the mental attitude relation of the first-order state being quite distinct from that of the HOT. In having the HOT, *S* is thinking *through* the first-order state as to its content, but thinking *of* the first-order state as to its mental relation.[12]

Telic higher-order thoughts.

In the case of a conscious belief that *p*, there must be on this account a first-order belief with the content *p*, and also a HOT with the content ⌐I believe that *p*⌐, their tokenings overlapping on a representation token with content *p*.[13] Now it is implausible that the direction of explanation is always from the existence of the first-order thought to the existence of the HOT. Suppose the belief that *p* is the product of careful deliberation, in which *S* is explicitly and consciously concerned with whether *p* is something he should believe. For example, S consciously deliberates whether the canons of rational belief forma-tion require or at least allow him to believe that the famous P=NP statement in complexity theory is false (as is widely conjectured), and decides, as we say, that it is false. In such a case, at least, it is plausible that the first-order belief $P=NP$ *is false* causally depends on the HOT *I believe that P=NP is false.*

The issue may be phrased as follows. Does the representation-of-p's playing the functional role of belief explain the representation in the HOT of p as some-thing believed, or does the representation in the HOT of p as something believed explain the representation-of-p's playing the functional role of belief? If the former, then the force of the HOT is assertoric: in virtue of having the HOT, S merely registers that p is something he believes. But if the latter, then the force of the HOT is telic; the HOT has desire-like or act-like force, and in having the HOT S (normally) makes it the case, as it were, that p is something he believes.

In my view HOTs are telic just when the conscious attitude involves some-thing like personal endorsement or commitment, as it does in the case of con-scious beliefs and conscious intentions, plans, goals, and the like. The HOT is telic in cases in which S promotes a conscious first-order state to behavioral effi-cacy, or identifies a conscious first-order state as his will.[14] The contrast is with such states as conscious appearances or conscious desires that S does not (or does not yet) endorse. In these latter sorts of cases the HOT has only assertoric force.

Even in routine conscious perceptual belief, when there is no reason to question the veridicality of perception, the status of the perceptual belief as a belief depends on its having been in some sense screened. An anomalous percep-tion might not pass muster; a perception that does is implicitly endorsed. On Rosenthal's view, routine and non-introspective but conscious perceptual beliefs are accompanied by HOTs that are not themselves conscious. To this I add: such HOTs have telic force, and their having telic force consists in their playing a certain role in the screening of conscious perceptual beliefs. Thus a conscious belief always depends for its status as a belief (in a sense of 'belief' appropriate to conscious reflective beings) on the existence of a HOT with telic force.

It is unclear how a representation's playing the causal role of belief could cause or explain p's being represented in the HOT as something believed. For it is the very nature of belief to play a characteristic role in the causation of behavior, as writers such as Alexander Bain, R. B. Braithwaite, Bayesian epistemologists, and functionalists in the philosophy of mind have emphasized. Thus, according to a preliminary formulation, to believe that p is to be disposed to behave in ways that would satisfy one's desires if it were the case that p.[15] But how could a content-representation's playing *that* causal role explain p's being represented in the HOT as something believed? How could such a complex *relational* property be detected or registered by the HOT?[16] How could the HOT, as it were, tell? And if it could, how would a merely assertoric HOT get beyond the content, ⌜There is a belief that p operating within me⌝—which falls short of the commitment implicit in the content ⌜I believe that p⌝?

By contrast, part of the causal role of a conscious appearance is its *tendency* to cause judgements of form ⌐I believe that p⌐; part of the causal role of a conscious desire is its *tendency* to cause judgements of form ⌐I will do A⌐. Registering such a tendency is fully sufficient for registering the presence of an appearance or a desire as such. So it is not implausible that a conscious appearance or a conscious desire's playing its characteristic causal role explains its being represented in an assertoric HOT as an appearance or as a desire.[17] With appearance and desire the positive suffices: there may be some other appearance or desire that over-rides it, but that won't matter to its being registered in the HOT as an appearance or desire. But beliefs and intentions have an all-things-considered character. They depend for their status on not being over-ridden, and it is difficult to see how this negative element could be detected or registered in the HOT. More plausible is that p's being represented in a telic HOT as something believed or intended explains (in reflective conscious creatures, under normal conditions) the content-representation's playing the role appropriate to belief or intention—explains, that is, there *being* a belief or intention.

It is true that belief formation is not under our simple voluntary control, as imagination by contrast is; and this may seem to conflict with the idea that our conscious beliefs are associated with telic HOTs. For if a telic HOT is an exercise of epistemic will, why should the thinker not be able on any occasion he wishes to withhold his epistemic will, or direct it to any proposition he might wish? But there is a plausible explanation, I think, for our inability to believe simply at will, based on the idea that conscious reflective believers must embed their telic HOTs in certain preferences about belief that are constitutive of it as a mental relation. Crudely, conscious reflective believers must want their beliefs to be true, on pain of not having *beliefs*. For if I try to believe that p for what I consciously reckon to be non-truth-relevant motives (believing, for example, that I am loved because so believing would be conducive to my happiness, or believing in ontological conventionalism because so believing would be a boon to my career), then my very consciousness of those motives will make it difficult for me to sustain it as a belief, as opposed to a wish or fantasy or pretense.[18]

An explanation along these lines of belief not being simply voluntary is compatible with conscious beliefs being embedded in telic HOTs, which are then directly responsive only to a restricted range of possible conscious motives for believing, namely, "alethic" (that is, truth-relevant) motives. This still allows for a range of voluntary control, as for example in deciding whether to be epistemically cautious or daring—whether to believe only on strong evidence or to take epistemic risks. Other examples displaying a voluntary element in belief could be constructed by exploiting the fact that beliefs come in packages. An epistemic package that includes the belief that p might also include general beliefs about what counts as evidence for items in the package (including p)—about, in effect, what counts as a truth-relevant motive. The package may be epistemically ratifiable: once my belief in it gets going, it may sustain itself. If we have even a restricted degree of direct voluntary control over our beliefs, then that is evidence for epistemic volition, and hence for telic HOTs. But telic HOTs are present, in my view, even when belief is not to any degree voluntary—when the facts seem to stare me in the face and I can do no other.

The restriction of conscious motives for telic HOTs to the alethic helps explain why normally no question arises about their efficacy. Thinking telically ⌜I believe that p⌝ isn't simply *identical* to believing that p. One could conceivably discover, on the basis of one's linguistic and non-linguistic behavior, that one didn't really believe that p after all. A telic HOT might fail, due to consciousness of non-alethic motives. A case of this sort might be imagined if the telic HOT is a product of peripherally conscious non-alethic motives. On one hand, if non-alethic motives are wholly unconscious, then they present no obstacle to belief formation, and the telic HOT succeeds. On the other hand, if non-alethic motives are fully conscious, they will preempt the telic HOT itself, for the "project" of believing that p as a simple volition will be transparently incoherent to the thinker. With peripherally conscious non-alethic motives, the HOT might exist but neither create nor reflect the stable behavioral dispositions that would be required in a thinker who genuinely believes that p. Absent interference by peripherally conscious non-alethic motives, telic HOTs produce belief—this is a default position. The epistemic will is not free, but precisely that fact helps accounts for its power, as our inability to float free of the earth helps account for our ability to walk.

"Outward-looking" self-knowledge.

In merely registering passively my inner states my focus is inward; but my saying what I believe is not like this. Rather, my saying what I believe is identical to my trying, carefully and under mildly idealized conditions, to say what's true.[19] Suppose I am asked whether or not I believe that the human race will survive for another million years. The questioner may be interested in my mind or in the human race, but in either case, his question is strictly and literally about my mind. But in saying what I believe, my focus is typically outward, and I construct something that may have been only implicitly present in me from the start, or not present in me at all prior to deliberation. Similarly, my thinking about what I believe is identical to my trying to think, carefully and under mildly idealized conditions, what's true. So these activities are not directly autobiographical. I do not focus my attention inward and report what I find there; rather, I focus my attention outward, and say or think something aimed at truth with respect to outer matters. By contrast, in reporting sensory experience, for example, I am concerned that my report correspond to inner matters.

The outward-looking nature of self-knowledge of belief may suggest that in gaining self-knowledge of belief I move from a state with content p to a state with content ⌜I believe that p⌝. The temptation is to explain the failure to glance inward as evidence of a move from a mental state with first-order content (a belief about the world) to a state with second-order content (a belief about myself). And this suggests a model of self-intimation of beliefs: first a belief about the world is formed, then that belief intimates itself, manifests itself to the thinker. But this would be a mistake. No clear sense can be made of such a process of self-intimation. The operation of a general rule of inference of form $\ulcorner p$, therefore I believe that $p\urcorner$ would lead the thinker into gross error when reasoning in conditional, indirect, or temporally or modally embedded contexts. (E.g., suppose for *reductio* that Clinton has an even number of hairs on his head. Then, by the inference rule, I believe this. But I am agnostic as to the parity of the Clinton hair count—a contradiction, etc.) Instead of using such an inference rule the thinker would have to detect the presence in himself of an actual and antecedently existing belief of form p in order to arrive at one of form $\ulcorner$I believe that $p\urcorner$. But this seems to require precisely the kind of inward glance that is missing in outward-looking self-knowledge.

A defender of the self-intimation model might postulate a rule or process that is activated or triggered sub-personally by the presence of a belief that p, and directly results in the thought $\ulcorner$I believe that $p\urcorner$. Then we could avoid the imputation of an inward glance, on the grounds that the rule or process is not something wielded at the personal level. The rule or process would be triggered by an actual belief that p, but the *thinker* would not detect the belief that p as part of the application of the rule. But this sub-personal process model of self-intimation is not very plausible. For one thing, it is hard to see how a sub-personal rule could be triggered by the presence of a belief without being triggered by a mere appearance. Recall the essentially relational nature of belief, and the all-things-considered element in belief: unlike an appearance, a belief would have to play a certain role in the production of behavior, without being over-ridden by a contrary appearance. It is difficult to see how the trigger for such a hard-wired rule could be sensitive to these relational and negative elements.

Moreover, the phenomenology of self-knowledge of belief is not the phenomenology of having a thought $\ulcorner$I believe that $p\urcorner$ well up within me as the result of the operation of such a sub-personal rule or process. For on that picture I would be passive with respect to the subject matter of my self-beliefs in just the way that I am passive with respect to the subject matter of my first-order beliefs. But in fact in constructing beliefs about the world I seem to myself to be actively engaged; it is a kind of personal project rather than something I undergo. My beliefs *per se* don't feel like they simply happen to me; rather, *the world*, often enough, feels like it simply happens to me, and this suffices to explain whatever sense I might have of being passive with respect to both belief and self-belief. I am not doubly a bystander, first in that much of the world happens independently of my action or will, and second in that my belief about the world also happens independently of my action or will. I do have the phenomenology of not being able to believe at will, just like that, anything I choose, but I do not have an additional, distinct sense of inhabiting an objective world that is largely independent of my will. Rather, to experience my beliefs as not under my simple voluntary control is already to experience the world as objective. So there does not appear to exist the extra element of passivity that would be required by the sub-personal rule model of self-intimation of belief.

Reporting what one consciously, occurrently believes, like reporting what one consciously, occurrently intends, is therefore not just a matter of reporting autobiographical fact, as it might be with reporting a sensory experience. A sign of this is that I cannot find myself "saddled" with a conscious, occurrent belief whose object I regard as inappropriate for that mental relation, as I can find myself saddled with a mood, a fear, or a desire that I regard as inappropriate.[20] I might find myself plagued by the thought that my many powerful enemies are scheming against me, but as long as I regard this as the product of a pathology, and resist it, it is not a belief but only a troublesome appearance or compulsive thought. It only becomes a belief when it receives my epistemic imprimatur, when I act doxastically on the pathological impulse. In contrast, I can feel a depression that I regard as quite inappropriate to my situation, or a fear of a rabbit that I acknowledge to be harmless, or a desire for a form of sleazy or vicious entertainment that I regard as unworthy of my desire.

The lack of inward glance reflects a sense in which both belief and self-belief are dynamic. In second-order inquiry I never simply coast on previous first-order epistemic work done. Each time I am asked or ask myself whether I think that p, I am epistemically engaged on the question of whether or not p. The outward-looking nature of self-knowledge is a matter of direction of fit, rather than a transition from the content p to $\ulcorner$I believe that $p\urcorner$. It's a matter of the goal governing a mental process, the goal of characterizing an objective world. The orders of the intentional contents involved in the mental process cannot be read off in any simple way from that goal, for the goal may just as well govern a process involving telic HOTs as a process involving first-order thoughts. Asked whether I believe that p, I reflect on whether p; I think telically $\ulcorner$I believe that $p\urcorner$ (say), with the aim of characterizing an objective world. This telic thought simultaneously yields a self-belief with the same content. In the case in which I deliberately and consciously apply canons of rational belief formation, performing conscious inferences of form, $\ulcorner$I believe that p, and anyone who believes that p ought to believe that q, therefore let me believe that $q\urcorner$, my goal is still faithfully to reflect an objective world, not my inner epistemic life. This outward-looking goal governs the conscious thinking of the premise $\ulcorner$I believe that $p\urcorner$ itself.

Sincerely saying $\ulcorner$I believe that $p\urcorner$ *normally* expresses a telic HOT or an associated assertoric HOT with the same content. But it could also express a third-personal self-belief, that is, a self-belief based on observation (by oneself or by an authority) of one's own behavior.[21] This must be intelligible, since S must think of $\ulcorner$believe(s) that $p\urcorner$ as a predicate that he could apply to others as well as to himself, and as a predicate that others could apply to himself. So S should be able to detect in his own behavior exactly those clues that others would use to ground the application of the predicate to himself. Moreover, if our earlier discussion is correct then telic HOTs can fail. In that case S does not believe that p despite thinking telically, $\ulcorner$I believe that $p\urcorner$. Actually believing that p, as opposed to just having the relevant telic HOT, is a matter of being in a state that plays a characteristic causal role in the production of behavior. Since the belief S ascribes to himself with the predicate $\ulcorner$believe(s) that $p\urcorner$ has the same behavioral manifestations as the belief that others ascribe to him with the same predicate, his own lack of belief that p may be something that S could detect by third-personal self-observation. Third-personal self-observation may serve a checking function, and it may help "calibrate" S's telic HOTs, so that telic thoughts of that type remain efficacious. But whenever third-personal self-belief does not cohere with self-belief derived in the normal outward-looking way there is a failure of epistemic will—or so I shall argue.

Spontaneous belief.

Stuart Hampshire argues in his book *Freedom of the Individual* that in having an intention to A an agent often has a spontaneous belief that he will A.[22] A spontaneous belief is a belief not derived or causally based on anything else that the believer takes as premise for the belief, but resulting rather from an exercise of the will or intention to act. If I am contemplating whether to buy flowers on my way home from work, for example, and then form the intention to do so, I normally have a spontaneous belief that I will buy flowers on my way home from work—a belief not derived or causally based on anything else that I take as premise for the belief.

For me to have an intention to A, in a case in which I think A-ing within my power, I have to think of it as up to me, as something I can make happen. Intention is or involves a commitment to act, and as soon as I am so committed I have a special kind of epistemic right to the belief that I will A. If in having the intention to A I do not believe that I'll A (in a case in which I think A-ing fully within my power, and possess no special reason to doubt that I will carry out the intention), then there is some defect in my commitment or its expression in my self-belief: I intend it half-heartedly, or I am of two minds in the matter, or my commitment has not yet manifested itself in my self-beliefs in the normal way. I have a right to believe and normally do believe that I will A, just in virtue of *exercising* or, as I shall sometimes say, flexing my commitment to A-ing—or, to vary the metaphor, tuning my mind to it, allowing it its normal expression elsewhere in my mind—and not in virtue of knowing about the *existence* of my intention to A together with general knowledge about the likelihood of succeeding in my intention.

Granted, I might also reason that I will A based on my knowledge of the existence of my intention, together with the generalization that I always or almost always follow through on such intentions. I may be in a position to step back from my practical commitment, acknowledge it third-personally, and noting my frequency of success, come to the conclusion that I will A. Such arguments would bolster a belief that I may, however, already have through a more fundamental channel. For if I argue from the existence of my intention together with a general premise about my record of following through on intentions of this kind, then my intention must exist prior to and independently of my carrying out this train of thought. And frequently my knowledge that I will A is coeval with and a concomitant of the sheer exercise of my intention to A.

Spontaneous beliefs are often justified. In general, if I believe with justification that doing A is fully within my power, and I fully intend to do A, and possess no special reason to doubt that I will carry out my intention in this case, then my spontaneous belief that I will A is justified. It is true that if I think or ought to think that I often change or abandon intentions of this kind, or that in this case circumstances are likely to arise that will cause me to fail in or abandon my intention, then I cannot be said to be justified in my belief that I am A-ing or will A. If my spontaneous belief could not withstand such scrutiny then it is unjustified. But these are only defeating conditions. The relevant necessary condition for spontaneous belief to be justified is the absence of such defeating conditions, not that the believer have checked or know that they are absent.

The justification of S's spontaneous belief does not depend on its being the case that, if S were to consider the matter from a third-personal standpoint, he would be justified in believing it. That would be to make its status as justified depend on the result of a counterfactual third-personal inquiry; the fact that it is counterfactual just reflects the familiar fact that we cannot expect a finite person actually and explicitly to carry out the justification of each of his beliefs. Instead, the justification of S's spontaneous belief depends on its not being the case that, if S were to reflect on the matter from a third-personal standpoint, he would not be justified in believing it. The justificational status of a spontaneous belief depends only on the absence of third-personal defeat, not the (would-be) presence of third-personal confirmation.

If S were to have doubts about whether or not he will A, he could meet those doubts by reflecting telically; he could consciously flex his commitment to A-ing ("*I will A!*"), and he might supplement this by explicitly noting the absence of defeating conditions. Thus he could settle his own epistemic doubt in a characteristically first-person way, without appeal to anything, such as the existence of the intention, that could be taken as a premise for the conclusion that he will A. It is a combination of a flexed telic state, together with the observation of the lack of any defeating conditions, that resolves his epistemic doubt.

The same ideas apply to the case of conscious belief that p. If the foregoing discussion is correct, then a conscious belief that p is one accompanied by a HOT with content ⌜I believe that p⌝, a content to which S bears a telic, that is, act-like or desire-like, mental relation. But a telic relation is relevantly like an intention, so that there will normally be a spontaneous belief on S's part, also with the content ⌜I believe that p⌝. This will be the self-belief that one typically has in having a conscious belief that p. Let us call a spontaneous belief of this sort, arising from the telic HOTs of consciousness, a "hot" (lower case) self-belief—the contrast will be with "cold", or third-personal self-belief. In consciously believing that p, if S does not have the hot belief ⌜I believe that p⌝, then there is a defect in his telic relation to the content ⌜I believe that p⌝. This is not to say S does not genuinely have the conscious belief that p, or does not genuinely have a telic relation to the content ⌜I believe that p⌝, but only that the telic HOT is not having its normal spontaneous effects.

Hot beliefs are typically justified. For telic HOTs reliably produce the relevant first-order beliefs; this was argued for above on the grounds that if the conscious motives behind a telic HOT are non-alethic, then the failure of the HOT will be transparent to the thinker, and the HOT itself cannot be sustained, while if the conscious motives are alethic, then the telic HOT will produce first-order belief. If HOTs were not typically reliable, then if S were to consider the matter coldly, he would not be justified in the hot self-belief ⌜I believe that p⌝. But HOTs are reliable, so the spontaneous self-beliefs accompanying conscious beliefs are typically not coldly defeated.

Moore's paradox and hot self-knowledge.

There is a connection between Hampshire's thesis about first-person knowledge of action and Moore's paradox.[23] If someone makes a putative assertion of the form, ⌜p, but I do not believe that p⌝, he is incoherent in a special way. He is not semantically incoherent, for the Moore sentence will in fact be true of him for indefinitely many values of 'p'. The thinker himself acknowledges that there are many true propositions that he fails to believe, and he knows that Moore's sentence will be true of him for any such proposition. The incoherence of Moore's sentence is pragmatic: the first conjunct purports to express a (conscious, occurrent) belief, and the second conjunct asserts that he lacks the belief. The first conjunct is an expression of epistemic commitment, and that commitment ought to be manifested in his self-beliefs in a characteristic way; but the second conjunct says that it is not. So there is some incoherence going on of a broadly pragmatic sort. (I do not intend thereby to suggest that there was no genuine assertion.)

A similar pragmatic incoherence can be identified in a Hampshire case. Imagine that someone says, ⌜I *will* A, but I don't believe that I shall A⌝. (The speaker follows the old rule, now moribund, according to which 'I will' expresses determination or consent, while 'I shall' expresses simple futurity. So the first conjunct has telic force: it expresses a resolution, or assurance, or promise.) One who thinks A to be within his power, and intends to A, and lacks special reason to doubt that he will succeed in his intention, has a defect in his will if he then fails to believe that he will A. The defect is not semantic, for people often do things that they didn't believe they would do. Rather, the defect is pragmatic: the commitment expressed is not manifested in the thinker's self-beliefs in the way that such commitments naturally are. (I do not intend thereby to suggest that there was no genuine intention.)

We must distinguish the *omissive* form of Moore's paradox, ⌜p, but I do not believe that p⌉, from the *commissive* form, ⌈p, but I believe that not-p⌉. The omissive form is such that it (as thought or spoken by S), plus the proposition that S himself believes it, entails by uncontroversial principles a contradiction. The commissive form is such that it (as thought or spoken by S), plus the proposition that S himself believes it, entails by uncontroversial principles that S has contradictory beliefs.[24]

Contrary to what many writers have assumed or argued, it is semantically and pragmatically possible for a linguistically competent speaker to assert a Moore-paradoxical sentence. I believe, and shall argue below, that the assertion of a Moore-paradoxical sentence may be sincere and literal. But nothing this controversial is needed to demonstrate the possibility of asserting an omissive Moore sentence. To see this it is sufficient to note that, even if the speaker is insincere, he may be counting on his auditors just to believe the proposition expressed by the Moore sentence and not to notice that the speaker doesn't himself believe it. The speaker of an insincere Moore sentence might not even realize that it is easy for his auditors to tell that he himself does not believe it. After all, the propositional content of the sentence is easy for others to believe.[25] Alternatively, the speaker may merely think, rightly or wrongly, that his auditors will think that he is sincere, whether or not he also thinks that his auditors will believe him. Or, believing his auditors to have a low opinion of his own intellectual capacity, he may think, rightly or wrongly, that his auditors will think that he thinks that his auditors will think he is sincere. That is, he thinks his auditors will think he is trying to deceive them about his sincerity. In any of these cases it seems plain that the speaker could genuinely assert something of form ⌈p, but I do not believe that p⌉.

A simplifying assumption may be introduced by way of the following example. Suppose that about once a year, in the middle of the night, and only when there is no one else around, and only when in bed in total darkness, with no one to communicate with and no way to record my thoughts, I enter a brief state of lucid discernment about my world and myself. In normal states I have no recollection of the lucid state, but in the lucid state I recollect both normal states and previous occurrences of the lucid state, and realize that these lucid states are brief, rare, and not recollected except during other lucid states. Then I can think, ⌈p, but I believe that not-p⌉, or ⌈p, but I don't realize that p⌉. If we grant the thinker a present tense for 'believe' or 'realize' that is "fatter" than the window of lucidity, then these are genuine, sincere, even true Moorean thoughts, both commissive and omissive. In order to put this case and others like it to one side, I will assume that the contextually determined "fatness" of the present tense of the psychological verb in a Moore sentence is locked into the time frame by which we judge the sincerity of the thought or utterance.

One way to try to get at the oddity of a Moore-paradoxical sentence is to try to specify a range of things at least one of which must have gone wrong when the sentence is asserted or thought. In the case of an omissive Moore sentence, this is not difficult to do.

Any assertion by S of an omissive Moore sentence is either false, or true by (good or bad) luck but insincere.

and

Any conscious belief or sincere assertion by S of an omissive Moore sentence must be false; and a full grasp of the natures of the relevant concepts, plus adequate reflection, would put S in a position to know that it is false.

It is more difficult, in the case of a commissive Moore sentence, to specify a reasonably concise and interesting range of things one of which must have gone wrong when the sentence is asserted or thought. I propose the following:

Any assertion by S of a commissive Moore sentence is either false, or true by (good or bad) luck but insincere, or true and sincere and S has contradictory beliefs (perhaps because S has a disunified mind that he thinks about, at least partly, third-personally).

and

Any conscious belief or sincere assertion by S of a commissive Moore sentence is either false and such that a full grasp of the natures of the relevant concepts, plus adequate reflection, would put S in a position to know that it is false; or false and S has an empirical belief that he has a disunified mind; or true and S has contradictory beliefs (perhaps because S has a disunified mind that he thinks about, at least partly, third-personally).

I conjecture that no significantly more concise and interesting ranges than these can be specified for what has gone wrong in Moore-paradoxical thoughts and assertions (even with the above simplifying assumption). In particular, insincere assertion, and even belief and sincere assertion of both omissive and commissive Moore sentences, are all psychologically and pragmatically possible, without semantic contradiction either on the part of those who attribute such beliefs and assertions or on the part of the Moore-paradoxical speaker or thinker himself.

The thought ⌜I believe that p⌝ usually expresses the telic HOT associated with a conscious belief that p, or the corresponding hot assertoric self-belief with the same content. But it can express a cold self-belief. When hot and cold conflict, or are believed to conflict, a Moore-paradoxical thought may result. Such a thought will reflect either a conceptual confusion, or a breach of the unity of the self, or a belief that such a breach exists.

Under the broad rubric of conceptual confusion, one kind of commissive Moorean thought may occur when the thinker openly has directly contradictory beliefs, or takes himself to openly have directly contradictory beliefs. Thus a believer in Hegelian dialectic, or paraconsistent logic, might take himself to have directly contradictory beliefs. Perhaps in virtue of his credulous reading or misreading of Hegelian dialectic or paraconsistent logic he actually does openly have directly contradictory beliefs.[26] Finding what he believes to be a pair of his own directly contradictory beliefs, he may splice belief and self-belief to construct, believe, and assert a sincere (perhaps even true) sentence of form ⌜p, but I believe that not-p⌝. It cuts no ice to hold that I am wrong in thinking that someone might openly have some particular pair of directly contradictory beliefs. For to hold that I am wrong is to agree that I think that someone might openly have such beliefs. But if I can believe that someone can have such beliefs, what is to stop someone from believing just that about himself, namely, that he himself has some particular pair of directly contradictory beliefs?[27] And this is sufficient for the possibility of his constructing and sincerely believing a commissive Moore sentence.

The case of lucid discernment described above involves what we may call a diachronically disunified or fragmented self. For what may be a case of a synchronically disunified self, suppose I have a state of lucid discernment that occurs as I go about my ordinary business, but that isn't attached to any of my behavior, including my verbal behavior. Even as I think to myself that *p* I find myself helplessly asserting with every sign of sincerity ⌜not-p⌝, and generally behaving in a way that would satisfy my desires in a world in which not-*p*. Perhaps we could describe the case such that the thinker is a single fragmented self—one who can sincerely and truthfully think, ⌜p, but I believe that not-p⌝. The thought that *p* is lucid and unequivocal, yet there may be enough in common between "thinker" and "behaver" that we should speak of a single fragmented self. But the case is not fully clear. As Jane Heal remarks about a similar case, there is also a contrary temptation either to speak of *my body* as the true subject of the belief that not-*p*, or to see the case as trading on an ambiguity in the word 'believe'.[28] The case is underdescribed as it stands; what to say about it may depend on details of what happens when the thinker of the lucid interior thought that *p* exerts great effort to make his thought that *p* control his behavior in matters of importance to him, and whether after doing so the thinker still thinks that *he himself* believes that not-*p*.

We can construct what I think are stronger cases of sincere Moorean thoughts by trading on social persuasion rather than phenomena resembling those of clinical neurology. For example, suppose a Harvard psychiatrist, as part of an enterprise called the Gullibility Project, convinces *S* that he, *S*, believes that he was abused as a child. As a result, *S* avows (that is, sincerely asserts the sentence[29]), "I believe I was abused." Now as a matter of fact *S* does *not* believe that he was abused as a child; he believes, and avows, "I was not abused", and he does not avow, "I was abused." It is no part of the Gullibility Project, unethical though it no doubt is, to convince *S* that he was abused. However, the psychologist is very forceful and persuasive, and puts forward a theory and a great deal of spurious evidence according to which people can readily believe such false propositions which they are in no way aware of believing. The psychologist's theory is entirely false, but S believes it, and believes its application to his own case. S conceives of many of his own actions and emotions as caused, in a way that eludes first-person awareness, by the belief that he was abused. So S believes third-personally, and avows, on the basis of the psychologist's theory and (alleged) evidence, "I believe that I was abused."

In Version 1 of this case, S puts these together and avows the commissive Moorean sentence, "I was not abused, but I believe I was abused." Since S avows, "I was not abused", he also believes, first-personally, "I believe I was not abused." He thinks he has two directly contradictory beliefs, namely, the belief that he was abused, and the belief that he was not abused. Note that he does not *in fact* have two directly contradictory beliefs, for he does not in fact believe that he was abused; he attributes this belief to himself only third-personally and erroneously. Note also that 'I' gets its referent in the usual way. S denies, we may suppose, that someone else cohabiting his body believes that he was abused. What the psychiatrist has convinced him of is that *he himself* believes that he was abused. He also denies, we may suppose, that he has some other belief-like relation to the proposition that he was abused. What the psychiatrist has convinced him of is that he *believes* that he was abused. So this is a case of sincere commissive Moorean belief without either contradictory belief or linguistic incompetence, and without any such degree of irrationality as would tempt us to withdraw the literal attribution of a commissive Moorean belief.

A commissive Moorean thought associated with the (true or false) belief that one has directly contradictory beliefs is only a mild epistemic defect, for this Moorean thinker also thinks the corresponding un-Moorean thought $\ulcorner p$ and I believe that $p \urcorner$. (If one *correctly* believes that one has directly contradictory beliefs, then of course the directly contradictory beliefs themselves are a more serious epistemic defect.) But there is nevertheless a defect, and it can be construed as a defect of epistemic will. For S thinks he has a belief that he cannot endorse; he therefore has an epistemic obligation to rid himself of the belief that he thinks he has and that he thinks is false, thus restoring to himself an epistemic unity that he thinks has been violated. S ought to attend to the belief that he endorses and his reasons for it, and suppress the behavioral efficacy of the "belief" he thinks he has but does not endorse—not let it take control.

This exercise in epistemic integrity will have one of two results: either i. the conscious belief, the belief that receives his personal epistemic endorsement, over-rides ("over-writes") the belief (as it seems to him) that he does not endorse, so that he no longer has (or seems to himself to have) the belief he does not endorse, or ii. he will feel himself powerless in this regard. But in the latter case, precisely as a result of the exercise of his epistemic will, he will come to see the putative belief that he does not endorse as alien to him—as not really *his*, or as something to which he bears some relation other than belief. A self-belief not under the control of his epistemic will can be exorcised by treating its subject as alien. And this result too restores him to epistemic integrity, by the back door as it were, for he will no longer literally and sincerely think the commissive Moorean thought. So it is possible to see the sincere thinking of a commissive Moorean thought as manifesting a defect of epistemic will, the normal exercise of which helps constitute him as a unified thinker.

In Version 2 of the Gullibility Project, S again sincerely avows, "I believe I was abused" even though he does not in fact believe that he was abused. But this time the psychiatrist has also convinced S that he lacks the belief that he was not abused. S does, however, believe consciously that he was not abused, and avows, "I was not abused." But even though he consciously asserts the relevant content, as a result of the psychiatrist's persuasion he thinks, wrongly, that he lacks the corresponding belief. That is, he avows, "I do not believe I was not abused", and he refuses to avow, "I believe I was not abused", despite consciously avowing, "I was not abused." He recognizes that there is a nearly universal linguistic habit, when one avows p, of also avowing ⌜I believe that p⌝. But he thinks that this linguistic habit is not universally correct—that the linguistic habit is based on normal or usual sorts of cases but that it leads to error in certain cases, such as this one. He himself adheres to the linguistic habit on every topic except that of whether he was abused. So there is no gap in his linguistic abilities as such, nor any error in his knowledge of what the linguistic practices are. He simply does not accept the linguistic practice of his cohorts as applying entirely without exception. Putting pieces together, he thinks and sincerely asserts the omissive Moorean sentence, "I was not abused, but I do not believe that I was not abused."

What is the nature of S's epistemic deficit in Version 2 of the Gullibility Project? Although it is severe, it is important to see first that S is neither mad nor stupid, and he is not unintelligible. He may have reflected on his epistemic situation. He is, in a sense, and on one topic alone, a linguistic non-conformist, but he thinks of this not as adherence to a different convention but as the result of seeing that a widespread linguistic habit would lead to error in this instance. In his own opinion all his beliefs are consistent, and indeed there is no direct contradiction in what he avows. His epistemic impairment is not such as to call into question the literal attribution of the sincere omissive Moorean thought. In fact, we may suppose, he insists that we interpret him as avowing an omissive Moore sentence literally construed. He resists reinterpretation; it is not someone else, he says, but he himself who lacks the relevant belief, and it is not some other belief-like relation, but belief itself that he lacks. If a subject as sophisticated as he is demands to be interpreted a certain way then it is uncharitable not to so interpret him.[30]

S's epistemic impairment consists partly in the massive empirical error into which the Gullibility Project has induced him. We could challenge S on empirical grounds: "If, as you claim, you fail to believe that you have not been abused, then how can you explain your assertion, which you heard yourself make just now, that you have not been abused?" S might admit that he does not know how this happens; or he might have a complicated empirical theory about why he asserts things that he fails to believe. *S* may claim that he has tried to believe that he was not abused, but that third-personal evidence pointed out to him by the Harvard psychiatrist convinces him that he has failed—a pity, says *S*, since the belief, if only he could acquire it, would be true.

S's auditors will get the distinct impression of dealing, just on this topic, with two selves, one the author of the assertion that he was not abused, the other the author of the assertion that he does not believe that he was not abused. But *S* himself may resist this reading. Given the facts of the case, there is here I think less temptation to ascribe the assertions to two distinct selves than in the well-known "split brain" experiments, say, where there is an organic basis to the alleged distinction between selves. However, *S* does seem to have violated an epistemic rule whose normal operation helps constitute him as a unified self.

A broadly conceptual impairment stems from the fact that *S consciously* avows, "I was not abused". Since this belief is conscious, on the higher-order thought theory of consciousness presented above it is accompanied by the perhaps unconscious telic HOT, and perhaps also its spontaneous assertoric sister, "I believe I was not abused." But *S* also avows, "I believe I was abused". So, as in Version 1 of the Gullibility Project, *S* attributes to himself two beliefs that are directly contradictory. Unlike Version 1, though, one of the self-attributions now remains unconscious, and *S* does not think of his beliefs *as* directly contradictory. And although this is not yet to say that *S* actually has directly contradictory beliefs, it may already be a kind of epistemic impairment merely to attribute to oneself beliefs that would contradict each other. Moreover, since *S* also avows, "I do not believe I was not abused", he has a conscious belief that directly contradicts the previously noted unconscious telic HOT and its spontaneous assertoric sister, "I believe I was not abused." So *S* has two beliefs that are directly contradictory. And although there is no direct contradiction either among his conscious beliefs or among the beliefs he consciously ascribes to himself, this is nevertheless plainly an epistemic defect. But the irrationality of thus having directly contradictory beliefs is mitigated by the fact that one of the relevant beliefs is and remains unconscious.

These aspects of *S*'s epistemic impairment can be described and accounted for at a more fundamental level. The empirical implausibility of *S*'s third-personal theory of himself, and the direct contradiction in his beliefs one of which remains unconscious, do not go to the heart of the matter. The fundamental incoherence is one of epistemic will, rather than of theoretical understanding. Because of the psychiatrist's cruel misinformation, *S* has an impaired conception of what his epistemic rights and obligations are in this instance, and so he does not exercise his epistemic will in the way that he normally does in connection with his conscious beliefs. The problem is not *per se* that *S* takes the third-personal stance toward himself, but rather that he allows that stance to preempt the exercise of his own epistemic will. In consciously believing on good evidence "I was not abused", he has a right to the conscious spontaneous belief "I believe

I was not abused", not basing it on anything he could take as premise. He has an epistemic right, almost universally exercised, to bring his conscious self-belief into alignment with his conscious belief—he has a right, that is, to form a conscious self-belief as to whether he thinks that p just by consciously thinking about whether p. But S's exercise of these epistemic rights is blocked, and his epistemic will hobbled, in just this instance, by his false third-personal theory about his own state of belief.

What is hobbled is an aspect of S's epistemic will which, when working normally, helps constitute two related unities. One is the unity of particular conscious belief and conscious self-belief, and the other is the unity of S as a conscious believer. According to our theory of conscious belief, in consciously believing that p—that he was not abused—S makes one content-representation token do double duty. It appears in the HOT which represents p as something believed, and in consequence it plays the functional role of belief, thus constituting the first-order belief that p. By an exercise of epistemic will it should also be made to help constitute a conscious self-belief (in Version 2), which in turn should be made to trump any contrary third-personal self-belief (in Version 1).

S's failure in respect of the second, personal unity is reflected in his interlocutor's sense of apparently dealing with two persons. If S allows himself to go on believing or failing to believe in a way that he can't wholly endorse, then that is to tolerate his own epistemic fragmentation. The concept of a single self can tolerate some slack in this regard, especially when, as in the Gullibility Project, the fragmentation of the self has its basis not in organic fragmentation but in social indoctrination. There can be an imperfectly unified self. Yet S lacks the coherence of a normally unified self, due to a defect in the commitment characteristic of belief. Integrity of epistemic will is part of ontological integrity.[31]

Many aspects of epistemic integrity remain to be limned. The nature of public integrity in assertions of fact and intention, and its connections to integrity of belief, need to be described. Interesting questions can be raised about the relation of a thinker to the body of his beliefs, as contrasted with particular beliefs. Is it merely a contingent fact about us that we cannot believe entirely at will, and for that matter cannot forget entirely at will, or is this a necessary part of the relation of a thinker to the body of his beliefs? The sense of inescapable risk in deliberative conscious belief, and its role in belief revision, has had some play in epistemology but remains isolated from philosophical theories of consciousness.[32] I believe that the present picture of conscious belief and epistemic agency as involving telic higher-order thoughts will prove a fruitful starting point for such inquiries.

Notes

Acknowledgements: I thank Stewart Cohen, Derk Pereboom, David Rosenthal, and Roy Sorensen for helpful discussions. Support from an Arizona State University Faculty Grant-in-Aid is hereby gratefully acknowledged.

1. *Night and Day* (The Hogarth Press, 1966), p. 239.
2. I use 'conscious' to mean approximately what Ned Block means by 'access-conscious' in his "On a Confusion About a Function of Consciousness", *Behavioral and Brain Sciences*, forthcoming. See further my accompanying comment on Block in that journal, "Access and What It's Like".
3. This use of 'telic' is borrowed from Lloyd Humberstone's "Direction of Fit", *Mind* 101, 401 (January 1992), pp. 59-83.
4. See David M. Rosenthal, "Two Concepts of Consciousness", *Philosophical Studies* 94, 3 (May 1986), pp. 329-359; reprinted in David M. Rosenthal, ed., *The Nature of Mind* (Oxford University Press, 1991), pp. 462-477; and "Thinking That One Thinks", in Martin Davies and Glyn W. Humphreys, eds., *Consciousness* (Basil Blackwell Ltd., 1993), pp. 197-223. See also Rosenthal, "Why Are Verbally Expressed Thoughts Conscious?", Report No. 32, Center for Interdisciplinary Research (ZiF), University of Bielefeld, 1990; "A Theory of Consciousness", in Ned Block, Owen Flanagan, and Guven Guzeldere, eds., *The Nature of Consciousness: Philosophical Debates* (MIT Press, 1995); "Explaining Consciousness", unpublished manuscript; and "Moore's Paradox and Consciousness", this volume.
5. I prefer the term 'cognizant of' where Rosenthal uses 'conscious of', but in discussing his view directly I conform to his usage. Note that Rosenthal's explanatory strategy assumes that we can get an account of the transitive construction 'conscious of', and an account of intentionality, independent of our account of consciousness.
6. "Thinking that One Thinks", note 18, p. 219. This represents a change from the view of his 1986 paper, according to which "conscious states are simply those states to which we have noninferential and nonsensory access" ("Two Concepts of Consciousness", p. 464 in the reprinting in *The Nature of Mind*).
7. "Thinking that One Thinks", p. 205, and note 18, p. 219. Note that the presence of the words 'of which I am conscious' in the explanans does not introduce any obvious circularity. The idea is to explain the grammatically intransitive 'conscious', as a predicate of mental states, in terms of the grammatically transitive 'conscious of'.
8. Here I am indebted to some remarks of Richard Hall.
9. Fred Dretske, "Conscious Experience", *Mind* 102, 406 (April 1993), p. 280, note 22.
10. These more general worries also afflict Rosenthal's earlier view ("Two Concepts of Consciousness", 1986), which required that the HOT not result from any inference or observation.
11. The token-constituency requirement has affinities with other views in the literature. David Sanford, "Armstrong's Theory of Perception", in Radu J. Bogdan, ed., *D. M. Armstrong* (D. Reidel Publishing Co., 1984), pp. 55-78, argues that David Armstrong's "distinct existences" argument is no threat to the view that a situation scanned might be a proper part of an operation of scanning. Sydney Shoemaker argues that in a sufficiently rational thinker a first-order mental state's playing an appropriate functional role entails its simultaneously playing the role appropriate to the thinker's thought that he is in that state. See his "On Knowing One's Own Mind", in James E. Tomberlin, ed., *Philosophical Perspectives, 2, Epistemology* (Ridgeview Publishing Co., 1988), pp. 183-209; "Rationality and Self-Consciousness", in K. Lehrer and E. Sosa, eds., *The Opened Curtain: A U.S.-Soviet Philosophy Summit* (Westview Press, 1991), pp. 127-149; "Self-Knowledge and 'Inner Sense', Lecture II: The Broad Perceptual Model", *Philosophy and Phenomenological Research* 54, 2 (June 1994), pp. 271-314.

12. Rosenthal requires the HOT always to have assertoric force, regardless of the attitude of the first-order state. Below I argue that the HOT sometimes has telic (desire-like or act-like) force.

    Tyler Burge, "Individualism and Self-Knowledge", *Journal of Philosophy* 85, 11 (November 1988), pp. 649-663, argues that in "basic self-knowledge" the thought that p is "thought and thought about in the same mental act", and that the content of the HOT is inherited from that of the first-order thought. Whether he would endorse a formulation in terms of token constituency is unclear. Burge is certainly not giving an account of what it is for a thought to be conscious.

13. I use quasi-quotes in an extended way, such that the quasi-quotation:

    $\ulcorner$I believe that $p\urcorner$

    designates the thought or intentional content that would be expressed in the relevant context by the result of putting in the (unspecified) expression p for 'p' in 'I believe that p'. (I do not mean thereby to commit myself to thoughts themselves, as contrasted with ascriptions of them, having a language-like structure.) In the standard linguistic case, variables within quasi-quotes are used, not mentioned, and quasi-quotation of a single variable is vacuous, so that the expression $\ulcorner p\urcorner$ is just the expression p. By analogy and to reduce clutter I will speak of the thought p, the thought that p, and the thought with content p.

14. This last phrase is from Harry G. Frankfurt, "Freedom of the Will and the Concept of a Person", *Journal of Philosophy* 68, 1 (January 14, 1971), pp. 5-20; reprinted in David M. Rosenthal, ed., *The Nature of Mind* (Oxford University Press, 1991), pp. 441-449. My word 'endorse' needs qualification; in some cases S may, as Frankfurt puts it, wish that he had a different will.

15. Roughly this formula occurs in Jonathan Bennett, "Why is Belief Involuntary?", *Analysis* (1992), p. 97. Bennett credits the idea to Alexander Bain.

16. Cf. Paul A. Boghossian, "Content and Self-Knowledge", *Philosophical Topics* 17, 1 (Spring, 1989), pp. 5-26.

17. In saying this I am not committed to self-knowledge of appearances or desires involving an inner analog of ordinary perception. Cf. Gareth Evans, *The Varieties of Reference* (Oxford University Press, 1982), pp. 227-228.

18. Cf. Bernard Williams, "Deciding to Believe", in *Problems of the Self: Philosophical Papers 1956-1972* (Cambridge University Press, 1973), pp. 136-151. See also Barbara Winters, "Believing at Will", *Journal of Philosophy* 76, 5 (May 1979), pp. 243-256.

    The preference for true belief, which I allege all conscious reflective believers must have, can I believe be formulated without entailing that believers have a sophisticated notion of truth, and without entailing that if they come to believe bad news then they come to want that bad news to be true. It is also compatible with the phenomena of self-deception, and with wanting, all things considered, to have a false belief. The issues here are complex and I hope to deal with them elsewhere.

19. This point is made by Gareth Evans in *The Varieties of Reference* (Oxford University Press, 1982), p. 225.

20. See Stuart Hampshire, *Freedom of the Individual (expanded edition)* (Princeton University Press, 1975) p. 76 for this idea; see also page 79 for a comparison to a distinction in Spinoza's *Ethics* between active and passive emotion, pp. 86-87 for

the idea that self-belief is not merely autobiographical, and p. 97 for the idea that I cannot dissociate myself from the contents that I believe myself to believe.

21. The adverbial form 'third-personally' is not uncommon; I use the adjectival form 'third-personal', instead of the more common 'third-person', to remind us that it can describe self-knowledge in which there is not even apparently another person; i.e., self-knowledge in which the subject term 'I' gets its referent in the usual first-person way.

22. Stuart Hampshire, *Freedom of the Individual (expanded edition)* (Princeton University Press, 1975).

23. The connection is very near the surface in Hampshire, op. cit.; see p. 70, and pp. 86-87. Bas C. van Fraassen makes the connection explicitly in section 10 of his "Belief and the Problem of Ulysses and the Sirens", *Philosophical Studies* 77, 1 (January 1995), pp. 7-37; he and also argues that someone who violates van Fraassen's Principle of Reflection is similarly pragmatically inconsistent. I am much indebted to van Fraassen's paper. In particular, though without endorsing Reflection, I take van Fraassen's "forewarned as I am" defense of Reflection against certain counterexamples, in which the thinker adjusts his present belief about his future belief by steeling himself against the onset of a future belief he cannot currently endorse, to be a paradigmatic and illuminating invocation of what I call epistemic will.

24. J. N. Williams, "Moore's Paradox: One or Two?", *Analysis* 39, 3, New Series No. 183 (June 1979), pp. 141-142.

25. Rogers Albritton made this point in his contribution to the symposium "Moore's Paradox and Self-Knowledge", APA Pacific Division meeting, April 1, 1994. Albritton also notes that Moore does not say in his original discussions that his peculiar sentences cannot be used to make assertions.

26. Cf. Roy Sorensen, *Blindspots*, op. cit., pp. 26-27.

27. Cf. Roy Sorensen, "Modal Bloopers", forthcoming.

28. Jane Heal, "Moore's Paradox: A Wittgensteinian Approach", *Mind* 103, 409 (January 1994), pp. 5-24; see especially p. 15. I regard Heal's cases, as well as mine of this paragraph, as underdescribed.

29. Thus I do not use 'avow' in Ryle's sense, as a first-person utterance that is not an ordinary assertion but part of the behavior that characterizes being in the state to which it refers. In my usage, avowals with 'I' as subject may be third-personal.

30. Cf. Tyler Burge, "Intellectual Norms and the Foundations of the Mind", *Journal of Philosophy*, in which it is argued that a thinker may think a thought correctly described with 'sofa' in oblique context even though he "questions the meaning" of the word. In version 2 of the Gullibility Project case, however, *S* does not question the meaning of any lexical item, nor does he think of himself as questioning the linguistic or conceptual import of any syntactic construction.

31. See Robert Van Gulick, "A Functionalist Plea for Self-Consciousness", *The Philosophical Review* Vol. 97, No. 2 (April 1988), esp. pp. 179-181, for a discussion of being a self as the mutual bootstrapping of functioning as a unified agent and possessing psychological information about the self. Assuming Van Gulick's picture, I would argue that the latter component requires the exercise of epistemic will.

32. See, for example, Richard Foley, *Working Without a Net: A Study of Egocentric Epistemology* (Oxford University Press, 1993).

*Philosophical Perspectives, 9, AI, Connectionism, and
Philosophical Psychology, 1995*

MOORE'S PARADOX AND CONSCIOUSNESS†

David M. Rosenthal
City University of New York Graduate School

I. Moore's Paradox and Transparency

As G. E. Moore famously observed, sentences such as 'It's raining but I don't think it is', though they aren't contradictory, cannot be used to make coherent assertions.[1] The trouble with such sentences is not a matter of their truth conditions; such sentences can readily be true. Indeed, it happens often enough with each of us that we think, for example, that it isn't raining even though it is. This shows that such sentences are not literally contradictory. But even though such sentences have unproblematic truth conditions, we cannot say the same about their conditions of assertibility. There are no circumstances in which one can use such sentences to perform coherent assertoric speech acts. Situations exist in which these sentences would be true, but none in which anybody could use them to say so.

This phenomenon is known, following Wittgenstein,[2] as Moore's paradox. As some authors have noted, the difficulty arises not only with assertions, but also with speech acts whose illocutionary force is not assertoric.[3] Thus I cannot coherently say 'Thank you but I feel no gratitude' or 'Rain is likely, but I don't expect it'. If somebody were to produce such an utterance, we would automatically try to interpret the words nonliterally, or as having been used ironically or with some other oblique force. Only by doing so could we regard the speaker as having performed any speech act at all.[4]

One reason to trace the absurdity of Moore's paradox to the impossibility of performing any coherent speech act is that the absurdity may vanish when the very words of such sentences are embedded in a larger sentence.[5] Consider, for example, 'Suppose it's raining but I don't think it is'. If, instead, the trouble lay with the semantic content of those words, it would pursue the words even when they're embedded in such larger contexts.

It has not generally been noted that there's an important kinship between Moore's paradox and Descartes's *cogito*. The sentence 'I don't exist' has unproblematic truth conditions. Not only is it possible for the sentence to be true; it once was true for each of us. Nonetheless, the sentence has no coherent conditions of assertibility; no circumstances exist in which one could coherently perform a speech act by assertively producing that sentence. It's arguably that which underwrites Descartes's claim in Meditation II that "the statement 'I am, I exist' is necessarily true every time it is produced by me, or mentally conceived."[6]

Like Moore's paradox, the *cogito* is a function not of the truth conditions of sentences, but rather of the performance conditions of speech acts and, possibly, the mental analogue of these performance conditions for the corresponding propositional attitudes. A useful test is to see whether a change of grammatical tense or person relieves the difficulty. There's no problem about saying 'I *didn't* exist' (or '*won't* exist'), or 'It's raining but *you* don't think it is'.[7]

The sentence 'I am not thinking' resembles the sentence 'I don't exist' in exactly these ways. Just as 'I exist' is true every time I think it or assert it, so also is the sentence 'I am thinking'. This led Descartes to conclude that the "I" whose existence he had established is essentially a thinking thing. And this appears to point to a certain kind of self-knowledge. I cannot, when I'm thinking, doubt that I am thinking. So it's tempting to suppose that my being engaged in thinking is enough for me to know that I'm thinking. And because this conclusion rests on just the kind of reasoning that underwrites Moore's paradox, Moore's paradox seems to be relevant at least to a certain sort of self-knowledge.

If being engaged in thinking is enough to know that one is thinking, then to that extent at least the mind is transparent to itself. As Descartes put it, "nothing can be in our mind of which we are not at that time conscious."[8] But this thesis of transparency is untenable. Not all of our thinking is, in fact, conscious thinking. This is clear in part from results in clinical and cognitive psychology, but it's also obvious from everyday, commonsense considerations. We often consciously puzzle over a problem, for example, only to have the solution occur to us later, apparently spontaneously, without the problem having in the meantime been in any way consciously before our mind. It's hard to see how this could happen unless problem solving thinking sometimes occurs without being conscious. Such nonconscious problem-solving sometimes occurs, moreover, when we're not even aware that any thinking is going on, for example, when we're asleep. Many other commonsense considerations support the same conclusion. Simply being engaged in thinking plainly isn't sufficient for that thinking to be conscious.

What, then, went wrong with the reasoning that seemed to show otherwise? It's undeniable that, just as I cannot sensibly assert 'It's raining but I don't think it is', so I cannot assert that I'm not thinking, or perform the mental act of thinking that I'm not thinking. But this hardly shows that whenever I do think, I automatically think that I'm thinking. The question of whether I'm thinking may simply not come before my mind, consciously or otherwise. Indeed, though thinking does occur during sleep, we have no reason to suppose that, when it does, the question of whether one is thinking ever occurs to us as well.

That thinking can occur without one's being aware of it is evident also from consideration of nonhuman cases. It's overwhelmingly likely that some creatures have the capacity to think despite their having no concept of thinking. Such creatures would therefore be unable ever to think that they think.

Descartes and, in a somewhat similar spirit, Donald Davidson both deny that such a thing is possible. But it's hard to see any reason for that denial that doesn't beg the question. Descartes insists that "in order to know what doubting is, and what thinking is, only doubting or thinking is needed,"[9] but he gives no reason for that claim. Davidson, by contrast, argues for his view that one cannot believe things without having the concept of believing, maintaining that unless one understands the difference between true and erroneous believing one cannot have beliefs at all. But his argument shows at best that the ability to distinguish between truth and error is needed to have the concept of belief, not that it's also needed simply to have beliefs. Davidson offers no argument to bridge that gap.[10]

Humans, of course, do often engage in thinking of a kind that would be impossible without a concept of thinking. We sometimes think about the thinking that we or others are engaged in. Indeed, I've argued elsewhere that our being conscious of our conscious mental states is due to our having higher-order thoughts about those states.[11] But often our thinking isn't in any way conscious. And such consciousness apart, it's relatively seldom that we think about anybody's thoughts, our own or anybody else's. So why couldn't there be creatures whose thinking is always like our nonconscious thinking, and who moreover never think about anybody's thoughts? Such creatures might well have no concept of thinking. Though their mental lives would plainly be far less rich than ours, if the concept of thinking applies in our case both to thinking that we think about and to thinking that we don't, it should apply also to the more limited thinking that these other creatures engage in.

Sydney Shoemaker has developed a different argument for the view that we cannot straightforwardly apply our concepts for human mental phenomena to nonhuman animals. The reason, according to Shoemaker, is that many features of human mental phenomena are central to the very concepts of those phenomena. Minimal rationality, for example, is central to many such concepts. Since nonhuman animals apparently lack minimal rationality, Shoemaker concludes that applying these concepts to nonhuman animals is "problematic."[12]

But Shoemaker's principle about when we can apply various mental concepts leads to untenable results. The concepts whose application to nonhuman creatures Shoemaker sees as problematic are human folk-psychological concepts. And it would be unsurprising if these concepts were tailored to human mental phenomena. But the distinctive features of human mentality that these concepts embody may show relatively little about mind generally. For one thing, there could be creatures whose mental states exhibited important features not shared by human mental states, for example, rationality superior to our own. Concepts for human mental phenomena should apply unproblematically to corresponding states of such superior creatures. But on Shoemaker's view, such beings could not have a concept of mind, in our sense of the word.[13]

There's also reason to doubt Shoemaker's claim that minimal rationality is essential to human mentality. Human mental states don't always manifest the ties with other states that subserve such rationality and hence, on Shoemaker's view, self-knowledge. But our mental concepts plainly apply to human states, even when they lack those ties. So we have no reason not to apply these concepts to states of creatures, even when those states never exhibit the connections that subserve minimal rationality.

Whatever we say about nonhuman creatures, not all human thinking is conscious, nor can it always readily become conscious. So it's a mistake to expect the analogue of Moore's paradox that underlies the *cogito* to help establish any thesis about transparency. All it shows is that when creatures with the concept of thinking are actually thinking, they cannot sensibly deny, in speech or in thought, that they are thinking.

It's worth taking note of another thesis about transparency that's arguably related to Moore's paradox. It's often held that knowing something is sufficient for one to know that one knows. And if so, knowing is in effect transparent to itself. Consider the sentence ⌜I know that *p* but I don't know that I know it⌝. Though not contradictory, it seems that there cannot be coherent conditions for asserting the sentence.

Such sentences are not strictly cases of Moore's paradox,[14] since even if one didn't know that one knew one might still believe that one did. But Moore's paradox does help us understand what's wrong with that sentence. By Moore's paradox, saying I know that *p* makes it incoherent to deny that I believe that I know it. And saying I believe that I know that *p* would make it incoherent to deny that it's true that I know it. As for justification, if I say I know that *p*, I take my assertion to be justified; so I can't then coherently deny knowing that I know on the basis of my not being justified in thinking I know. Similarly, if I say I know that *p*, it would be incoherent to deny that I've tracked my knowing that *p*.[15] Nonetheless, this cousin of Moore's paradox no more warrants concluding that knowing actually implies knowing that one knows than the *cogito* entitles us to hold that all thinking is conscious. All it shows, rather, is that we cannot coherently assert that we know something and at the same time deny knowing that we know it.[16]

II. Language and Consciousness

I'll return in section IV to the question of whether Moore's paradox does help establish some form of self-knowledge about one's own mental states. But whatever the case about that, I want now to argue that Moore's paradox does point to factors that help explain a special case in which our thinking is almost without exception conscious thinking.

Whenever we say anything sincerely, we express some intentional state that we're in. If I sincerely say, for example, that it's raining, I express my thought that it's raining. Similarly with other sorts of speech act and the mental attitudes that correspond to them. If I say thank you, I express my gratitude; if I say it will probably rain I express my expectation that it will. And so forth. Every sincere speech act expresses an intentional state with the same content as the speech act and a mental attitude that corresponds to the illocutionary force of the speech act.

Moore's paradox reflects this connection between our speech acts and the intentional states they express. I cannot use the sentence 'It's raining but I don't think it is' to make a coherent assertion precisely because the assertion that the first conjunct purports to make expresses the very intentional state that the second conjunct denies I'm in. To be used in performing a conjunctive speech act, the first conjunct of a Moore's-paradox sentence must express a correspond-ing thought. But the second conjunct denies that any such thought exists, thereby denying that the whole sentence can be used to make any coherent assertion.[17] The same holds for the sentences 'Thank you but I'm not grateful' and 'It'll probably rain but I don't expect it to'; thanking somebody expresses one's gratitude, and saying something will probably happen expresses one's expectation. Similarly for versions of Moore's paradox derived from other illocutionary forces and the mental attitudes that correspond to them.

Many of our intentional states are not in any way conscious states. But when we express our intentional states in speech, those states are always conscious, or almost always. Suppose I think it's raining. My thought may or may not be conscious. But if I verbally express that thought by asserting that it's raining, the thought is invariably conscious. Indeed, with an exception that I'll mention in closing, any intentional state that I express with a speech act will be a conscious intentional state.

Intentional states are expressed not only by speech, but also by many forms of nonverbal behavior. Taking an umbrella may express my belief that it will rain, or my desire not to get wet, or both. Facial expressions and bodily movements of various kinds may express my delight in something or my dislike of it, my fear of something or my anticipation of some future event. In all these cases the intentional state my nonverbal behavior expresses may well be conscious; but it may also fail to be. I may take the umbrella absently, "without thinking," as we might say—that is, without thinking consciously. And one's facial expressions and bodily movements often betray delight, distaste, fear, and expectations of which one is, oneself, wholly unaware.

This difference between expressing intentional states verbally and expressing them by one's nonverbal behavior is striking. When an intentional state is expressed in speech, it's always conscious, but when it's expressed nonverbally it needn't be. Doubtless this contrast helped to persuade Descartes and others that language and consciousness are both essential to mentality. It's tempting to think and talk about intentional states in terms of the speech acts that would express them, since doing so enables us to describe the content and mental attitude of intentional states with an accuracy and precision not otherwise available.[18] And if we describe our own intentional states and those of others by reference to speech acts that would express those states, we may take the further step of thinking about all intentional states as though they are expressed in speech, and hence conscious. But as we've seen, there is ample evidence that our commonsense, folk-psychological conceptions don't require that all intentional states are conscious, and indeed ample evidence that many of them are not.

It might be argued that slips of the tongue, such as those said to occur in Freudian parapraxis, cause difficulty here. Such slips, it may seem, express thoughts of which we're not conscious. If so, the thoughts our speech acts express sometimes aren't conscious. But there would also be another problem. The latent content such slips supposedly express is typically distinct from the manifest content that matches the semantic meaning of the speech act. So the content of these speech acts would diverge from the content of the intentional states they express. Of course, the latent thought expressed by one's slip is often conscious; witness the conscious embarrassment sometimes caused by realization of what one's slip reveals. Even so, it's arguable that the content of the speech acts involved in such slips corresponds not to the latent content, but to the manifest content.

But in fact things are more complicated. Suppose an unintended word intrudes into one's performing of a speech act, thereby revealing some nonconscious thought that one has. The occurrence of that word is best construed not as an integral part of the speech act, but in effect as a piece of nonverbal behavior. It's on a par with cases in which one's tone, or other aspects of one's utterances, unintentionally betray one's nonconscious intentional states. The way we utter things often manifest intentional states without thereby expressing them verbally. The latent thought in these cases is simply a causal factor, somewhat like an external noise, which interferes with the correct expression of the conscious thought corresponding to the speech act. So the slips that occur in parapraxis are not counterexamples to the foregoing generalizations.

It's important here to distinguish between verbally expressing an intentional state and reporting that state. Although verbally expressing our intentional states and reporting them are both ways of conveying to others what intentional states we're in, there are important differences between these two ways. When I think it's raining, I verbally express my thought by saying that it's raining. My verbal expression has the same content as the intentional state it expresses and an illocutionary force that corresponds to the mental attitude of the intentional state. By contrast, I report my thought that it's raining when I explicitly say that I have that thought, for example, when I say 'I think it's raining'. And the content of my thought differs from the speech act that reports it.

The contrast between reporting and expressing one's intentional states emerges most decisively, however, with intentional states that have a nonassertoric mental attitude. If I wonder whether it'll rain, I express my state of wondering by saying 'Will it rain?', whereas I report my wondering by saying 'I wonder whether it'll rain'. Here the illocutionary force of the speech act that verbally expresses my intentional state is that of a question, corresponding to the mental attitude of wondering. By contrast, the illocutionary force of my report is assertoric, as it is with all reports of intentional states.

Again, Moore's paradox is helpful. I cannot assertively produce the sentence 'It's raining but I don't think it is' because asserting the first conjunct would express an intentional state that the second conjunct denies I am in. Suppose, now, that there were no difference between reporting an intentional state and verbally expressing it. Then my denial that I am in the intentional state of thinking that it's raining would be tantamount simply to expressing the thought that it's not raining. Accordingly, the Moore's-paradox sentence would be equivalent to 'It's raining and it's not raining', which is an actual contradiction. But Moore's paradox is not literally contradictory. To avoid this result, therefore, we must distinguish reporting our intentional states from verbally expressing them.

Ordinary usage of verbs of propositional attitude may sometimes seem to run together reporting with expressing of our intentional states. For example, when one says ⌜I doubt (or suppose) that *p*⌝, 'I choose this one', or 'I sympathize with you', it may seem that one expresses one's doubt, supposition, choice, or sympathy, rather than reports those states. But this appearance results from focusing exclusively on performance conditions. Once we take into consideration the truth conditions of such sentences, it's clear that these speech acts report the relevant attitudes. Indeed, as just noted, Moore's paradox would otherwise be an outright contradiction.

Distinguishing between reporting our intentional states and expressing them allows us to formulate a second connection between consciousness and speech. Verbally expressing an intentional state is, with a certain type of exception, a sufficient condition for that state to be conscious. But also, when a creature has the requisite concepts and linguistic ability, a mental state's being conscious is sufficient for the creature to be able to report being in that state.

This second connection between language and consciousness is to be expected. Conscious mental states satisfy two conditions: we're conscious of being in them, and the way we're conscious of them seems to us to be immediate. We needn't, of course, be conscious of our conscious states in a way that's at all attentive or focused; we're only peripherally conscious of the vast majority of our conscious states. But when mental states occur of which we are not in any way conscious, those states are not conscious states. And, given the requisite concepts and linguistic ability, being conscious of something is sufficient for being able to report about it.

What about the other way around? Being able to report about a mental state is not sufficient for that state to be conscious, because a state's being conscious requires not just that one is conscious of that state, but also that one is conscious of it in a way that's from an intuitive point of view immediate. Being able to report some mental state one's in solely because of behavioral evidence one has that one is in that state is not sufficient for the state to be a conscious state.

This intuitive immediacy may not amount to much. It's enough for our consciousness of our own mental states to be intuitively immediate that we're conscious of them in a way that doesn't rely on any inference, at least not on any inference of which we're aware.[19] So, although being able to report on a state doesn't suffice for that state to be conscious, being able to report on it noninferentially does.

III. Verbally Expressed Thoughts

We are now in a position to explain why verbally expressed intentional states are invariably conscious. Moore's paradox is absurd because the speech acts of asserting that p and asserting that I think that p, though they differ in respect of their truth conditions, have roughly the same conditions of assertibility. Any circumstances in which I could say that p are circumstances in which I could say I think that p. And with a qualification[20] that won't affect the argument here, the converse holds as well.

More important, this performance-conditional equivalence is second nature for us. We automatically take saying $\ulcorner p \urcorner$ and saying $\ulcorner$I think that $p \urcorner$ to amount to much the same thing insofar as conditions of assertibility are concerned. Indeed, we ourselves tend insensibly to slip between saying the one and saying the other; we may even have difficulty recalling on specific occasions which of the two forms we used. It's a matter of well-entrenched linguistic habit that the two are, for practical purposes, interchangeable. It's because this performance-conditional equivalence is second nature to us that Moore's paradox is not just absurd, but intuitively jarring. We know automatically that no circumstances can exist in which somebody could sensibly say that p but deny thinking that p.

The relevant performance-conditional equivalence emerges in the absurdity of the following conversation. Suppose I ask you whether it's raining, you say 'I think so', and I remonstrate that I asked not about your intentional states but about the weather. That's a bad joke in roughly the way Moore's paradox is, though it's harder here to imagine any charitable reinterpretation that would save things. And it's jarring in just the way Moore's paradox is, because in that context we automatically regard your saying 'I think so' as performance-conditionally equivalent to your saying that it's raining. Indeed, it's so automatic as to be second nature.

Suppose I think that it's raining, and I express my thought by saying 'It's raining'. Because saying 'It's raining' is performance-conditionally equivalent to saying 'I think it's raining', I could equally well have said that I think it's raining. And because that equivalence is second nature for us, I might as easily have said the other; in most circumstances it's likely to be a matter of complete indifference to me which I say.

Now put performance conditions aside for a moment, and think instead of truth conditions. What makes the sentence 'I think it's raining' true isn't the rain, but my being in a certain intentional state. Its being true requires that I think it's raining. So if I were to say 'I think it's raining', however we may take that remark in respect of performance conditions, I am literally telling you about one of my intentional states. I am reporting a certain thought.

So, when I express my thought that it's raining by saying 'It's raining', I could equally well have reported my thought that it's raining. Moreover, because it's second nature for us that saying 'It's raining' is performance-conditionally equivalent to saying 'I think it's raining', if I had instead said 'I think it's raining', my report would have not have been based on any inference, at least not on any inference of which I was conscious.[21] So, whenever I actually say 'It's raining', I could equally well have noninferentially reported my thought that it's raining.

But noninferential reportability is sufficient for a state to be a conscious state. So, given that it's second nature for us that saying 'It's raining' is perform-ance-conditionally equivalent to saying 'I think it's raining', whenever I verbally express any intentional state, that state will be conscious. And, since Moore's paradox is a reflection of that performance-conditional equivalence, we have used the factors that underlie Moore's paradox to explain why verbally expressed intentional states are always conscious.

Let me again briefly rehearse the argument. I've urged that Moore's paradox is absurd because saying $\ulcorner p \urcorner$ is performance-conditionally equivalent to saying $\ulcorner$I think that $p \urcorner$. And it's intuitively jarring because that equivalence is so automatically a part of how we use these words. Given the equivalence, whenever I say $\ulcorner p \urcorner$, I could equally well have said $\ulcorner$I think that $p \urcorner$. But to say $\ulcorner$I think that $p \urcorner$ is, literally, to report one's thought that p. And because it's second nature that saying $\ulcorner p \urcorner$ is performance-conditionally equivalent to saying $\ulcorner$I think that $p \urcorner$, saying $\ulcorner$I think that $p \urcorner$ would be reporting one's thought noninferentially. Being able to report an intentional state noninferentially, however, is sufficient for that state to be conscious. So the factors underlying Moore's paradox also explain why all verbally expressed intentional states are conscious.

The explanation applies equally to intentional states whose mental attitude is not assertoric. If I ask, 'Is it raining?', for example, the performance-conditional equivalence revealed by Moore's paradox shows that I could just as well have said 'I wonder whether it's raining'. If I say 'Close the door', I could instead have said in so many words that I want you to close it. Whenever I verbally express these intentional states, I'm able also to report those states noninferentially; similarly for states with other mental attitudes. A intentional state's being verbally expressed is sufficient for its being conscious.

The connection between an intentional state's being expressed and its being conscious holds only, as we've seen, when the state is expressed in speech. States expressed by nonverbal behavior often aren't conscious. It will reinforce the foregoing explanation if we can use it to show why things are different in the two kinds of case.

Unlike speech acts, the pieces of nonverbal behavior that express our intentional states do not have established performance conditions. Taking my umbrella may in certain circumstances be odd or irrational or inappropriate, but these things don't define performance conditions for my action. Because taking my umbrella has no performance conditions, even if that action nonverbally expresses, say, my desire not to get wet, the action cannot have the same performance conditions as a speech act that reports the desire I nonverbally express. So taking the umbrella will not be interchangeable, as a matter of well-entrenched linguistic habit, with the making of such a report. I might well perform the action of taking the umbrella even when I could not readily report the desire my action expresses. Similarly with other cases of nonverbally expressing our intentional states. An intentional state's being nonverbally expressed is not, therefore, sufficient for that state to be conscious.

We could, perhaps, imagine a piece of nonverbal behavior becoming so well-entrenched in our social practices that we came to see that behavior as having performance conditions. For example, taking an umbrella might come not simply to indicate the likelihood of rain,[22] but also actually to mean that it's going to rain, that is, to have that semantic content. Taking an umbrella would then be performance-conditionally equivalent to reporting one's thought that it's going to rain. It's arguable that if that equivalence also became second nature, one would be unable to take an umbrella without one's thought that it's going to rain being conscious. Intuitions about this kind of case, however, are unlikely to be firm enough to test this idea, since that kind of thing is unlike anything that actually happens.

I've argued that Moore's paradox is absurd because every speech act is roughly equivalent, in respect of performance conditions, to a report of the intentional state that the speech act expresses. But one might wonder whether the trouble with Moore's paradox is simpler than this. Perhaps all that's wrong is that one cannot say 'It's raining but I don't think it is' without betraying one's insincerity in saying it. In effect, Moore's paradox would then be simply self-defeating. Indeed, Moore himself at one point suggests this kind of diagnosis.[23]

On such an account, we need to explain why it is that saying 'It's raining but I don't think it is' automatically betrays one's insincerity.[24] One possibility is suggested by Paul Grice's idea that my meaning something involves intending that my hearer believe that I believe what I say. On this proposal, I couldn't mean that p if in the same breath I said I don't believe it. So I couldn't say it sincerely.[25] But this is implausible as an explanation of what's wrong with Moore's paradox. Moore's paradox is absurd independent of any context of communication. It's absurd even in soliloquy, where no betrayal of insincerity is relevant; one cannot say even to oneself 'It's raining but I don't think it is'.[26] The best explanation of this independence from any context of communication will arguably appeal to the performance-conditional equivalence I've been relying on.

I suggested earlier that this equivalence holds because of a connection between intentional states and the speech acts that express them. All speech acts express corresponding intentional states; we cannot coherently assert 'It's raining but I don't think it is' because what the first conjunct purports to assert expresses the intentional state that the second conjunct denies I am in.

Earlier I described the regularity concerning speech acts' expressing intentional states solely in terms of sincere speech. But how about insincere speech? When my utterance of 'It's raining' is a lie, none of my assertoric intentional states has the content *it's raining*; so my words can't express any such actual state. Still, don't I *say* it's raining? Only in a qualified way. 'Say' and related verbs of illocutionary act are sometimes used in a weak sense, as roughly equivalent to 'utter'; saying in this sense involves no illocutionary act. For example, when we recite lines in a poem or play, we seldom if ever produce them with illocutionary force, though typically we pretend to; we say things then in only the weak sense. When an actor utters 'My heart is in the coffin there with Caesar', nobody would take him to perform an actual illocutionary act, despite his pretense to do so. As Frege remarked, "stage assertion is only sham assertion."[27]

Insincere speech also operates this way. When we speak insincerely we pretend to be in intentional states that don't exist, and thereby pretend to perform the relevant illocutionary acts. Lying and play acting differ, of course, in the motives we have for pretending; so in lying my pretense isn't candid, as it is in play acting. Moreover, in lying the character I play is a fictional version of myself, one who actually believes the things I pretend to assert. So when I speak insincerely, it's only in the reciting sense that I say anything.

One might reject this account of insincere speech on the ground that it treats sincere and insincere speech differently. But a uniform treatment has significant disadvantages. Since no corresponding intentional state causes insincere utterances, a uniform treatment must require that the connection between thought and speech generally is oblique. And that oblique connection is almost certain to appeal to a context of communication, even though speech, sincere and insincere alike, often occurs independently of any such context. We can conclude that insincere speech notwithstanding, all illocutionary acts express corresponding intentional states.[28]

What, then, is the status of the regularity about speech acts' expressing corresponding intentional states? It cannot be purely a conceptual matter, a matter of nothing more than the meanings of the relevant words. If it were part of the meaning of 'assert' that assertions express corresponding beliefs, Moore's paradox would not simply have problematic performance conditions, but would be an outright contradiction.[29] Nonetheless, it's somehow a part of the way we automatically think about asserting and other speech acts. The only alternative is that the connection between speech acts and corresponding intentional states is a particularly well-entrenched part of our folk-psychological conceptions.[30]

Those who diagnose Moore's paradox as being conceptually defective sometimes urge that the only alternative to that view is an account on which Moore's paradox "merely...depict[s] situations which we take to be extremely unlikely."[31] But here as elsewhere, the dichotomy between conceptual and merely empirical misleads. Much that's intuitively impossible runs counter not to established semantic connections, but only deeply entrenched background beliefs about the way things are.

For a speech act to express an intentional state is, in part, for that state to be among the causal factors leading to the speech act. When I say that it's raining, many things causally contribute to my saying it. But if my speech act verbally expresses my thought that it's raining, my having that thought is one of the causal factors that lead to my saying it. I've argued that this connection between speech and thinking is, for us, so strongly second nature that simply saying that *p* inevitably makes it obvious to one that one thinks that *p*. And the very same connection is responsible for there being no coherent performance conditions for asserting Moore's paradox.

IV. Moore's Paradox and Self-knowledge

It's impossible, even speaking to oneself, to assert 'It's raining but I don't think it is'. Moreover, it's no less impossible to think that thing assertorically. Just as there are no coherent conditions for asserting 'It's raining but I don't think it is', so there's no coherent mental analogue of assertibility conditions for thinking 'It's raining but I don't think it is'.

But the tie between speech acts and the intentional states they express can't by itself explain why it's impossible to think Moore's paradox. Nor does that tie have any suitable mental analogue. Because asserting expresses a corresponding belief, it's impossible to assert anything without believing it. But it's plainly possible to think something without thinking that we think that thing. Indeed, it's arguable that that typically happens when our thoughts aren't conscious. We can't explain the impossibility of thinking Moore's paradox by appeal to the same factors that explain the impossibility of saying it.

It's sometimes held that a satisfactory explanation of Moore's paradox must explain in a uniform way why we cannot say it and why we cannot think it. This requirement would preclude explaining the linguistic version of Moore's paradox by reference to performance conditions. Proponents of a uniform treatment typically also insist that semantic contradictoriness somehow underlies Moore's paradox. Speech acts and intentional states literally share their content; so, if we must give an uniform explanation, it will have to be in semantic terms.[32] But we can use the uniformity requirement to undermine the performance-conditional explanation only if we have independent reason to adopt that requirement. And it's unlikely that any reason exists apart from the claim that Moore's paradox demands a semantic explanation, which in this context is question begging.

How, then, can we explain the impossibility of thinking Moore's paradox? Here, it seems, we must appeal to a certain rationality that governs many of our thoughts. We can perfectly well have the thought that *p* without thinking that we have it. But it's irrational both to think that *p* and to think that one doesn't think it. So, if the question arises about whether one thinks that *p* and one does actually think that *p*, it would be irrational to conclude that one doesn't think it.

Rationality does not of course dictate that this question will arise. And when it doesn't, it's generally possible to think that *p* without thinking that one thinks that *p*. In that kind of case, the first-order thought arguably will not be a conscious thought. But insofar as we are rational in this particular way, if one has some particular thought and it's possible for the question to arise as to whether one has it, it must also be possible for the relevant higher-order thought to occur. As Kant insisted, in the case of rational beings "the representation '*I think*'...must be capable of accompanying all other representations... ."[33]

Sydney Shoemaker has argued for an even stronger connection between rationality and our having thoughts about our thoughts. Adopting the functionalist view that believing and desiring are defined in terms of certain connections with actions, sensory input, and other mental states, Shoemaker argues that these connections actually constitute a certain minimal rationality. Moreover, he urges that beliefs and desires do more than simply cause the behavior with which they're rationally connected; they also "rationalize" that behavior. And to rationalize a course of action, beliefs and desires must refer to it.

But rationality applies not merely to overt actions, but also to the very mental activities of believing and desiring, themselves. Just as having certain beliefs and desires may make a certain course of action rational, so too it may be rational to adopt certain beliefs and desires given that we have certain others. But as with overt courses of action, we do not count as rational a person's adopting or changing certain beliefs or desires unless others of the person's beliefs and desires rationalize that adoption or change of beliefs and desires. And the beliefs and desires that do this rationalizing will have to refer to those which are rationally adopted. The rational fixation of beliefs and desires requires one to have higher-order beliefs about the first-order beliefs and desires one rationally fixes. Accordingly, such rationality cannot occur without our being conscious of our first-order beliefs and desires.[34]

As Shoemaker notes, one could deny that rationality in the adopting of beliefs and desires is due to explicit rationalizing by higher-order beliefs and desires. Perhaps rationality here requires only that the causal relations that hold among our first-order beliefs and desires conform to rational standards.[35] It's far more plausible that beliefs and desires are states whose causal ties tend to conform to patterns we count as rational than that they are definitionally states whose rational fixation requires the causal influence of higher-order beliefs and desires. Perhaps, then, rationality doesn't require us to have higher-order beliefs.

But even if rationalization of the sort Shoemaker describes does occur, there's another difficulty with his argument. Beliefs and desires are sometimes occurrent, but often they're dispositional. In their dispositional versions, belief and desire are simply dispositions to be in the relevant occurrent intentional states. And the beliefs and desires that rationalize actions will often be dispositional in just this way. But simply being disposed to have an occurrent belief or desire about something doesn't make us conscious of that thing. So, when the higher-order thoughts and desires that rationalize our adoption of certain first-order beliefs and desires are merely dispositional, they won't make us conscious of the first-order states. So they won't make those first-order states conscious states. Moreover, there could be creatures for which that's how it always happens. In the human case, the higher-order beliefs and desires that rationalize other intentional states are often occurrent. But rationality would not be compromised if the higher-order states were always dispositional. Intentional states can be rational without being conscious; indeed a creature could exist for which all rationality among its intentional states was that way.[36]

Connections between rationality and consciousness to one side, Shoemaker has developed an ingenious and probing argument that links Moore's paradox to one's having first-person access to one's mental states.[37] He defines as self-blind a being that has our concepts of mental phenomena and can therefore ascribe to itself mental states, but which has no first-person access to its mental states. A self-blind individual could come to believe that it's in some particular mental state, but only in a characteristically third-person way. Such an individual, moreover, might be presented with highly compelling third-person evidence both that it's raining and also that it doesn't believe that it's raining. Since the self-blind creature lacks any first-person access, this third-person evidence would give it good reason to assert 'It's raining but I don't think it is'.

Shoemaker argues, however, that Moore's paradox would be absurd even for a self-blind creature, so defined. He urges that such an individual, simply by being conceptually unimpaired, would recognize the absurdity of Moore's paradox; on my account, that would mean recognizing the performance-conditional connections between saying that p and saying $\ulcorner$I think that $p\urcorner$. But then, Shoemaker urges, our ostensibly self-blind individual would be indistinguishable from somebody that does have ordinary first-person access. And if this is so, self-blindness is not a possibility, after all; any creature with our mental concepts and the ability to ascribe mental states to itself in a third-person way would also be able to do so in a first-person way as well. First-person access to one's own mental states would follow from that conceptual capacity alone.[38]

For creatures relevantly like us, all verbally expressed intentional states are conscious. So any such creatures will have first-person access to all their verbally expressed intentional states. The factors that explain Moore's paradox, I've argued, also underlie this connection between verbal expression and consciousness. But very few of our intentional states are actually expressed in speech; indeed, few come close to being so expressed. Moore's paradox, moreover, arguably pertains in the first instance to whether certain speech acts can be performed. So even if a self-blind creature does have first-person access to its verbally expressed intentional states, it's unclear why merely recognizing the absurdity of Moore's paradox would extend such first-person access to intentional states that aren't expressed in speech.

Moreover, even a self-blind individual that recognized the absurdity of Moore's paradox might not be like us in the ways required for it to have first-person access even to its verbally expressed intentional states. By the definition of self-blindness, such an individual would have our mental concepts, and be able to believe of itself that it's in various mental states. And, as Shoemaker's argument makes clear, it will have the ability to express its intentional states in speech. But on the argument I put forth earlier, that's not sufficient for all the self-blind individual's verbally expressed thoughts to be conscious. It's also necessary that the performance-conditional equivalence between saying ⌜p⌝ and saying ⌜I think that p⌝ is second nature to that individual.

This is important because, if that connection is not second nature, the access an individual has to its verbally expressed thoughts will be based on some conscious inference. And access that's thus consciously mediated would be characteristically third-person access, even if it's access to the individual's own states. It would therefore not make one's verbally expressed thoughts conscious. And since genuine self-knowledge requires conscious first-person access, it would not result in self-knowledge, either.

Shoemaker often writes as though sensitivity to the absurdity of Moore's paradox would be a direct result of having unimpaired conceptual capacities.[39] If so, the relevant performance-conditional equivalences would presumably be conceptual truths; they would thus be second nature for us. I've argued against this idea. It's difficult to see how to explain Moore's paradox by appeal to the meanings of words like 'assert' and 'think' without construing it as an outright contradiction. It's more plausible, I think, to see the connection between asserting and believing as part of our folk-psychological knowledge about these things— part of a folk theory so well-entrenched as to constitute commonly shared background knowledge. The relevant conceptual competence is necessary, but not sufficient, for the performance-conditional equivalence. If this is right, our self-blind creature's access to its own mental states would be mediated by a conscious inference that relies on the relevant folk-theoretic connection.

But even if the relevant tie between thinking and asserting were an exclusively conceptual matter and not part of folk theory, our self-blind individual might still have to rely on some conscious inference for access to its own mental states. Conceptual truths function in effect as null premises in inference. So any inference that relies solely on such truths would be automatic. But the self-blind individual's inference would rely on more than the conceptual connection between speech and thinking. That inference would go from that conceptual connection plus the fact that the individual asserts that p to that individual's thinking that p. Indeed, Shoemaker sometimes seems to envisage the need for some conscious inference. "[I]t ought to possible," he writes at one point, "to get [our self-blind creature] to recognize that the assertive utterance of Moore-paradoxical sentences involves some sort of logical impropriety."[40]

Perhaps, however, the relevant inference would after a time come to be second nature, and would therefore no longer be conscious. The resulting access that the self-blind individual would have to at least those of its thoughts which are verbally expressed would then not be based on any inference of which it was aware. Such access would therefore be indistinguishable from the first-person access we have to our conscious states. But the concept of self-blindness does not ensure that the required inference would ever stop being conscious. And if it didn't, the self-blind individual would continue to be limited to having only third-person access to its mental states.

Shoemaker argues that any individual with mental concepts "will be aware of having [mental states] when it does, or at least will become aware of this under certain conditions (e.g., if it reflects on the matter)."[41] Shoemaker may be assuming here that "reflect[ing] on the matter" is enough to raise the question whether one is in a certain mental state. And that, along with the particular kind of rationality discussed earlier (pp. 324-5) would be sufficient for one to be aware that one is in that state.

But reflection will not, in general, raise the question of whether one is in a particular mental state unless, independently of reflection, one already has access to the state. If one's access to the state is characteristically third-person, reflection cannot transform that into first-person access, since that would mean making one unaware of the relevant third-person considerations. And it begs the question at hand to invoke reflection if one must already have first-person access.

According to Wittgenstein, Moore's paradox is absurd because "the statement 'I believe it's going to rain' has a meaning like, that is to say a use like, 'It's going to rain'."[42] In effect, this is to construe the speech act 'I believe it's raining' as expressing my belief that it's raining, rather than as reporting that belief. This diagnosis of Moore's paradox can be seen as having consequences about self-knowledge. If I make no claim about my mental states when I say 'I believe it's raining', my remark cannot be challenged on that score. And that would help us understand the air of incorrigibility such remarks have, even though they would not then express knowledge about one's beliefs.[43]

This view notoriously faces serious difficulties. On it, for example, I cannot literally deny another person's claim that I don't believe that it's raining.[44] Shoemaker's argument, by contrast, appeals to no such diagnosis, and he countenances both genuine self-knowledge and the semantic difference between ⌜p⌝ and ⌜I think that p⌝. Still, it's not clear exactly what the semantic difference between these two amounts to if conceptual competence alone is enough to take one automatically from one to the other.

I've argued that Moore's paradox sheds light on our first-person access by pointing to those factors which explain why all verbally expressed intentional states are conscious. But as I also mentioned, there's an exception to that regularity. Suppose I assert 'I think it's raining'. Speech acts express intentional states with the same content; so here my speech act expresses my thought that I think it's raining. It expresses, that is, a higher-order thought to the effect that I have the thought that it's raining. But that's not the thought I'm typically aware of having when I say I think it's raining. Rather, when I say I think it's raining, the thought I'm ordinarily conscious of is my first-order thought that it's raining. When I perform a speech act whose content is that I'm in some intentional state, the state that's conscious is not the state my speech act expresses, but the state it reports.

This is an important exception. It's doubtless this kind of case that has encouraged some to assimilate the reporting of mental states to the verbal expression of those states. As I remarked earlier, Moore's paradox helps resist that tendency; if reports and verbal expressions weren't different, Moore's paradox would be an actual contradiction, which it isn't. Still the exception demands explanation. That, however, is a task for another occasion.[45]

Notes

†This is an expanded version of a paper read at the American Philosophical Association, Pacific Division, Symposium on Moore's Paradox and Self-Knowledge, April 1994, in Los Angeles. The shorter version appears, slightly revised, in *Philosophical Studies* (77, 2-3 (March 1995): 195-209), under the title "Self-Knowledge and Moore's Paradox," along with the contributions of the other symposiasts, Sydney Shoemaker, "Moore's Paradox and Self-Knowledge," 211-228, and Rogers Albritton, "Comments on 'Moore's Paradox and Self-Knowledge,'" 229-239.

1. G.E. Moore, "A Reply to My Critics," in *The Philosophy of G.E. Moore*, ed. Paul Arthur Schilpp (New York: Tudor Publishing Company, 1942) [2nd ed. 1952]: 533-677, p. 543; "Russell's 'Theory of Descriptions'," in *The Philosophy of Bertrand Russell*, ed. Paul Arthur Schilpp (New York: Tudor Publishing Company, 1944): 175-226, p. 204.

2. Ludwig Wittgenstein, *Philosophical Investigations*, translated by G.E.M. Anscombe (New York: Macmillan, 1953), II, §X; *Remarks on the Philosophy of Psychology*, vol. I, edited by G.E.M. Anscombe and G.H. von Wright, translated by G.E.M. Anscombe (Oxford: Basil Blackwell, 1980), pp. 91f.

   Rogers Albritton has urged that what Wittgenstein regarded as paradoxical was not that such sentences as 'It's raining but I don't think it is' are troubled, but that they are troubled even though counterparts not in the first-person present tense are not. ("Comments," p. 229. This view recalls *Remarks on the Philosophy of Psychology*, vol. I, ¶490.) But even if that's so, we could understand this paradoxical contrast only if we first understand what's defective about the first-person, present-tense case, and the correct account of those might then make the contrast no longer seem paradoxical.

3. Max Black, "Saying and Disbelieving," *Analysis*, 13, 2 (December 1952): 25-33, pp. 32-3; David M. Rosenthal, "Intentionality," *Midwest Studies in Philosophy*, X (1986): 151-184; p. 154; John R. Searle, *Intentionality: An Essay in the Philosophy of Mind* (Cambridge: Cambridge University Press, 1983), p. 9; and Sydney Shoemaker, "On Knowing One's Own Mind," *Philosophical Perspectives, 2, Epistemology, 1988*, 183-209, pp. 204-5. D.H. Mellor claims, to the contrary, that Moore's paradox "has no analogue for the other attitudes" ("What Is Computational Psychology?", *Proceedings of the Aristotelian Society*, Supplementary Volume LVIII [1984]: 37-53, p. 38).

4. Roy A. Sorensen has argued that we can assert certain indirect versions of Moore's paradox, e.g., 'The atheism of my mother's nieceless brother's only nephew angers God', which implies 'God exists but I believe that God does not exist'. (See his

Blindspots [Oxford: Oxford University Press, 1988], p. 28; I am grateful to Sorensen for calling this argument to my attention.) But one can assert Sorensen's sentence only if one doesn't fully understand its content; it's as though one asserts a certain sentence to be true, without really asserting its content.

5.   As Wittgenstein in effect noted and, more explicitly, Albritton.

6.   "Necessarily" because 'I don't exist' necessarily lacks conditions of assertibility. *Oeuvres de Descartes*, ed. Charles Adam and Paul Tannery (Paris: J. Vrin, 1964-75), VII, p. 25; my translations here and below. See *The Philosophical Writings of Descartes*, by René Descartes, translated by John Cottingham, Robert Stoothoff, Dugald Murdoch, and Anthony Kenny, 3 volumes (Cambridge: Cambridge University Press, 1984-91), which gives the Adam and Tannery page numbers.

7.   I develop this explanation of the *cogito* briefly in "Will and the Theory of Judgment," in *Essays on Descartes' Meditations*, ed. Amélie O. Rorty (Berkeley: University of California Press, 1986), pp. 405-434, §IV, and more extensively in "Judgment, Mind, and Will in Descartes," Report No. 29/1990, Center for Interdisciplinary Research (ZiF), University of Bielefeld, §VII.

8.   *Fourth Replies*, Adam and Tannery, VII, p. 232. Descartes is aware that his reasoning establishes transparency only with respect to what mental attitudes our intentional states exhibit, and not also with respect to the content of those states, and thus explicitly qualifies his claim in the quoted passage (see also VII, pp. 246-246).

9.   *The Search for Truth*, Adam and Tannery, X, p. 524.

10.   "Thought and Talk," in *Mind and Language*, ed. Samuel Guttenplan, (Oxford: Oxford University Press), 1975, pp. 7-23.

11.   E.g., in "Thinking that One Thinks," in *Consciousness*, ed. Martin Davies and Glyn W. Humphreys (Oxford: Basil Blackwell, 1993), pp. 197-223, and "A Theory of Consciousness," in *The Nature of Consciousness: Philosophical Debates*, ed. Ned Block, Owen Flanagan, and Güven Güzeldere (Cambridge, Mass.: MIT Press, forthcoming)

12.   "Rationality and Self-Consciousness," in *The Opened Curtain: A U.S.-Soviet Philosophy Summit*, ed. Keith Lehrer and Ernest Sosa (Boulder, Colorado: Westview Press, 1991): 127-149; p. 145, see §§IV-V.

13.   Shoemaker evidently also thinks that the only alternative to using our concepts of human folk psychology would be to use concepts of subpersonal states "describable in the terminology of neurophysiology" ("Rationality and Self-Consciousness," p. 147). But that's far from obvious. We can avoid discredited aspects of our commonsense conception of mentality without restricting ourselves to subpersonal description; we could simply strip the unwanted features away. Similarly, if human folk-psychological concepts embody parochial features special to human mentality, we may well be able to subtract them, and use the resulting concepts to talk equally well about both our mental states and those of other creatures.

14.   Nor, *pace* John Koethe, are sentences of the form ⌜p but I don't know that p⌝, of which the target sentence is a substitution instance, since I may unequivocally believe that *p* even if I don't know it. (See Koethe, "A Note On Moore's Paradox," *Philosophical Studies*, 34 (1978): 303-310, p. 303.)

15.   Robert Nozick, *Philosophical Explanations* (Cambridge, Mass.: Harvard University Press, 1981), pp. 245-247.

16.   Knowing can be either active or latent; active knowing is conscious, and latent knowing is, roughly, being disposed to have active knowledge. It's typically not

noted that only when the relevant knowing is uniformly conscious is there intuitive appeal to the claim that knowing implies knowing that one knows; when knowing is latent, that intuitive appeal vanishes. This reinforces the suggestion that knowing appears to imply second-order knowing only because one cannot coherently represent oneself as knowing while at the same time denying that one know that one knows.

17. So on my view the trouble does not result, as Albritton suggests, from one's being conscious of the belief the first conjunct purports to express.

18. Indeed, it's likely that when we describe intentional states in terms of the content and illocutionary force of speech acts that might express those states, we draw more fine-grained distinctions among those states than their nature warrants. We project distinctions among our words back onto the intentional states those words express, even though nothing about the intentional states themselves would allow us to distinguish them so finely.

19. There's no circularity in this last qualification, since we're explaining what it is for a state to be conscious in terms of what it is we're conscious *of.* A state is conscious just in case one is conscious of being in that state, and conscious of that in a way that's independent of any inference of which one is, in turn, conscious.

20. ⌐I think that p⌐ can, of course, be used to qualify the firmness of one's conviction that p is the case, in ways that simply asserting ⌐p⌐ doesn't.

21. I take that qualification for granted in what follows.

22. As with Paul Grice's "natural" meaning; see his "Meaning," *The Philosophical Review* LXVI, 3 (July 1957), 377-88.

23. "A Reply to My Critics," pp. 542-43.

24. Many speech acts telegraph their insincerity; what's allegedly different about Moore's paradox is that it does this solely as a result of its semantic properties, and not, e.g., because of the way it's uttered.

25. Paul Grice, "Utterer's Meaning and Intentions," *The Philosophical Review*, LXXVIII, 2 (April 1969): 147-177. Mellor endorses this explanation. See "Conscious Belief," *Proceedings of the Aristotelian Society*, New Series, LXXXVIII (1977-78): 87-101, pp. 96-7, and "Consciousness and Degrees of Belief," in his *Matters of Metaphysics*, Cambridge: Cambridge University Press, 1991, 30-60, p. 38. See also M.F. Burnyeat, "Belief in Speech," *Proceedings of the Aristotelian Society*, New Series, LXVIII (1967-68): 227-48.

26. For more shortcomings of the appeal to sincerity, and of a Gricean explanation, see Jay David Atlas, "What is Paradoxical about Moore's Paradox?: Rationality, Sincerity, Implicature, and the Self-Limitations of Belief," Claremont, California: Pomona College, MS.

27. Gottlob Frege, "Thoughts," in *Logical Investigations*, translated by P.T. Geach and R.H. Stoothoff (New Haven: Yale University Press, 1977): 1-30, p. 8.

28. Cf. J.L. Austin's claim that if I insincerely say 'I promise' I don't strictly speaking promise, but only say I do ("Other Minds," in *Philosophical Papers*, second edition [Oxford: Oxford University Press, 1970], pp. 101-3 [first edition, pp. 69-71]). Similarly, Black notes that "[a] man who lies is trying to deceive his hearers by behaving like somebody who makes an honest assertion." Thus "the making of an utterance [in a certain tone of voice] in the absence of the corresponding knowledge or belief is properly treated as a violation of the language" ("Saying and Disbelieving," pp. 116-7). I argue this at some length in "Intentionality," §V, and

the postscript to it in *Rerepresentation: Readings in the Philosophy of Mental Representation*, ed. Stuart Silvers (Dordrecht: Kluwer, 1989), pp. 341-344 (§V of the article was radically truncated there).

29. One might argue that, even if 'assert' had such a meaning, the sentence isn't an outright contradiction because it doesn't actually use the word 'assert'. Compare one's at once running and saying 'I'm not moving fast'; there's no contradiction there, even though 'run' in part means to move fast. Similarly with 'It's raining but I'm not asserting it', which purports to combine the act of asserting with the denial that I'm performing that act.

But these considerations are not decisive. If 'assert' meant in part that one thinks the relevant content, then the sentence 'I assert that it's raining but I don't think it is', which uses both 'assert' and 'think', would be a contradiction. That it's instead an instance of Moore's paradox argues against the meaning hypothesis.

30. It's worth noting that we speak not only about speech acts' expressing intentional states, but also about their expressing abstract thoughts, i.e., propositions. And we sometimes describe both in the same terms. Thus to say an assertion expresses a particular belief may mean either that it expresses an intentional state or that it has a certain content and an assertoric illocutionary force. Because Moore's paradox is cast in terms of the speaker's intentional states, it's only the expressing of those states that's relevant here.

31. Jane Heal, "Moore's Paradox: A Wittgensteinian Approach," *Mind*, CIII, 409 (January 1994): 5-24, p. 6. Cf. Albritton's contrast between sentences that involve some "linguistic malpractice" and those which are just very surprising.

32. E.g., Heal, who bases her claim that a common explanation is required on her observation that "the idea that someone realises the sentences to be true of him or herself" is just as strange as the idea of somebody's asserting such a sentence (p. 6). But this misrepresents the purely mental version of Moore's paradox; thinking that p is not the same as thinking that the sentence ⌜p⌝ is true of something. Thinking a sentence is true is tantamount to considering asserting that sentence; one can't think the sentence ⌜p but I don't believe it⌝ is true of oneself, precisely because one can't consider asserting it. By contrast, the mental version of Moore's paradox has to do with my thinking the content that p but I don't believe it, independently of any overt sentences. And it may be possible to do that even if it's impossible to think that the corresponding sentence is true.

Shoemaker argues that explaining what's wrong with thinking Moore's paradox would automatically explain what's wrong with saying it ("Moore's Paradox and Self-Knowledge," §I). But this ignores the possibility, argued for here, that believing Moore's paradox is less defective than asserting it; asserting something may well require more than just believing it.

33. *Critique of Pure Reason* B132, translated by Norman Kemp Smith (London: Macmillan & Co. Ltd, 1958), p. 153.

In section I, I argued that the factors that explain Moore's paradox also underlie the *cogito*. But Descartes's demon can cause doubt by undermining rationality. So, if the impossibility of thinking Moore's paradox rests on rationality and the *cogito* relies on the same factors, then there is some question about whether the *cogito* can, after all, effectively resist the Demon.

34. "On Knowing One's Own Mind," pp. 188-191; see also "Rationality and Self-Consciousness," p. 126, and "First-Person Access," *Philosophical Perspectives, 4,*

Action Theory and Philosophy of Mind, 1990, 187-144, p. 206.

35. "On Knowing One's Own Mind," p. 193.
36. If self-knowledge could be latent (see fn. 16), then rationalizing dispositional states might yield latent self-knowledge. It's likely, however, that only active, conscious knowing can count as self-knowledge. Similarly, nothing counts as first-person access unless we're conscious of having the access.
37. The most extensive development of this provocative argument occurs in "On Knowing One's Own Mind," esp. pp. 193-198.
38. This conclusion recalls a remark of Wittgenstein's, though he and Shoemaker rely on very different arguments. Wittgenstein claimed that "it is possible to think out circumstances in which...someone [could] say 'It is raining and I don't believe it'." Such a situation, he thought, would be one in which one could say: "Judging from what I say, *this* is what I believe." But I could say this, he insisted, only if my "behavior indicat[ed] that two people were speaking through my mouth" (*Philosophical Investigations*, II, p. 192). In effect, he held, one cannot be a unified individual and also be in a position to say such a thing, and thus to judge from the outside what beliefs one has.
39. E.g., "Rationality and Self-Consciousness," p. 134.
40. "On Knowing One's Own Mind," p. 194. Elsewhere he describes a plainly conscious inference that would take the putatively self-blind individual from believing that *p* to having a motive for saying, indifferently, ⌜*p*⌝ or ⌜I believe that *p*⌝. Arguably, Shoemaker begs the question there, since the individual's conscious reasoning from its having the belief that *p* presumably presupposes that the belief is conscious.
41. "On Knowing One's Own Mind," p. 19.
42. *Philosophical Investigations*, II, p. 190. Indeed, Wittgenstein understands Moore's paradox exclusively in terms of use:

> Moore's paradox can be put like this: the expression "I believe that this is the case" is used like the assertion "This is the case"; and yet the *hypothesis* that I believe this is the case is not used like the hypothesis that this is the case (p. 190).

Cf. *Remarks on the Philosophy of Psychology*, vol. I, pp. 91-96.
43. Cf. Wittgenstein's better known claim that saying 'I'm in pain', like crying 'ouch', expresses rather than reports my pain (*Philosophical Investigations*, §§244, 256). And if no speech act reports our states of pain, we cannot be said to have knowledge of them (§246). Here the sense of incorrigibility is stronger, since one can deny 'It's raining', but not 'ouch'.
44. Or that I'm not in pain. Moreover, as noted above, collapsing the distinction between reporting and expressing leads to construing Moore's paradox as an outright contradiction.
45. I address this question in "Why Are Verbally Expressed Thoughts Conscious?", Report No. 32/1990, Center for Interdisciplinary Research (ZiF) University of Bielefeld.

Philosophical Perspectives, 9, AI, Connectionism, and
Philosophical Psychology, 1995

THE CONCEPT OF MANIPULATIVENESS

Felicia Ackerman
Brown University

Unlike such psychological concepts as psychopath or superego that (despite their popularity in contemporary everyday life) were originated by psychologists as theoretical concepts, the concept of manipulativeness has always played its major role in laymen's informal day-to-day explanations and assessments of people's characters, motives, and behavior. This may be part of why this concept has received relatively little philosophical attention. This essay aims at remedying that lack.

'Manipulative' is of course defined in the dictionary, and the concept also has obvious importance for writers on business, salesmanship, and management. Accounts from such sources provide a useful starting point, as follows.

(1) Manipulate: To influence or manage shrewdly or deviously...to influence, manage, use, or control to one's advantage by artful or indirect means. (*American Heritage Dictionary*, 1993, pp. 1093-4.)

(2) To manipulate someone...involves a subtle influence on that person's actions, beliefs, desires, feelings, or values, which in turn inhibits rational deliberation. It may involve the falsification or omission of information, or it may involve a play on one's nonrational impulses. But it is widely characterized by an element of subtle and often deceptive persuasiveness. (Pfeiffer, 1979.)

(3) Manipulation generally implies secret or ulterior motives. It's extremely hard to accuse anyone of being manipulative if he puts all his cards on the table... . More important, manipulation often suggests getting another person to do something differently from what he or she is already doing. (Levering, 1994, p. 145.)

(4) [To call something manipulative] implies there's something unethical about it. (Levering, 1994, p. 123.)

All these accounts have problems. To start with the first account, manipulation can be done shrewdly, but it can also be done stupidly (and still work on a particularly susceptible person). Manipulation also need not be aimed at one's own advantage. A parent may, purely for the child's own good, manipulate a small child out of a tantrum or a teenager into staying in school, even in a situation where it would be to the parent's advantage if the small child continued the tantrum or the teenager quit school and got a job. And manipulation need not be artful or indirect. A white mother who says to her son, 'If you marry that black woman, I'll kill myself' is being manipulative, but there is nothing artful or indirect about it. Nor is it shrewd or (if she intends to carry out the threat) devious. There is nothing subtle about it either, which undermines the second account; nor is there anything subtle about the traditional salesman's manipulative sort of "close" to a wavering prospect: 'Now would you like this blue widget, or should I wrap up the green one for you?'

Especially interesting is the second account's claim that successful manipulation inhibits rational deliberation. Certainly this is true of many cases of manipulation, such as the "subliminal advertising" cases of the 1950's, where moviegoers were allegedly motivated to buy popcorn by having 'Buy popcorn' flashed on the screen at levels they could not detect consciously. But a parent who manipulates a small child out of a tantrum (e.g., by saying, 'Big boys don't act that way. You want to be a big boy, don't you? Suppose Uncle Joe could see you now. He wouldn't think you're big enough for that new tricycle he promised you.') is clearly not trying to inhibit a process of rational deliberation. In fact, rational deliberation can itself be a tool of manipulation, as in the case of a newly discovered unfaithful husband who tries to deflect his wife's fury by criticizing her emotionality and getting her to discuss the situation calmly.

The second and third accounts also invoke deceptiveness, although neither goes so far as to call it a necessary condition. Clearly, it is not. A genuine intention to carry out her suicide threat does not prevent the racist mother from being manipulative, any more than a genuine intention to deliver on a bribe prevents a parent who bribes a teenager to stay in school from being manipulative. Deflecting a screaming toddler with a toy may be manipulative but involves no deception, nor does the salesman's manipulative "close" mentioned above, unless one tries to stretch the case by claiming that the salesman is trying to seduce the prospect into thinking he has already agreed to buy (which seems implausible). It is not "extremely hard to accuse [the racist mother] of being manipulative" even though "[she] puts all [her] cards on the table," making it implausible to call her motive "ulterior." And there seems to be no reason to suppose that manipulation is any more associated with getting another person to do something differently from what he is already doing than with getting him to continue what he is already doing. Manipulation does involve getting someone to do, feel, or believe something one is not certain that he would otherwise (with these notions understood broadly enough to apply to continuing doing, refraining from doing, etc.), but so do such nonmanipulative ways of changing behavior or beliefs as sincerely telling a driver that the light has changed, a fifth-grader that 12x12=144, or a hiker that an avalanche is rapidly approaching his destination.

The fourth account does not pretend to be a definition. Obviously, many nonmanipulative acts (such as stealing and murder) are unethical. Still, it is worth considering whether it is necessarily true that manipulativeness is *prima facie* unethical. (The '*prima facie*' is to cover such cases as manipulating someone out of pushing a button that would destroy the world.)

One possible response is to hold that the term 'manipulative' is pejorative, so that no one who understood the term correctly could sincerely call another person manipulative and yet sincerely deny the relevance of the question, 'What's *prima facie* morally wrong with what he's doing?'[1] and it would be self-contradictory to say 'Manipulativeness is *prima facie* morally acceptable.' But consider an ethical egoist who says that manipulating others is a perfectly morally acceptable way of achieving one's own ends. This egoist seems to be expressing a consequence of his non-contradictory ethical egoism rather than contradicting himself (even though, of course, what he is saying may be necessarily false and synthetic). Moreover, one does not have to be an ethical egoist to hold that manipulating a toddler out of a tantrum is not even *prima facie* unethical. Another consideration complicates matters here. This is the fact that terms that apply to things people generally disapprove of are apt to take on a pejorative cast because one way to denigrate something is to equate it with another thing already deemed bad. An initially neutral term may also develop both pejorative and nonpejorative senses, like the term 'discrimination'.[2] I am not claiming that 'manipulative' has *no* pejorative sense; the above examples show only that it has a nonpejorative one.

Another way in which calling something manipulative could imply that there is something unethical about it is that the *prima facie* wrongness of manipulation of rational beings could be a synthetic *a priori*. Deciding this issue requires a return to our original question: just what is the concept of manipulativeness?

I have argued that none of the above accounts gives necessary and sufficient conditions for manipulativeness. This obviously does not imply that the conditions these accounts mention are irrelevant to the question of whether someone is being manipulative. A natural suggestion is that the concept of manipulativeness has what Alston calls combinatory vagueness, which is present in cases where "we have a variety of conditions, all of which have something to do with the application of the term, yet are not able to make any sharp discriminations between those combinations of conditions which are, and those which are not, sufficient and/or necessary for application" (Alston, 1967, p. 220).[3] This imprecision is hardly surprising in view of the concept's roots in the casual discourse of daily life.[4] The above accounts of manipulativeness yield the following list of conditions (which are not mutually exclusive).

> influence
> shrewdness
> deviousness
> indirect means
> artfulness
> aim is to benefit the manipulator
> subtlety

> inhibition of rational deliberation
> falsification or omission of information
> play on nonrational impulses
> deceptiveness
> ulterior motives
> getting someone to do something differently from what he is already doing
> unethicalness

My counterexamples to the four quoted accounts suggest the following additional conditions.

> inhibition of action, belief, emotion, etc. that the "manipulatee" finds
>   natural or appropriate (or is otherwise inclined to engage in)
> pressure/making it awkward for the manipulatee to say no

The first of these additional conditions characterizes the cases of the screaming child and the betrayed wife; the second is found in the salesman's "close."

Testing an account of a combinatorily vague term is complicated, since no condition on the list is sufficient, and it is compatible with the notion of combinatory vagueness that no single condition on the combinatory list is even necessary. But one can give test cases where it is the presence or absence of some particular condition or conditions that is crucial to determining whether the case is a case of manipulativeness.

The case of the racist mother, for example, illustrates the relevance of unethicalness, inhibition of rational deliberation, and play on nonrational impulses. To see this, imagine a society where intermarriage is universally deplored and where it is considered appropriate for parents to have a large say in whom their children marry. In such a society, the mother would not count as manipulative, because she would be deemed as introducing a relevant consideration of the sort society assumes should affect her son's decision. Her threat to kill herself might even be seen as a noble example of self-sacrifice in pursuit of a higher good, like Gandhi's hunger strikes. Whether Gandhi's hunger strikes are to count as manipulative does seem to rest on whether they are counted as unethical (an illegitimate play on others' emotions) or virtuous (a paragon of the force of conscience and self-sacrifice). Similarly, imagine the racist mother downgrading her threat to an accurate 'If you marry that black woman, I'll be miserable for the rest of my life.' This seems manipulative only if we believe that the mother should not try to make her misery a factor in the son's marital decision. Contrast this case with that of a wife who tells her husband, 'If you take that job in Phoenix, I'll be miserable, because I'd be miserable apart from you, and I hate the Southwest.' Most Americans nowadays would probably consider this the nonmanipulative introduction of a relevant consideration, but in a more male-dominated society, this wife might be considered as manipulative as the racist mother is in ours.

The conditions of subtlety and deviousness can also be revealed as important in particular cases. Thus, compare 'Your money or your life' with a case of subtle pressure that makes someone feel intimidated into giving another money. The first case is not clearly manipulative (the people I asked disagreed), but the second clearly is. Similarly, telling an outright lie to a real estate prospect about whether there is a leak in the basement of a house seems less manipulative (although at least as reprehensible) than keeping up a running commentary about the prestige of the neighborhood all the time one is in the basement with the prospect, in the hope he will not notice the leak. (As this example illustrates, manipulativeness resembles many psychological concepts in that its applicability is sometimes a matter of degree, rather than simply an all-or-none matter.)

For a case where self-interested ulterior motives are important in making it a case of manipulativeness, suppose J insincerely replies, 'You look wonderful in it' to a woman who asks how she looks in a particular dress. If J is a saleswoman working on commission, the reassurance counts as manipulative. But if J is the woman's husband, and his sole aim is to ensure her happiness once they are on their way to a party and it is too late for her to change outfits, he is not being manipulative.

The importance of falsification of information can be illustrated by a used-car salesman who turns back the odometer. But the factor of getting someone to do something differently from what he is already doing should be dropped from the list of conditions, as it seems no more relevant to manipulativeness than is getting someone to continue what he is doing.

Now for the two conditions I introduced. The first–getting someone to go against what he finds natural or appropriate or is otherwise inclined to do–unlike the condition of getting someone to go specifically against *rational deliberation*, actually seems necessary for manipulation. But it is certainly not sufficient, as is illustrated by such nonmanipulative injunctions as 'Stop! There's a car coming,' 'Don't burp in public; it's bad manners,' and 'Brush your teeth before going to bed.' And the importance of pressure/making it awkward for someone to say no is illustrated by the salesman's "close" example.

The role of the concept of unethicalness in the concept of manipulation is threefold. First, as Ernest Sosa has suggested in conversation, there may be a pejorative sense of 'manipulative' just as there seems to be a pejorative sense of 'discrimination.' Second, as the above examples suggest, the judgment that an action is unethical is often a factor in the judgment that it is manipulative, i.e., unethicalness is an element in the cluster of conditions that form the concept of manipulativeness. Finally, many of the other conditions of the cluster–deviousness, inhibition of rational processes or processes deemed appropriate by the "manipulatee," use of others for one's own personal benefit, deceptiveness, etc.–are things it is quite reasonable to think of as *prima facie* unethical.

By definition, a combinatorily vague concept will have possible indeterminate cases. Some I have already mentioned. Others are as follows: a house-seller simply fails to mention the leak in the basement, rather than either lying about it or trying to deflect the prospect's attention from evidence of its existence; a newcomer to town dresses shabbily and never invites his new acquaintances over to his house because he fears they would resent him and not want to be his friend if they knew he was rich; a parent exaggerates statistics about teenage unemployment in order to convince his teenager to stay in school for the teenager's own good. All these are cases whose manipulativeness most of my informants either disagreed about or found unclear.[5]

Notes

1. This account of the notion of a pejorative term is adapted from Alston, 1964, ch. 2.
2. I owe this example to Ernest Sosa.
3. Note the similarity of this notion to Searle's view of proper names (Searle, 1958 and 1967), which in effect equates the sense of a proper name with a sufficient but unspecified number of the descriptions backing it up.
4. This is not to deny that many scientific, supposedly precise concepts also have combinatory vagueness. See Alston, 1964, ch. 5. The notion of a cluster concept is essentially the same as Alston's notion of combinatory vagueness.
5. I thank Ernest Sosa and James Van Cleve for helpful discussions of this material.

References

Alston, W.P.: 1964, *Philosophy of Language*, Prentice-Hall, Englewood Cliffs.
Alston, W.P.: 1967, "Vagueness" in P. Edwards (ed.) *The Encyclopedia of Philosophy*, New York, Collier-Macmillan, v. 8, pp. 218-221.
American Heritage Dictionary of the English Language, 1993, Boston, Houghton Mifflin.
Levering, R.: 1988, *A Great Place to Work*, Random House, New York.
Pfeiffer, R.M.: 1979, *Working for Capitalism*, Columbia University Press, New York.
Searle, J.R.: 1958, "Proper Names," *Mind*, LXVII, 166-73.
Searle, J.R.: 1967, "Proper Names and Descriptions," in P. Edwards (ed.), *The Encyclopedia of Philosophy*, New York: Collier-Macmillan, v. 6, pp. 487-491.

Philosophical Perspectives, 9, AI, Connectionism, and
Philosophical Psychology, 1995

PROPOSITIONAL ATTITUDES AND
COMPOSITIONAL SEMANTICS

Steven E. Boër
The Ohio State University

0. Introduction

In recent years a number of prominent philosophers (e.g., Schiffer 1987a, 1991; Horgan 1989; Crimmins and Perry 1989) have argued that the presence in a natural language L of propositional attitude constructions makes it impossible to provide L with a correct compositional truth theory, i.e., a finitely axiomatizable theory of truth-in-L (relative to a context c) which canonically yields a true and "interpretive"[1] theorem of the form (T) for each disambiguated sentence type S of L (in which, for $n{\geq}0, \mathcal{I}_1,...,\mathcal{I}_n$ are the context-dependent terms occurring in S and $\ulcorner Ref_c(\mathcal{I}_i)\urcorner$ is written for ⌜the object assigned to $\mathcal{I}_i$ by c⌝):

(T) S is true$_c$ in $L \equiv (\exists x_1)...(\exists x_n)(x_1 = Ref_c(\mathcal{I}_1)$ &...& $x_n = Ref_c(\mathcal{I}_n)$ & $\phi(x_1,...,x_n))$.

No doubt the best proof that something can indeed be done is simply to *do* it. Unfortunately, we lack *inter alia* the sort of comprehensive and agreed-upon syntactic theories for natural languages upon which any such ambitious semantic project would ultimately have to rely. My aim in this paper is, however, to do the next best thing: that is, (a) to construct a regimented language L_1 which, though having an artificially simple vocabulary and syntax, is nevertheless like English in those respects which count for the problem at hand and (b) to provide and defend a particular finitely axiomatized truth theory for L_1. In this way a very powerful argument by analogy can be mounted against the truth-theoretic skeptic.

The layout of the territory to be scouted is as follows. In section 1, we become informally acquainted with an axiomatic theory Z of a certain family of abstract objects (the A-objects) and their connection with belief; Z will provide the technical resources for our semantical metalanguage. Section 2 introduces two object-languages: the structurally univocal language L_0 and the structurally ambiguous language L_1, showing how the latter can be disambiguated via the former. Section 3 shows how A-objects may be deployed to construct a plausible, finitely axiomatizable sense-reference semantics for L_1 along broadly Fregean lines, issuing in the desired T-sentences for L_1. Section 4 explores the question of whether a finitely axiomatizable semantics can in turn be constructed for languages of thought. Section 5 illustrates how our theory disposes of some well-known puzzles about belief ascription that have been alleged to support the truth-theoretic skeptic. Finally, Section 6 demonstrates that our theory is immune to the battery of powerful objections which Stephen Schiffer has recently lodged against various versions of Fregean semantics.

1. A-Objects: An informal exposition of the theory Z.

Z–an extension of the system ILAO of Zalta (1988) developed in Boër (1994)–is a theory about the ontology of the propositional attitudes, realistically construed as relations between persons and propositions, and the connection between possession of such attitudes and inner discourse in one's language of thought. Z takes as primitive and seeks axiomatically to characterize both the notion of *n-ary relation* (including *properties* as unary relations and *propositions* as 0-ary relations) and a special intensional notion of *encoding*. Encoding is a way of "having" a property F which neither necessitates nor rules out exemplifying it. For anyone willing to allow that *there are* non-actual things–the existential quantifier here being objectual, not merely substitutional–encoding provides a model for understanding sentences which predicate properties of such things. For example, a fictional entity like Sherlock Holmes does not exemplify the property lives-in-19th-century-London, nor is it clear what sense it would make to say that Holmes might have exemplified it, but the property still "belongs" to him in intuitively the *same* sense that the property lives-in-14th-century-China does *not* belong to him–a sense captured by regarding Holmes as an entity which encodes the former but not the latter. So conceived, the properties which such non-actual things encode are essential to their identity.

In our informal meta-metalanguage, we will be discussing Z as itself a semantical metalanguage both for languages of thought and for the promised target language L_1. To help keep track of the players, we adopt the following notational conventions. Lowercase Greek letters are variables in our meta-metalanguage ranging over expressions of Z, which expressions themselves are couched in familiar logical notation employing italicized words of English as non-logical terms. For each person u, M_u is u's language of thought (u's "Mentalese"). With the exception of 'Z' and 'M', boldface Roman letters are metavariables in Z interpreted as follows: '**P**' and '**S**' range respectively over Mentalese propositional terms and sentences; '**a**',...,'**w**' range over Mentalese names of various Mentalese types; '**x**', '**y**' and '**z**' range over Mentalese variables of various Mentalese types (the Mentalese types of items in their ranges being indicated, where relevant, by a left superscript). The guillemets '**«**' and '**»**' are devices in Z for forming structural-descriptive names of Mentalese expression-types[2]; and other boldface symbols are names in Z for their Mentalese counterparts (e.g., '**[**' and '**&**' respectively denote the Mentalese expression-types *left bracket* and *conjunction sign*; for typographical reasons, boldface '∃' and '∀' appear below as '**A**' and '**E**'). Uppercase Greek letters (with the exception of '**Π**' and '**Φ**' as introduced below) are restricted variables in our meta-metalanguage ranging over Z's boldface metavariables for Mentalese expressions. Finally, script expressions are variables in Z ranging over expressions of the object-languages L_0 and L_1, whose own expressions will be written in plain Roman. Where useful, we will tolerate in our meta-metalanguage the sort of contextually harmless use-mention conflations involved in writing ⌜the belief relation $[\lambda x^i y^p\ Believes^{<ip>}(x,y)]$⌝ and ⌜the A-object $[THAT\ \phi]$⌝ instead of the strictly correct but cumbersome locutions ⌜the relation denoted in Z by the λ-abstract ⌜$[\lambda x^i y^p\ Believes^{<ip>}(x,y)]$⌝⌝ and ⌜the A-object denoted in Z by the propositional term ⌜$[THAT\ \phi]$⌝⌝.

The theory Z formally articulates these ideas in a typed intensional logic whose basic Types are i (individual) and p (proposition), where $<t_1,...,t_n>$ counts as a Type if $t_1,...,t_n$ do.[3] (Type indices appear as right superscripts.) The encoding of F by x and the exemplification of F by x are respectively represented in Z's two primitive forms of predication 'xF' and 'Fx' (also written '$F(x)$'). (Since tense and modality are irrelevant to our topic, the tense and modal operators of Z will be ignored in what follows.) The propositional connectives are treated classically. '$\exists$' is defined as usual in terms of Z's primitive quantifier '$\forall$', which in turn is so restricted as to ensure a "free logic" for definite descriptions–viz., where τ contains no definite descriptions save those whose nonemptiness is assured by the axioms, $\phi(\tau/\alpha)$ may be inferred from ⌜$(\forall\alpha)\phi$⌝; but ⌜$\psi(\tau/\beta) \rightarrow \phi(\tau/\alpha)$⌝ may be inferred from ⌜$(\forall\alpha)\phi$⌝ for any term τ substitutable for both α and β, provided that the formula ψ is atomic.

The variables of Z in a given Type range over both "ordinary" objects (O-objects) and "abstract" objects (A-objects) of that Type. O-objects are *actual* items such as the concrete individuals of our world and the n-ary relations that might hold among them, including propositions as 0-ary relations. For each admissible[4] condition ϕ and Type t other than i, Z posits the existence of a relation of Type t which is necessarily-always coextensive with ϕ. O-objects of any Type are essentially incapable of encoding. In contrast, A-objects are *non-actual* items which essentially encode various properties. A-objects are the only non-actual items posited in Z. In particular, for any admissible condition, Z posits an A-object x of Type t such that x encodes a property of Type $<t>$ iff that condition obtains. Z incorporates a redundancy theory of truth for propositions in the form of the proper axiom ⌜$(\forall x^p)(Tr(x) \equiv x)$⌝.

O-objects of Type i (*O-individuals*) are identical iff they share all properties of Type $<i>$, whereas A-objects of Type i (*A-individuals*) are deemed identical iff they encode the same properties. Properties of various Types $<t>$ are themselves held to be identical iff they are encoded by the same A-objects of Type t. The identity of relations (and propositions as 0-ary relations) is then defined in terms of identity of the associated relational and propositional properties. ('$=$' is used for the defined notion of numerical identity between objects of a given Type, while '$=_E$' is used to express community of properties; *only* for O-individuals do the two notions of identity coincide.) For any Type $<t>$ property F we can legitimately specify, Z thus assures us of the existence of a *unique* A-object x of Type t which encodes a property G iff $G = F$. (Given our free logic for descriptions, however, we cannot prove that this A-object x *does* encode F unless ⌜$(\forall G)$⌝ can be instantiated to our description of F.)

Despite the heavy-duty intensional apparatus, Z enshrines the principle of Substitutivity of Identity: subject to the usual restrictions on free variables, every instance of ⌜$\alpha^t = \beta^t \rightarrow (\phi \equiv \phi(\beta^t//\alpha^t))$⌝ is an axiom. (Note that the axiom scheme uses '$=$' rather than '$=_E$': Z allows that numerically distinct A-objects might *exemplify* the same properties.) So all genuine term-occurrences in formulas of Z are open to substitution of codesignative terms and to "existential" quantification (the scare-quotes being a reminder that since Z quantifies over non-actual objects, the sense of existence conveyed by '$\exists$' does not imply actuality, which is conveyed instead by the typed predicate '$E!^{<P>}$'.) Adherence to the substitutivity of identity is required for our project, for the sense-reference semantics to be formulated in Z for our target language L_1 is intended to provide a *reductive* explanation of L_1's opacity phenomena, which it could not do if it exhibited such phenomena itself!

Beyond its borrowed account of relations in general, Z provides a theory of the binary relation $[\lambda x^i y^p \, Believes^{<i,p>}(x,y)]$ of (occurrent) believing which is at once propositionalist, functionalist, and sententialist. Z's account of the belief relation is *propositionalist* because it takes the objects of the belief relation to be propositions (albeit of a special sort); *functionalist*, because it regards standing in the belief relation to a proposition as coextensive with being in a certain functionally defined relation to something (itself functionally defined[5]) which is internal to the believer; *sententialist*, because it construes that "something internal" as a sentence in the subject's language of thought. (We make the simplifying and idealizing assumption that each language of thought M has a type-structure like that of Z and possesses counterparts of Z's logical apparatus–in particular, its own sentential complementizer, referred to in Z as '**THAT**^{M}'. Given such a theory of what beliefs are, we may then employ Z as a semantical metalanguage in which to articulate the truth conditions of belief *ascriptions* in the target language. The core of Z's theory of belief lies in the complex axiom schemes [*That*=] and [*Belief*], about which we must now say a few words.

For any Type $<t,i,<i>>$ relation R, Z defines R's *proxy* (written 'PROX(R)'), as the corresponding Type t property $[\lambda x^i \, (\exists y^i)(\exists z^{<i>})Rxyz]$ and further defines 'x^i *proxy-encodes* relation $R^{<t,i,<i>>}$' (written '$x{:}R$') as short for 'x^i encodes R's proxy' (i.e., as abbreviating 'xPROX(R)'). As objects of the belief-relation Z then posits certain A-objects of Type p–called *proxy-encoding abstract propositions* (*PEAPs*)–each of which proxy-encodes just a special semantical relation R of Type $<p,i,<i>>$ between PEAPs, persons, and sentence types[6] of those persons' Mentalese. Where ϕ is any propositional formula of Z, these PEAPs are canonically named in Z by propositional terms of the form $\ulcorner[THAT \, \phi]\urcorner$ or $\ulcorner[THAT_{v+} \, \phi]\urcorner$ for some '+'-marked[7] individual variable $\ulcorner v^+ \urcorner$ occurring free (but nowhere bound) in ϕ. In its fully general form, the axiom scheme [*That*=] which characterizes these PEAPs requires an extremely complicated stipulation about the relation between the structure of the formula ϕ in question and that of a certain expression Φ used to describe a related Mentalese sentence. Fortunately, our present purposes do not require the full generality of the original axiom scheme, so we can make do here with a weaker version of it which is restricted to propositional terms $\ulcorner[THAT \, \phi]\urcorner$ and $\ulcorner[THAT_{v+} \, \phi]\urcorner$ in which ϕ contains no *complex* terms other than propositional terms of these same two sorts[8], no primitive propositional variables, and no boldface semantical metavocabulary. For each such ϕ, let $\alpha_1,...,\alpha_k$ and $v_1,...,v_m$ be respectively the distinct simple names and (unmarked) variables from which it is composed, let v^+ be its sole free '+'-marked variable (if any), and (where n is the number of occurrences of simple names in ϕ) let $\beta_1,...,\beta_n$ be that sequence of its simple names in which (for $1 \leq i \leq n$ and $1 \leq j \leq k$) $\beta_i = \alpha_j$ iff the ith name-occurrence in ϕ is an occurrence of α_j. Then we define ϕ's counterpart-expression Φ as any expression so constructed from n distinct boldface name-metavariables $\Delta_1,...,\Delta_n$, $m+1$ distinct boldface variable-metavariables $\Omega,\Omega_1,...,\Omega_m$ and various bold-face logical symbols in Z's metavocabulary for Mentalese that (A) no *name*-meta-variable among $\Delta_1,...,\Delta_n$ occurs more than once in Φ and (B) ϕ itself could be obtained from Φ by simply de-boldfacing the boldface logical symbols in Φ and then simultaneously substituting $\beta_1,...,\beta_n,v^+, v_1,...,v_m$ for $\Delta_1,...,\Delta_n,\Omega,\Omega_1,...,\Omega_m$ respectively in the result. Thus, e.g., ϕ and Φ might respectively be '$(\exists x)(Runs(x)$ & $Sings(x))$' and '**(Ex)(r(x) & s(x))**', or '*Loves(Tom,Tom)*' and '**f(a,b)**'.

With the foregoing restrictions in place, [*That*=] may be semi-formally stated as the stipulation that every (suitably formalized) instance of the following schema is an axiom:

[*That*=] [*THAT* ϕ] (*or* $\ulcorner[THAT_{v^+}\ \phi]\urcorner$) = the PEAP proxy-encoding just that relation between a proposition P, person u and term **P** of M_u which consists in its being the case that, for some $\Delta_1,...,\Delta_n$, $\Omega_1,...,\Omega_m$ (*and* Ω): (i) **P** is of the sort **«[THAT Φ]»** (*or* **«[THAT$_\Omega$ Φ]»**); (ii) **P** denotes P in M_u; (iii) $R(\alpha_j, u,\Delta_j)$, if α is an A-object proxy-encoding only the relation R ($1 \leq j \leq k$); (iv) Δ_j denotes α_j and is not of the sort **«Δ°»** for any Δ, if α is not an A-object proxy-encoding only the relation R ($1 \leq j \leq k$); and (v) $\Delta_i =_E \Delta_j$ if the relation proxy-encoded by $\alpha_i =_E$ the relation proxy-encoded by α_j.[9]

(The parenthetical remarks supply the qualifications for the case involving '+'-marked variables; Δ is to be a boldface name-metavariable distinct from any of $\Delta_1,...,\Delta_n$; the symbol '°' is Z's name for the Mentalese "opacity marker", a functionally defined device which marks a term-occurrence as opaque.[10]) The propriety of the definite description '*the* PEAP...' is guaranteed by the existence- and identity-conditions for A-objects in general. Since the only proxy-encoding A-objects explicitly mentioned in Z are given special names like $\ulcorner[THAT\ \phi]\urcorner$–names which are descriptively defined using encoding predication–the propriety of speaking of *the* relation proxy-encoded by one of these distinguished A-objects is secured by the axiom scheme [!:]:

[!:] Where τ is any Type t sense-term, every instance of the following is an axiom:
$$(\forall \rho^{<t,i,<i>>})((PROX(\rho) = (\iota\theta^{<t>})\tau\theta) \rightarrow (\rho = (\iota\xi^{<t,i,<i>>})\tau{:}\xi)).$$

All *other* names in Z are to be taken as denoting objects which are *not* proxy-encoders. This is provided for in the axiom-scheme [~:]:

[~:] For any primitive name, definite description or λ-abstract α' devoid of encod-ing predications and expressions defined thereby (i.e., where α' is not a sense-term), every instance of the following is an axiom:
$$\sim(\exists G^{<t,i,<i>>})\alpha'{:}G$$

To this are added two (provisional[11]) assumptions about the semantical features of languages of thought. On the one hand, it is assumed that any suitably formalized instance of the following schema is an axiom (where ϕ and Φ are as in [*That=*] and σ, ρ, and ζ are respectively clauses (iii), (iv) and (v) of [*That=*]):

[DEN$_M$] If σ and ρ and ζ, then «[**THAT Φ**]» (*resp.* «[**THAT$_\Omega$ Φ**]») denotes in M_u
the PEAP [*THAT* ϕ] (*resp.* ⌐[*THAT$_{v+}$* ϕ]⌐).

On the other hand, where ⌐Θ*⌐ is shorthand in Z for ⌐the result of *removing* all occurrences of the opacity marker in Θ *except* those in terms of the sort «[**THAT S**]»⌐, it is assumed that every instance of

[TRUE$_M$]   For any sentence **S** of M_u: if «[**THAT S**]» denotes in M_u the PEAP
[*THAT* ϕ], then **S*** is true in M_u iff ϕ*.

will be an axiom *provided that* ϕ is a propositional formula and ϕ* is the result of erasing all underlining in ϕ *except* that occurring within terms of the form ⌐[*THAT* ψ]⌐.[12]

Since, e.g., we have seen that '$(\exists x)(Runs(x)$ & $Sings(x))$' and '(**Ex**)(**r(x)** & **s(x)**)' are appropriately related, the following instance of [*That=*] (suitably formalized) will be an axiom of Z:

> [*THAT* $(\exists x)(Runs(x)$ & $Sings(x))$] = the PEAP proxy-encoding just that
> relation H between a proposition P, person u and term **P** of M_u which consists
> in its being the case that: (a) **P** is of the sort «[**THAT (Ex)(r(x)** & **s(x))**]»; (b)
> **P** denotes P in M_u; (c) $R(Runs,u,\mathbf{r})$ if *Runs* is an A-object proxy-encoding
> only the relation R, and $R(Sings,u,\mathbf{s})$ if *Sings* is an A-object proxy-encoding
> only the relation R; (d) **r** denotes *Runs* and is not of the sort «**n°**» for any **n**, if
> *Runs* is not an A-object proxy-encoding only the relation R; and **s** denotes
> *Sings* and is not of the sort «**n°**» for any **n**, if *Sings* is not an A-object proxy-
> encoding only the relation R; and (e) **r** $=_E$ **s** if the relation proxy-encoded by
> *Runs* = the relation proxy-encoded by *Sings*.[13]

Since other axioms of Z–viz., instances of [DEN$_M$] and [~:]–ensure that (b), (c) and (e) are redundant in this particular case, the relation H which the PEAP [*THAT* $(\exists x)(Runs(x)$ & $Sings(x))$] is said to proxy-encode will (necessarily-always) obtain between P, u, and **P** iff **P** is of the sort «[**THAT (Ex)(r(x)** & **s(x))**]» in which **r** denotes the property of running and **s** denotes the property of singing.

The point of taking PEAPs of the sort [*THAT* ϕ] as the objects of the relation *Believes* emerges in the axiom [*Belief*], which connects the propositionalist aspect of the theory to its sententialist and functionalist aspects by way of certain necessary and sufficient conditions for being belief-related to a PEAP. The axiom may be informally stated as follows (the parenthetical qualifications being required to handle self-ascriptive (*de se*) beliefs):

[*Belief*]   *Believes*(x^i,y^p) iff, for some formula-type **S** of M_x such that the ternary relation proxy-encoded by y obtains among y, x and «**[THAT S]**» (*or* «**[THAT_x S]**»), x mentally affirms a token of **S**[*] (in which the self-demonstrative in M_x supplants all occurrences of **x** in **S**).[14]

Given functionally defined analogues of mental affirmation for the cases of intending and desiring, we could obviously formulate analogous axioms [*Intends*] and [*Desires*].

Since the object-languages L_0 and L_1 will contain semantically *context-dependent* terms, we must say something about how "contexts" figure in **Z** in its capacity as semantical metalanguage for L_1 and L_0. Informally, an utterance context c may be thought of as something which provides the following items (where *Int* is the set of positive integers):

> an utterer, $[I]_c$, together with a sequence PI_c of $[I]_c$-based percept species $[PI_1]_c,[PI_2]_c,...$;
> an utterance time, $[now]_c$;
> an utterance location, $[here]_c$;
> an "addressee" assignment A_c with domain $\mathrm{Dmn}(A_c) \subseteq Int$, together with a function PA_c such that $\mathrm{Dmn}(PA_c) = \mathrm{Dmn}(A_c)$ and, for each $i \in \mathrm{Dmn}(PA_c)$, $PA_c(i)$ is an $A_c(i)$-based percept species (the expressions $\ulcorner[you_i]_c\urcorner$ and $\ulcorner[PA_i]_c\urcorner$ will be our canonical abbreviations for the (possibly empty) descriptions $\ulcorner(\iota y)(<i,y> \in A_c)\urcorner$ and $\ulcorner(\iota y)(<i,y> \in PA_c)\urcorner$ respectively);
> a "demonstrated objects" assignment O_c with domain $\mathrm{Dmn}(O_c) \subseteq Int$, together with a function PO_c such that $\mathrm{Dmn}(PO_c) = \mathrm{Dmn}(O_c)$ and, for each $i \in \mathrm{Dmn}(PO_c)$, $PO_c(i)$ is an $O_c(i)$-based percept species (the expressions $\ulcorner[this_i]_c\urcorner$ and $\ulcorner[PO_i]_c\urcorner$ will be our canonical abbreviations for the (possibly empty) descriptions $\ulcorner(\iota y)(<i,y> \in O_c)\urcorner$ and $\ulcorner(\iota y)(<i,y> \in PO_c)\urcorner$ respectively);
> a "demonstrated males" assignment M_c with domain $\mathrm{Dmn}(M_c) \subseteq Int$, together with a function PM_c such that $\mathrm{Dmn}(PM_c) = \mathrm{Dmn}(M_c)$ and, for each $i \in \mathrm{Dmn}(PM_c)$, $PM_c(i)$ is an $M_c(i)$-based percept species (the expressions $\ulcorner[he_i]_c\urcorner$ and $\ulcorner[PM_i]_c\urcorner$ will be our canonical abbreviations for the (possibly empty) descriptions $\ulcorner(\iota y)(<i,y> \in M_c)\urcorner$ and $\ulcorner(\iota y)(<i,y> \in PM_c)\urcorner$ respectively);
> a "demonstrated females" assignment F_c with domain $\mathrm{Dmn}(F_c) \subseteq Int$, together with a function PF_c such that $\mathrm{Dmn}(PF_c) = \mathrm{Dmn}(F_c)$ and, for each $i \in \mathrm{Dmn}(PF_c)$, $PF_c(i)$ is an $F_c(i)$-based percept species (the expressions $\ulcorner[she_i]_c\urcorner$ and $\ulcorner[PF_i]_c\urcorner$ will be our canonical abbreviations for the (possibly empty) descriptions $\ulcorner(\iota y)(<i,y> \in F_c)\urcorner$ and $\ulcorner(\iota y)(<i,y> \in PF_c)\urcorner$ respectively);
> for each primitive name α in **Z**, a sequence $[{}^{\bullet}\alpha^{\bullet}{}_1]_c,[{}^{\bullet}\alpha^{\bullet}{}_2]_c,...$ of Type $<<i>,i>$ relations which are variously restricted versions of the relation ${}^{\bullet}\alpha^{\bullet}$ that **n** bears to u when **n** in M_u is *cognate with* α.

Some explanation of these ingredients is now in order.

For any ordinary individual x, an *x-based percept species* is a *kind* to which only x-based percepts–i.e., perceptual representations *of* x, can belong. Note that identities obtaining among utterer, addressees or demonstrated items do *not* require matching identities to obtain among the correspondingly based percept species: even if, e.g., $[you_i]_c = [he_j]_c$ it need not be the case that $[PA_i]_c = [PM_j]_c$. This fact is crucial to what follows. Expressions of the form $\ulcorner\Pi_x\urcorner$ are restricted variables of Z-Type $<i>$ ranging over x-based percept species; these special variables, together with $\ulcorner PI_k\urcorner$, $\ulcorner PA_k\urcorner$, $\ulcorner PM_k\urcorner$, $\ulcorner PF_k\urcorner$ and $\ulcorner PO_k\urcorner$ $(k \geq 1)$ are the *percept species terms* of Z. Thus, e.g., for a given context c in which, say, $[this_3]_c = $ Fido, the Fido-based percept-species $[PO_3]_c$ might be something as general as the property of being a visual representation of Fido, or as particular as the property of being a visual representation of Fido *qua* excited slobbering brown Dachshund clinging to one's left leg (i.e., a *sight* of that sort, grounded in Fido). The parenthetical remark about "sights" is a reminder that our calling something a perceptual representation of x "*qua F*" is not meant to imply that the owner of the representation does or even can *conceptualize* x as an F, nor is there any commitment to the idea that the content of all perceptual representations must be linguistically expressible in some favored idiom. Hence, there is no commitment to the linguistic expressibility of what various such perceptual representations might have in common: percept species need not be descriptive properties.

Our relational notation $\ulcorner[{}^{\bullet}\alpha^{\bullet}{}_k]_c\urcorner$ admits of a variety of possible interpretations. In the original presentation of Z (Boër 1994), $\ulcorner[{}^{\bullet}\alpha^{\bullet}{}_k]_c(\mathbf{n},u)\urcorner$ was interpreted as expressing a requirement that u's Mentalese name $\mathbf{n}$ should be a "cognate" of the Z-term α– where the cognate-relation ${}^{\bullet}\alpha^{\bullet}$ is spelled out in terms of the genetic notion of "Least Types" found in Millikan (1984)–and that $\mathbf{n}$ should satisfy the kth contextually supplied restriction on ${}^{\bullet}\alpha^{\bullet}$ (e.g., a restriction on how admissible cognates must be acquired). (Such restrictions might, of course, be vacuous: it might be that case that $[{}^{\bullet}\alpha^{\bullet}{}_k]_c = {}^{\bullet}\alpha^{\bullet}$ in a given context c.) We will assume this genetic interpretation here. The only formal constraints Z imposes are that $\ulcorner[{}^{\bullet}\alpha^{\bullet}{}_k]_c(\mathbf{t},u)\urcorner$ does not obtain when $\mathbf{t}$ is a complex Mentalese name of the sort «$\mathbf{n}^\circ$» and (much more importantly) that, for any name $\mathbf{n}$ in any Mentalese idiolect M_u and any *distinct* names α and β, it is possible that $\ulcorner[{}^{\bullet}\alpha^{\bullet}{}_k]_c(\mathbf{n},u)\urcorner$ obtains but $\ulcorner[{}^{\bullet}\beta^{\bullet}{}_k]_c(\mathbf{n},u)\urcorner$ does not. (The reader may supply any favored interpretation consistent with these.)

We may now introduce our final ingredient: Z's context-dependent *sense-names*. The sense-names of a given Type t in Z are of two sorts: (i) *ordinary sense-names* of the form $\ulcorner[\underline{\alpha}_k]_c\urcorner$ $(k \geq 1)$, where the underlined term α is one of Z's primitive context-independent names in Type t, and (ii) *deictic sense-names* of the form $\ulcorner[\underline{\delta}_k]_c\urcorner$, where the underlined term δ is one of Z's primitive context-dependent names in Type t. Ordinary sense-names are characterized by the stipulation that every (suitably formalized) instance of the schema [*OSN=*] is an axiom:

[*OSN=*] $[\underline{\alpha}_k{}']_c = $ the A-object proxy-encoding just that relation between an object of Type t, a person u and a name $'\mathbf{a}$ which consists in $\mathbf{a}$ having the form «$\mathbf{n}^\circ$» for some name $'\mathbf{n}$ such that $\mathbf{n}$ both denotes α in M_u and $[{}^{\bullet}\alpha^{\bullet}{}_k]_c(\mathbf{n},u)$.

Here the clause $\ulcorner [\,\!^{\bullet}\alpha^{\bullet}{}_{k}]_{c}(\mathbf{n}, u)\urcorner$ locates the contextually supplied "extra something" that a term of the sort «n°» in Mentalese sentence **S** must have if placing **S** in one's belief-box is to constitute having a belief (at least partly) *de dicto*.

The treatment of deictic sense-names–viz., $\ulcorner [\underline{I}_{k}]_{c}\urcorner^{15}$, $\ulcorner [\underline{you}_{k}]_{c}\urcorner$, $\ulcorner [\underline{he}_{k}]_{c}\urcorner$, $\ulcorner [\underline{she}_{k}]_{c}\urcorner$ and $\ulcorner [\underline{this}_{k}]_{c}\urcorner$ ($k \geq 1$)–is more complicated, since it involves the notion of a "Mentalese demonstrative". We may briefly gloss the notion as follows.[16] Let $\ulcorner \mathbf{this}^{M_u}\urcorner$, $\ulcorner \mathbf{you}^{M_u}\urcorner$, $\ulcorner \mathbf{he}^{M_u}\urcorner$ and $\ulcorner \mathbf{she}^{M_u}\urcorner$ be names in Z for certain special uninterpreted expression-kinds of u's Mentalese–the so-called *demonstrative tags*–and let $\ulcorner \mathbf{d}^{M_u}\urcorner$ (with or without subscripts) be a restricted variable in Z ranging over the demonstrative tags of M_u; these boldface names and variables are the M_u-*tag-terms* of Z. A Mentalese demonstrative-token is a demonstrative tag token whose employment is controlled by its owner's being appeared-to in such-and-such a way: it is the inner counterpart of a public-language demonstrative *cum* successful demonstration. Thinking of a perceived object is not automatic but requires that certain items of the perceiver's language of thought–viz., the demonstrative tags–should be suitably related to the perceiver's perceptual representation(s) of the object. Let '*Index*$^{<i,i>}$' be that predicate of Z whose intended interpretation is this special causal/computational indexing relation between tokens of Mentalese demonstrative tags and perceptual representations, whereby the percepts become elements of thought. Then, where $\boldsymbol{\delta}$ is a M_u-tag-term and $\boldsymbol{\pi}$ is a percept species term, we stipulate that their juxtaposition $\ulcorner \boldsymbol{\delta}\boldsymbol{\pi}\urcorner$ is a complex name in Z of the corresponding demonstrative *type* in M_u, which our theory identifies with the property of being a token of the demonstrative tag $\boldsymbol{\delta}$ in M_u which is indexed by some perceptual representation belonging to the species named by $\boldsymbol{\pi}$.[17] We make the natural assumption that an object y is the denotation in c of a Mentalese demonstrative $\mathbf{d}\Pi_x$ iff $y = x$. Finally, where (for $k \geq 1$) $\boldsymbol{\delta}_k$ is $\ulcorner I_k\urcorner$, $\ulcorner you_k\urcorner$, $\ulcorner he_k\urcorner$, $\ulcorner she_k\urcorner$ or $\ulcorner this_k\urcorner$, let $\boldsymbol{\pi}_k$ be respectively $\ulcorner PI_k\urcorner$, $\ulcorner PA_k\urcorner$, $\ulcorner PM_k\urcorner$, $\ulcorner PF_k\urcorner$ or $\ulcorner PO_k\urcorner$. Then we may state the appropriate axioms for the deictic sense-names $\ulcorner [\underline{I}_k]_c\urcorner$, $\ulcorner [\underline{you}_k]_c\urcorner$, $\ulcorner [\underline{he}_k]_c\urcorner$, $\ulcorner [\underline{she}_k]_c\urcorner$ and $\ulcorner [\underline{this}_k]_c\urcorner$ ($k \geq 1$) via the stipulation that every (suitably formalized) instance of the following schema is an axiom:

[DSN=] $[\boldsymbol{\delta}_k{}^i]_c$ = the A-individual proxy-encoding just that relation between an individual, a person u and a Mentalese term $^i\mathbf{t}$ which consists in $\mathbf{t}$ being of the sort $\mathbf{d}°[\boldsymbol{\pi}_k]_c$ for some $\mathbf{d}^{M_u}$.[18]

(Note that it follows from our definitions that $[\boldsymbol{\delta}_k]_c$ (if it exists) is the object of any perceptual representation belonging to the corresponding species $[\boldsymbol{\pi}_k]_c$: e.g., $[you_k]_c$ (if it exists) is the object of any perceptual representation belonging to the species $[PA_k]_c$, and so on. The A-individual $[\boldsymbol{\delta}_k{}^i]_c$ exists even if $[\boldsymbol{\pi}_k]_c$ does not, but one cannot prove in Z that $[\boldsymbol{\delta}_k{}^i]_c$ proxy-encodes the relation in question unless the existence of $[\boldsymbol{\pi}_k]_c$ is assumed.) All that we take to be contextually determined is the identity of the indexing percept species $[\boldsymbol{\pi}_k]_c$–the question of how (if at all) the "style" of the mental demonstrative (i.e., the value of $\ulcorner \mathbf{d}^{M_u}\urcorner$) is further determined is not germane to the opacity-transparency issue and will be ignored here.

The importance of sense-names in Z is that they allow us to capture at the propositional level the difference between the truth conditions of *de re* and *de dicto* interpretations of an object-language belief ascription in terms of different PEAPs believed, and to do so in a way that correctly tracks the corresponding differences at the functional/sentential level in terms of different sorts of Mentalese sentences tokened. Consider, e.g., the pure *de dicto* reading of (1) and let c be a context in which a demonstrated object is assigned to the sole occurrence of 'this'; then (2) represents the truth condition of this reading of (1) in c:

(1) I believe that this is red.

(2) $Believes([I]_c, [THAT\ [\underline{Red}_1]_c([\underline{this}_1]_c)])$.

Where M is $[I]_c$'s Mentalese, we can easily prove in Z that (2) is equivalent to (3):

(3) $(\exists z')(\exists^{<\cdot>}\mathbf{n}^M)(\exists \mathbf{d}^M)(E!^{<\cdot>}z\ \&\ \text{«}\mathbf{n}°(\mathbf{d}°[PO_1]_c)\text{»}^\circledast z\ \&\ Affirms([I]_c,z)\ \&$
$Denotes_M(\mathbf{n},red)\ \&\ [\mathbf{\cdot}red^{\cdot}_1]_c(\mathbf{n},[I]_c))$.

In other words, it is provable in Z that the utterer in c bears the relation *Believes* to the PEAP $[THAT\ [\underline{Red}_1]_c([\underline{this}_1]_c)]$ iff the utterer affirmatively tokens *in foro interno* a Mentalese sentence of the sort $\text{«}\mathbf{n}(\mathbf{d}[PO_1]_c)\text{»}$ whose predicate term $\mathbf{n}$ bears $[\mathbf{\cdot}red^{\cdot}_1]_c$ to the utterer and denotes the property of being red, and whose subject term is a Mentalese demonstrative $\mathbf{d}[PO_1]_c$ (which, by definition, denotes the object $[this_1]_c$ represented by all members of the percept species $[PO_1]_c$).

By way of contrast, consider the partly *de re* reading of (1) on which 'this' but not 'red' occurs transparently. Relative to the same context c, the truth condition of this reading of (1) is given by (4), which is equivalent in Z to (5):

(4) $Believes([I]_c, [THAT\ [\underline{Red}_1]_c([this_1]_c)])$

(5) $(\exists z')(\exists^{<\cdot>}\mathbf{r}^M)(\exists^{<\cdot>}\mathbf{t}^M)(E!^{<\cdot>}z\ \&\ \text{«}\mathbf{r}°(\mathbf{t})\text{»}^\circledast z\ \&\ Affirms([I]_c,z)\ \&$
$Denotes_M(\mathbf{r},red)\ \&\ [\mathbf{\cdot}red^{\cdot}_1]_c(\mathbf{r},[I]_c)\ \&\ Denotes_M(\mathbf{t},[this_1]_c))$

(M now being the utterer's Mentalese). That is, it is provable in Z that the utterer in c bears the relation *Believes* to the PEAP $[THAT\ [\underline{Red}_1]_c([this_1]_c)]$ iff he/she affirmatively tokens *in foro interno* a Mentalese sentence of the sort $\text{«}\mathbf{r}(\mathbf{t})\text{»}$ whose predicate term $\mathbf{r}$ bears the relation $[\mathbf{\cdot}red^{\cdot}_1]_c$ to him/her and denotes the property of being red, and whose subject term $\mathbf{t}$ denotes the (first) contextually demonstrated object, $[this_1]_c$.

None of this, of course, presupposes or entails any *systematic* connection between the formulas of Z and the sentences of any real or artificial public language L. It is one thing to have a formal theory of belief *qua* relation to PEAPs and quite another to have a formal theory–let alone a finitely axiomatizable one–of the truth-conditions of belief *ascriptions* in L. To this latter task we now belatedly turn.

2. The target language L_1.

Our model language L_1 will be constructed in two stages. First we will specify a (univocal) base language L_0, a typed first-order quantificational language with identity and deictic terms. Second, we will transform L_0 to the desired (ambiguous) language L_1 by adding various indexicals, demonstratives and proper names from English, and we will show how to define a structural disambiguation mapping from L_1's sentences onto corresponding sets of L_0-formulas. The philosophical point of the procedure is to enable us to represent the possible *de re*/*de dicto* ambiguities of any propositional attitude sentence in L_1 via the unique meanings of the various L_0-formulas which correspond to it under this mapping.

Types in L_0 are as for Z. The lexicon of L_0 has three subdivisions. First, there are the typed logical expressions: viz., the identity predicate 'is$^{<i,i>}$', the universality predicate 'All$^{<<i>>}$', and the variables 'X$_1$', 'X$_2$',... and personal parameters 'X$_1^+$', 'X$_2^+$',... (all of L_0-type i). Second, there are the untyped logical syncategoremata: viz., the sentential connectives 'not' and 'If...then...', the abstraction operator $\ulcorner[\mathcal{V}\lfloor..\mathcal{V}...]\urcorner$, and the primitive complementizer 'that'. Third, there are the typed non-logical expressions. These will include the deictic names–viz., for each k, $\ulcorner u_k\urcorner$, $\ulcorner a_k\urcorner$, $\ulcorner h_k\urcorner$, $\ulcorner s_k\urcorner$, $\ulcorner d_k\urcorner$ (all of L_0-type i)–together with a suitably finite array of primitive ordinary names of L_0-types i, $<i,p>$, $<i>$ and $<i,i>$ alone. In L_0-type $<i,p>$ will be the verb $\ulcorner$believes$_k\urcorner$ for $k \geq 1$ (cf. note 28). In L_0-type i will be the similarly subscripted individual constants 'A','B',...,'W'. As regards the remaining two non-empty classes of names–those of L_0-types $<i>$ and $<i,i>$–it makes no difference to our project which predicative items we borrow from English to fill them, provided that the names of type $<i>$ are English words signifying properties of individuals and that the names of type $<i,i>$ are English words signifying relations between individuals. Since the language of Z itself is just a highly regimented extension of English in which there are finitely many univocal names $\alpha_1^{<i>},...,\alpha_k^{<i>}$ and $\beta_1^{<i,i>},...,\beta_n^{<i,i>}$ meeting these criteria, it will be convenient to suppose that ordinary names of L_0-types $<i>$ and $<i,i>$ are simply the de-italicized and numerically subscripted[19] versions of $\alpha_1^{<i>},...,\alpha_k^{<i>}$ and $\beta_1^{<i,i>},...,\beta_n^{<i,i>}$ in Z, and to label the corresponding name sets $\{\alpha_1^{<i>},...,\alpha_k^{<i>}\}$ and $\{\beta_1^{<i,i>},...,\beta_n^{<i,i>}\}$ as '*NAMES*$^{<i>}$' and '*NAMES*$^{<i,i>}$'.

The syntax for L_0 involves (in addition to the usual recursive formation rules for atomic and compound formulas) the special formation rules (FR1) and (FR2) for complex terms (viz., abstracts and 'that'-clauses):

(FR1)   For any formula S and variable $\mathcal{V}$ of L_0, $\ulcorner[\mathcal{V}\lfloor S]\urcorner$ is a complex term of L_0-type $<i>$.

(FR2)   Where C is the result of subscripting 'that' with at most one personal parameter and S is a formula of L_0, $\ulcorner C\,S\urcorner$ is a complex term of L_0-type p.

Even apart from its simple syntax, L_0 is still pretty distant from English. On the one hand, the deictic names of L_0 are primitive items which are not borrowed from English. On the other hand, L_0 possesses none of the indexical or demonstrative words of English, nor any ordinary-looking proper names.

To approach English more closely in these respects–and to ameliorate the suspicion that we are deliberately ignoring potential troublemakers–we now specify a related language L_1 differing from L_0 only in three ways. First, the deictic names of L_1 are just the familiar 'I', 'you', 'he', 'she', and 'this'. Second, L_1's ordinary names of type i are precisely the ordinary-looking 'Alice', 'Bob',...,'Wanda'. Third, the remaining names it shares with L_0 will appear without subscripts. Formulas and complex terms of L_1 are specified, *mutatis mutandis*, as for L_0. Closed formulas of L_1 will be called sentences.

We now show how to correlate each sentence of L_1 with the class of L_0-formulas which will eventually be used to interpret it. First, we define a function # from expressions $\mathcal{E}$ of L_1 such that $\#(\mathcal{E})$ is the expression which results from $\mathcal{E}$ when the kth occurrence in left-to-right order ($k \geq 1$) of each name η of type i in S is replaced by its subscripted counterpart, η_k. (Of course, when the expression $\mathcal{E}$ is an L_1-formula, $\#(\mathcal{E})$ will not itself be a formula of L_1 but is merely a formula-surrogate which will be useful in specifying $\mathcal{E}$'s interpretation.) Second, for each subscripted expression η_k formed from an L_1-name η of type i, we define its L_0-counterpart η_k' as follows:

> (i) if η_k is formed from the alphabetically n^{th} *ordinary* name of L_1-type i, then η_k' is the k-subscripted alphabetically n^{th} ordinary name of L_0-type i.
> (Thus, e.g., for any k: $\ulcorner Alice_k' \urcorner$ is the name $\ulcorner A_k' \urcorner$ of L_0; $\ulcorner Bob_k' \urcorner$ is the name $\ulcorner B_k' \urcorner$ of L_0;...; and $\ulcorner Wanda_k' \urcorner$ is the name $\ulcorner W_k' \urcorner$ of L_0.)
> (ii) if η_k is formed from the *deictic* name 'I', 'you', 'he', 'she' or 'this' of L_1, then η_k' is respectively the L_0-term $\ulcorner u_k \urcorner$, $\ulcorner a_k \urcorner$, $\ulcorner h_k \urcorner$, $\ulcorner s_k \urcorner$ or $\ulcorner d_k \urcorner$

Let $\ulcorner (-\eta_k-) \urcorner$ be any expression containing just one occurrence of η_k and let $\ulcorner (-\mathcal{V}-) \urcorner$ be the expression which results from substituting the variable $\mathcal{V}$ for η_k in $\ulcorner (-\eta_k-) \urcorner$, $\mathcal{V}$ being alphabetically the first variable foreign to $\ulcorner (-\eta_k-) \urcorner$. Then we can contextually eliminate η_k from $\ulcorner (-\eta_k-) \urcorner$ by the definition (CD):

(CD) $\ulcorner (-\eta_k-) \urcorner =_{def.} \ulcorner [\mathcal{V} | (-\mathcal{V}-)](\eta_k') \urcorner$ if η_k in $\ulcorner (-\eta_k-) \urcorner$ lies within the scope of an occurrence of 'that' or $\ulcorner that_p \urcorner$ for some personal parameter p; $\ulcorner (-\eta_k'-) \urcorner$ otherwise.

Now it is well-known that the presence of logical structure in a sentence containing contextually defined expressions may allow those expressions to be eliminated in a variety of logically *inequivalent* ways. We exploit this familiar fact in order to define, for each sentence S of L_1 the following set $Rdg(S)$ of L_0-formulas which constitute its *readings*:

> For any L_0-formula S_0: $S_0 \in Rdg(S)$ iff either (i) $S = S_0$ or (ii) $\#(S)$ may be transformed into S_0 by repeated applications of (CD).

We may now define a *structural disambiguation* for L_1 as any function D from the sentences S of L_1 such that $D(S) \in Rdg(S)$. (By speaking of arbitrary L_0- and L_1-type t in clause (i) above, this way of relating certain terms of L_1 to those of L_0 can clearly be applied to terms of types *other* than i as well; but since our present concern is with singular terms, we will not bother with the obvious extension of the technique to other terms. As can be seen from the results in the next section, this means that occurrences of terms of types other than i in 'that'-clauses of L_1 will always be treated as opaque. When the technique is extended to terms of these other types, the full range of possible pure and mixed *de re/de dicto* ambiguities can be generated for these other terms as well.)

The overall picture, then, is this. To the naked eye, L_1 is a regimented fragment of English, containing lots of familiar singular and general terms and, like the mother tongue, having sentences which hide (what will turn out to be semantically significant) structural ambiguities that in principle could be unpacked in a related but univocal idiom. If we like, we may think of a sentence S of L_1 as standing to the L_0-formulas in $Rdg(S)$ in a relation relevantly like that between ordinary sentences and their "logical forms".

3. A Sense-Reference Semantics for L_0 and L_1.

Where f is a an assignment of O-objects to free variables and c is a context (as characterized in section 1), our semantics for L_0 will provide each term or formula $\mathcal{E}$ of L_0 with two sorts of semantical values relative to c and f: to wit, $\mathcal{E}$ will express a sense $Sen_{c,f}(\mathcal{E})_{L_0}$ and denote a referent $Ref_{c,f}(\mathcal{E})_{L_0}$. (Where its value is contextually obvious, the language-identifying final subscript will be omitted.) In the case of terms and formulas containing the second- or third-person demonstratives of L_0, the assignment of senses and references is conditional upon the provision by c of appropriate demonstrata. Formally, the two expressions $\ulcorner Ref_{c,f}(\mathcal{E})\urcorner$ and $\ulcorner Sen_{c,f}(\mathcal{E})\urcorner$ are defined in Z as follows:

$$Ref_{c,f}(\mathcal{E})_{L_0} =_{def} (\imath x^t) Denotes_{L_0}^{<<i>,i,i,t>}(\mathcal{E},c,f,x)$$
$$Sen_{c,f}(\mathcal{E})_{L_0} =_{def} (\imath x^t) Expresses_{L_0}^{<<i>,i,i,t>}(\mathcal{E},c,f,x)$$

–where, for each of the finitely many L_0-types t occupied by L_0-expressions, $Denotes_{L_0}^{<<i>,i,i,t>}$ is the appropriate relativized denotation-relation and $Expresses_{L_0}^{<<i>,i,i,t>}$ the appropriate relativized expression-relation.

The names '$Denotes_{L_0}^{<<i>,i,i,t>}$' and '$Expresses_{L_0}^{<<i>,i,i,t>}$' are *primitives* of Z: no attempt will be made here to reduce them–i.e., to equate $Denotes_{L_0}^{<<i>,i,i,t>}$ or $Expresses_{L_0}^{<<i>,i,i,t>}$ with relations specified in other terms. Since our current project is semantical rather than metasemantical, it requires only that we specify the *extension* of these relations *via-a-vis* L_0, not that we provide a reductive–let alone a naturalistic–account of them. Importantly, our theory will allow that what is expressed by $\mathcal{E}$–viz., its sense–can always be identified *apart* from the expression-relation $Expresses^{<<i>,i,i,t>}$.

The senses of primitive terms of L_0 are specified by the semantical postulates[20]

$$Sen_{c,f}(\text{`All}^{<<i>>\text{'}}) = Ref_{c,f}(\text{`All}^{<<i>>\text{'}})$$
$$Sen_{c,f}(\text{`is}^{<i,i>\text{'}}) = Ref_{c,f}(\text{`is}^{<i,i>\text{'}})$$
$$Sen_{c,f}(\ulcorner believes_k \urcorner) = [\underline{believes_k}]_c$$
$$Sen_{c,f}(\mathcal{V}) = Ref_{c,f}(\mathcal{V})$$
$$Sen_{c,f}(\ulcorner \mathcal{V}^+ \urcorner) = Ref_{c,f}(\ulcorner \mathcal{V}^+ \urcorner)$$
$$Sen_{c,f}(\ulcorner u_k \urcorner) = [L_k]_c$$
$$(\forall x^i)(x = Sen_{c,f}(\ulcorner a_k \urcorner) \equiv ((\exists y^i)(y = [you_k]_c) \,\&\, x = [\underline{you_k}]_c))$$
$$(\forall x^i)(x = Sen_{c,f}(\ulcorner d_k \urcorner) \equiv ((\exists y^i)(y = [this_k]_c) \,\&\, x = [\underline{this_k}]_c))$$
$$(\forall x^i)(x = Sen_{c,f}(\ulcorner h_k \urcorner) \equiv ((\exists y^i)(y = [he_k]_c) \,\&\, x = [\underline{he_k}]_c))$$
$$(\forall x^i)(x = Sen_{c,f}(\ulcorner s_k \urcorner) \equiv ((\exists y^i)(y = [she_k]_c) \,\&\, x = [\underline{she_k}]_{c,}))$$
$$Sen_{c,f}(\ulcorner A_k \urcorner) = [\underline{Alice_k}]_c$$

.

.

.

$$Sen_{c,f}(\ulcorner W_k \urcorner) = [\underline{Wanda_k}]_c$$

and by the finitely many postulates which are instances of the schema

$$Sen_{c,f}(\tau_k^x) = [\underline{\tau_k}]_c$$

in which τ_k^x is the subscripted and de-italicized version of $\tau \in NAMES^{<i>} \cup NAMES^{<i,i>}$. (E.g., the equations $\ulcorner Sen_{c,f}(\ulcorner red_k \urcorner) = [\underline{red_k}]_c \urcorner$ and $\ulcorner Sen_{c,f}(\ulcorner kicks_k \urcorner) = [\underline{kicks_k}]_c \urcorner$ will be semantical postulates courtesy of this schema.) Since, by hypothesis, the only occupied relational types in L_0 are $<i>$, $<i,i>$, and $<i,p>$, the senses of the possible atomic predications $\ulcorner \mathcal{I}_0(\mathcal{I}_1) \urcorner$ and $\ulcorner \mathcal{I}_0(\mathcal{I}_1,\mathcal{I}_2) \urcorner$ are compositionally supplied by the following three postulates, in which left superscripts on variables indicate the L_0-type of the L_0-terms in their range:[21]

$$(\forall x^p)(\forall^{<i>}\mathcal{I}_0)(\forall^i \mathcal{I}_1)\,(x = Sen_{c,f}(\ulcorner \mathcal{I}_0(\mathcal{I}_1) \urcorner) \equiv$$
$$x = [\lambda\; Sen_{c,f}(\mathcal{I}_0)(Sen_{c,f}(\mathcal{I}_2))]).$$
$$(\forall x^p)(\forall^{<i,i>}\mathcal{I}_0)(\forall^i \mathcal{I}_1)(\forall^i \mathcal{I}_1)(x = Sen_{c,f}(\ulcorner \mathcal{I}_0(\mathcal{I}_1,\mathcal{I}_2) \urcorner) \equiv x =$$
$$[\lambda\; Sen_{c,f}(\mathcal{I}_0)(Sen_{c,f}(\mathcal{I}_1),Sen_{c,f}(\mathcal{I}_2))]).$$
$$(\forall x^p)(\forall^{<i,p>}\mathcal{I}_0)(\forall^i \mathcal{I}_1)(\forall^p \mathcal{I}_2)(x = Sen_{c,f}(\ulcorner \mathcal{I}_0(\mathcal{I}_1,\mathcal{I}_2) \urcorner) \equiv x =$$
$$[\lambda\; Sen_{c,f}(\mathcal{I}_0)(Sen_{c,f}(\mathcal{I}_1),Sen_{c,f}(\mathcal{I}_2))]).$$

The senses of complex terms and compound formulas of L_0 likewise hold no surprises, being provided for by the following postulates, in which $'p'$ ranges over personal parameters of L_0 and $f[x/\mathcal{V}]$ is the result of semantically substituting the object x for the variable $\mathcal{V}$ in the assignment f:

$$(\forall y^{<i>})(\forall \mathcal{V})(\forall S)(y = Sen_{c,f}(\ulcorner [\mathcal{V}\, |S] \urcorner) \equiv y = [\lambda x\; Sen_{c,g}(S)]) \text{ (where } g = f[x/\mathcal{V}])$$
$$(\forall x^p)(\forall S_1)(\forall S_2)(x = Sen_{c,f}(\ulcorner \text{If } S_1 \text{ then } S_2 \urcorner) \equiv x = [\lambda\; Sen_{c,f}(S_1) \rightarrow Sen_{c,f}(S_2)])$$
$$(\forall x^p)(\forall S)(x = Sen_{c,f}(\ulcorner \text{not} S \urcorner) \equiv x = [\lambda\; {\sim} Sen_{c,f}(S)])$$
$$(\forall x^p)(\forall S)(x = Sen_{c,f}(\ulcorner \text{that } S \urcorner) \equiv x = [THAT\; Sen_{c,f}(S)])$$

$(\forall y^p)(\forall S)(y = Sen_{c,f}(\ulcorner that_p S\urcorner) \equiv y = [THAT_x Sen_{c,f}(\ulcorner P \vert S\urcorner)(x)])$

The salient reference-postulates for the primitive terms of L_0 are

$Ref_{c,f}(`All`^{<<i>>>}) = [\lambda F^{<i>} (\forall x^i)(E!^{<i>}x \to Fx)]$

$Ref_{c,f}(`is`^{<i,i>>}) = [\lambda x^i y^i (\forall F^{<i>})(Fx \equiv Fy)]$

$Ref_{c,f}(\mathcal{V}) = f(\mathcal{V})$

$Ref_{c,f}(\ulcorner \mathcal{V}^+\urcorner) = f(\ulcorner \mathcal{V}^+\urcorner)$

$Ref_{c,f}(\ulcorner u_k\urcorner) = [\Pi]_c$

$(\forall x^i)(x = Ref_{c,f}(\ulcorner a_k\urcorner) \equiv x = [you_k]_c)$

$(\forall x^i)(x = Ref_{c,f}(\ulcorner h_k\urcorner) \equiv x = [he_k]_c)$

$(\forall x^i)(x = Ref_{c,f}(\ulcorner s_k\urcorner) \equiv x = [she_k]_c)$

$(\forall x^i)(x = Ref_{c,f}(\ulcorner d_k\urcorner) \equiv x = [this_k]_c)$

$Ref_{c,f}(\ulcorner believes_k\urcorner) = believes$

$Ref_{c,f}(\ulcorner A_k\urcorner) = Alice$

.

.

.

$Ref_{c,f}(\ulcorner W_k\urcorner) = Wanda$

and the finitely many instances of the schema

$$Ref_{c,f}(\tau_k^x) = \tau$$

in which, as before, τ_k^x is the subscripted and de-italicized version of $\tau \in NAMES^{<i>} \cup NAMES^{<i,i>}$. (E.g., $\ulcorner Ref_{c,f}(\ulcorner red_k\urcorner) = red\urcorner$ and $\ulcorner Ref_{c,f}(\ulcorner kicks_k\urcorner) = kicks\urcorner$ will be semantical postulates courtesy of this schema.) The referents of the possible atomic predications $\ulcorner \mathcal{I}_0(\mathcal{I}_1)\urcorner$ and $\ulcorner \mathcal{I}_0(\mathcal{I}_1,\mathcal{I}_2)\urcorner$ are compositionally supplied by the following three postulates:

$(\forall x^p)(\forall^{<i>}\mathcal{I}_0)(\forall^i \mathcal{I}_1)(x = Ref_{c,f}(\ulcorner \mathcal{I}_0(\mathcal{I}_1)\urcorner) \equiv$
$\quad x = [\lambda Ref_{c,f}(\mathcal{I}_0)(Ref_{c,f}(\mathcal{I}_1))]).$

$(\forall x^p)(\forall^{<i,i>}\mathcal{I}_0)(\forall^i \mathcal{I}_1)(\forall^i \mathcal{I}_2)(x = Ref_{c,f}(\ulcorner \mathcal{I}_0(\mathcal{I}_1,\mathcal{I}_2)\urcorner) \equiv$
$\quad x = [\lambda Ref_{c,f}(\mathcal{I}_0)(Ref_{c,f}(\mathcal{I}_1),Ref_{c,f}(\mathcal{I}_2))]).$

$(\forall x^p)(\forall^{<i,p>}\mathcal{I}_0)(\forall^i \mathcal{I}_1)(\forall^p \mathcal{I}_2)(x = Ref_{c,f}(\ulcorner \mathcal{I}_0(\mathcal{I}_1,\mathcal{I}_2)\urcorner) \equiv$
$\quad x = [\lambda Ref_{c,f}(\mathcal{I}_0)(Ref_{c,f}(\mathcal{I}_1),Ref_{c,f}(\mathcal{I}_2))]).$

The postulates specifying the referents of abstracts and compound formulas parallel those specifying their senses:

$(\forall y^{<i>})(\forall \mathcal{V})(\forall S)(y = Ref_{c,f}(\ulcorner [\mathcal{V} \vert S]\urcorner) \equiv$
$\quad y = [\lambda x Ref_{c,g}(S)])$ (where $g = f[x/\mathcal{V}]$.

$(\forall x^p)(\forall S_1)(\forall S_2)(x = Ref_{c,f}(\ulcorner If S_1 then S_2\urcorner) \equiv$
$\quad x = [\lambda Ref_{c,f}(S_1) \to Ref_{c,f}(S_2)]).$

$(\forall x^p)(\forall S)(x = Ref_{c,f}(\ulcorner not S\urcorner) \equiv x = [\lambda \sim Ref_{c,f}(S)]).$

The crucial difference between our account and a traditional Fregean account is that we identify the referent of a 'that'-clause with the sense of a certain *transform* of the 'that'-clause itself, and *not* (as Frege does) with the sense of the embedded sentence. Let $\ulcorner S_0(\mathcal{J}/V)\urcorner$ denote the result of uniformly substituting $\mathcal{J}$ for V in S$_0$. Further, let $\ulcorner S'\urcorner$ denote the result of replacing every occurrence in S of a formula having the form $\ulcorner[V\,|S_0](\mathcal{J})\urcorner$ with an occurrence of $S_0(\mathcal{J}/V)$. Then we take the following as our postulates:

$$(\forall x^p)(\forall S)(x = Ref_{c,f}(\ulcorner \text{that } S \urcorner) \equiv x = Sen_{c,f}(\ulcorner \text{that } S' \urcorner))$$
$$(\forall x^p)(\forall S)(\forall P)(x = Ref_{c,f}(\ulcorner \text{that}_p\, S \urcorner) \equiv x = Sen_{c,f}(\ulcorner \text{that }_p S' \urcorner))$$

The *referent simpliciter* of a formula S of L_0 in a context c (in symbols: $Ref_c(S)_{L0}$) is the proposition (if any) that S denotes in c relative to every assignment f–i.e., we have the postulate

$$(\forall S)(\forall x^p)(x = Ref_c(S) \equiv (\forall f)(x = Ref_{c,f}(S)))$$

Bearing in mind that our basic notion of truth, viz. truth for propositions, is defined in redundancy fashion by the axiom $\ulcorner(\forall x^p)(Tr(x) \equiv x)\urcorner$ of Z, we may define our truth predicate for L_0 by

$$TRUE_c(S)_{L0} =_{def.} Tr(Ref_c(S)_{L0}),$$

according to which S's being true-in-L_0-in-a-context-c is just S's referent *simpliciter* in c being a true proposition. The redundancy account of truth for propositions ensures that the sense- and reference-talk can ultimately be eliminated from the right-hand side of our T-sentences for L_0. Notice also that

$$\sim(\exists x^t)(x = Ref_c(\mathcal{J})) \rightarrow (\sim TRUE_c(S)_{L0} \;\&\; \sim TRUE_c(\ulcorner \text{not} S \urcorner)_{L0})$$

is provable for any sentence S and term $\mathcal{J}$ of L_0-type t occurring therein.

Since L_1, like English but unlike L_0, is an *ambiguous* language, it is natural further to relativize sense and reference in L_1 to a structural disambiguation D–i.e., to allow for the interpretation of L_1's sentences only *relative* to a semantically possible disambiguation. L_1 may then be given a simple proxy-semantics in terms of our base semantics for L_0 by adopting the following two postulates:

$$(\forall x^p)(\forall S_{L1})(x = Sen_{c,f,D}(S)_{L1} \equiv x = Sen_{c,f}(D(S))_{L0})$$
$$(\forall x^p)(\forall S_{L1})(x = Ref_{c,f,D}(S)_{L1} \equiv x = Ref_{c,f}(D(S))_{L0}).$$

The *univocal referent* of a sentence S of L_1 in a context c (in symbols: $Ref_c(S)_{L1}$) is the proposition (if any) that S denotes in c relative to every assignment f and every structural disambiguation D. This notion is introduced by the postulate

$$(\forall S_{L_1})(\forall x^p)(x = Ref_c(S)_{L_1} \equiv (\forall f)(\forall D)(x = Ref_{c,f,D}(S)_{L_1})).$$

It should be clear that the L_1-sentences with univocal referents are precisely the closed ones which are devoid of 'that'-clauses containing singular terms.[22] The *D-disambiguated referent* of a sentence S of L_1 in a context c (in symbols: $Ref_{c,D}(S)_{L_1}$) is the proposition (if any) that S denotes in c relative to every variable-assignment f and the particular structural disambiguation D. This notion is introduced by the postulate

$$(\forall S_{L_1})(\forall x^p)(x = Ref_{c,D}(S)_{L_1} \equiv (\forall f)(x = Ref_{c,f,D}(S)_{L_1})).$$

Closed L_1-sentences with 'that'-clauses which contain singular terms may have a variety of D-disambiguated referents in a given context, but will have no univocal referent in that context. Finally, S's being *true in L_1 under a disambiguation D* (or: *D-true in L_1*) in a context c may be defined as its D-disambiguated referent in c being a true proposition; and S's being *univocally true in L_1 in c* may be defined as its being D-true in c for every D: accordingly, we stipulate

$$D\text{-}TRUE_c(S)_{L_1} =_{def.} Tr(Ref_{c,D}(S)_{L_1});$$
$$TRUE_c(S)_{L_1} =_{def.} (\forall D)(D\text{-}TRUE_c(S)_{L_1}),$$

in consequence of which we will have as theorems the desired equivalences

$$(\forall S_{L_1})(\forall D)(D\text{-}TRUE_c(S)_{L_1} \equiv TRUE_c(D(S))_{L_0});$$
$$(\forall S_{L_1})(TRUE_c(S)_{L_1} \equiv (\forall D)TRUE_c(D(S))_{L_0}).$$

This completes our sketch of the sense-reference semantics for L_1 and its account of truth-in-L_1.

By way of illustration, let us briefly examine the consequences of the foregoing for the truth conditions of a sample belief ascription in L_1. Consider, e.g., the context-dependent sentence (6) of L_1:

    (6) believes(I, that red(this))

Restricting our attention to singular terms, (6) will be ambiguous as between the *opaque L_0-reading* (7) and the *transparent L_0-reading* (8):

    (7) believes$_1$(u$_1$, that red$_1$(d$_1$))
    (8) [X$_1$ | believes$_1$(u$_1$, that red$_1$(X$_1$))](d$_1$)

Where $D_{6/7}$ and $D_{6/8}$ are structural disambiguations assigning the readings (7) and (8) respectively to (6), our semantical theory yields as theorems the T-sentences (TS-1) and (TS-2):

(TS-1) $D_{6/7}$-$TRUE_c$('believes(I, that red(this))') $\equiv$ $(\exists x^t)(x = Ref_c(\ulcorner\text{this}_1\urcorner)$ &
        $Believes([I]_c, [THAT [\underline{red}_1]_c([\underline{this}_1]_c)]))$.

(TS-2) $D_{6/8}$-$TRUE_c$('believes(I, that red(this))') $\equiv$ $(\exists x^t)(x = Ref_c(\ulcorner\text{this}_1\urcorner)$ &
        $Believes([I]_c, [THAT [\underline{red}_1]_c(x)]))$.

Via the axiom schemes [*That*=] and [*Belief*], it can be shown that the truth condition laid down in (TS-1) obtains just in case $Ref_c(\ulcorner\text{this}_1\urcorner) = [this_1]_c$ and the utterer u in c affirmatively tokens a sentence of the sort «$\mathbf{n}(\mathbf{d}[PO_1]_c)$» in his/her Mentalese idiolect M_u such that $\mathbf{n}$ denotes *red*, $\mathbf{n}$ bears the relation $[^{\bullet}\text{red}^{\bullet}_1]_c$ to u, and $\mathbf{d}[PO_1]_c$ is a demonstrative in M_u denoting the object $[this_1]_c$ (which is represented by all members of the percept species $[PO_1]_c$). It can similarly be shown that the truth condition laid down by (TS-2) obtains just in case $Ref_c(\ulcorner\text{this}_1\urcorner) = [this_1]_c$ and the utterer u in c affirmatively tokens a sentence «$\mathbf{r}(\mathbf{t})$» in his/her Mentalese idiolect M_u such that $\mathbf{r}$ denotes *red*, $\mathbf{r}$ bears the relation $[^{\bullet}\text{red}^{\bullet}_1]_c$ to u, and $\mathbf{t}$ denotes $[this_1]_c$.

    For an *iterated* belief ascription of L_1 like the sentence

(9) believes(Bob, that believes(Alice, that red(Spot)))

matters are considerably more complicated. Restricting our attention again to singular terms, our account of structural disambiguation gives the six L_0-readings (10)-(15):

(10) believes$_1$(B$_1$, that believes$_2$(A$_1$, that red$_1$(S$_1$)))
(11) [X$_2$ | believes$_1$(B$_1$, that believes$_2$(X$_2$, that red$_1$(S$_1$))))](A$_1$)
(12) believes$_1$(B$_1$, that [X$_1$ | believes$_2$(A$_1$, that red$_1$(X$_1$))](S$_1$))
(13) [X$_2$ | believes$_1$(B$_1$, that [X$_1$ | believes$_2$(X$_2$, that red$_1$(X$_1$))](S$_1$))](A$_1$)
(14) [X$_1$ | believes$_1$(B$_1$, that believes$_2$(A$_1$, that red$_1$(X$_1$))))](S$_1$)
(15) [X$_2$ | [X$_1$ | believes$_1$(B$_1$, that believes$_2$(X$_2$, that red$_1$(X$_1$))))](S$_1$)](A$_1$)

Now (10) is the fully opaque attribution having as referent (hence as truth condition) in c the proposition

(A) $Believes(Bob,[THAT [\underline{Believes}_2]_c([\underline{Alice}_1]_c,[THAT [\underline{red}_1]_c([\underline{Spot}_1]_c)]]))$.

It is easily provable that $Ref_{c,f}((12)) = Ref_{c,f}((10))$. As regards (11), we have the chain of identities

$Ref_{c,f}('[X_2 | \text{believes}_1(B_1, \text{that believes}_2(X_2, \text{that red}_1(S_1)))](A_1)')$
$= [\lambda \; Ref_{c,f}('[X_2 | \text{believes}(B_1, \text{that believes}_2(X_2, \text{that red}_1(S_1)))]')(Ref_{c,f}('A_1')]$
$= [\lambda \; Ref_{c,f}('[X_2 | \text{believes}_1(B_1, \text{that believes}_2(X_2, \text{that red}_1(S_1)))]')(Alice)]$
$= [\lambda \; [\lambda y \; Ref_{c,f[y/'x_2']}('\text{believes}_1(B_1, \text{that believes}_2(X_2, \text{that red}_1(S_1)))')(Alice)]$
$= [\lambda \; [\lambda y \; Believes(Bob, Ref_{c,f[y/'x_2']}('\text{that believes}_2(X_2, \text{that red}_1(S_1))'))](Alice)]$
$= [\lambda \; [\lambda y \; Believes(Bob, [THAT \; Sen_{c,f[y/'x_2']}('\text{believes}_2(X_2, \text{that red}_1(S_1))')])](Alice)]$
$= [\lambda \; [\lambda y \; Believes(Bob, [THAT [\underline{Believes}_2]_c(y, Sen_{c,f[y/'x_2']}('\text{that red}_1(S_1)')))])](Alice)]$
$= [\lambda \; [\lambda y \; Believes(Bob, [THAT [\underline{Believes}_2]_c(y, [THAT [\underline{Red}_1]_c([\underline{this}_1]_c)]))])](Alice)]$.

By λ-conversion, the last member of this chain is strictly equivalent to the proposition

(B) *Believes(Bob, [THAT [Believes₂]ᵪ(Alice, [THAT [Red₁]ᵪ([Spot₁]ᵪ)])])*.

Since the postulate for ⌜that S⌝ yields the chain of identities

$Sen_{c,f_{y/}·x_2·}$('that $[X_1 \mid believes_2(X_2, that\ red_1(X_1))](S_1)$')
$= [THAT\ Sen_{c,f_{y/}·x_2·}('believes_2(X_2, that\ red_1(S_1))')]$
$= [THAT\ [\underline{believes_2}]_c(y, Sen_{c,f_{y/}·x_2·}('that\ red_1(S_1)'))]$
$= [THAT\ [\underline{believes_2}]_c(y, [THAT\ Sen_{c,f_{y/}·x_2·}('red_1(S_1)')])]$
$= [THAT\ [\underline{believes_2}]_c(y, [THAT\ [\underline{red_1}]_c([\underline{Spot_1}]_c)])]$,

$Ref_{c,f}((13))$ will be strictly equivalent to (B) as well. Similarly, we may show that $Ref_{c,f}((14))$ is strictly equivalent to the proposition

(C) *Believes(Bob, [THAT [Believes₂]ᵪ([Alice₁]ᵪ, [THAT [Red₁]ᵪ(Spot)])])*.

Finally, $Ref_{c,f}((15))$ can be shown to be strictly equivalent to the proposition

(D) *Believes(Bob, [THAT [Believes₂]ᵪ(Alice, [THAT [Red₁]ᵪ(Spot)])])*.

Where $D_{9/10}$ through $D_{9/15}$ are structural disambiguations assigning the readings (10) through (15) respectively to (9), our semantical theory accordingly yields the corresponding T-sentences:

(TS-3) $D_{9/10}\text{-}TRUE_c$('believes(Bob, that believes(Alice, that red(Spot)))') $\equiv$
Believes(Bob,[THAT [Believes₂]ᵪ([Alice₁]ᵪ,[THAT [red₁]ᵪ([Spot₁]ᵪ)])]).

(TS-4) $D_{9/11}\text{-}TRUE_c$('believes(Bob, that believes(Alice, that red(Spot)))') $\equiv$
Believes(Bob, [THAT [Believes₂]ᵪ(Alice, [THAT [Red₁]ᵪ([Spot₁]ᵪ)])]).

(TS-5) $D_{9/12}\text{-}TRUE_c$('believes(Bob, that believes(Alice, that red(Spot)))') $\equiv$
Believes(Bob,[THAT [Believes₂]ᵪ([Alice₁]ᵪ,[THAT [red₁]ᵪ([Spot₁]ᵪ)])]).

(TS-6) $D_{9/13}\text{-}TRUE_c$('believes(Bob, that believes(Alice, that red(Spot)))') $\equiv$
Believes(Bob, [THAT [Believes₂]ᵪ(Alice, [THAT [Red₁]ᵪ([Spot₁]ᵪ)])]).

(TS-7) $D_{9/14}\text{-}TRUE_c$('believes(Bob, that believes(Alice, that red(Spot)))') $\equiv$
Believes(Bob, [THAT [Believes₂]ᵪ([Alice₁]ᵪ, [THAT [Red₁]ᵪ(Spot)])]).

(TS-8) $D_{9/15}\text{-}TRUE_c$('believes(Bob, that believes(Alice, that red(Spot)))') $\equiv$
Believes(Bob, [THAT [Believes₂]ᵪ(Alice, [THAT [Red₁]ᵪ(Spot)])]).

Just as in the case of the two inequivalent propositions associated with (6) by (TS-1)-(TS-2), the four inequivalent propositions (A)-(D) can be shown to encapsulate possible truth conditions which do not involve A-objects, although the proof of this fact is long and complicated. The key to the proof lies in facts about the semantics of Mentalese discussed in the next section.

4. Semantics for Mentalese?

The semantical theories we have provided for L_0 and L_1 are finitely axiomatized and compositional. Now it is important to distinguish between (i) the demand for finite axiomatization of some subject-matter in the language of a theory T and (ii) the demand for a finite axiomatization of T itself. Thus, e.g., the demand for a finitely axiomatized compositional semantics for a standard extensional first-order language L may be met by within the language of a formal set theory like ZFS; but the fact that ZFS is not finitely axiomatizable does not detract in the least from our having met the initial demand regarding L. Similarly, the fact that our semantics for L_0 and L_1 are finitely axiomatized in the language of a theory Z whose own proffered axiomatization is not finite but essentially employs axiom schemata does not in itself show that we have failed to provide the desired sort of semantics for L_0 and L_1.

However, there is a special feature of our semantics for L_0 and L_1 which might occasion a related suspicion: viz., our account overtly and essentially appeals to the semantic properties of items in various languages of thought. It might be argued that (a) we have purchased the desired result for L_0 and L_1 at the cost of tacitly assuming that some finitely axiomatized compositional story can be told about these Mentalese semantic properties, and (b) no such story is possible, so that (c) our victory over the skeptic is hollow. Now we obviously cannot refute this argument by giving here a finitely axiomatized compositional semantics for every thinker's Mentalese idiolect! But there is no need to. For the skeptic's premiss (a) is false: nowhere have we relied upon any assumption about the existence of any particular sort of semantical *theory* for languages of thought. On the contrary, we have made—and our project anent L_0 and L_1 requires—only the following idealizing assumptions about languages of thought: (i) that they have the same basic syntactic structure as L_0; (ii) that they contain counterparts of L_0's logical vocabulary among their primitives[23]; (iii) that their primitive terms have determinate denotations identifiable in Z or some specifiable extension thereof; (iv) that a Mentalese demonstrative $\mathbf{dII}_x$ denotes the object x; and (v) that Mentalese terms of the sort «[**THAT** Φ]» obey the schemes $[\text{DEN}_M]$ and $[\text{TRUE}_M]$[24]. Of these, only (iii)-(v) are semantical assumptions. Of course, *if* every language of thought had a finitely axiomatized semantics of the sort we have explored, it is not hard to see how it might yield (iii)-(v) as theorems. But this hardly shows that assuming (iii)-(v) amounts to presupposing the existence of such a theory! Nor is the skeptic's premiss (b) very plausible, as may be seen by briefly sketching what a denotational semantics for languages of thought might look like from the standpoint of Z.

To begin with, we can directly identify the denotation of each ordinary perceptual demonstrative type $\mathbf{dII}_x$ in M_u by the obvious axiom

$$(\forall y^i)(\forall u^i)(\forall x^i)(\forall \mathbf{d}^{M_u})(\forall \mathbf{II}_x)(y = Ref_c(\mathbf{dII}_x)_{M_u} \equiv y = x).$$

The special self-demonstratives invoked by our account of *de se* belief will be provided for by the axiom

$(\forall u^i)(Ref_c(\mathbf{I}^{M_u})_{M_u} = u)$.

We can identify the denotation $Ref_c(\mathbf{«d°»\Pi_x})_{M_u}$ of an opacity-marked Mentalese perceptual demonstrative type by the axiom

$$(\forall x^i)(\forall v^i)(\forall \mathbf{d_1}^{M_v})(\forall \mathbf{\Pi}_x)(Ref_c(\mathbf{«d_1°»\Pi_x})_{M_v} = (\iota w^i)((\forall F^{<i>})(wF \equiv F =$$
$$PROX([\lambda y^i u^i z^{<i>} (\exists \mathbf{d_2}^{M_u})(z =_E \mathbf{«d_2°»\Pi_x})]))).$$

And for each primitive *non*-demonstrative name **n** in M_u-type t, we identify the denotation $Ref_c(\mathbf{«n°»})_{M_u}$ of its opacity-marked counterpart $\mathbf{«n°»}$ by taking as axioms exactly those instances of the scheme

(16) $(\forall k \in Int)(\forall u^i)(([\mathbf{°\alpha°}_k]_c(\mathbf{n},u) \ \& \ Ref_c(\mathbf{n})_{M_u} = \mathbf{\alpha}) \equiv Ref_c(\mathbf{«n°»})_{M_u} = [\mathbf{\alpha}_k]_c)$

for which the corresponding formula

(17) $Ref_c(\mathbf{n})_{M_u} = \mathbf{\alpha}$

is an axiom. Since M_u presumably has a finite primitive vocabulary, assumption (iii) assures us that there will be at most finitely many axioms of the sort (17), hence at most finitely many axioms of the sort (16). Then, *provided* we could specify the referent of each primitive name **n** in M_u-type t *via* a codesignative term $\mathbf{\alpha}$ of Z which was properly cognate with it (i.e., such that $[\mathbf{°\alpha°}_k]_c(\mathbf{n},u))$—thus allowing us to use (16) to prove all the relevant theorems of the form $\ulcorner Ref_c(\mathbf{«n°»})_{M_u} = [\mathbf{\alpha}_k]_c\urcorner$—we could readily give a finitely axiomatized denotational semantics for M_u in which the notion of sense plays no role at all. For, given assumptions (i)-(iii), the referents of Mentalese atomic predications, abstracts, and compound sentences could obviously be given axioms that mimic our postulates for the referents of the counterpart constructions in L_0. Mentalese terms of the form $\mathbf{«[THAT\ S]»}$ or $\mathbf{«[THAT_x\ S]»}$ would, however, require a different treatment than the 'that'-clauses of L_0; this difference is reflected in their characterizing axioms:

$$(\forall x^p)(x = Ref_c(\mathbf{«[THAT\ S]»})_{M_u} \equiv x = [THAT\ Ref_c(S)_{M_u}])$$
$$(\forall x^p)(x = Ref_c(\mathbf{«[THAT_x\ S]»})_{M_u} \equiv x = [THAT_x\ Ref_c(\mathbf{«[x\ S]»})_{M_u}(x)])$$

As one would expect, accounts of $\ulcorner Ref_c(S)_{M_u}\urcorner$ and $\ulcorner TRUE_c(S)_{M_u}\urcorner$ which are parallel to those for $\ulcorner Ref_c(S)_{L_0}\urcorner$ and $\ulcorner TRUE_c(S)_{L_0}\urcorner$ could then be given. Moreover, assumption (v) would be vindicated, for all the relevant instances of $[DEN_M]$ and $[TRUE_M]$ would now be theorems. That is, we would be able to prove the likes of

$$(Ref_c(\mathbf{r})_{M_u} =_E red \ \& \ ['red^{\bullet}_k]_c(\mathbf{r},u) \ \&$$
$$Ref_c(\mathbf{s})_{M_u} =_E Spot \ \& \ ['Spot^{\bullet}_k]_c(\mathbf{s},u)) \rightarrow$$
$$Ref_c(\text{«}[\textbf{THAT r}^\circ(\textbf{s}^\circ)]\text{»})_{M_u} =_E [THAT \ [\underline{red_k}]_c([\underline{Spot_k}]_c)])$$

and

$$Ref_c(\text{«}[\textbf{THAT r}^\circ(\textbf{s}^\circ)]\text{»})_{M_u} =_E [THAT \ [\underline{red_k}]_c([\underline{Spot_k}]_c)] \rightarrow$$
$$(TRUE_c(\text{«}\textbf{r}(\textbf{s})\text{»})_{M_u} \equiv red(Spot))$$

directly from the reference-axioms for M_u, without invoking Z's provisional axiom schemes [DEN$_M$] or [TRUE$_M$].

The technical obstacle to providing such a semantics for *each* person u's Mentalese is, of course, the proviso regarding (16), which requires that we specify the referent of each primitive name $\mathbf{n}$ in M_u via a codesignative term $\boldsymbol{\alpha}$ of Z for which $\ulcorner['\boldsymbol{\alpha}^{\bullet}_k]_c(\mathbf{n},u))\urcorner$ holds. For the relation $['\boldsymbol{\alpha}^{\bullet}_k]_c$ requires (*inter alia*) that $\mathbf{n}$ should be *cognate* with $\boldsymbol{\alpha}$, but there is no *a priori* reason why Z should antecedently contain any such $\boldsymbol{\alpha}$. If a thinker's inner and outer languages were sufficiently alien to Z (most of whose vocabulary comes from ordinary English), we would not, by the lights of our theory, be able fully to specify in Z the truth conditions of those languages' sentences. How, then, could we ever describe in Z the sense of a primitive term in a *non*-cognate public language L, or the referent of an opacity-marked term in an alien form M of Mentalese? Suppose, e.g., the word denoting $[\lambda x \ red(x)]$ in L were 'dool'. Then although we could have

$$(18) \qquad Ref_c(\ulcorner\text{dool}_k\urcorner)_L = red,$$

as a correct denotation-axiom in Z, the parallel sense-claim

$$Sen_c(\ulcorner\text{dool}_k\urcorner)_L = [\underline{red_k}]_c$$

would *not* be correct, since the A-object $[\underline{red_k}]_c$ proxy-encodes a cognateness relation to *our* (i.e., Z's) word '*red*', which, by hypothesis, 'dool' does not enjoy!

Very briefly, one possible solution can be sketched as follows. If we are entitled to (18) then we can add '*dool*' to Z (accompanied by an axiom '*dool = red*' in the extended version of Z) in the same spirit that ordinary English has adopted so many catchy foreign words and phrases (even when it already possesses a co-referring native word or phrase). Once we have done so, we can have as a correct axiom

$$Sen_c(\ulcorner\text{dool}_k\urcorner)_L = [\underline{dool_k}]_c$$

since the A-object $[\underline{dool_k}]_c$ will now proxy-encode being cognate to *our* (i.e., extended Z's) adopted word '*dool*', which itself will be cognate in the appropriate way with the foreigners' use of 'dool'. Accordingly, there would be no problem about how an

English-speaker x's Mentalese might contain a name **n** such that $[^\cdot dool^\urcorner_k]_c(\mathbf{n},x)$. Since (at least on our genetic interpretation) a Mentalese word will presumably be cognate in the relevant way to its public counterpart, we can make analogous sense of "borrowing" from an alien Mentalese idiolect M provided that the person who thinks via M-formulae expresses his/her thoughts in the sentences of some public language L (disambiguated in some regimentation L_r). In this case, we could borrow a word **w** of M by adopting an italicized version of **w**'s overt counterpart N in L, stipulating $\ulcorner$N $= \tau\urcorner$ for some term τ of Z (as we imagined doing with '*dool*' above) and identifying **w** as the Mentalese item standardly associated with the indexed version N_k of N in sentence S of L_r (formally: '$(\iota\mathbf{n})Assoc(\mathbf{n},N_k,S)$'). Then we could lay down the finitely many instances of the schemes (19) and (20) as axioms:

(19) $(\forall\mathbf{w})(\forall N_k, S{\in}L_r)(\mathbf{w} = (\iota\mathbf{n})Assoc(\mathbf{n},N_k,S) \to Ref_c(\mathbf{w})_M = \tau)$

(20) $(\forall\mathbf{w})(\forall N_k, S{\in}L_r)(\mathbf{w} = (\iota\mathbf{n})Assoc(\mathbf{n},N_k,S) \to Ref_c(\text{«}\mathbf{w}^\circ\text{»})_M = [\mathbf{\underline{\tau}}_k]_c).$

5. Applications: Some Puzzles Solved

Several philosophers have contended that indexicals and demonstratives in belief contexts generate certain opacity-phenomena which belie the existence of compositional semantical theories for the languages containing them. The opacity-phenomena in question have to do with the fact that the truth conditions of *de dicto* belief ascriptions whose 'that'-clauses contain indexicals and demonstratives appear to be sensitive to the way in which the *believer* is designated and to contextual facts about relations among speaker, addressee(s) and other parties, contrary to the assumption in standard compositional semantical theories that the subject position in belief ascriptions is always transparent, sensitive only to the reference of the term which occupies it. It therefore behooves us to see how our theory can accommodate the data without abandoning this standard assumption.

It is important to distinguish the troublesome opacity-phenomena from the quite different—and already explained—kind of truth-conditional shift which attends the passage from one to another of the various pure or mixed *de re/de dicto* readings of belief ascriptions in L_1. That one such reading of a belief ascription rather than another—hence one truth condition for it rather than another—is the favored one in such-and-such cases no doubt has a plausible pragmatic explanation in terms of certain contextual factors suggesting (*à la* Grice) the intended identity of the structural disambiguation parameter. This may be illustrated as follows.

Suppose it is claimed that, relative to the distinct contexts indicated below, the occurrences of the deictic 'he' in

(21) Mary believes that he is a jerk. (Uttered by someone *other than* Mary while demonstrating Tom as 'he' is pronounced.)

and

(22) I believe that he is a jerk. (Uttered by someone who demonstrates Tom as 'he' is pronounced.)

require different semantical treatment on the ground that (22), in virtue of its first-person character, *semantically* implies that its subject thinks of Tom under a certain demonstrative mode of presentation whose content is determined by the particular way that the subject is perceptually related to Tom on that occasion, whereas the third-person ascription (21) is supposedly noncommittal regarding its subject's way of thinking of Tom. Now (21)-(22) translate into L_1 as the (a)-sentences of (23)-(24) respectively, where the corresponding (b)- and (c)-formulas are respectively their opaque and transparent readings in L_0 with respect to the embedded pronoun 'he':

(23) a. believes(Mary,that jerk(he))
      b. believes$_1$(M$_1$,that jerk$_1$(h$_1$))
      c. [X$_1$ | believes$_1$(M$_1$,that jerk$_1$(X$_1$))](h$_1$)
(24) a. believes(I, that jerk(he))
      b. believes$_1$(u$_1$, that jerk$_1$(h$_1$))
      c. [X$_1$ | believes$_1$(u$_1$, that jerk$_1$(X$_1$))](h$_1$)

Our theory allows that the readings (23c) and (24b) would indeed have the alleged special implications and be the ones L_1-speakers would often tend to hear. But it is important to realize that *the other reading of each (a)-sentence is semantically legitimate and capable of being the pragmatically favored one when the utterance situation is of a suitable kind*. In this respect, the difference between the two readings of each (a)-sentence is like that between the reading we would accord to an utterance of 'Yes, visiting relatives can be boring' which occurred in response to 'I hate visiting my relatives' and the reading we would accord to it when it occurred in response to 'I hate visits from relatives'. To confirm this, let us consider the examples in the order given (it being assumed throughout that all parties are L_1-speakers).

Not surprisingly, which way a hearer is likely to disambiguate an utterance of (23a) depends on his/her antecedent beliefs about the parties involved and their relations to one another. On the one hand, (23b) is likely to be the favored reading of (23a) when it is (or the hearer takes it to be) mutually obvious to speaker and hearer/addressee that Mary is present and currently perceiving Tom. Thus, e.g., imagine that Alice and Bob are seated together at a cocktail lounge idly watching the other patrons. An anonymous drunk at the bar (Tom) has begun to scream at the bartender and is attracting everyone's attention. Suddenly Alice and Bob notice their friend Mary sitting alone in a distant booth staring at Tom and visibly being upset at his drunken behavior. Alice nudges Bob, discreetly gestures at Tom and whispers (23a). In these surroundings, surely Bob—or virtually any L_1-speaker so situated—would hear the utterance as ascribing to Mary a (visual/auditory) demonstrative belief of the sort she might express in L_1 by uttering 'jerk(he)' while pointing at Tom. On the other hand, a more typical scenario would *not* have all the salient characters and special overt perceptual links between them simultaneously in place, in which case an utterance of

(23a) would likely be heard as having (23c) as its intended reading. Thus, e.g., imagine that (unbeknownst to Bob) Mary has recently said to Alice 'jerk(he)' while angrily brandishing a copy of Tom's new book. Later, Alice and Bob visit the book store and happen upon an author's book-signing party starring Tom, who is touting his new book. Alice discreetly points at Tom and whispers (23a). Since Mary is not present and Alice has given Bob no clues about Mary's connection with this author, there is nothing to suggest that Mary has the alleged belief under any particular mode of presentation of Tom. Bob—or virtually any L_1-speaker so situated—would hear the reading (23c), which transparently ascribes to Mary a belief *de* Tom.[25]

That intuitions about (24a) would work in the opposite direction, favoring the opaque over the (equally legitimate) transparent reading, should not be surprising. Normally, one who demonstrates an object x in the course of an utterance act cannot help thinking of x via a token of some Mentalese demonstrative type $\mathbf{dII}_x$ in the course of performing the demonstration. But in an utterance of (24a), not only are utterer and subject identical, but the use of 'I' in subject position conventionally indicates the utterer's *awareness* of that identity, thus suggesting that $\mathbf{dII}_x$ or something relevantly like it is also the Mentalese demonstrative type tokened by the subject in having the belief about Tom. This explains our normal inclination to the reading (24b)—on which, according to our theory, (24a) would be true in a context c just in case Alice mentally affirms a sentence token of the sort «$\mathbf{j}(\mathbf{dII}_{Tom})$» in which $\mathbf{j}$ bears $['jerk'_1]_c$ to her and denotes $[\lambda x \, jerk(x)]$ and in which $\mathbf{dII}_{Tom}$ denotes Tom in virtue of being a Mentalese demonstrative tag $\mathbf{d}$ indexed by a contextually supplied Tom-based percept species $\mathbf{II}_{Tom}$ (in consequence of which her token of $\mathbf{dII}_{Tom}$ will consist of a demonstrative tag token indexed by some Tom-based percept belonging to the species $\mathbf{II}_{Tom}$). But however natural it might be to think that the utterer's demonstrative way of picking out Tom *for us* is also incorporated in his/her *own* way of thinking of it, this conclusion is not inevitable. It is perfectly possible to bring the transparent reading (24c) to the fore by imagining a rather unusual demonstrative setting—e.g., an "over-the-shoulder" demonstration, involving a conventional gesture towards a person (Tom) with whom the utterer is not in perceptual contact. Suppose Alice, who already thinks that Tom is a jerk, believes on purely general grounds that Tom is now standing directly behind her (she's at a party and Tom is always lurking behind her at parties). Asked by Mary whether there is anyone present whom she holds in low esteem, Alice uses a thumb-over-the-shoulder gesture to point to the person standing behind her, uttering (24a) while so doing. Suppose further that it is a matter of *mutual knowledge* between Mary and Alice that Alice's belief that Tom is now standing directly behind her is based only on the general ground indicated. Then it is most likely that Mary will hear the transparent reading (24c) as the intended one, and (24a) thus disambiguated will be true in the envisaged context if and only if Alice mentally affirms a sentence token of the sort «$\mathbf{j}(t)$» in which $\mathbf{j}$ is a $['jerk'_1]_c$ in her Mentalese denoting $[\lambda x \, jerk(x)]$ and t is merely some Mentalese term or other denoting Tom.

In contrast, the potentially troublesome semantic differences arise in connection with what are stipulated to be purely *de dicto* readings of belief ascriptions. That is, the contexts are so described that no other reading is intuitively plausible, and it is then argued that analogous truth-conditional asymmetries still arise. Let us look now at a version of Mark Richard's classic example—aptly called by Crimmins and Perry ((1989): 695-6) "the ultimate doxastic puzzle case".

Consider the occurrences of 'I' in (25) and (26), which seem in certain contexts to have divergent semantic implications about how the believer thinks of the utterer:

(25) Mary believes that I am watching her. (Uttered by someone other than Mary to a third party or in soliloquy).

(26) You believe that I am watching you. (Uttered to Mary over the telephone.)

(25)-(26) translate into L_1 as the (a)-sentences of (27)-(28) respectively, the corresponding (b)- and (c)-formulas being their opaque and transparent disambiguations in L_0 with respect to the embedded pronouns:

(27)   a. $\text{believes}(\text{Mary}, \text{that}_{X_1+} \text{watch}(I, X_1^+))$
       b. $\text{believes}_1(M_1, \text{that}_{X_1+} \text{watch}_1(u_1, X_1^+))$
       c. $[X_2 \,|\, \text{believes}_1(M_1, \text{that}_{X_1+} \text{watch}_1(X_2, X_1^+))](u_1)$

(28)   a. $\text{believe}(\text{you}, \text{that}_{X_1+} \text{watch}(I, X_1^+))$
       b. $\text{believe}_1(a_1, \text{that}_{X_1+} \text{watch}_1(u_1, X_1^+))$
       c. $[X_2 \,|\, \text{believe}_1(a_1, \text{that}_{X_1+} \text{watch}_1(X_2, X_1^+))](u_1)$

The only significant difference between (27a) and (28a) lies in their having distinct but hypothetically coreferential subject terms (the difference in grammatical person between the reflexive pronouns 'her' and 'you' is not semantically significant given their co-reference), yet it seems that an utterance of (27a) would be *true* while an utterance of (28a) would be *false* given the following sort of scenario. Mary is at the airport talking on a public telephone to someone whom she supposes to be far away and whom she does not know by sight; at the same time she is looking at the bank of telephones on the opposite side of the terminal building, where she notices a strange man who is staring intently at her while speaking into one of the telephones. Unbeknownst to her, of course, the man with whom she is having the telephone conversation is the very man she sees watching her from across the room. Now suppose [Case 1] the stranger utters (28a) to Mary through the telephone: she presumably would sincerely deny having any such belief, in consequence of which the ascription would seem to be false. But if [Case 2] the stranger, covering the mouthpiece of his handset, were to mutter (27a) to himself (or to a suitably knowledgeable third party), it seems he would be speaking truly; for Mary is by hypothesis *watching him* watch her. Since in Case 1 (27a)'s occurrence of 'I' would be heard as opaque, as would (28a)'s occurrence of 'I' in Case 2, the only readings pragmatically at issue in these two cases are (27b) and (28b).

Our theory accommodates these semantic intuitions through its contextual parameter. The interpretive question for the hearer is which (if any) of the admissible contexts for this utterance type is involved here. The facts of Case 1 and Case 2 respectively raise to salience *different* percept species: viz., the property of being an auditory representation of the speaker *qua* telephoner in the former and the (distinct) property of being a visual representation of the speaker *qua* gawking stranger in the latter. This makes it wholly appropriate to think of (27b) and (28b) as being evaluated *with respect to different contexts c* and *c'* such that $[PI_1]_c \neq [PI_1]_{c'}$—contexts which will deliver different sense-values $Sen_c('u_1')$ and $Sen_{c'}('u_1')$ despite the fact that $Ref_c('u_1') = Ref_{c'}('u_1')$. Our semantics then delivers the desired truth$_c$-condition for (28b) and truth$_{c'}$ condition for (27b).

Semantics, of course, is not epistemology. A semantic theory for demonstratives does not have to predict exactly *which* contexts *c* and *c'*—hence exactly which utterer-based percept species $[PI_1]_c$ and $[PI_1]_{c'}$—are involved here: all it is required to do is to tell us what the sense or referent of sentences would be relative to any admissible context. How, for a particular agent *X*, the hearer *knows* which context involving *X* as speaker provides *X*'s "intended" reading of an ambiguous sentence is a question for the theory of knowledge—a subproblem of the problem of Other Minds.

Crimmins and Perry claim that the telephone case, suitably embellished, shows that there can be a *single* context *c* relative to which (30) would be false even though (29) were true and the utterer in *c* = the man watching the addressee in *c*:

(29)   The man watching you believes that you are in danger.
(30)   I believe that you are in danger.

This, they claim, shows that the prospects are dim for even a context-relativized dox-astic logic. Consider our original scenario anent Mary, the stranger, and the telephone. Suppose in addition, however, that (a) *each* fails to realize that the one he/she sees is the one with whom he/she is conversing on the phone, and (b) that the man watching her does in fact believe that she (the woman he is watching from afar) is in danger (he sees a runaway baggage cart hurtling towards her from behind). Given (b), the man waves frantically at Mary; but given (a), he says nothing on the phone. Then Mary, seeing the stranger's urgent waving, says into the phone, 'The man watching me believes that I am in danger' whereupon the stranger, hearing this but not realizing that she refers to *him*, simply echoes her by uttering (29). Yet, given (a), he still would not utter (30) over the phone: indeed he would deny it if the voice on the phone were to ask 'Do you think that I am in danger?'

What are we to make of this? Questions about (finitely long) arguments can of course be paraphrased as questions about their corresponding conditionals. Is there, then, a problem for our theory about how the corresponding conditional

(31)   If the man watching you believes that you are in danger, then I
        believe that you are in danger.

could be *false* relative to a context of the sort envisaged above? Since the pure *de dicto* readings of both embedded belief ascriptions are stipulated, consider (31)'s L_0-counterpart (32) (in which idle subscripts have been suppressed):

(32)   If believes(the-man-watching-a$_1$,that in-danger$_1$(a$_2$)) then
        believe(u$_1$,that in-danger$_2$(a$_3$)).

Allowing for the introduction into L_0 of definite descriptions as terms—the details of which are irrelevant here—our semantics provides (32) the context-relativized truth condition

(33) $Believes((\iota x)(Man(x)$ & $Watching(x,[you_1]_c),[THAT$ $[\underline{In\text{-}danger_1}]_c([\underline{you_2}]_c)])$
    $\rightarrow Believes([I]_c,[THAT$ $[\underline{In\text{-}danger_2}]_c([\underline{you_3}]_c)])$.

Even without cranking through the details, it should be clear by now that the demonstrative sense $[\underline{you_2}]_c$ need not coincide with the demonstrative sense $[\underline{you_3}]_c$ despite the stipulation that $[you_2]_c = [you_3]_c$ = Mary. So there is no obstacle to (33) being a false proposition, hence no obstacle to (32) being false in the envisaged context. The story about what the stranger would or would not say into the phone or shout to Mary does indeed pragmatically suggest which context c is at issue, viz., one in which (*inter alia*) the Mary-based percept species $[PA_2]_c$ and $[PA_3]_c$ are distinct.

As the example stands, our theory *does* happen to allow that there can be a single context c at which (30) is false, (29) is true and the utterer = the man watching the addressee—but only because of an inessential feature of the verbal setup, viz., that the crucial occurrences of 'you' are respectively the *second* one in (29) and the *first* one in (30), thus allowing us to exploit the fact that the Mary-based percept species $[PA_2]_c$ and $[PA_1]_c$ might be distinct. But if we provide the stranger with a word or phrase which refers to Mary but does *not* contain any occurrences of 'you', then the problem can be reinstated. Thus, suppose we alter the case merely by replacing (29) with

(34)   He believes that you are in danger.

and stipulating that the occurrence of 'He' is to be understood, echo-fashion, as an intersentential anaphor anchored in Mary's prior token of 'The man watching me'. What now?

In our technical sense of "context", the unique occurrences of 'you' in (34) and (30) must be assigned the same sense $[\underline{you_1}]_c$ for *every* context c in which Mary = $[you_1]_c$ and so our theory indeed cannot allow that there can be a "single context" c at which (30) is false, (29) is true and the referent of 'He' in c is $[I]_c$. But this need not be a concession of defeat, for our technical notion of context, being designed to include percept species, is considerably more fine-grained than the preanalytic notion of context or "utterance situation" on which the puzzle trades. Granted, the puzzle situation specifies a variety of visual and auditory relations as simultaneously obtaining among the parties, but the sense of 'context' employed in the statement of the puzzle is one which makes no discriminations between contexts on the basis of which corresponding perceptual representations might be operative in Mentalese indexing or otherwise raised to salience. In short, what Crimmins and Perry count as a single context is in our sense at least two distinct contexts—precisely *because* different percept species can be invoked depending on whether, e.g., the utterer is prompted by visual or auditory facts to address Mary. Nevertheless, our notion of context still has the usual array of desirable features: where 'context' is understood in our sense, no disambiguated sentence of L_1 can be both true and false at the same context, and every disambiguated sentence of L_1 is assigned a truth condition relative to any given context. (Even so, however, anyone desiring a *context-relativized* doxastic logic will have to accommodate the failure of argument-validity to square with the status of the corresponding conditional.) So in the end we can explain the felt shift in truth-values via a shift in truth conditions occasioned by a tacit change of context—a phenomenon which in no way threatens the compositional semantics we have offered.

6. Why our theory is immune to Schiffer's critique.[26]

Schiffer complains that Fregeans never get past their "functional" definition of senses to an *intrinsic* characterization of them. But surely it cannot reasonably be required that sense-candidates be empirically given objects as opposed to theoretical posits: senses are officially *abstracta* of some sort, and (barring a magical Inner Eye) the only access we have to such entities is through the theories that characterize them. It would, e.g., be unreasonable to insist that the notion of a *set* is somehow illegitimate unless sets are "intrinsically describable" if that meant "characterizable in other than set-theoretic terms", since (as Schiffer admits) *being a set* is an essential and individuating property of sets. However, it would be perfectly reasonable to ask about the existence- and identity-conditions for sets, and these are questions for which set-theories provide answers. Similarly, it would be unreasonable to complain that the A-objects we propose as sense-candidates are given only through the theory Z, since being an A-object is an essential and individuating property of A-objects, but it would be perfectly reasonable to ask about their existence- and identity-conditions—which, as we have seen, are fully specified in Z.

The real substance of Schiffer's worry derives from Russell's famous complaint that a Fregean sense can only be "specified through the phrase", i.e., only *as* the (actual or potential) *sense* of an expression of some language. For at least some of our sense-candidates—viz., the senses of those primitive terms $\mathcal{J}$ of L_0 for which it was stipulated that $Sen_{c,j}(\mathcal{J}) = Ref_{c,j}(\mathcal{J})$—it is obvious that this objection fails. Thus, e.g., the sense of 'All$^{<<i>>}$' in L_0 is precisely identified in Z via the theorem

$$Sen_{c,j}(\text{'All}^{<<i>>}\text{'}) = [\lambda F^{<i>} (\forall x')(E!x \rightarrow Fx)] \,,$$

on whose right-hand side there is no mention of any words. It might, however, be objected that although the axiom

$$(35) \qquad Sen_{c,j}(\ulcorner \text{red}_k \urcorner) = [\underline{red_k}]_c$$

mentions no words of L_0 on its right-hand side, the A-object $[\underline{red_k}]_c$ thus invoked is itself defined in Z via the axiom

(36) $[\underline{red_k}]_c = (\iota w^{<i>})((\forall R^{<<i>,i,<i>>})(wR \equiv R = \text{PROX}([\lambda y^{<i>}u^iz^{<i>} (\exists n^{Mu})(z =_E \text{«}n°\text{»} \&$
$['red^{\bullet}_k]_c(\mathbf{n},u) \& Ref_{M_u}(\mathbf{n}) =_E red)])))$,

which indirectly involves mention of the *metalinguistic* term 'red' of *Z* because (as it happens) this term is mentioned in specifying the intended interpretation of the predicate ⌐$['red^{\bullet}_k]_c$⌐ in (36). In short, it might be objected that our description of $Sen_{c,i}(\ulcorner red_k \urcorner)$ is still somehow *metalinguistically* "through the phrase".

How serious is this? Well, there is certainly no problem of ineliminable *sense*-talk in *Z*. Neither (35) nor (36) identifies the sense of 'red' in L_0 with the *sense* of anything! On the contrary, the sense of 'red' in L_0 is held to be a certain *A-object* whose specification involves no sense-talk but may indirectly involve mention of the metalinguistic term 'red' in the aforementioned way. So if there is anything objectionable here, it must be that the sense of a word in an object language has been identified with another entity defined (*sans* sense-talk) in terms of a word in some metalanguage. It is hard to see why anyone should take offense at this, even in the special case where the metalanguage *contains* the object-language. Thus, e.g., a theory (in meta-English) which, for some equivalence relation *R* defined without sense-talk, contains the set-theoretic claim

> The sense of the English word 'red' = $\{x \mid R(x, \text{'red'})\}$.

may well be false and wrongheaded but certainly is not cognitively vacuous in the way Russell and Schiffer allege sense-theories to be. The harmlessness would be even more apparent if the object-language were, say, German and claim were

> The sense of the German word 'rot' = $\{x \mid R(x, \text{'red'})\}$.

But, except for the use of A-objects instead of sets, this is essentially the situation *vis-a-vis* $[\underline{red_k}]_c$ and 'red' in *Z*!

According to Schiffer, the Fregean has trouble with belief ascriptions like

(37)   Everyone who hears her believes that Mary is musical.

because, on the plausible assumption that (37)'s 'that'-clause is univocal, a Fregean semantics would have the wildly implausible consequence that (37) is true only if all the people who hear Mary hold this belief about her under exactly the *same* mode of presentation. It is easily demonstrated, however, that our theory has no such consequence. Since we are not presently concerned with the nature of the connection between 'her' and 'Mary' in (37), it will simplify matters to suppose that 'Everyone who hears her/Mary' is expressed in L_0 by some complex higher-order predicate $\mathcal{E}$ such that $Ref_{c,i}(\mathcal{E}) = [\lambda F^{<i>} (\forall x^i)((E!x \& person(x) \& hears(x,Mary)) \rightarrow Fx)]$. Then (37)'s counterpart in L_1 would be

(38) $\mathcal{E}([X \mid believes(X, that\ musical(Mary))])$.

For the sake of argument, let us suppose that the fully opaque reading of the belief-clause is contextually at issue, so that (38) will paraphrase into L_0 as

(39) $\mathcal{E}([X \mid believes_1(X, that\ musical_1(M_1))])$.

Now the belief property $Ref_{c,f}('[X \mid believes_1(X, that\ musical_1(M_1))]')$ is, according to our axioms, identical with $[\lambda x\ Ref_{c,f[x/'X']}('believes_1(X, that\ musical_1(M_1))')]$, which —since $Sen_{c,f}('M_1') = [\underline{Mary}_1]_c$ and $Sen_{c,f}('musical') = [\underline{musical}_1]_c$—is in turn identical to the property $[\lambda x\ [\lambda\ believes(x, [THAT\ [\underline{musical}_1]_c([\underline{Mary}_1]_c)])]]$. So (39) is true just in case all the people in question exemplify this property, i.e., just in case the proposition

$$(\forall x')((E!x\ \&\ hears(x,Mary)) \rightarrow believes(x, [THAT\ [\underline{musical}_1]_c([\underline{Mary}_1]_c)])).$$

is true. And, to cut a long story short, this will be the case—given our axiom *[Belief]*—if and only if each person x who hears Mary affirmatively tokens a sentence **«m(n)»** of x's own *Mentalese*(!) in which **m** bears $['musical'_1]_c$ to x and **n** bears $['Mary'_1]_c$ to x. There is here manifestly no requirement that the Mentalese sentence tokened *in foro interno* by one person should *intrinsically* resemble that tokened by any other! A similar result obtains, *mutatis mutandis*, for a demonstrative version of (37) such as (40a), whose counterpart in L_1, opaquely construed, paraphrases into L_0 as (40b) and hence inherits the truth condition (40c):

(40) a. Everyone who hears her believes that *she* is musical.
     b. $\mathcal{E}\ ([X \mid believes_1(X, that\ musical_1(s_2))])$
     c. $(\forall x')((E!x\ \&\ hears(x,[she_1]_c)) \rightarrow believes(x, [THAT\ [\underline{musical}_1]_c([\underline{she}_2]_c)]))$.

For, relative to a context c in which $[she_1]_c = [she_2]_c = $ Mary, the condition (40c) obtains iff each person x who hears Mary mentally affirms a token z of a sentence type **«m(d[PF_2]_c)»** of M_x in which **m** bears $['musical'_1]_c$ to x and **d** is a demonstrative tag indexed by the Mary-based percept species $[PF_2]_c$—in consequence of which z will, by definition, consist of a token of **m** concatenated with a token of **d** which stands in the indexing relation to *some* perceptual representation Π_{Mary} belonging to the percept species $[PF_2]_c$. But—and this is the crucial point—Π_{Mary} need not be the *same* Mary-based perceptual representation for each such person x! Thus, e.g., $[PF_2]_c$ might be the very general property of being-an-auditory-representation-of-Mary, while the various persons who hear Mary might enjoy quite different auditory representations of her.

Schiffer further maintains that a problem about "believed identity" arises for hybrid theories which (a) construe propositions as structured entities composed of individuals and relations, (b) invoke languages of thought and (c) identify senses with the functional roles of Mentalese expressions. Since our theory does neither (a) nor (c), the problem does not arise for us in its original form. It is important, however, to see why no analogue of it can be used against us. In a nutshell, the problem is this. Suppose Tom, a prolific novelist, writes only under the pen-name 'Ugo'. Suppose that Lloyd, who is Tom's publisher and a fully rational person to boot, is the only other person who is aware of Ugo's identity. In particular, Lloyd is aware that his friend Alice has read the Ugo novels but has never met their author. Then (41)-(43) would, it seems, be simultaneously true on their fully opaque readings:

(41)　Lloyd believes that Tom is Ugo.

(42)　Lloyd believes that Alice believes that Ugo is a novelist.

(43)　Lloyd believes that Alice *doesn't* believe [i.e. fails to believe] that Tom is a novelist.

The challenge is to accommodate this fact. The functional-role theorist, Schiffer argues, is thwarted by an inherent commitment to the following rationality principle (where «$S(a)$» is a Mentalese sentence containing the term a and «$S(b)$» is the result of replacing a in «$S(a)$» by b):

(RP)　If X is rational and affirms both «$S(a)$» and «$\sim S(b)$» then X affirms «$\sim(a = b)$».

Be that as it may, our theory is not similarly thwarted. By the lights of Z, the following triad is consistent:

(44)　*Believes(Lloyd,[THAT [$\underline{Tom}_1$]$_c$ =$_E$ [$\underline{Ugo}_1$]$_c$])*

(45)　*Believes(Lloyd,[THAT [$\underline{Believes}_2$]$_c$([$\underline{Alice}_1$]$_c$,[THAT [$\underline{Novelist}_1$]$_c$([$\underline{Ugo}_1$]$_c$)])])*

(46)　*Believes(Lloyd,[THAT $\sim$[$\underline{Believes}_2$]$_c$([$\underline{Alice}_1$]$_c$,[THAT [$\underline{Novelist}_1$]$_c$([$\underline{Tom}_1$]$_c$)])])*

For the principle (RP) need not hold in Z with full generality. Since we are not committed to the idea that senses are functional roles, we can freely allow that (RP) does not hold when, e.g., «$S(a)$» is a Mentalese belief-ascription in which a lies within the scope of the Mentalese complementizer **THAT** *and carries an opacity-marker*, as would be the case on our theory if (46) and (45) were true. Since, as we have seen, languages of thought can in principle be given a denotational semantics in terms of A-objects, such a failure of (RP) is only to be expected.

According to Schiffer, sense-theorists also face a serious problem about meaning and intending. Stated in terms of our language L_1, the difficulty would supposedly arise as follows. Suppose Dora (an L_1-speaker) assertively utters the L_1-sentence

(47)　believes(Lloyd, that snores(Fido)).

and means what she thereby says. Any theory which posits as sense of (47) a proposition P containing additional senses or sense-modifying elements $e_1,...,e_n$ having no linguistic counterpart in (47) will be unable to provide Dora with an appropriate completion of ⌜meant-by(I, (47), that S)⌝ in which ⌜that S⌝ explicitly refers to P.[27] The idea behind the complaint is that if such a proposition P were the sense of (47) and Dora meant what she said in uttering (47), then she must thereby have meant P. If so, then it must be possible for her to *say* what she meant in a way that makes explicit the involvement of $e_1,...,e_n$. But by the lights of any "hidden elements" theory she supposedly could *not* do this by asserting (a suitably tensed version of) the corresponding L_1-sentence

> (48)   mean-by(I, (47), that believes(Lloyd, that snores(Fido))).[28]

This task could only be accomplished by supplanting the higher 'that'-clause in (48) with some other clause ⌜that S⌝ such that every constituent in the sense of (47) is determined by some *overt* constituent(s) of S. But, Schiffer argues, plausible candidates for S do not seem to be available.

Whatever the case may be with other theories, our proposal faces no such embarrassment. It must be kept in mind that our semantics is importantly different from standard Fregean approaches in three relevant respects. First, it identifies the referent of ⌜that S⌝ *not* with the sense of S itself but rather with the sense of the phrase ⌜that S'⌝ in which S' is the result of replacing every occurrence in S of a formula having the form ⌜$[\mathcal{V}|S_0](\mathcal{I})$⌝ with an occurrence of $S_0(\mathcal{I}/\mathcal{V})$. Second, PEAPs do not in any literal sense have constituents: they do not "*contain* additional senses or sense-modifying elements". Third, proxy-encoded items of the sort $[\mathbf{\cdot\alpha\cdot}_k]_c$ add no descriptive material to one's thought: the intrinsic character of the Mentalese sentence at issue is not affected by variations in the strength of the cognateness requirement.

Assuming that a fully opaque reading of (48) is at issue, the referent in a given context c of its higher 'that'-clause will be the PEAP

$$[THAT\ [\underline{Believes}_1]_c([\underline{Lloyd}_1]_c,[THAT\ [\underline{Snores}_1]_c([\underline{Fido}_1]_c)])].$$

Admittedly, this PEAP is not identical with the object our theory supplies as sense in c of (47); but we have seen that our theory, unlike Frege's, requires *no* such identity to vouchsafe the truth in c of a fully opaque reading of (48). On the contrary, restricting our attention to L_1 (and suppressing temporal parameters), we may provide the following axiom for the triadic predicate '*Say-by*':

[*Say-by*] $(\forall x')(\forall S\in L_1)(\forall c)(\forall D)(\forall z^p)(Say\text{-}by(x,<S,c,D>,z) \equiv (ActLang(L_1,x)$
    $\&\ Utters(x,<S,c,D>,L_1)\ \&\ [I]_c = x\ \&\ [THAT\ Sen_{c,D}(S)_{L_1}] = z)).$

Here '$<S,c,D>$' denotes the contextual-structural disambiguation of S with respect to c and D (i.e., a "sentence-under-analysis"); '*Say-by*' denotes the relation whose obtaining between a person x, sentence-under-analysis y, and PEAP z makes it the case that x, in uttering y as such, conventionally counts as saying z; '*ActLang*' denotes the actual language relation; and '*Utters*' denotes the relation whose obtaining between a person x, sentence-under-analysis $<S,c,D>$, and language L constitutes x's tokening S *qua* sentence of L subject to c and D. (A more general version of [*Say-by*], not restricted to sentences of L_1, could no doubt be provided, but the current point requires no such generalization.) Consequently, we have no trouble passing from the hypothetical facts of the case—viz., that, for some D providing the fully opaque readings of (47) and (48) and some c in which $[I]_c$ = Dora, Dora uttered the sentence-under-analysis $<(47),c,D>$ of her actual language L_1, with respect to which the equation

$$[THAT\ Sen_{c,D}((47))] = [THAT\ [\underline{Believes}_1]_c([\underline{Lloyd}_1]_c,[THAT$$
$$[\underline{Snores}_1]_c([\underline{Fido}_1]_c)])]$$

holds—to the truth of

$$Say\text{-}by([I]_c,\ <(47),c,D>,\ [THAT\ [\underline{Believes}_1]_c([\underline{Lloyd}_1]_c,[THAT$$
$$[\underline{Snores}_1]_c([\underline{Fido}_1]_c)])]).$$

But this, together with the stipulated truth of

$$(\imath z^p)(Say\text{-}by([I]_c,<(47),c,D>,z) = (\imath z^p)(Mean\text{-}by([I]_c,<(47),c,D>,z)$$

(i.e., that what she meant by uttering (47) = what she said thereby), entails the truth of

$$Mean\text{-}by([I]_c,\ <(47),c,D>,\ [THAT\ [\underline{Believes}_1]_c([\underline{Lloyd}_1]_c,[THAT$$
$$[\underline{Snores}_1]_c([\underline{Fido}_1]_c)])]),$$

which is precisely the proposition assigned by our theory as the truth$_c$ condition (i.e., the referent$_c$) of the fully opaque reading of (48).

Related to the meaning-intention problem is another difficulty which, though not adduced by Schiffer, might be raised by a sympathizer (cf. Forbes 1993). It can be thought of as a version of the traditional Paradox of Analysis. To wit, if X's believing that P is analyzed as it's being the case that Q, then to believe *that X believes that P* must be to believe *that Q.* But then any account of the belief that P which invokes items not overtly mentioned in describing it as such will be doomed to failure, since one could believe (*de dicto*) that so-and-so believes that P without thereby believing that so-and-so is related to these additional items. Thus, in application to our own theory, one surely could believe that Lloyd believes that Fido snores *without* believing that Lloyd affirms such-and-such a Mentalese sentence.

So far, so good. But there is nothing in these considerations about iterated belief contexts which need worry us. For the axiom [*Belief*] which "analyzes" belief as affirmation of certain Mentalese sentences is only an equivalence-claim, *not* the outright equation of A-objects which Z requires to support substitution *salva veritate* in belief contexts. (That is to say, we have not claimed that the *property* of bearing the belief relation to a PEAP is *identical* to the *property* of affirming such-and-such a Mentalese sentence.) So far as Z is concerned, what is theoretically implied by the fact that one entertains the (pure *de dicto*) belief that Lloyd believes that Fido snores is merely that one's "belief box" contains a suitable Mentalese belief ascription to Lloyd. Objectionable beliefs about Mentalese itself are not imputed.

Nor will it be possible to object that Dora could believe that Lloyd believes that Fido snores without believing that Lloyd is related to the PEAP

$$[THAT \ [\underline{Snores_1}]_c([\underline{Fido_1}]_c)].$$

For our claim is only that the L_0-formula which is the fully opaque reading of

(49)   believes(Dora, that believes(Lloyd, that snores (Fido)))

is *true_c* in L_0 iff Dora bears the relation $[\lambda xy \ Believes(x,y)]$ to the PEAP

$$[THAT \ [\underline{Believes_2}]_c([\underline{Lloyd_1}]_c, [THAT \ [\underline{Snores_1}]_c([\underline{Fido_1}]_c)])],$$

which Dora will do when and only when she affirms a certain kind of Mentalese belief ascription, which ascription in turn is *true_c-in-her-Mentalese* iff Lloyd bears the relation $[\lambda xy \ Believes(x,y)]$ to the PEAP $[THAT \ [\underline{Snores_1}]_c([\underline{Fido_1}]_c)]$, which Lloyd will do when and only when he affirms a certain kind of Mentalese sentence predicating snoring of Fido. Nothing in this scenario has any unwelcome consequences about the *contents* of Dora's beliefs.

One might, however, complain that we have violated some independently plausible methodological constraint on semantical theories that invoke languages of thought. Where 'T' ranges over such theories, the envisaged constraint would presumably be something like

(MC)   For any sentence S of a language L, if reference to or quantification over Fs occurs in *every* ϕ such that T yields $\ulcorner L\text{-True}(S) \equiv \phi \urcorner$, then Fs must somehow be explicitly represented in any Mentalese sentence which T requires to be affirmed by one who satisfies the open formula $\ulcorner$believes $(X, \text{that } S)\urcorner$ of L.

One could certainly quibble about the plausibility of (MC). Thus, e.g., suppose T were a theory which (unlike Z) employed quantification over possible worlds, so that every T-sentence provable in T would have the form $\ulcorner L\text{-True}_w(S) \equiv \phi \ in \ w\urcorner$. Does this mean that T is duty-bound to regard all beliefs about modal matters as beliefs explicitly about possible worlds—in the sense of involving the affirmation of Mentalese sentences containing overt talk of possible worlds? An affirmative answer does not seem inevitable. Fortunately, we need not become enmeshed in this issue, for our theory directly avoids any confrontation with (MC) by rendering (MC) *vacuously* true for the case in which $T = Z$ and the Fs in question are A-objects. The reason is simple: our sense-reference semantics for L_0 and L_1, together with our denotational semantics for Mentalese, jointly ensure that every instance of (MC) for the case in question will have a *false* antecedent. For, via [DEN$_M$] and [*Belief*] , the references to A-objects can ultimately be eliminated so as to obtain T-sentences for iterated belief ascriptions in L_0 and L_1 which mention no A-objects at all—though of course they will mention Mentalese sentences whose parts might turn out to *denote* various A-objects, a fact which is irrelevant to satisfying (MC).

7. Conclusion.

We have seen how, with the aid of the theory Z of A-objects, we can construct a finitely axiomatized sense-reference semantics, hence a finitely axiomatized truth theory, for a first-order indexical language L_1 containing familiar verbs of propositional attitude and displaying the full range of pure and mixed *de re*/*de dicto* readings of its attitude-ascriptions. We have shown how this semantical theory solves the skeptic's puzzles and answers the skeptic's specific objections. Barring some revelation of a *relevant* disanalogy between L_1 and natural languages, the truth-theoretic skeptic has been refuted.

Notes

1. Intuitively , the truth theory in question is "interpretive" of its object-language when the indicated truth conditions are those that flow from the meaning of the sentences in question: this is the intuition that underlies the Davidsonian requirement that knowledge of such a truth theory for a language would enable one correctly to interpret (i.e., to *understand*) utterances of its (declarative) sentences.

2. Formally, the device for quasi-quoting Mentalese is defined by the following scheme, where $\Theta_1,...,\Theta_m$ are terms for Mentalese expression-types and '$^\wedge$' denotes a concatenation operation on Mentalese expression tokens:

    $$«\Theta_1,...,\Theta_m» =_{def.} [\lambda x^j \, (\exists y_1)...(\exists y_m)(\Theta_1(y_1) \, \& \, ... \, \& \, \Theta_m(y_m) \, \& \, x =_E y_1{}^\wedge...{}^\wedge y_m)].$$

3. To avoid confusion, the capitalized word 'Type' will be used in the text *only* in connection with the Simple Type Theory imposed on Z. In contrast, the word 'type', *sans* initial capital, will be used when invoking the type-token distinction; 'kind' will be used as a synonym of 'type' thus employed. The Simple Types of any typed language L *other* than Z will always be explicitly referred to as 'L-types'.

4. 'Admissible' here means "expressible in Z by means of a propositional formula", where a *propositional formula* is a formula which contains no encoding *sub*formulas and no subformulas of the sort $\ulcorner(\forall\alpha)\phi\urcorner$ in which α is an initial term somewhere in ϕ. (However, the matrix ψ of a definite description $\ulcorner(\iota\beta)\psi\urcorner$ does *not* count in Z as a subformula of a formula which contains $\ulcorner(\iota\beta)\psi\urcorner$, so encoding formulas can occur within propositional formulas *if* they are thus isolated within definite descriptions.) The restriction to admissible conditions means that non-isolated encoding formulas do not commit the theory to the existence of any new relations that it would not be committed to without such formulas.

5. The point here is just that the salient concepts of a compositional Mentalese syntax—e.g., "Mentalese sentence", "binary Mentalese predicate", "Mentalese sentential complementizer", etc.—can presumably be functionally defined. (See Brandom (1987).)

6. Intuitively, an expression type is a *kind* and an expression token is an individual belonging

to one or more such kinds. Since kinds are naturally assimilated to properties, Z uses terms of Type $\langle i \rangle$ for expression types and terms of Type i for expression tokens of its various object-languages.

7. '$+$'-marked individual variables are restricted variables ranging over persons and are subject to the syntactic restriction that they can occur in sentences only inside terms of the form $\ulcorner[THAT_{v+}\ \phi]\urcorner$, where $\ulcorner THAT_{v+}\urcorner$ functions as a variable-binding operator.

8. The context-relativized terms of the sort $\ulcorner[\alpha_k]_c\urcorner$ characterized below in the axiom schemes $[OSN=]$ and $[DSN=]$ are to be counted as *simple* for the purpose of laying down the conditions on $[That=]$.

9. Formally, and subject to the restrictions in the text, the axiom scheme is

$$[That=]\quad [THAT_{v+}\ \phi] = (\imath w^p)((\forall H^{\langle p \rangle})(wH \equiv H = \mathrm{PROX}([\lambda y^p u^i \mathbf{P}\ Denotes_{M_u}(\mathbf{P}, y)\ \& $$
$$(\exists \Omega)(\exists^{t_1} \Delta_1)...(\exists^{t_n} \Delta_n)(\mathbf{P} =_E \kappa[\mathbf{THAT}_\Omega\ \Phi]\!\ast \& \sigma \& \rho \& \zeta)])))$$

—where σ is the conjunction (for $1 \leq j \leq n$) of all conditionals

$$(\exists G^{\langle t_j,\ i,\ \langle p \rangle \rangle})G =_E (\imath F_j^{\langle t_j,\ i,\ \langle p \rangle \rangle})\alpha_j : F_j \to ((\imath F_j^{\langle t_j,\ i,\ \langle p \rangle \rangle})\alpha_j : F_j)(\alpha_j, u, \Delta_j)$$

and ρ is the conjunction (for $1 \leq j \leq n$ and Δ the first term-metavariable distinct from each of $\Delta_1,...,\Delta_n$) of all conditionals

$$\sim(\exists G^{\langle t_j,\ i,\ \langle p \rangle \rangle})G =_E (\imath F_j^{\langle t_j,\ i,\ \langle p \rangle \rangle})\alpha_j : F_j \to (Denotes_{M_u}(\Delta_j, \alpha_j)\ \& (\exists \Delta)(\Delta_j =_E \kappa\Delta°\!\ast))$$

and ζ is the conjunction (for $1 \leq j, k \leq n$ and $j \leq k$) of all conditionals

$$(\imath F_j^{\langle t_j,\ i,\ \langle p \rangle \rangle})\alpha_j : F_j =_E (\imath F_k^{\langle t_k,\ i,\ \langle p \rangle \rangle})\alpha_k : F_k \to \Delta_j = \Delta_k.$$

10. Since one's Mentalese is supposed to be a disambiguated idiom, X's mentally ascribing to Y a *de dicto* belief and X's mentally ascribing to Y a corresponding *de re* belief must involve *different* mental representations on X's part, a conclusion equally supported by the well-known Formality Constraint in light of the differing causal powers of X's beliefs about Y's *de dicto* beliefs and X's beliefs about Y's corresponding *de re* beliefs. The role of the opacity marker in Z is to provide for the requisite formal differences in Mentalese sentences *qua* content-clauses of Mentalese attitude ascriptions.

11. See section 4 for a discussion of how this provisional axiom might be obtained as a theorem at least for certain languages of thought.

12. Formally, the two schemata are as follows:

$$[DEN_M]\quad (\sigma \& \rho \& \zeta) \to Denotes_{M_u}(\kappa[\mathbf{THAT}\ \Phi]\!\ast, [THAT\ \phi])$$
$$[TRUE_M]\quad Denotes_{M_u}(\kappa[\mathbf{THAT}\ \Phi]\!\ast, [THAT\ \phi]) \to (TRUE_{M_u}(\mathbf{S}^\circledast) \equiv \phi^*)$$

(Though inert in the examples we will discuss, the symbols '$\circledast$' and '$°$' do crucial work in *iterated* belief-formulas.) We count any subscripts attached to underlining as part of the underlining itself, hence to be erased whenever the latter is.

13. The logic of the λ-operator in Z—according to which $\ulcorner\rho = [\lambda v_1...v_n\ \rho(v_1,...,v_n)]\urcorner$ is an axiom for any primitive term ρ of type $\langle t_1...t_n \rangle$ and variables $v_1,...,v_n$ of respective types $t_1,...,t_n$—entitles us to write '*Sings*' and '*Runs*' interchangeably with '$[\lambda x^i\ Sings(x)]$' and '$[\lambda x^i\ Runs(x)]$'.

14. Formally, the axiom is

[Belief] $(\forall x^i)(\forall y^P)(Believes(x,y) \equiv ((\exists z^i)(\exists S^{M_x})(E!^{\triangleleft\triangleright}z$ & $S^{\circledast}z$ & $Affirms(x,z)$ &
$((\imath F^{\triangleleft p,i,\triangleleft\triangleright})y{:}F)(y,x,\ll[\mathbf{THATS}]\gg)) \vee (\exists z^i)(\exists S^{M_x})(\exists x^{M_x})(E!^{\triangleleft\triangleright}z$ & $S(\mathbf{I}^{M_x}/x)^{\circledast}z$ &
$Affirms(x,z)$ & $((\imath F^{\triangleleft p,i,\triangleleft\triangleright})y{:}F)(y,x,\ll[\mathbf{THAT_xS}]\gg))))$.

15. For purely syntactic reasons which will emerge later, we allow that 'Γ' may appear with subscripts, but we ensure that these subscripts are semantically inert by stipulating that $[I_k]_c = [I]_c$. Note, however, that the *sense* $[I_j]_c$ may not be identical with the *sense* $[I_k]_c$ for distinct j and k.

16. Mentalese demonstratives are not discussed in Boër (1994). The following account incorporates into Z the theory sketched in Levine (1988) in response to the nasty "Two Tubes" puzzle about demonstrative belief expounded in Austin (1990). For the record, Z thus extended avoids the puzzle by providing the following perfectly consistent set of truth conditions for the allegedly paradoxical claims made by the victim of the Two Tubes apparatus (where '*Spot*' rigidly designates the red spot in question):

$[this_1]_c =_E [this_2]_c =_E Spot$
$Believes([I]_\sigma[THAT\ Red([\underline{this}_1]_c)])$
$Believes([I]_\sigma[THAT\ Red([\underline{this}_2]_c)])$
$Believes([I]_\sigma[THAT\ [\underline{this}_1]_c =_E [\underline{this}_1]_c])$
$Believes([I]_\sigma[THAT\ [\underline{this}_2]_c =_E [\underline{this}_2]_c])$
$\sim Believes([I]_\sigma[THAT\ [\underline{this}_1]_c =_E [\underline{this}_2]_c])$

17. Formally, the definition-scheme is:

$$\delta^{Mu}\ \pi =_{def.} [\lambda x^i\ \delta(x)\ \&\ (\exists y^i)(\pi(y)\ \&\ Index^{<i,P>}(y,x))].$$

18. Formally, the axiom scheme is:

$$[DSN{=}]\ \ [\underline{\delta}_k]_c = (\imath w^i)((\forall H^{\triangleleft\triangleright})(wH \equiv H = \mathrm{PROX}([\lambda y^i u^{i\ i}t\ (\exists \mathbf{d}^{Mu})(t =_E \mathbf{d}^\circ[\pi_k]_c)])))$$

19. The numerical subscripting on 'A', 'B',..., 'W' and on the predicates adopted from English has no effect on these terms' denotations. Its function will emerge below in connection with the syntactic "counterpart relation".

20. The "semantical postulates" discussed hereafter are not axioms of Z itself: they are postulates of a semantical theory couched in Z.

21. Technical note: in Z, as in ILAO, terms of type p also count as (propositional) formulas, so (e.g.) where we have $\ulcorner Sen_c(S_1)=[\lambda\ \phi]\urcorner$ and $\ulcorner Sen_c(S_2)=[\lambda\ \psi]\urcorner$, the formula $\ulcorner Sen_c(S_1) \rightarrow Sen_c(S_2)\urcorner$ is strictly equivalent to $\ulcorner[\lambda\ \phi] \rightarrow [\lambda\ \psi]\urcorner$, which is a well-formed formula having the same significance in Z as $\ulcorner\phi\rightarrow\psi\urcorner$. The same holds, *mutatis mutandis*, for $\ulcorner Ref_c(S_1) \rightarrow Ref_c(S_2)\urcorner$ where we have $\ulcorner Ref_c(S_1) = [\lambda\ \phi]\urcorner$ and $\ulcorner Ref_c(S_2) = [\lambda\ \psi]\urcorner$. A minor complication arises when an expression of the sort $\ulcorner[\lambda\ \theta] \rightarrow [\lambda\ \psi]\urcorner$ occurs as a subformula of $\ulcorner[THAT\ \phi]\urcorner$ since the form of the corresponding Mentalese sentence posited by $[That{=}]$ is a function of the form of ϕ. Unwanted clutter in the posited Mentalese sentences can be easily avoided by so restricting the definition of Φ in the axiom scheme $[That{=}]$ that occurrences in ϕ of propositional λ-terms which are not arguments to predicates in ϕ will be treated as occurrences of the formulas which are their matrices insofar as construction of Φ is concerned.

22. If we had applied our contextual definition ploy to *all* names in L_1, all and only the closed

sentences of L_1 containing 'that'-clauses would have univocal meanings.

23. This assumption creates a slight discrepancy with our original (oversimplified) account of the relation between ϕ and Φ in the axiom [*That*⁼] inasmuch as, e.g., ⌜[*THAT* (**A**x)*Red*(*x*)]⌝ would correspond on the original account to «[**THAT (Ax)r(x)]**», which makes it look as if quantification in Mentalese would have to be handled differently than quantification in L_0. The discrepancy and the analogous problem regarding λ-abstracts are easily rectified by treating talk about Mentalese expressions of the sorts «($\forall$x)(¨¨x¨¨)» and «[λx ¨¨x¨¨]» as shorthand for talk about the corresponding Mentalese expressions of the sorts «**All([x ⊢x¨¨])**» and «[x ⊢x¨¨]» respectively.

24. It is this assumption which enables us to do two crucial things in conjunction with the axiom [*Belief*]: viz., (a) to capture the correct truth conditions for the Mentalese sentences posited by our semantics for iterated belief ascriptions in L_0 and L_1; (b) to ensure the ultimate eliminability of any clauses mentioning A-objects from our T-sentences for L_0 and L_1 (which eliminability protects us from certain objections canvassed in section 6.)

25. We note in passing that the transparent reading of (23a) can continue to dominate even when the utterer *is* Mary: e.g., for a hearer who is unaware of this identity! As a matter of convention, people are normally *supposed* to use the first-person form when consciously referring to themselves unless—as sometimes happens—there is some special reason for a different style of reference to oneself (as, e.g., when parents use 'Daddy' or 'Mommy' instead of 'I' in talking about themselves to small children, who presumably have not yet fully mastered the use of indexicals). Absent any indication of such a special stylistic reason, an utterance of (23a) by Mary would conversationally implicate that Mary takes herself to be ascribing a belief to *someone else*.

26. The following objections are gleaned from Schiffer (1987a, 1987b, 1990 and 1992). Those of his objections to other Fregean theories which have no analogue as regards our own are ignored here.

27. Schiffer's target here is the "Unarticulated Constituents" theory proposed in Crimmins and Perry (1989) and further developed in Crimmins (1992).

28. In specifying the vocabulary of L_0 and L_1, we included 'believes' as the only verb of propositional attitude; but, given our earlier remarks about how to add axioms [*Intends*] and [*Desires*] to Z, it should be clear that we could enrich L_0 and L_1 with 'intends' and 'desires', specifying their senses and references using the Z-terms ⌜[*intends$_k$*]$_c$⌝ and ⌜[*desires$_k$*]$_c$⌝ on the one hand and '*intends*' and '*desires*' on the other. The term 'mean-by' could then be thought of as introduced into L_0 and L_1 by a definition based on some Gricean belief-intention analysis. None of this would beg any questions currently at issue, since it is clearly some such analysis of speaker-meaning that Schiffer has in mind.

29. Assuming, of course, that

$$Ref_{c,D}(\ulcorner \text{'believes(Lloyd, that snores(Fido))'}\urcorner{}_{L_1})$$
$$= <\text{'believes(Lloyd, that snores(Fido))'},c,D>.$$

References

Austin, D. (1990): *What is the Meaning of "This"?*, Cornell University Press, Ithaca.

Boër, S. (1994): 'Propositional Attitudes and Formal Ontology', *Synthese*, **98**: 1-56.

Brandom, R. (1987): 'Singular Terms and Sentential Sign Designs', *Philosophical Topics*, **15**: 125-67.

Crimmins, M. and J. Perry (1989): 'The Prince and the Phone Booth: Reporting Puzzling Beliefs', *The Journal of Philosophy*, **86**: 685-711.

Crimmins, M. (1992): *Talk About Beliefs*, MIT Press/Bradford Books, Cambridge.
Forbes, G. (1993): 'Solving the Iteration Problem', *Linguistics and Philosophy*, **16**: 311-30.
Horgan, T. (1989): 'Attitudinatives', *Linguistics and Philosophy*, **12**: 133-65.
Levine, J. (1988): 'Demonstrating in Mentalese', *Pacific Philosophical Quarterly*, **69**: 222-40.
Richard, M. (1983): 'Direct Reference and Ascriptions of Belief', *Journal of Philosophical Logic*, **12**: 425-52.
Schiffer, S. (1987a): *Remnants of Meaning*, MIT Press/Bradford Books, Cambridge.
Schiffer, S. (1987b): 'The "Fido"-Fido Theory of Belief', in J. Tomberlin, ed., *Philosophical Perspectives, 1, Metaphysics, 1987* Ridgeview Publishing, Atascadero.
Schiffer, S. (1990): 'The Mode-of-Presentation Problem', in C. Anderson and J. Owens, eds., *Propositional Attitudes*, CSLI, Stanford.
Schiffer, S. (1991): 'Does Mentalese Have a Compositional Semantics?', in B. Loewer and G. Rey, eds., *Meaning In Mind: Essays on the Work of Jerry Fodor*, Blackwell, Cambridge.
Schiffer, S. (1992): 'Belief Ascription', *The Journal of Philosophy*, **89**: 499-521.
Zalta, E. (1988): *Intensional Logic and the Metaphysics of Intentionality*, MIT Press/Bradford Books, Cambridge.

*Philosophical Perspectives, 9, AI, Connectionism, and
Philosophical Psychology, 1995*

CONTEXTUALITY, REFLEXIVITY, ITERATION, LOGIC*

Mark Crimmins
University of Michigan

Mark Richard and I agree that attitude reports are heavily contextual in their literal import, but we disagree about the workings of this contextuality, and, as I have shown (in 'Context in the Attitudes'; hereafter '*CA*'), our disagreements surface in different predictions about reports involving reflexivity and iteration (I will rehearse these arguments soon). Although Richard, in his *Propositional Attitudes* (hereafter '*PA*'), and 'Attitudes in Context'; (hereafter '*AC*') has discussed these topics, I am not satisfied that he has adequately addressed them, and I am more convinced than ever that the issues are revealing of the manner in which speakers exploit conversational context in reporting attitudes. Richard also has argued quite correctly that his account, but not the account that I favor, accommodates a certain simple notion of the *logical validity* of arguments. I will argue that this is far from an advantage, and that, on my account, a notion of validity is in fact available that is better suited to the type of contextuality that the reflexivity and iteration considerations reveal.

The present issues arise in the attempt to explain belief reporting within the going project in philosophical semantics of systematically characterizing "what is said" or the "semantic content" or the "proposition expressed" in philosophically interesting sorts of utterance. Probably, the most important questions in this area concern the presuppositions and desiderata of this project, including questions about the relations of what-is-said to facts and intuitions about syntax, lexical meaning, truth conditions, inference, compositionality, understanding, cognitive architecture, and discourse. In particular, there are deep questions here about how best to explain the various kinds of contextual flexibility and indeterminacy that arise when "timeless" meaning far underdetermines (plausible candidates for) what is said in an utterance. I hope that exploring in detail one interesting variety of discourse will prove a reasonable way of chipping away at these big questions.

Richard's Account

According to Richard, the semantic value of a that-clause is a linguistic *RAM* (Russellian Annotated Matrix): a structured entity containing the expressions occurring in the clause paired with their referents. The cognitive objects of belief (the things to which agents bear the *Bel* relation) are cognitive RAMs, containing mental representations instead of expressions. In a true belief report, the RAM expressed by the that-clause must *translate* a RAM the agent *Bel*-believes. The crucial constraint on this relation of RAM translation is that, for a linguistic RAM to correctly translate a cognitive RAM, each name-type in the linguistic RAM must correspond to a representation in the cognitive RAM such that, in the context, the name-type correctly translates the representation.

For example, in the obvious sort of context it is false to report,

(1)   Lois believes that Clark can fly,

because the that-clause expresses a linguistic RAM that is not a contextually appropriate translation of any cognitive RAM that Lois *Bel*-believes, because in this context the name 'Clark' correctly translates only representations via which Lois does not attribute the ability to fly to Kent. The that-clause in (1) expresses this linguistic RAM (apologies for various simplifications):

(2)   <<'Clark', *Clark*, <'can fly', *ability to fly*>>,

which is a contextually appropriate translation of a RAM that Lois does not *Bel*-believe, namely:

(3)   <<r_C, *Kent*,>, <'can fly', *ability to fly*>>,

which involves her representation r_C (via which Lois represents Kent as a reporter, as named 'Clark', etc.). The linguistic RAM is not a contextually appropriate translation of a cognitive RAM that Lois does *Bel*-believe, namely:

(4)   <<r_S, *Kent*>, <'can fly', *ability to fly*>>,

which involves her representation r_S (via which Lois represents Kent as a super-hero, as named 'Superman', etc.).

On Richard's account of '*A* believes that *p*' (considered as uttered in a context *c*), the semantic value of '*A*' is the agent, that of '*p*' is a linguistic RAM, as we have seen, and that of 'believes' is, roughly, everything else that makes up the content of the belief ascription as a whole. So the content of 'believes' in a particular reporting context is a relation that builds in the context's standards of translation: it is a ternary relation (*Believes$_c$*) that holds between an agent, a linguistic[1] RAM, and a mapping from linguistic to cognitive RAMs just in case the mapping gives contextually appropriate translations and maps the linguistic RAM to a cognitive RAM that the agent *Bel*-believes. That is,

(5) *Believes$_c$(A,p,f)* iff:
    (i)   In *c*, *f* is an appropriate translation mapping, and
    (ii)   *Bel(A,f,(p))*.

The content of a belief report '*NN* believes that '*S*', in context *c* where '*NN*' stands for *A* and '*S*' expresses RAM p_S, is the following:

(6) (∃*f*) *Believes$_c$(A,p$_S$,f)*.

Reflexivity

According to Richard, the appropriateness of RAM *p* as a translation of RAM *q* (in a context) requires that the component expressions in *p* correctly translate the component representations in *q* (in that context). In fact, the translation mappings are given by mappings from such "atomic" expressions to representations; a RAM translation is built up compositionally from the translations, on the mapping, of its component expressions. Largely because of this, when there are two occurrences of a single name-type in a that-clause, the truth of the report requires that the agent *Bel*-believe a RAM that has two corresponding occurrences of a single representation of the name's referent. That is, using a name twice in the that-clause *always* attributes to the agent the cognitive analogue of using a name twice.

In *CA* I objected to this consequence of the semantics based on the following example:

(7) He's falling for it; Cyril believes that John is John's father.

In the obvious sort of context (John disguises his voice on the telephone to Cyril and says 'This is John's father'), this seems to make a true claim which does not require that Cyril believe that anything is a "self-father". I think Richard agrees that such intuitions of truth are relevant to assessing theories about semantic content. But Richard's semantics takes this statement to express what is surely false: a claim that is true only if Cyril *Bel*-believes a RAM that contains the same representation of John twice; to believe such a RAM, Richard agrees, is essentially to believe that John is a self-father.

I suggested as the lesson of this example that it is a mistake to think that translation standards are built up from standards of translating simple expression-types if these simple standards cannot change in mid-that-clause. I therefore recommended as a conservative amendment that Richard allow this kind of variation.[2]

But Richard (*AC*, 127-129) is not convinced by the example. He points out that in the case described we also would naturally make the following statement, which he regards as false:

(8)   Cyril believes that John is his own father.

Since the intuitions about this statement are very similar to those about (7), Richard takes it that the observation that this one is false should lead us to recognize (7) as false too, despite our intuitions to the contrary.

Now, certainly there is a reading of (8) that is false in the imagined circumstances: a reading which explicitly attributes to Cyril the belief that John is a self-father. This reading might be sketched as follows:

(9)   Cyril Believes $\lambda x(x$ is x's father)John.

This reading lets 'own' serve as a 'reflexivizer', which is as it should be, according to Richard (*AC*, 127). But it seems consistent with this feature of 'own' that there is a reading that might be sketched like this:

(10) λx(Cyril believes that x is x's father)John.

Or perhaps, if one is distracted by the repetition of variables, the following would be better[3]:

(11) $\lambda x((\exists y)(x=y$ & Cyril believes that x is y's father))John.

The difference is that, while (9) explicitly attributes to Cyril a belief that John has the property of self-fathering, (10) (or (11)) does not. Instead, (10) (or (11)) merely attributes to Cyril a belief the content of which is that an individual, namely John, is the father of an individual, namely John. Evidence that something like this reading is intended and understood is that the following, which is has exactly the content given in (9), is not in the least "natural":

(12)   Cyril believes that John is a self-father.

Richard's reaction to this suggestion[4] is as follows:

> The problem with this response is that it does not generalize to cases that seem perfectly parallel to the sort of case Crimmins has in mind. Consider this variation on Crimmins' example. We have pointed out John to Cyril and said 'that's John's father'. Cyril accepts this, and says things like 'that is John's father' while demonstrating John. We now have the following dialogue with a third party:
> —Ha! Cyril was taken in. He actually believes it.
> —What exactly does he believe?
> —That John is his own father.
> The last response is in no way strained. And it could be replaced by 'That John is John's father' without affecting the acceptability of the exchange. But by separating the propositional name from the attitude verb as the dialogue does,

we block the reading Crimmins has in mind. (*AC*, 128)

I think we do not block the reading I had in mind. The reading in question, very roughly, gives 'his own' *wide scope* over 'believes'. Richard's argument is that, by separating 'believes' from the that-clause with additional dialogue, the wide-scope reading is blocked. But consider the following example:

(13) Patrick believed that the forgery we showed him was real.

I think it is pretty clear that the description 'the forgery we showed him' takes wide scope in the natural reading here—or, if "wide scope" is not the proper label for this phenomenon, it at least is clear that the description is not attributed cognitively to Patrick. Now, I take it that we *cannot* block this reading as follows:

—He actually believed it.
—What exactly did he believe?
—That the forgery we showed him was real.

I take it that there is still the natural reading on which the description is not attributed cognitively to Patrick. What this shows is that the lack of an explicit use of an attitude verb does not block what have been called wide-scope readings.

A digression: We might explain the availability of "wide-scope" readings in such dialogues in at least two ways. First, we might take there to be a tacit or elliptical occurrence of an attitude verb, across which we *do* quantify, in front of the that-clause. Second, we might cast this phenomenon not so much a matter of scope with respect to attitude verbs, as a matter of *describing*, rather than *expressing* a proposition. A paraphrase of the that-clause ascribed to Patrick might be this:

(14) The proposition, concerning the forgery we showed him, to the effect that it is real.

There is no doubt a sense in which the proposal that that-clauses are descriptions of propositions is not an *alternative* to the apparatus of scopes, if Russell's theory of descriptions is right.[5] But taking that-clauses as themselves descriptions reduces the sense of oddity in "quantifying back in time" across an attitude verb. On Russell's theory, that kind of quantification-back happens even in this dialogue:

—He kicked it.
—What exactly did he kick?
—The ball.

A descriptive paraphrase of the relevant reading of the that-clause in Richard's example would be this:

> (15) The proposition, concerning John, attributing to him the property of being his father,

(where both pronouns are anaphoric on 'John'). Here the explicit 'reflexivity' shows up in our description of the proposition rather than in the proposition we describe. (End of digression.)

Perhaps another explanation of this phenomenon would be better. But nothing depends on the particulars of the explanation. It is clear that dialogue intervening between an attitude verb and a that-clause does not block the readings of descriptions in which the descriptive material is not attributed to the agent, and there is no reason to think that the "reflexivizing" character of 'own' is any different. Therefore, we have no reason to question the accuracy of our intuition that there is a legitimate reading of 'that John is his own father' which in the contexts we have been discussing correctly characterizes Cyril's belief. The word 'own' may indeed introduce explicit reflexivity, but like the content of a description, the reflexivity need not be attributed to the agent.

Because of this, concerns about (8) need not lead us to abandon the intuition that the described use of (7) is true. But perhaps the present discussion suggests the idea that, like (8), we should take (7) to involve scope-effects. In particular, we might hold that one of the two occurrences of 'John' in (7) takes wide scope, so that the logical form of the report is one of these:

> (16) λx(Cyril believes that John is x's father)John.
> (17) λx(Cyril believes that x is John's father)John.
> (18) $\lambda x,y$(Cyril believes that x is y's father)John,John.

If one of these is the correct reading, then Richard's apparatus—which applies the translation device only to narrow occurrences of names—can handle the case.[6] Now, perhaps the idea that names have variable scopes is not widely accepted; but I will let that pass. In any case, I think that none of the three candidates is a plausible suggestion as to (7)'s logical form, because each of the two uses of 'John' in (7) is quite clearly aimed at a particular representation (or kind of representation) that Cyril uses to represent John. To see this, note that (7) is an unexceptional member of two different families of true-seeming reports:

> (19) Cyril believes that John has called using an ordinary telephone.
> Cyril believes that John is the father of one of Cyril's students.
> ...
>
> (20) Cyril believes that John is a young student.
> Cyril believes that the person on the phone is John's father.
> ...

It seems clear that the natural way of describing in Richard's terminology the difference between the uses of 'John' in the two families is to say that they "translate" two different representations that Cyril has of John. Absent the motive of avoiding the present objection, a partisan of Richard's account surely would treat this as a paradigm of the contextual translational mechanics of belief reporting at work.[7] Thus all the occurrences of 'John' in the reports in both families are unremarkably narrow-scoped. But surely the first occurrence of 'John' in (7) does exactly the same semantic work as those in (19), and surely the second occurrence of 'John' in (7) does the same semantic work as those in (20). So it is entirely ad hoc to propose that one or both occurrences of 'John' in (7) are wide-scoped.[8] And thus the objection that Richard's account leads to a counterintuitive treatment of reports like (7) stands.

As I see it, we are not forced to abandon any intuitions whatever here, and the overwhelmingly natural conclusion is that, if belief reporting is a matter of using names to translate representations, different occurrences of a single narrowly-scoped name-type in a that-clause can, and sometimes must, translate different representations. A revision of Richard's theory that would accommodate this is fairly minor: we allow context to contribute different translation restrictions to different occurrences of names. The most natural way of achieving this seems to be to abandon the idea that translation restrictions keyed to name-types are built into the contents of attitude verbs, and instead to allow occurrence-specific restrictions to be contributed by no expression whatever—to allow these restrictions to be what John Perry calls 'unarticulated constituents' of the content of a belief report. Doing so is a good idea for another reason as well, involving iterated ascriptions.

Iterated Ascriptions

Because Richard builds the contextual restrictions on translation into the content of 'believes', the particular relations we express or think about when we talk or think about what people believe vary considerably from context to context. There is little reason to think that the translation restrictions operative in the present context are operative in the context of a speech by Clinton yesterday, or in Yeltsin's cognitive context right now. This raises a problem about iterated belief sentences. Consider the following sentence:

(21) Tom believes that Pierre believes that London is pretty.

If I were to make such a report, on Richard's account, the content of 'believes' in the reporting context (building in as it does the translation restrictions I am exploiting) would be very likely to differ from the content of 'believes' in Tom's cognitive idiolect (which builds in translation restrictions that he employs cognitively). So if we take the second occurrence of 'believes' to contribute the content of 'believes' (in the reporting context) to the RAM expressed by the largest that-clause in (21), then my report is very unlikely to be true. But the truth of this report should not be so easy to defeat.

Richard recognizes this in *PA*, and he finds a resourceful solution. When an attitude verb like 'believes' occurs *in* a that-clause, it contributes its *character* rather than its content to the RAM expressed by the that-clause. The character of 'believes' (*Believes^{char}*) is the relation obtained by abstracting over contexts in a *Believes$_c$* relation: it is the relation among an agent, a RAM, a mapping, *and a context*, that holds if the mapping both respects the translation standards of the context and maps the RAM to a cognitive RAM that the agent *Bel*-believes. So my use of (21) is given the following analysis:

(22) ($\exists f$) *Believes$_c$(Tom, p, f)*,

where *p* is the RAM expressed by the that-clause, 'that Pierre believes that London is pretty,' which is the following RAM (omitting details about the treatment of quantification):

(23) <(some treatment of '$\exists$g'), <'Pierre', *Pierre*>, <'believes', *Believes^{char}*>, <<'London', *London*>, <'is pretty', *being pretty*>>, (some treatment of 'g')>.

It is clear that the truth of my report, on this account, does not require that the content of 'believes' in the reporting context match the content of Tom's corresponding cognitive representation in his cognitive context. What is required for the truth of my report is that Tom *Bel*-believe a RAM that in our context translates the RAM (23). For this to be so, he only needs to have a representation with the same *character* as that of 'believes'. This move quite effectively eliminates the problem that iterated ascriptions become too rarely true.

The objection I raised in the earlier paper (*CA*) was that this move unfortunately misses needed readings of iterated ascriptions. I based my objection on the following circumstances in which (21) might naturally be used. Tom knows that Pierre has two representations of London (r_1 and r_2), and Tom himself has only a single representation of London. I assumed that such a situation would be possible because Tom is not confused in something like the way Pierre is. I argued that corresponding to Pierre's two representations of London there should be two readings of my (21): I may mean to attribute to Tom either of two beliefs: that Pierre thinks London pretty via r_1, or that Pierre thinks London pretty via r_2.

Given the contextual machinery of *PA*, there are contextually varying readings of (21) only if there is at least one constituent of the that-clause RAM (23) of which *Tom* has two representations—our recognizing these readings must reflect our at least tacitly understanding that in the case described Tom *must* have two such representations. But what constituent might this be? It is an explicit assumption of the example that Tom has but one representation of London. I argued (and Richard agrees for his own reasons in *AC*) that it is implausible to insist that Tom must have—and that we are conversationally distinguishing between—two cognitive representations with the character *Believes^{char}* (as Richard points out these would have to have distinct contents, and so would require distinct cognitive contexts; I don't think that this would be impossible, but it does not seem *necessary* to the example, for a reason I sketched in *CA* and which I will explain soon). The other constituents of (23) are still less plausible as entities such that we must know that Tom has two representations of them for the two readings to be available.

I suggested in the earlier paper that something like the restrictions on translation be admitted as unexceptional constituents of the semantic contents of belief sentences, so that in our iterated ascription I straightforwardly (though tacitly) *say* what sort of representation it is that Tom takes Pierre to employ. On this suggestion, what I am saying is that Tom believes, via such and such representations, the proposition that Pierre believes, via so and so representations, the proposition that London is pretty. My suggestion was based on the observations that (i) part of the content of Tom's belief (supposing he has it) has to do with restrictions on representations (because it has to do partly with *how* Pierre believes what he believes), and (ii) the truth of my report of Tom's belief seems sensitive to *how*, according to Tom's beliefs as I describe them, Pierre believes that London is pretty. I took the natural response to these observations to be that the "how-information" about Pierre's beliefs should be part of the content I am literally attributing to Tom. This way of amending Richard's account fits nicely, as it happens, with the suggestion of allowing different translation restrictions for different occurrences of a name, and, not coincidentally, would bring his theory closer to one developed by Perry and myself (in "The Prince and the Phone Booth" and in *Talk About Beliefs*).

In any case, Richard's response to my iteration worry (*AC*, pp. 129-142) is that on the understanding of 'representation' he now has in mind (which may have evolved since *PA*), I beg a question in stipulating that Tom has only one representation of London. While "[c]ertainly, there is *a* sense of 'representation' in which, provided Tom is not confused, all of Tom's tokenings of 'London' are tokenings of the same type of representation", nevertheless on the understanding of 'representation' relevant to the attitude-report semantics, "to think about what others think when they are confused may require minting new representations of the objects of their thought" (*AC*, p. 134). Richard's proposal is that (21) is not a problem for him because keeping track of Pierre's thoughts *does* require Tom to have two representations *of London*.

Now, *if* Tom has two representations of London, then of course one of them can serve in his cognitive context as a translation of Pierre's r_1 and the other can translate r_2, and so the two readings we want can be based on restricting 'London' in the reporting context to translate one or the other of Tom's two representations. So much is clear. But certainly we need a good reason to think that in reporting beliefs we employ a notion of representation such that it is *necessary*, if there are to be the two readings of (21), that (as the speaker) I think that Tom has *two* such representations—representations, moreover, that (as the speaker) I think he uses cognitively as translations of Pierre's representations.

Richard (in *AC*) tries valiantly to make this idea plausible. But I think that ultimately there is a very forceful objection to the move. It seems to me clearly consistent with the availability of the two readings of (21) for Tom to have, as his way of recording the relevant information about Pierre's belief, tokens that explicitly represent the following contents:

(24)   *Bel(Pierre, << r_1,London>, <r_p,being pretty>>)*
(25)   *¬Bel(Pierre, <<r_2,London>, <r_p,being pretty>>)*

That is, Tom can directly represent the *Bel*-believing states of affairs without relying on the strategy—which Richard thinks is used in English—of using different representations as translations.[9] I think that the two readings of (21) ought to be available (and that one reading is true, the other false) given these facts about Tom. So the question is whether Tom's having these explicit token beliefs *constitutes* his having two representations of London that he uses to translate Pierre's two representations of London. I cannot see any good reason to think that it does. In fact, for Tom to explicitly represent these two contents, he does not even need two concrete *tokens* of a representation of London, since a single token representation can occur in more than one token belief, just as a single letter-token can be part of two word-tokens in a crossword puzzle. Tom doesn't need two tokens here, not because he might accomplish some subtle representational trick, but rather because the only job that the token has to do in the two token beliefs is to represent London. What Richard has to show is that, despite appearances, this situation would *constitute* Tom's employing two different representations of London *as translations* of Pierre's representations of London. And I very much doubt that this could be made plausible.

In fact, it is easy to escape this predicament. We can simply take the ascription (21) to express a proposition to the effect that Tom believes, via such and such representations, that Pierre believes, via so and so representations, that London is pretty. The different readings correspond to different sorts of representations Pierre is believed by Tom (according to my report) to employ in his belief. Thus, we do not have to take ordinary speakers to presuppose that the way people represent what others believe *must* involve that-clauses and translation restrictions. This is good. At the same time, we get an argument that *English* does not build translation restrictions into the content of 'believes', since the way out of the iteration problem for ascriptions is to take such restrictions out of the semantic content of 'believes'.

To see the connection between the reflexivity and iteration problems, it may be helpful to see how the two issues arise in a single example. Before I set out the example, it would be useful to quote from Richard's paper (*AC*) a section in which he explains the kind of thoughts that might constitute Tom's "ambiguating" what had been a single representation of London so as to translate differently Pierre's representations. These thoughts are as follows:

> (H) Hmmh. Pierre has a way of thinking about London—he associates it with 'Londres'—and when he thinks that way of London, he thinks that London is pretty. (*AC*, 130)
>
> (H') Hmmh. Pierre has a way of thinking about London—he associates it with 'London'—and when he thinks that way of London, he thinks that London is not pretty. (*AC*, 135)

I think that these are indeed natural expressions of what Tom is supposed to think about Pierre. Richard writes that his way of modelling mental states "would naturally be voiced by things like (H) and (H')" (*AC*, 138). Now, Richard holds that the final occurrences of 'London' in (H) and (H') must count as *different representations* Tom's thought—in the sense of 'representation' relevant to Richard's semantics.

Now consider the following iterated ascription (with brackets for clarity):

> (26) Tom believes that [Pierre believes that London is pretty when he thinks of London as 'Londres', but believes that London is not pretty when he thinks of London as 'London'].

Apart from its length, this is a perfectly natural ascription in which I am attributing to Tom the conjunction of the very thoughts expressed by (H) and (H'). So Richard should agree that it is, as it seems, true. Since I use the name 'London' several times in the that-clause, then if Richard is right about reflexivity, that name is constrained to translate the same representation each time in Tom's cognitive RAM. Since the report is true, it follows that Tom has beliefs which he might express as follows, and which involve just a single representation of London:

> (27) Pierre believes that London is pretty when he thinks of London as 'Londres'.
> (28) Pierre believes that London is not pretty when he thinks of London as 'London'.

If Richard is right that such thoughts involve Tom's using a representation as a translation of Pierre's representations, then since Tom is using just one representation, in his context *it* cannot translate *different* ones of Pierre's representations. But Richard's treatment of the iteration problem *requires* that the very representations of London we attribute to Tom in the report be constrained in Tom's cognitive context to translate different ones of Pierre's representations.

It seems something has to go: the treatment of reflexivity, the treatment of iteration, or the idea that in believing (H) and (H') Tom employs different representations of London. I suggest that he abandon all three; no real harm to his account would result.[10]

Logic

Why would Richard resist the idea that the "how-information" in ordinary belief reports enters by way of unarticulated constituents of propositional content? One reason he mentions in (*AC*) is that he is uncomfortable with the result that we would have no explanation of the *logical validity* of arguments like this:

> Whatever Pierre believes Tom believes.
> Pierre believes that London is lovely.
> So Tom believes that London is lovely.

On Richard's account this is straightforwardly valid, by which he means that it is truth-preserving in every context. But exactly why is that a good result? Because the argument form has an intuitive air of validity about it? But perhaps that is simply a consequence of belief ascriptions having a "transitive" or "relational" surface form. Because we have some reason to think that it is a genuinely valid argument? I will argue that, if there is a useful notion of logical validity for context-sensitive discourse, then the above argument, supposing it has a valid reading, will present no special problems.

A brief aside: I wonder whether sentences like the first premise in this argument really have any definite, settled meaning in English. Granted, we can imagine using such sentences for certain rough and ready purposes, but the question is whether this use is creative or systematic. Consider our situation now in which we know a lot about Pierre's representations and beliefs (about London, at least). For us, right now, what exactly would 'Whatever Pierre believes Tom believes' *mean*? What would this require of Tom's beliefs and representations about London, for instance, given what we know about Pierre's beliefs and representations about London? I have only the foggiest idea.

Richard's idea is that the first premise of the above argument means that for every RAM that there is (in every possible language and cognitive system), if in our context it correctly translates a RAM that Pierre *Bel*-believes, then it also translates one that Tom *Bel*-believes. Whether this is true depends on the facts, about each RAM, as to whether *in our context* it could be used to translate RAMs that Pierre and Tom do or do not *Bel*-believe. Thus, the truth of the statement now depends on exceedingly subtle facts about the identity of our *context*—facts that determine just when in uttering a belief report, for instance, we would *change* the context we are in (changing rather than exploiting the translational standards in force in our context). I doubt that such questions genuinely have answers—I doubt that there are the relevant facts of the matter about this, and so I doubt that *our* context is sharply enough defined to settle what RAMS translate each other *in it*. If it is not, then on Richard's account of what it means, our use of 'Whatever Pierre believes Tom believes' does not have a truth value.[11]

Qualms about individuating contexts play another role here: on the notion of validity favored by Richard, for us to actually employ this argument validly, supposing we could at least understand its first premise, it would have to be the case that our context (in particular, the translation standards in force) did not shift between stating the premises and stating the conclusion; I do not believe that any real facts could determine whether this were so, either, and for the same reasons. To make an account like Richard's plausible, we have to allow that contexts are readily and subtly changeable (through mechanisms of "accommodation"); but then our intuitions about what sentences would be true considered as uttered in various actual and possible concrete conversational situations become poor data for individuating contexts and for assigning them to concrete conversational situations (but what other data is there?).

What these qualms about contexts suggest, I think, is that relying on the notion of a context in characterizing logical validity may merely sweep under the rug difficult issues about what logic is and what validity amounts to when subtle contextuality is at play. The issues peek back out at us as problems with the individuation of contexts and the determination of a context by facts about concrete conversational situations.

To get clearer about the issue of the validity of arguments like the one in question, I will now detour into a discussion of the validity of arguments involving demonstratives. This is relevant because in my view what the reflexivity and iteration considerations show is that the contextuality involved in belief reporting is *unlike* the rigid mechanics of true *indexicals* like 'today' and 'I'— whose interpretation is clearly fixed by robust features of concrete conversational situations—and rather more like the free play of *pure demonstratives* like 'this' and 'that'. I will rehearse some familiar arguments to show that fancy footwork is needed to make sense of a notion of logical validity as applied to arguments involving 'this' and 'that'. My goal is to argue that similar fancy footwork will be needed—and is readily available—if one wants a notion of logical validity that applies to language involving unarticulated propositional constituents.

Suppose that logical validity is, as Richard holds (following David Kaplan) truth-preservation in every context. Then, characterizing logical validity requires unravelling the notion of *contexts*. To play its role in characterizing validity, a context must determine the content of various expressions, including the sentences that figure in the arguments we need to evaluate. And to play its role in explaining the contextuality of language, a context must relate in some intimate way to real conversational situations.

Kaplan has noticed various problems in developing a useful notion of context adequate to a language containing pure demonstratives. One is the problem that a single expression (e.g., 'that') might be used more than once in a single sentence with a different referent on each occasion. Now, it is no help to decide, as might seem natural, that the two occasions of use of 'that' occur in different contexts, since for the purposes of characterizing validity we need there to be just *one* context in which the sentence as a whole can be considered to occur (along with the other sentences of the argument).[12] For this reason, Kaplan considers adopting in his formal language not one but several *words* corresponding to the English 'that': 'that$_1$', 'that$_2$', 'that$_3$', etc., each of which is assigned (at most) one referent at any given context.[13] Thus, the argument, 'That is heavier than that; so that is distinct from that', on its natural reading, is translated into 'That$_1$ is heavier than that$_2$; so that$_1$ is distinct from that$_2$'. This device, of course, is a tool in a formal language, not a proposal about English. But one might suggest that in reality our "word" 'that' is a tool for spontaneously creating new words—that every (or nearly every) use of 'that' is a use of a different word for the purposes of logic. This—call it the many-*that*'s move—may sound like a mere trick; surely we have not really discovered any new words (that is, 'that' is 'that'!). But stripped of its radical clothing, the genuine fact that we have discovered here is that where pure demonstratives are concerned, to retain a useful notion of validity as truth-preservation in every context we need to individuate arguments more finely than we intuitively individuate the uninterpreted sentences involved. The many-*that*'s move is one way of doing this; there are others. The insight is that there has to be more *input* to any useful notion of logical validity for this sort of discourse than simply the sequence of English sentences (as we intuitively individuate them).

Now, there may be problems with the many-*that*'s move; perhaps the question just which *that$_n$*'s are uttered in an actual or possible utterance will prove troublesome, as might the assignment contexts to real situations. These difficulties seem to me to favor abandoning the move in favor of a less dramatic but equally effective idea, such as the proposal that, to fully specify an argument, one must point out the demonstratives whose co-reference is *stipulated*. This idea will prove useful below, but I will not dwell on its advantages in the case of demonstratives.

One reason to be interested in moves like the many-*that*'s move and its less dramatic alternative is that the type of non-indexical contextuality that produces the problem that they are meant to solve is not the sole province of (explicit) demonstratives, but indeed is enormously widespread. Consider the following argument:

> (29) Bill's neighbor is big.
> Bill is not big.
> So Bill's neighbor is bigger than Bill.

Certainly there is a "reading" on which this argument is valid. But consider the following superficially similar argument:

(30) Bill's goldfish is big.
      Bill is not big.
      So Bill's goldfish is bigger than Bill.

On its natural reading, this is a poor joke—it had better come out *not* logically valid. The culprit: the word 'big' is context-sensitive, and (30), unlike (29), is guilty of contextual equivocation. Suppose we accept the idea (which may well not be correct) that the content of 'big' is fixed by some contextually given parameter (whether a comparison class, or something else). Thus, we will want to say that the two uses of 'big' in the latter argument have different contents, fixed by different contextual parameters. For the same reasons as in the case of pure demonstratives, if we want to retain a notion of validity on which the former argument really is valid but the latter is not, we will have to individuate these argument sufficiently finely that the uses of 'big' in the latter argument are treated in a different way from the uses of 'big' in the former argument. We could do this dramatically, by claiming the discovery of new words 'big$_1$', 'big$_2$', etc., or less dramatically, by claiming that *fully specifying an argument form involves not only giving a sequence of sentences, but also stipulating identities among contextually determined elements of propositional content.*[14]

The same issue arises for arguments involving unarticulated propositional constituents. If the location in question in a use of 'It's raining' is taken to be an unarticulated constituent of its propositional content (a constituent which is not part of the content of any expression in the sentence), then the question arises how to apply the notion of validity to arguments like this:

If it's raining, Georgians are in trouble.
It's raining.
So Georgians are in trouble.

We might worry about capturing the intuitive validity of this argument; after all, if there is no expression for a location whose content is varying according to context, then the context (as we have developed the notion for semantics and logic) does not settle the content of the premises, and as there is no guarantee that, considered at a single context, the two premises are logically related in subject matter, the argument comes out invalid. But the worry is easy to address. For one thing, we might postulate a silent, hidden indexical expression which can be sensitive to a contextual parameter (and if we want to allow different uses of 'It's raining' in a single argument to concern different locations, we could postulate a sequence of such hidden indexicals). Or, less dramatically, we might hold that specifying the argument that is the natural reading here involves stipulating that the premises are to be taken as concerning rain at the same location—once again, the argument involves as a *given* an identity of contextually provided constituents.

Let us return now to the argument at issue:

> Whatever Pierre believes Tom believes.
> Pierre believes that London is lovely.
> So Tom believes that London is lovely.

On the account of attitude reports that I favor, the full propositional content of the second premise includes as an unarticulated constituent a constraint on representations (restricting the representation of London that Pierre must have to make the report true). Equally, the propositional content of the conclusion involves an unarticulated constraint on representations. The first premise is a bit more complicated, involving as it does quantification over, rather than reference to, (types of) modes of presentation (at least, that is the gloss I would give to what I take to be the pretty loose grip our understanding has on this premise). Perhaps the rough idea conveyed by this premise can be put as follows: 'Whatever Pierre believes (on a relevant way of thinking) Tom believes (in the same way)'. On this construal, the great unclarity in this premise of which I complained above amounts at least in part to an unclarity in the domain of relevant ways of thinking (where these are certain *types* of cognitive representations). Now, to do justice to the intuition that the argument is valid, it seems enough to hold that in fully specifying the argument that is the natural reading here (to the extent that this really is determinate) we must stipulate (i) that the contextually provided unarticulated constraints are identical in the second premise and conclusion (the same "way of thinking about London" is in question in both), and (ii) that the unarticulated constraint in question is one of the "relevant ways of thinking" over which the first premise quantifies.

Thus construed, the argument is analogous to this one:

> Whenever it rained last week, it poured.
> It rained last Friday.
> So it poured last Friday.

(Note that no single place need be under discussion here; to see this, imagine that we are discussing a geographically scattered event like a war or World Cup tournament.) When the relativity to location of raining is taken into account, we notice that the following must be stipulated in fully specifying the argument that is the (or one) natural reading here: (i) that the same place is in question in the second premise and the conclusion, and (ii) that that place is one of the relevant places tacitly quantified over in the first premise. Stipulations (i) and (ii) are importantly analogous to the two stipulations needed to specify fully the argument about Pierre and Tom.

If one wants a notion of logical validity on which such arguments have a valid reading, I conclude, one is available. And notice that the way we have accommodated non-indexical contextuality does not rely on fiddling with the notion of *contexts*. While that notion is quite handy for explaining how true indexicals like 'I' and 'today' affect the validity of arguments, it may not figure into the best way of accommodating the more free-wheeling contextuality characteristic of demonstratives and (many) underarticulated constructions.

Notes

*   I presented a draft of this paper at the meetings of the Pacific Division of the American Philosophical Association in April of 1994. I have had the benefit of Mark Richard's detailed comments, which he presented on that occasion.

1.   There is actually no requirement that these RAMs be linguistic—in fact, they will be cognitive in the case of cognitive belief attributions (our thoughts and beliefs about what people believe); I return to such cases below.

2.   The alternative of taking contextually given translation standards to operate on whole sentences rather than atomic expressions would seem more or less to abandon—or at least not to accomplish—the project of *explaining* how belief reports require more of beliefs than match of Russellian content, for the resulting account would be little beyond the bare statement that they *do* require more. I am not sure how deep an objection this would be, however.

3.   See *AC*, note 5, p. 128.

4.   I made this suggestion in response to a draft of *AC*

5.   This strategy does not suffer in iterations. The three wanted readings of '*A* believes that *B* believes that P(the ϕ)' are captured as follows:

> *A* believes the proposition that *B* believes that P(the Q),
> *A* believes the proposition that *B* believes the proposition, concerning the Q, that P(it),
> *A* believes the proposition, concerning the Q, that *B* believes the proposition that P(it).

6.   Richard in fact made this suggestion in his comments on the earlier draft of this paper.

7.   One should also note that the wide-scope move here, given other features of Richard's account, requires that (7) be given (in part) essentially Naive Russellian truth conditions. That is, its truth will not be sensitive to just *how* Cyril thinks of John (in his mode of presentation corresponding to one or both occurrences of 'John' in (7)). This result encounters the usual problems with Naive Russellian truth conditions: it shouldn't be that easy for (7) to be true.

8.   One might protest that the first occurrence of 'John' is plausibly wide-scoped (or "*de re*"), since it is meant to correspond to a perceptually-based representation, or to a fairly informationally thin representation. But those features of the example are entirely irrelevant. Suppose, e.g., that John has successfully disguised himself as an adult for Cyril on many occasions, and that Cyril has only a passing acquaintance with John as a student; and suppose, as you like, that Cyril thinks that both, either, or neither of the "two" are named 'John'. Still, we can set up the conversational context so that it seems quite unambiguous and true to say that Cyril believes that John is John's father.

9.   In doing this, he can directly represent Pierre's representations (as I have shown in the examples in the text), or instead directly represent conditions on them, as he

would in explicitly representing the following content:

$$(\exists r,s)[C(r) \ \& \ D(s) \ \& \ Bel(Pierre, \ <<r, London>, \ <s, \ being \ pretty>>)].$$

10. In his comments on an earlier draft of this paper, Richard suggested that the uses 'London' in (26) are uses of different names, as far as semantics is concerned, which translate different of Tom's representations—and so his treatment of iteration does not apply. But this suggestion is both ad hoc and (independently) unpalatable. Surely the only semantically significant jobs that the two occurrences of 'London' are doing in (26) are precisely identical: standing for London. The "how-information" is introduced into the content of (26) not indirectly by a choice of term for London, but directly and explicitly.

11. There are other reasons for concern about Richard's analysis of the first premise:

> i. There may be beliefs of Pierre's and Tom's that we do not have the concepts to express—and so (one presumes) which are not differentially translated by any RAMs in our context. Surely such beliefs might matter to the truth of (what we would likely mean by) the first premise in some context, and just as surely more might be needed for their identity (for that purpose) than identity of Russellian content.
>
> ii. There may be beliefs for which we simply do not happen to have appropriate translations. For example, imagine that we know about the difference between the two sorts of belief about Venus, but that we do not in our context have names (or cognitive representations) set up to do the needed translating; still we might want to count the two kinds of belief with the Russellian content that Venus is bright as *different* for the purpose of the first premise.
>
> iii. We might, in some one context, for very different and unrelated reasons have 'Venus' set up to translate two utterly different representations of Venus belonging to two different agents (say, the 'Hesperus' representation of one Babylonian and the 'Phosporus' representation of another). Suppose the agents believe with their different representations the Russellian content that Venus is the home of a god. It seems wrong for this situation necessarily to *constitute* their believing the *same thing*, for the purposes of the first premise.

The upshot of all this seems to be that, while perhaps we do use talk like that in the first premise to require more fine-grained identities between beliefs than mere identity of Russellian content, it is not plausible that the identity in question always coincides with identity of contextual RAM translations. Our available translations do not seem to *index* the intuitive "things believed" we are getting at in this sort of talk. My inclination, by the way, is to regard the language of the first premise—like 'believes the same thing' locutions—as somewhat unsystematic, open-textured, creative use of English. A fortiori, I do not have an account of its semantic analysis. But I will sketch below a sort of approximate analysis of one likely use.

12. Actually, I am not sure that this idea could not, with some fiddling, be made to work to as well as some of the other artificialities we will consider. The main difficulties, probably, would be to individuate "sub-contexts" of demonstratives (especially with respect to sentences that are not in fact used in the larger context), to explain how it is determined in which subcontext a demonstrative occurs when

it is part of a sentence that occurs in a given (full, sentential) context, and to explain the assignment of the resulting (full, sentential) contexts to real conversational situations. But these difficulties are quite similar to those encountered by the "many-*that's* move", soon to be discussed in the text.

13. Kaplan, 'Demonstratives', p. 528 and 'Afterthoughts', pp. 582-590.
14. Of course, we could also take as "input" the actual interpretations of the uses of 'big' here, but it seems to me that the thinner the input the better, if we are aiming at a notion of logical validity that is as close as possible to the usual ones. On the latter alternative mentioned in the text, we need not specify the exact interpretation of 'big' to specify what comes out as the single, valid reading of the following argument:

> X is big.
> Y is not big.
> So X is bigger than Y.

References

Crimmins, Mark: 1992, *Talk About Beliefs*, Cambridge, MA: MIT Press.

Crimmins, Mark: 1992, 'Context in the Attitudes', *Linguistics and Philosophy* **15**, 185-198.

Crimmins, Mark and John Perry: 1989, 'The Prince and the Phone Booth', *Journal of Philosophy* **86**, 685-711.

Kaplan, David: 1989, 'Demonstratives', in Almog, J., Perry, J., Wettstein, H., eds., *Themes from Kaplan*, New York: Oxford University Press.

Kaplan, David: 1989, 'Afterthoughts', in Almog, J., Perry, J., Wettstein, H., eds., *Themes from Kaplan*, New York: Oxford University Press.

Richard, Mark: 1990, *Propositional Attitudes*. Cambridge University Press, Cambridge.

Richard, Mark: 1993, 'Attitudes in Context', *Linguistics and Philosophy* **16**, 123-148.

Philosophical Perspectives, 9, AI, Connectionism, and
Philosophical Psychology, 1995

CONCEPTUAL STRUCTURE AND
THE INDIVIDUATION OF CONTENT

Derk Pereboom
University of Vermont

Current attempts to understand psychological content divide into two families of views. According to externalist accounts such as those advanced by Tyler Burge and Ruth Millikan, psychological content does not supervene on the physical features of the individual subject, but is fixed partially by the nature of the world external to her.[1] In the rival functional role theories developed by Ned Block and Brian Loar, content does supervene on the physical features of the individual, and is, in addition, determined solely by the role it plays in the causal network of an individual's sensations, behavior, and mental states.[2] Over the past fifteen years, criticism of these two types of views has often focussed on their capacity to individuate content in an acceptable way, and both seem to be deficient in this respect.

A satisfactory theory must individuate content at a level that captures the generalizations in psychological explanation we want to make. Functional role theory allows for an extremely fine-grained specification of content, since any difference in associated belief can make for a difference in content. However, this type of theory seems to provide no principled criteria for individuating content in a way coarse-grained enough to explain how it might remain the same despite differences in associated beliefs, and thus content determined by functional role would seem to be incapable of sustaining the right psychological generalizations.[3] Externalist theories, by contrast, furnish anchors for content by linking the cognitive value of concepts to entities in the external world, entities which retain their identity through variation in associated beliefs. But critics have argued that in some cases externalist theories nevertheless cut content too finely, and furthermore, that on other occasions externalist individuation is too coarse.[4] In some cases, contents that externalist theories distinguish need to function in the same type of role for explaining inference and behavior, whereas in other situations contents that they render equivalent must account for significantly different patterns of inference and behavior.

I believe that the force of these criticisms persists, despite attempts to mitigate their impact, but that there is a strategy for individuating content that might well not suffer from deficiencies in fineness or coarseness of grain. This approach takes its cue from the individuation of natural kinds in sciences such as chemistry and biology. In these sciences, structural features of entities play a prominent role in characterizations of the natural kinds of which they are members. Recent studies in cognitive psychology suggest that psychological content also has various structural features. I shall argue that these features can be appropriated for the individuation of content, and furthermore, that such individuation has a reasonable prospect of capturing fundamental intuitions about psychological explanation, and of providing principled criteria for identity of content and concept.

I

In psychological explanation of inference and behavior, propositional attitudes such as beliefs, desires, and wishes have a key role. Part of the explanatory power of a propositional attitude is attributable to its being the kind of attitude it is, for example, its being a belief rather than a desire or a wish. The remaining explanatory role of an attitude, by one taxonomy, is played by its *content*, for example, its being a belief *that is it raining*, rather than *that it is not raining*. But this taxonomy is not universal. In David Kaplan's semantic theory, for example, 'content' refers to the proposition expressed by the 'that' clause, where the proposition *Socrates is wise* is the same proposition as *he is wise*, given that 'Socrates' and 'he' are coreferential.[5] In his taxonomy, besides content and type of attitude, a propositional attitude includes *character*, which includes features of how a subject represents a proposition. In Jerry Fodor's system, besides type of attitude and content in Kaplan's sense, propositional attitudes include *vehicle*, the symbol by means of which one's contents are represented, and *functional role*, the causal role a vehicle plays in a system of inference patterns.[6] A discussion of content, therefore, requires that one set out the definition of the notion one is using. Here I shall be using 'content' in a way closely related to the first and broadest sense discussed, as the features of an attitude other than the kind of attitude it is. But as we shall see, the distinctions that Kaplan and Fodor make are important.

Any view about the content individuation must sustain the capacity of content to function in the psychological explanation of individual subjects' inferences and behavior. Individuation of content must be fine-grained enough to account for differences in inference and behavior, but it must also be coarse-grained enough to capture salient similarities in the production of inference and behavior from subject to subject, and for a single subject across time.[7] Frege's test is strongly evidential for fineness of grain in the intrapersonal case.[8] 'Hesperus' and 'Phosphorus' refer to the same entity, but if the identity statement *Hesperus = Phosphorus* would be informative for a subject, then an acceptable psychological theory must make a distinction between the concepts 'Hesperus' and 'Phosphorus' for that subject (supposing she has both concepts), which is to say that in her case it must make a distinction between the contributions to content (i.e. the cognitive value) of these concepts. In general, if a subject has the concepts 'A' and 'B,' and if 'A = B' would be informative for her, then 'A' and 'B' are different concepts for that subject, and thus for her they differ in cognitive value.

Let us recall why Frege's test provides strong evidence for differences in contribution to content in the intrapersonal case. Content plays the pivotal role in the psychological explanation of inference and behavior. If *Hesperus = Phosphorus* would be an informative identity for a subject, then for that subject beliefs and desires involving the concept 'Hesperus' can make significantly different contributions to explanations of inference and behavior from those involving 'Phosphorus.' If Ariane does not know that Hesperus = Phosphorus, her belief that Hesperus is a planet cannot be regarded as having the same content as the belief that Phosphorus is a planet, because she might infer that Hesperus revolves around a star from her belief that Hesperus is a planet, and yet fail to infer from this same belief that Phosphorus revolves around a star. And her desire to visit Hesperus just once cannot be counted the same as her desire to visit Phosphorus just once, because supposing her desire to visit Hesperus just once has caused her to make arrangements to land on Hesperus, this would not preclude her from making further plans to land on Phosphorus. Thus a psychological theory that aims to track significantly different contributions to explanations of inference and behavior must distinguish Ariane's concept 'Hesperus' from her concept 'Phosphorus,' despite the fact that these concepts are coreferential.

One might worry that Frege's test is inadequate because it threatens to distinguish cognitive value wherever there is any difference in functional role, and that thus this test will also undermine the psychological generalizations we want to make. But this worry can be set aside. Although, for example, the functional roles of my concepts 'fourteen days' and 'fortnight' are different, Frege's test does not distinguish them. My thoughts involving 'fortnight,' are more likely to make me think 'what a quaint thought!' and to call to mind Burge's article "Belief and Synonymy" than are my thoughts involving 'fourteen days.' But nevertheless, *a fortnight = fourteen days* is not informative for me. Hence, there are differences in functional role where Frege's test will not distinguish cognitive value.

Frege's test poses a problem for some externalist theories of content. Consider, for example, the Millian account of proper names discussed by Saul Kripke, according to which coreferential proper names are intersubstitutable in belief contexts *salve veritate*, and make the same contribution to semantic content.[9] In an extension of this semantic view to the explanation of inference and behavior, coreferential proper names would make the same contribution to psychological content. Kripke's puzzle about belief provides a persistent difficulty for such an account, and also, he argues, for any theory of belief attribution.[10] Pierre comes to have a belief which he expresses as "*Londres est jolie.*" By the rules of translation and disquotation, we English-speakers attribute to him the belief that London is pretty. But Pierre lands up in London, in a bad part of town, and he acquires a belief that he expresses as "London is not pretty," which, by the rule of disquotation (and perhaps translation from Pierre's idiolect) we attribute to him as the belief that London is not pretty. He all the while maintains the belief '*Londres est jolie*,' and thus we would continue to attribute to him the belief that London is pretty. Accordingly, we attribute contradictory beliefs to him, but this would seem to involve a mistake. The anti-Millian point of this case is that attributing a contradiction in belief to Pierre seems unavoidable if coreferential proper names make the same contribution to content. But Kripke argues that the puzzle raises a problem not just for a Millian view, but for all theories of belief attribution, because they all would endorse the rules of translation and disquotation, and it is not obvious that any other conceivably controversial elements are required to construct the puzzle.

As Loar has shown, the anti-Millian point of Kripke's puzzle can be expressed without using the notion of contradiction. Even if we conceive of Pierre landing up in an upscale part of London, and forming the belief that he expresses as "London is pretty," we could not count this new belief to be the same as the belief he acquired in France, since they are not inferentially identical. It seems to follow that coreferential proper names must sometimes make different contributions to content.[11] And as Akeel Bilgrami argues, Loar's argument allows us to see that the anti-Millian point of Kripke's case can be expressed by a Fregean puzzle. For Pierre *Londres* = *London* would be informative, and thus for him, these proper names differ in cognitive value.[12] Hence, Frege's test provides strong evidence that for Pierre '*Londres*' and 'London' make distinct contributions to content.

Another example of Kripke's reveals that an informative identity can be constructed even when the coreferential proper names are the same (when the vehicles, in Fodor's sense, are the same). A subject may not realize that Paderewski the statesman is identical to Paderewski the pianist, and therefore the identity *Paderewski* = *Paderewksi* may be informative for her. In addition, when the Millian view is applied to demonstratives, coreferential demonstrative expressions make the same contribution to content. Burge points out, however, that Fregean puzzles can be constructed not only for coreferential and identical proper names, but also for coreferential and identical demonstrative expressions.[13] *This* = *this* can be informative if the first 'this' is accompanied by a demonstration of the svelte Orson Welles in *The Lady from Shanghai* and the second by a demonstration of a more corpulent Welles in *Touch of Evil*.

Accordingly, in each of these cases, we have strong evidence that the two expressions flanking the identity sign indicate different contributions to content. As the "Paderewski" example shows, the divergence in cognitive value between the two expressions cannot always be explained by a difference in vehicles. Moreover, even when vehicles are distinct, it is dubious that the distinction between vehicles always or even typically accounts for differences in cognitive value. Plausibly, a further contribution is sometimes provided by the beliefs associated with the expressions. For example, in Kripke's case, the beliefs Pierre associates with '*Londres*' might well be different from the beliefs he associates with 'London.' But even if we make this move, Kripke would argue that the problem for belief attribution remains unsolved. We can imagine that many French people have just the information about London that Pierre acquired in France, and that counterfactually, they would be in Pierre's predicament. Yet we would want to make unembellished attributions, like 'Madeleine believes that London is pretty,' to them. So if we were to apply our standards for belief attribution consistently, we would still want to attribute to Pierre the belief that London is pretty, and this is what generates Kripke's puzzle.

A common objection to Burge's view about content individuation is that it sometimes renders contents equivalent when they must explain significantly different patterns of inference and behavior, and at other times distinguishes contents that must explain very similar patterns of inference and behavior. To illustrate, let us examine a case Burge has used to argue for his view.[14] Alfred is a member of the English-speaking linguistic and social community, and he correctly applies the term 'arthritis' in many situations. But he has recently developed a pain in his thigh, and he has come to believe "I have arthritis in my thigh," even though in his community arthritis is classified by the experts as a disease solely of the joints. Now imagine a counterpart to Alfred, who is identical to him in every non-intentional individualistic feature, but in his community the word 'arthritis' refers to certain rheumatoid ailments, including arthritis, but also including certain ailments of the muscles and tendons, and in this community his belief (expressed in his language) "I have arthritis in my thigh" is true. We English-speakers would attribute a belief involving our concept of arthritis (with our word 'arthritis' in oblique position) to Alfred, but not to his counterpart, even though there are no non-intentional individualistic differences between them. To attribute a belief in our language to the counterpart, we would have to devise a translation, such as 'tharthritis,' for his term 'arthritis.' Hence, the content of Alfred's attitude, and more specifically, his concept of arthritis, is dependent not simply on non-intentional individualistic facts about him, but also on facts about his social environment.

For the thought-experiment to support Burge's view, it must be plausible to attribute contents including the concept 'arthritis' to Alfred, just as to an expert on earth, and to deny the concept 'arthritis' of Alfred's counterpart. But many report the individualist intuition that the behavior and inferences of Alfred and his counterpart are explained by the same psychological states. Furthermore, although the differences in behavior between Alfred and the expert might some-times be explained by the different 'arthritis' beliefs they hold, a significant enough divergence in such beliefs could conceivably force us to attribute different concepts to them. For the view that concepts, when attributed in psychological explanations, are completely independent of surrounding beliefs is implausible.[15]

Burge and others have developed theories that disavow such individualist intuitions. My aim is to develop a view that preserves these intuitions while explaining the considerations that pull in the opposite direction, and in addition supplies a solution to Kripke's puzzle, and provides a method of content individuation that can sustain the psychological generalizations we want to make. Such a view will not obviously undermine an externalist position of the sort that Burge has advocated. But it will provide an alternative to such a position, and its plausibility will derive from the force of the individualist intuitions, and from the attractive ways in which it can meet the other desiderata of a theory of content.

II

Both Kripke's puzzle and Burge's thought-experiments depend crucially on taking ordinary attribution practice to be strongly indicative, if not definitive, of the nature of the content of an attitude. Hence, in developing an alternative to their externalist theories, one might attempt to undermine this confidence in ordinary attribution practice. One might begin by differentiating two perspectives from which attributions can be evaluated. Burge himself, in a discussion of Frege's views on the sense of beliefs involving proper names and indexicals, distinguishes the *public* from the *psychological* functions of attribution. What is "*communicated* through ordinary language when proper names, or other indexicals are used" is distinct from what is required "to solve the problems of cognitive value and oblique belief contexts."[16] John Perry, Donald Davidson, and Michael Devitt have also suggested a distinction of this sort, and Davidson and Devitt have argued that it can be brought to bear on Burge's thought-experiments.[17] Devitt argues that in attribution, the purpose of psychological explanation can be distinguished from the aim of learning about the world:

> Folk ascribe thoughts not only for psychological purposes but also to learn about the world. This dual purpose raises the possibility that the folk do not regard all the content they ascribe as relevant to the explanation of behavior.[18]

I shall attempt to develop this type of suggestion in greater detail.

Belief attributions have various purposes. One goal of belief attribution is to communicate to others evidence about features of the world represented by a belief. That this is an important function of belief attribution is clear. People's beliefs are a significant source of evidence about what they represent, and public attribution of beliefs is an important means for communicating this evidence. If, however, communication of evidence about the world is one's aim in attributing a belief to a subject, the exact way the subject represents that evidence might well not be pertinent. For example, even if a subject cannot distinguish elms from most other deciduous trees, and even if she believes that elms and beeches are the same type of tree, the attribution of her belief as "She believes that elms are subject to epidemics" can still communicate evidence about elms. Despite the subject's meager conceptual ability, if her beliefs have certain contextual relations to elms, perhaps involving a causal chain, attributions of her beliefs as being about elms can still provide evidence about elms to an audience.

Belief attribution has another fundamental purpose, the part it plays in the psychological explanation of inference and behavior. And when this is the main goal, attribution will tend to have different emphases than it does when the aim of communication of evidence about the world dominates. When communication of evidence about the world is the chief aim, carefully delineating all aspects of a subject's attitudes may be irrelevant. But specifying the nature of a subject's attitudes very precisely may be critical for psychological explanation, because the exact nature of the attitude can make a difference for her inferences and behavior.

When communication of evidence about the world is at issue, belief attribution can prescind from the details of the ways in which entities are represented. *De re* belief attributions often fit this description. When I make the *de re* attribution of Pierre's belief, 'London is such that Pierre believes it not to be pretty,' the mode by which Pierre represents London might be of no concern to me because in attributing this belief I am interested mainly in communicating evidence about London. And that the mode by which Pierre represents London is of no concern to me may be indicated by the fact that in my attribution coreferential expressions are substitutable for 'London' *salva veritate*. Moreover, although in *de dicto* attributions delineating the subject's mode of representation is always an aim, communication of evidence about the world might function as an additional purpose there as well, and might have an effect on the character of the attribution. My attribution 'Pierre believes that the capital of England is pretty' may come close to specifying Pierre's actual mode of representation of London, while 'Pierre believes that the largest city in England is pretty' does not, and, accordingly, substitution of coreferential expressions *salva veritate* in my attribution fails. But nevertheless the precedence taken by the goal of communication of evidence about the world might render my specification of further details about the way Pierre represents London unnecessary.

Let us now reexamine Kripke's puzzle with these reflections in mind. The attribution to Pierre of the belief that London is pretty can communicate evidence that London is pretty. And further, the attribution to him of the belief that London is not pretty can communicate evidence that London is not pretty. But although these attributions might communicate conflicting evidence, and thus provide evidence for incompatible states of affairs, we have yet no reason to believe that there is a contradiction in the way Pierre represents London. For if Pierre's psychological states were more accurately specified—described more precisely than is required for the aim of communication of evidence about the world—any such contradiction might well disappear.

Furthermore, distinct tasks in psychological explanation may demand different levels of precision in the specification of psychological states. If we want to explain why Pierre, while still in France, says to the travel agent "*Je voudrais vogayer à Londres,*" we can do so partly by attributing to him the belief that London is pretty. If we want to explain why Pierre, now in England, chooses to get over his bad mood by listening to music rather than by taking a walk, we can do so partly by attributing to him the belief that London is not pretty, or in French, *que Londres n'est pas jolie*. Given our typical explanatory interests in such contexts, we need not qualify our attribution of the concept 'London' or of the concept '*Londres*' to Pierre, and indeed so far—and this is often the case—psychological explanation does not demand greater precision in the specification of content than does communication of evidence about the world. But when we must explain how he can believe both '*Londres est jolie*' and 'London is not pretty,' our characterizations of Pierre's attitudes must become more detailed and precise. In particular, more must be said about the way in which he is thinking about London—his mode of presentation of London. One way to accomplish this is to hedge our attribution of the concept 'London' by specifying that he has not realized that *Londres* = London, and therefore Pierre's beliefs involving his use of '*Londres*' are inferentially isolated from those involving his use of 'London.'

Throughout his article, Kripke stresses the point that there is some terminology that suffices to explain Pierre's situation. He argues, however, that this does not solve his puzzle.

> But beware of one source of confusion. It is no solution in itself to observe that some *other* terminology, which evades the question whether Pierre believes London is pretty, may be sufficient to state all the relevant facts... . But none of this answers the original question. Does Pierre, or does he not, believe that London is pretty? I know of no answer to *this* question that seems satisfactory.[19]

As we have seen, our attribution of beliefs to Pierre can communicate evidence that London is pretty and evidence that London is not pretty. We can legitimately make such attributions, given the understanding that they reflect not the precise nature of Pierre's psychological states, but the evidence about the world that his beliefs can provide, as well as the requirements of many cases of psychological explanation. But in Kripke's case, psychological explanation requires a more precise specification of how Pierre represents London, and thus we would not attribute his French belief simply as "Pierre believes that London is pretty." Rather, we would stress the details of his mode of presentation by hedging any less precise attributions. As a result, there will not be an unqualified yes/no answer to Kripke's question. But this raises no intractable problem for belief attribution. Just as for answers to "Was French foreign policy responsible for the geopolitical decline of Spain in the seventeenth century?" and "Is the ocean blue?" an answer to Kripke's question must be qualified. Reality is too complex for simple yes/no responses to such questions to be satisfactory. The content of Pierre's attitude is too intricate, perhaps both in its conceptual and indexical features, for Kripke's question to have an unqualified yes/no answer.[20]

We can also use these observations to explore an alternative analysis of the issues raised by Burge's example. Burge provides good reason to believe that ordinary belief attribution is often non-individualistic in the sense that our ordinary attributions of content are dependent on facts about a subject's physical and social environment. From this fact about ordinary attributions he concludes that belief contents themselves have externalist individuation-conditions. Let us, however, attempt to develop an account of content that takes seriously the individualist intuitions that psychological explanation could require the cognitive value of Alfred's and his counterpart's concepts to be the same, and the cognitive value of Alfred's and the expert's concepts to differ. Rather than concede an externalist position about content individuation, we might then instead regard these intuitions as providing evidence against taking ordinary attribution as determinative of cognitive value. Throughout his writings, Burge assumes that ordinary attribution practice yields a notion of content adequate for psychological explanation.[21] But while ordinary attribution practice may be adequate to psychological explanation in typical cases, it might be that in more challenging cases, those that more accurately disclose the real nature of attitude contents, ordinary practice is inadequate.

Let us reexamine Burge's thought-experiment to see whether the intuitions that oppose his view can be accommodated, while keeping in mind the distinction between attribution aimed at communication of evidence about the world and attribution geared to psychological explanation. Alfred and his counterpart are identical with respect to all non-intentional, individualistic characteristics. Alfred's English-speaking society uses 'arthritis' to refer to a rheumatoid ailment of the joints, while in the counterpart's society this term is used to refer not only to this ailment of the joints, but also to ailments of the muscles and tendons. Burge argues convincingly that we would ordinarily attribute beliefs using our term 'arthritis'—without qualification—not only to the expert, but to Alfred as well. But this fact might be explained by our interest in communicating, by means of belief attribution, evidence about the features of the world represented by a belief, and by the requirements of psychological explanation in many ordinary contexts. First, the goal of communication of evidence about the world through attribution requires that we use terms that have public linguistic meanings, and that we use these terms in accordance with their public linguistic meanings. And thus this goal gives us reason to make attributions of Alfred employing the term 'arthritis' with its public linguistic meaning, and not using 'arthritis' while intending a linguistic meaning other than the public one, or using a made-up term not in the public language—even if the term 'arthritis' fails to capture the nature of his concept accurately. Further, even though Alfred's knowledge of arthritis is too limited to preclude even fairly elementary errors—measured against the standard of public linguistic meaning—the combination of his conceptual and contextual relations to arthritis might well be sufficient for attribution of his beliefs as being about arthritis to communicate evidence regarding the rheumatoid ailment of the joints. Given Alfred's conceptual and contextual relations to arthritis, therefore, attributions using the term 'arthritis,' unhedged, with its public linguistic meaning, might well be sufficient to satisfy the aim of communication of evidence about the world, even if psychological explanation could require that we not attribute to him the same concept as the expert. Moreover, attribution to Alfred using our term 'arthritis,' unhedged, would likely be sufficient for many cases of psychological explanation. But if we want to specify the nature of his concept more precisely—and perhaps we must do so in order to explain some of the differences between the inferences and behavior of Alfred and the expert—attributions of our concept 'arthritis' to Alfred might well have to be qualified.

Our predisposition to deny attribution of our concept 'arthritis' to Alfred's counterpart might also be explained by the aim of communication of evidence about the world. In his thought-experiment, Burge specifies that the public linguistic meaning of 'arthritis' in the counterpart's community is not the same as the linguistic meaning of 'arthritis' in our community. Hence, to attribute a belief using our term 'arthritis' to Alfred's counterpart would be to attribute to him a term intending a linguistic meaning foreign to his community. Most often communication of evidence about the world by attribution is directed towards the subject's own community. Typically, therefore, attribution using the linguistic meanings of the subject's community facilitates communication of evidence about the world, while such communication is frustrated by attribution using linguistic meanings foreign to the subject's community. Consequently, our attribution practice is strongly disinclined to attribute to a subject terms intending linguistic meanings alien to his community, and we are accordingly averse to using 'arthritis' with our linguistic meaning in making attributions to Alfred's counterpart. Nevertheless, if our aim is psychological explanation, our attributions, together with our hedgings and qualifications, may yet be forced to exhibit a convergence of the concepts of Alfred and his counterpart.

Many philosophers, such as Loar, Block, and Fodor, have argued that variation in standards of attribution indicate that there are two types of content—wide, externalist content, and the narrow content required for psychological explanation of inference and behavior. In the view I am developing here, as in Bilgrami's, content is unitary, and its true character is most accurately approximated in the context of psychological explanation. The arguments of Burge and others do not, all by themselves, show that "wide content" qualifies as a separate kind of real psychological content. "Wide content," it would seem, is derived from attributions that in part aim to facilitate communication of evidence about the world. But this purpose might be viewed as having a tendency to deflect the aim at truth about the attitudes of the subject in the interest of communicating evidence about the features of the world that the attitude represents. Thus when our interest is in communication of evidence about the world, we attribute to Pierre the belief that London is pretty, disregarding the more complex nature of his representation of London. In this case, we, as attributors, might regard ourselves as not engaged solely in specifying what is in Pierre's mind—in describing the real nature of his attitudes—but also by the additional and potentially conflicting goal of communicating evidence about the features of the world that Pierre's beliefs are about. When, by contrast, our interest is psychological explanation, our focus is solely on Pierre's psychology, and on representing Pierre's attitudes accurately, or as accurately as the particular task in psychological explanation requires. In this picture, therefore, attribution of "wide content" incorporates a tendency to represent the content of a subject's attitudes imprecisely, whereas when our interest is psychological explanation, attribution is seen as approaching content as it really is.

Correlatively, in this view it is not the case that there are two different types of truth-conditions for content attribution. When one aims at communication of evidence about the world, there may be good reasons for attributing a "content" that diverges from the real nature of the attitude. Such divergence may have genuine pragmatic value, but it does not aim solely at truth about the content of the attitude. And thus success in the pursuit of communication of evidence about the world might quite readily conflict with the satisfaction of the truth-conditions of content attribution. Since pursuit of the goal of communication of evidence about the world has a tendency to motivate an imprecise characterization of the contents of subjects' attitudes, it would be a mistake to posit an additional sort of truth-condition that corresponds to this purpose. When, by contrast, one's quest in attribution is psychological explanation, one aims more directly and less equivocally at the truth about subject's attitudes, and therefore also at the satisfaction of the truth-conditions of attribution.

Furthermore, if ordinary content attribution serves partially to communicate evidence about the world, and this purpose tends to conflict with representing content as it really is, then concepts as they are employed in ordinary content attribution do not have externalist individuation-conditions of the sort we have examined. For if the factors in thought-experiments that generate externalist conclusions can be explained as a function of the goal of communication of evidence about the world, and if this purpose deflects the aim at truth about attitude contents, then we should not look to attributions part of whose purpose is communication of evidence about the world for the individuation-conditions of concepts. These individuation-conditions are not best revealed by instances of pragmatically valuable attribution practice which has a tendency to generate false attributions, but rather by attributions that aim at truth about attitude contents.

In summary, our objective was to develop a view that solves Kripke's puzzle and explains the results of Burge's thought-experiments while preserving the key individualist intuitions. In the picture we have constructed, attitude attributions have (at least) two aims, communication of evidence about the world and psychological explanation. Ordinary attribution typically combines both purposes. But ordinary attribution need not be regarded as unequivocally tending to accuracy about the nature of attitudes. For while the goal of psychological explanation inclines to subserving truth in attribution, the purpose of communication of evidence about the world has a tendency to deflect the aim at truth about attitudes. In addition, psychological explanation typically does not require maximal precision in specification of attitudes. Thus the ordinary attributions of Kripke's puzzle and Burge's thought-experiments need not be viewed as representing attitudes accurately. Consequently, there might well be room for the concepts of Alfred and his counterpart being the same, and perhaps also for the concepts of Alfred and the expert being different, and Pierre's beliefs might really not be puzzling after all.

III

Our account must now provide a method for content individuation that can support the psychological generalizations we want to make. Let us first consider the causal theories, developed by Dretske, Millikan, and Fodor, which supply a method for content individuation that has become prominent in recent years.[22] The common element in these causal theories is that the cognitive value or psychological meaning of representations is provided by entities or properties that cause them. Causal theories differ in their ways of handling what is perhaps their deepest difficultly, the disjunction problem, which has been outlined by Fodor.[23] To illustrate, 'cow' representations are caused not only by cows but also by bushes on dark nights, and thus a simple causal theory would have 'cow' mean not just *cow* but rather *cow or bush-or-a-dark-night*. The disjunction problem forces causal theories to provide a way of selecting the right causes from all the possible causes of a representation. In Millikan's theory, the right causes are singled out by the notion of proper biological function. In one statement of this view, the content of a belief is C just in case the role that beliefs of this type play, when the mechanisms that produce this belief are fulfilling their proper functions as determined by evolutionary biology, involves being caused by C's.[24] In Fodor's asymmetrical dependence theory, 'cow' means *cow* and not *cow or bush-on-a-dark-night* because 'cow' tokens are caused by things in virtue of being cows, and the existence of 'cow' tokens caused by things in virtue of their being bushes on dark nights depends on the existence of 'cow' tokens caused by things in virtue of their being cows, and not vice-versa. Fodor's idea is that there is a hierarchy of causal dependence among causes of tokens of a mental representation-type, and the property that specifies the psychological meaning or cognitive value of that representation is causally most fundamental.

Many difficulties have been raised for each of these theories.[25] A problem from the perspective of someone swayed by individualist intuitions is that causal theories would seem to acquiesce to Burge's analysis of his thought-experiments. For example, by a causal theory, the 'arthritis' concepts of Alfred and his counterpart would have to differ, since their external-world causes differ—the disease called "arthritis" on earth is not the same disease as the disease called "arthritis" on twin earth. In addition, the 'arthritis' concepts of Alfred and the expert would seem to be identical, no matter how different the associated beliefs were, as long as these concepts were caused by the same disease. Causal theories, therefore, seem unable to preserve the individualist intuitions.

A further problem for causal theories would concern anyone, whether or not her intuitions are individualist. One of the major difficulties for causal views is that they fail to accommodate the results of Fregean tests. Loar's revised version of Kripke's puzzle about belief is especially illustrative here. Pierre acquires the belief '*Londres est jolie*' in France, and then lands up in a pretty part of London, where he acquires the belief 'London is pretty,' without realizing that *Londres* = London. By Frege's test, his concept '*Londres*' is distinct form his concept 'London.' Psychology must hold them distinct, because they play significantly different roles in Pierre's inferences and in the production of his behavior. But their causes might be precisely the same—indeed, the views of London that caused the 'Londres' concept might be the very same as those that caused the 'London' concept.[26]

Fodor proposes to handle this objection by saying that although the *belief contents* of Pierre's beliefs '*Londres est jolie*' and 'London is pretty' are the same, nonetheless the *beliefs* differ.[27] Hence Fodor hopes to retain a causal theory of content, while eschewing a causal theory of belief. As we have seen, Fodor's view is that a belief is a function of four factors, type of attitude, content, vehicle, and functional role. According to his analysis of Kripke's puzzle, the contents and type of attitude of Pierre's two beliefs are the same, whereas their vehicles, or the functional roles of their vehicles, differ.

Such a solution would be satisfactory, if, among other things, Fodor provided us with an account of the individuation of vehicles and their functional roles that would sustain plausible generalizations in psychological explanation. But surprisingly, Fodor argues that psychological explanation can dispense with vehicle and functional role, and embrace only content in his own sense and, presumably, type of attitude.[28] Fodor hopes to exclude vehicles and functional roles from psychological explanation precisely in order to avoid their messy individuation-conditions, while he retains causally individuated content and type of attitude because their individuation-conditions are less problematic. Limited by the resources of type of attitude and content in Fodor's sense, however, psychology will be unable to explain the differences in inference and behavior that emerge from Pierre's failure to identify London and *Londres*. By Fodor's characterization of content, the contents of Pierre's beliefs '*Londres est jolie*' and 'London is pretty' are the same, and they therefore play the same role in psychological explanation. Fodor does have elements in his theory that could explain the differences in inference and behavior resulting from Pierre's failure to identify London and *Londres*. But since he lacks a way to specify when these elements are the same and when they are different, his theory fails to solve one of the fundamental problems for accounts of psychological explanation.

One of the main reasons why theorists have been drawn to causal views about content is to provide a theory that meets the requirements of naturalism, and causal theories are regarded as sufficiently naturalistic in virtue of their capacity to incorporate reductionism. But naturalist requirements, I believe, can be met without any type of reductionism. In my view, furthermore, reductionist theories of content should be rejected for the reason that they cannot individuate content with the accuracy required for psychological explanation. While I will not argue for this general claim here, it is well-illustrated by one of Fodor's counterexamples to Millikan's biological theory of the content of desires.

According to Millikan's view, the content of a desire is provided by its proper biological function. In one formulation of her account, the content of a desire is C just in case the role that desires of this type play, when the mechanisms that produce this desire are fulfilling their proper functions as determined by evolutionary biology, is to cause the organism to secure C's.[29] Fodor's counterargument examines our desire for sweets. By evolutionary biology's account of the proper function of the mechanisms that produce the desire for sweets, the role of this desire is to get the organism to ingest sugars. Consequently, on Millikan's theory, the desire for sweets is correctly described as a desire for sugars. But the desire for sweets is satisfied by saccharine and Nutra-Sweet, and thus, the content of the desire for sweets is just what it seems to be, *for sweets*, and not *for sugars*. The content of the desire for sweets, therefore, cannot be derived from its proper biological function.[30]

Millikan might respond that the desire for sweets might really be the desire for sugars despite Fodor's counterexample, because the possibility of a desire for A being satisfied by something that only appears to be A provides no reason to believe that the desire is really for something that appears to be A. The desire for something sweet being satisfied by Diet Coke (which contains Nutra-Sweet) is much like a desire for a Vermeer painting being satisfied by a van Meegeren forgery. The desire for the Vermeer being satisfied by the forgery does not mean that the desire for a Vermeer is really just a desire for a painting that looks like a Vermeer. Hence, the possibility of our system's being fooled by Nutra-Sweet is not adequate reason to reject the biological account of desire content.

One odd consequence of this response is that despite appearances, Diet Coke *really* fails to satisfy the desire for sweets, just as the forgery *really* doesn't satisfy the desire for a Vermeer. This is counterintuitive, perhaps because if one were asked if one's desire for sweets was satisfied after it was pointed out that the Diet Coke one just consumed contained no sugars, one might well say "yes," whereas if one were asked if one's desire for a Vermeer was satisfied after it was pointed out that the painting one just acquired is a forgery, one would say "no." This provides reason to believe that Fodor's "desire for sweets" case is not one of being fooled by appearances.

But a further counterexample might prove more convincing. By evolutionary biology's account of the proper functions of the mechanisms that produce the desire for sex, the role of this desire is to get the subject to reproduce. Thus on Millikan's account, desire for sex must actually be the desire for reproduction. An unintuitive consequence of this view is that desire for sex would not really be satisfied unless reproduction were attained. One might hold out for the claim that desire for sex is only apparently satisfied when reproduction is not achieved, but this view is far from plausible.

At the root of the difficulty for Millikan's view is that desire for sex plays a role in psychological explanation that is systematically different from the role played by desire for reproduction, despite the fact that the evolutionary purpose of the desire for sex is to get the organism to reproduce. This problem, one might note, is generated not by assuming intrinsic intentionality, or supposing a privileged introspective point of view, or assuming that causal powers cannot be relationally individuated, but solely by reflection on the actual practice of psychological explanation. And thus the relation between evolutionary biology and psychology is not as close as Millikan makes it out to be. Evolution can achieve its aims by granting us a system of beliefs and desires—a psychology. But this psychology is significantly independent of evolutionary theory for the individuation of its kinds. In the case of sexual desire, we form a desire not for reproduction, but for the intimacy and sensory pleasures associated with sex. This strategy is perhaps a better way for evolution to secure reproduction than by having us form a desire to reproduce *per se*. Similarly, given our natural environment, a desire for the sensory pleasure provided by sweet tastes may well be a more efficient way to make us ingest sugars than would a desire for sugars *per se*, especially if this alternative would involve representing their chemical structure. In both cases, psychological content cannot be determined by evolutionary biological considerations alone.

These reflections suggest that it is advantageous to regard individuation of psychological content as largely independent of evolutionary biological considerations. A reductionist evolutionary biological theory seems unable to individuate psychological states with the accuracy required for psychological explanation. More generally, I favor the nonreductive view according to which content individuation is largely independent of all more basic scientific theories.[31] In recent papers, Stephen Stich and Michael Tye have argued convincingly that the nonreductive strategy can be applied to a theory of content.[32] They maintain, correctly, I believe, that for content to be naturalistic, it need not be reduced to the non-intentional, for if psychology meets the criteria of a true *scientia* in its own right, and the entities it posits are constituted by entities over which physics quantifies, worries about its naturalistic credentials can be laid to rest.

IV

If one wishes to reject the various well-known externalisms, such as the views of Burge and Millikan, and if one wants to provide adequate foundations for psychology, one must provide reason to believe that a satisfying alternative theory of psychological content individuation is in the offing. Externalist theories provide a workable, although perhaps imperfect theory of content individuation, and if one has no indication of a better option, it would be best to appropriate some form of externalism despite its counterintuitive features. Psychology is very likely to require some method of content individuation, and it might have to settle for the best one available despite imperfections. I shall argue that there is a promising alternative to the foremost externalist theories, and that this alternative that does not suffer from the difficulties faced by the functional role theories that have been advanced.

According to functional role theories, the content of a mental state is a function of the perceptual inputs, behavioral outputs, and the other mental states to which the state is causally related. The main problem for this type of view is that it appears to lack any principled and satisfying method for classifying token-distinct psychological states as having the same content. My belief that it is raining likely has a somewhat different causal role than your belief that it is raining, and so functional role theory might well class them as being beliefs of different types. But this method of individuation precludes the kinds of generalizations in psychological explanation that we want to make.

A strategy for content individuation within a framework that rejects certain well-known externalisms has recently been developed by Bilgrami. According to his proposal, the cognitive value of a subject's concept is individuated solely by the beliefs associated with that concept.[33] His strategy, as he himself points out, must have the resources to solve three problems.[34] The first of these we have already explored: A theory in which the cognitive value of a concept is individuated solely by the beliefs associated with the concept (at a time) will cut cognitive value too finely, since when cognitive value is determined in this way it will not sustain plausible psychological generalizations. Second, if all of a subject's associated beliefs were relevant to individuating the cognitive value of a concept, any change in belief would amount to a change in the cognitive value of a concept. And if any change in belief would amount to a change in cognitive value, then a subject could not deepen or broaden her grasp of any one concept. Third, if the cognitive value of a concept were determined by associated beliefs, then concepts that these beliefs involve would constitute the psychological meaning (although perhaps not the linguistic meaning) of that concept, and hence, they would be analytic of it (in one traditional sense).[35] A theory of this sort, therefore, would seem to reintroduce a version of the analytic/synthetic distinction, which, for Quinean reasons, might be unappealing.

Bilgrami proposes to solve these problems by an appeal to context. Only in some abstract sense is the cognitive value for some term individuated by all of the subject's beliefs associated with it. In any specific situation, the context will select a subset of those beliefs to determine the cognitive value for the term. Alfred and the expert may share the belief that Alfred's mother has arthritis in her fingers, in part because in the context of attribution all of the beliefs relevant to individuating the cognitive value for 'arthritis' are possessed by both subjects. In addition, change of belief is possible without change of cognitive value because the beliefs that a context designates as relevant to individuating the cognitive value for a term may not include those that change.[36] Finally, since distinct beliefs are selected to provide the cognitive value or psychological meaning for a term in different contexts, it could well be that no particular concepts provide the psychological meaning for a term in all contexts, and thus no particular concepts would be analytic of a term.[37]

Bilgrami does not tell us in any detail, however, how context might play the role he envisions, for example, how context indicates which beliefs of Alfred and the doctor would be relevant to individuating the cognitive value for the term 'arthritis.' The details of his contextual theory are important, because they would constitute the principles that determine how generalizations in psychology are to be made, and how cognitive value can remain stable despite variation in associated beliefs. The seriousness of the problem becomes clear when we bring to mind that a theory of attribution, at minimum, must meet two requirements. First, it must illuminate, rather than merely reduce to, our intuitions about attribution in particular cases. Second, the theory must be testable against such particular intuitions about attribution. If, however, Bilgrami fails to provide principles that specify the relations between contexts and attributions, the theory does indeed threaten to reduce to our intuitions about particular cases. If he insists that nevertheless the theory does more work than such intuitions do, but he supplies no principles that specify the relations between contexts and attributions, we will have no clear way of distinguishing between the deliverances of the theory and our intuitions. And if we cannot make these distinctions, we will have no way of testing whether the theory is true.

It is doubtful, however, that the principles Bilgrami needs to supplement his contextual theory can be provided. Perhaps the relations between contexts and attributions are much too complex to be formulated in a useful way. One might thus argue that a contextual account without general principles for individuation of content might be the best theory available. But one should agree that if there were a theory that supplied such principles, then there would be some reason to favor such a view.

V

Practices in other sciences suggest a more promising strategy for individuating content. When we classify entities as members of the same or different kinds in chemistry and biology, we often look to structural features of these entities. The stuff in streams and the stuff in oceans is of the same type because it has the same chemical structure. We consider different human beings to be members of the same species partly because of similar genetic structure. Recent work in cognitive psychology indicates that many concepts also have structure of various sorts, and consequently there might be a basis, similar to those in other sciences, for evaluating questions about sameness and difference of these concepts, and also of the content of which these concepts are components. In the last two decades, significant insight into conceptual structure has been achieved. But much more remains to be done, and accordingly, what follows is not meant to constitute an actual theory of content individuation, but rather a suggestion for the direction such a theory might take.

Conceptual structure will be valuable for individuating concepts and content if from among the beliefs associated with a concept it provides a way of selecting some as more weighty than others. Since concepts are essentially connected with a complex of abilities that includes classification, identification, and recognition, one might aim to isolate the associated beliefs that are most salient for these abilities.

Cognitive psychologists have recently argued for what has come to be known as *psychological essentialism*.[38] This is not the view that things have essences, but rather that our representations of things of some kinds are structured by beliefs of them as having essences. According to this theory, these experimentally identifiable beliefs play a much more important part than others in our classification of such things. For example, many natural kind and some artifact concepts are structured by an assumption that internal properties of the things falling under those concepts are causally responsible for their surface properties, and that these internal properties are more important than their surface properties for the things being what they are. Hence, when we classify such things, their internal properties have a much more influential function in carrying out these tasks than do their surface properties. Sometimes actual concepts of the internal properties play the crucial part in the structure of the concept, but often a *placeholder conception*, like 'whatever the experts believe to cause the symptoms of the disease called "arthritis"' or 'whatever internal properties really cause the symptoms of the disease called "arthritis"' has the decisive role.[39]

One of the most significant features of psychological essentialism is that it provides a principled and empirically testable way to determine which beliefs play the central role in structuring certain concepts. Let us consider two examples. In one experiment performed by Susan Gelman and Henry Wellman, four- and five-year olds were asked for items like dogs and cars whether their insides or their outsides were more important for being what they are. For example, they were asked to consider the following situations: "What if you take out the stuff inside a dog, the blood and bones and things like that and got rid of it and all you have left are the outsides?" and "What if you take the stuff outside of the dog, you know, the fur and got rid of it and all you have left are the insides?" They were asked two kinds of questions about the transformed entity, an *identity* question like "Is it still a dog?" and a *function* question such as "Can it still bark and eat dog food?" For the identity question, 72% of the responses indicated that the entity is no longer what it was when the insides are removed, while 35% indicated that it is no longer what it was when the outsides are removed. 92% indicated that the functions are lost when the insides are removed, 29% when the outsides are removed.[40] Experiments of this sort provide evidence that young children's conceptions of internal properties of dogs and cars—despite their lack of detailed knowledge of these properties—play a more crucial role in classifying such things than do conceptions of surface properties.

In another study, Gelman and Wellman told four-year olds about an animal that was brought up in an environment suited to a different species, and questioned the children in order to determine whether they believed the animal developed innate potentialities, or instead displayed the properties associated with the environment of upbringing. For example, they asked about a cow who was raised by pigs what her mature physical features would be like, for example whether her tail would be straight or curly, and what her mature behavior would be like, for instance whether she would say "moo" or "oink." Overall, children answered on the basis of innate potential 85% of the time. Experiments like this provide evidence that young children's conceptions of internal properties of animals figure more prominently in inferences about category membership—how it is to be classified—than do conceptions of environment and nurture.[41]

If psychological essentialism can be established, then from among the many beliefs associated with certain types of entities, we can experimentally isolate a core group that is most significant for classification. One should note that psychological essentialism does not specify that the only beliefs at the core of the structure of a concept, even for natural kind concepts, are about essences. Psychological essentialism marks only the beliefs especially important for one type of conceptual ability, classification. Similar research might be carried out for other abilities associated with concepts, such as identification and recognition, and it might reveal specific types of core beliefs connected with these abilities as well.

In addition, not every classificatory concept has the sort of psychological essentialist structure we have encountered. Functional concepts, for example, are not likely to involve supposition of an internal essence that is causally responsible for surface properties. But at the core of the structure of such concepts we might well find a belief about a functional definition or about a corresponding placeholder conception. At the core of the concept 'carburetor' we might discover the belief that a carburetor is a device that mixes air with gasoline for internal combustion, and for those who cannot produce such a definition, we might find the belief that nevertheless there is a definition for a carburetor and that mechanics know what it is.

But still, psychological essences of the sort that Gelman and Wellman have investigated provide a paradigm for individuating the cognitive value of concepts by structural features. By appealing to similarities and differences in the core group of beliefs associated with certain concepts we can judge the cognitive value of various instantiations of these concepts to be the same or different. The kinds of tests Gelman, Wellman and others have developed can be used to confirm hypotheses about similarity in conceptual structure both within persons over time and across different persons. Psychological essentialism, therefore, provides us with a good example of the type of structure a concept may have, a model for individuating the cognitive value of concepts by such structure, and empirical procedures for determining structural intra- and interpersonal similarity.

Further reflection indicates how individuation of the cognitive value of concepts by their structural features might illuminate the three difficulties Bilgrami raises for theories that individuate content by associated beliefs: first, the problem of finding a method for avoiding individuation of content that is too fine-grained, and, more broadly, of finding a method for individuating content in just the right way; second, the specter of losing the distinction between change in belief and change in meaning; and third, the threat of reintroducing analyticity.

On the first issue, individuation by conceptual structure remedies functional role theory's lack of a principled and satisfying method for classifying token-distinct psychological states as having the same content. We might endorse, for example, the principle that beliefs about essential properties carry more weight for individuation than do beliefs about accidental properties, as well as similar principles derived from a study of identification and recognition. Suppose, then, that two scientists are thoroughly knowledgeable about arthritis, but yet the functional roles of their 'arthritis' concepts differ somewhat. We can nevertheless attribute the same concept to them at least in part because they agree on the defining properties of arthritis, and they use a similar set of core beliefs to identify and recognize arthritis.

Individuation by conceptual structure can also help account for the intuition that, in Burge's case, psychological explanation could require that Alfred and the expert be attributed distinct 'arthritis' concepts. Suppose that Alfred has some beliefs about arthritis, but does not know its defining properties. He also has a placeholder conception constituted by the belief that arthritis is a disease characterized by whatever internal properties explain the symptoms of what people in his society call "arthritis". In addition, he has some false beliefs about arthritis, and he lacks a significant measure of the beliefs that would enable him to identify and recognize arthritis at the expert level. In this situation, the difference between the core structures that function in Alfred's and the expert's conceptions of arthritis might well be significant enough to constitute a distinction in their concepts' cognitive value. Individuation by conceptual structure might, therefore, distinguish between concepts' contributions to content where some externalist views would prescind from such a difference. And thus this method potentially provides a better account of certain key intuitions about the kinds of generalizations we need to make in psychological explanation.

In addition, individuation by conceptual structure can also account for the intuition that in Burge's case, psychological explanation could require that Alfred and his counterpart be attributed the same 'arthritis' concepts. Suppose again that Alfred and his counterpart do not differ with respect to any non-intentional individualistic feature. Both believe that the word 'arthritis' refers to certain rheumatoid ailments not only of the joints but also of the muscles and tendons. Both lack a significant proportion of the beliefs that would enable them, in their respective societies and environments, to classify, identify, and recognize arthritis at the expert level. And each has a placeholder conception that he would express as "a disease characterized by whatever internal properties explain the symptoms of what people in my society call "arthritis"." Under these circumstances, individuation by structural features of concepts would authorize attribution of the same 'arthritis' concepts to each, despite the fact that the standards of ordinary attribution practice would prevent us from doing so.

But how could an attribution practice indicate the similarity in their belief contents? It would be misleading to do so by attributing to each the unqualified belief that he has arthritis in his thigh. For as we have argued, although attributing to Alfred the belief that he has arthritis in his thigh would be warranted by ordinary practice, it might well be mistaken to take it as an accurate report of his attitude. To capture Alfred's concept precisely, we might need to hedge our attribution as we just did, by specifying that although Alfred has such and such a placeholder conception, he lacks a significant measure of the beliefs at the core of the 'arthritis' concept.' And thus the similarity in their attitude-contents would not be captured accurately by attributing to each the unqualified belief that he has arthritis in his thigh.

But perhaps attributing to each a qualified 'arthritis' concept, in a single language, might indicate the similarity accurately enough. For the purposes of communication of evidence about the world it would not be pragmatically valuable to attribute to Alfred or to his counterpart a concept in a language that the audience—typically his own community—does not speak. But if we prescind from that purpose, the peculiarity vanishes. For the purpose of psychological explanation, we may need to attribute the same concept to Alfred and his counterpart, and there could well be different languages by which to characterize that concept.

These claims have implications for the truth-conditions of beliefs. In Burge's view, the content of Alfred's belief, which one might ordinarily express by 'that he has arthritis in his thigh,' makes a contribution to a truth-condition that is context-dependent only for the indexical components specified by 'he' and 'his.' But if we suppose that the beliefs of Alfred and his counterpart have the same content, and that Alfred's belief is false whereas the counterpart's is true, then the truth-condition of Alfred's belief cannot be context-dependent only to this degree. For nothing else besides a context-dependent element of the truth conditions of the two beliefs could make the difference in their truth-values, and what makes the difference in these truth values is independent of the contribution of the indexicals 'he' and 'his.' It clearly would have to be the contribution to truth conditions of 'arthritis,' or whatever words or phrases occupy the position of this term in an accurate attribution, that makes for the additional context-dependence in the truth conditions.

A good candidate for a context-sensitive component in Alfred's 'arthritis' concept is the placeholder conception. In the placeholder conception 'a disease characterized by whatever internal properties explain the symptoms of what people in my society call "arthritis"' there is indeed a context-sensitive element. For Alfred, the description 'what people in my society call "arthritis"' will refer to the disease called "arthritis" in English, whereas for the counterpart this description will refer to the disease called "arthritis" in twin-English. Or if the placeholder conception makes explicit reference to experts, in Alfred's conception the term 'the experts' will refer to the experts on earth, whereas in the counterpart's conception the term 'the experts' will refer to the experts on twin earth. Hence, concepts that in Burge's scheme do not introduce context-dependence into truth conditions do introduce such context-dependence in the view we are considering.

Let us now turn to the second difficulty Bilgrami raises. If a concept is to retain its cognitive value despite change in associated beliefs, some anchor must be available to provide stability for cognitive value when such change occurs. The reason that functional role theories have failed to supply such anchors is that the required distinctions among the beliefs associated with a concept—distinctions that would allow some of these beliefs to play a more prominent role than others in determining the cognitive value of a concept—have not been made in a principled way. But psychological essentialism's illumination of classification, and similar results for identification and recognition, would allow for principled distinctions based on conceptual structure. If we individuate the cognitive value of a concept by core beliefs, then it can remain the same despite change in the beliefs other than those at the core. Change of cognitive value would occur only when change occurs in the beliefs at the core of the concept's structure.

The third problem Bilgrami points out is that individuating the cognitive value of a concept by the beliefs of the subject risks making certain concepts analytic of that concept. And indeed, individuation in accord with structural features like those posited by psychological essentialism entails this result, for concepts involved in beliefs found at the core of a concept would constitute its psychological meaning, and would, in one sense, be analytic of it. But as Hilary Kornblith points out, this admission does not contravene the Quinean opposition to analyticity.[42] Quine's opposition focusses on the connection between analyticity and apriority, but the type of investigation into the structural core of a concept we have considered is decidedly empirical. In the view we have been developing, conceptual analysis is a significant and fruitful project, but it does not manifest the objectionable features that are challenged by Quine's arguments.

Thus we can see how an appeal to conceptual structure might solve the kinds of problems that arise for a theory of content in which individuation by associated beliefs plays a central role. An account of this kind provides criteria for conceptual identity and difference, allows us to distinguish between change of psychological meaning and change of belief, and shows how a theory of content can accommodate a plausible notion of analyticity. A rejection of recent externalist views about content, therefore, might well be compatible with a psychology that is plausible, principled, and empirical.

Let us now consider two objections to the view we have been developing. First, one might argue that the belief attributions made in the psychological essentialist experiments themselves have as purposes both psychological explanation and communication of evidence about the world. And thus these attributions cannot be assumed to indicate psychological content unequivocally. Much that may seem to be of psychological interest in these attributions may subserve the goal of communication of evidence about the world, and not of psychological explanation, and hence, by my own conjecture, they may deflect the aim at truth about psychological content. Consequently, I have not shown that a theory of psychological content can avail itself of the claims about conceptual structure made by theorists like Gelman and Wellman.

But this objection is mistaken. As became clear in our discussion of Kripke's puzzle, our attributions might aim (mainly) at one goal rather than the other, and differences in purpose will result in differences in attribution. Since the dominant purpose of the psychological essentialist experiments is to provide instruments for explaining inference and behavior, and not to communicate evidence about the objects used in the experiments to an audience, we have reason to believe that the attributions in the experiments are aimed at specifying psychological content. Moreover, it is difficult to see how the crucial features of the experiments, for example, the attribution to the children of the view that internal properties of animals are more important than surface properties for being what they are, might be understood as a function of the aim to communicate evidence about these animals to an audience. The implausibility of this conjecture provides further reason to take the crucial attributions in the psychological essentialist experiments to illuminate real psychological content.

A further objection derives from an anti-individualist argument for prototype theory developed by Bernard Kobes.[43] Kobes points out that, in general, psychology aims to explain not only behavior, but also a subject's classificatory successes and failures. But, he argues, this normative dimension cannot be facilitated if a concept's range of correct application is explained solely in terms of the individual subject's articulations and dispositions. A subject's articulations and dispositions are often insufficient for specifying the range of correct application of the concepts she has, while she is yet committed to there being such a range of correct application. This background commitment, then, should lead us to fix the range of her concept's application non-individualistically: "it is fixed in part by the subject's natural and social environment."[44]

This objection transfers easily to the psychological essentialist view we have been considering: although the articulations and dispositions of the subjects in the psychological essentialist experiments are insufficient to specify the range of correct application of their concepts, these subjects are yet committed to there being such a range. We must therefore individuate the subjects' concepts non-individualistically, and we are thus led back to an externalist account of the sort Burge has advocated. But, in reply, there is an account of the range of correct application of the relevant concepts for which the articulations and dispositions of the subject do suffice. For the commitment of the subjects to a range of correct application, and the deference to experts and to the world that this commitment involves, will be reflected in such articulations and dispositions. This commitment can be explained by the sort of placeholder conception we have been discussing. A placeholder conception does not specify the range of correct application in the way that a completed science would, but rather with the aid of conceptions like 'whatever the experts believe to cause the symptoms of the disease called "arthritis"' or 'whatever internal properties really cause the symptoms of the disease called "arthritis."' To discover the *extension* of a placeholder conception we must certainly examine the world beyond the individual, just as is the case for conceptions like 'the first person born in the twentieth century' and 'that man over there.' But we have encountered no reason to think that a placeholder conception *itself* is to be individuated with reference to factors beyond the individual subject's articulations and dispositions.

Let me make three points of clarification about the account as it has been developed so far. First, individuation of content by structural features may serve as a welcome supplement to functional role theory. Such a view about individuation might well supply the principled criteria for sameness of content that functional role theories require. But one might also accept individuation by structural features and reject functional role theory if one were to deny that content is solely a function of relations to perceptual inputs, behavioral outputs, and other states.[45] Second, it is consistent with this account, which focusses on the psychological explanation of inference and behavior, that there are other branches of psychology for which attributions of content should be externalist in one or more of the senses we have discussed. Perhaps the psychology of perception is one of those branches, but I shall not take a stand on this issue here.[46] Third, for all I have argued so far, there may be externalist factors relevant to content attribution even when psychological explanation of inference and behavior is at issue. I have argued that for the psychological explanation of such phenomena, *certain prominent* externalisms may well be inappropriate, and that in order to specify sameness and difference of content, one might turn instead to structural features of concepts. This leaves room for the appropriateness of other sorts of externalist characterizations of content for this type of psychology. But I shall not pursue this issue any further here.

VI

In summary, several prominent externalist theories of content conflict with some of our intuitions about psychological explanation. And thus, although individuation of content in accord with these externalisms could suffice for most epistemic and psychological purposes, such views might well be inadequate when certain recalcitrant cases of psychological explanation are at issue. Furthermore, functional role theories seem to lack any principled and satisfying method of classifying token-distinct psychological states as having the same type of content. Recent exploration of the structural features of concepts, however, potentially supplies the kinds of resources needed to individuate content in a way that yields the generalizations in psychological explanation we want to make. At this stage a theory of content individuation along these lines can be neither fully spelled out nor confirmed. But such a theory does underwrite an ongoing empirical research program that will ultimately determine its prospects.[47]

Notes

1.   Hilary Putnam, "The meaning of 'meaning'," in Hilary Putnam, *Philosophical papers*,

v. 2 (Cambridge: Harvard University Press, 1975), pp. 215-271; Saul A. Kripke, *Naming and Necessity* (Cambridge: Harvard University Press, 1980); "A Puzzle About Belief," in *Meaning and Use*, ed. A. Margalit (Dordrecht, D. Reidel, 1979); Tyler Burge, "Individualism and the Mental," in *Midwest Studies in Philosophy* v. VI, eds. P. French, T. Uehling, H. Wettstein (Minneapolis: University of Minnesota Press, 1978), pp. 73-121; see also, his "Other Bodies," in *Though and Content*, ed. A. Woodfield (Oxford: Oxford University Press, 1979), pp. 97-120; "Two Thought Experiments Reviewed," *Notre Dame Journal of Formal Logic*, 23 (1982), pp. 284-293; "Individualism and Psychology," *Philosophical Review* 95 (1986), pp. 3-45; "Individuation and Causation in Psychology," *Pacific Philosophical Quarterly* 70 (1989), pp. 303-322; Lynne R. Baker, *Saving Belief* (Princeton: Princeton University Press, 1987); Ruth Millikan, *Language, Thought, and Other Biological Categories* (Cambridge: MIT Press, 1984), "Thoughts Without Laws: Cognitive Science Without Content," *Philosophical Review* 95 (1986), pp. 47-80; Daniel Dennett, "Evolution, Error, and Intentionality," in *The Intentional Stance* (Cambridge: MIT Press, 1987), pp. 287-321.

2.	Ned Block, "An Advertisement for a Semantics for Psychology," in *Midwest Studies in Philosophy*, v. X, ed. P. French, T. Uehling, H. Wettstein (Minneapolis: University of Minnesota Press, 1986, pp. 615-678; Brian Loar, "Conceptual Role and Truth Conditions," *Notre Dame Journal of Formal Logic* 23 (1982), pp. 272-283, "Social Content and Psychological Content," in *Contents of Thoughts*, ed. R. H. Grimm and D. D. Merill (Tucson: The University of Arizona Press, 1985), pp. 99-110. In some functional role theories content does not supervene on the physical features of the individual; see, for example, Gilbert Harman, "Functional Role Semantics," *Notre Dame Journal of Formal Logic* 23 (1982), pp. 242-256, and "Wide Functionalism," in *The Representation of Knowledge and Belief*, eds. R. Harnish and M. Brand (Tucson: University of Arizona Press, 1986).

3.	Ned Block, "An Advertisement for a Semantics for Psychology;" Jerry Fodor, "Banish DisContent," in *Language, Mind, and Logic*, ed. J. Butterfield (Cambridge: Cambridge University Press, 1986), reprinted in *Mind and Cognition*, ed. William G. Lycan (Oxford: Blackwell, 1990), pp. 420-438, "Meaning Holism," in *Psychosemantics* (Cambridge MIT Press, 1987), "Substitution Arguments and the Individuation of Beliefs," in *A Theory of Content and Other Essays* (Cambridge: MIT Press, 1990), pp. 161-176, at pp. 161-2.

4.	See, for example, Brian Loar, "Social Content and Psychological Content;" Akeel Bilgrami, *Belief and Meaning* (Oxford: Blackwell, 1992), pp. 1-63.

5.	David Kaplan, "Demonstratives," in *Propositions and Attitudes*, eds. Nathan Salmon and Scott Soames (Oxford: Oxford University Press, 1979).

6.	Jerry Fodor, "Substitution Arguments and the Individuation of Beliefs," 167-8.

7.	See, for example, Fodor, "Banish DisContent" and Bilgrami, *Belief and Meaning*, pp. 30-1.

8.	Gottlob Frege, "On Sense and Reference," in *Translations of the Philosophical Writings of Gottlob Frege*, eds. P. Geach and M. Black (Oxford: Blackwell, 1966).

9.	Saul A. Kripke, *Naming and Necessity*; "A Puzzle About Belief," at pp. 241-2.

10.	Ibid. pp. 241-2.

11.	Brian Loar, "Social Content and Psychological Content."

12.	Bilgrami, *Belief and Meaning*, 16-19.

13.	Tyler Burge, "Sinning Against Frege," *Philosophical Review* (1979), pp. 398-432.

14. Tyler Burge, "Individualism and the Mental."

15. In "Social Content and Psychological Content" Loar argues that a Fregean puzzle reinforces these sorts of problems for Burge's anti-individualist theory of cognitive value. The following case illustrates Loar's contention. Suppose that Alfred is French, and he believes '*J'ai de l'arthrite à ma cuisse*,' and we therefore attribute to him the belief that he has arthritis in his thigh, using our concept of arthritis—a concept which we also attribute to the experts. On one occasion he travels to England, where he learns, in English, the meaning of the experts' conception of 'arthritis,' including that it refers to a disease of the joints. Reflecting on the pain in his thigh, and the fact that the thigh is not a joint, he comes to believe the English sentence 'I do not have arthritis in my thigh.' But he maintains the belief '*J'ai de l'arthrite à ma cuisse*' for many months, not realizing that *arthrite* = arthritis. But then one day he makes the connection that *arthrite* = arthritis, which is informative for him. This belief has profound effects on his inferences, the first of which is the abandonment of the belief '*J'ai de l'arthrite à ma cuisse*.' This is intended to show that the cognitive value of the expert's concept is distinct from that of Alfred's original 'arthritis' concept. One might imagine a similar example, all in English, in which for a time after Alfred learns from the experts that arthritis is a disease of the joints, he believes that there are two diseases called arthritis. (Perhaps he believes that 'arthritis' is like 'fruit,' a word with two distinct definitions whose extensions overlap. By both definitions apples are fruits, but peas are so by only one.) But then he comes to believe that arthritis = arthritis, which for him, at that time, is informative.

    This type of Fregean puzzle does not, however, help to show that the cognitive value of Alfred's and the expert's concepts are distinct. One should note that it departs from the form of Frege's original puzzle, since it aims to demonstrate an interpersonal rather than an intrapersonal difference in cognitive value—a difference in cognitive value between Alfred and the expert rather than within Alfred. But such extension of Frege's test would draw distinctions in cognitive value where they do not exist. Consider this counterexample. Suppose Alfred's French counterpart has precisely the same beliefs about arthritis that Alfred has, except that the counterpart would express them in French, and that the inference and behavior associated with these 'arthritis' concepts are as similar as they can be for people who speak different languages. We would want to make psychological generalizations that regard these concepts as having the same cognitive value. But we could imagine Alfred travelling to France, learning his counterpart's '*arthrite*' beliefs, believing, for a time, that he has two different ailments in his thigh, and later coming to the informative realization that arthritis = *arthrite*. Hence, this interpersonal Fregean test would illegitimately distinguish the concepts of Alfred and his counterpart.

16. Tyler Burge, "Sinning against Frege," at p. 419; see also his "Individualism and Psychology," p. 7, and "Belief *De Re*," *Journal of Philosophy* 56 (1978), pp. 338-362.

17. John Perry, "Belief and Acceptance," *Midwest Studies in Philosophy* V (Minneapolis: University of Minnesota Press, 1980), pp. 533-542; Donald Davidson, "Knowing One's Own Mind," Presidential Address, Pacific Division Meeting of the American Philosophical Association, March 28, 1986, *Proceedings of the American Philosophical Association*, pp. 441-458, at p. 449; Michael Devitt, "A Narrow Representational Theory of the Mind" in *Mind and Cognition*, ed. William G. Lycan (Oxford: Blackwell, 1990), pp. 371-398.

18. Devitt, p. 389.

19. "A Puzzle About Belief," p. 259.

20. In the "unarticulated constituent" account of Mark Crimmons and John Perry ("The Prince and the Phone Booth: Reporting Puzzling Beliefs," *The Journal of Philosophy* 86 (1989), pp. 685-711) and in the "hidden indexical" theory of Stephen Schiffer ("Belief Ascription," *The Journal of Philosophy* 89 (1992), pp. 499-521), ordinary belief attributions are construed as always making implicit reference to modes of presentation. Thus 'Pierre believes that London is pretty' specifies not simply a two-place relation between Pierre and the proposition *that London is pretty*, but a three-place relation among Pierre, the proposition, and an unarticulated mode of presentation under which Pierre believes the proposition. If the unarticulated modes of presentation for Pierre's two beliefs are different, then we have a solution to Kripke's puzzle. These semantical accounts are compatible with my views, but a thorough examination of essentially semantical issues is beyond the scope of this article.

21. See, for example, "Individualism and Psychology," p. 7.

22. Fred Dretske, *Knowledge and the Flow of Information* (Cambridge: MIT Press, 1981); Ruth Millikan, *Language, Thought, and Other Biological Categories* (Cambridge: MIT Press, 1984), "Thoughts Without Laws: Cognitive Science Without Content," *Philosophical Review* 95 (1986), pp. 47-80; Jerry Fodor, *A Theory of Content and Other Essays* (Cambridge, MIT Press, 1990), pp. 51-136; see also Mohan Matthen, "Biological Functions and Perceptual Content," *Journal of Philosophy* 85 (1988), pp. 5-27.

23. Jerry Fodor, *A Theory of Content and Other Essays*, pp. 59-61.

24. Ruth Millikan, "Thoughts Without Laws, Cognitive Science Without Content," pp. 67-71.

25. Fodor provides a splendid catalogue of these problems in his *A Theory of Content and Other Essays*, pp. 51-136. See also William Seager, "Fodor's Theory of Content," *Philosophy of Science* 60 (1993), pp. 262-277.

26. Bilgrami, *Belief and Meaning*, pp. 58-60.

27. Jerry Fodor, "Substitution Arguments and the Individuation of Beliefs."

28. Ibid, pp. 168, 174-5.

29. Ruth Millikan, "Thoughts Without Laws, Cognitive Science Without Content," pp. 63-67. The view cited here is similar to Fodor's refinement of Millikan's idea in *A Theory of Content* (pp. 69-70). Daniel Dennett remarks, citing Millikan "...so evolution can select an organ *for* its capacity to oxygenate blood, can establish it *as* a lung. And it is only relative to such design "choices" or evolution-"endorsed" purposes—*raisons d'être* that we can identify behaviors, actions, perceptions, beliefs, or any of the other categories of folk psychology" ("Evolution, Error, and Intentionality," in *The Intentional Stance* (Cambridge: MIT Press, 1987), pp. 287-321, at p. 300).

   One might suggest that a biological account of psychological content avail itself of Millikan's device of a *most proximate Normal explanation* (Ruth Millikan, *Language, Thought, and Other Biological Categories*, Chapter 6, at p. 100). But it is difficult to see how this device can solve the problems that Fregean puzzles raise for causal theories. For example, it would seem unable to differentiate in a satisfactory way between Pierre's 'London' and '*Londres*' concepts, since even the very same views of London might be the most proximate cause of each of them (while the mechanisms that produce the attitude in question are fulfilling their proper function as determined by evolutionary biology).

30. Jerry Fodor, *A Theory of Content and Other Essays*, p. 77.

31. Richard Boyd, "Materialism Without Reductionism: What Physicalism Does Not

Entail," in *Readings in the Philosophy of Psychology*, v. 1, ed. Ned Block (Cambridge: Harvard University Press, 1980), pp. 67-106; Jerry Fodor, "Special Sciences," in *Readings in the Philosophy of Psychology*, v. 1, pp. 120-133; Hilary Putnam, "The Nature of Mental States," in *Readings in the Philosophy of Psychology*, v. 1, pp. 223-231, "Philosophy and Our Mental Life'" in *Readings in the Philosophy of Psychology*, v. 1, pp. 134-143; Derk Pereboom and Hilary Kornblith, "The Metaphysics of Irreducibility," *Philosophical Studies* 63 (1991), pp. 125-145.

32. Stephen Stich, "What is a Theory of Mental Representation?" *Mind* 101 (1992), pp. 243-261; Michael Tye, "Naturalism and the Mental," *Mind* 101 (1992), pp. 421-441.

33. Bilgrami, *Belief and Meaning*, pp. 10-13.

34. Ibid, pp. 10-13, 83-129.

35. In one Kantian sense, a judgment is analytic in virtue of concept-containment; cf. *Critique of Pure Reason*, A6/B10-A10/B14.

36. Bilgrami, *Belief and Meaning*, pp. 122-9.

37. Ibid, pp. 83-113.

38. Douglas Medin and Andrew Ortony, "Psychological Essentialism," in *Similarity and analogical reasoning*, eds. S. Vosniadou and A. Ortony (Cambridge: Cambridge University Press, 1989) pp. 179-195; Douglas Medin, "Concepts and Conceptual Structure," *American Psychologist*, v. 44, n. 12, pp. 1469-1481.

39. For a notion similar to the placeholder conception, see Georges Rey's "Concepts and Stereotypes: A Reply to Smith, Medin, and Rips," *Cognition* 19 (1985), pp. 197-303.

40. Susan A. Gelman and Henry M. Wellman, "Insides and essences: Early understandings of the non-obvious," *Cognition* 38 (1991), pp. 213-244, at pp. 223-229.

41. Ibid, pp. 229-234.

42. Hilary Kornblith, *Inductive Inference and Its Natural Ground* (Cambridge: MIT Press, 1993), p. 80.

43. Bernard W. Kobes, "Semantics and Psychological Prototypes," *Pacific Philosophical Quarterly* 70 (1989), pp. 1-18.

44. Ibid, p. 10. Dispositions and articulations of the sort that Kobes discusses, and an anti-individualist argument based on them, are examined in depth in Tyler Burge's "Wherein is Language Social," in *Propositional Attitudes: the Role of Content in Logic, Language, and Mind*, eds. C. Anthony Anderson and Joseph Owens (Stanford: Center for the Study of Language and Information, 1990), pp. 113-130, esp. 122-130.

45. Derk Pereboom, "Why a Scientific Realist Cannot Be a Functionalist," *Synthese* 88, (1991), pp. 341-358.

46. See Tyler Burge, "Individualism and Psychology;" Bernard W. Kobes, "Individualism and Artificial Intelligence" in *Philosophical Perspectives, 4, Action Theory and Philosophy of Mind, 1990*, ed. James Tomberlin (Atascadero, CA: Ridgeview Publishing Company, 1990); "Cartesian Error and the Objectivity of Perception," in *Contents of Thoughts*, ed. R. H. Grimm and D. D. Merrill (Tucson: The University of Arizona Press, 1985); Gabriel Segal, "Seeing What is Not There," *The Philosophical Review* 98 (1989), pp. 189-214; Frances Egan, "Must Psychology Be Individualistic?" *The Philosophical Review* 100 (1991), pp. 179-203.

47. I want to thank Lynne Rudder Baker, David Christensen, Hilary Kornblith, and Bernard Kobes for enlightening commentary and discussion.

Philosophical Perspectives, 9, AI, Connectionism, and Philosophical Psychology, 1995

LAW AND ORDER IN PSYCHOLOGY

Louise Antony
University of North Carolina, Chapel Hill

There's an old Yiddish joke that my husband tells better than I do and that goes like this: this guy walks up to his rabbi and says "Rabbi, I have a question. Why should there be a *gimmel* in 'eretz'?" The rabbi looks puzzled: "But there is no *gimmel* in 'eretz'." "Well, then," continues the man, "why *shouldn't* there be a *gimmel* in 'eretz?'" "Well, why *should* there be a *gimmel* in 'eretz?'" "Rabbi, that's what I asked *you*!"

This pretty much sums up, *mutatis mutandis*, the debate about laws in psychology. The burden of proof flies like a volley ball back and forth between those who insist that there *can't* be any laws in psychology and those who think that there *must* be laws in psychology. What makes the issue such a hot potato is this: certain undeniable facts about human life and experience appear to imply the existence of laws governing mental activity. At the same time, there are well-known reasons for doubting the existence of such laws. No one wishes to be caught having to deny the obvious facts, and in that case, one must either impugn the inference from truisms to laws ("why *should* there be laws in psychology?") or refute the arguments against them ("well, why *shouldn't* there be laws in psychology?")

I'd like, in this essay, to go a couple of rounds on this issue. I cannot here consider all the arguments in favor of positing mental laws, nor all the arguments against them.[1] Instead, I shall try to chart the contours of one specific area of philosophical controversy, namely, the metaphysics of mental causation.

The starting point here is a set of mundane observations about the role of mentalistic attributions in the everyday characterization, explanation, and prediction of the behavior of our fellow human beings. We frequently appeal to people's beliefs and desires in order to explain their actions, we cite their "states of mind" as causes or partial causes of a variety of phenomena, and we use our apparent knowledge of others' psychologies to predict how they'll behave: Hermione wrote the letter because she wanted to make amends; her embarrassment at having to do so caused her to blush; we knew she'd write it, though, despite the awkwardness, because she has such integrity. Such casual psychologizing as this is ubiquitous in human life, and, notwithstanding the prognostications of the more evangelical eliminativists, looks likely to stay that way.

The question of lawfulness usually arises when we commence philosophical reflection on these undeniable facts, or when we begin to consider what might be required as part of a scientific account of them. On the face of it, our propensity to psychologize suggests that we are robustly realistic about the mental; it suggests that we not only believe in mental things, but that we think of these mental things as active elements in the causal order. The fact that our psychologizing works as well as it does suggests that this naive metaphysics is roughly *true*. That means that there are mental events, and that these mental events cause, and are caused by, other events. But causation involves laws; hence, commitment to the reality of mental causation appears to entail commitment to the existence of *mental laws*.

Donald Davidson, of course, has argued that this particular reasoning is fallacious:[2] causation does involve laws, he says, but the laws that are entailed by the occurrence of individual causal transactions needn't utilize the same vocabulary (or needn't advert to the same properties)[3] that we happen to use in picking out the causally related events. The requirement that there be a law backing each true claim of the form '*c* caused *e*' is satisfied as long as there is *some* description of *c* and *e* that supports generalization.

How we choose to identify events depends on pragmatic factors: what we know, what our audience knows, and what we all find interesting, and these are things that have nothing to do, necessarily, with nomic structure. To illustrate the point, Davidson draws an analogy:

> Suppose a hurricane, which is reported on page 5 of Tuesday's *Times*, causes a catastrophe, which is reported on page 13 of Wednesday's *Tribune*. Then the event reported on page 5 of Tuesday's *Times* caused the event reported on page 13 of Wednesday's *Tribune*. Should we look for a law relating events of these kinds?[4]

Certainly not. It is, therefore, an error to suppose that "singular causal statements necessarily indicate, by the concepts they employ, the concepts that will occur in the entailed law."[5] Thus, the fact that some events that happen to be mental cause other events is not reason in and of itself to think that there are mental laws.

But hold on—we've not yet done justice to the undeniable facts. Mental events don't just *cause* other events—they sometimes *explain* them. And while it may not matter for the truth of a singular causal *claim* how the cause is described, it does matter for the adequacy of a causal *explanation*. Causation may be extensional; explanation surely isn't. Davidson's own example makes the point. If I tell you that the event reported on page 13 of Wednesday's *Tribune* was caused by the event reported on page 5 of Tuesday's *Times*, I've spoken the truth, but I haven't thereby explained the occurrence of the catastrophe.[6,7]

So it's not enough to causally explain an event simply to pick out its cause—the cause must be characterized in a certain way. Which way? Let's put this question in the context of another: why think that laws are involved in causation at all? Laws carry, at the very least, the notion of generality. Hume tells us in the *Enquiry* that a cause is "an object, followed by another, and where all the objects similar to the first are followed by objects similar to the second."[8] If we agree with Hume, we think that in any causal transaction, each of the individual events is of some *kind* such that any event of the first kind is followed by some event of the second kind. The law entailed by a true causal claim is then simply that universal statement that reveals the relevant kinds, that exposes the correct parameters of generalization.

All this suggests an answer to our first question: for a causal explanation to be adequate, the cited cause must be characterized in terms that support generalization. If this answer is correct, then the adequacy of causal explanations in terms of events characterized as mental entails the truth of generalizations involving mental kinds. One could, of course, avoid this conclusion either by denying that mental events are causes at all (in which case one must show how to avoid the *prima facie* implications of the undeniable facts), or by denying that explanations that appeal to mental events are *causal explanations*. But if one agrees with Davidson that "rationalization is a species of causal explanation," it looks like we might be stuck with mental laws after all.[9]

Stephen Schiffer, however, explicitly rejects this argument. He agrees that it is incumbent upon us to account for what he calls the "explanatory role" of psychological properties in addition to accounting for the truth of singular causal claims, but denies that this requires positing psychological laws. According to Schiffer, we can fully account for the explanatory role of psychological properties if we can explain how such properties can occur in true "because" statements,[10] and this can be done without appeal to laws. All that is required (in addition to the truth of the relevant singular causal claim) is that certain crucial counterfactuals be true, and–importantly–that certain pragmatic constraints be satisfied. Thus, according to Schiffer, to say that the property G has an explanatory role in the causal-explanatory statement "x F'ed because x G'ed" is to say that, first, that x's G-ing caused x's F'ing, second that x wouldn't have F'ed if x had not G'ed, and third, that G "satisf[ies] the relevant pragmatic interests."

But while Schiffer's account makes no explicit appeal to laws, a close look at his discussion of these "pragmatic interests" reveals that the existence of law-like regularities involving psychological properties is nonetheless presupposed. Schiffer reasonably declines to offer a complete and precise list of the pragmatic constraints, but he does offer a set of conditions satisfaction of which he regards as sufficient for a property to satisfy the pragmatic concerns. Thus, he says, any pair of properties K and K' can occur acceptably in true 'because'-statements if:

> (a) events having a property of kind K' are typically caused by events having a property of kind K, (b) the latter events wouldn't have caused the former events without their kind K properties, (c) there is a reliable practice of predicting events having properties of kind K' on the basis of events having

properties of kind K, and (d) properties of kind K are relatively manipulable and epistemically accessible. (Schiffer 1991, 14)

I quite agree that satisfaction of these conditions would certify the explanatory relevance of a pair of properties. But I do not see how any pair of properties could satisfy these conditions–especially (a), (c), and (d)–without there being lawful regularities involving those properties.

The notions of "typicality" and "reliability" are so closely allied to the notions of "generality" and "regularity" that conditions (a) and (c) seem almost to be glosses of the claim that adequate causal explanations must invoke properties that support generalization. Take (c). For a pair of properties K and K' to satisfy (c), it would have to be the case that K's being instantiated gives one good reason to believe that K' will be instantiated, i.e., that '$K \rightarrow K'$' is, roughly, true. (I'll discuss the significance of the "roughly" soon.) The conditional can't, at any rate, be merely accidentally true–otherwise the practice of predicting K' on the basis of K wouldn't be *reliable*. Now how could it be that the conditional '$K \rightarrow K'$' is roughly true without there being a lawful connection between K and K'? Perhaps Schiffer's thought is that the predictive power of K could depend on its having either an accidental or an epiphenomenal association with some *other* property, which is lawfully connected to K'. But in the first case, there would be no explanation for the reliability of the practice of predicting K' on the basis of K. And in the second case, while we could explain the reliability of the predictive practice, it would turn out that the pair of properties K and K' would fail the counterfactual condition, (b)–for to say that K is epiphenomenal is precisely to say that it is causally inert, and thus not causally necessary for the production of any effect.[11]

When Schiffer speaks of "pragmatic" factors that influence the acceptability of a particular way of designating a cause in a causal explanation, one immediately thinks of subject-relative factors, considerations such as the interest or the salience of the properties cited, or of the information value of the candidate descriptions. But the conditions Schiffer gives us are not of this sort–they are metaphysical conditions, conditions that the *world* must meet independently of any interest any subject has in their being met. Even though condition (d) adverts to the nature and interests of the audience, its conditions of satisfaction are still perfectly objective, for it is a fact independent of us which properties are epistemically accessible to and manipulable by creatures with our particular complex of endowments and embedded in our particular circumstances.

Indeed, condition (d) raises a whole new set of considerations that, on their face at least, provide support for the existence of psychological laws. Consider what must be true of the world for a property K to be "epistemically accessible" to or "manipulable" by us. In the first place, it is necessary that K (or instantiations of K), interact with our sensory and cognitive equipment in regular ways. So if K is a mental property, its epistemic accessibility entails the existence of a regularity in which a mental property participates. But secondly, the very notions of "epistemic accessibility" and "manipulability" entail the possibility of regularities involving the mental, bringing in mental properties, as it were, at the other end. Note that these two notions are thoroughly *intentional*: no device can be said to have *epistemic* access to any aspect of its environment unless it is a device that *represents* its environment. (Of course there may be many other conditions necessary for epistemic access–but this much at least is necessary.) Nor can a device be said to be *manipulating* aspects of its environment–as opposed to merely interacting with it–unless it is capable of forming intentions regarding its environment, so represented. The claim, then, that certain properties are epistemically accessible to (e.g.) us presupposes the possibility of regular connections between those properties (or their instantiations) and certain *intentional*, hence mental, states in us.

What Schiffer has done, in effect, is to remind us of one of the undeniable facts that has gone hitherto unremarked in our focus on mental causation and intentional explanation. The fact is this: our everyday psychological practice, which everyone agrees to be sound, *essentially involves treating psychological properties as nomic*. We routinely generalize along psychological lines, and, generalizing along these lines, get by remarkably well. We are constantly calculating on the basis of psychological ascriptions, and have such enormous confidence in these calculations that we regularly bet our lives on them. I will, for example, sometimes walk behind a car with its engine running and its back-up lights on. (My friends in New Jersey find this audacious.) Why? Because sometimes I believe I have succeeded in getting a car's driver to realize that I'm there, and this belief, together with background assumptions about the minimal rationality of drivers and the general benignity of their intentions, satisfies me that this particular driver will refrain, at this particular time, from backing up.[12]

The point is not that we can't get rid of folk psychology–the same could be true, for all we know, of a host of superstitions, prejudices, and otherwise unwholesome human reflexes. Folk psychology is not some bad habit we just can't break–it is rather an extraordinarily useful tool for negotiating our way through our environment. But if it works for us to project psychological predicates, then, *ipso facto*, psychological predicates *are projectible*. The fact that Schiffer's constraints can be satisfied by mental properties (and in the case of (d), the fact that the constraint can be satisfied *at all*) demonstrates that reliable psychological regularities *exist*. Why don't these regularities simply *count* as laws? What's wrong with mental laws, anyway? Why *shouldn't* there be laws in psychology?

Tougher Laws–No Exceptions

Davidson, as we saw, was anxious to resist the inference from the existence of mental causes to the existence of mental laws. Many of his interpreters (including me), took this as evidence that he did not believe in psychological laws at all. Recently, however,[13] Davidson has averred he that never meant to impugn mental laws *per se*, and that all he ever said was that psychological laws were not the right *kind* of laws to back causal claims. Psychological generalizations, he says, are not, and cannot be made *strict*.

> ....In fact, I have said repeatedly that if you want to call certain undeniably important regularities laws–the familiar regularities that link the mental with the mental...or the mental with the physical–I have no objection; I merely say these are not, and cannot be reduced to, *strict* laws.[14]

Moreover, he says, his critics are mistaken if they think that he means to single out the domain of the *mental* in this regard. On the contrary, he says: the recognition that the laws of psychology are not strict merely puts that discipline on the same footing as all the other *non*basic sciences:

> Most, if not all of the practical knowledge that we (or engineers, chemists, geneticists, geologists) have that allows us to explain and predict ordinary happenings does not involve strict laws....(Davidson, 1993)

So there now appears the possibility of *rapprochement*.[15] I've been pushing the line that there are mental laws *of some sort*; Davidson only denies that those laws are strict. I say we can't explain intentional explanation without intentional laws; he says only that causation requires *strict* laws as well.

But–not to make trouble or anything–this proposed division of labor just raises a new question: *why* does causation require strict laws? Why cannot the generalizations drawn from our own folk psychological practice serve as the backing laws for singular causal claims about, *inter alia*, reasons and actions? In "Actions, Reasons, and Causes," Davidson considers and rejects this suggestion, apparently on the grounds, first of all, that such generalizations are hopelessly *imprecise*: "generalizations connecting reasons and actions are not–and cannot be sharpened into–the kind of law on the basis of which accurate predictions can reliably be made."[16]

It should be noted, incidentally, in support of his recent disclaimers, that Davidson draws no distinction in this regard between the concepts of folk psychology and everyday categories of any other sort. He clearly finds all quotidian taxonomies to be inferior, in terms of predictive utility, to scientific ones. Remember how silly it would be to look for a law relating "events reported on page 5 of Tuesday's *Times*" with "events reported on page 13 of Wednesday's *Tribune*?" Well, Davidson insists, it would be

> ...only slightly less ridiculous to look for a law relating hurricanes and catastrophes. The laws needed to predict the catastrophe with precision would, of course, have no use for conceptions like hurricane and catastrophe. The trouble with predicting the weather is that the descriptions under which events interest us...have only remote connections with the concepts employed by the more precise known laws.[17]

But what is Davidson saying? That ordinary classifications–folk psychological classifications among them–are not *useful*? That would be patently false–we agreed, after all, that the overall success of folk psychological predictions was one of the undeniable facts.

And why all this emphasis on precision? If we're really interested in the *utility* of a generalization, we ought to acknowledge that precision in our categories is not always a boon. Indeed there's typically a tradeoff between utility and precision. Let's talk about that darned weather. Meteorologists predicted in the fall of 1989 that Hurricane Hugo would hit Raleigh, NC. It struck Charlotte, instead, with unexpectedly serious results. Now I trust that these folks at the National Weather Service knew the laws of thermodynamics, and what with supercomputers and satellite observatories, I imagine that they were able to learn virtually everything they wanted to in the way of factual detail. But had they tried to predict Hugo's path by computing the trajectories of his component molecules I doubt that they would have had more success. it would have been foolhardy in the extreme. Supercomputers and satellite observatories may have improved the predictive capabilities of meteorologists, but only by making available more of the relevant information about macro patterns, and not by feeding them precise parameters to plug into the antecedents of fundamental physical laws.

It's not just that the computational task here is monumental (although if we really are interested in the utility of a generalization, this consideration is hardly trifling). It's also important to remember that when we are interested in predicting *disasters*, we want our predictions to read in terms of "disasters" and not in terms of, say, distributions of basic physical magnitudes over regions of space-time. Full knowledge of such distributions, together with full knowledge of physical laws, might or might not yield precise predictions about subsequent such distributions,[18] but it won't tell us *nada* about *hurricanes*, much less about disasters. This is just the point familiar from the early work on functionalism by Putnam and others: groupings that interest us at one level of description may dissolve at the next level down.

But even if we were to concede that folk psychological generalizations were not ideally precise, what bearing would that have on their ability to back singular causal claims? After all, precision and accuracy are relative matters. Why are generalizations in intentional terms beyond the pale? And even if there could be established some required threshold of precision that folk psychological generalizations fail to meet, whence this confidence that ordinary generalizations could not be refined into more adequate forms? Another passage from "Actions, Reasons and Causes" suggests an answer:

> The practical syllogism exhausts its role in displaying an action as falling under one reason; so it cannot be subtilized into a reconstruction of practical reasoning, which involves the weighing of competing reasons.[19]

Davidson's idea appears to be this: explanation via reasons involves the *ex post facto* selection of but *one* of the psychological states that was causally determinative of the action. Serious prediction, however, would require our knowing the rest of the agent's contending desires and beliefs. Since intentional explanations give no hint about the nature of these competitor states, we have no basis for thinking that the connection discerned in this instance between a desire of type *n* and an action of type *m* is one that holds in general.

This picture connects the *hedged*, or *ceteris paribus* character of psychological generalizations with the defect in predictive utility that supposedly makes them unsuitable for backing causal claims: the link is given by the fact that intentional generalizations specify *incomplete* causal antecedents. This explains both why these generalizations inevitably have exceptions (and so why they can't be relied on for prediction), and also how and why they inevitably break down.

But if these are indeed Davidson's assumptions about what is required for prediction, they appear once again to fly in the face of the undeniable facts. Predictions made in ordinary life are never made in full knowledge of the operation of all causally relevant factors, only in the confidence that such factors as are not known won't scuttle the prediction, and this is as true outside the psychological domain as within it. There's no reason to think that predictions about what an agent will do require a complete "reconstruction of practical reasoning," when predictions about matches lighting and baseballs shattering windows are made in analogous states of ignorance. Our everyday predictive practice works to the extent that we do manage, somehow or other, to find salient those elements of the total cause that normally do suffice for the production of that type of effect.

Davidson's complaint connects with the more traditional worry about laws with *ceteris paribus* clauses, *viz.*, that "laws" thus qualified are empirically *vacuous*. For a law to be testable, it's been argued, it is required that we be able to determine whether the antecedent conditions are satisfied in a given situation, independently of determining whether the consequent conditions are satisfied. But if the antecedent always contains the escape clause "all else being equal," then the non-occurrence of the consequent could always be taken as evidence that things were not equal, rather than as evidence that the causal generalization is false.

I am not inclined, however, to give this objection much weight either. Anyone who accepts the holism of confirmation must be prepared to give up this clear, but naive criterion of empirical meaningfulness. We know that any generalization may be preserved, whatever the evidence, provided one is prepared to be suitably flexible elsewhere. In fact, in the case of laws, empirical vulnerability is inversely related to centrality. The more central the law that's at stake, the less likely it is that apparent counter-evidence will be credited.

J.A. Coffa[20] has even argued that the laws paraded as paradigm cases of appropriate backing generalizations by Carnap, Hempel and others must themselves be treated as hedged laws. For example, in the canonical D-N explanation of the expansion of a metal rod, the law cited is the standard law of thermal expansion:

$$\Delta L = k \cdot L_0 \cdot \Delta T$$

where L_0 is the original length of the metal rod, k is the coefficient of thermal expansion for the material out of which the rod is composed, and T is the amount by which the temperature of the rod was altered. But, Coffa argues, this putative law is false as it stands. Bodies do not always expand when heated; they do not expand if there is, for example, a sufficient compressive force present. The correct statement of the law, therefore, must be qualified by what Coffa calls an "extremal clause"–essentially a *ceteris paribus* clause stated negatively rather than positively. The final law then would read: *In the absence of other changes relevant to length,* an increase in temperature T is physically sufficient for an increase in length k $\cdot L_0 \cdot \Delta T$." The D-N explanation must then be emended; to it must be added a statement to the effect that the extremal clause is satisfied. Coffa goes on to argue that every law involves an extremal clause, and every D-N explanation contains a premise asserting that the extremal clause is satisfied.[21,22]

In response to the objection that this simply renders *all* laws vacuous, Coffa points out that our response to experimental test is never determined by the logic of the experimental situation; that whenever we are dealing with a law stated in conditional form we are always free to deny the antecedent upon the failure of the consequent. The relevant issue, according to Coffa, is whether or not we are in fact able to use the laws in predictions–that we are able to use such laws as the law of thermal expansion, or Newton's law of motion, demonstrates that we are sometimes prepared to stipulate that the extremal clause is fulfilled, *in advance of* the occurrence of the predicted effect. The suggestion, apparently, is that we treat the issue of the empirical significance of our lawlike claims less as turning less on the content or logical form of the law *statements*, and more on the overall cogency of our epistemic practice with regard to that law. The law's ability to function in a successful epistemic practice speaks both for the reality of the nomic connections explicitly posited by the law, and also for the objectivity and determinacy of the conditions denoted by the extremal clause. I would go on to add that our own ability to identify–ultimately–the posited interfering factors in those cases in which we're inclined to make use of the escape clause can testify to the determinacy of the extremal clause.

Coffa's insight also has bearing on the issue Schiffer raises about *ceteris paribus* laws. Less tolerant than Davidson, Schiffer utterly denies the existence of "hedged laws"–he thinks that statements of such putative laws fail to express any determinate proposition. Schiffer says, of a sentence like "If a person wants something, then, all other things being equal, she'll take steps to get it," that it

looks as though it's expressing a determinate proposition, because it looks as

> though 'all other things' is referring to some contextually determinate things and
> 'equal' is expressing some determinate relation among them. But one would be
> hard pressed to say what the 'other things' are and what it is for them to be
> 'equal.' (Schiffer 1991, 2)

But on Coffa's analysis, it is not the *context* in which the law is asserted that
determines the content of the extremal clause, but rather the nomic patterns in
which the terms of the law participate. The extremal clause refers to the absence
of factors *relevant to* the causal transaction characterized by the law. By the same
token, there is no reason why anyone who asserts the law must be in a position
to specify the factors that go into the extremal clause; the clause involves an
existential generalization, and one can be in a position to know that an existential
generalization is true without being able to specify its true instances.

Coffa's arguments may show that there are no strict laws. At the very least,
they show that there's nothing in our actual scientific practice that lends support
to the idea that the laws backing causal claims must be strict–there's nothing
inadequate or insufficient about *ceteris paribus* laws from a *pragmatic* point of
view. But the demand for strict backing laws is not just unmotivated–in the
context of Davidson's overall agenda, it's actually self-defeating. If ordinary
intentional generalizations can't serve as the backing laws for singular causal
claims because they are *irremediably* hedged, then it can be shown that there is
no strict law in any other vocabulary that covers the very same set of events.

Suppose that we observe Hermione typing "DN1" into her computer, and
want to know why. Hermione tells us that she wants to play *Duke Nukum*, and
believes that typing "DN1" into her computer will enable her to do so. We
would, in such circumstances, rightly conclude that Hermione's desire to play
Duke Nukum caused her to type "DN1." Davidson wants to insist that there is no
strict law connecting desires-to-play-Duke-Nukum with typings-of-"DN1" and
yet that there will be some descriptions of the *very same events* as the ones that
instantiate these descriptions, such that the law stated in terms of those other
descriptions will be strictly true. He can't have both of these things.

Consider the factors that account for the existence of exceptions to hedged
laws: why doesn't every match striking result in a match lighting? There are a
couple of reasons. First, the ignition of a match that has been struck depends
upon the presence of certain *background conditions*–a struck match won't light
in the absence of oxygen. Second, ignition also depends on the *absence* of certain
interfering factors–there must not be a strong wind blowing as the match is being
struck.[23]

These same problems are going to turn up in the intentional case.
Obviously, Hermione's desire to play Duke Nukum needs to occur in a particular
sort of context in order to cause her to actually enter the magic letters into her
computer. First is needed the right sort of psychological context: Hermione must
lack countervailing desires (she must not want to do any work, nor must it move
her that the children haven't had a chance to play) and she must possess a belief

of the right kind (she must think that that's a computer in front of her) and she can't be in possession of beliefs of another sort (she mustn't think the electricity has gone out). Then there are the broader physical requirements. Hermione has to stay alive and functioning long enough after the onset of the desire for the neurological signals to travel down to the muscles of her fingers, so we need oxygen, an ambient temperature within the range that will support human life and so forth, and we need Hermione's body to be in overall good working order. (This will also ensure satisfaction of another condition, which is that Hermione's muscles must respond properly to the signals from the nerves.) On top of this, there must be an absence of interfering events: nothing must occur that would distract Hermione, nothing that would kill her or incapacitate her. No one must yank the computer out from beneath her fingers.

Now it's supposed to be the case that there's some physical predicate that applies to the event that is the onset of Hermione's desire in one of those cases in which it is efficacious, and such that that physical predicate figures in a strict law. Call it P1. Whatever the spatio-temporal boundaries of the onset of Hermione's desire, those must also be the spatio-temporal boundaries of the P1 event. So if Hermione's desire occurs, say, within the spatial region occupied by Hermione, then so must the P1 event. That is, "P1" must express a physically intrinsic property of Hermione; to be in a P1 state, it should be sufficient to be a body in the state Hermione's body is in at the moment she is beset with the urge to play Duke Nukum. But now notice that any such state is going to be independent of the presence or absence of oxygen around the body. Hence, if the absence of oxygen in the environment would engender an exception to the intentional generalization, it would similarly defeat the generalization stated in terms of P1. (If we assume that the onset of Hermione's desire involves a smaller region than the space occupied by her entire body, then the P1 event will be independent of even more background conditions.[24])

Then there's the problem of interfering events. If the onset of Hermione's desire is over before the fingers actually begin to type, then so is the P1 event. But then the occurrence of a P1 event couldn't be strictly sufficient for the occurrence of a P2 event (where this is the physical type instantiated by the actual typing in the case where it *was* brought about), since a racking abdominal pain, or even a sharp call of "Are you ever coming to bed?" emanating from Hermione's husband, can always intrude between the occurrence of the P1 event and the initiation of the act of typing.

I can imagine two responses here–one is to say that the *exceptionless* law is not the one that relates the P1 event to the P2 event, but rather one that relates the P1 event to a minimally proximate effect, say a P1.5 event. That's OK, except that the desire still did cause the *typing*, and we're supposed to have a strict law that subsumes *those two events*. (I presume that no one is going to be tempted to go on and insist that the desire didn't actually cause the typing, but only the finger signals that led to the typing.) The other response I can think of is to suggest that we temporally stretch out the P1 event so as to bring it up to the instant just before the occurrence of the typing event, thus "capturing" the non-occurrence of the various potential intruder events. One could make an analogous move in response to the problem about background conditions that arises due to the spatial dimensions of the event–stretch out the location of the event to just far enough from Hermione's body to capture all the air she needs to complete the causal transaction.

These moves strike me as *ad hoc*–I can't think of any other reason to hold that the onset of Hermione's desire occurs partly outside her body, or that it lasts until precisely the moment her fingers begin to move, but I confess to having extremely few intuitions about event identity, and pretty weak ones at that, so maybe I'm just wrong. Perhaps it could be motivated like this: it could be argued that the *particular* event that's identical to Hermione's wanting to play in this case is an event consisting in Hermione's *healthy* body seated in a *salutary* environment *without* pains or disgruntled husbands anywhere about. That's a particular *type* of event, and that's the type of type P1 is. But at any rate, the important point is this: if any such stretching strategy works for the physical type, *it can work for the intentional type, too.* Whatever it takes to contrive a strict law at the physical level can be pressed into service at the intentional level, too.

Back to Basics

Where does this leave us? I think I know what's really behind the opposition to psychological laws, and the feeling that such laws can't be the bottom line when it comes to causation. The fact that psychological laws have exceptions is really beside the point–the fact that they are nonstrict is an artifact of what really affects people, namely the fact that they are *nonbasic.* I claimed, back near the beginning, that we look for laws behind causal claims because of our interest in prediction and explanation–we want to know the lines along which generalization is apt to work. But perhaps there are two different roles for laws to play in causal explanation: first, to state the pragmatically important generalization that subsumes a particular causal transaction, but second, *to point to the causally efficacious features of the situation.* It is with respect to this second role that higher-order laws seem to disappoint.

It's a basic presumption of physicalism that causation is ultimately grounded in the goings-on of fundamental physical entities, which goings-on are, of course, governed by fundamental physical laws. Mental causation, if it exists (and of course the same can be said for biological causation, chemical causation, meteorological causation, etc.) must therefore be shown somehow to be really a species of physical causation. It's a fairly natural next step to think that this requires subsuming mental causes and their effects under physical laws.

But I think the physicalistic intuition that causation has to "bottom out" in basic physical transactions can be accommodated without making the requirement that every causal interaction be backed by some basic physical law. In fact, we'd better not have to make that requirement, or we will certainly get the result that there is no causation anywhere *except* at the level of fundamental physics. As both Jaegwon Kim,[25] and Ernest LePore and Barry Loewer[26] have pointed out, if we do assume that every case of (e.g.) mental causation is subsumed by a strict physical law, then it appears that there is no work left for a posited higher-level causal power to do. (Not unless we posit some kind of "strong emergent" that appears to be incompatible with the assumption, shared by most parties to this debate, that the physical is comprehensive.) But as we've seen, it's not the case that there is guaranteed to be a strict law covering every singular causal transaction; indeed, if the cause-and-effect pair is subsumed by a non-strict law, chances are good that there is guaranteed *not* to be a strict law covering those two particular events. What this means is that there are causal *regularities* that cannot be apprehended at more basic levels of description, that require reference to higher-level properties (like "red blood cell," "hurricane," "wanting a cup of coffee") and that involve events which are essentially tied to the higher level of description.

What we ought to say, instead of saying that every causal interaction is backed by some strict physical law, is that causal interactions that are backed by non-strict laws entail the existence of some–ultimately physical–*mechanism*. By a mechanism, I mean, roughly, a pattern of lower-level events that guarantees, contingent on features of the background, the emergence of some higher-level regularity. I think that talk of mechanisms in connection with causation, rather than laws, can organize the swirl of objections and misgivings philosophers have expressed about nonstrict laws in general and psychological laws in particular.

In the first place, notice that virtually everything Davidson has said about strict laws and their involvement in causation is actually true of mechanisms. Davidson says that we're frequently ignorant of the laws that govern a particular causal interaction, and that we don't need to know such laws in order to be warranted in making singular causal claims. I've argued, on the contrary, that the adequacy of a causal explanation depended upon our picking out nomic features of the situation. Clearly it's not the *regularities* we're innocent of when we make causal judgments–it's rather the mechanisms that secure and explain those regularities that we don't know, or don't know in detail.

Similarly, the fact that our causal explanations frequently isolate only one of the features of the total sufficient cause, with the result that any generalization based on that feature is liable to exception, does not show that the "real" nomic connections lay at a different or deeper level. It shows rather that the maintenance of the particular nomic connection that we are discerning is accomplished by some mechanism. Mechanisms may break down, and mechanisms don't work unless they're embedded in an appropriate environment. More complete understanding of mechanisms and their requirements, rather than more thorough knowledge of the laws that govern the mechanism's primitive operations, is what affords us greater and greater accuracy in prediction.

The connections we discern among phenomena in our environments are connections that hold only against certain backgrounds, and not against others.

But as Jerry Fodor has been recently emphasizing,[27] the fact that the existence of a regularity depends on other contingencies does not impugn its nomic status. As Coffa's model recognizes, if the *backgrounds* are ones we can count on, the connections will be reliable, too. The traffic light turns red, the car approaching the intersection from my right draws to a stop. Had the state legislature voted to make green the color that meant 'stop,' this regularity would not have existed. Had the driver been bent on suicide, the car would not have stopped, and similarly if the driver had been blind. But given that red was the agreed-upon signal for "Stop" and given that drivers, by and large, possess decent eyesight and a reasonably healthy interest in self-preservation, the generalization, "cars stop at red lights" is something you can bank on. (As you do.)

When we think of the role of "backing" causal claims in terms of our practical needs for prediction and explanation, it isn't going to matter to us whether the laws mention genuinely causally potent properties, or only properties that "point to" or are contingently, but reliably connected to such properties. Indeed, as far as prediction goes, properties that encode stable contingencies may be far more useful than properties that do not. But it's not just in the domain of everyday explanation that this point holds. Science, too, can exploit stable contingencies in the construction of its taxonomies. In closing, let me say briefly how appreciation of this point can shed light on another hot potato issue: the controversy over "narrow" vs. "wide" taxonomies in psychology.

The main argument for positing narrow semantic or intentional content, due to Jerry Fodor[28] has always been this: science taxonomizes by causal powers, and causal powers are individualistic. Hence if psychology is a proper science, it must taxonomize individualistically. But on the other hand, there are good and well-known reasons for thinking that intentional content is *wide*, i.e., that a mental state possesses its intentional content in virtue of not only properties intrinsic its thinker, but also in virtue of factors that lay outside its thinker. It was then argued, by Stephen Stich among others, that if the taxonomy of scientific psychology must be narrow, then it can't taxonomize in terms of ordinary intentional properties.[29] And this seems to entail that the psychology that's really science, and that contains real laws, can't be the "folk psychology" of everyday life.

The error, I think, came at the first step, as Fodor now recognizes. Scientific taxonomies don't have to be narrow–what has to be true is that any wide properties that are taxonomic for a given science have to be reliably attached to narrow properties. Evolutionary biology taxonomizes in terms of wide properties– whether something is literally a horse depends on the creature's history and not on its current physical structure. And yet, any object that, *per impossibile*, shared a horse's precise physical structure and yet lacked its history, though not a *horse*, would be causally indistinguishable from one. That's OK. As long as there are no such creatures actually around, and to the extent that there's a reason why there are none around, we can collapse the narrow causally potent properties together with the wide, causally inert ones, and nothing untoward will happen.

So too in psychology. I can concede that the narrow, individualistic properties that supervene on my neurology effectively "screen off" the wide elements, and that wide intentional content is, in this sense, causally inefficacious, while at the same time preserving the desired relation between folk psychological intentional laws, which must be wide, and the laws of a finished scientific psychology.[30]

Notes

1. Most conspicuously, I will neglect the arguments for the anomalism of the mental that appeal to either indeterminacy, holism, or normativity. I do address such arguments in Antony (1989), Antony (1991) and Antony (1994).
2. See Davidson (ARC) and (ME) in Davidson (1980).
3. In what follows, I will probably forget to keep to the formal mode, which Davidson prefers. Nothing will turn on it if I do.
4. Davidson 1980, p. 17.
5. Davidson 1980, p. 17.
6. It might be objected that there *are* contexts in which this would be an adequate explanation. You might accept such a statement as an explanation if, for example, you happened to know which event it was that was reported on page 5 of Tuesday's *Times*. But by the same token, you might foresee bad times for Oedipus upon learning that he wants to marry Jocasta *if* you happen to know who Jocasta is. The context "...because ___ " is just as intensional as "Oedipus wanted..."
7. Note, by the way, for the sake of what follows, that "the catastrophe was caused by a hurricane" *is* an adequate explanation.
8. One might also be attracted to the notion of law as a way of bringing in some kind of objective *necessity* or *efficacy* as an ingredient in causation. Hume would, of course, repudiate this idea.
9. As I read Davidson, he thinks it's sufficient to account for the causal explanatory force of appeals to reasons by appending to the old Verstehen account of rational explanation the token-materialist thesis that every reason is individually identical with some physical event that is the cause of the action being explained. I've argued that this kind of account can't work without interlevel laws linking the rationalizing, intentional properties of the reason with its causally efficacious physical properties, and, further, that Davidson's commitment to the indeterminacy of intentional content precludes his developing an adequate causal account of rational explanation. See Antony (1989).
10. This is because, Schiffer tells us, "the explanatory role, the 'causal relevance' of psychological properties is nothing over and above their ability to occur in true 'because'-statements." I must say that I'm not sure what Schiffer has in mind here. Schiffer has strong deflationist tendencies, and likes to recast what appear to be metaphysical issues about the nature of mental and semantic phenomena in terms of the nature and ground of linguistic practices. But I find that I cannot understand the questions, so revised, except by importing my understanding of the original metaphysical questions. That is, I feel that I understand what might be required when someone asks for an explanation of certain *facts*, like "why (or how) did his stepping on a banana peel cause him to slip?" I would answer such a question by saying what it is about banana peels that makes stepping on them treacherous.

(They're slippery, of course. More on this sort of thing below.) Were someone to ask, however, what enables "slipperiness" to occur in a true "because"-statement, I wouldn't know what she meant unless she had in mind either a question about English vocabulary (which is clearly not an adequate replacement for the causal relevance question), or else the metaphysically loaded question just mentioned. In the latter case, the move to the formal mode certainly provides no economy.

11. I'd like to thank Geoff Sayre-McCord for helpful discussions on this point.

12. It's important to note that, as this example shows, we use psychological ascriptions and generalizations to make predictions not only about other psychological phenomena, but also about the behavior of unalloyedly physical phenomena (and highly heavy ones, at that). For these purposes, the reference to intentional states is ineliminable. For further discussion and additional examples, see Rey 1991.

13. In "Thinking Causes," Davidson 1993.

14. Davidson 1993, p. 9.

15. I am unconvinced that this is an accurate picture either of Davidson's early view or of his current commitments; I believe that he does mean to make an invidious distinction between the intentional and the non-intentional sciences, and that, as a result, he is committed to a much stronger form of the anomalism thesis than he here admits. We'll get into that later.

16. Davidson 1980, p. 15.

17. Davidson 1980, p. 17.

18. Indeed, as Mark Bedau has demonstrated with an elegant example, it is possible for one to have perfect knowledge of all the laws governing a system, perfect knowledge of the system's initial conditions, and still be unable to predict facts about the system couched in terms of macro-features. See Bedau 1994.

19. Davidson 1980, p. 16.

20. Coffa 1973. I was unable to obtain a copy of Coffa's dissertation, and thus I am following Wesley Salmon's exposition. See Salmon, p. 84.

21. Coffa 1973, 210. Quoted in Salmon 1989, 84.

22. Coffa's view of laws is quite in tune with the view Jerry Fodor has recently articulated. The only difference appears to be that while Coffa would have the satisfaction of the extremal clause be explicitly announced as a premise in the D-N explanation schema, Fodor makes satisfaction of the *ceteris paribus* clause a precondition of the evaluation of a hedged law or of an explanation containing one:

> Strict laws and [ceteris paribus] laws with satisfied ceteris paribus conditions operate alike in respect of their roles in covering causal relations and in respect of their roles in covering law explanations... . Strict laws are just the special case of [ceteris paribus] laws where the ceteris paribus clauses are discharged *vacuously*...(Fodor, 1989)

23. There is another source of exceptions that I should acknowledge, and that is the fact that match striking is *multiply realizable*–there are many different kinds of matches, and many different ways of striking them. The kind of problem multiple realizability raises for the viability of a notion of *ceteris paribus* law is somewhat different from the issues I want to discuss here, and so I will set it aside. The problem is set out quite compellingly in Schiffer (1991), and I do not, at any rate, have anything much to add to Fodor's reply, given in Fodor (1991).

24. Davidson is vague on the location of mental events. He explicitly endorses the whole-body view in "The Individuation of Events:" "Aside from a few dubious cases, like pains, itches, pricks, and twitches, we have no reason to locate mental events more precisely than by identifying a person..." (Davidson 1980, 176) On the other hand, in the same essay, he articulates a principle that suggests that perhaps we should locate mental events in the brain or in the nervous system: he says it is an error to assume "that if an event is a change in a substance, the location of the event is the entire space occupied by the substance. Rather, the location of the event at a moment is the location of the smallest part of the substance a change in which is identical with the event."
25. See Kim 1989, 1990, and forthcoming.
26. See LePore and Loewer, 1989.
27. See Fodor 1994.
28. See Fodor 1987. Also see Baker 1987
29. See Stich 1983.
30. My thinking on the issues treated in this paper was much influenced by lectures given by Jerry Fodor over two summers at Rutgers, during an NEH Summer Seminar in 1992, and an NEH Institute in 1993. These lectures formed the basis of his book, *The Elm and the Expert*. So I thank Fodor, and all my fellow seminarians and institutians for stimulating discussion of issues surrounding intentional laws. I would also like to acknowledge my debt to the work of Terrence Horgan and Robert van Gulick, especially Horgan (1993) and van Gulick 1993. Thanks also for conversations and correspondence above and beyond the call of duty, to Lynne Rudder Baker, Simon Blackburn, Stephen Leeds, Hal Levin, Barry Loewer, Bill Lycan, Brian McLaughlin, and Georges Rey. Extra special thanks to Joe Levine and Geoff Sayre-McCord.

References

Antony, Louise (1994) "The Inadequacy of Anomalous Monism as a Realist Theory of Mind," forthcoming in *Zeitschrift Protosoziologie*: special issue entitled "Language, Mind, Action: On Donald Davidson's Philosophy".

Antony, Louise (1989) "Anomalous Monism and the Problem of Explanatory Force," *The Philosophical Review*, **XCVIII**, 153-187.

Antony, Louise (1991) "The Causal Relevance of the Mental," *Mind & Language*, 6: 295-327.

Baker, Lynne Rudder (1987) *Saving Belief: A Critique of Physicalism* (Princeton: Princeton University Press).

Bedau, Mark (1994) "Strong and Weak Emergentism: Comments on O'Conner," commentary on Timothy O'Conner, "Emergent Properties" at the APA Central Division Meetings, 1994.

Coffa, J. Alberto (1973) *The Foundations of Inductive Explanation*. Doctoral Dissertation, University of Pittsburgh.

Davidson, Donald (1980) *Essays on Actions and Events*. (Oxford: Oxford University Press).

Davidson, Donald (1993). "Thinking Causes", in Heil and Mele (1993).

Fodor, Jerry (1994) *The Elm and the Expert: Mentalese and Its Semantics*. (Cambridge, Ma.: Bradford Books of MIT Press).

Fodor, Jerry (1989) "Making Mind Matter More" *Philosophical Topics*, 17: 59-80.

Fodor, Jerry (1987a) *Psychosemantics*. (Cambridge, Ma.: MIT Press).

Fodor, Jerry (1991) "You Can Fool Some of the People All of the Time, Everything Else Being Equal: Hedged Laws and Psychological Explanation" *Mind*, 100: 19-34.

Heil, John and Alfred A. Mele (1993). *Mental Causation*, Oxford: Clarendon Press.

Horgan, Terence (1993). "From Supervenience to Superdupervenience: Meeting the Demands of a Material World", *Mind*, 102, 555-586.

Kim, Jaegwon (1989). "Mechanism, Purpose, and Explanatory Exclusion," *Philosophical Perspectives, 3, Philosophy of Mind and Action Theory, 1989*: 77-108.

Kim, Jaegwon (1990). "Explanatory Exclusion and the Problem of Mental Causation," in Enrique Villenueva, ed., *Information, Semantics and Epistemology* (Oxford: Basil Blackwell, 1990).

Kim, Jaegwon (Forthcoming). "What Me Worry?" presented at the 1994 conference of SOFIA, Lisbon Portugal, and to be included in a volume edited by Enrique Villenueva.

LePore, Ernest and Barry Loewer (1989). "More on Making Minds Matter," *Philosophical Topics*, 17: 175-91.

Lewis, David (1973). "Causation", *Journal of Philosophy*, **70**, 556-67.

McLaughlin, Brian MS. "Epiphenomenalism." Unpublished Manuscript.

Rey, Georges (1991). "An Explanatory Budget for Connectionism and Eliminativism," in Terry Horgan and John Tienson, eds., *Connectionism and the Mind*, Dordrecht: Kluwer Publishers.

Salmon, Wesley (1989). *Scientific Explanation. Minnesota Studies in the Philosophy of Science*, Vol. XIII. (Minneapolis: University of Minnesota Press).

Schiffer, Stephen (1991). "Ceteris Paribus Laws," *Mind*, **100**, 397, 1-17.

Stich, Stephen (1983). *From Folk Psychology to Cognitive Science: the Case Against Belief.* (Cambridge, Ma.: MIT Press).

van Gulick, Robert (1993). "Who's in Charge Here? And Who's Doing All the Work?" in Heil and Mele.

Philosophical Perspectives, 9, AI, Connectionism, and
Philosophical Psychology, 1995

CAUSALLY RELEVANT PROPERTIES

David Braun
University of Rochester

In this paper I present an analysis of causal relevance for properties. I believe that most of us are already familiar with the notion of a causally relevant property. But some of us may not recognize it "under that description." So I begin below with some intuitive explanations and some illustrative examples.

A causally relevant property is a certain kind of property of causes. Every cause of an effect has many different properties. But many properties of a cause appear to have no role in causing its effect. Those properties of the cause are causally *irrelevant* to the effect. The properties of a cause that do have some role in causing its effect are causally relevant to the effect.

Here are some more rough-and-ready explanations of the idea. If a cause causes an effect in part *because* it has a certain property, then that property of the cause is causally relevant to the effect. The causally relevant properties of a cause are those *in virtue of which* it causes its effect. A cause's causally relevant properties are those it *needs* to cause its effect. They are the properties that *make a difference* to the effect.

An illustration: Suppose a rock collides with a window, causing the window to break. The collision causes the window to break (in part) because the rock has a certain momentum and because the window is made of a certain fragile sort of glass. So the collision causes the breaking partly because the rock and the window have those properties. So those properties are causally relevant to the window's breaking. But not every property of those entities is causally relevant to the breaking. For instance, the window does not break because the rock has a red spot on it, or because the collision occurs simultaneously with George's sneeze (which occurs 10 miles away). Those properties of the rock and the collision are causally irrelevant to the breaking.

Consider another example (this one adapted from Dretske, 1989). Suppose Wilma is a skilled soprano. Suppose she sings the word 'shatter' at a high pitch and amplitude, causing a nearby glass to vibrate and shatter. Wilma's singing causes the glass's shattering because of its high pitch and amplitude. So those properties of her singing are causally relevant to the shattering. However, the shattering does not occur because Wilma's singing means *shatter*. That property is causally irrelevant to the shattering.

We are clearly able to make judgments about causal relevance. Admittedly, there are some cases about which we lack strong intuitions. But it's also undeniable that we have strong intuitions in many cases. Thus we have good reason to believe that there is a real difference between causally relevant and irrelevant properties. Therefore I believe it is worthwhile attempting to find an analysis of causal relevance. (If we cannot find an analysis, then it is worthwhile trying to obtain clearer explanations of causal relevance, or at least more information about it.)

This is what I try to do below. To be precise, I attempt to give a set of modally necessary and sufficient conditions for being a causally relevant property. Before presenting my analysis, I criticize another analysis of causal relevance that relies heavily on counterfactuals. I then present and criticize an alternative analysis that relies on essential properties. This last analysis serves as a basis for my final analysis.

Many philosophers who have written about causally relevant properties have been especially concerned with the causal relevance of mental properties to actions.[1] This was also my main interest when I began thinking about causally relevant properties. In this paper, however, I am concerned with the metaphysics of causally relevant properties in general. But in the last section I do attempt to apply my analysis to mental properties.

1. Preliminaries: Events, Causation, and Properties

I will assume here that causes and effects are always individual (token) events. The collision of the rock with the window, and the window's breaking, are events; so are Wilma's singing and the glass's shattering. I include among events such "uneventful events" as the window's retaining a certain composition and shape throughout the day preceding its breaking.

I will also assume a liberal view of which events count as causes. I will assume that an "uneventful event" can be a cause. For instance, the window's retaining its shape and composition throughout the day preceding the breaking is one cause of its breaking. I will furthermore assume that any event that occurs in the causal history of an event is a cause of that later event. For instance, Wilma's birth is a cause of Wilma's singing.[2]

Events, like other individuals, have properties. Some of these properties are essential and some not. (A property is essential to x iff it is metaphysically necessary that if x exists, then x has that property.) For instance, it's plausible to suppose that Wilma's singing has its pitch essentially. But the property of taking place simultaneously with Sylvester's cough (suppose Sylvester is very far from the scene) seems not to be essential to the singing — the singing could have occurred even if the cough had never occurred.

Some philosophers hold that an event just *is* something like an instance of a property, or a property of a region, or a property of a substance at a time.[3] I think these attempts at analyzing the notion of an event are useful as rough explanations of what an event is. But I do not accept them as analyses.

Nevertheless, much of what I say in this paper about events and causally relevant properties is compatible with these views.

At the beginning of this essay, I said that properties of various *objects* were causally relevant to the window's breaking. For instance, I said that the momentum of *the rock* was causally relevant to the window's breaking. But from here on I will be concerned only with properties of *events*, and with the analysis of the notion of an event's causally relevant properties. This restriction is justified by my assumption that causation is a relation between events: if this assumption is correct, and we are interested in the properties of causes in virtue of which they cause their effects, then we should concentrate on properties of events. My restriction to properties of events is not so severe as it may seem. If an object involved in causing an effect seems to have a causally relevant property, then this property can always be "viewed as" a property of an event. For instance, if the rock has a certain momentum M when it collides with the window, then the collision (that *event*) has the property of being-a-collision-with-an-object-that-has-momentum-M. This seems to be a causally relevant property of the collision.

2. A Counterfactual Analysis

Let's turn to Wilma's singing and the glass's shattering to motivate our first analysis of causal relevance. The meaning of Wilma's singing is, in some sense, unnecessary to the shattering, whereas the pitch and amplitude are, in that same sense, necessary. So it's very natural to say the following: If Wilma's singing had meant something different, or meant nothing at all, then the shattering would still have occurred; but if Wilma's singing had lacked that pitch and amplitude, the shattering would not have occurred.[4]

LePore and Loewer (1987, 1989), Horgan (1989), and others try to elevate remarks like these into an analysis of causal relevance.[5] LePore and Loewer's (1987) attempt at such an analysis is the following (with slight changes in wording):

> If c and e are events, and F is a property, then *c's being F is causally relevant to e's being G* iff
> (1) c causes e.
> (2) c is F and e is G.
> (3) If it were not the case that c is F, then it would not be the case that e is G.
> (4) That c is F and that e is G are metaphysically and logically independent.

A few remarks about this analysis. One might wonder whether LePore and Loewer have fixed on the right analysandum. If we are concerned with analyzing causal relevance, should the analysandum be c's being F is causally relevant to e's *being G*

or

c's being F is causally relevant to e's *occurrence*?

The first analysandum mentions some property of the effect.[6] The second analysandum seems more "minimal," since in order for an event e to be G, e must at least occur. In what follows, I concentrate on the task of analyzing the more minimal notion of a property's being causally relevant to an event's occurrence. We can modify LePore and Loewer's analysis to get an analysis of this more minimal analysandum in the following way.

If c and e are events, and F is a property, then *c's being F is causally relevant to e* (or e's occurrence) iff

(1)   c causes e.
(2)   c is F.
(3)   If it were not the case that c is F, then it would not be the case that e occurs.
(4)   That c is F and that e occurs are metaphysically and logically independent.

Call this the *Counterfactual Analysis*.

There is a second question one might have about the analysandum: to what do we refer when we say "c's being F"? We don't merely refer to the event c; but we shouldn't refer to some other event, either. Do we, perhaps, refer to a fact or state of affairs? To avoid these worries, we should view the analysandum here as a *three-place relation* between a property and two events (taken in a certain order). We can more perspicuously state the analysandum as "property F *is causally relevant with respect to* c *and* e". But I will continue to use the more convenient, if slightly misleading, "c's being F" terminology.

The Counterfactual Analysis is very intuitive — these counterfactuals fairly leap to mind when we think about causal relevance. It's also an intuitive advantage for the Counterfactual Analysis that it links causal relevance to counterfactual dependence, since event causation itself seems to have *some* sort of connection with counterfactual dependence. Nevertheless, the Counterfactual Analysis has serious problems, which I believe make it unacceptable.[7]

3. Criticisms of the Counterfactual Analysis
3.1 Pre-emption

Counterfactual analyses of event causation have well-known problems with pre-emption.[8] The Counterfactual Analysis of causally relevant properties has similar problems with pre-empting causes.

Consider Wilma again, a moment before she begins to sing. Suppose that her friend Betty is in the same room. Betty has also decided to try to break the glass by singing. Wilma begins to sing, and the glass begins to vibrate. Betty begins to sing also, but before her singing becomes audible, the glass shatters.

It's clear that Wilma's singing causes the shattering, and that the pitch of her singing is causally relevant to the shattering. But the counterfactual analysis entails that the pitch of Wilma's singing is causally irrelevant. For in these circumstances, the following counterfactual is false:

If Wilma's singing had not had pitch P, then the shattering would not have occurred.

If Wilma's singing had not had pitch P, then Betty's singing would have caused the glass to shatter. So on the counterfactual analysis, the pitch of Wilma's singing is causally irrelevant.[9]

3.2 Closely Related Properties

If we want to determine whether the amplitude of Wilma's singing is causally relevant to the shattering, the Counterfactual Analysis urges us to imagine a situation in which Wilma's singing lacks its actual amplitude. We are then supposed to imagine what other properties Wilma's singing would have in this situation. One seemingly appropriate situation to imagine is one in which Wilma's singing has an amplitude that's only slightly different from its actual amplitude. This sort of situation seems closer to actuality than any situation in which her singing differs dramatically in its amplitude.

If this is right, then there is a problem for the Counterfactual Analysis. For if Wilma's singing had had only a slightly different amplitude, then the glass (probably) would still have broken. So by the Counterfactual Analysis, the actual amplitude of Wilma's singing is causally irrelevant.

I call this 'the problem of closely related properties'. In many cases where some property is causally relevant to an effect, another closely related property would have done the job as well. Furthermore, if the event had lacked its actual property, it might well have had the closely related property. This problem afflicts the Counterfactual Analysis's handling of many examples. For instance, the Counterfactual Analysis has a problem with the various, slightly different, momenta that the rock could have had as it collided with the window.[10]

3.3 Negative Properties

The Counterfactual Analysis has problems with at least some properties which we might naturally call "negative properties." Consider Wilma's case again, and consider the property of *not*-occurring-next-to-a-soundproof-wall. Wilma's singing has this property, since Wilma is not singing near a soundproof wall. But if she had been next to a soundproof wall, placed between her and the glass, then the glass would not have shattered. So it seems that the following counterfactual is true:

> If Wilma's singing had lacked the property of not occurring next to a (suitably placed) soundproof wall, then the shattering would not have occurred.

So on the Counterfactual Analysis this negative property is causally relevant to the glass's shattering. But this seems wrong. Furthermore, it's easy to generate many other negative properties, one for each "interfering factor" that might have been present, and the Counterfactual Analysis will count each of these as causally relevant. For instance, the glass does not have a blanket over it; if it had, the shattering would not have occurred. So the property of not-occurring-as-the-glass-had-a-blanket-over-it is causally relevant by the counterfactual test. Similarly, there was no person who grabbed the glass, there was no machine generating counteracting sound waves, and so on. But surely not all of the corresponding negative properties are causally relevant to the shattering.[11]

3.4 Universal Properties

Let's say that a *universal property* is one which every object (in a world) either has or lacks. There are at least two sorts of universal properties that raise problems for the counterfactual analysis.[12]

Consider the rather odd property of being such that force equals mass times acceleration. An object has this property as long as F=ma; so Wilma's singing has this property (if F=ma). In fact, for every natural law, there is a property which an object has just in case that law holds, and Wilma's singing has all those properties, too. Let P, Q, R,... be the various natural laws which "cover" the events that occur when Wilma's singing causes the shattering, and consider the following counterfactual:

> If Wilma's singing had lacked the property of being such that P, Q, R,...., then the shattering would not have occurred.

This says, in effect, that if some of the laws had not held, then the shattering would not have occurred. It seems to be true. If it is true, then on the Counterfactual Analysis, a property of having a law hold is causally relevant. But this is counterintuitive. The properties mentioned by a law are likely candidates for being causally relevant. Not so for the property of a law's holding.

Here is another case involving universal properties. Suppose that Wilma's singing occurs at time t, and that the shattering occurs at t'. Now consider the property of being such that some object exists at t'. Wilma's singing has this property, since some object exists at t'. But if her singing had lacked that property, then the glass's shattering would never have occurred. So by the counterfactual analysis, this property is a causally relevant property of Wilma's singing. Again, this is counterintuitive.[13]

This ends my criticisms of the Counterfactual Analysis. I do not maintain that these criticisms are conclusive. But the number and variety of problems are sufficient to motivate looking for a different sort of analysis of causal relevance.

4. The Essentialist Analysis

To obtain our next analysis, let's begin with the relation of causal relevance between *events*, and then build on this to get a relation of causal relevance between properties and events. When should we say that one event is causally relevant to another event? One obvious answer is, "when the first is a cause of the second." So we get

> (E)   If c and e are events, then *c is causally relevant to e* iff c is a cause of e.[14]

Now let's return to our original notion, that of an event's having a property that is causally relevant to another event. (A three-place relation, as I mentioned above.) Let's consider the following proposal: a property is causally relevant to an effect iff it is *essential* to an event that is causally relevant to that effect. Or, in other words, causally relevant properties are essential properties of causes.

> (E3)   If c and e are events, and F is a property, then *c's being F is causally relevant to e* iff
> (1) c is causally relevant to e (i.e., c is a cause of e).
> (2) c is essentially F.

Call this the '*Essentialist Analysis*'. (I have labeled it 'E3' because it is an essentialist analysis of a three-place relation.)

The Essentialist Analysis might be surprising, but I think it is intuitively plausible (on reflection).[15] The notion of a causally relevant property is, very roughly, that of a property which is "needed," in some sense, for an effect to occur, and which is involved somehow in causing the effect. Both of these intuitive desiderata are met by the Essentialist Analysis. Take some effect. That effect "needs" its causes in order to occur. Those causes also "need" their essential properties in order to occur. So an effect does, in a sense, "need" the essential properties of its causes in order to occur.

We are also inclined to say that a causally relevant property is a property that "makes a difference" to whether or not an effect occurs. On the Essentialist Analysis, a causally relevant property makes a difference to whether or not a cause occurs, for a cause cannot occur without having its essential properties. A cause, in turn, makes a (causal) difference to whether its effect occurs. So there is a strong sense in which a causally relevant property makes a difference to whether an effect occurs.

The Essentialist Analysis can also explain the successes of the Counter-factual Analysis, and our natural inclination to use counterfactuals when thinking about causal relevance. On the Essentialist Analysis, a counterfactual of the form "if the cause had not had that property, then the effect would not have occurred" is true, when the property is causally relevant. For if the property is causally relevant on the Essentialist Analysis, then it is essential to the cause, and so the counterfactual has an impossible antecedent. On standard (Stalnaker-Lewis) accounts of counterfactuals, counterfactuals with impossible antecedents are vacuously true. So assuming this standard account, the counterfactual will be true whenever the property mentioned is essential to the cause.[16] Therefore, if a property is causally relevant according to the Essentialist Analysis, then it is also causally relevant according to the Counterfactual Analysis.[17]

The converse holds in many cases, but not all. The differences allow the Essentialist Analysis to handle some cases that are problematic for counterfactual analyses. Pre-emption is no problem; if the property is essential to an actual cause, then the fact that the cause might have been pre-empted does not matter. Closely related properties do not present a difficulty. If the amplitude of Wilma's singing is essential to it, then the existence of closely related amplitudes is unimportant. The universal properties and negative properties that I mentioned above are not essential properties of the causes, so the Essentialist Analysis does not entail that they are causally relevant.[18]

We can existentially generalize on the Essentialist Analysis to get analyses of (i) the notion of a property that is causally relevant to an event (a two-place relation between properties and events); and (ii) the notion of a causally relevant property *tout court* (a one-place property of properties).[19]

> (E2) If e is an event and F is a property, then *F is causally relevant to e* iff: there is an event c such that
> (1) c is causally relevant to e (c is a cause of e).
> (2) c is essentially F.

> (E1) If F is a property, then *F is a causally relevant property* iff: there are events c and e such that
> (1) c is causally relevant to e (c is a cause of e).
> (2) c is essentially F.

5. The Essentialist Analysis and Event Individuation

There is another strong motivation for the Essentialist Analysis that I want to mention. It has to do with event individuation and causation. I can best explain it by example.[20]

Suppose that Fred says 'hello' rather too loudly. It is plausible to think that there are at least two events occurring as Fred utters 'hello'. One event is essentially a saying-'hello' and essentially loud. The other event is also essentially a saying-'hello', but only accidentally loud. Both occur in the same location, and both are loud, but they are distinct, since only the second could have been soft. Though distinct, these events are closely related. For instance, the first *necessitates* the second: it is necessary that if the first occurs, then so does the second.

One good reason for thinking that there are two such non-identical events is that they seem to differ in their causes and effects. The first event (the essentially loud event) is caused by Fred's being nervous. The second is not. Our counterfactual judgments support this conclusion. If Fred had not been nervous, the second event would still have occurred — Fred would still have said 'hello', but softly. These events also seem to differ in their effects. The second event (the accidentally loud one), but not the first, causes Barney to say 'hello' in return. For if the essentially loud event had not occurred, the accidentally loud event still might have occurred, but softly, and in that case, Barney would still have said 'hello'.

This example, and the above analysis of it, lend some support to the Essentialist Analysis. For it seems that it is the difference in the events' *essential* properties that allows them to differ in their effects. The reason that one event causes Barney's response and the other does not is that one possesses a certain property accidentally, whereas the other has it essentially. The property of being a saying-'hello' is causally relevant to Barney's response because it is an essential property of a cause of Barney's response; the property of being loud is not causally relevant to Barney's response, even though it is possessed by a cause of his response, because that property is not possessed essentially by that cause (or any other cause). So this example, and others, give us reason to think that the Essentialist Analysis is on the right track.[21]

6. Problems With the Essentialist Analysis

But the Essentialist Analysis is not quite right. Sometimes a cause has an essential property that is not causally relevant to its effects. The cases I know of involve modal properties, universally essential properties, "necessitated properties," and negative essential properties.[22]

6.1 Modal Properties

Consider Wilma's singing and its property of occurring-as-Sylvester-sneezes (Sylvester being some 20 miles away). Wilma's singing has that property contingently. But consider the property of *actually*-occurring-as-Sylvester sneezes. This "rigidified" property is essential to Wilma's singing.[23] So on the Essentialist Analysis the property of actually-occurring-as-Sylvester-sneezes is causally relevant to the glass's shattering. But that is counterintuitive. Obviously, *any* other contingent property of Wilma's singing could be "actualized" to get another essential property.

A similar problem occurs with *possibility* properties. Suppose that Wilma's singing does not occur as Fred coughs, but that it might have. So Wilma's singing has the property of possibly-occurring-as-Fred-coughs. Wilma's singing has that property essentially. So on the Essentialist Analysis, that property is causally relevant property to the shattering.

Let's say that if F is a property, then the properties of being possibly F, being necessarily F, and being actually F are *modal properties*. The above examples show that the Essentialist Analysis has problems with at least some modal properties.

6.2 Universally Essential Properties

There are non-modal properties that everything has essentially. For example: being self-identical, being F-or-not-F (for any F), being such that $2 + 2 = 4$, being such that four colors are sufficient to color every map. On the Essentialist Analysis, all of these properties are causally relevant properties of every cause. But they are not.

6.3 Necessitated Properties

The property of having pitch P is essential to Wilma's singing, and also (intuitively) causally relevant. But if having-pitch-P is essential to Wilma's singing, then so is the property of having-pitch-P-*or*-occurring-as-Sylvester-sneezes. So according to the Essentialist Analysis, this *disjunctive property* is a causally relevant property of Wilma's singing. In general, if F is essential to c, then so is F-or-G, for *any* G whatsoever — even if G is clearly not causally relevant, and even if G is not instantiated by c. So on the Essentialist Analysis, being F-or-G is causally relevant. But surely not all such disjunctive properties are causally relevant.

This disjunctive property of Wilma's singing is what I call a 'necessitated property'. Suppose that c's being F is causally relevant to e and that the Essentialist Analysis agrees: that is, c is essentially F, and c causes e. Now suppose further that it's necessary that anything that is F is also H. Then H is necessitated by an obviously causally relevant property, and qualifies as a necessitated property. By the Essentialist Analysis, H is also causally relevant to e.

Disjunctive properties are not the only troublesome necessitated properties. If Wilma's singing has pitch P essentially, then it also has the property of having *some* pitch essentially; and it also has the property of having *some property* essentially; and so on. All of these are causally relevant on the Essentialist Analysis.[24]

6.4 Negative Essential Properties

Wilma's singing is essentially a singing. It is also essentially *not* an explosion, not a kick, not a brown cow, not green, and not triangular. According to the Essentialist Analysis, all of these negative properties are causally relevant to the shattering. But that is very counter-intuitive.

7. A Final Analysis

So the Essentialist Analysis is incorrect. But it is still well motivated by examples, by plausible arguments, and by plausible views concerning event causation and individuation. So perhaps all the analysis needs is an amendment that will exclude the above problematic properties. I think that there is such a way of amending the analysis. This amendment appeals to the notion of a *natural property*.

As a matter of fact, I will present below *two* amended versions of the Essentialist Analysis. The first one will be rather uninteresting, but will almost certainly exclude the problematic properties. I will then present the analysis that appeals to natural properties. Finally, I will argue that these two amended analyses are equivalent. I will later discuss the advantages and (alleged) disadvantages of appealing to the notion of a natural property in an analysis of causal relevance.

7.1. Potentially Causally Relevant Properties

One way to rule out the problematic properties is to add a clause to the Essentialist Analysis requiring that F be a *potentially causally relevant* property. In other words, we could require that F be a property that *can* be causally relevant. Call the analysis that includes this requirement the '*Relevant Essentialist Analysis*' (or the 'Relevant Analysis', for short). This analysis would exclude the problematic properties because none of them is potentially causally relevant (or so it seems).

Notice that the property of being a potentially causally relevant property is a one-place property (of properties), whereas the relation of causal relevance that we are analyzing is a three-place relation (among a property and two events). So the analysandum does not appear on the right hand side of the analysis, and neither does any synonym. So the analysandum and the analysans are not synonymous, and the analysis is not completely trivial. But one might nevertheless think that we now need an analysis of the notion of a potentially causally relevant property. Or if we cannot have an analysis of it, then we deserve some further explanation of it.

We could turn around and explain potential causal relevance in terms of the three-place relation of causal relevance: a property is potentially causally relevant iff it is possible for there to be events c and e such that c's being F is causally relevant to e. This would give us a very tight circle of interdefinables—perhaps too tight to be very interesting.

We might also appeal to causal laws in order to get at least a sufficient condition for potential causal relevance. It's plausible to think that if a genuine causal law ascribes property F to causes, then F is potentially causally relevant. Perhaps this could be strengthened into a necessary condition—I consider this possibility below.

In any case, the Relevant Essentialist Analysis is disappointing, but effective in dispensing with the problematic properties.

7.2. Natural Properties

We can understand the second way of ruling out the problematic properties by noticing that all of those properties seem to be a bit strange or a bit "derivative." Our expressions for referring to them are complex, and we may suspect that the properties themselves are, in some way, complex. Furthermore, and more importantly, these properties do not seem to divide things into genuine kinds, and possession of them does not make for genuine resemblance. For instance, two things may share a disjunctive property without (intuitively) being members of the same kind and without genuinely resembling each other. Two events may share the property of being-a-singing-or-an-explosion without genuinely resembling each other. Two events (or objects) may both be not-green without resembling each other in the least.

These points hold not only for the properties mentioned in the earlier examples, but also for many others. For instance, two objects may both be shorter than the Eiffel Tower, or grue, without having anything significant in common. Two events may both be fifty miles north of a burning barn, or simultaneous with George's sneeze, or longer than World War II, without really resembling each other.[25]

So we have strong (independent) motivation for making a distinction between those properties that make for genuine resemblance and significant kinds, and those that do not. Let's say that the properties that make for genuine resemblance, and for membership in significant kinds, are *natural* properties.[26,27]

How might this distinction help us in amending the Essentialist Analysis? I believe we can exclude the properties that raise problems for the Essentialist Analysis by requiring that a causally relevant property be natural.

> (NE3) If c and e are events, and F is a property, then *c's being F is causally relevant to e* iff:
> (1) c is causally relevant to e (c is a cause of e).
> (2) c is essentially F.
> (3) F is a natural property.

Call this the '*Natural Essentialist Analysis*' (or the 'Natural Analysis', for short).[28]

This modification should help deal with negative properties and the problematic disjunctive properties. Negative properties and disjunctive properties are not natural, because they do not make for genuine resemblance. So these properties do not count as causally relevant on this modified account.[29] Similarly, many items that share universally essential properties do not genuinely resemble each other, and so these properties are neither natural nor causally relevant. The same thing goes for the troublesome modal properties.[30]

So much for how natural properties can help the Essentialist Analysis. One might still want to know more about how we can tell whether a property is natural. Thus far I have been appealing to intuitions about genuine resemblance. Intuitions about genuine resemblance are a strong motivation for making the distinction, and they do give us a good grip on the notion. But is there some further criterion for, or explanation of, naturalness? I believe there are rather severe limits on how far such explanations can go, because I believe that the property of naturalness is a metaphysically fundamental property of properties. But I think we can appeal to causal laws in order to state a sufficient condition for naturalness. Unnatural properties are not mentioned in any causal laws that we know of; only properties that make for genuine resemblance appear in them. So, plausibly, a sufficient condition for a property's being natural is that it be mentioned in a causal law. The causal law need not be strict, since properties that appear in *ceteris paribus* laws also appear to be natural.

We can now see how the Relevant Analysis and the Natural Analysis are related (and why I mentioned the Relevant Analysis first). Earlier I gave the following sufficient condition for potential causal relevance: if a causal law ascribes F to causes, then F is potentially causally relevant. But, obviously, if a law ascribes F to causes, then the law mentions F. And if a law mentions F, then F is natural, according to the preceding paragraph. So we get an analogous sufficient condition for naturalness: if a causal law ascribes F to causes, then F is natural.

This makes the following conjecture plausible: a property is natural iff it is potentially causally relevant. If this is so, then the Relevant Analysis and the Natural Analysis are equivalent.

There is a fairly plausible argument for this conjecture by way of causal laws. Assume that if a causal law mentions F as a property of causes, then F is natural. Now assume that the converse is also true. And assume, furthermore, that a causal law mentions property F as a property of causes iff it is potentially causally relevant.[31] Then a property is natural if and only if it is potentially causally relevant.

So the natural properties may well be all and only the potentially causally relevant properties. Thus the Relevant and Natural Analyses may well be equivalent. Since the Relevant Analysis almost certainly excludes the properties that are problematic for the Essentialist Analysis, we can conclude that the Natural Analysis does so also.[32]

Thus I conclude that the Natural Essentialist Analysis provides modally necessary and sufficient conditions for the three-place relation of causal relevance. As before, we can existentially generalize on this analysis to get analyses of two-place and one-place relations of causal relevance.

8. Remarks on, and Objections to, the Natural Analysis

The Natural Essentialist Analysis ties together many subjects in metaphysics. It informs us directly of relations between causal relevance, event causation, essential properties of events, and natural properties. It also tells us indirectly about how these are connected with genuine resemblance, event individuation, counterfactual dependence, and causal laws. So the Natural Analysis is, in that sense, highly informative. This is one of its virtues.

One might well have suspected, before looking for an analysis of causal relevance, that some of these properties and relations are closely connected. In fact, others have remarked on some of these connections (though not in discussions of three-place causal relevance). For instance, Armstrong, Lewis, and Shoemaker have maintained that the natural properties (the properties that make for genuine resemblance) are those that are potentially causally relevant.[33] And, as I mentioned earlier, some philosophers have explored the connection between the essential properties of events and their causal relations. (See notes 15 and 20.) The Natural Essentialist Analysis describes how these matters relate to three-place causal relevance for properties. So it confirms our (pre-theoretic) hunches that these connections exist. I take this to be another virtue of the Natural Analysis, and to be some confirming evidence for it.

But these very virtues may prevent the Natural Analysis from satisfying expectations that some may have for an analysis of causal relevance. For the rest of this section, I will try to anticipate some objections that may arise from these unsatisfied expectations. Abstracting away from the details, my response is that the Natural Analysis is interesting and informative even if it does not meet these expectations. Furthermore, these expectations are unreasonably high. We have no reason to think that any (correct) analysis could satisfy them.

For instance, it might be objected that the Natural Analysis has very limited usefulness, because in order to use it, one must make certain judgements about essential properties and their naturalness, and these judgments may be as difficult to make as judgments about causal relevance itself. I agree that this may happen in some cases. But how serious an objection to the Natural Analysis is this? Some may take this to be a serious objection because of their (commonly held) expectations for such analyses. They may, for instance, expect an analysis to give us an easily applicable "decision procedure". The Natural Analysis does not. It merely purports to give us an informative set of modally necessary and sufficient conditions for causal relevance. But there's little reason to think that there is an analysis of causal relevance which constitutes a "decision procedure". Moreover, the (alleged) limited usefulness of the Natural Analysis is no objection to its truth; nor does it detract from the interest of the analysis.

It's also easy to exaggerate the limits on the usefulness of the Natural Analysis. We have various (somewhat independent) judgments about event individuation, causation, essential properties, naturalness, and, finally, causal relevance. When we are more confident in our judgments regarding the former than we are in our judgments about causal relevance, then the Natural Analysis may help us form judgments concerning causal relevance. When we are more confident in our judgments about causal relevance than in our judgments about the other properties, then the Natural Analysis may serve as a guide to, or at least as a constraint on, our forming judgments about these other matters.

This first objection leads quite naturally to a second potential objection having to do with *circularity*, of a broadly epistemic sort. Applying the analysis (the objection goes) may easily lead us into a circle. For instance, to determine whether a property is natural, we may need to consider whether a property is mentioned by a causal law, which may lead us to ask whether that property is ever causally relevant to an effect. A similar point holds for attempts to use the analysis to justify our judgments of causal relevance.

In fact, one might think this sort of epistemic circularity emerged earlier, before we considered natural properties. Consider Fred's saying 'hello' again. Why did I maintain that there are two 'hello's, one that is accidentally loud and another that is essentially loud? Perhaps I *first* judged that the loudness of Fred's 'hello' was causally irrelevant to Barney's response. So I *then* inferred that there must be a 'hello' that is only accidentally loud. Thus I concluded that there are two distinct 'hello's. So perhaps my judgments about the events' individuation and their essential properties were determined by my judgments about the causal relevance of certain properties to Barney's response. Wouldn't this sort of circularity occur in all attempts to use the (Natural) Essentialist Analysis?

I reply that the Natural Essentialist Analysis *may* lead one in a circle. But it also may not, if one has (what one takes to be) reliable judgments about event individuation, essential properties and the naturalness of those properties. Typically, one will have to "balance" one's judgments about all these matters. Again, this epistemic point does not detract from the virtues of the Natural Analysis. It does not show that the Natural Analysis is useless, or uninformative, or false. If anything, it raises the question of why we should think that the traditional requirement, that an analysis should always avoid this sort of epistemic circularity, can be satisfied.

According to a third objection, the Natural Analysis is *uninformative* because the above circles are "too tight". This objection is particularly wide of the mark. Firstly, as I said above, there is an obvious sense in which the Natural Essentialist Analysis is informative: it informs us of some of the relations between properties and relations like causation and naturalness. (In fact, some may think that the Natural Analysis is so informative that it is misinformative.) Secondly, tightness of epistemic circles is not a good criterion for informativeness. Synonymy is clearly a better criterion; but the two "sides" of the Natural

Analysis are not synonymous. Finally, the circles are not so tight as the objection suggests, for we have several different notions at work here. Essentiality, causation, naturalness, and causal relevance are directly involved, while others are indirectly involved.

Finally, one might be worried by what might be called a *metaphysical* circularity. We've seen that three-place causal relevance might be analyzed partly in terms of potential causal relevance. But one might also be able to analyze potential causal relevance in terms of the three-place relation; and perhaps we could analyze naturalness in terms of potential causal relevance. And in fact, it might be hard to avoid mentioning three-place causal relevance if one attempted to analyze naturalness or potential causal relevance. So we may have a set of "inter-analyzable" properties and relations here. But this is a sign that none of these relations is more "basic", in a metaphysical sense, than any other. Thus (one might conclude) the Natural "analysis" does not analyze causal relevance into metaphysically "more basic" properties and relations, or tell us what the three-place causal relevance relation metaphysically consists in (whatever that may mean), and so it fails as an analysis.[34]

I agree that the "inter-analyzability" of these properties and relations is a sign that we have reached metaphysical "bedrock". But we might have suspected, even before we began looking for an analysis, that causal relevance is a metaphysically basic relation. If it is basic, then it does not "decompose", and so a traditional analysis of it is impossible. Furthermore, there is no reason (of which I am aware) to think that causal relevance is not basic, and that a more traditional analysis is possible. But if causal relevance is basic, then the most we can hope to obtain in an analysis is information about how it is related to other metaphysically important matters. That is, the most we can hope for is an informative set of necessary and sufficient conditions for causal relevance — which is just what the Natural Essentialist Analysis is (or purports to be).

Perhaps it is misleading to call the Natural Analysis an "analysis", if it does not satisfy the traditional expectations for an analysis. However, the Natural Analysis does satisfy one traditional requirement: it is an informative set of modally necessary and sufficient conditions. If that is not enough for it to be an analysis, then we should take it be merely such a set of conditions — which is, after all, enough to make it interesting.

This ends my attempt to present and defend an analysis of causal relevance. For the remainder of this paper I criticize an alternative line of analysis, and then attempt to apply the Natural Essentialist Analysis to two cases, one involving a semantic property of a mental state.

9. On Nomological Analyses

I have suggested that there are some close connections between causal relevance and causal laws. So one might suspect that the notion of a causally relevant property can be analyzed in terms of causal laws, while entirely bypassing the Natural Essentialist Analysis. Several philosophers have offered such *nomological analyses* of causal relevance. Fodor (1989) proposes the following:

> F is a causally relevant property *if* it is a causal law that F-instantiations are sufficient for G-instantiations.

But this won't do as a replacement for the Natural Essentialist Analysis for two reasons. For one thing, the analysandum is wrong. Fodor is analyzing the notion *F is causally relevant*, whereas the Natural Essentialist Analysis analyzes *c's being F is causally relevant to e*. Secondly, Fodor provides at best a sufficient condition for his analysandum.[35,36]

To get a nomological analysis of the three-place causal relevance relation, we need the notion of a property that is a necessary part of a set of properties that is causally sufficient for an effect. A bit more precisely: a property of a cause is causally relevant to an effect if it is a member of a minimal set of properties which is sufficient, under the laws, to bring about the effect. Still more precisely:

> If c and e are events, and F is a property, then *c's being F is causally relevant to e* iff
>
> (1)   c is a cause of e.
> (2)   c is F.
> (3)   There is a set of true law propositions L, and one of L mentions F as a property of causes.
> (4)   L, and a set of true propositions of particular fact P, together with the proposition that c occurs and is F, entail that e occurs; but L and P, together with the proposition that c occurs and is *not* F, do not entail that e occurs.

This is a rough, first attempt, but it is explicit enough for me to say why I am unhappy with it. First, I doubt that it is a necessary truth that all causation falls under laws. I think it is possible for there to be a cause and an effect whose causal transaction is not "covered" by a law. Perhaps such causal transactions occur in completely lawless worlds. But even in these cases, there may be a difference between the causally relevant and causally irrelevant properties of the cause. Say that these causally relevant properties are "lawlessly causally relevant." Nomological analyses entail that lawless causal relevance is impossible. Now perhaps there are no actual lawlessly causally relevant properties. But do we want to say they are impossible?[37]

I have a second, more specific, worry about the nomological analysis. Clause (4) requires that the laws, the proposition that c is F, and some set of particular fact propositions, together entail that e occurs. I am sure that such premises can entail that a certain *kind* of event occurs. But the premises can entail that e itself occurs only if they can entail some (modally) sufficient condition for an *individual* event e to exist. Whether they can is a hard question in the metaphysics of events. But I doubt that they can.

10. Content Properties

I will now try to apply the Natural Essentialist Analysis to two examples. I will first consider Wilma's singing. This will allow us to see that the analysis can deliver the right results, and it will give us some practice in making judgments about event individuation and causation. I then want to apply the analysis to a case involving a mental state and a mental property. In particular, I want to consider a belief and its property of expressing a certain proposition. (I am counting this *content property* as a mental property.) I want to argue that this property is causally relevant to some action.

In order to apply the analysis, I must make judgments about the causes of certain effects, the essential properties of those causes, and the naturalness of those properties. Though I think my judgments (and arguments for them) are correct, one could reasonably question them, even if one accepted the Natural Essentialist Analysis. This should not be surprising. We should expect some cases to be hard and controversial, even given a plausible analysis. (Would the analysis be more plausible if it made all the hard cases easy?)

Let's turn to Wilma's singing, and its property of meaning *shatter*. To determine whether the singing's having this meaning is causally relevant to the glass's shattering, we must (among other things) determine whether there is an event that has that meaning essentially, and, if there is, whether it is a cause of the glass's shattering. Here is a quick summary of what I think: There is a singing which has that meaning essentially.[38] But no singing that has that meaning essentially is a cause of the shattering. So it is not the case that there is a singing whose possession of that semantic property is causally relevant to the shattering.

Let me elaborate and explain. There are many events occurring in Wilma's time and location when she sings. For instance, there is a singing which essentially means *shatter*, essentially is an utterance of 'shatter', and essentially has a certain pitch and amplitude. There is also a distinct singing event which has only the pitch and amplitude essentially. The first event could not occur without meaning *shatter*, whereas the second could. (The second event could also fail to be an utterance of the sound 'shatter' — it might instead be an utterance of 'matter' or 'hatter', or an utterance of some fairly similar non-English sound, like 'atter'). Call the first event the 'rich singing' since it has a rich set of essential properties; call the second event the 'poor singing'.

The poor singing (the singing that accidentally means *shatter*) is a cause of the shattering; the rich singing (the singing that essentially means *shatter*) is not. I think this is intuitively plausible. But in any case, the following counterfactuals seem to support my view. If the rich singing had not occurred, the poor singing still might have. But if the poor singing had occurred, then the shattering would (still) have occurred. So if the rich singing had not occurred, the shattering still might have occurred. Therefore, the rich singing is not a cause of the shattering.

I think this counterfactual reasoning is strong support for my claim that the rich singing is not a cause of the shattering. But one might wonder whether the first counterfactual is true. How, one might ask, could the rich singing occur without the poor singing? And is this very "likely" to occur? Is it only a "remote" possibility, insufficient to make the counterfactual true? To use possible worlds talk: are the worlds in which the poor singing occurs without the rich singing at least as similar to actuality as those worlds in which neither occurs?

Well, just before Wilma sings, she has various intentions. Let's suppose she intends to break the glass, to impress her audience, and to pretend that she is ordering the glass to shatter. These intentions cause her to have intentions to say *shatter*, to utter 'shatter', and to sing with a certain pitch and amplitude. But Wilma could have sung without intending to pretend to order the glass to shatter, and so without intending to say *shatter*. She could merely have intended to break the glass, and thus merely intended to sing with a certain pitch and amplitude. In that case, her intention to sing at a certain pitch and amplitude would still have occurred. This intention would still have caused a sound with the same pitch and amplitude as her actual sounds. So the poor singing would still have occurred. But the rich singing would not have occurred. For Wilma's intention to say *shatter* is a cause of the rich singing, and the rich singing means *shatter* because it is caused by that intention.[39] So without the intention to say *shatter*, the sound that she produced would not mean *shatter*, and the rich singing would not occur.

So there are worlds in which the following occurs: Wilma intends to break the glass and impress her audience and sing with a certain pitch and amplitude, but she doesn't intend to say *shatter*. So the poor singing occurs but the rich singing does not. And still the glass breaks. I say that these worlds are no more remote from actuality than those in which neither the rich singing nor the poor singing occurs. (Those latter worlds are worlds in which Wilma does not sing at all, or she sings at a different pitch and amplitude.) So the counterfactual is true.

So the rich singing is not a cause of the shattering. The same goes for any other singing-event that essentially means *shatter*. (Similar counterfactual reasoning would apply.) So the property of meaning *shatter* is not causally relevant to the shattering.

Let's turn now to mental states. Suppose Wilma believes that there is champagne before her. Suppose she wishes to drink the champagne, and then does so. Her beliefs and desires have certain semantic properties or content properties: they express certain propositions. Are these properties causally relevant to her drinking the champagne? I think the answer is 'yes'.

A quick summary of my reasons: When Wilma believes that there is champagne before her, there is a mental event occurring in her that I will call a 'belief'. That event is a cause of her champagne drinking. It essentially has the property of having the propositional content that there is champagne before Wilma. That property is a natural property. So by the Natural Essentialist

Analysis, the belief's having that content is causally relevant to the champagne drinking.

Now more about the details. Those who think the content property is not essential are perhaps forgetting that there may be more than one mental event involved, just as there was more than one singing involved in the previous case. I think that there is at least one belief event in Wilma that essentially has the content that there is champagne before her. That event could not have occurred without having that content. I will call it the 'rich mental event'. But it is also plausible to hold that there is another belief-like event that has the content only accidentally. Call that the 'poor mental event'. (Whether this last event is a *belief*, I will not try to judge, but I am inclined to think that beliefs have their contents essentially. The poor mental event might be something like what others have called 'narrow mental states'.)

As for the naturalness of the content property: Beliefs that share the property of expressing the proposition that there is champagne before Wilma seem to be genuinely similar. Furthermore, this property seems to figure in certain (*ceteris paribus*) laws. For instance, anyone who believes that there is champagne before Wilma will be caused thereby to believe that there is champagne before someone. So this property seems to be natural.[40]

The rich mental event (the belief that has the content essentially) is a cause of the champagne drinking. So it is correct to say that Wilma's belief that there is champagne before her causes her to drink it. It is hard to resist this judgment. And it is also supported by the following, seemingly true, counterfactual:

(1)   If the rich mental event (the essentially contentful belief) had not occurred, then the champagne drinking would not have occurred.

In more ordinary terms: if Wilma had not believed that there was champagne before her, she would not have drunk the champagne.

Now someone could question this last counterfactual, and my causal claim, in a way that is analogous with the singing case. Such an objector might reason as follows:

(2)   If the rich mental event had not occurred, then the poor mental event still might have.

Furthermore,

(3)   If the poor mental event had occurred (without the rich one), then the champagne drinking would still have occurred.

If (2) and (3) are correct, then (the objector might maintain) the rich belief is not a cause of the drinking.

I reject this reasoning because I doubt that (2) is true.[41] First of all, (2) is not very plausible. It is difficult to imagine how the poor mental event could occur without the rich event. That is, it is difficult to imagine how the poor event could occur without having its actual content.

Difficult, but not impossible. I admit that it is *possible* for the poor event to occur without having its actual content. Imagine that Wilma grows up in a world (a "Twin Earth") where there is no champagne, but where there is a superficially similar liquid, *schmampagne* (which is, for instance, not made from grapes). Suppose she nevertheless is molecularly the same as she actually is, and receives all the surface stimuli she actually does. I suppose the poor mental event could occur in such a situation. Then it would not have its actual *champagne* content — it might instead have the propositional content that there is *schmampagne* before Wilma. So in this situation, the rich mental event would not occur. So it is possible for the poor mental event to occur without the rich mental event.

But all this shows is that it is possible for the antecedent and consequent of (2) to be true together. This is *not* enough to show that (2) is true, since the compossibility of a counterfactual's antecedent and consequent is never enough to show that it is true. For instance, it is possible that: I am not a philosopher and I live on Mars. But it is false that if I were not a philosopher, then I might live on Mars. On the contrary, if I were not a philosopher, I would still live on Earth (working as a chemist or a plumber or whatnot). The "Martian possibility" is a possibility, but it is too "remote" to make the counterfactual true. Similarly for (2). The "Twin Earth possibility" is too remote a possibility to make (2) true. To use worlds talk: the worlds in which neither the poor nor the rich mental event occurs are more similar to actuality than those worlds in which the poor mental event occurs without its actual *champagne* content.[42]

So I conclude that counterfactual (1) is true. And thus I conclude that the rich mental event (the belief that has the content essentially) causes Wilma's champagne drinking.[43] The content property is natural. Therefore, the Natural Essentialist Analysis entails that the content property of Wilma's belief is causally relevant to her champagne drinking.[44]

Notes

1. See, for example, Block (1990), Dretske (1989), Fodor (1989), Heil and Mele (1991), Horgan (1989), Kim (1979, 1984, 1989), LePore and Loewer (1987, 1989), Segal and Sober (1991), Sosa (1984), and Yablo (1992b).

2. The events that we ordinarily call 'causes' are causes which are remarkable or salient in some way (in some context, given the reasons for thinking about causation in that context). They are causes that, for instance, are out of the ordinary, or are morally reprehensible. That is why, in most conversational contexts, we would not say that Wilma's birth is a cause of her singing, or that the window's having a certain shape is a cause of its breaking. See Lewis (1986b, pp. 214-6) for further discussion.

3. See Lewis (1986c) and Kim (1973, 1974, 1976).

4. Dretske (1989, pp. 1-2) says about this case, "...the fact that these sounds have a

meaning is surely irrelevant to their having this effect. The glass would shatter if the sounds meant something completely different, or if they meant nothing at all."

5. Horgan's (1989) analysis of what he calls '*quausal* relevance' strongly resembles LePore and Loewer's (1987), in that it is motivated by counterfactual considerations. Block (1990) seems to endorse a counterfactual analysis of causal relevance without explicitly providing one.

6. Of course, I mean some property other than existence or occurrence. LePore and Loewer (1987) fix on the first analysandum because they wish to defend Davidson against the charge of making mental properties epiphenomenal. Davidson holds something like a nomological theory of causation, and the first analysandum seems appropriate for a nomological theory of causal relevance.

7. I am indebted to correspondence with Joseph Almog and Noa Goldring in the following criticisms of the Counterfactual Analysis.

8. See the postscripts to Lewis (1973) in Lewis (1986a).

9. Horgan, and LePore and Loewer, are aware of this problem. They respond by restricting their analyses to cases that do not involve pre-emption.

    The Wilma-Betty example must be modified somewhat to show that certain variants of the Counterfactual Analysis have problems with pre-emption. One variant analysis modifies the crucial counterfactual to:

    If c had not been F, then c would not have caused e.

    The Wilma-Betty example in the text does not constitute a counterexample to this variant. If Wilma's singing had not had the right pitch, Betty's singing would have caused the shattering—but the counterfactual

    If Wilma's singing had not had that pitch, then Wilma's singing would not have caused the shattering

    is still true. Here is a counterexample to this variant analysis: Betty listens to Wilma to determine whether Wilma is singing at the right pitch to shatter the glass. Betty has decided to sing if Wilma's pitch is not correct. So if Wilma's singing had not had that pitch, it would still cause the glass to shatter, by first causing Betty to sing.

10. Horgan (1989, p. 60) is aware of the problem of closely related properties. He responds by forbidding consideration of counterfactual situations in which the cause has a property that is (1) of the same "general type" as the actual property, and (2) is causally relevant "in essentially the same way." Horgan realizes that this exclusion makes his analysis circular, but he does not try to break out of the circle.

11. Notice that "instantiations" of these negative properties are (usually) not sufficient for the occurrence of an event that is a genuine cause of the effect. For instance: there is some air where a soundproof wall might have been. The presence of air is a genuine cause of the shattering. One might initially think that the absence of a soundproof wall is the same as the presence of air in that spot. This might lead one to think that the property of not-being-located-near-a-soundproof-wall is causally relevant to the shattering. But the presence of air and the absence of a soundproof wall are not the same—the absence of the wall would "occur" if there were no air at all, or if there were a blanket where there is actually air, or if there were a sound-generating machine where there is actually air, and so on.

12. The universal properties mentioned below are different sorts of properties, and may raise problems for different reasons. One might refuse to recognize some of them as properties. I agree with this reaction to this extent: we must distinguish between these rather un-natural properties and others in order to distinguish between causally relevant and irrelevant properties. See section 7.

13. One might suspect that this example does not satisfy clause (4) of the Counterfactual Analysis. But it does. The proposition that Wilma's singing is such-that-some-object-exists-at-t′ does not logically or metaphysically entail that the shattering occurs. Also, the proposition that the shattering occurs (at t′) does not entail that Wilma's singing occurs; thus it does not entail that Wilma's singing has the above property. We can construct further counterexamples of the same sort by finding propositions entailed by the proposition that e occurs, but which do not entail that Wilma's singing occurs. For instance, that the shattering occurs metaphysically entails that some glass exists at some time or other. But this latter proposition does not entail that Wilma's singing occurs. So by the Counterfactual Analysis, the singing's having the property of being-such-that-some-glass-exists-at-some-time is causally relevant to the shattering.

14. I assume that the "right to left" direction of (E) is uncontroversial: if c is a cause of e, then c is causally relevant to e. But some might reject the converse, that is, some might maintain that an event may be causally relevant to e, and yet not be a cause of e. Yablo (1992b, pp. 273-4) may hold this view. I cannot review all the different reasons one might have for holding this view. But one possible reason is this: one might think that a real cause must not only be causally relevant to an effect, but must also be causally sufficient (or nearly so) for the effect. I reject this reason, because many events that we judge to be causes are nowhere close to being causally sufficient. In any case, I accept (E), and I assume it in my analyses. Someone who rejects (E) could still accept my analyses of causal relevance *for properties*, by ignoring the remarks that assume (E) and substituting her preferred analysis (if any) of causal relevance between *events*.

15. Lewis (1973, 1986c) and Yablo (1992a, 1992b) also see many connections between the essential properties of events and their causal properties.

16. To be precise, the counterfactual "If c had not had that property, then e would not have occurred" is ambiguous, and will be *vacuously* true on only one reading.

   (1) If it were the case that (c occurs and is *not* F), then it would not be the case that e occurs.

   (2) If it were *not* the case that (c occurs and is F), then it would not be the case that e occurs.

The difference is in the scope of the negation in the antecedent. Suppose F is essential to c. Then the antecedent of (1) is false in every world because there is no world where c occurs and is not F. So it is impossible, and (1) is vacuously true. But there are worlds where c does not occur. In those worlds, the antecedent of (2) is true. So the antecedent of (2) is possible, and (2) is not vacuously true.

   Nevertheless, (2) will almost always be true if the Essentialist Analysis says that c's being F is causally relevant to e. For then F is essential to c, and so the second counterfactual is equivalent to

(3)   If it were not the case that c occurs, then it would not be the case that e occurs.

This counterfactual is true if c causes e, if there is no pre-emption or redundant causation going on. But c does cause e, if c's being F is causally relevant to e.

The counterfactual in the Counterfactual Analysis has the form of (2) above. But the counterfactuals we appeal to when thinking about causal relevance informally often seem to have the form of (1). I have been using both freely. In most cases, this makes no difference.

17.   Horgan (1989) realizes that according to some counterfactual analyses of causal relevance, any essential property of a cause will be causally relevant to its effects. Horgan thinks that this is undesirable, but he does not say why. In response to this "problem," Horgan replaces the counterfactual analysis with an analysis that talks explicitly about pertinently similar events (roughly, counterparts) in pertinently similar worlds.

18.   Some might argue that the "law properties" I mention in section 3.4 are essential to Wilma's singing. For they may think that the laws of nature are necessary. Or they may think that an actual event could not occur in a world where the natural laws are different from the actual laws. I reject both claims, and I furthermore think Wilma's singing could occur in a world with different laws. Imagine a world in which forces, masses and accelerations satisfy 'F=ma' up until Wilma sings. A millisecond after she sings, they begin to satisfy the equation '$F=ma^{1.01}$'. So our laws don't hold at that world. But (it seems to me) Wilma's actual singing occurs there. If I am wrong about this, and the law properties are essential to Wilma's singing, then I cannot exclude them until I have the Natural Analysis at hand. (The Natural Analysis excludes law properties because they are not natural properties.)

19.   The analysis of "F is causally relevant to e" (analysis (E2)) has a consequence which some may find strange. Every actual event e has a long causal history. The events in that history are all causes of e. So on (E2), the essential properties of events in that history count as causally relevant to e. For instance, the Big Bang is a cause of the glass's shattering. If the property of having an extremely high temperature is an essential property of the Big Bang, then that property is causally relevant to the shattering. I think this last claim is as acceptable as the claim that the Big Bang is a cause of the shattering. We could, if we wish, try to distinguish between an event's *direct* causes, and its *indirect* causes. If we did so, we could make a similar distinction between direct and indirect causal relevance. The property of having extremely high temperature would then be only indirectly causally relevant.

One might also think that the analysis of "F is a causally relevant property" is too restrictive. Couldn't there be a property which is causally relevant but which has never actually been instantiated? Or one which has been instantiated, but never by a cause of another event? I prefer to call such a property 'causally potent' or (better) '*potentially* causally relevant'. See section 7 for more on this property.

20.   I have borrowed the following example from Goldman (1971, p. 3) and Lewis (1986c). I follow Lewis, for the most part, in my analysis of the example.

21.   Some apparent counterexamples to the Essentialist Analysis can be "turned aside" if we keep in mind that two events with different essential properties can occur in the same place and time. For instance, suppose Wilma sings at exactly 80 decibels, and this causes a needle in a sound-level meter to point at exactly '80'. The exact

amplitude of Wilma's singing seems to be causally relevant to the needle's pointing at exactly '80'. Yet one might think that the exact amplitude is not essential to Wilma's singing — it could have occurred and been only 78 decibels, for instance. So one might conclude that according to the Essentialist Analysis, the exact amplitude of Wilma's singing is not causally relevant to the pointing. But there are (arguably) at least two events occurring as Wilma sings. One occurs essentially at exactly 80 decibels. The other occurs only accidentally at exactly 80 decibels; it could have occurred at 78 decibels. (The first necessitates the second.) The first event's being exactly 80 decibels is causally relevant to the pointing according to (E3). So by (E2) the property of being at exactly 80 decibels is causally relevant to the pointing.

22. The following examples also raise problems for the Counterfactual Analysis, and for any counterfactual analysis that does not require that the relevant counterfactual be non-vacuously true.

23. Here is why, using possible worlds talk: in any possible world where the singing exists, that singing has the property of occurring-in-the-actual-world-at-the-time-that-Sylvester-sneezes.

24. Second-order, existential properties may, in some sense, be disjunctive. I will not attempt to determine this here. The above examples seem quite powerful, but I am not entirely sure that they are successful. The intuition that these properties are causally irrelevant may be due to the (accurate) judgment that these properties are not usually causally *sufficient*.

25. See Kim (1973, 1974, & 1976), Geach (1969), Lewis (1983), and Shoemaker (1984) for discussion and further examples.

26. Strictly speaking, naturalness, as I will think of it here, is not an all-or-nothing affair. Some properties are more natural than others. So naturalness is a matter of degree. For instance, a property that is a disjunct of two (quite different) properties is less natural than its disjuncts, but more natural than a disjunction of infinitely many varied disjuncts. But some properties are sufficiently unnatural to be labeled as plain 'unnatural'. The properties that I claim in the text are not natural are, strictly speaking, not natural *enough*.

My distinction, and my arguments in favor of it, are strongly influenced by Kim, Shoemaker and especially Lewis (see previous note). I have chosen to use Lewis's term 'natural' (because it seems natural), but I strongly suspect that the notion I have in mind is not the same as Lewis's. (It may be closer to Shoemaker's and Kim's.) Lewis wants the *perfectly*, or *maximally*, natural properties to be intrinsic. I am not sure that the maximally natural properties in my sense are intrinsic. In any case, I want some extrinsic, or relational, properties to be natural *enough* to be causally relevant. Lewis also holds that only the fundamental properties of physics are perfectly natural. I do not know whether this holds for the notion I have in mind, but in any case, I want non-fundamental properties to be natural enough to be causally relevant.

27. Both objects and events have natural properties. For instance, being-two-inches-in-diameter is a natural property of objects; being-a-collision is a natural property of events. There are difficult questions about how these are related. Suppose, for instance, that a rock has the natural property of being-two-inches-in-diameter. If the rock is involved in a collision, then the collision will have the property of being-a-collision-with-an-object-2-inches-in-diameter. Is this a natural property of the event? I am inclined to say 'yes', for there seems to be a genuine similarity between

collisions involving 2-inch-wide objects (and a genuine dissimilarity between those events and collisions involving 2-mile-wide objects). But I hesitate to endorse a general principle, such as "if a property of an object involved in an event is natural, then the 'corresponding' property of the event is also natural." In any case, I am concerned here with the natural properties of events, whether or not these are "inherited" from objects' natural properties.

28. Since naturalness comes in degrees, perhaps the amendment should explicitly mention degrees of naturalness. Perhaps we should develop a theory of degrees of naturalness, and then replace (3) with "F is natural to degree D or greater." Alternatively, perhaps causal relevance itself should be viewed as a matter of degree. Suppose c causes e, and c is both essentially F and essentially G. Suppose also that F is more natural than G. Then perhaps F is causally relevant to e to a greater degree than G. I must, however, leave these intriguing possibilities aside.

29. But some necessitated properties, including some disjunctive and existential properties, may be natural (enough). Consider, for instance the property of being-exactly-60-decibels-*or*-between-60-and-62-decibels, and the property of having-*some*-pitch-between-440-and-442-Hz.

30. The universally essential properties are not natural because they do not divide objects into genuine kinds. The same goes for many possibility properties, but perhaps not all. Consider the property of being-possibly-a-sound. Perhaps only sounds can have this property, and so perhaps all events that have this property will genuinely resemble each other. Some actuality and necessity properties may also be natural, for example, actually-having-pitch-P. So perhaps we should say this: the properties of being-actually-F and being-necessarily-F are natural iff F is. (This principle won't work with possibility properties: being-green may be natural, but not being-possibly-green.)

31. Are there potentially causally relevant properties that are not mentioned by laws? I believe that "in the actual world", every potentially causally relevant property that is instantiated is mentioned in some law. But perhaps "in other worlds" there are potentially causally relevant properties that are instantiated but not mentioned by laws. This might happen in worlds where some causation is lawless. If this is possible, then the argument in the text for the equivalence of the Natural and Relevance Analysis shows only a material, not a modal, equivalence. See section 9.

32. There may be yet another way of amending the Essentialist Analysis to yield an analysis equivalent to the Relevant and Natural Analyses. This amendment appeals to the idea that some essential properties of an object are (what I will call) *constitutive*, whereas other are not. For instance, I am essentially red-or-not-red, and also essentially human, but only the latter is a constitutive property of me. The problematic properties of Wilma's singing are not constitutive properties of the singing. So perhaps an amendment to the Essentialist Analysis that excluded non-constitutive properties would exclude causally irrelevant properties. (This appeal to constitutive properties is inspired by Almog's [1991] account of *primal traits*; see Fine [1994] for a similar notion.)

33. I am stating their views using my own vocabulary, at the risk of distorting their views. Armstrong (1978) uses the term 'universal' in much the same way that I use 'natural property'. Armstrong (1978 2: pp. 44-5) says that every universal bestows some causal power upon the particulars that instantiate it, and that the causal powers of a particular are determined by the universals it instantiates. This amounts to the

claim that all, and only, the natural properties of an object determine its causal powers. And that seems to entail that all and only the natural properties are potentially causally relevant. Lewis agrees with Armstrong on the connection between naturalness and causal powers. He says (1983, p. 347), "Natural properties [are] the ones whose sharing makes for resemblance, and the ones relevant to causal powers."

Shoemaker's (1984) distinction between "real" and "mere-Cambridge" properties corresponds roughly to my distinction between natural and unnatural properties. (But Shoemaker's real properties are properties of objects, not events.) Shoemaker says (1984, p. 212) that two real properties are identical iff they make the same contribution to the causal powers of things that have them. He also says (1984, p. 214) that all real properties make some contribution to the causal powers of things that have them. Together, these seem to entail that all real, or natural, properties are potentially causally relevant. If we suppose that any property that does contribute to objects' causal powers is real (in Shoemaker's sense), then we end up again with the view that all and only natural properties are potentially causally relevant.

34. The objection supposes that a putative "analysis" may provide a set of modally necessary and sufficient conditions for items' bearing a relation, and yet not tell us "what the relation is". So it seems to presuppose that two relations can be necessarily co-extensive without being identical. This seems correct: the universally essential properties I mentioned earlier are necessarily co-extensive, but seem to be distinct.

35. Fodor's sufficient condition is also too stringent to be illuminating. For on his analysis, a property is not counted as causally *relevant* unless it is causally *sufficient* for occurrences of another property. But there seem to be properties that are causally relevant but which are not causally sufficient in this sense. For instance, having-amplitude-A is causally relevant to the shattering. But it is unclear whether having that property is causally sufficient for any other sort of event. It is not causally sufficient for glass shatterings (for a certain pitch is also needed), or even sound-level meter readings (for certain conditions must hold inside the sound-level meter). Perhaps Fodor would nevertheless maintain that there is a causal law that says that sounds with amplitude A cause glass breakings, but it's a law that is *very* "ceteris-paribus-y". (Thanks to Lynne Baker for discussion of this.)

36. Segal and Sober (1991) have also proposed a nomological analysis of causal relevance. It builds various conditions on top of Fodor's, to obtain a sufficient condition for the one-place property of being a causally relevant (efficacious) property. Segal and Sober's proposal, however, seems to presuppose a three-place relation of causal relevance for microphysical events. (See their [1991], p. 10, clause (ii) of (P4).) So they may intend to give a sufficient condition for causal relevance for macroscopic properties only. Thus they may intend their proposal to have a more limited scope than Fodor's.

37. If all actual causal transactions are governed by causal laws, then perhaps a nomological analysis gives a *materially* necessary and sufficient condition for causal relevance. But then nomological analyses must count *ceteris paribus* laws as real laws, or else they will count too few properties as causally relevant.

38. I am occasionally inclined to think that there is no singing event that means *shatter* essentially. If there is not, then there is no need to go any further — the Natural Essentialist Analysis entails that the meaning property is not causally relevant to the shattering.

39. To see this, suppose that Wilma's singings sound like the German noun 'Schatten', which means (roughly) *shadow*. Clearly her singings do not mean *shadow* just because they happen to sound like a German word with this meaning. Similarly, if Wilma does not intend to say *shatter*, then her singings do not mean *shatter*, even if her singings sound like an English word that means *shatter*.

40. I do more to defend the view that content properties figure in *ceteris paribus* causal laws in Braun (1991). "Twin Earth" cases show that content properties of mental events are determined by their relational properties. Nevetheless, I think they are natural enough to be causally relevant. This may show that my notion of naturalness is from different from Lewis's (1983) notion. See note 26.

41. My argument in the next four paragraphs resembles arguments given by Horgan (1989, pp. 61-3) and Heil and Mele (1991, pp. 68-9) when they consider whether Twin Earth cases show that content is causally irrelevant.

42. I also doubt that counterfactual (3) is true. As I say in the main text, it is possible for the poor mental event to occur without the rich mental event. Let's suppose that it is also *possible* for the actual champagne *drinking* to occur in some such cases. Nevertheless, it is "unlikely" that the actual token champagne drinking would occur in such a case. And it is at least as "likely" that a schmampagne drinking would occur instead. That is, it is as least as "likely" that Wilma would drink schmampagne as a consequence of having a *schmampagne* belief. In possible worlds talk: the worlds in which Wilma has a *schmampagne* belief and drinks schmampagne are at least as similar to actuality as the worlds in which she has a *schmampagne* belief and her *actual* champagne drinking occurs. Therefore (3) is false.

43. The poor mental event is also (arguably) a cause of Wilma's behavior, for if it had not occurred, Wilma's behavior would not have occurred. So the poor mental event and the rich mental event are distinct causes of Wilma's behavior, occurring at the same place and time. I believe this conclusion is correct, but it raises various issues, some of which are discussed by Kim (1989) and Yablo (1992b).

44. Thanks to the following people for many helpful discussions, and for comments on earlier versions of this paper: Joseph Almog, Lynne Rudder Baker, Earl Conee, Noa Goldring, Stephen Yablo, the members of my metaphysics seminar at the University of Rochester in the fall of 1991, and the members of the philosophy of mind discussion group at Cornell University in the spring of 1992 (especially Mark Crimmins, Joe Moore, Richard Miller, and Sydney Shoemaker). My work on this paper was partly supported by NEH grant FT-32125-89. I am grateful for the support.

References

Almog, Joseph. 1991. "The What and the How." *Journal of Philosophy*, *88*, pp. 225-44.

Armstrong, D. M. 1978. *Universals and Scientific Realism* (in two volumes). Cambridge: Cambridge University Press.

Block, Ned. 1990. "Can the Mind Change the World?" In George Boolos (ed.), *Meaning and Method: Essays in Honor of Hilary Putnam*, pp. 137-170. New York: Cambridge University Press.

Braun, David. 1991. "Content, Causation, and Cognitive Science." *Australasian Journal of Philosophy*, *69*, pp. 375-389.

Dretske, Fred. 1989. "Reasons and Causes." *Philosophical Perspectives, 3, Philosophy of Mind and Action Theory, 1989,* edited by James E. Tomberlin, pp. 1-15.

Fine, Kit. 1994. "Essence and Modality." *Philosophical Perspectives, 8, Logic and Language, 1994,* edited by James E. Tomberlin, pp. 1-16.

Fodor, Jerry. 1989. "Making Mind Matter More." *Philosophical Topics, 27,* pp. 59-79. Reprinted in Jerry Fodor, 1990, *A Theory of Content and Other Essays.* Cambridge, MA: MIT Press.

Goldman, Alvin I. 1970. *A Theory of Human Action.* Englewood Cliffs, NJ: Prentice-Hall.

Heil, John and Mele, Alfred. 1991. "Mental Causes." *American Philosophical Quarterly, 28,* pp. 61-71.

Horgan, Terence. 1989. "Mental Quausation." *Philosophical Perspectives, 3, Philosophy of Mind and Action Theory, 1989,* edited by James E. Tomberlin, pp. 47-76.

Kim, Jaegwon. 1973. "Causation, Subsumption, and the Concept of Event." *Journal of Philosophy, 70,* pp. 217-36.

Kim, Jaegwon. 1974. "Noncausal Connections." *Nous, 8,* pp. 41-52.

Kim, Jaegwon. 1976. "Events as Property Exemplifications." In Myles Brand and Douglas Walton (eds.), *Action Theory,* pp. 159-77. Dordrecht: D. Reidel.

Kim, Jaegwon. 1979. "Causality, Identity, and Supervenience in the Mind-Body Problem." *Midwest Studies in Philosophy, 4,* pp. 31-50.

Kim, Jaegwon. 1984. "Epiphenomenal and Supervenient Causation." *Midwest Studies in Philosophy, 9,* pp. 257-70.

Kim, Jaegwon. 1989. "Mechanism, Purpose, and Explanatory Exclusion." *Philosophical Perspectives, 3, Philosophy of Mind and Action Theory, 1989,* edited by James E. Tomberlin, pp. 77-108.

LePore, Ernest and Loewer, Barry. 1987. "Mind Matters." *Journal of Philosophy, 84,* pp. 630-642.

LePore, Ernest and Loewer, Barry. 1989. "More on Making Mind Matter." *Philosophical Topics, 27,* pp. 175-191.

Lewis, David. 1973. "Causation." *Journal of Philosophy, 70,* pp. 556-67. Reprinted, with new postscripts, in Lewis (1986a), pp. 159-214.

Lewis, David. 1983. "New Work for a Theory of Universals." *Australasian Journal of Philosophy, 61,* pp. 343-77.

Lewis, David. 1986a. *Philosophical Papers,* Volume II. New York: Oxford University Press.

Lewis, David. 1986b. "Causal Explanation." In Lewis (1986a), pp. 214-40.

Lewis, David. 1986c. "Events." In Lewis (1986a), pp. 241-269.

Segal, Gabriel and Sober, Elliot. 1991. "The Causal Efficacy of Content." *Philosophical Studies, 63,* pp. 1-30.

Shoemaker, Sydney. 1984. *Identity, Cause, and Mind.* Cambridge: Cambridge University Press.

Sosa, Ernest. 1984. "Mind-Body Interaction and Supervenient Causation." *Midwest Studies in Philosophy, 9,* pp. 271-81.

Yablo, Stephen. 1992a. "Cause and Essence." *Synthese, 93,* pp. 403-449.

Yablo, Stephen. 1992b. "Mental Causation." *Philosophical Review, 101,* pp. 245-280.

Philosophical Perspectives, 9, AI, Connectionism, and
Philosophical Psychology, 1995

SINGLING OUT PROPERTIES[1]

Stephen Yablo
University of Michigan, Ann Arbor

Colors have characteristic causes and effects–
that we do know.

Wittgenstein, *Remarks on Color*

I.

Who can forget the story of how epistemologists used to do business? Having offered to help you clarify *how* you know that *p*, they would gasp at your reasoning and declare that you *don't* know it—or rather *wouldn't*, if not for a reconstruction of your procedures invented by themselves. Then they would be gone, leaving you struggling to reconceive your relations to *p* along recommended lines.

Of course this, the style of epistemology Putnam once satirized as "intellectual Walden Two,"[2] is now defunct. But the spirit animating it lives on. What the metaphysician offers to clarify is not how *p*'s truth is *known*, but what *makes p* true. Trouble is (you can guess the rest), a review of all likely truth-makers reveals that *nothing* does. Or rather nothing *would*, if not for a certain *substitute* truth-maker identified by the metaphysicians themselves. Whoever would persist in counting *p* true is thus forced to reconceive its truth as flowing from unexpected sources.

With apologies to Putnam, this approach to metaphysics might be called "ontological 1984," in view of the Party's penchant for tampering with the truth-grounds of everyday statements. Statements about the past, O'Brien explains, are true in virtue of what is preserved in records and memories; numerical claims owe their truth values to the Party's stipulations. "You are no metaphysician, Winston," O'Brien says when his prisoner boggles at some such revelation. Using the term in O'Brien's sense, this paper explores some strategies for not being a metaphysician.

II.

Here is the scenario. There is a predicate "F" and we have various things we want to say with it—things we regard as quite likely true, or even certainly true. But we are troubled. Granted that "F" applies to roughly the objects we suppose, what property or relation or condition or what have you does it apply *in virtue of*? Information about the property is not lacking; there are the various statements we are inclined to make using "F", and these, being presumably correct, add up to a considerable data base. What bothers us is that the information feels *circumstantial*; we learn what the property is *like*, not what it *is*. The urge thus arises to *identify* Fness,[3] to single it out and elucidate its nature. Only then will we know what makes our predications true.

This sort of scenario is enacted everywhere in philosophy, as a few examples will bring out. Naturalized semanticists have charged Tarski with promising, but failing, to explain what truth is. Tarski *partly* explained truth when he reduced it to denotation; it falls to us, though, to complete Tarski's task by finding the relation, presumably naturalistic, that words bear to the objects they denote.[4] Or take the debate in the philosophy of mind as to which feature of a person makes her correctly describable as "believing that *p*." Is it a relation she bears to a sentence of mentalese, or the attribution's making best sense of her behavior, or the fact that we, in a similar state, would declare that *p*? The pattern even extends to ethics, where the search is on for the property that "perfectly deserves the name 'value.'"[5] Whether value attributions can be true is disputed, of course, but if they can, the thought is, it ought to be possible to produce for inspection the property that gives them this status.

So: by the looks of things, there are lots of properties standing in need of further identification. However it's in connection with *qualitative* proper-ties—secondary and phenomenal—that the identification problem becomes really acute. This is because qualitative properties can seem not merely undiscovered but positively *hidden*.[6]

According to one way of drawing the primary/secondary distinction, primary qualities are well represented by our ideas of them. When veridical, which is not always, these ideas portray shape, size, number and so on as they really are. With secondary qualities, it is nearly the reverse: our ideas of taste, smell, color, and so on, though seldom false,[7] convey a very *poor* sense of their associated properties. Thus Reid:

> our senses give us a direct and distinct notion of the primary qualities, and inform us what they are in themselves: but of the secondary qualities...[they] inform us only, that they are qualities that effect us in a certain manner...as to what they are in themselves, our senses leave us in the dark.[8]

For this reason, "the nature of the secondary qualities is a proper subject of philosophical disquisition."[9] Happily, "philosophy has made some progress" in the matter.[10] But philosophy would not be needed if experience had not left these qualities' identities so obscure.

Now for Reid, the problem about secondary qualities grows out of a contrast between the qualities themselves, which are unknown, and the sensations they produce in us, which are known full well. So he would not himself see the problem as extending to *phenomenal* properties, like that of sensing greenly or suffering pain. Others however find the cases analogous—some, like Descartes, mentioning them in the same breath:

> If someone says he sees color in a body or feels pain in a limb, this amounts to saying that he sees or feels something of which he is wholly ignorant...[11]

Pain-experience, though generally veridical in the sense of occurring only when one is really in pain, gives little indication of what that condition really amounts to. But if we cannot know pain just on the basis of our experience of it, how to proceed? Research will have to be conducted into pain's identity; somewhere a state lies waiting such that identifying pain with *it* honors, in Dennett's words, "all, or at any rate most, of our intuitions about *what pain is*."[12]

III.

These examples remind us of what is fast becoming standard operating procedure in metaphysics: gather a body of more or less central preconceptions associated with some predicate, and then, guided by whatever clues philosophy and science have to offer, strike out in search of the associated state or property. That a procedure is standard doesn't make it right, of course. But there *do* seem to be reasons for wanting to know the worldly correlates of our predicates.

Nothing counts as a theory of *pain*, Dennett says, unless it honors enough of our intuitions about what pain is. Intuitions being the impromptu, unexamined things they are, though, "a prospect that cannot be discounted is that these intuitions do not make a consistent set."[13] How might we ward that prospect off? The obvious strategy would be to *produce* a state making the intuitions come true. And this seems little different from identifying pain itself.

Rather more worrisome, because less remote, is the prospect that our intuitions clash not among themselves, but with views we hold about the larger world. There is nothing *internally* incoherent, according to Mackie, in the idea of "objectively prescriptive" value properties, or "colors as we see them belong[ing] intrinsically to the...surfaces of objects";[14] it's just that other things we think rule out anything's actually *possessing* such properties. Again, the obvious response would be to identify redness with (say) R_{295}, a property conspicuously at peace with our larger theory. This is a second reason we might want Fness identified.

"[D]oes it not appear a contradiction," Reid asks, "to say we know that fire is hot, but we know not what heat is?"[15] Even to *understand* the statement that fire is hot, some would say, requires knowledge of what heat is.[16] These formulations can be faulted, no doubt, for treating knowledge and understanding as all-or-nothing affairs. But the underlying idea seems right: the *better* one knows what Fness is, the better one understands "X is F," and the less superficial one's knowledge that it is F. This gives a third motive for the project of singling Fness out.

Next is the motive of simple curiosity. Questions may arise about a property whose answers depend, or seem to depend, on the property's further identification. Is pain *essentially* painful? Kripke says yes and concludes that pain is not identical to anything physical. But matters arguably belong the other way around: "an opinion on [the] truth or falsity [of the essential painfulness claim] waits upon a theory of what pain *is*."[17]

What finally if we have *no* intrinsic interest in Fness, and want only to *communicate* using the predicate "F"? Not even this, it seems, can excuse us from the identificatory project. For communication has a metaphysical side; unless both parties are using "F" in reference to *the same property*, they are talking past each other. Whether this proviso holds, however, depends on (i) the property that we ourselves attribute by use of "F," and (ii) the property that our interlocutors do. This gives us an interest in (i); and an interest in (i) is an interest in the identity of Fness.

With so many reasons for seeking after Fness's identity, how could anyone object? Nonetheless I do object, if not to the project's goal, then in some cases to the project itself. Seeking after a property's identity makes sense only if its identity is not yet known. That is, there has to be a *better* way of conceiving Fness than what we have already, such that knowing what Fness is means conceiving it like *that*. *But the existence of a better idea of Fness is not something that can be assumed in advance.* The next three Sections look at some of the trouble this assumption can cause; the rest of the paper experiments with dropping the assumption and getting out of the identification racket.[18]

IV.

Remember the scenario: we have a body of doctrine involving some predicate "F," and we seek a better idea of the property we attribute with it. Asked what's wrong with our existing idea, we'd complain of knowing the property only indirectly, as the whatever-it-is meeting certain conditions. These conditions might take a number of forms, but in the usual examples they are causal. Pain is the state that is brought about by tissue damage, that prevents concentration, that prompts avoidance behavior, and so on. Red is the property producing a certain type of experience in suitably placed observers. While all of this is useful information, the complaint goes, none of it tells us what the property *is* as opposed to what it *does*.

To which the obvious reply is, given enough information about what something *does*, it ought to be possible to track it down and make a positive identification. This is the strategy Armstrong employs in *A Materialist Theory of Mind*. Having argued on philosophical grounds that "the concept of a mental state is the concept of a state of the person apt for the production of certain sorts of behavior," he proceeds to ask, "What in fact is the nature of these inner states?" This last is said to be a matter not for philosophy but "high-level scientific speculation."[19] Armstrong envisages a two-part procedure then. Calling a property *F-ish* if it satisfies the main presumptions about Fness, philosophical analysis reveals that

(1) Fness = the F-ish property,

Next, the scientists are brought in to tell us which property is in fact F-ish. Not that we can't make an educated guess. Armstrong himself thinks that "the identification of [mental] states with physico-chemical states of the brain is, in the present state of knowledge, nearly as good as the identification of the gene with the DNA molecule."[20] And "from the standpoint of total science, the most *plausible* answer is that redness is a purely physical property."[21]

Now though we run into a famous problem. When Armstrong says that the red-role is played by a physical property, he is only playing a scientific hunch; there *could*, he admits, be "*irreducibly* diverse causes in the physical surfaces bringing about identical colour-appearances for human observers."[22] But where Armstrong puts this forward as a sort of a doomsday scenario in which colors are reduced to the status of pseudo-qualities, nowadays it is thought to be more or less the situation: "apart from their radiative result, there is nothing that blue things have in common..."[23] Something similar is of course the standard line on suffering things—they too have nothing but a causal syndrome in common. It begins to seem that Armstrong-style concepts of sensations and colors are concepts of precisely nothing.

V.

What is the property that red things, suffering things, or what have you possess in common, and in virtue of which they are rightly called by those names? While we know, or think we do, how the intended property *behaves*—its causal role—we cannot seem to find a property that covers all and only the cases where the role is actually played.

Or can't we? If what is wanted is a property covering just the cases where a causal role gets played, why not the property of having a property that plays it? This is the solution urged by *dispositionalism* in the philosophy of color,[24] and the souped-up dispositionalism called *functionalism* in the philosophy of mind. The general format is

(2) Fness = the property of having an F-ish property.

Because (2) represents Fness as the property of having a property playing a certain role, let's call it the *role theory* of Fness. ((1) was the *realizer* theory.) Redness, this theory claims, is the property of having a property playing the red-role; pain is the state of being in a state playing the pain-role; etcetera.

Having been crafted with an eye to just this result, the properties championed by the role theory have a large advantage over those championed by the realizer theory, viz. satisfaction of the following key preconception about Fness:

> *commonality*: it is shared by all and only Fs.

But this is not the only preconception in play. The thing we know best about Fness, our main intuitive grip on the property, is that Fness is *F-ish*, with all the causal powers that entails. Hence a second key preconception is

> *causality*: it has F-ish causal powers.

The question is whether the property of *having* an F-ish property—the property that Fness *is* according to the present theory—is *itself* in relevant respects F-ish.[25]

When Reid refers to the colors as the causes of well-known experiential effects, he is only echoing common sense. Unschooled by philosophy, anyone would say that our experiences of a ripe tomato as red are caused by the tomato's *redness*. But is this a view that the dispositionalist can accept? Experiences of color are, for her, *manifestations* of color; they stand to it as sleep stands to dormitivity or death to deadliness. While we may indeed cite dormitivity in the *explanation* of sleep, to indicate that the sleep occurred not by chance but thanks to a sleep-inducing property of the dormitive substance, it is famously *not* plausible to say that the sleep-inducing feature was the dormitivity itself. Still less would we seek a place for the mushroom's *deadliness* in the causal ancestry of the ensuing death.

Is the claim that dispositions lack causal powers altogether? Not at all; the mushroom's deadliness might well influence the property-owner to post warning signs. The claim is not even that dispositions cannot be responsible for the effects they are dispositions to produce. There could be a sleeping potion that worked partly, or even entirely, through our recognition of its dormitivity.[26] And part of the magic of the true charmer is his ability to win you over by his very charmingness. (This is to say nothing of the phenomenon of being famous for being famous.) But the lengths one must go to to find such cases brings it home that, special fiddling aside, dispositions do not cause their manifestations.[27] Dispositions to produce color-sensations are no exception; sensations of redness might be due to various properties of an object, but the property of having a property productive of such sensations is not one of them.[28]

Sure as common sense might be about the causal powers of colors, it is adamant about those of occurrent mental states: pain causes avoidance behavior, itchiness makes us scratch, and so on. Part of the knock against Rylean behaviorism was its reluctance to acknowledge such facts. And part of the attraction of early functionalism was the way it seemed to welcome them and indeed build them into the essences of the relevant states.

But although this is a story functionalists love to repeat, it doesn't really hang together; given the difficulty of getting a state to *cause* the effects by which it is defined, the part about building various outcomes into pain's essence sits ill with the part about preserving pain as their causal basis. What really happened is that the functionalist succeeded rather too well. Determined not to slight pain's effects, she created a state so tightly bound up with those effects that it could no longer bring them about.[29]

VI.

Back to the original problem. When Armstrong proposed to identify Fness as *the* state playing a certain role, the reply came that such a thing might not exist, different states playing the role on different occasions. But why did we assume that a *single* state was required? Is it written in stone that "F" must be attributable for the same reason in every case? No, says Lewis. Pain might be

> one brain-state in the case of men, and some other...in the case of mollusks. It might even be one brain state in the case of Putnam, another in the case of Lewis... . The seeming contradiction (one thing identical to two things) vanishes once we notice the tacit relativity to context in one term of the identities.[30]

That is, we can agree with the realizer theory that

(1) Fness = the F-ish property

always holds true,[31] without supposing that it expresses the *same* truth in connection with different objects.[32] Rather (1) resembles "the winner = whoever came in first" in maintaining a constant truth value through coordinated fluctuation in the references of its parts. But then, just as it would be clearer to say "the winner of a given race = whoever came in first in that race," we should clarify (1) to

(1*) Fness in a given thing = the property that is F-ish w.r.t. that thing.

This is Armstrong's original realizer theory amended to take account of the fact that different properties might play the F-role with respect to different objects. But as written the theory is incomplete.

Imagine that itchiness in Pam is I-fiber firing while itchiness in Sam is I-sac fibrillation. Are we to conclude that there is nothing that Pam and Sam have in common when both feel itchy? No such conclusion follows, says Lewis. What is true is that Pam and Sam don't have their *realizer*-properties in common. But there is also (and still) the *role*-property of having *some* property or other playing the itchy-role for a creature like yourself. This latter property may not be itchiness, but it is a related property, and it's one that Pam and Sam share. For the sake of a label, why don't we call it *the property of having itchiness?*[33] And in general why don't we contrast *Fness*, the realizer-property that varies from object to object, with *the property of having Fness*, the role-property that Fs share? Then in addition to replacing (1) with (1*), Lewis would replace (2) with

(2*) the property of having Fness = the property of having an F-ish property.

By this distinction between the property of Fness and that of having Fness, Lewis appears to get the best of both worlds. For whatever names you call them by, he has an itchiness-property that makes him scratch, and an itchiness-property he shares with all itchy creatures of whatever physiological make-up.[34]

Where are we? Armstrong's realizer-properties had the right causal powers but were not common to all of the right things; the role theory (once) championed by Putnam had the opposite virtues. Only with Lewis's mixed theory, it seems, do we get both *commonality*—properties shared by all and only F-things—and *causality*—properties with F-ish causal powers. What could be better?

Here is what. Better than a theory offering *two* F-properties, one shared by all and only Fs and the other with the intuitive causal powers of Fness,[35] would be a theory offering a *single* F-property, common to all and only Fs *and* possessing the intuitive causal powers of Fness. Otherwise we cannot say that Pam is scratching for the same reason Sam is, viz. itchiness. The closest that a Lewisian can come to this is: Pam and Sam both scratch because both have the property of having itchiness. But this is like saying that mescaline and Audrey Hepburn movies are enjoyable for the same reason, viz. possession of properties conducive to enjoyment.[36] I conclude that the mixed theory is giving us the reverse of what we want. Rather than similar effects due to a common property, we are getting a common property built around the fact of similar effects.[37]

VII.

Originally we sought to identify "F"'s referent as *the F-ish property*, whatever that might turn out to be. This is recognizably a descendant of Kripke's method in *Naming and Necessity*, except that where we speak of F-ishness, Kripke speaks of the conditions fixing "F"'s reference.[38] That the method works more or less as advertised in connection with terms like "hot" and "gold" can be taken for granted here. But the attempt to extend it to color terms—to identify the referent of "yellow" as

that (manifest) property of objects which causes them, under normal circumstances, to be seen as yellow (i.e., to be sensed by certain visual impressions)[39]

—runs, it appears, into a familiar sort of trouble; for, as Crispin Wright puts it,

> there may simply fail to be any interesting physical essence underlying the
> manifestations which have a salient similarity for us...we hold out a hostage to
> fortune in attempting reference fixing of this kind, and the hostage may not be
> redeemed.[40]

Reference fixing is pointing where one *hopes* an interesting physical essence lies.
But some hopes are better founded than others, and it is all too easy to believe
that objects making a similar impression on human color sense do so for
physically different reasons.

How could Kripke have missed this problem? A possible reply is: what
problem? To speak of the "manifest property of objects which causes them...to
be seen as yellow" is not to say *anything* about physical essences; the issue of
physicality is not addressed.[41] Kripke does tell us that "it is up to the physical
scientist to identify the property so marked out in any more fundamental physical
terms that he wishes."[42] But this sounds more like a burden shifting remark
("identify it if you can") than a profession of faith that the scientist will succeed,
much less an insistence on physical specifiability as a condition of successful
reference fixing.

Whether handing the identificatory ball off to appropriate experts is sound
methodology is not the question; we can assume it is. The question is: what if
the experts can make no yardage, and the ball is handed back? Emboldened by
their reading, or misreading, of Kripke, many philosophers would take a hard
line on this, rejecting not-further-identifiable properties as unreal. ("If there is no
saying what Fness is, most likely it isn't *anything*"). But this is because they
have allowed the sensibly unpretentious policy of deferring to expert opinion
where it exists to harden into the absurdly self-effacing one of *automatically*
discounting ordinary, nonexpert, ways of conceiving properties as superficial.
Assume that all properties possess hidden depths, and Fness, which refuses to
reveal any (or indeed to reveal much of anything about itself not already imputed
by common opinion), takes on the feel of a projective fantasy.

Well, suppose we do *not* allow the sensible policy to harden into the absurd
one. Then the fact that Fness is impervious to experts admits of a new interpretation: the way the rest of us conceive Fness is the *right* way if you want to know
what Fness is. (The rest of us *become* the experts, if you like.) This is what the
"hostage to fortune" line overlooks. Fortune might have had a hand to play if
yellowness were a theoretical posit, an I-know-not-what postulated to explain the
familiar and known. (Depending on whether the explanation could be made to
work, yellowness's claim to reality might or might not hold up.) But the claim
here is that yellowness is *itself* something familiar and known; our ordinary,
nonexpert ways of conceiving it tell as good a story as any about what it is.

So, then: yellowness is the intrinsic, categorical feature that objects *appear* to have when they look yellow to us, that *makes* them look yellow to us, that yellow things have in common, and so on. Pressed for its "true identity," the best we can do is reiterate the preconceptions (intrinsic, categorical, yellow-look-making, etc.) while insisting that it is not laziness or any other human failing that prevents a fuller answer, but the property itself.

"Naive objectivism" is the usual name for a view like this—the word "naive" functioning partly to identify the view and partly to mark it as ludicrously simple-minded. This assessment is so deeply ingrained that it is surprising to realize how little explicit argument there is to back it up. "What is beyond dispute," Dennett says,

> is that there is no simple, nondisjunctive property of surfaces such that all and only the surfaces with that property are red...[43]

His evidence boils down to the fact that science offers no simple, nondisjunctive, conception of redness. But this is agreed all around. The most that follows is something else agreed all around: naive redness, if it exists, is not a property that scientists have much truck with.

That they should present an attractive face to science is hardly a core presumption about the colors. But it *is* generally presumed that objects *look* colored as a result of being so; and this might seem equally damaging:

> One view about [secondary qualities] seems clearly ruled out. Colors, for example, can't be properties of substances over and above the microstructural properties of them that account for the ways they influence the physical features of the light that impacts on our visual systems...To suppose [otherwise] is either to embrace a view about the causation of our perceptual experiences which is known to be false, namely the view that they are caused by something other than the microstructural physical properties of objects, or to embrace the view that secondary qualities are epiphenomenal and play no role in the production of our perceptual experiences...[44]

Because our color experiences are fully accounted for in terms of the relevant microstructure, colors understood as over and above that microstructure would be causally otiose. (At best they could aspire to "seconding" whatever causal messages were being sent by the underlying physics.[45]) Moral: if you want your colors causally active, better make them microphysical.[46]

Before accepting this result, consider a parallel argument. The scale at a certain weigh-station is adjusted to sound an alarm whenever a truck weighs in at over 70,000 pounds—in a word, whenever a truck is *heavy*. Enter yourself, on an overloaded semi, and the buzzer sounds. Given how the scale is adjusted, it would seem that your truck's property of being heavy was highly relevant to the alarm's sounding. But think again. I forgot to mention that your truck was *barely* heavy, in the sense of weighing *just* over 70,000 pounds. With the truck's *bare* heaviness being *itself* sufficient for the effect, every *other* aspiring cause is left with nothing to do. Apparently then the truck's heaviness ("another" aspiring cause after all) made no causal difference to the buzzer's sounding. Moral: if you want your weight-properties causally relevant, make them as determinate as possible.

How can this be, though? To be heavy is *part of what it is* to be barely heavy; and how can a part be crowded out by its containing whole? What the truck story really shows is that when properties are so related that to possess one is part of what it is to possess the other—when they are related as determinable to determinate—they do not compete for causal honors.[47]

Imagine that the scale is constructed on a balance-beam model; if a truck weighs enough to lift the 70,000 pound counterweight, then a circuit is broken and the buzzer sounds. So the mechanism is absolutely insensitive to weight differences above 70,000 pounds. With this in mind, what is the property of the truck whose instantiation resulted in the buzzer's sounding? While it is true that the truck's bare heaviness was sufficient for the effect, if we had to name a property as the one responsible, it would be the heaviness pure and simple.[48] For only the latter is *commensurate* with the effect, in the sense of including what the effect needed with a minimum of irrelevant extras.

So a determinable property, far from being preempted by its determinate, is often *better* placed to function as cause. Couldn't this be how it is with the tomato's surface microstructure and its surface redness? If colors were nonphysical determinables of the microproperties thought to preempt them, then no causal competition would be possible. And because color-properties would be *better* proportioned to our perceptual responses than their microphysical determinates—a rose whose color were otherwise microphysically implemented would look as red—they'd be better placed to play the role of cause.[49]

Does it even make sense, though, to think of redness as a determinable of its physical underpinnings? Normally determinates are taken to *entail* their determinables as a conceptual matter. So even if, as seems plausible, colors are *necessitated*, in the metaphysical sense, by their microphysical underpinnings, talk of determinates and determinables is out of place. For plainly, no microphysical state conceptually entails redness.

Yet on second thought, it's the conceptual entailment requirement that's out of place. Determination is above all a relation between *properties*. But as we know from Kripke's examples of "synthetically identical" properties, conceptual entailment is not; a single property, conceived in alternative ways, will have different conceptual consequences. (To put the point in the usual misleading way, entailment relates not properties, but properties-under-a-conception.) Accordingly we drop the entailment condition and explain determination in wholly metaphysical terms: Fness is a determinate of Gness iff to be F is a *way* of being G. To have your molecules arranged *thusly* is a *way* of being red, so redness is a determinable of the given microproperty.

VIII.

Standing back for a minute from the example of color, what is the picture we have arrived at? The goal was a property Fness that was common to all Fs, and that played an F-ish causal role. Surmising that only a physical property could play the desired role, we were dismayed to learn that *different* physical properties P_1, P_2, etc. played it in different objects. But the surmise was wrong: the F-role is best played by a nonphysical determinable with P_1, P_2, etc. as determinates. Surmising that coverage of the Fs required a higher-order property existentially generalizing over P_1, P_2, etc., we were dismayed to learn that this property had the wrong causal powers. But the second surmise was also wrong: a determinable with P_1, P_2, etc. as determinates covers the same extensional ground as its higher-order alternative.

Notice that the very same property, what we might call *Fness as such*, gets overlooked both times, despite offering the only real hope of harmonizing some fairly basic convictions, e.g., that red objects have something in common on account of which they *look* red. The tempting conclusion is that philosophers don't really like this property; they dislike it to the point of suppressing it even in contexts where nothing else will do. Because the reasons for such an attitude will be different in different cases, let's consider the reasons for hostility to properties like *redness* as such, that is, to the naive colors. And let's start with the worry that, despite my optimistic noises above, what these *are* remains to be explained.

IX.

Zinc is explained by showing where it falls in the table of elements; radio waves are explained by pointing to a segment of the electromagnetic spectrum; pokeweed is explained by locating it in the kingdom of plants. To explain what a thing is, then, apparently, one blocks off its ontological neighborhood, enumerates the inhabitants according to some illuminating principle, and indicates which of the enumerated items it is. All that remains is to apply this model to the case of the colors. Explaining what they are would be a matter of spelling out "which properties colors are...in a particular set that is acknowledged on both sides to exhaust the properties of material objects."[50]

But there is no such set, that I know of. To assume that there is is to assume that the colors can be caught in a net designed with other sorts of properties in mind. And why should the naive objectivist accept this? *Sui generis*, unscientific, and of minuscule causal impact, colors as she conceives them have nothing to draw the enumerator's attention.

If redness isn't to be picked out on a master list of properties, what *can* be done to calm our concerns about what it is? Attempting to *define* those concerns would be a good start. Wh-questions notoriously require a *context*: some sort of gap or defect in one's information that one is seeking to remedy. This is why it makes little sense to wonder, apropos of nothing, who Frank Sinatra is, or where North America might be found. But suppose that one's information about Sinatra was hearsay from what turned out to be a defective source. Then it *would* make sense to wonder who Sinatra was. Similarly, it would make sense to wonder what redness was if our "source" on it proved defective. But this is exactly the situation, according to some philosophers: our "source" on the colors is color experience, and color experience does not portray the colors as they really are. Either it *conceals* the colors, or (worse) it *deceives* us about them.

Does our experience of color fall short in either of these ways? The charge of deception is leveled by Mackie in his book on Locke. Science has left us with only so many candidates for the role of color, Mackie thinks, and the colors as presented by color experience are not among them. Since there are no properties that *are* as the colors *look*, color experience tells a false story. How the story goes can be gleaned from Mackie's remark that

> it is most improbable that there is any single quality, an objective 'resemblance' of, say, my sensation of a particular shade of green, in all the things...that give me this sensation.[51]

What forest green *looks* to be, then, is

(a) the common cause of our experiences of forest green, and
(b) an objective resemblance of those experiences.

But if this is the story experience tells, it is not obvious why it should be thought false. The only argument offered against (a), that science does not *postulate* a common cause, applies equally to our experiences of things as jagged, loopy, heaped, frizzy, or tangled[52]; science does not postulate common causes here either. The worst that follows is that scientifically speaking, color is in the same boat as these. (And why should the naive objectivist not agree?) How to interpret "resemblance" in (b) is famously unclear, but suppose we take it Mackie's way: "an objective quality resembles the idea of that quality [iff] in this respect things are just as they look."[53] Then to say that reality contains no property "resembling" my experience of forest green is to say that it contains no property that is as forest green looks. This is not an argument for the deception thesis but just a restatement of it.

What about the charge that, while color experience may not lie, it leaves out important parts of the truth? That this should be raised against objectivism is ironic. Dispositionalism and physicalism would seem far more natural targets. Not even Locke thought that red *looked* like a power to produce experiences,[54] and still less does it look microstructural in nature. But what is the argument that redness does not look to be what the naive view says it is: an intrinsic nondispositional *sui generis* color property? This would seem to be *exactly* how it looks.

Not so fast, you might say. Even if naive objectivism does not make the colors microphysical, they do come out *determinables* of microproperties. And redness does not *look* like a determinable of microproperties. This invites the question of how determinables of microproperties may be *expected* to look. It is true that the experience of a color does not suggest the myriad ways in which that color is liable to be microphysically implemented. But if a property's liability to be implemented in thus and such ways is the kind of thing a revealing experience of the property ought to register, then *primary* quality experience is unrevealing too. For: roundness, no less than redness, is implementable in myriad microphysical ways (having outermost molecules arranged like *so*) of which the experience of roundness gives no hint. Yet roundness is the paradigm of a *revealed* property, the kind that redness was supposed to be contrasted with.

X.

So far we have found no basis for the complaint that color experience is unrevealing. Neither though have we attached much content to the contrary claim: that the experience of a color gets the color *right*.

What standard experiences of color *do* seem to suggest is that redness (e.g.) is intrinsic and categorical. But this much is true of lots of properties—roundness, for instance. To be revealing, shouldn't our experience of a color inform us of features *peculiar* to it? There is even the view that it should lay the color's nature completely bare. Yet as expectations rise about our experience's power to reveal, so too do doubts about the intelligibility of the corresponding feature. Can we really make sense of an *objective* property that is, in Evans's phrase, "exactly as we experience redness to be"?[55]

Here is a way of making the worry sharper. Redness and greenness are fundamentally different, perhaps fundamentally opposed. If color experience is revealing, this ought to be reflected somehow in our different experiences of them. But the only relevant experiential difference would seem to be in qualitative feel. And what can qualitative feel possibly tell us about the nature of an intrinsic, categorical property of external objects, a property that is "there anyway," regardless of the impression it makes on human observers? No wonder Evans complains, against other-than-dispositional conceptions of redness, that "what one conceives when one conceives that objects which appear red to us are in addition really red...is quite opaque."[56]

The challenge is to think what redness could be, that the right way to conceive it is in terms of experiences of such and such a qualitative type. Dispositionalists and physicalists have ready replies. If redness were a disposition to produce red-type experiences, then *clearly*, those experiences would be peculiarly apt to redness, and an invaluable guide to its nature. And although red-type experiences would *not* be peculiarly apt if redness were microphysical, neither would we expect them to be; science, not color experience, would be our guide to the nature of redness. It is only on the naive account that a certain type of experience is *needed* for knowledge of what redness is (science isn't going to help) at the same as it is *prohibited* (redness being objective). This seeming paradox is our final topic.

XI.

Near the beginning of "Values & Secondary Qualities," McDowell declares that the colors are not "adequately conceivable except in terms of how their possessors would look."[57] By an "adequate" conception of X, let's take him to mean a conception whereby one knows what X is. Then McDowell's claim is that whoever does not conceive redness in terms of how it makes things look does not know what redness is—or, as we might put it, that it is *epistemically essential* to red to make things look that way. But is this true of red?

With surprising regularity, paranormal perception buffs report the existence of "color-touchers," or individuals capable of detecting color by tactile means. Whether the reports are true doesn't matter;[58] the issue for us is the conceptual one of whether someone who accessed color by touch alone could still be said to conceive them adequately.[59] Take for instance the subjects discussed in "Seeing Color With The Fingers," a story in the June 1964 issue of *Life* on "dermo-optical perception:"

> Yellow, they said, felt slippery, soft and lightweight. Blue, while not so slippery as yellow, was smoother and the hand could move more freely over it. Red was sticky and clinging. Green was stickier than red but not so coarse. Indigo was very sticky but harder than red or green. Orange was hard and rough, and inhibited movement... . Black was very inhibiting and clinging, almost gluey, while white was quite smooth, though coarser than yellow.[60]

How shall we describe these people? They have a *way of thinking* about yellowness—an *idea* of it if you like—but that is all. What yellowness *is* they do not know.[61]

The epistemic essentiality claim seems right, then. But McDowell puts a *construal* on the claim that I want to raise a question about. Properties that are "not adequately conceivable except in terms of certain subjective states," he says, are "subjective themselves in a sense that that characterization defines."[62] The question is whether "that characterization" defines a sense of "subjective" at all. To call a property "subjective" is to comment in an ontological vein about what it is. But to say that it is not adequately *conceived* except (e.g.) in terms of how it makes things look is to applaud certain ways of *thinking* of the property. Unless standards of adequate conception are dictated *by the property and it alone*, no ontological conclusions follow.

Now, it may seem *obvious* that the property sets the standards. All that we mean by an adequate idea of X, recall, is one marking its possessor as knowledgeable about what X is. And surely, the standards for knowing what a thing is flow from *what it is*! To have a name for this view, let's call it *absolutism* about knowing what. *Anti-absolutism* holds that standards for knowing what are sensitive to (so far unspecified) additional factors. Some examples will help us to decide which view is closer to the truth.

Imagine a person who because of some sort of agnosia is unable to recognize presented squares: not by touch nor by sight nor in any other way. Asked whether she knows what a square is, we'd be hard put to say she did. On the one hand, she does have an idea of squareness; she may even know that squares are four-sided regular polygons. On the other, here she is with a square in her hands and she can't ascertain its shape!

Now switch to the property of being a milliagon, here defined as a million-sided regular polygon. With respect to milliagons, all of us are in the position of our agnosic friend, the position of not being able to recognize them either by sight or touch. By parity of reasoning, shouldn't we suspect ourselves of not knowing what a milliagon is? Yet we do not; somehow, to know what a milliagon is, the ability to recognize one is not required. To the absolutist, this can only mean that as n decreases, the property of n-sided regular polygonhood puts stronger and stronger demands on those would seek to know it. But the truth is surely that since *most* people can recognize squares perceptually but not milliagons, the ability is required in the one case but not the other.[63]

Listening to the summer weather report, you may hear, in addition to tomorrow's *temperature*, the expected *heat index*—a function of temperature and humidity that is supposed to predict how hot the day will *feel*. Poor Henry ignores this figure; for him, every day is a 100% humidity day, because Henry is unable to perspire. The humidity normally being quite a bit less than 100%, Henry spends much of the summer feeling considerably hotter than we do; on a day when we might be out enjoying the breeze, Henry will be huddled next to the air conditioner.

Of course, Henry appreciates, in a sense, that it's merely warm out there, not hot. Even so, given how he feels on such days, one wants to say: poor guy, he doesn't know what it is for a day to be (merely) warm. How will the absolutist explain this? She must say that Henry's idea is objectively wrong; the *right and true* way to feel when it's warm out is the way that *we* feel. This is wildly implausible, however. Perspiration functions to drop our skin temperature *below* that of the surrounding air, so if anyone is appreciating the temperature "as it really is," it's Henry.[64] (Except for the historical accident of our greater numbers, it would have been wetskins like ourselves that were under suspicion of experiencing the temperature incorrectly.)

Absolutists say that standards of adequate conception are dictated by the (nature of the) thing conceived. But if so, then the following clearly possible thing should *not* be possible: knowing what X_1 is without knowing what X_2 is, even though X_1 and X_2 are identical.[65] All that most people know about sodium chloride (e.g.) is that it is some sort of chemical; what *salt* is, however, they *do* know. And while few have led such sheltered lives as to be ignorant of what cold is, ignorance of low random kinetic energy abounds.[66] (Note that it could have been the other way around.[67]) Since different things count as knowing what X is depending on how it is picked out, responsibility for the line between adequate ideas of X and inadequate ones does not lie with X alone.

So much is to challenge an influential *argument* for the visual nature of the colors. Now let me raise a doubt about the argument's conclusion. The color-touchers, let's imagine, evolved in isolation from those accessing color in other ways; they found the tactile mode of color perception as natural and inevitable as we do the visual one. Bananas and canaries they called "silft" ("slippery, soft and lightweight"), ripe strawberries were "styngy" ("sticky and clinging"), and so on. To know what silftness and so on *were*, one had to know how they made things *feel*. Only later, when contact was made with the likes of us, was it realized that silftness, to fix on that example, was none other than yellowness. Whereupon some of the more philosophical color-touchers reasoned as follows: since silftness is tactile by nature, yellowness has a tactile nature as well.

Now, the fact that this conclusion is drawn in a counterfactual world doesn't make it any more tolerable. If yellowness *could* have been tactile by nature, then, given the modal fixity of natures, it *is* tactile by nature; and as we know, it is no such thing. This turns the color-touchers' modus ponens into a modus tollens; since yellowness is not of a tactile nature, neither is silftness. But of course, two can play this game. By whatever authority *we* are able to vouch for the non-tactile nature of yellowness, the color-touchers affirm that silftness is not of a visual nature. It follows that yellowness isn't visual either.

XII.

Yellowness is *supposed* to be conceived in terms of how it makes things look. But the connections between the way a thing is supposed to be conceived, and the way it is, are complicated. Even the obvious-looking principle that "one is not obliged to conceive X as F unless it *is* F" may be doubted. And the stronger one that substitutes "unless X is F by nature" is definitely mistaken.

But our story has a lacuna exactly here. If the ways we are supposed to think of things need not reflect anything metaphysically important about them, why on earth are we supposed to think of them in these ways?[68]

Start with a reason going back in essence to Frege. Agreement, testimony, dispute—all of these depend on words being used in reference to the same items. The Frege point is that that is not enough. Take the case where you say, "Aristotle is amazing," speaking of the philosopher, and I hear "Aristotle is amazing," understanding our friend Aristotle Sundog Greenglass. Obviously, we have failed to communicate; and this remains so even if, unbeknownst to anyone, the philosopher's private researches into generation and corruption were so successful that the two Aristotles are in fact the same. The point applies on the property side as well; if you say, "Zemly is all charged up," meaning that she is excited, and I hear you as talking about Zemly's electrical condition, then the exchange is not saved if future science reveals that to be excited *is* to be electrically charged.

Along with speaking of the same items, then, communicators aim to think of these items in related ways. (Of course—communication would not be worth the effort unless it had guessable effects on the participants' states of mind.) But how better to arrange for this result than by indexing standards of conception to the pieces of public language that they exchange? So denoted, the Morning Star is to be understood in terms of its morningish appearance, and the Evening Star in terms of how it appears in the evening; the road from Thebes to Athens asks to be envisaged as traveled Athens-ward, the one from Athens to Thebes as traveled the other way. So denoted, salt is a condiment, the Sun is the preeminent celestial body, and sound is something to be heard; sodium chloride, meanwhile, is a chemical, Sol is one star among many, and compression waves are particles in motion.

Now, that it aids communication if different words carry with them different standards of right ideation was *supposed* to be a *non*-metaphysical reason for playing favorites. But any sort of favoritism among ideas stands as a temptation to the metaphysician. What is the relation between the Athens-Thebes road and the Thebes-Athens road? Naively, identity. But when one thinks of these roads in the ways their names prescribe, certain subtle "differences" emerge; one of the roads runs uphill, the other down, one offers better views, and so on. And now Leibniz's Law appears to show that the roads are not identical after all. Or consider the following. Science identifies sound with compression waves—a type of motion. But motion is perceived visually or by touch, while sound is perceived through the ears. So the wave theory of sound is wrong. Both arguments have had their advocates.

Still harder not to read metaphysical meaning into is a second sort of favoritism among ideas. Imagine that the color-touchers' verdicts agree with ours until chemists devise a substance which, although "yellow to the fingers," is blue to the eye. Who would, or should, win the ensuing argument seems clear. (I assume that the story is not filled out in prejudicial ways.) The visual perspective on color is *privileged*; judgments framed from it are, other things equal, dialectically weightier than those framed from other perspectives.[69] But this privilege surely testifies to some sort of *special rapport* between color and vision. And now it begins to seem that the colors *of their nature* favor vision over the other senses.

Everything here depends on what we make of the bruited special rapport. The first interpretation that comes to mind is simply that vision is a superior *detector* of color; those who look make fewer mistakes than those who touch. But so what if it is? After all, vision is also a superior detector of faces; animals do a remarkable job of recognizing each other by smell; and coastlines are best judged from the air. This hardly suggests that faces are of a visual nature, or that animals and coastlines are olfactory and aerial.[70] The most that follows from a perspective's greater statistical reliability is that if reliability is your goal, that is the perspective to adopt.

Yet such a reply, although correct within its limits, is superficial. This comes out when we press the question of *why* the colors are most reliably accessed by sight. With coastlines, the reasons are clear: due to their great size they are best viewed from afar; because they are (more or less) planar, the ideal viewing angle is from above or below; because air is transparent and rock is opaque, the view from above is better. Facts about coastlines thus explain *why* the aerial perspective should track the truth about them especially closely. But we have cited no facts about the naive colors that would give the visual perspective a truth-tracking advantage over that of the color touchers. And in fact it is consistent with our fantasy that the color touchers, unbothered by variation in lighting conditions, make *fewer* mistakes than ourselves. Somehow, though, this does not seem to rob the visual perspective of its dialectical advantage. Were a brute conflict to arise in which neither judgment could be written off to ambient lighting, sensory fatigue, or what have you, the visual perspective would prevail.

So color's special rapport with vision runs deeper than statistics. As deep as metaphysics, perhaps? I think we can explain the added depth in another way.[71] Let the color-touchers' idea track yellowness as accurately as you like, this remains a *de facto* connection which both sides stand ready to sacrifice in the interests of protecting the property's *de jure* connection to the visual idea. Silftness, meanwhile, is signified *de facto* by the visual idea, *de jure* by the tactile one; both sides would surrender the first connection to protect the second.[72] So if, contrary to what we suppose, the properties are distinct, the visual idea goes with yellowness and the tactile one with silftness. There are ways of putting this that lend it a metaphysical air; for instance, "the price of cognitive access to *yellowness* is to think of it visually or else in a way that agrees with the visual idea," or, the logical next step, "yellowness is *empirically* visual even if not noumenally so." But the point is just that an idea cannot denote yellowness without denoting the same property as our yellowness-idea, which is visual. And this is no more than a truism.

XIII.

Remember our paradox: to know what yellowness is, one must know how it makes things look; yet if yellowness is objective, the impression it makes on human observers should not be *relevant* to what it is. The paradoxical answer is that there can be perfectly objective properties such that to know what they are, one has to understand them in subjectivity-involving ways.[73] I take these properties to include, in addition to the colors, qualitative properties like feeling itchy and suffering pain; perceptual properties such as that of being shaped like *so*; and normative properties like rationality and goodness. To illustrate with the last example, it may well be that no one who appreciates what goodness is can remain indifferent to it. But if so, the reason is not that goodness exerts an irresistible magnetic pull; it's that you have to care about goodness to qualify as appreciating what it is.

Notes

1. This paper began life as comments on Mark Johnston's contribution to the 1989 Colloquium on Color at the University of Michigan. Later versions were read at Queensland University, Australian National University, Monash University, UC Riverside, and UC San Diego; thanks to all who participated, especially Andre Gallois, Peter Menzies, Philip Pettit and Michael Smith. Closer to home I had help from Mark Crimmins, Allan Gibbard, Sally Haslanger, Ted Hinchman, David Hills, Joseph Levine, Gideon Rosen, David Velleman and José Zalabardo. I learned of John Campbell's related ideas ("A Simple View of Color") from Crispin Wright.
2. "Why Reason Can't Be Naturalized" in Putnam 1983. Perhaps I'm not using the phrase in exactly his sense.
3. I use "Fness" stipulatively as the property in virtue of which "F" applies; it's not a foregone conclusion that this'll be the same property in every case.
4. Field 1972. Field might not endorse this project now.
5. Lewis 1989, 136. See also Railton 1986, Boyd 1988, Johnston 1989, and Smith 1989.
6. Oddly, they can also seem entirely open to view; see Campbell 1993.
7. Aristotle says, "I call that sense-object special that does not admit of being perceived by another sense and *about which it is impossible to be deceived*, as sight is connected with color, hearing with sound, and taste with flavor" (*De Anima*, II, 6, my emphasis). Likewise Locke: "blue and yellow, bitter or sweet can never be false ideas" (*Essay Concerning Human Understanding*, II, 32, 16). This view of Locke's is noted in Curley 1972, 463.
8. *Essays on the Intellectual Powers of Man*, II, 17. According to Locke, "the ideas produced in us by these secondary qualities have no resemblance of them at all" (*Essay*, II, 8, 15).
9. *Essays*, II, 17.
10. *Essays*, II, 17.
11. *Principles*, I, 68. Note that Descartes speaks not of pain, the feeling, but pain the thing felt; I ignore the many issues this distinction raises.
12. Dennett 1978, 224.
13. Dennett 1978, 224.
14. Mackie 1977, 35; Mackie 1976, 19.
15. *Essays*, II, 17.
16. See the literature on Russell's principle that lack of acquaintance with any constituent of a proposition prevents understanding; for instance, Russell 1912, 58, and Evans 1985b, chapter 4.
17. Jackson et al 1982, 216.
18. This oversimplifies the eventual proposal; see section VII.
19. Armstrong 1968, 89-90. He treats color similarly. Redness is identified "by reference to the way it happens to affect us and by mentioning objects that happen to be red" (*ibid.*, 276). And "just as there arises the question what, as a contingent matter of fact, a mental state is, so there arises the question what, as a contingent matter of

fact, the property of redness actually is" (*ibid.*, 277).

20. *ibid.*, 91.
21. *ibid.*, 277
22. *ibid.*, 289.
23. Hardin 1984, 496; he bases the conclusion on Nassau 1980. Campbell 1969 made the point earlier.
24. I assume the widely accepted second-order property treatment of dispositions; see Prior 1985. Alternative theories treat dispositions as counterfactual properties or as categorical ones. Against the first alternative see Shope 1978 and Wright 1992; Johnston 1993 attempts a fix. Against the second see Prior et al 1982 and Prior 1985.
25. Here we ask whether the role property is F-ish in causal respects, but the question could be generalized. Part of the role of evaluative properties, for instance, is to merit an appreciative response. But does the property of having an appreciation-meriting property *itself* merit appreciation?
26. Block's nice example; see his 1990.
27. This is also the conclusion of Prior et al 1982, Prior 1985, Jackson & Pargetter, 1988, and Block, 1990. Based on his and Jackson's "program model" of causal relevance, Pettit holds dispositions to be causally relevant to their manifestations (Jackson & Pettit 1990). But this model, which counts a higher-level property causally relevant if it "effectively ensures" the instantiation of some causally efficacious lower-level property, seems overly permissive; it makes Brutus's property of being Caesar's killer causally relevant to Caesar's death, and Drano's property of being plumber-recommended causally relevant to the unclogging of my drain.
28. Some dispositionalists embrace this result gladly. Secondary qualities, McDowell says, "cannot be credited with causal efficacy" (1985, 188). See also McGinn 1983, 15.
29. On the causal powers of functional states see Block 1990.
30. Lewis 1980, 233.
31. Provided that context supplies a unique F-ish property.
32. Or different objects at different times—I ignore this complication.
33. "I mean to deny all identities of the form ⌜*a* is identical with the attribute of having *a*⌝ where *a* is an experience-name definable as naming the occupant of a specified causal role...I take 'the attribute of having pain'...as a noncontingent name of that state or attribute Z that belongs, in any world, to whatever things have pain in that world" (Lewis 1983, 101).
34. Similarly, in addition to the pencil's redness, which causes redness's intuitive effects, there is also its higher-order property of having redness, the property it shares with other red things.
35. Lewis 1986, xi: "...there is a state common to all who are in pain—"being in pain," I call it—but it is not pain, and it does not itself occupy the role of pain."
36. A similar point applies to Jackson and Pargetter on color. For them, "when I say that an object in [circumstances] C3 is red and another in C4 is red also, I am saying that they...have something in common. Both have what is redness for me now in their circumstances" (1988, 135). But given their Lewisian framework, *that* commonality consists merely in the fact that both are such as to cause red experiences—which cannot be the reason *why* they would cause red experiences.
37. That is what we are getting if we insist on commonality. Insist on causality and the

problem is different: itchiness does not cause scratching because it's *itchiness*, rather it qualifies as itchiness because (among other things) it causes scratching. This is on top of the fact that it is not shared.

38. Reference fixing conditions are generally conceived as concise (this is suggested by the examples), indefeasible (so as to enable a priori knowledge), antecedently graspable (on pain of circularity) specifications of a term's referent. I'm not sure that any of these conditions is strictly demanded by what Kripke says. As characterized on pp. 34ff., for example, a priority looks quite *compatible* with defeasibility. And Kripke seems to show ambivalence about antecedent graspability when he describes as "independent of any view argued in the text" the view that "such terms as 'sensation of yellow', 'sensation of heat', 'sensation of pain', and the like, could not be in the language unless they were identifiable in terms of external observable phenomena, such as heat, yellowness, and associated human behavior" (footnote 71 on p. 140).

39. Kripke 1980, 140.

40. Wright 1992, 131.

41. Not in this passage, anyway; see note 66 on p. 128. *Perhaps* Kripke's use of "physical" in note 66 can be read as expressing commitment to an "interesting physical essence" underlying manifestations of yellowness. But so little weight is put on the word that it is hard to feel sure; it might equally be functioning to bring out yellowness's objectivity or intrinsicness. "Perhaps I am rather vague about these questions, but further precision seems unnecessary here."

42. *ibid.*, 140.

43. Dennett 1991, 376.

44. Shoemaker 1990, 116.

45. Johnston 1992 speaks of "a bizarre pre-established harmony of redundant causes of our visual experience" (227-8).

46. Likewise, apparently, for nonphysical *mental* properties. If neurophysiology sufficed to explain behavior, "we would be forced to say that the extra mental properties postulated...are causally idle; and that the characteristically Parallelist thesis that the mental is unable to affect the physical order in any way is completely correct" (Armstrong 1968, 47). This is a particular theme of Malcolm 1968.

47. This is not to say that determinables *inherit* their determinates' causal powers; see Yablo 1992, note 32. The claim is that determinables are not *preempted* by their determinates.

48. To speak of a property as causing, or being causally sufficient, for an effect, is short for a similar claim about the property's instantiation; so the truck's *bare* heaviness was sufficient, but its *heaviness* was the cause.

49. "The position is inconsistent; properties with physical determinates are themselves physical, yet you say color is *not* physical." I deny the assumption that only physical properties can have physical determinates. *Determinates* are properties such that to have them is to have the original property, not simpliciter, but in a certain way; and *physical* properties are properties whose actual and possible possessors have something physical in common, or form a physically natural class. The assumption in question is therefore this: if for at least one way G of being F, the Gs have something physical in common, then the Fs do too. This is wildly implausible. And it remains so even if we strengthen the premise to: every x that is F at all is F in some specific way G_x, where the G_xs have something physical in common. Why

shouldn't a physically unnatural class decompose into physically natural subclasses? (Analogy: Whenever a first-order statement is provable, it is provable in some specific way. But although provability-in-such-and-such-a-way is decidable, provability is not; the decidable parts add up to an undecidable whole.)

50. Boghossian & Velleman 1991, 67.

51. Mackie 1976, 36.

52. "Sesquiary" qualities these might be called. Thanks to David Hills for making me see their relevance.

53. Mackie 1976, 49.

54. Although compare McDowell: "What would one expect it to be like to experience something's being such as to look red, if not to experience the thing in question (in the right circumstances) as looking, precisely, red?" (1985, 112). What bothers me here is the substitution of "experience a thing *as looking red*" for "experience it as *red*." If these are different, then the unrevealingness charge—which concerned the experience of things *as red*—goes unanswered. But to assume their identity is to prejudge one of the main questions before of us, namely, does our experience of redness represent it as ontologically visual?

55. Evans 1985a, 272.

56. *ibid.*, 273.

57. McDowell 1985, 113.

58. They are not true. See Gardner 1966.

59. "By touch alone" because I propose to ignore the fact that most reputed color-touchers, including those about to be discussed, have had normal color vision.

60. Rosenfeld 1964, courtesy of David Hills' paranormally good memory. Duplessis 1975 contains a discussion of color-touching among the blind. See Cytowic 1989 and 1993 for the related, and apparently genuine, phenomenon of synesthesia, or cross-modal perception. See also Churchland 1979, chapter 2, for a nicely elaborated fable about temperature-seeing.

61. The remainder of the paper is greatly indebted to Crimmins 1989. Note that I speak of "knowing what X is" rather than "having the concept of X." These are different. Astrophysicists have the concept of dark matter but they don't know what satisfies it, that is, what dark matter is. And one needn't have the concept of a Platonic solid to know what the Platonic solids are.

62. McDowell 1985, 113. Though compare this, from the same paper: "I have written of what property-ascriptions are *understood* to be true in virtue of, rather than what they *are* true in virtue of" (112, my emphasis).

63. Consider in this connection Oliver Sacks' "twins": "A box of matches on their table fell, and discharged its contents on the floor. '111' they both cried simultaneously...I counted the matches—it took me some time—and there were 111. 'How could you count the matches so quickly?' I asked. 'We didn't count,' they said. 'We see the 111'" (Sacks 1990, 199). Knowing what 111 is would be a different and more demanding thing if more of us had this ability. Mark Crimmins gives a related example: "Some objects reflect light primarily in the infra-red spectrum—outside the band of visible light. Suppose we are given one. This object has a certain color-like property, call it *infra-mauve*, of reflecting such and such frequencies of light to such and such degrees. We cannot recognize visually when an object is infra-mauve, but clearly we know what property it *is*. And isn't our situation with respect to infra-mauve just like [the sightless person's] with regard to red?" (Crimmins 1989).

64. This is based on a remark of Kripke's at the 1989 Color Symposium.
65. And indeed known to be identical. See Hintikka 1962, 149, note 9, for an evasion of the point.
66. Using "cold" in the sense of low temperature.
67. See Crimmins 1989.
68. What may be the deepest reason I don't feel ready to discuss; we valorize certain styles of conception as part of an ongoing project of grooming ourselves to respond similarly to new cases. (See Pettit 1990 for a congenial account of rule following, especially pp. 16ff.)
69. Not that this privilege could never be lost—a point urged on me by Philip Kitcher and Paul Churchland. Similar privilege accrues to the first-person perspective on sensations as against the third-person, and to the interpretive perspective on intentional states as against that afforded by physics plus (alleged) bridge laws. Here too metaphysical conclusions have been thought to follow, e.g., by Davidson in his attack on psychophysical identities.
70. Another form of the argument is this. The visual idea of yellowness is in closer rapport with it than the tactile one, while with silftness it is the other way around; since identicals stand in the same relations, yellowness can't be silftness. But all the supposed difference in relations comes to is that *attributions* of yellowness and silftness respond differently to the same evidence. Of course—they are different attributions! The properties attributed can still be one and the same. They can even be *believed* to be the same, albeit with probability less than one. Admittedly, if visual and tactile evidence were to push in opposite directions, and push very hard, the identity-belief would come under pressure. But that recalcitrant experience *would* force us to distinguish "two things" doesn't force us to distinguish them *now*. (A good thing too, or few identity claims would be left standing.)
71. Compare Wittgenstein's criteria/symptoms distinction in 1953, para. 354.
72. So we are using an intensionalized version of Wittgenstein's distinction; different things can be criterial for X and Y even though X *is* Y.
73. Someone might say that the objectivist has won a hollow victory; for even if an objective property makes F-attributions true, the property's status *as* truth-maker is owing to subjective factors. This is something I am still pondering, but I agree to this extent: objectivist metaphysics is one thing, objective discourse another.

References

Aristotle, 1986. *De Anima* (New York: Penguin)

Armstrong, D. 1968. *A Materialist Theory of the Mind* (London: Routledge)

Baxandall, M. 1985. *Patterns of Intention* (New Haven: Yale)

Block, N., ed. 1980. *Readings in the Philosophy of Psychology*, vol. 1 (Cambridge: MIT Press)

Block, N. 1990. "Can the Mind Change the World?" in G. Boolos, ed., *Meaning and Method: Essays in Honor of Hilary Putnam* (Cambridge: Cambridge University Press), 137-170

Boër, S. and W. Lycan. 1986. *Knowing Who* (Cambridge: MIT Press)

Boghossian, P. and D. Velleman. 1989. "Colour as a Secondary Quality," *Mind* 98, 81-103

Boghossian, P. and D. Velleman. 1991. "Physicalist Theories of Color," *Philosophical Review* 100, 67-106

Boyd, R. 1988. "How to Be a Moral Realist," in Sayre-McCord 1988, 181-228

Campbell, J. 1993. "A Simple View of Colour," in Haldane & Wright 1993

Campbell, K. 1969. "Colours," in R. Brown and C.D. Rollins, ed. *Contemporary Philosophy in Australia* (London: Allen & Unwin)

Churchland, P. 1979. *Scientific Realism and the Plasticity of Mind* (Cambridge: Cambridge University Press)

Cottingham, J., R. 1984. Stoothoff, and D. Murdoch, *Philosophical Writings of Descartes* (Cambridge: Cambridge University Press)

Crimmins, M. 1989. "Having Idea and Having the Concept," *Mind & Language* 4, 280-294

Curley, E. 1972. "Locke, Boyle, and the Distinction Between Primary and Secondary Qualities," *Philosophical Review* 81, 438-464

Cytowic, R. 1989. *Synesthesia: A Union of the Senses* (New York: Springer-Verlag)

Cytowic, R. 1993. *The Man Who Tasted Shapes* (New York: Putnam)

Dennett, D.1978. *Brainstorms* (Montgomery: Bradford Books)

Dennett, D. 1991. *Consciousness Explained* (Boston: Little, Brown & Company)

Duplessis, Y. 1975. *The Paranormal Perception of Color* (New York: Parasychology Foundation)

Evans, G. 1985a. "Things Without the Mind," in G. Evans, *Collected Papers* (Oxford: Clarendon Press)

Evans, G. 1985b. *The Varieties of Reference* (Oxford: Oxford University Press)

Field, H. 1972. "Tarski's Theory of Truth," *Journal of Philosophy* 69, 347-375

Gardner, M. 1966. "Dermo-optical Perception: A Peek Down the Nose," *Science*

Haldane, J. and C. Wright. 1993. *Reality, Representation, and Projection* (Oxford: Oxford University Press)

Hardin, C. 1984. "Are 'Scientific' Objects Coloured?" *Mind* 93, 491-500

Hardin, C. 1988. *Color for Philosophers* (Indianapolis: Hackett)

Hintikka, J. 1962. *Knowledge and Belief* (Ithaca: Cornell University Press)

Jackson, F. and R. Pargetter. 1987. "An Objectivist's Guide to Subjectivism About Color," *Internationale Revue de Philosophie*, 127-141

Jackson, F., R. Pargetter, and E. Prior. 1982. "Functionalism and Type-Type Identity Theories," *Philosophical Studies* 42, 209-225

Jackson, F. and P. Pettit. 1990. "Program Explanation: A General Perspective," *Analysis* 50, 107-117

Johnston, M. 1989. "Dispositional Theories of Value," *Proceedings of the Aristotelian Society*, supp. volume 63, 139-174

Johnston, M. 1992. "How to Speak of the Colors," *Philosophical Studies* 68, 221-263

Johnston, M. 1993. "Objectivity Refigured," in Haldane & Wright 1993

Kripke, S. 1980. *Naming and Necessity* (Cambridge: Harvard University Press)

Lewis, D. 1966. "An Argument for the Identity Theory," *Journal of Philosophy* 63, 17-25, reprinted in Lewis 1983

Lewis, D. 1980. "Review of Putnam," in Block 1980

Lewis, D. 1983. *Philosophical Papers*, vol. 1 (Oxford: Oxford University Press)

Lewis, D. 1986. *Philosophical Papers*, vol. 2 (Oxford: Oxford University Press)

Lewis, D. 1989. "Dispositional Theories of Value," *Proceedings of the Aristotelian*

Society, supp. volume 63, 113-137

Mackie, J. 1976. *Problems from Locke* (Oxford: Clarendon Press)

Mackie, J. 1977. *Ethics: Inventing Right and Wrong* (New York: Penguin)

Malcolm, N. 1968. "The Conceivability of Mechanism." *Philosophical Review* 87, 45-72

McDowell, J. 1983. "Aesthetic Value, Objectivity and the Fabric of the World," in E. Schaper, ed. *Pleasure, Preference, and Value* (Cambridge: Cambridge University Press)

McDowell, J. 1985. "Values and Secondary Qualities," in T. Honderich, ed., *Morality and Objectivity* (London: Routledge and Kegan Paul), reprinted in Sayre-McCord 1988.

McGinn, C. 1983. *The Subjective View* (New York: Oxford University Press)

Millikan, R. 1994. "On Unclear and Indistinct Ideas," *Philosophical Perspectives* 8, 75-100

Nassau, K. 1980. "The Causes of Color," *Scientific American*

Pargetter, R. and E. Prior, 1982. "The Dispositional and the Categorical," *Pacific Philosophical Quarterly* 63, 366-370

Peacocke, C. 1989. "Perceptual Content," in J. Almog, J. Perry and H. Wettstein, ed., *Themes from Kaplan* (New York: Oxford University Press)

Pettit, P. 1990. "The Reality of Rule-Following," *Mind* 99, 1-21

Pettit, P. 1991. "Realism and Response-Dependence," *Mind* 100, 587-626

Prior, E., R. Pargetter, & F. Jackson, 1982. "Three Theses About Dispositions," *American Philosophical Quarterly* 9, 251-257

Prior, E. 1985. *Dispositions* (Aberdeen: Aberdeen University Press)

Putnam, H. 1983. *Realism and Reason* (Cambridge: Cambridge University Press)

Railton, P. 1986. "Moral Realism," *Philosophical Review* 95, 163-207

Reid, T. 1969. *Essays on the Intellectual Powers of Man* (Cambridge: MIT Press)

Rosenfeld, A. 1964. "Seeing Color with the Fingers," *Life*, 102-113

Russell, B. 1912. *Problems of Philosophy* (Oxford: Oxford University Press)

Sacks, O. 1990. *The Man Who Mistook His Wife For A Hat* (New York: Harper)

Sayre-McCord, G., ed. 1988. *Essays on Moral Realism* (Ithaca: Cornell University Press)

Shoemaker, S. 1990. "Qualities and Qualia: What's in the Mind?" *Philosophy and Phenomenological Research* 1 (supplement), 109-131

Shoemaker, S. 1986. "Review of McGinn, *The Subjective View*," *Journal of Philosophy* 83, 407-413

Shope, R. 1978. "The Conditional Fallacy," *Journal of Philosophy* 75, 397-413

Smith, M. 1989. "Dispositional Theories of Value," *Proceedings of the Aristotelian Society*, supp. volume 63, 89-111

Wittgenstein, L. 1953. *Philosophical Investigations* (Oxford: Blackwell)

Wright, C. 1992. *Truth & Objectivity* (Cambridge: Harvard University Press)

Yablo, S. 1992. "Mental Causation," *Philosophical Review* 101, 245-280

Philosophical Perspectives, 9, AI, Connectionism, and Philosophical Psychology, 1995

Corrections to "HOP, SKIP, AND JUMP: THE AGONISTIC CONCEPTION OF TRUTH" by Stephen Yablo which appeared in *Philosophical Perspectives, 7, Language and Logic, 1993*

[Editorial note: A variety of serious errors appeared in Yablo's paper in *Philosophical Perspectives, 7, Language and Logic, 1993*. The errors are of several different sorts. The first are relatively straighforward typographical errors. For the most part, corrected whole lines and some entire corrected passages are shown, but lines from volume 7 will not end at the right margin in this volume for a variety of reasons. In addition, the typography is, in general, different throughout since the typesetting for this volume was not done on the same machine as volume 7. The second sort of error involves formatting. The worst of the formatting errors concerns boldface. Though we did not know it (and, worse, did not notice in the final camera-ready copy), the typesetting machine we used for volume 7 would not produce boldface symbols or Greek letters. The codes for bold are actually in the file, but without a specific font for bold symbols and bold Greek letters the printer would not produce such boldface items. We are also unable to produce such bold items with the typesetting machine used for this volume. Yet Yablo does make crucial use of boldface Greek letters. As you will see below, we have solved this problem by replacing bold Greek letters by their bolded English name, e.g., **sigma**.]

Pages 373 and 374, tables 6 and 8: the letters 't' and 'f' (with their appropriate overlining) should be adjacent, e.g.,

tf

Page 375, line 7 in section **IV** should read:

be true (false) of in a given fact-situation–or, what comes to the same given our

Page 375, third line from the bottom should read:

(D2) $\|\phi \vee \Psi\| \approx f \Leftrightarrow \|\phi\| \approx f$ and $\|\Psi\| \approx f$.

Page 376, the second line on the righthand side of the definition of $\rho(\alpha)$ should read:

$jump(\rho(\alpha\text{-}1))$ if $\alpha \neq 0^{21}$

Page 381, the lefthand sides of the definitions near the top of the page should read:

$$\rho_\alpha$$

$$\rho^\alpha$$

Page 382, in the righthand side of the quantifier clause of the definition, in both phrases

$\phi^{\ulcorner\phi\urcorner}$ should read: $\phi^{\ulcorner\alpha\urcorner}$

Page 382, the first line in section **VII** should read:

Now the above ought to sound somewhat familiar. For near the end of his

Page 385: no occurrence of 'ϕ' should be italicized.

Page 386, the eighth line from the end of **Appendix 1** should read:

and $\theta \in \Gamma$.[59] Tree $\mathfrak{F}$ is a *proof* of θ in Σ iff[60]

Page 387, the pertinent parts of the first and second full paragraphs should read:

Surprisingly much of the above can be repeated, *mutatis mutandis*, in the context of the strong theory. Where Kripke's smallest fixed point σ was obtained from the null set by repeated application of *jump*, our **sigma** comes from the empty set by repeated application of *skip*. Provided that the extension of each predicate P other than T is disjoint from its antiextension, σ is included in **sigma**: that is, *every truth value assigned by Kripke's minimal fixed point is assigned by ours*. Usually in fact **sigma** assigns *more* truth-values than σ. ... More controversially, **sigma** finds the Truth Teller K to be *false* rather than gappy.[67] This again seems to be the right result. Since 'I am true' is not, in and of itself, true, any sentence *calling* it true must be considered false. But K is itself such a sentence, so K is false.

Just now I said that **sigma** assigns every truth value that σ does. This does not mean that **sigma** assigns every *semantic* value that σ does, for not every σ-gap is a **sigma**-gap. Sometimes the σ-gap receives a truth value, true or false, in **sigma**; this is how it is with K, the Truth Teller. Other times **sigma** leaves the σ-gap's semantic value undecided.

Page 387, third full paragraph: each occurrence of 'χ' should be '**chi**'.

Page 387, seventh line of fourth full paragraph should read:

> this fixed point **iota** contains attributions that the least fixed point **sigma** omits. Define the

Page 387, the second line in **Appendix 3** should read:

> our language $\mathcal{K}$ will be the set $\{\,\|\phi\| \approx \mathbf{v} \mid \phi$ is a sentence of $\mathcal{L}$ and $\mathbf{v}$ is a truth-value$\}$ of

Page 388 and following: all occurrences of '$\|$' should be uniform throughout.

Page 388 and following (including note 75): all occurrences of '**v**' with any overline should be uniform throughout.

Page 388, the sixth line from the bottom should end:

> inconsistent to do so").

Page 389, the part of rule [I] before the dash should read:

> [I]   from $\varnothing$, infer $\|\phi\| \approx \mathbf{v}$

Page 390, the full sentence before rule [**T2**] should read:

> System Σ_{S} takes over rules [A]-[∀] and [T1] from Σ_{S}, but [T2] is modified to

Page 390, (**P4**) on: each occurrence of 'σ' from here on should be '**sigma**'.

Page 391, (**P5**) on: each occurrence of 'χ' from here on should be '**chi**'.

Page 391, (**P6**) on: each occurrence of 'ι' from here on should be '**iota**'.

Page 391, from rule [V] on: all occurrences of 'Σ_{S}' should be uniform.

Page 393, note 12, line 6 should start:

> no further ahead.

Page 394, note 42, the first sentence should read:

> Suppose that $\|\cdot\|$ is a solution.

Page 394, note 45, the second line should read:

operation he calls "almost closing off."

Page 395, note 56, the last line should read:

$$\bigcap_{\beta<\lambda} \bigcup_{\beta<\alpha<\lambda} \Theta_\alpha.$$